TADATOSHI FUJIMAKI

I have a lot of fun drawing Riko. Her movements are always so lively, and I happen to like women like that in real life.

Kuroko, on the other hand, gives me trouble. He barely speaks, and to this day, I have no idea what he's actually thinking.

—2010

Tadatoshi Fujimaki was born on June 9, 1982, in Tokyo. He made his debut in 2007 in *Akamaru Jump* with *Kuroko's Basketball*, which was later serialized in *Weekly Shonen Jump*. *Kuroko's Basketball* quickly gained popularity and became an anime in Japan in 2012.

BASKETBALL

9 & 10

SHONEN JUMP Manga Edition
BY TADATOSHI FUJIMAKI

Translation/Caleb Cook
Touch-Up Art & Lettering/Mark McMurray
Design/Sam Elzway
Editor/John Bae

KUROKO NO BASUKE © 2008 by Tadatoshi Fujimaki
All rights reserved.
First published in Japan in 2008 by SHUEISHA Inc., Tokyo.
English translation rights arranged by SHUEISHA Inc.

The stories, characters and incidents mentioned in this
publication are entirely fictional.

Printed in the U.S.A.

Published by VIZ Media, LLC
P.O. Box 77010
San Francisco, CA 94107

10 9 8 7 6 5 4 3 2 1
First printing, April 2017

PARENTAL ADVISORY
KUROKO'S BASKETBALL is rated T for Teen and
is recommended for ages 13 and up. This volume
includes mild langueage.
ratings.viz.com

www.viz.com

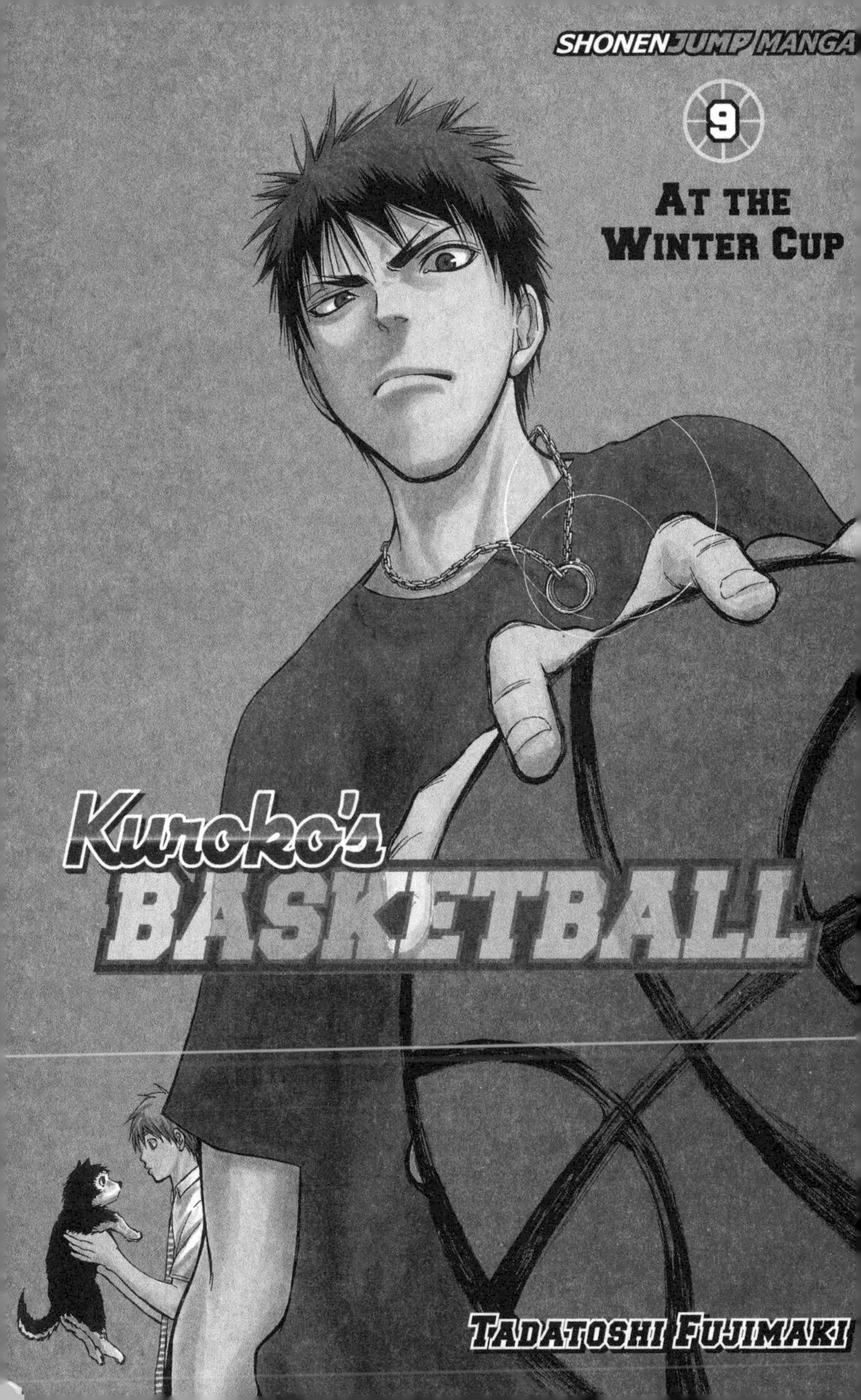
SHONEN JUMP MANGA
9
AT THE WINTER CUP
Kuroko's BASKETBALL
TADATOSHI FUJIMAKI

Characters

TAIGA KAGAMI

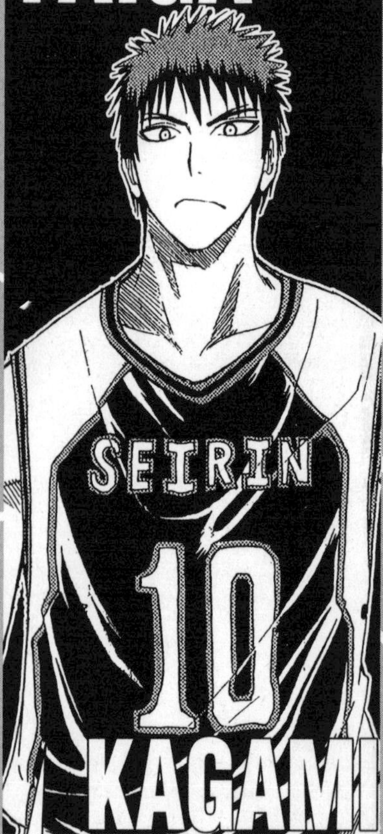
SEIRIN
10

A first-year on Seirin High's basketball team. Though he's rough around the edges, he's a gifted player with a lot of potential. His goal is to beat the Miracle Generation.

TETSUYA KUROKO

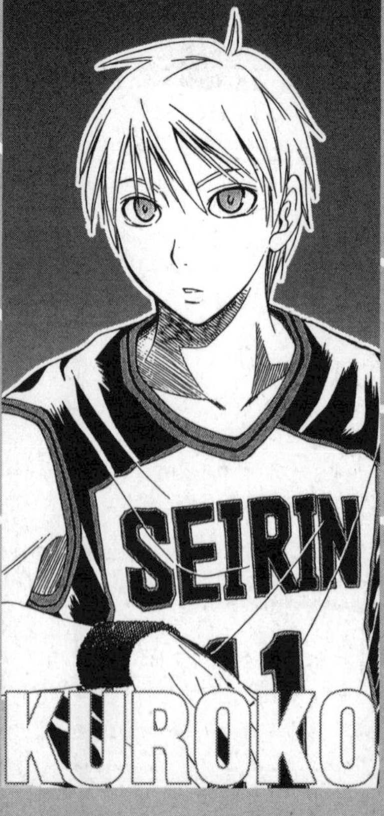
SEIRIN

A first-year on Seirin High's basketball team. Gifted with a natural lack of presence, he utilizes misdirection on the court to make nearly invisible passes.

KUROKO'S BASKETBALL

RYOTA

KISE

One of the Miracle Generation. Any basketball move he sees, he can mimic in an instant.

SHINTARO

MIDORIMA

A first-year at Shotoku High, he's the top shooter of the Miracle Generation.

DAIKI

AOMINE

The ace of the Miracle Generation and Kuroko's former friend, he's now a first-year at To-oh Academy.

TEPPEI

KIYOSHI

A second-year on Seirin High's basketball team and the club's founder. He was hospitalized but returned shortly after Inter-High.

RIKO

AIDA

A second-year and coach of the Seirin High basketball team.

JUNPEI

HYUGA

A second-year on Seirin High's basketball team. As captain, he led his team to the Finals League last year despite only playing first-year players.

Teiko Middle School is an elite championship school whose basketball team once fielded five prodigies collectively known as "the Miracle Generation." But supporting those five was a phantom sixth man—Tetsuya Kuroko. Now Kuroko's a first-year high school student with zero presence who joins Seirin High's basketball club. Though his physical abilities and stats are well below average, Kuroko thrives on the court by making passes his opponents can't detect!

Seirin suffers a loss during the Finals League of Inter-High. With their eyes set on the next prize, the Winter Cup, they dive into summer training camp. While there, they run into Shutoku, and Kagami receives some unexpected help from Midorima!

Meanwhile, Kaijo's Kise clashes with To-oh's Aomine at the Inter-High quarterfinals. He finally manages to copy Aomine's style, but will it be enough to win?!

STORY THUS FAR

TABLE OF CONTENTS

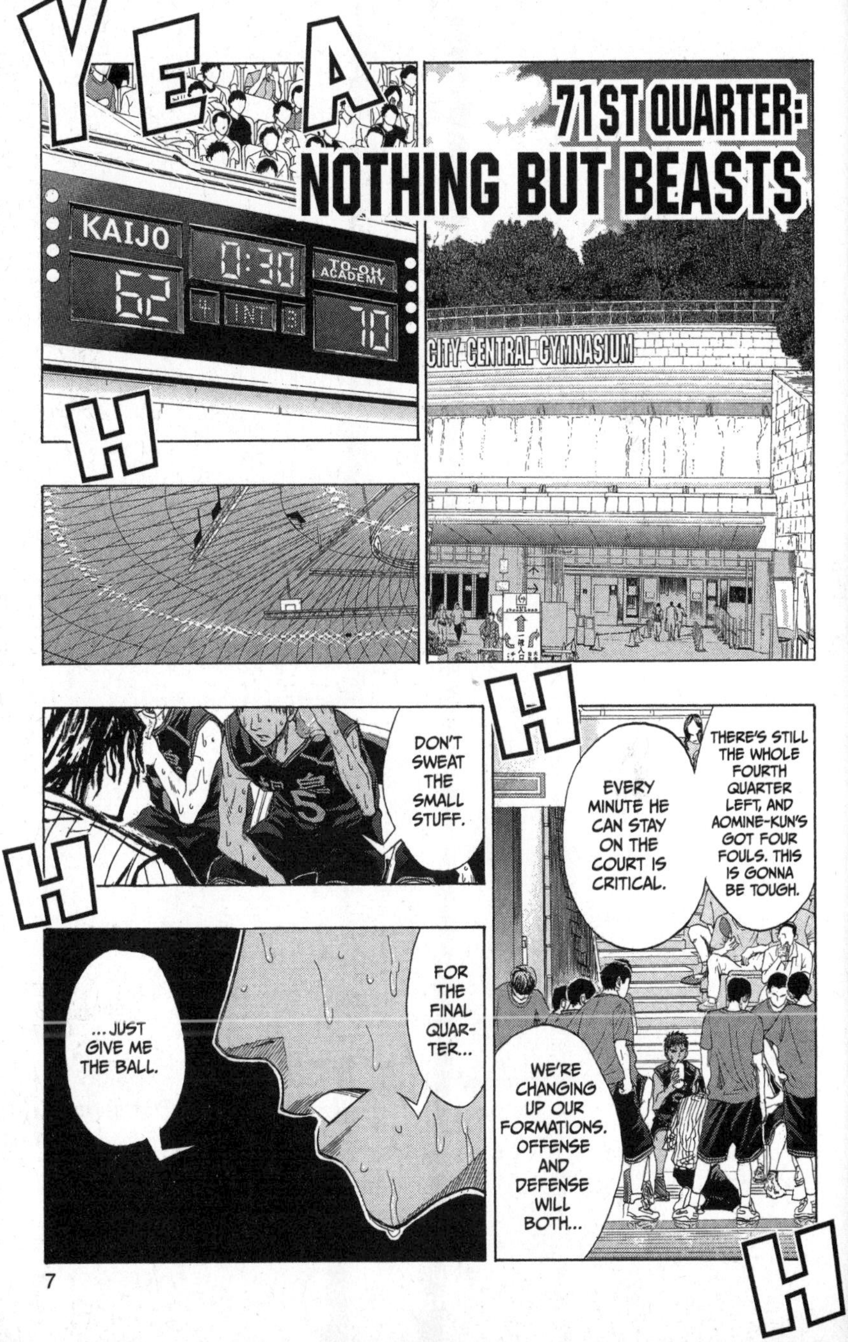
YEAHHHH
71ST QUARTER: NOTHING BUT BEASTS
CITY CENTRAL GYMNASIUM
KAIJO 62
0:30
TO-OH ACADEMY 70
THERE'S STILL THE WHOLE FOURTH QUARTER LEFT, AND AOMINE-KUN'S GOT FOUR FOULS. THIS IS GONNA BE TOUGH.
EVERY MINUTE HE CAN STAY ON THE COURT IS CRITICAL.
WE'RE CHANGING UP OUR FORMATIONS. OFFENSE AND DEFENSE WILL BOTH...
DON'T SWEAT THE SMALL STUFF.
FOR THE FINAL QUAR-TER...
...JUST GIVE ME THE BALL.

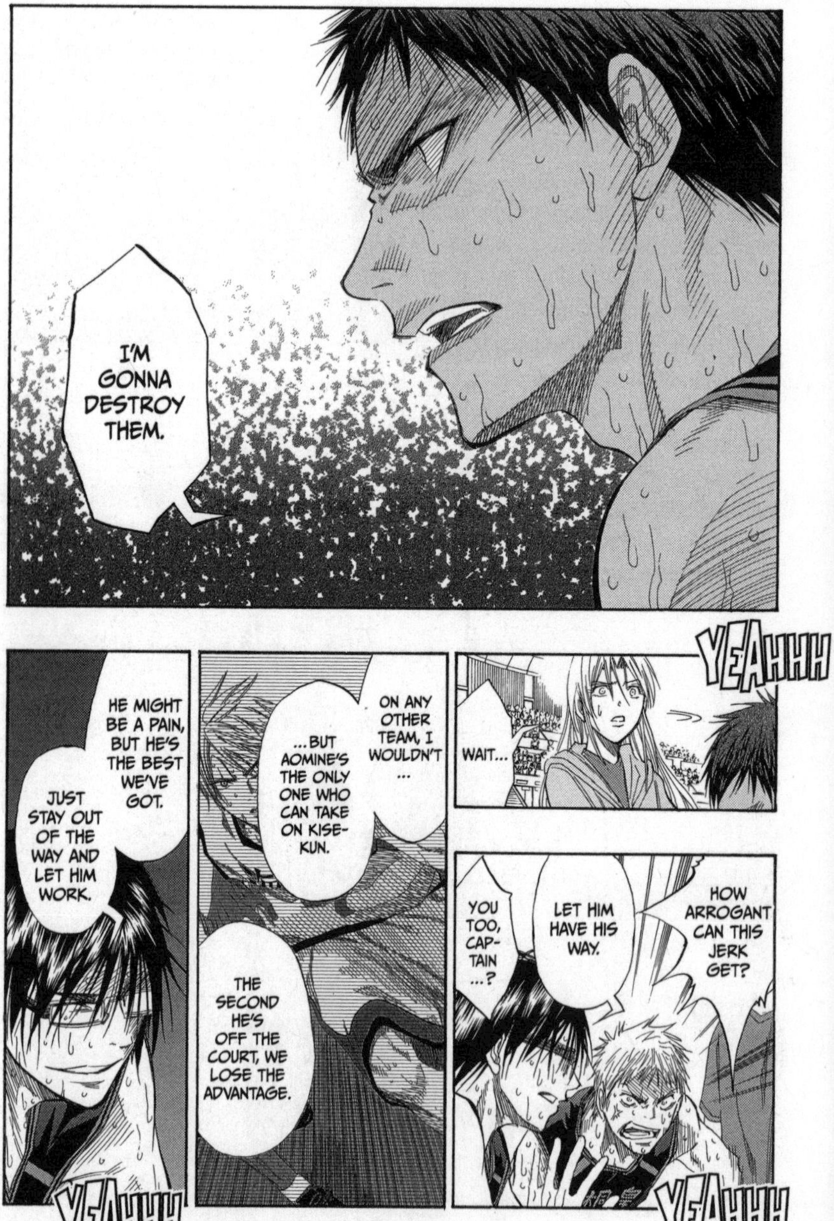
I'M GONNA DESTROY THEM.
YEAHHH
WAIT...
HOW ARROGANT CAN THIS JERK GET?
LET HIM HAVE HIS WAY.
YOU TOO, CAPTAIN...?
YEAHHH
ON ANY OTHER TEAM, I WOULDN'T...
...BUT AOMINE'S THE ONLY ONE WHO CAN TAKE ON KISE-KUN.
THE SECOND HE'S OFF THE COURT, WE LOSE THE ADVANTAGE.
HE MIGHT BE A PAIN, BUT HE'S THE BEST WE'VE GOT.
JUST STAY OUT OF THE WAY AND LET HIM WORK.
YEAHHH

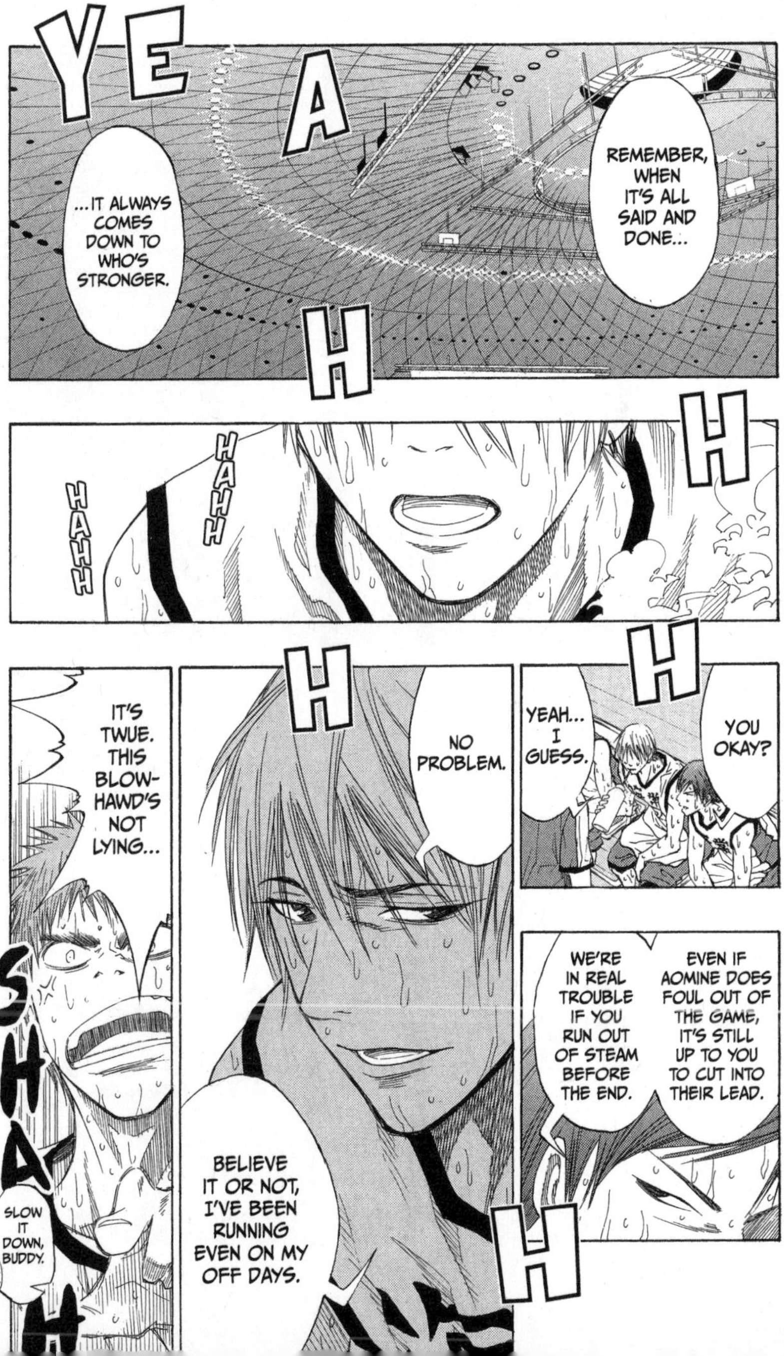

YEAHHHHH
REMEMBER, WHEN IT'S ALL SAID AND DONE...
...IT ALWAYS COMES DOWN TO WHO'S STRONGER.
HAHH HAHH
YOU OKAY?
YEAH... I GUESS.
EVEN IF AOMINE DOES FOUL OUT OF THE GAME, IT'S STILL UP TO YOU TO CUT INTO THEIR LEAD.
WE'RE IN REAL TROUBLE IF YOU RUN OUT OF STEAM BEFORE THE END.
NO PROBLEM.
BELIEVE IT OR NOT, I'VE BEEN RUNNING EVEN ON MY OFF DAYS.
IT'S TWUE. THIS BLOW-HAWD'S NOT LYING...
SHAHH
SLOW IT DOWN, BUDDY.
MORI-YAMA

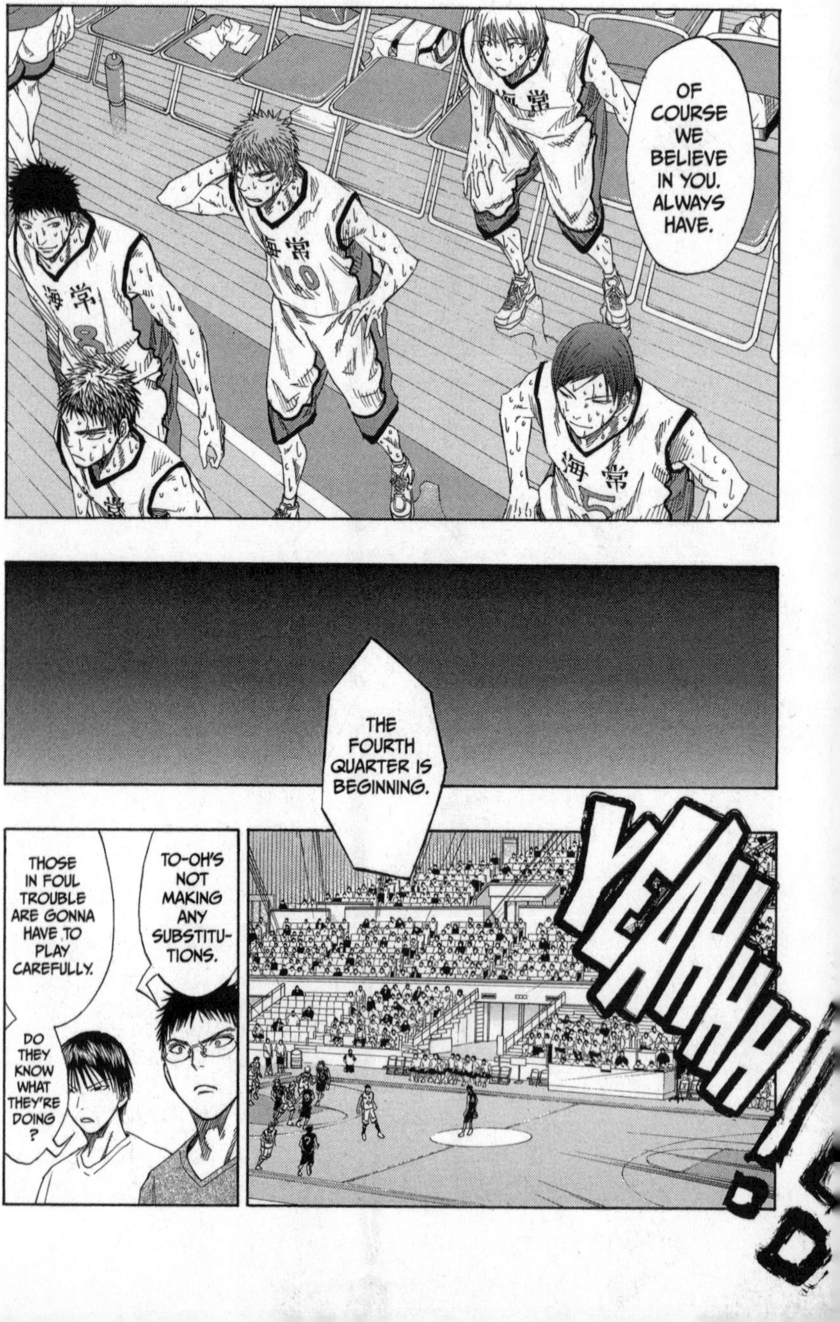
OF COURSE WE BELIEVE IN YOU. ALWAYS HAVE.
THE FOURTH QUARTER IS BEGINNING.
YEAHHH!!
TO-OH'S NOT MAKING ANY SUBSTITU-TIONS.
THOSE IN FOUL TROUBLE ARE GONNA HAVE TO PLAY CAREFULLY.
DO THEY KNOW WHAT THEY'RE DOING?

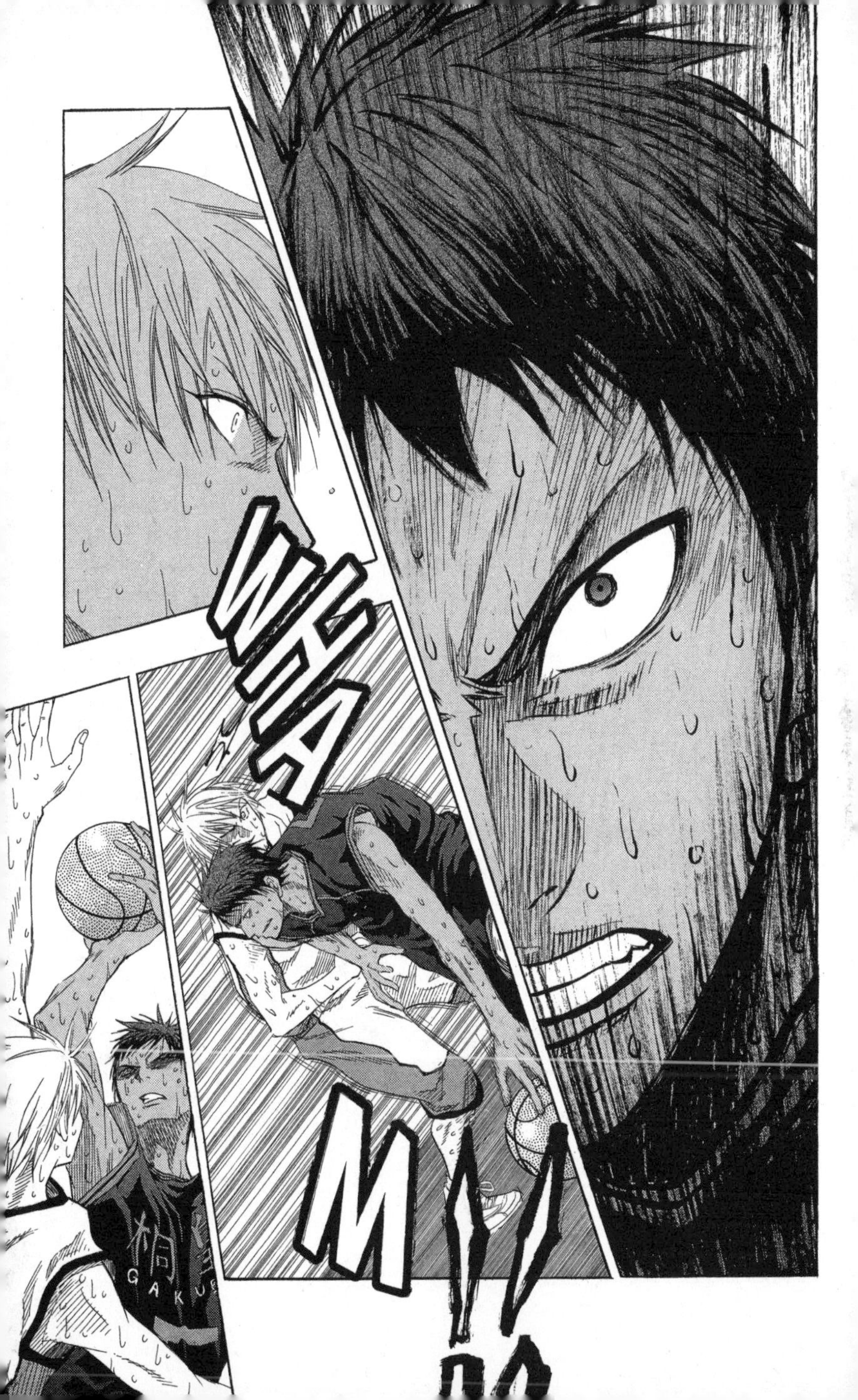
WHA
M
GAKU

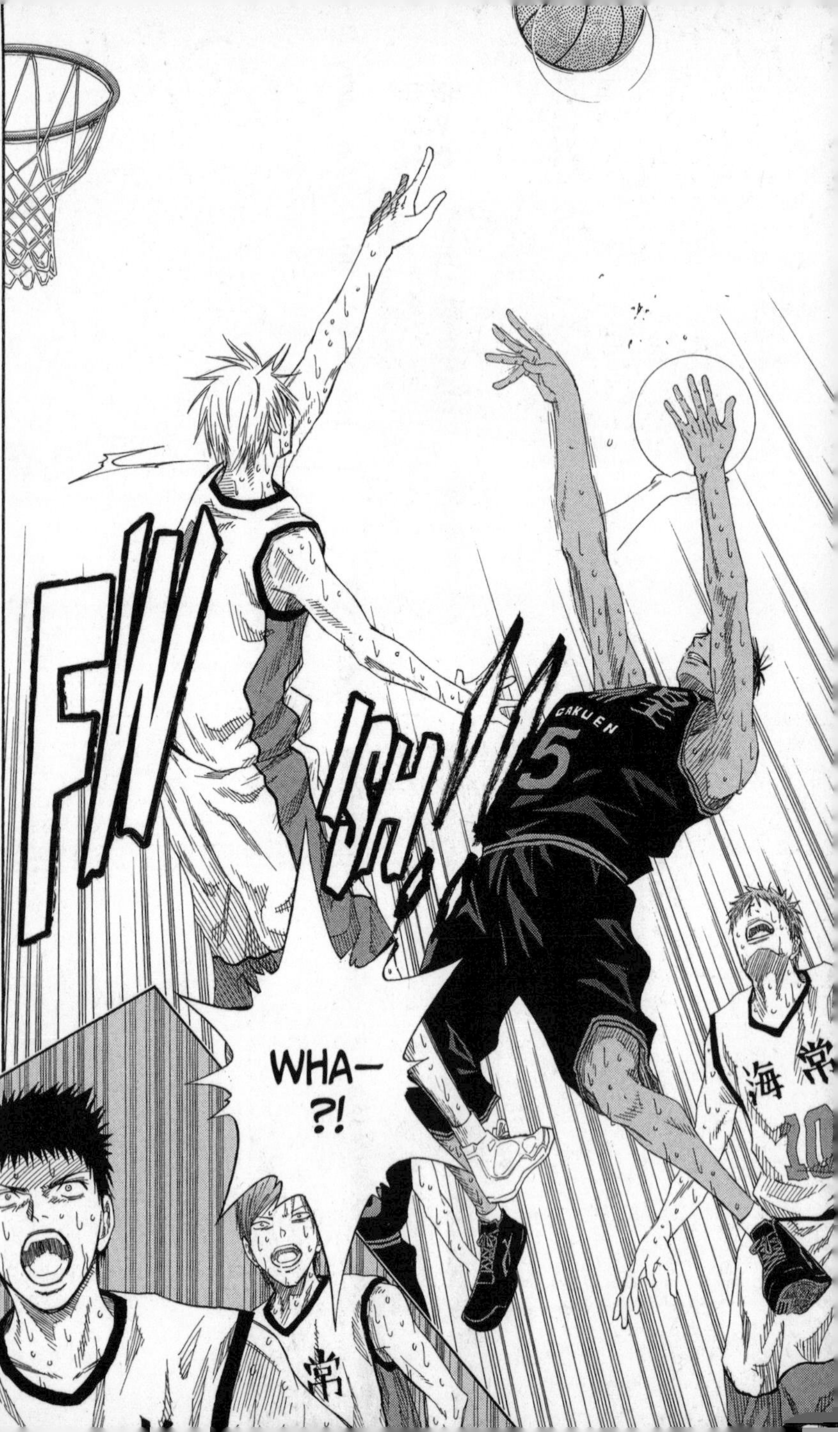
FWISH
WHA-
?!
GAKUEN
5
海常
10
常

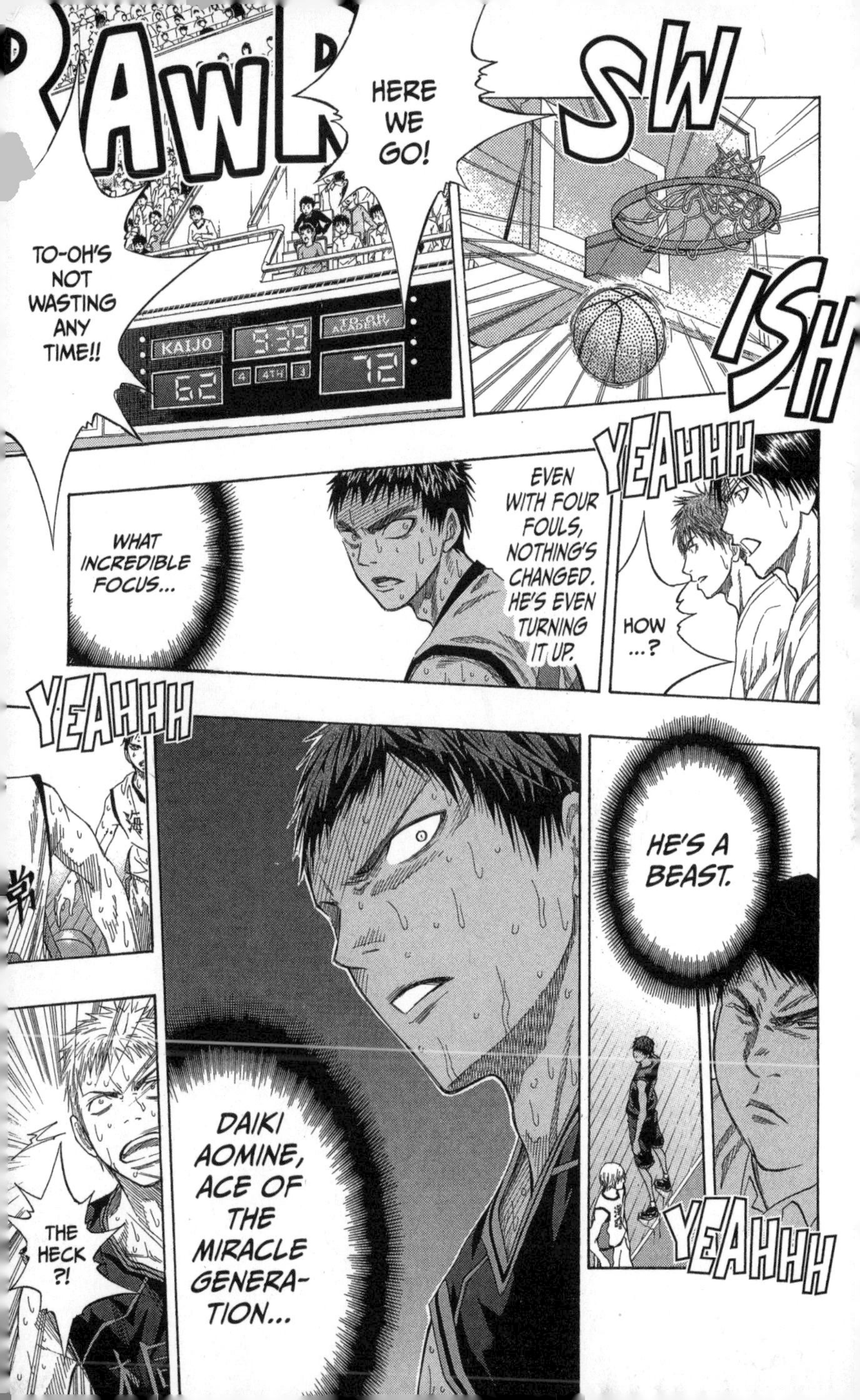
SW
ISH
HERE WE GO!
KAIJO
5:39
TO-OH ACADEMY
62
4TH
72
TO-OH'S NOT WASTING ANY TIME!!
YEAHHH
HOW ...?
EVEN WITH FOUR FOULS, NOTHING'S CHANGED. HE'S EVEN TURNING IT UP.
WHAT INCREDIBLE FOCUS...
HE'S A BEAST.
YEAHHH
DAIKI AOMINE, ACE OF THE MIRACLE GENERATION...
YEAHHH
THE HECK ?!

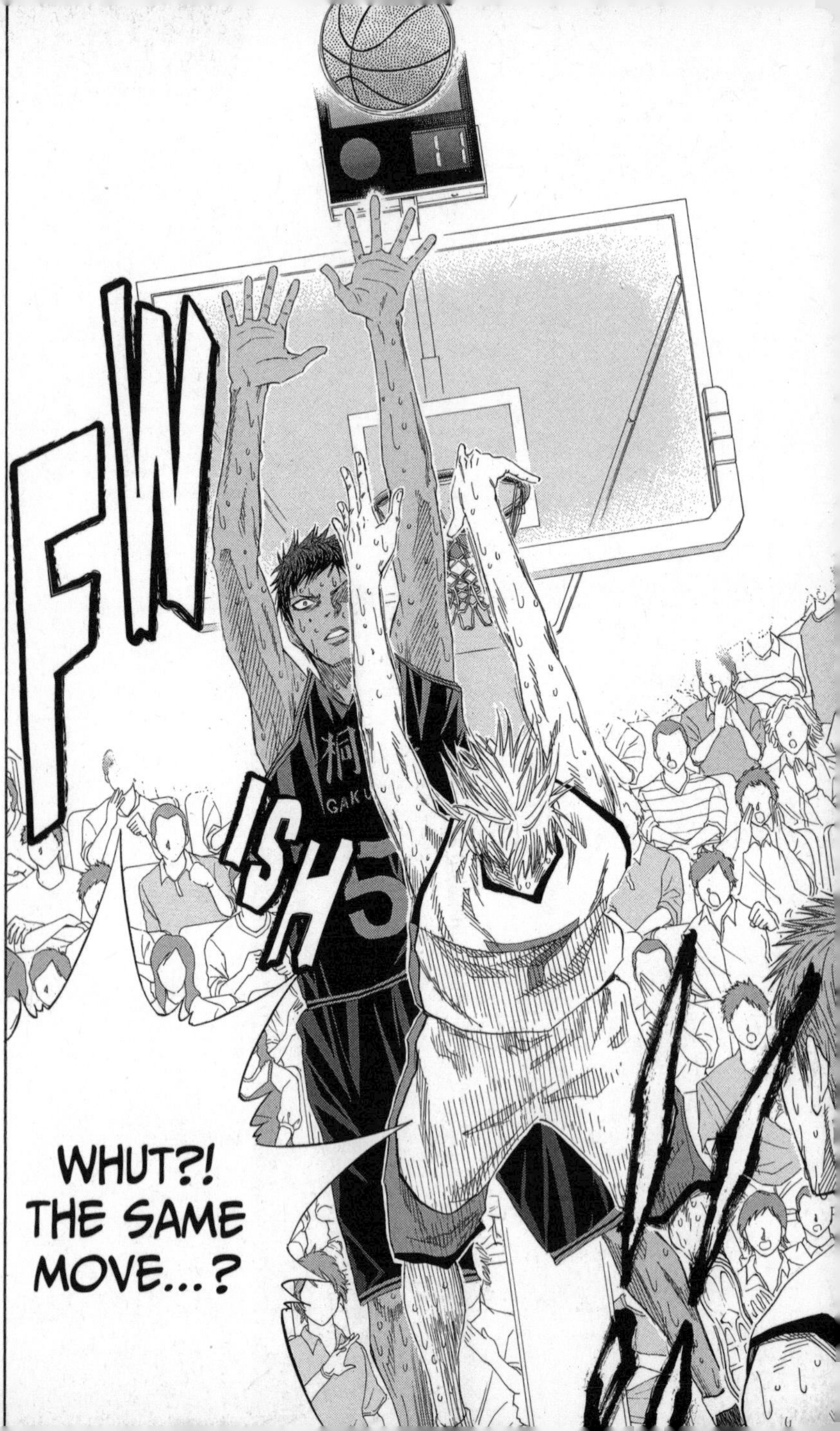
FWISH
WHUT?! THE SAME MOVE...?

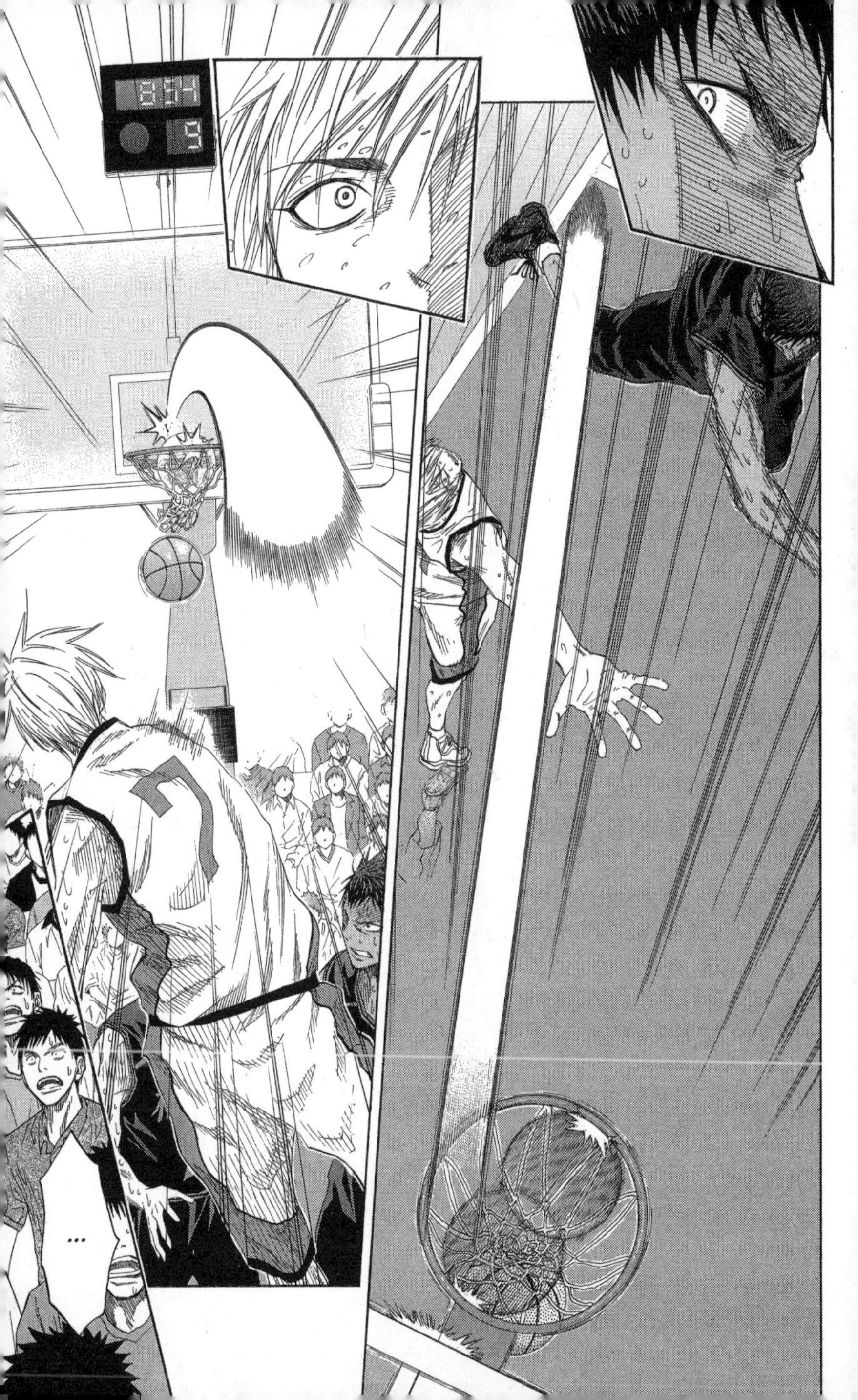
...

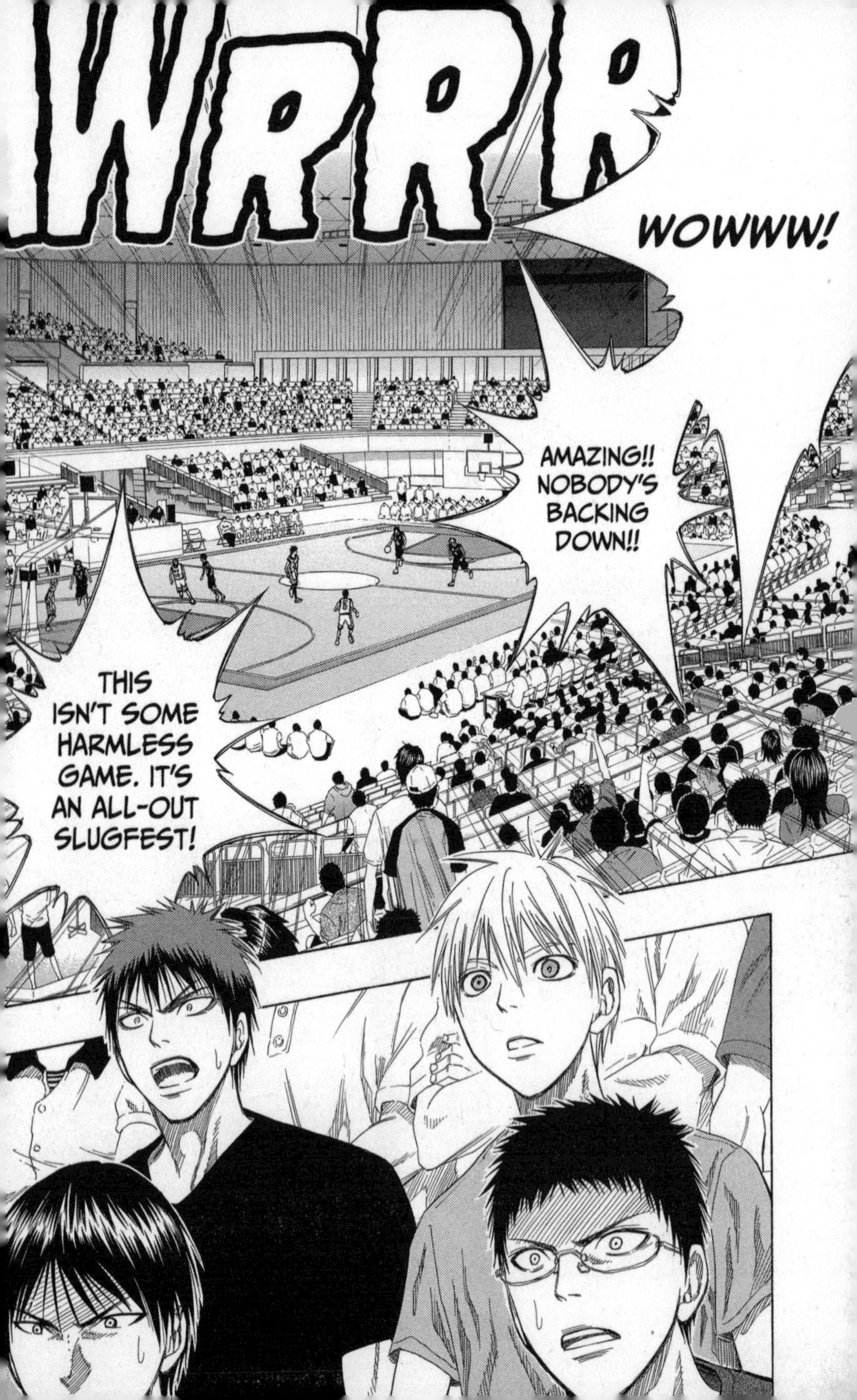
WRRR
WOWWW!
AMAZING!! NOBODY'S BACKING DOWN!!
THIS ISN'T SOME HARMLESS GAME. IT'S AN ALL-OUT SLUGFEST!

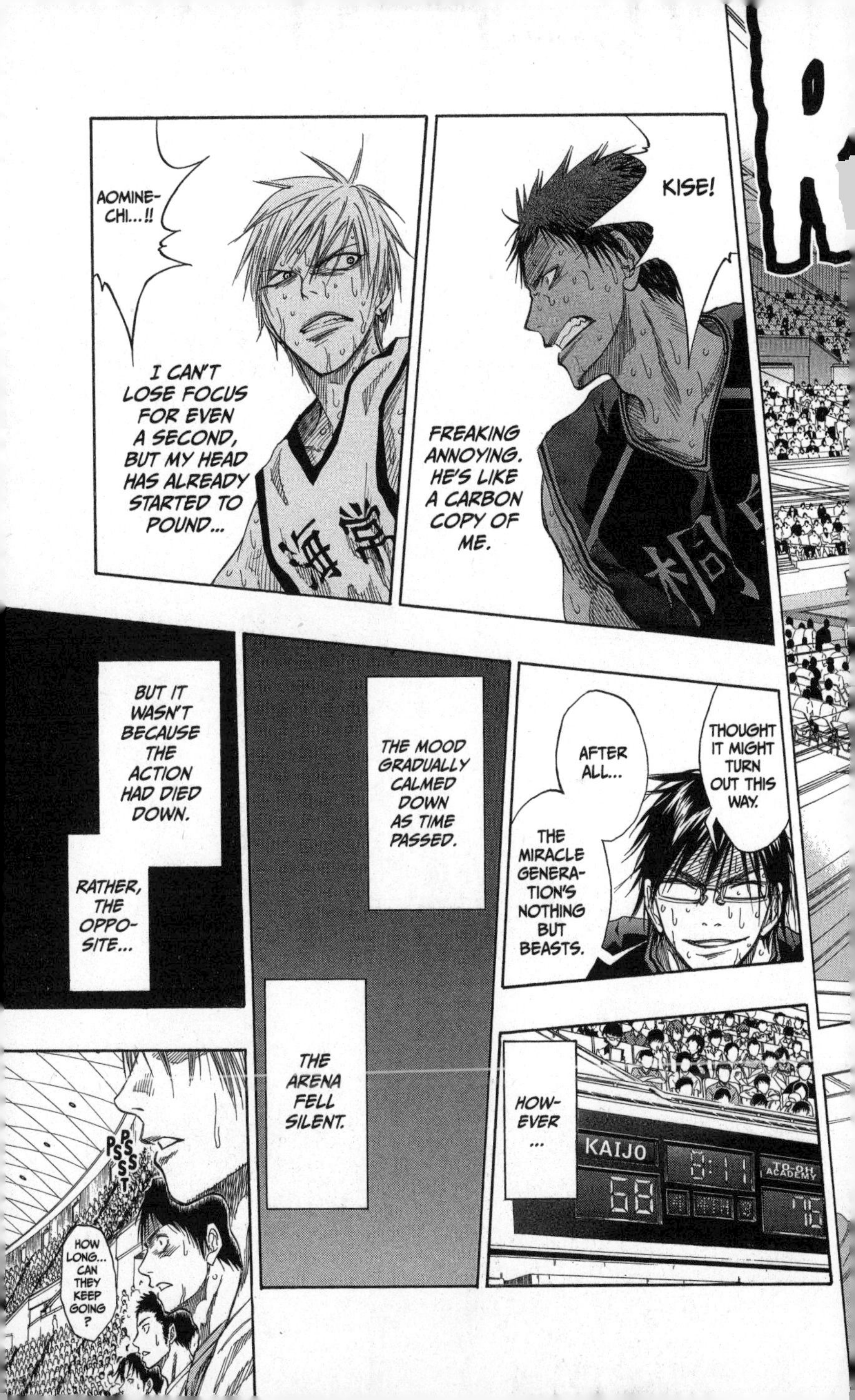
KISE!
FREAKING ANNOYING. HE'S LIKE A CARBON COPY OF ME.
AOMINE-CHI...!!
I CAN'T LOSE FOCUS FOR EVEN A SECOND, BUT MY HEAD HAS ALREADY STARTED TO POUND...
THOUGHT IT MIGHT TURN OUT THIS WAY.
AFTER ALL...
THE MIRACLE GENERATION'S NOTHING BUT BEASTS.
THE MOOD GRADUALLY CALMED DOWN AS TIME PASSED.
BUT IT WASN'T BECAUSE THE ACTION HAD DIED DOWN.
RATHER, THE OPPOSITE...
HOW-EVER...
KAIJO
TO-OH ACADEMY
THE ARENA FELL SILENT.
PSSST
HOW LONG... CAN THEY KEEP GOING?

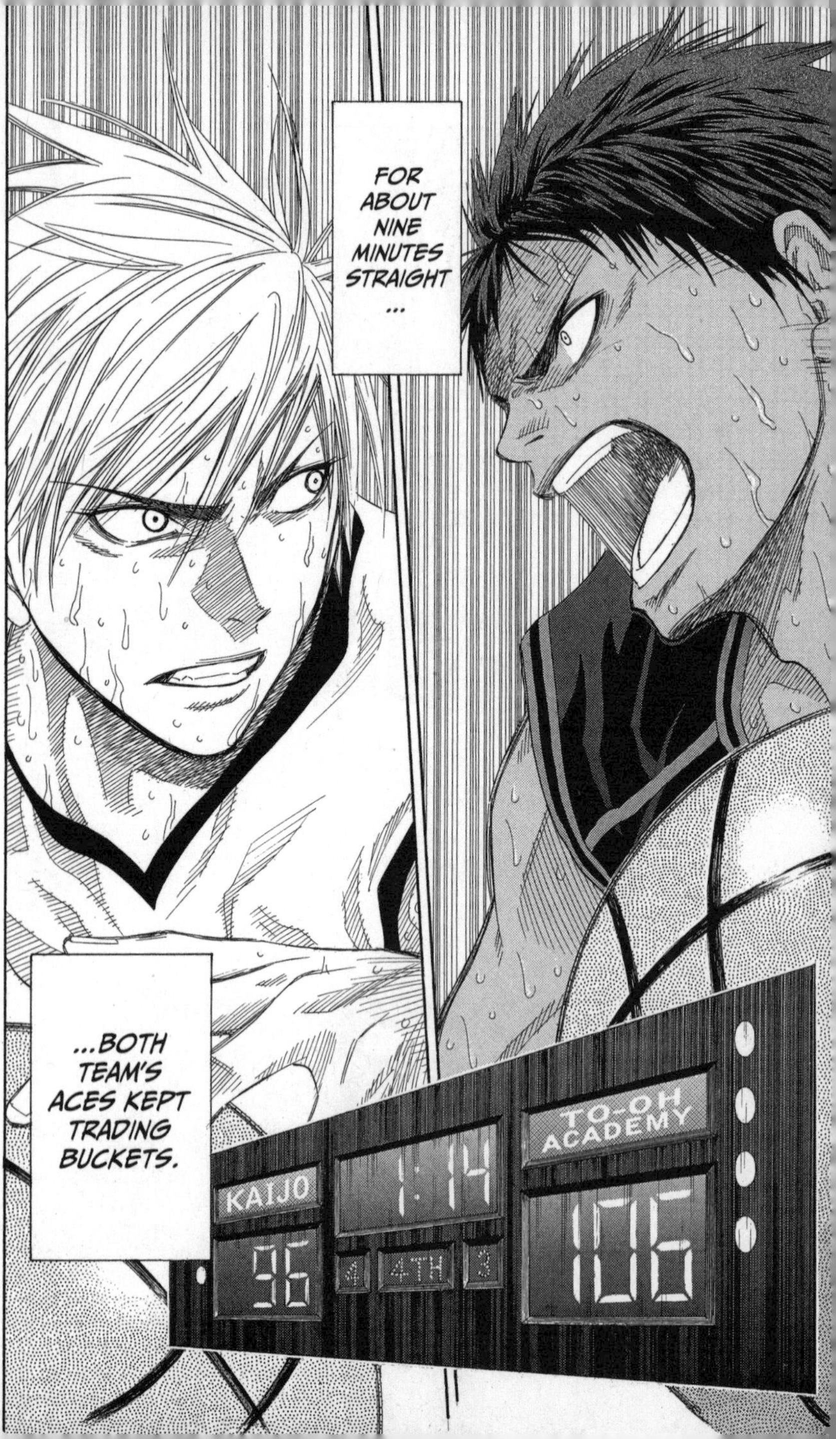
FOR ABOUT NINE MINUTES STRAIGHT ...
...BOTH TEAM'S ACES KEPT TRADING BUCKETS.
TO-OH ACADEMY
106
1:14
KAIJO
95
4
4TH
3

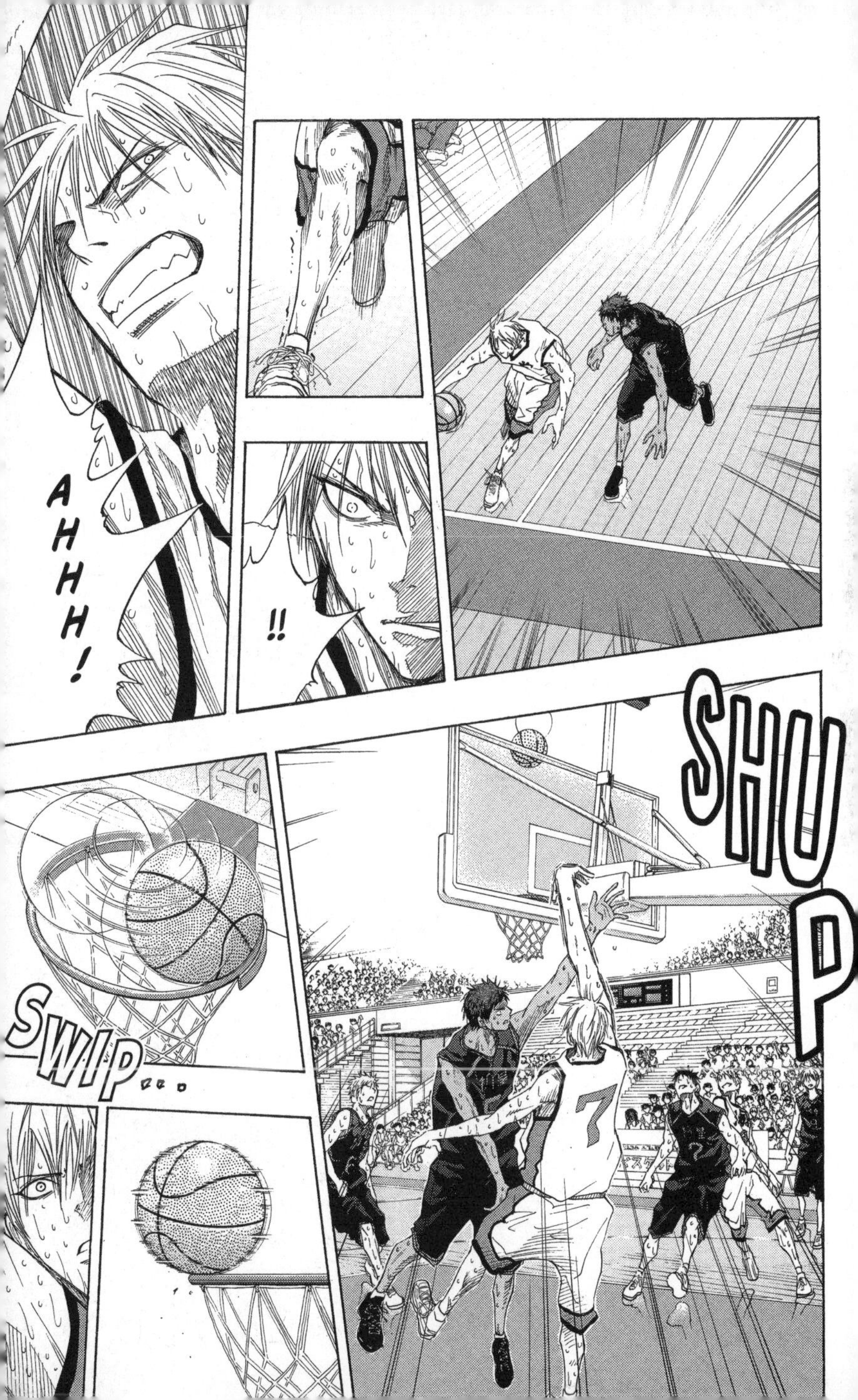
!!
AHHHH!
SHUP
SWIP...

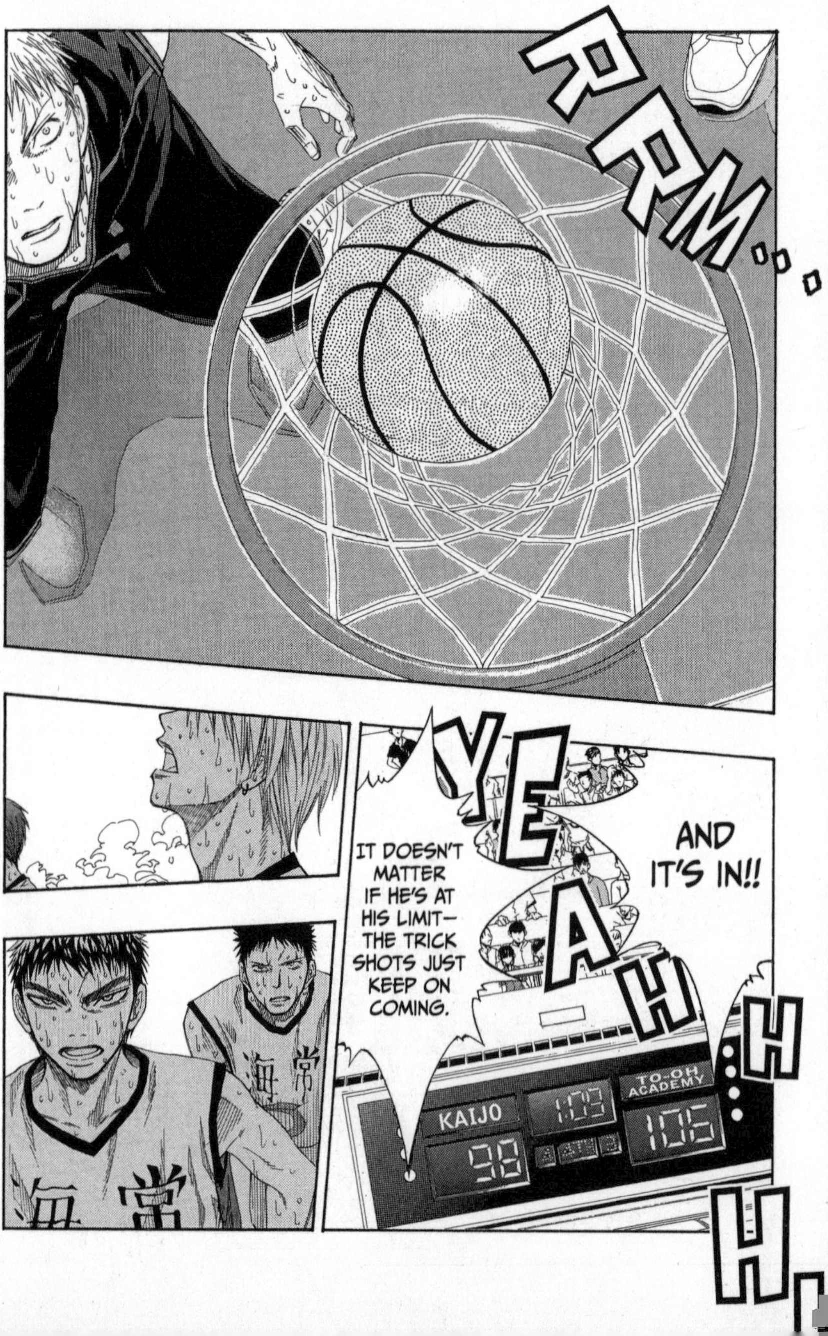
RRM...
AND IT'S IN!!
YEAHHHH!
IT DOESN'T MATTER IF HE'S AT HIS LIMIT—THE TRICK SHOTS JUST KEEP ON COMING.
TO-OH ACADEMY
1:03
106
KAIJO
98

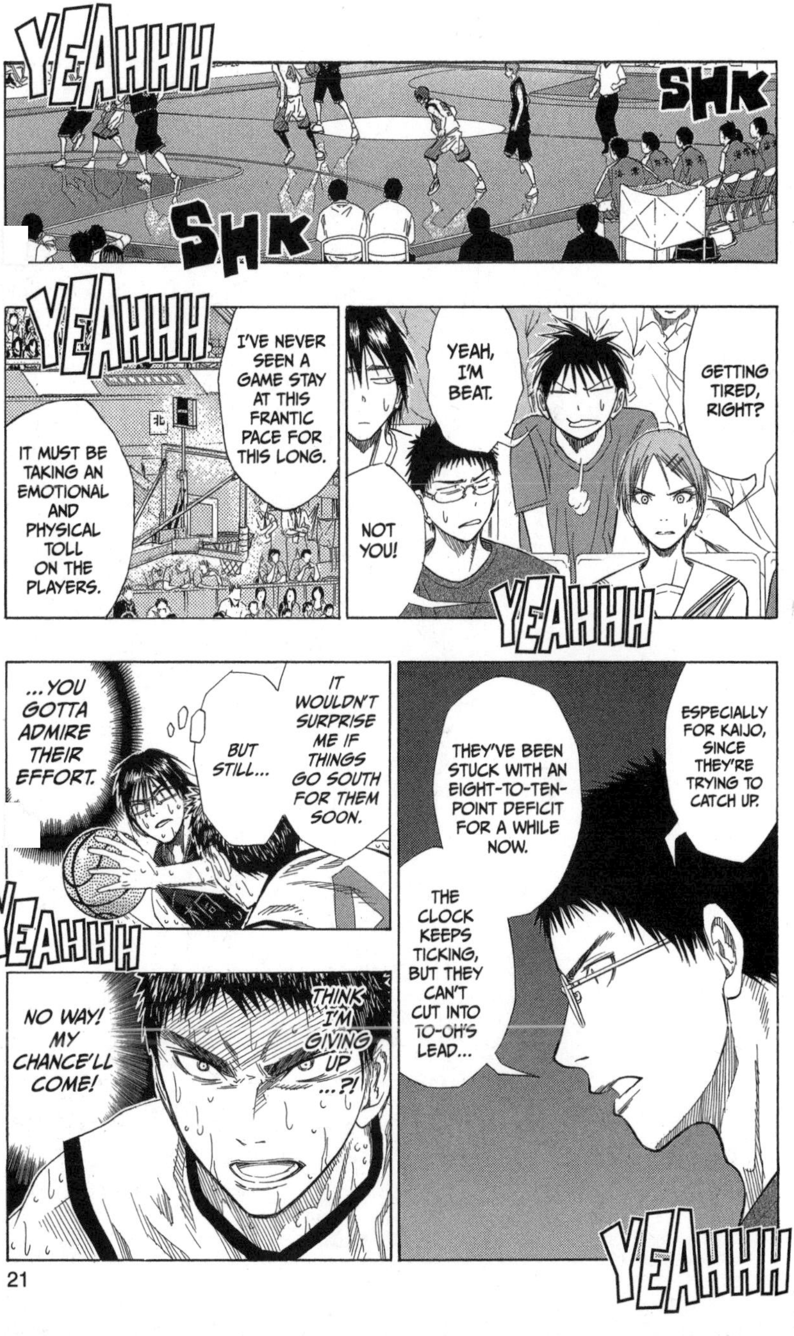
YEAHHH
SHK
SHK
GETTING TIRED, RIGHT?
YEAH, I'M BEAT.
NOT YOU!
YEAHHH
I'VE NEVER SEEN A GAME STAY AT THIS FRANTIC PACE FOR THIS LONG.
IT MUST BE TAKING AN EMOTIONAL AND PHYSICAL TOLL ON THE PLAYERS.
YEAHHH
ESPECIALLY FOR KAIJO, SINCE THEY'RE TRYING TO CATCH UP.
THEY'VE BEEN STUCK WITH AN EIGHT-TO-TEN-POINT DEFICIT FOR A WHILE NOW.
THE CLOCK KEEPS TICKING, BUT THEY CAN'T CUT INTO TO-OH'S LEAD...
YEAHHH
IT WOULDN'T SURPRISE ME IF THINGS GO SOUTH FOR THEM SOON.
BUT STILL...
...YOU GOTTA ADMIRE THEIR EFFORT.
YEAHHH
THINK I'M GIVING UP ...?!
NO WAY! MY CHANCE'LL COME!

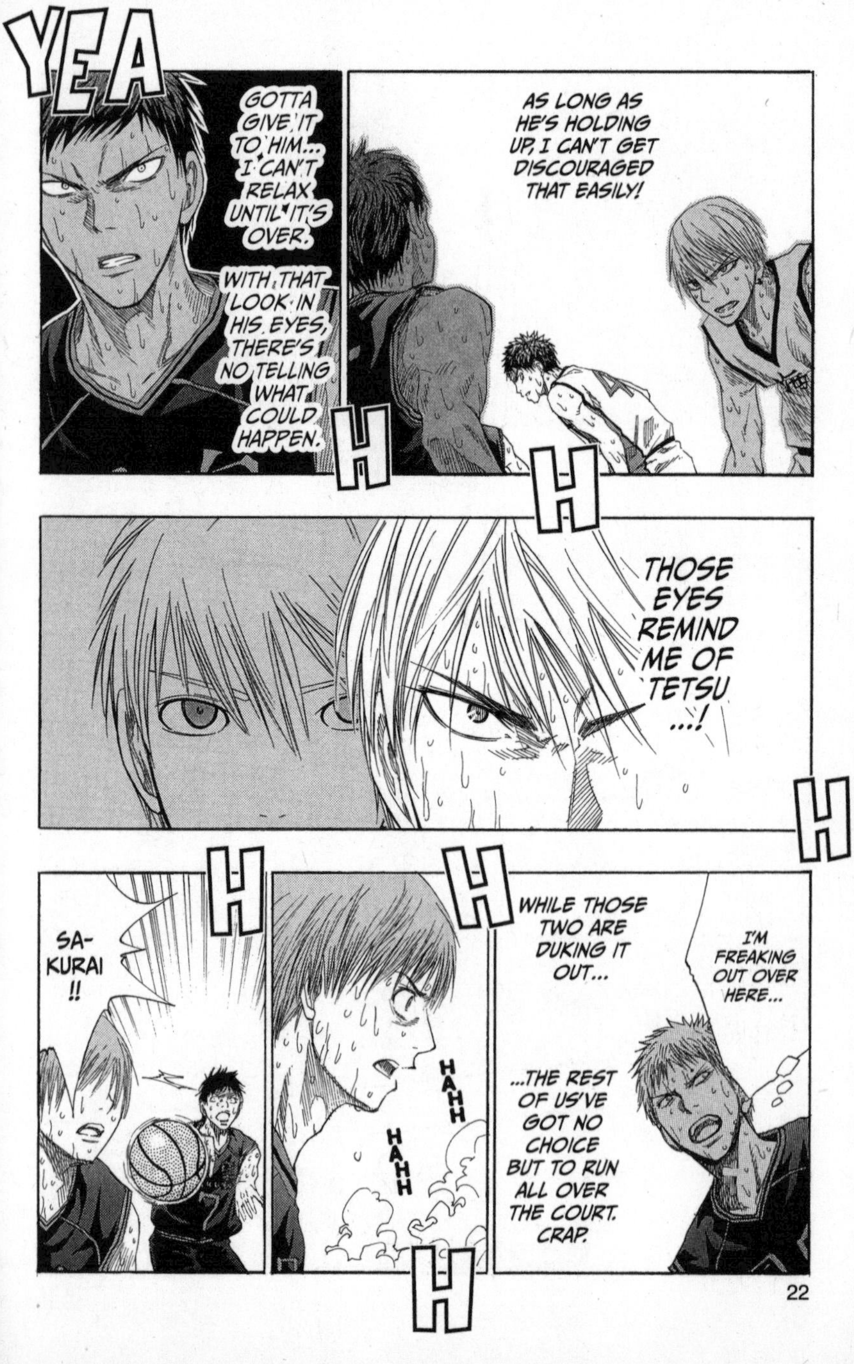
YEA
AS LONG AS HE'S HOLDING UP, I CAN'T GET DISCOURAGED THAT EASILY!
GOTTA GIVE IT TO HIM... I CAN'T RELAX UNTIL IT'S OVER.
WITH THAT LOOK IN HIS EYES, THERE'S NO TELLING WHAT COULD HAPPEN.
H
H
THOSE EYES REMIND ME OF TETSU ...!
H
H
H
WHILE THOSE TWO ARE DUKING IT OUT...
I'M FREAKING OUT OVER HERE...
...THE REST OF US'VE GOT NO CHOICE BUT TO RUN ALL OVER THE COURT. CRAP.
HAHH
HAHH
H
SA-KURAI !!

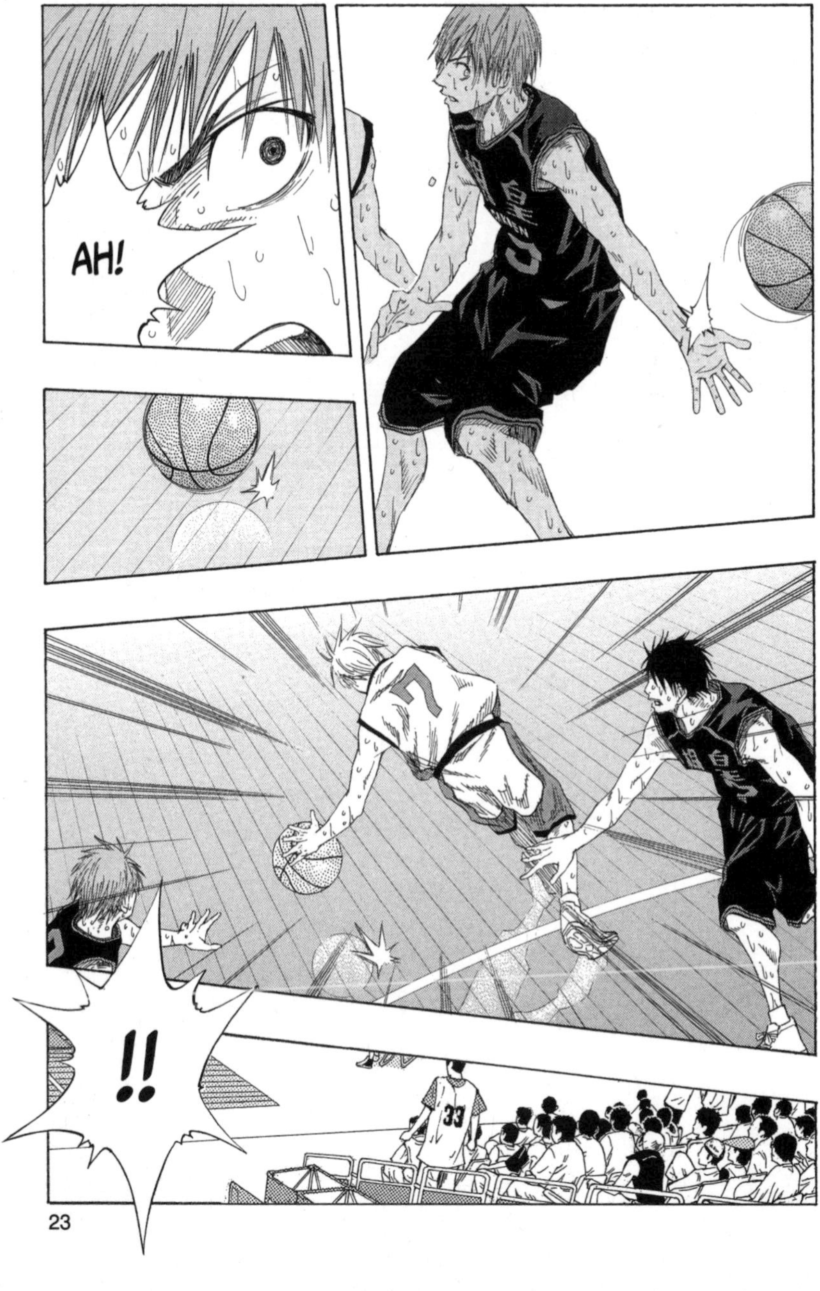
AH!
!!

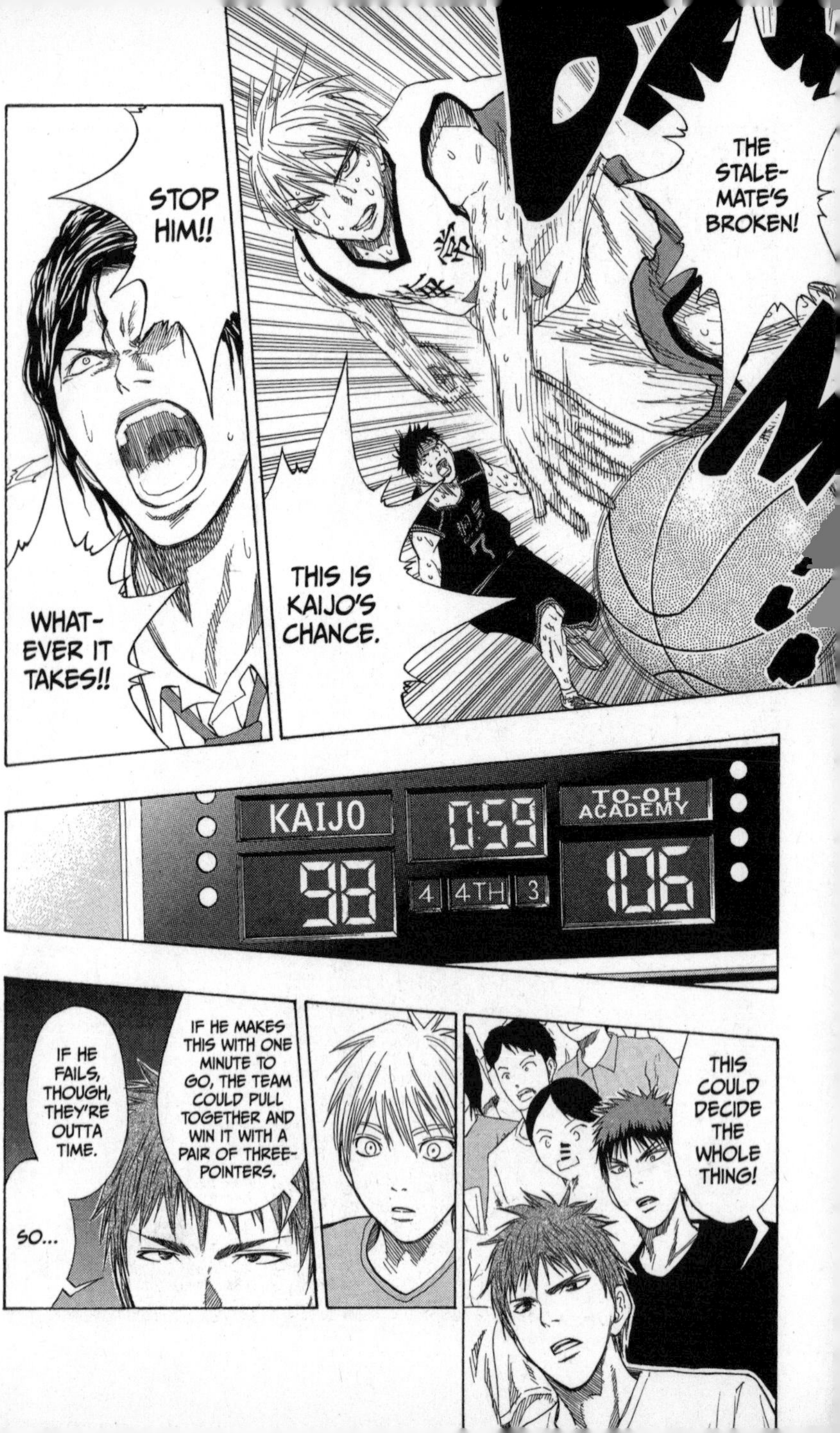
THE STALE-MATE'S BROKEN!
THIS IS KAIJO'S CHANCE.
STOP HIM!!
WHAT-EVER IT TAKES!!
TO-OH ACADEMY
0:59
KAIJO
106
3
4TH
4
98
THIS COULD DECIDE THE WHOLE THING!
IF HE MAKES THIS WITH ONE MINUTE TO GO, THE TEAM COULD PULL TOGETHER AND WIN IT WITH A PAIR OF THREE-POINTERS.
IF HE FAILS, THOUGH, THEY'RE OUTTA TIME.
SO...

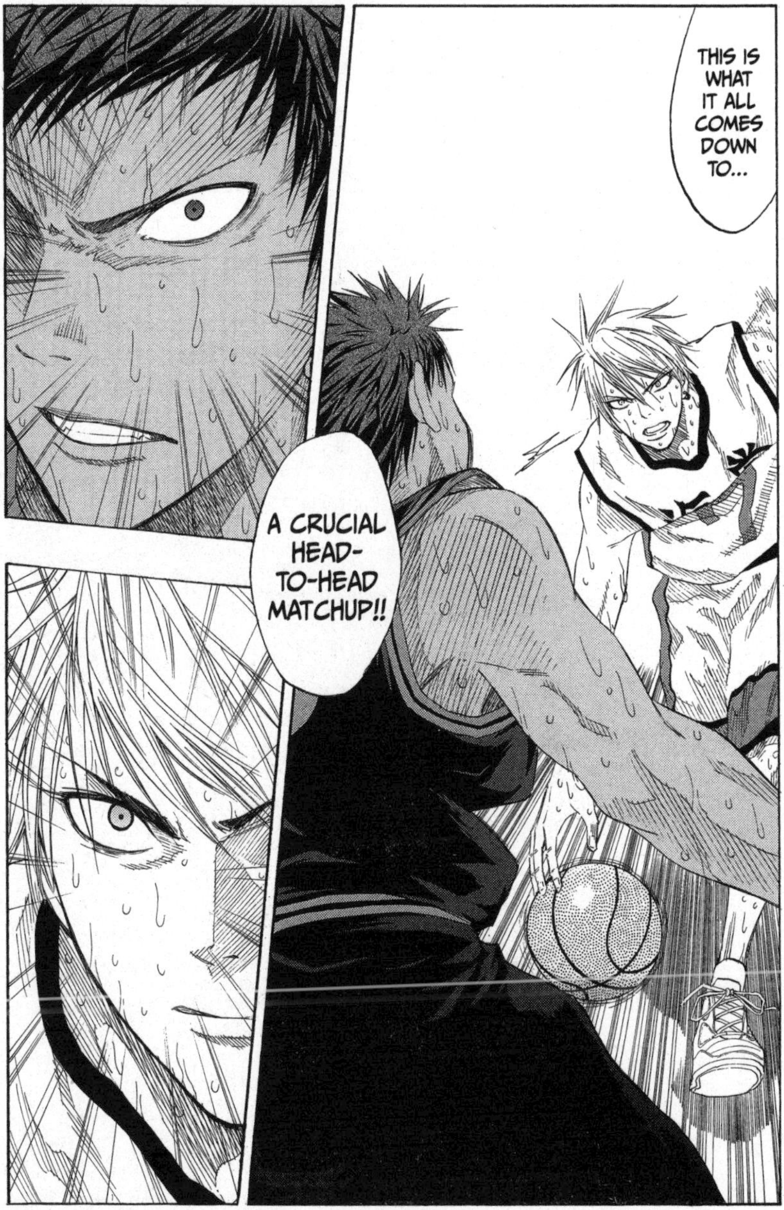
THIS IS WHAT IT ALL COMES DOWN TO...
A CRUCIAL HEAD-TO-HEAD MATCHUP!!

KUROKO'S BASKETBALL BLOOPERS TAKE 11

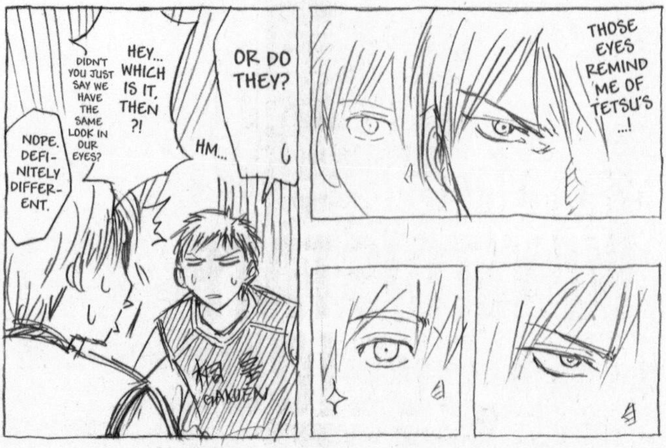
THOSE EYES REMIND ME OF TETSU'S ...!
OR DO THEY?
HM...
HEY... WHICH IS IT, THEN ?!
DIDN'T YOU JUST SAY WE HAVE THE SAME LOOK IN OUR EYES?
NOPE. DEFINITELY DIFFERENT.
GAKUEN

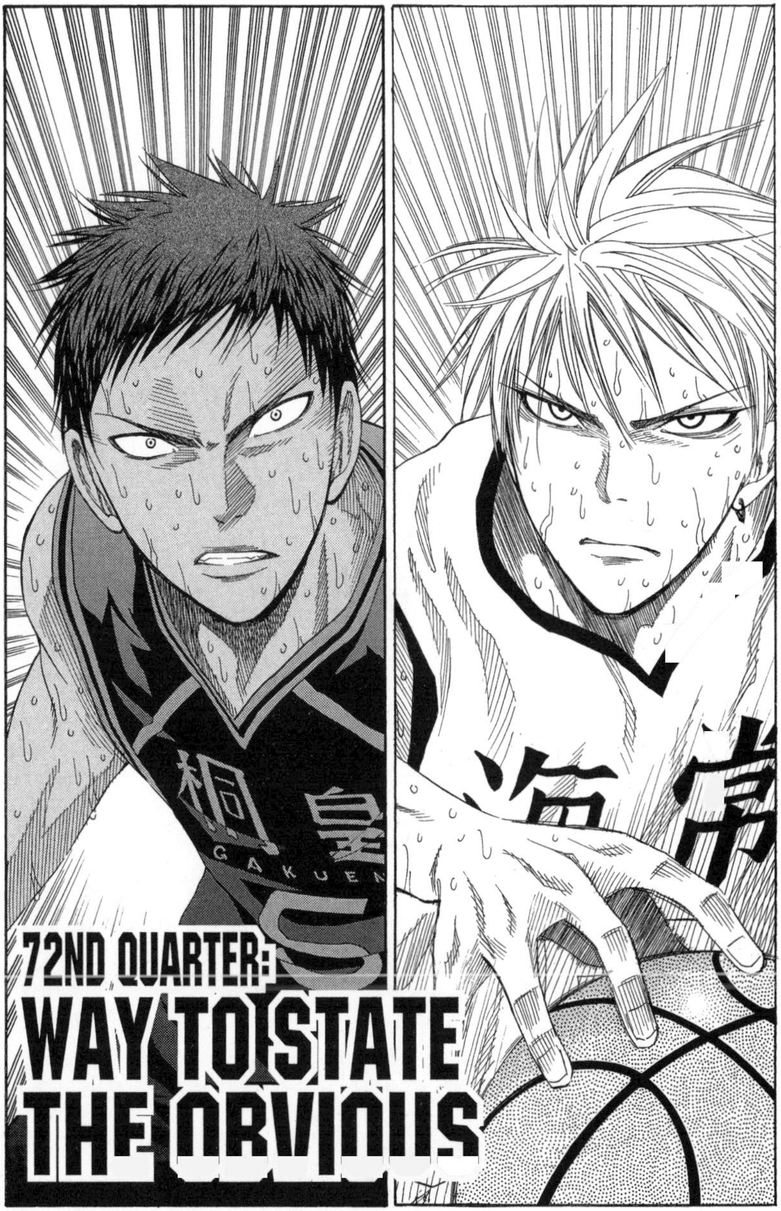
海常
桐皇
GAKUEN

72ND QUARTER: WAY TO STATE THE OBVIOUS

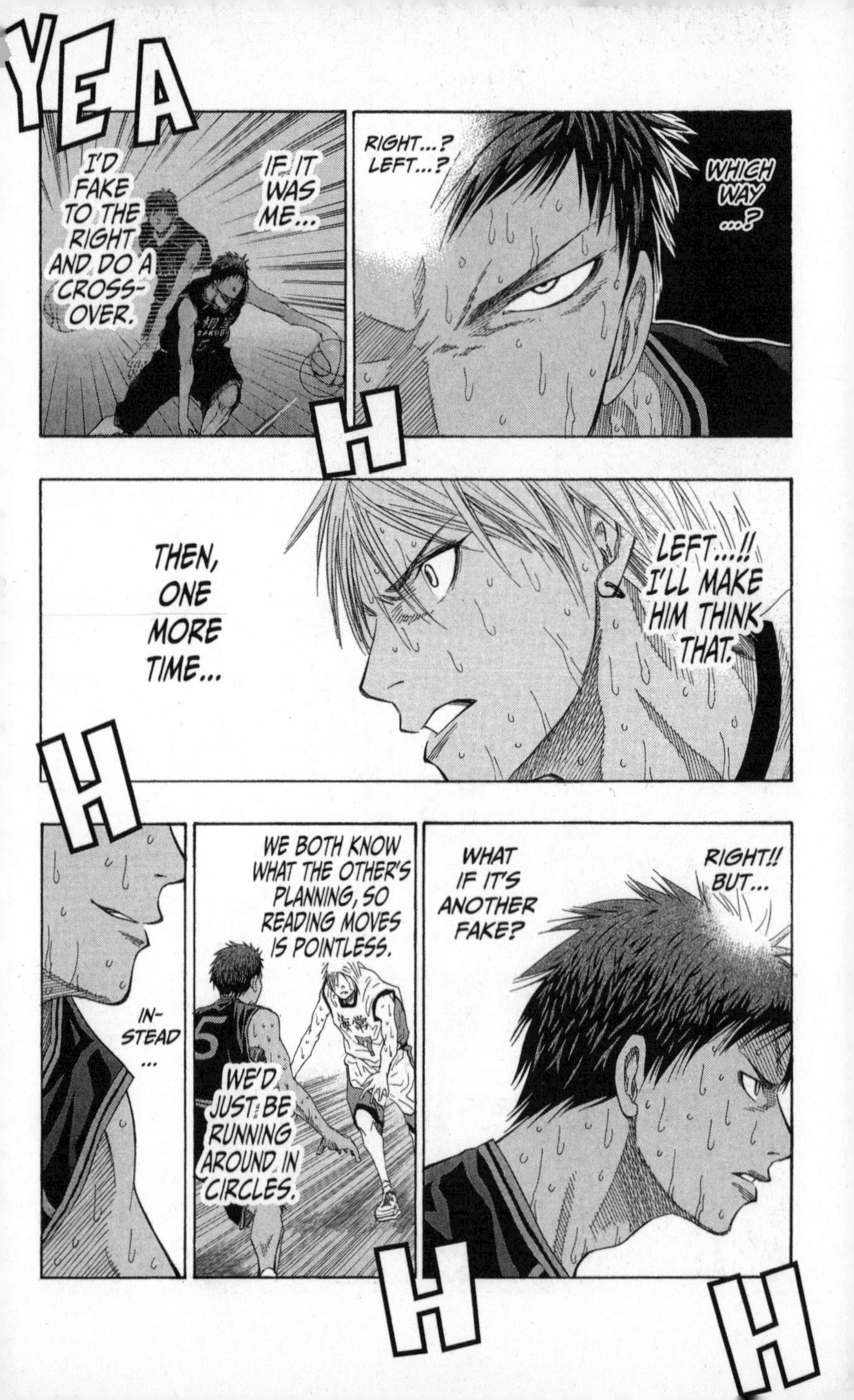
YEA
WHICH WAY ...?
RIGHT...? LEFT...?
IF IT WAS ME...
I'D FAKE TO THE RIGHT AND DO A CROSSOVER.
H
LEFT...!! I'LL MAKE HIM THINK THAT.
THEN, ONE MORE TIME...
H
RIGHT!! BUT...
WHAT IF IT'S ANOTHER FAKE?
WE BOTH KNOW WHAT THE OTHER'S PLANNING, SO READING MOVES IS POINTLESS.
WE'D JUST BE RUNNING AROUND IN CIRCLES.
INSTEAD...
H
H

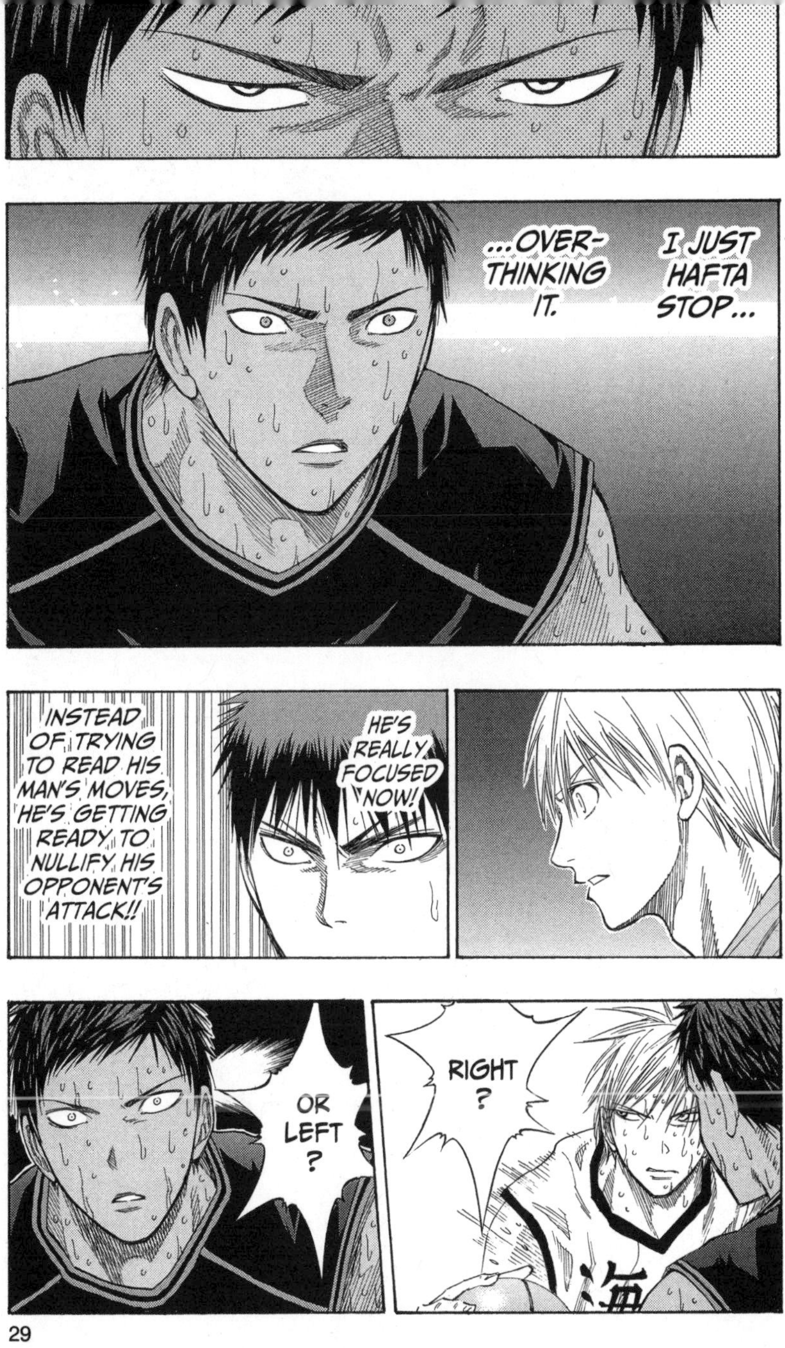
I JUST HAFTA STOP...
...OVER-THINKING IT.
HE'S REALLY FOCUSED NOW!
INSTEAD OF TRYING TO READ HIS MAN'S MOVES, HE'S GETTING READY TO NULLIFY HIS OPPONENT'S ATTACK!!
RIGHT?
OR LEFT?

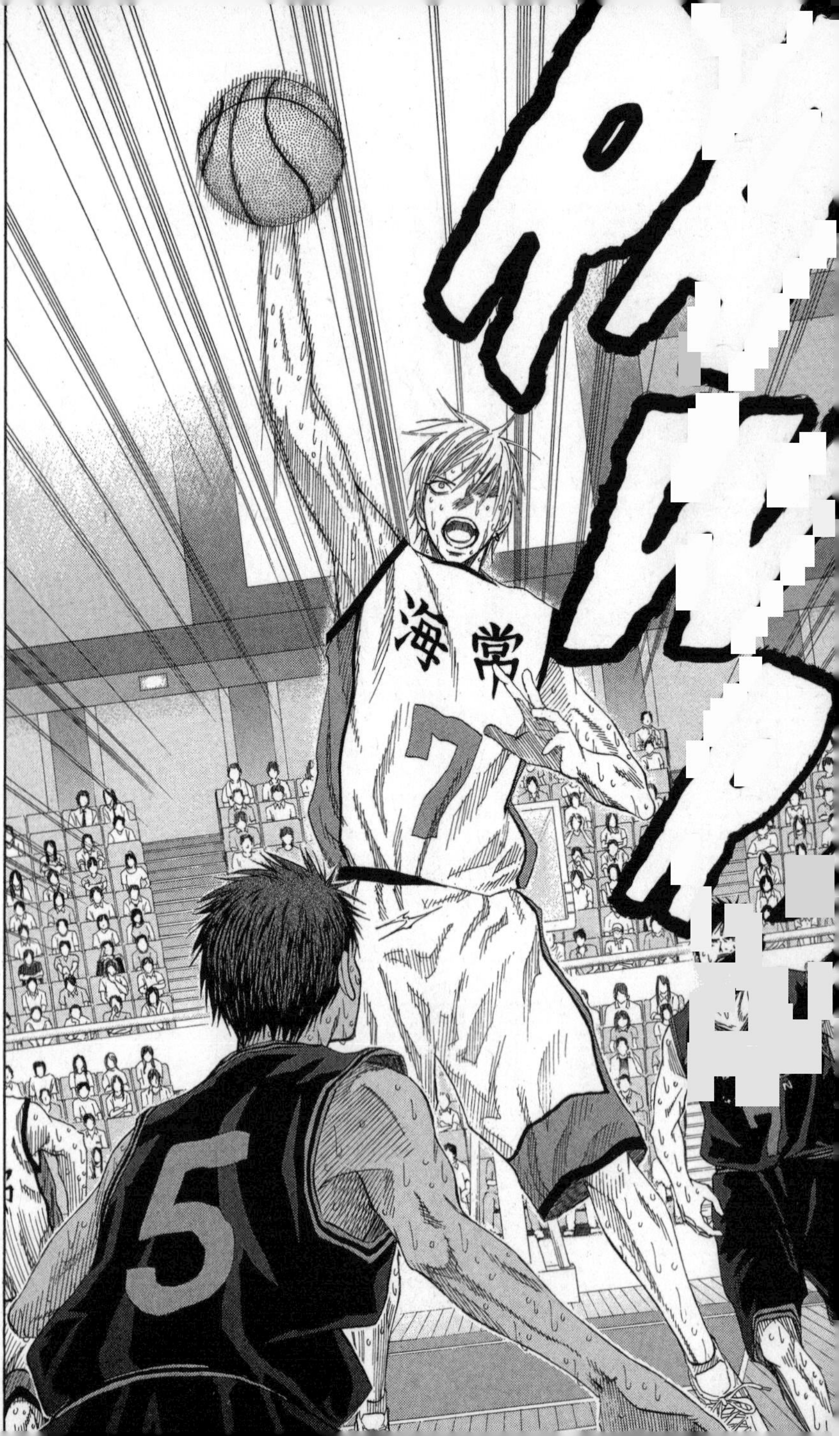
海常

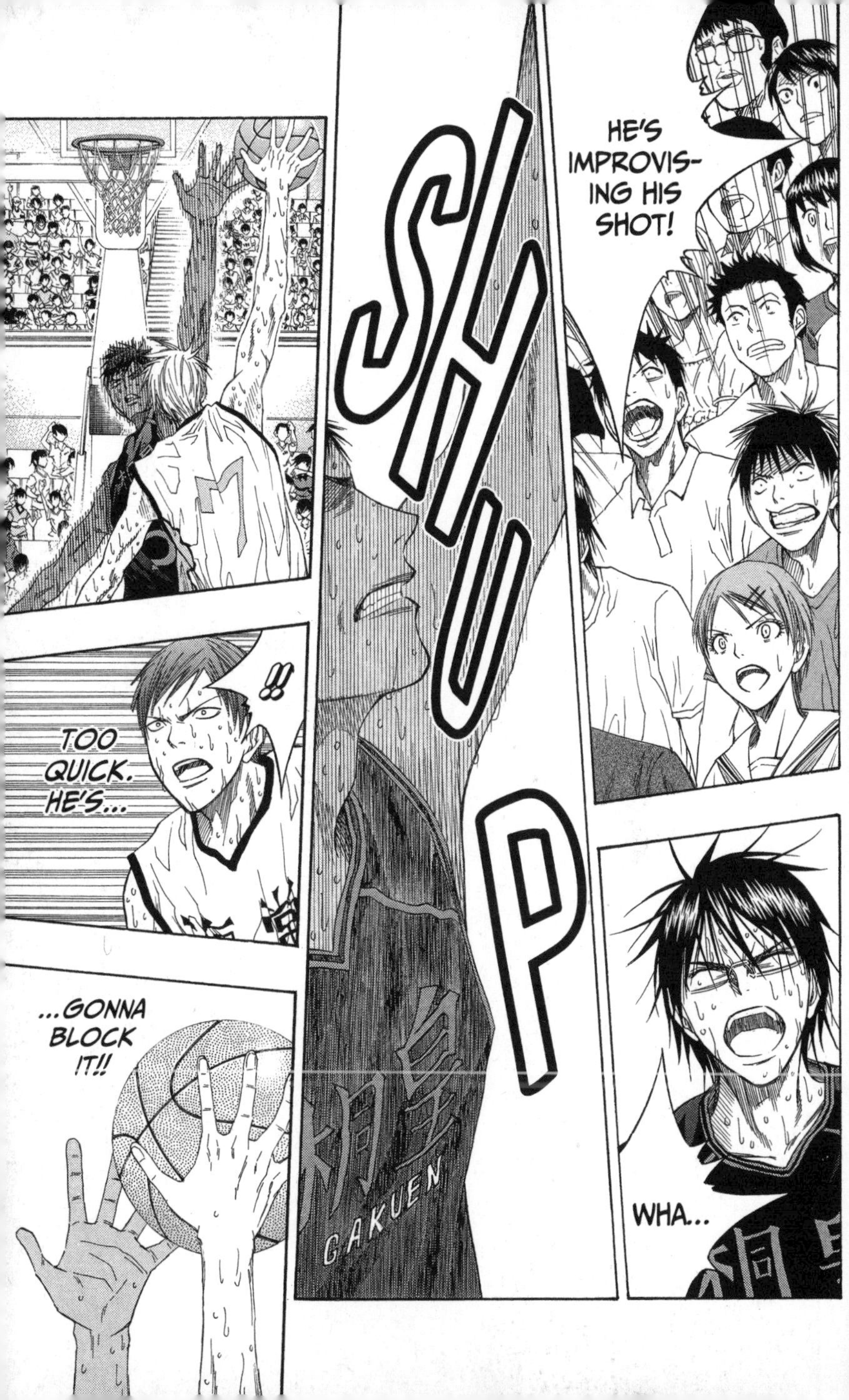
HE'S IMPROVIS-ING HIS SHOT!
WHA...
SHUP
GAKUEN
!!
TOO QUICK. HE'S...
...GONNA BLOCK IT!!

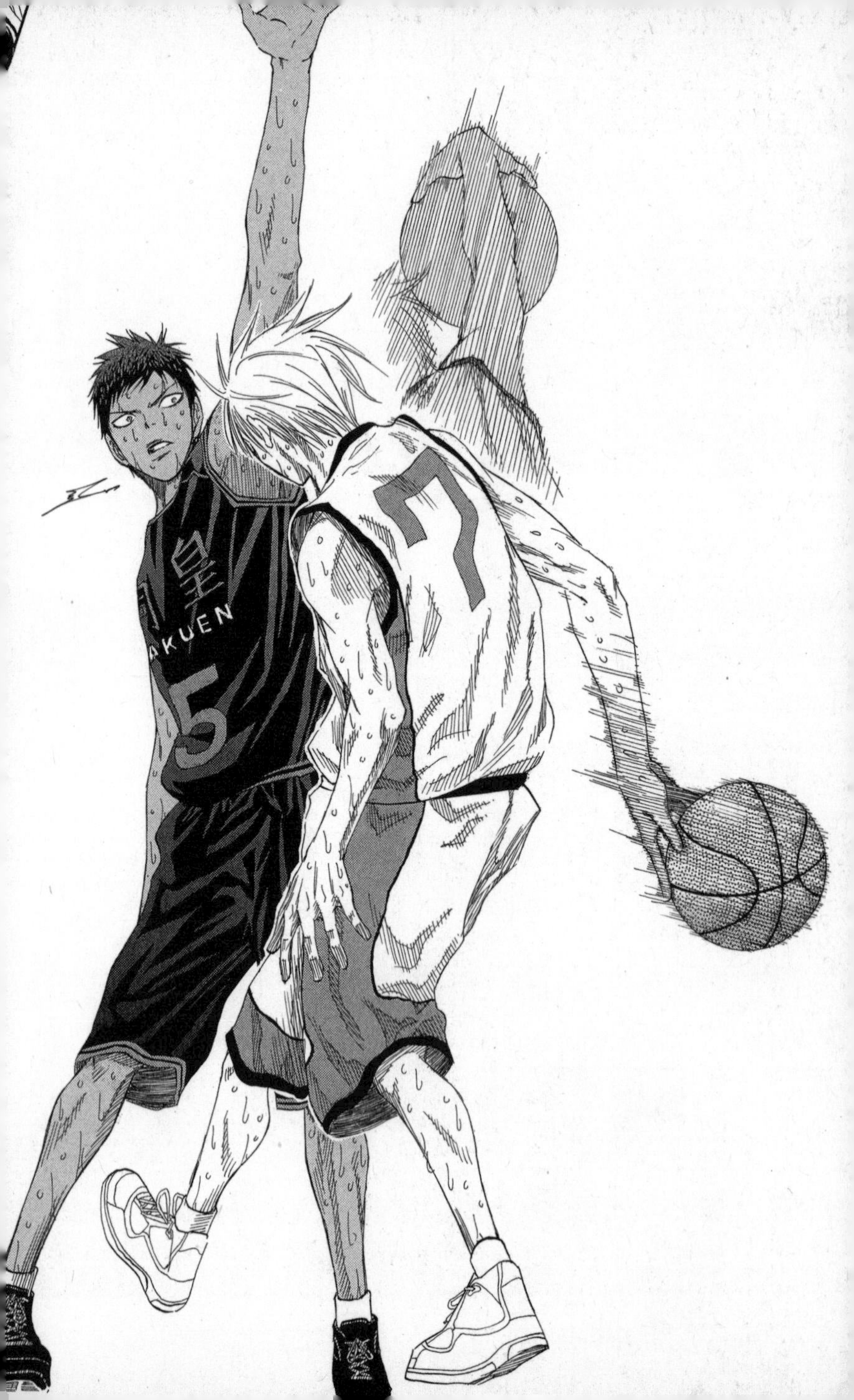
皇
AKUEN

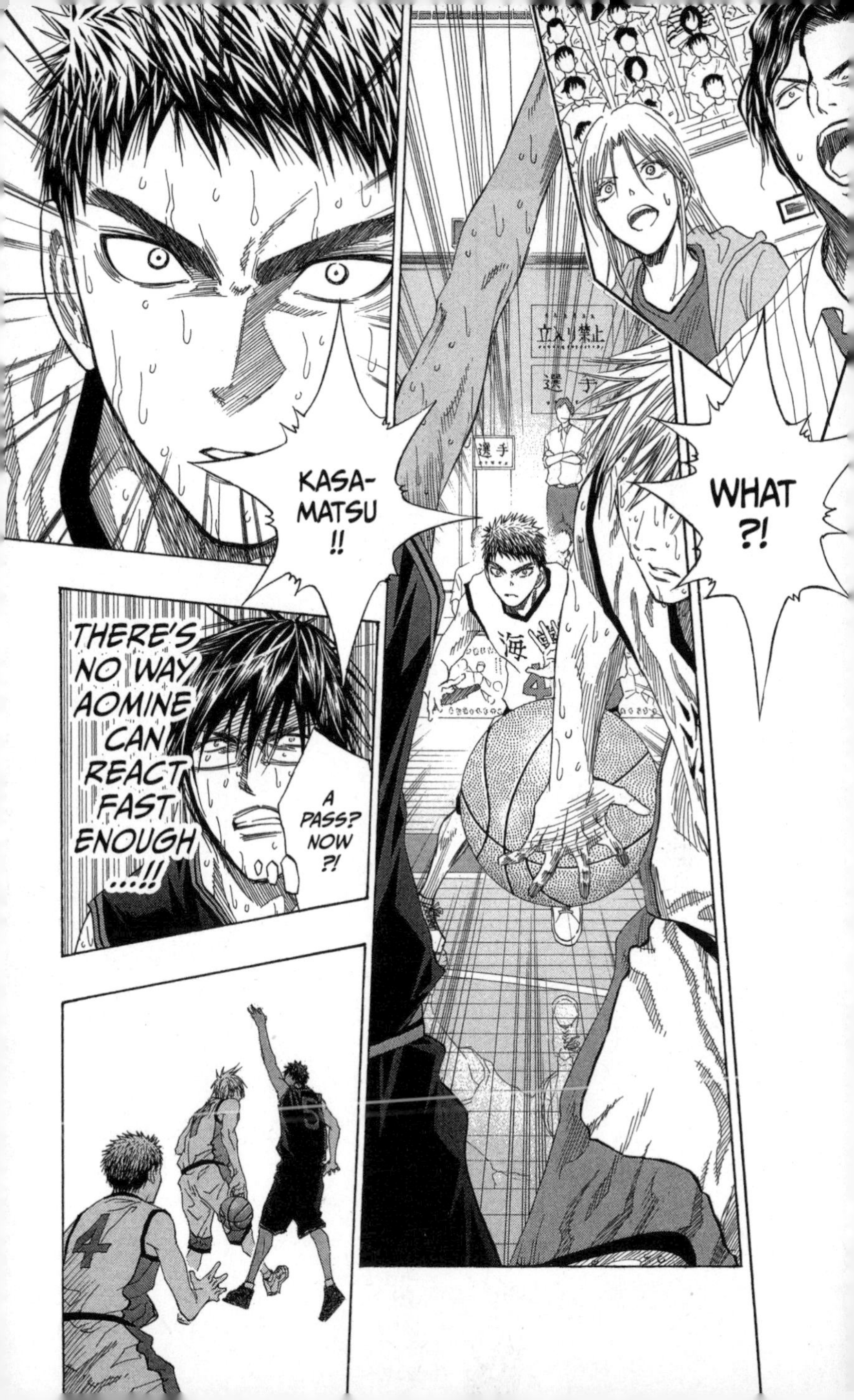
WHAT ?!
立入り禁止
選手
KASA-MATSU !!
A PASS? NOW ?!
THERE'S NO WAY AOMINE CAN REACT FAST ENOUGH ...!!

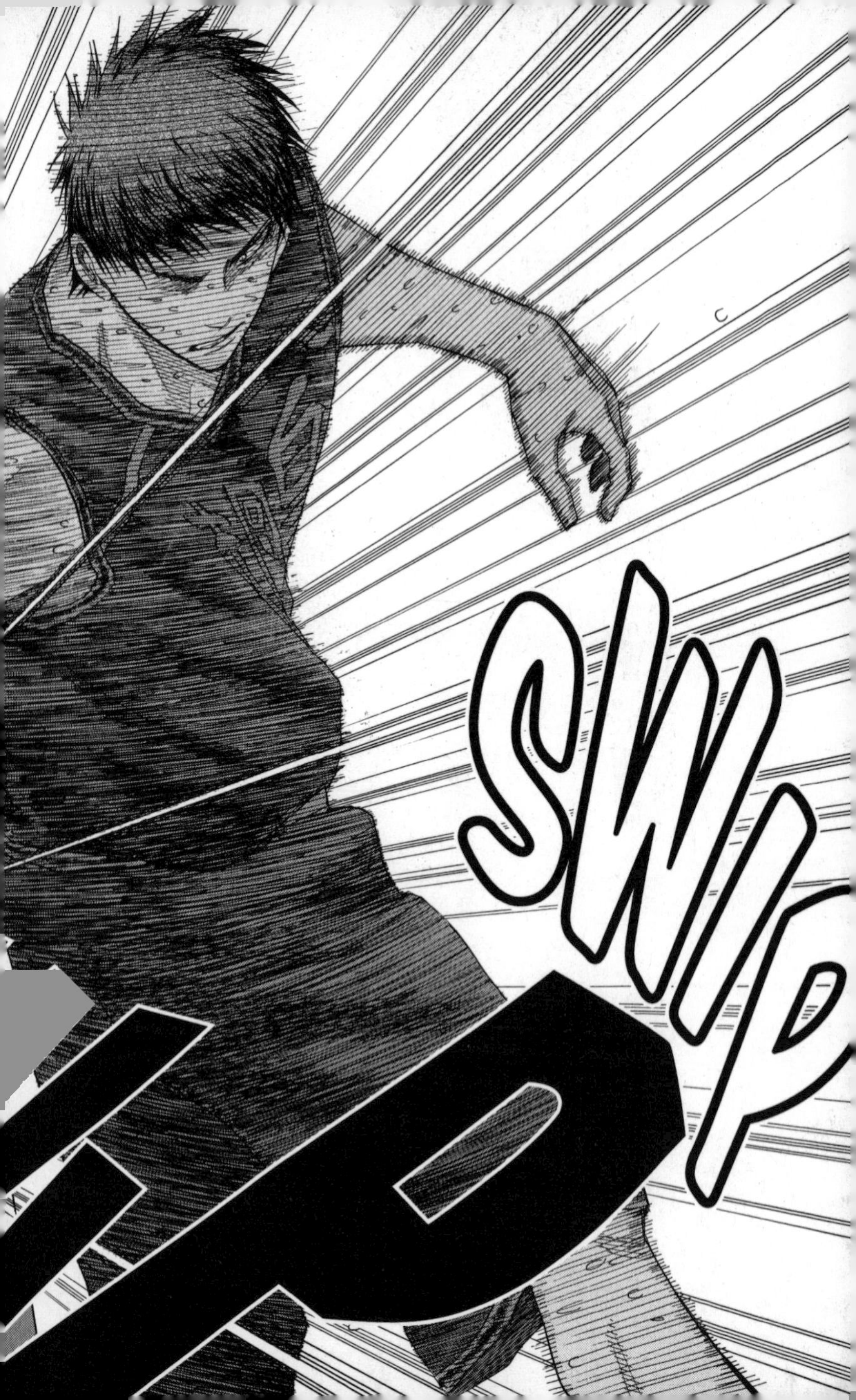
SWIP

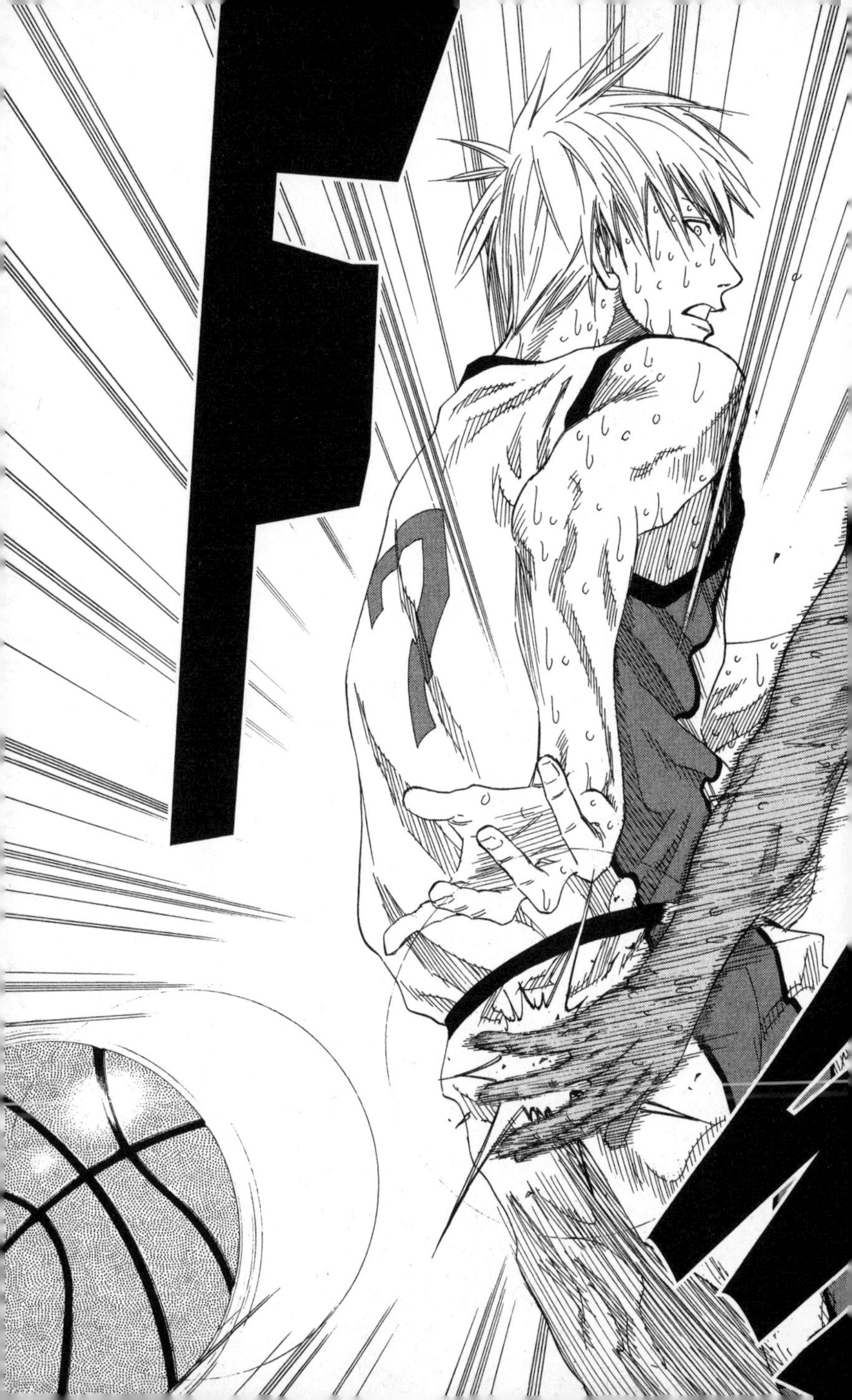

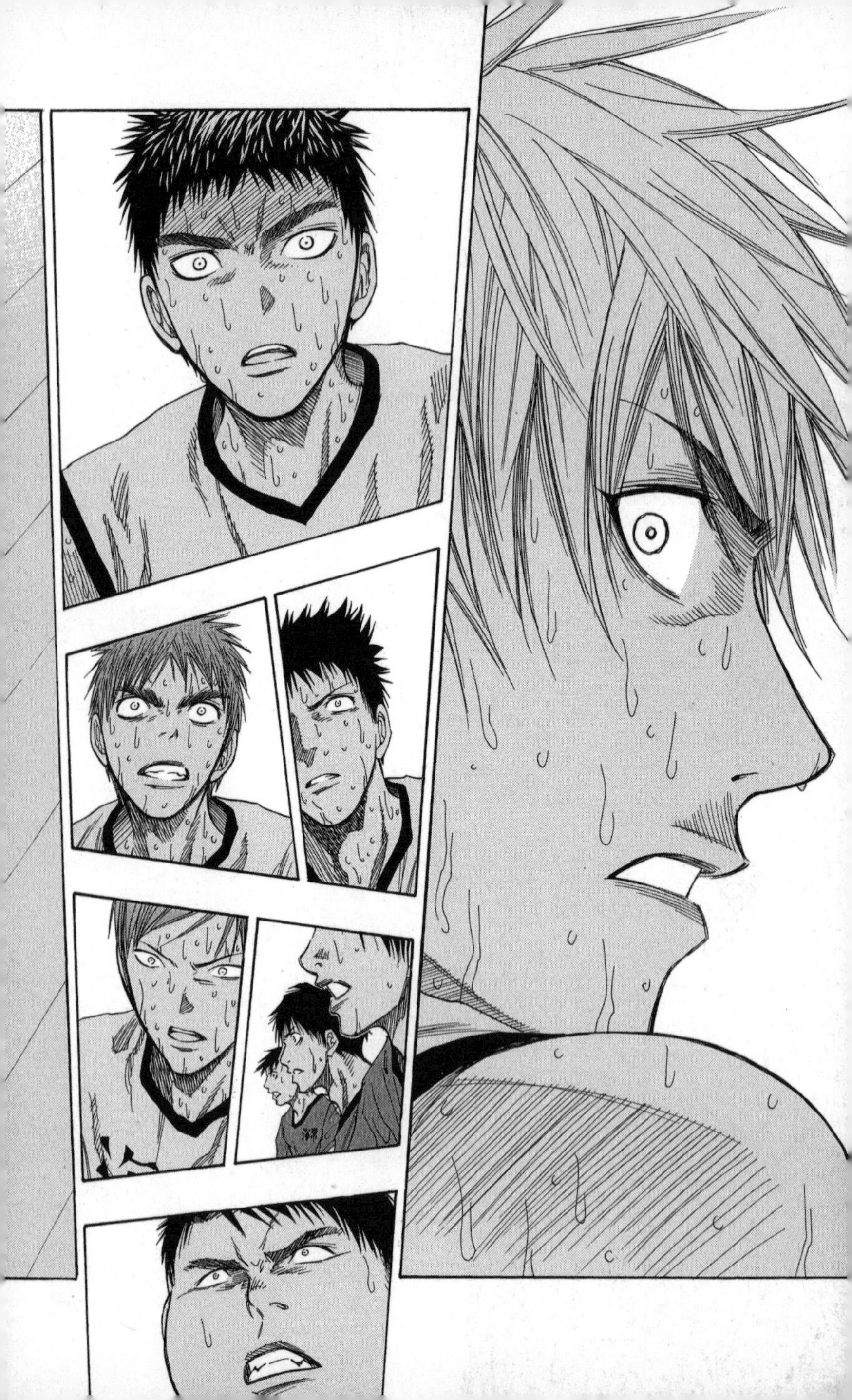

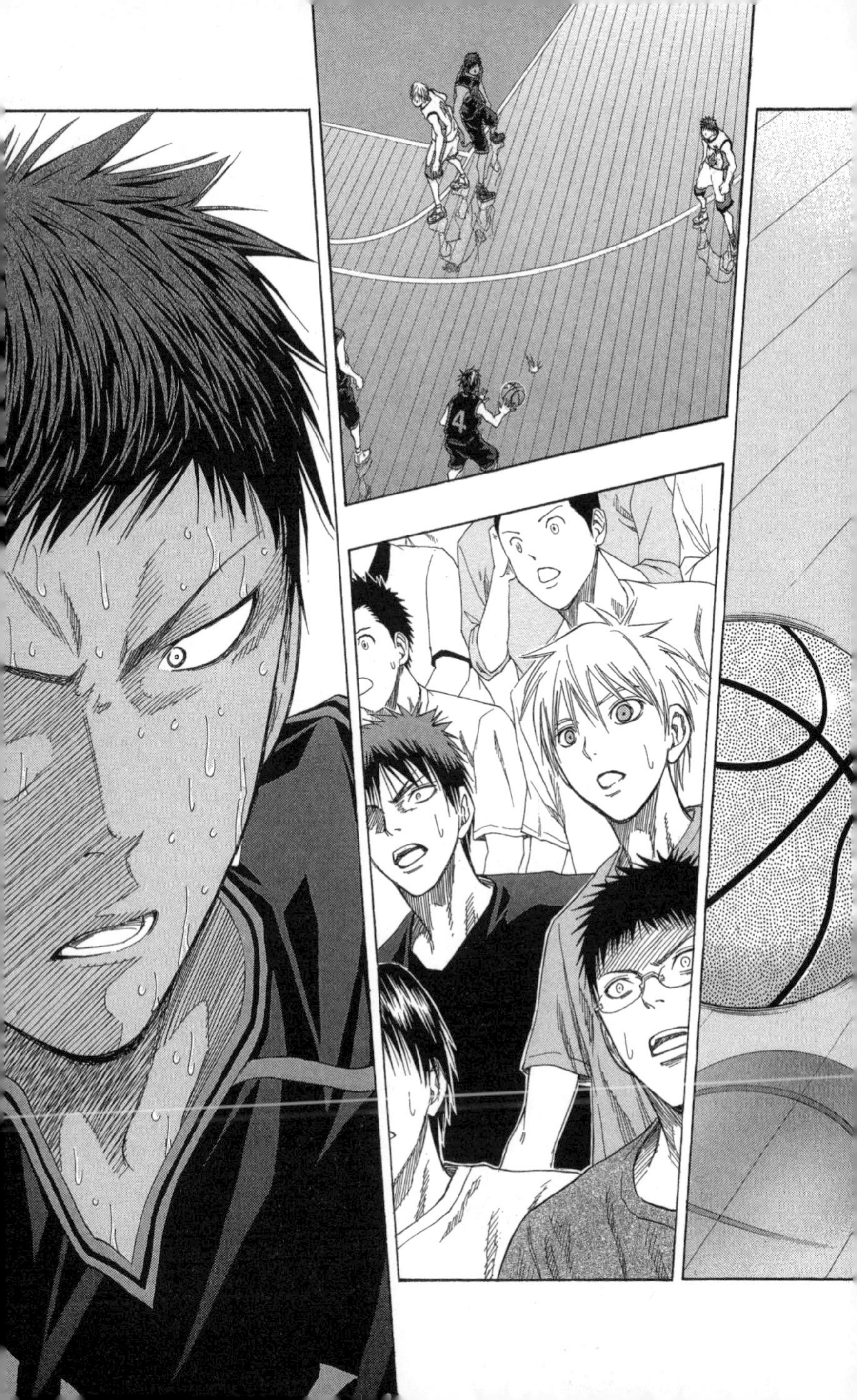

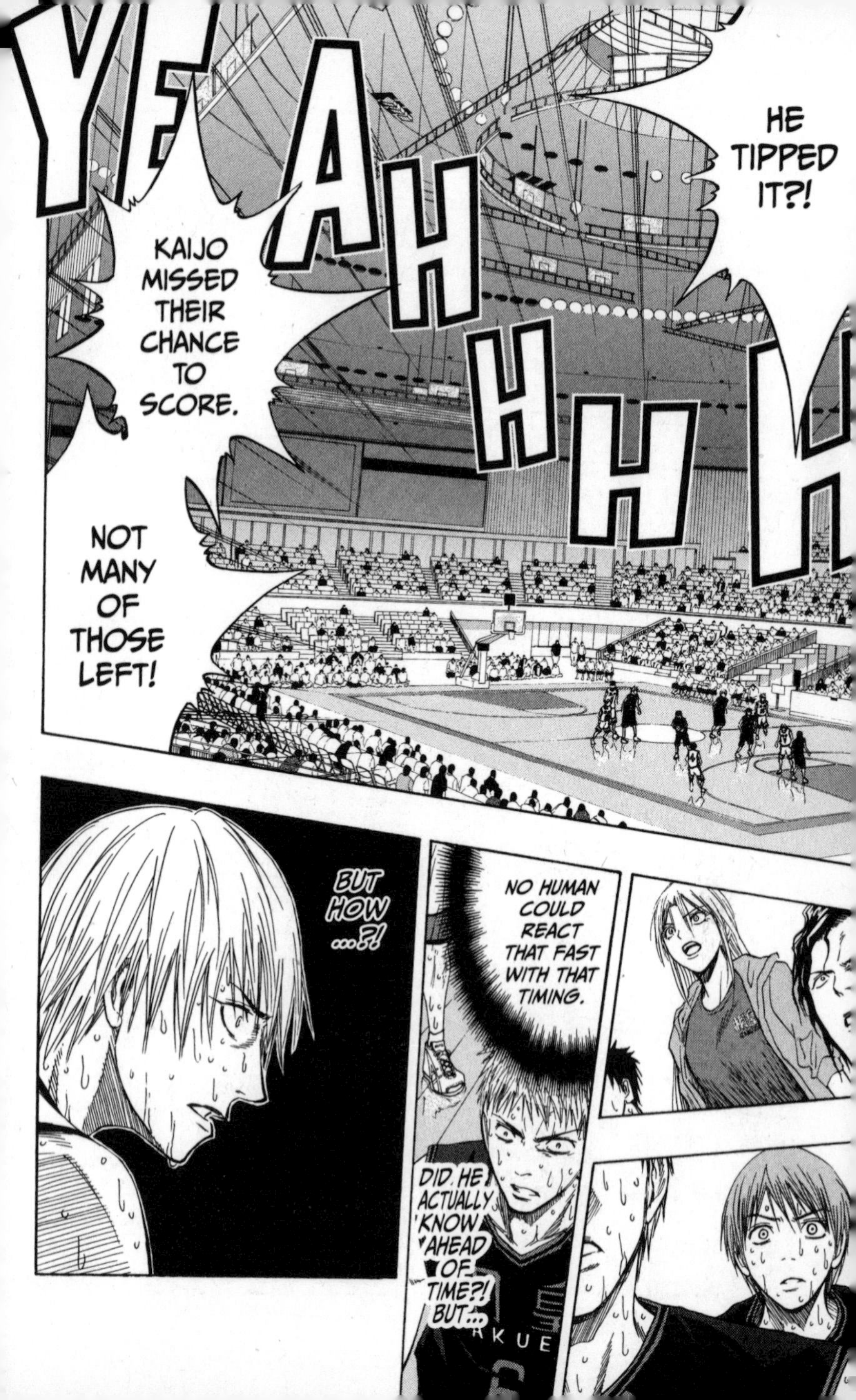
HE TIPPED IT?!
YEAHHHH
KAIJO MISSED THEIR CHANCE TO SCORE.
NOT MANY OF THOSE LEFT!
NO HUMAN COULD REACT THAT FAST WITH THAT TIMING.
DID HE ACTUALLY KNOW AHEAD OF TIME?! BUT...
BUT HOW ...?!

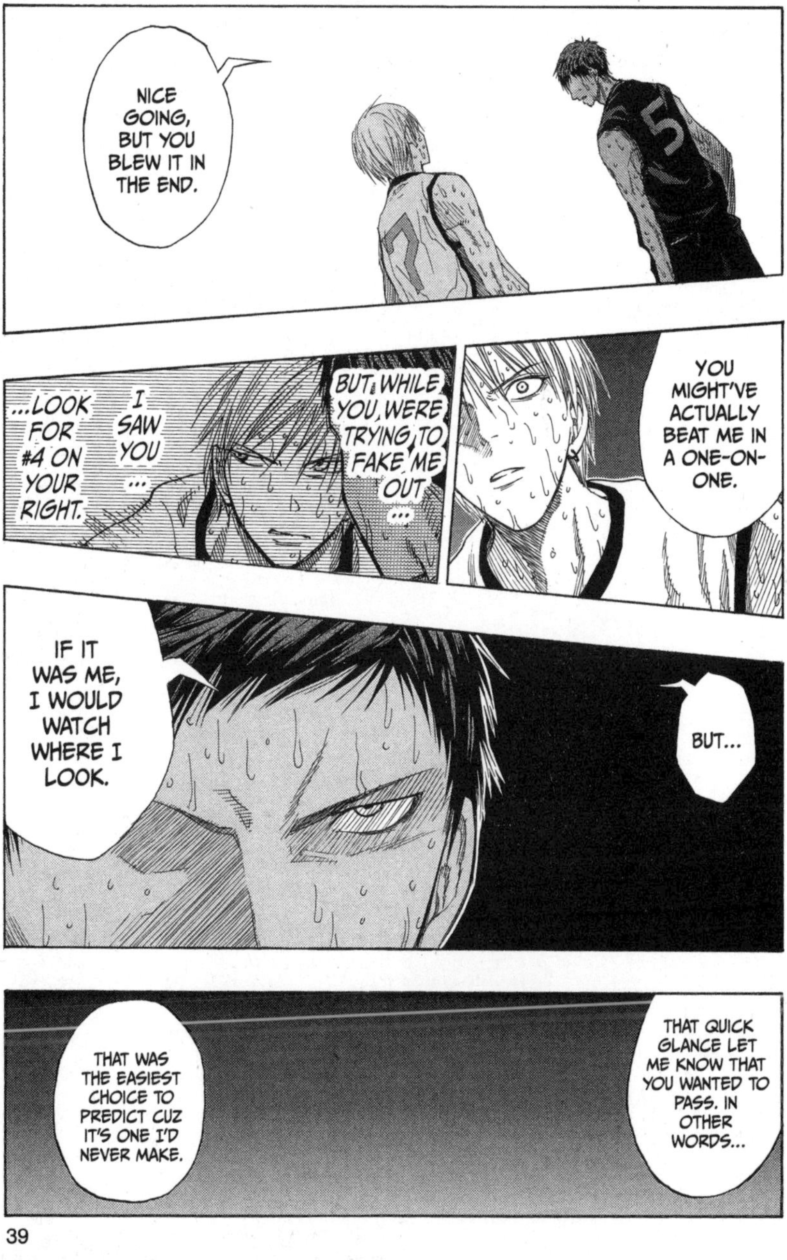
NICE GOING, BUT YOU BLEW IT IN THE END.
YOU MIGHT'VE ACTUALLY BEAT ME IN A ONE-ON-ONE.
BUT WHILE YOU WERE TRYING TO FAKE ME OUT...
I SAW YOU...
...LOOK FOR #4 ON YOUR RIGHT.
BUT...
IF IT WAS ME, I WOULD WATCH WHERE I LOOK.
THAT QUICK GLANCE LET ME KNOW THAT YOU WANTED TO PASS. IN OTHER WORDS...
THAT WAS THE EASIEST CHOICE TO PREDICT CUZ IT'S ONE I'D NEVER MAKE.

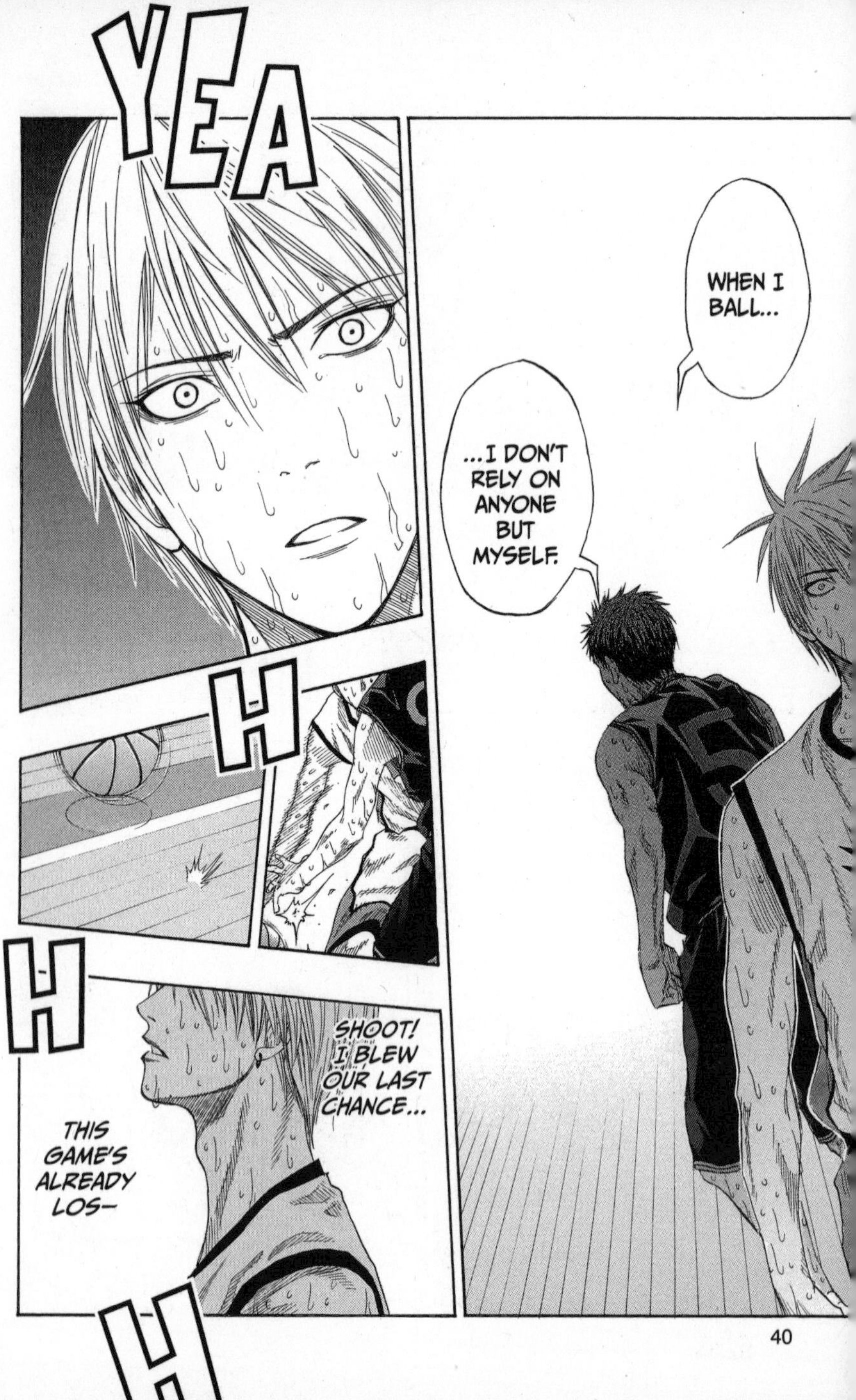
WHEN I BALL...
...I DON'T RELY ON ANYONE BUT MYSELF.
YEA
H
H
SHOOT! I BLEW OUR LAST CHANCE...
THIS GAME'S ALREADY LOS—
H

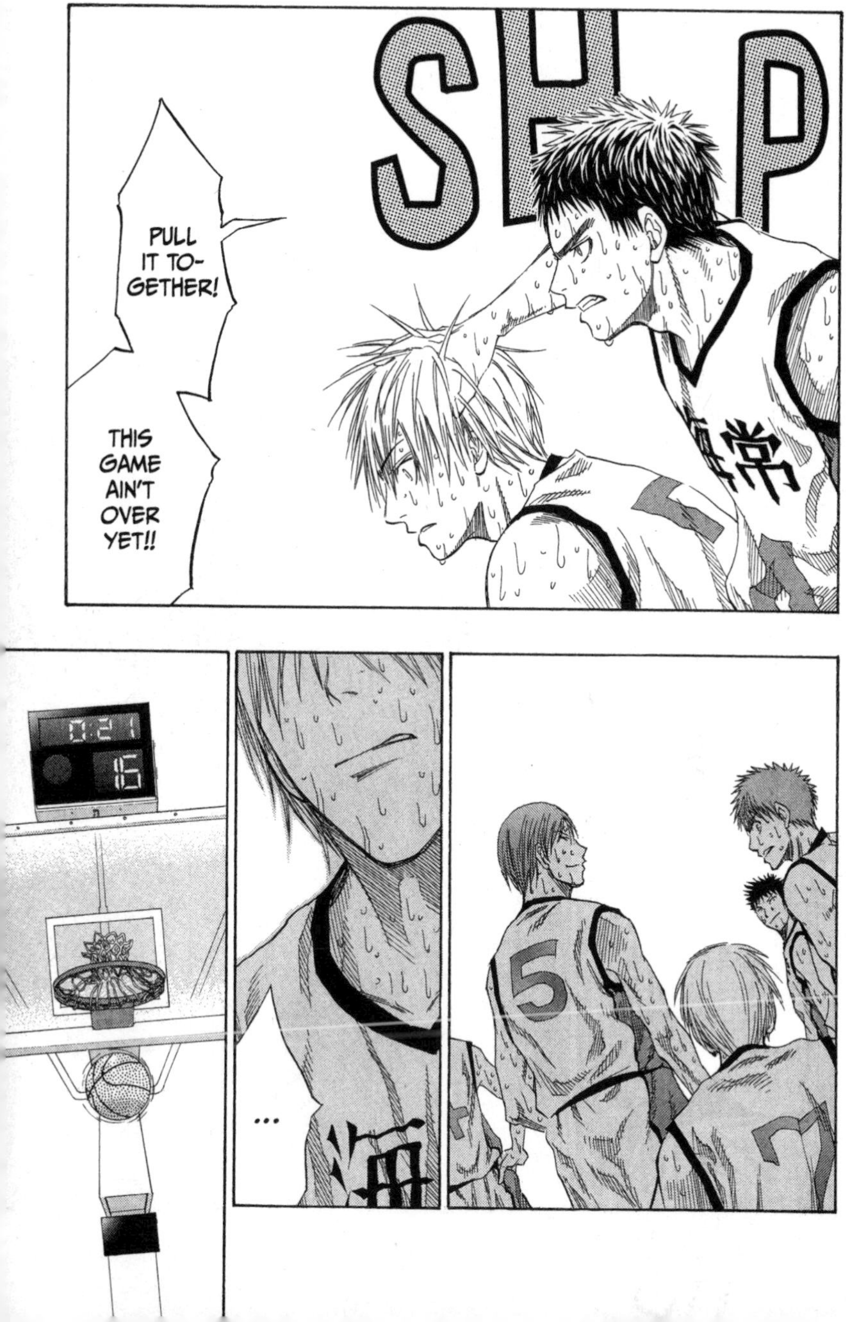
PULL IT TO-GETHER!
THIS GAME AIN'T OVER YET!!
...
0:21
15

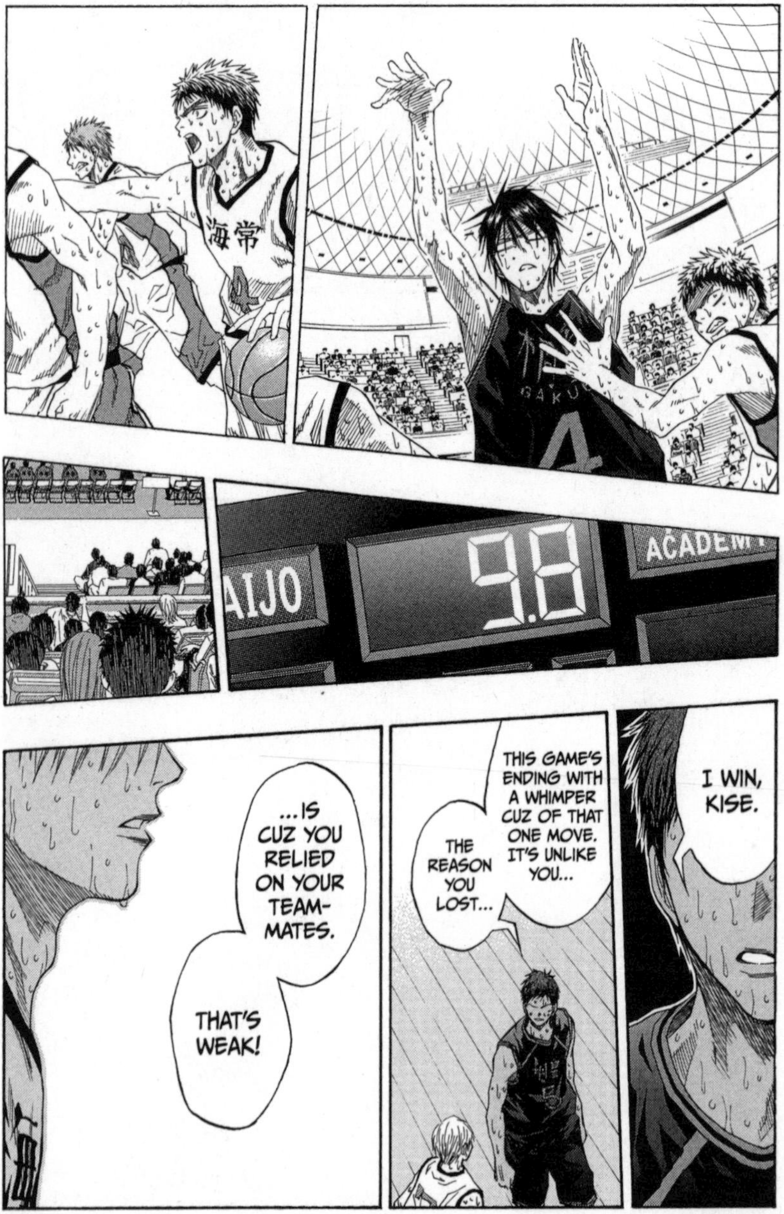
AIJO
9.8
ACADEM
I WIN, KISE.
THIS GAME'S ENDING WITH A WHIMPER CUZ OF THAT ONE MOVE. IT'S UNLIKE YOU...
THE REASON YOU LOST...
...IS CUZ YOU RELIED ON YOUR TEAMMATES.
THAT'S WEAK!

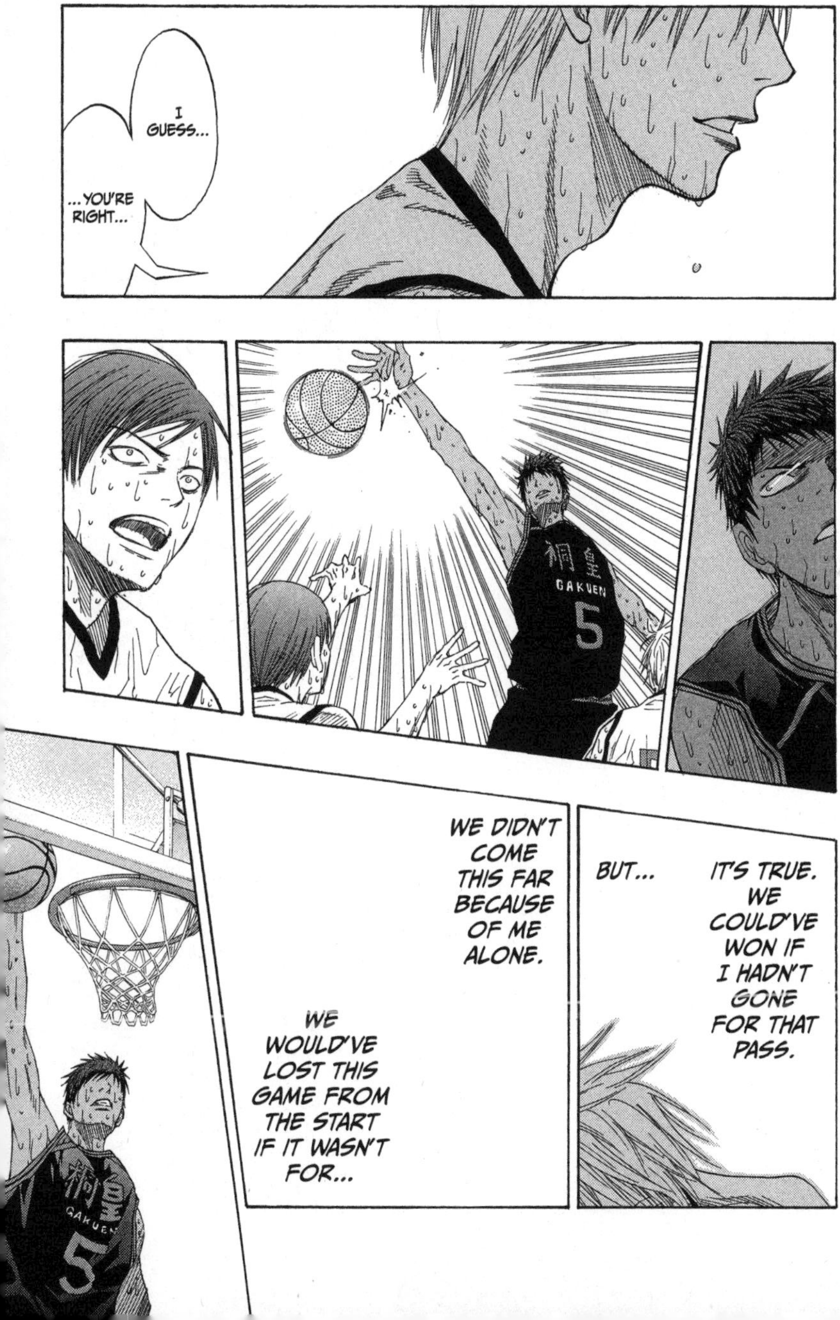
I GUESS...
...YOU'RE RIGHT...
IT'S TRUE. WE COULD'VE WON IF I HADN'T GONE FOR THAT PASS.
BUT...
WE DIDN'T COME THIS FAR BECAUSE OF ME ALONE.
WE WOULD'VE LOST THIS GAME FROM THE START IF IT WASN'T FOR...

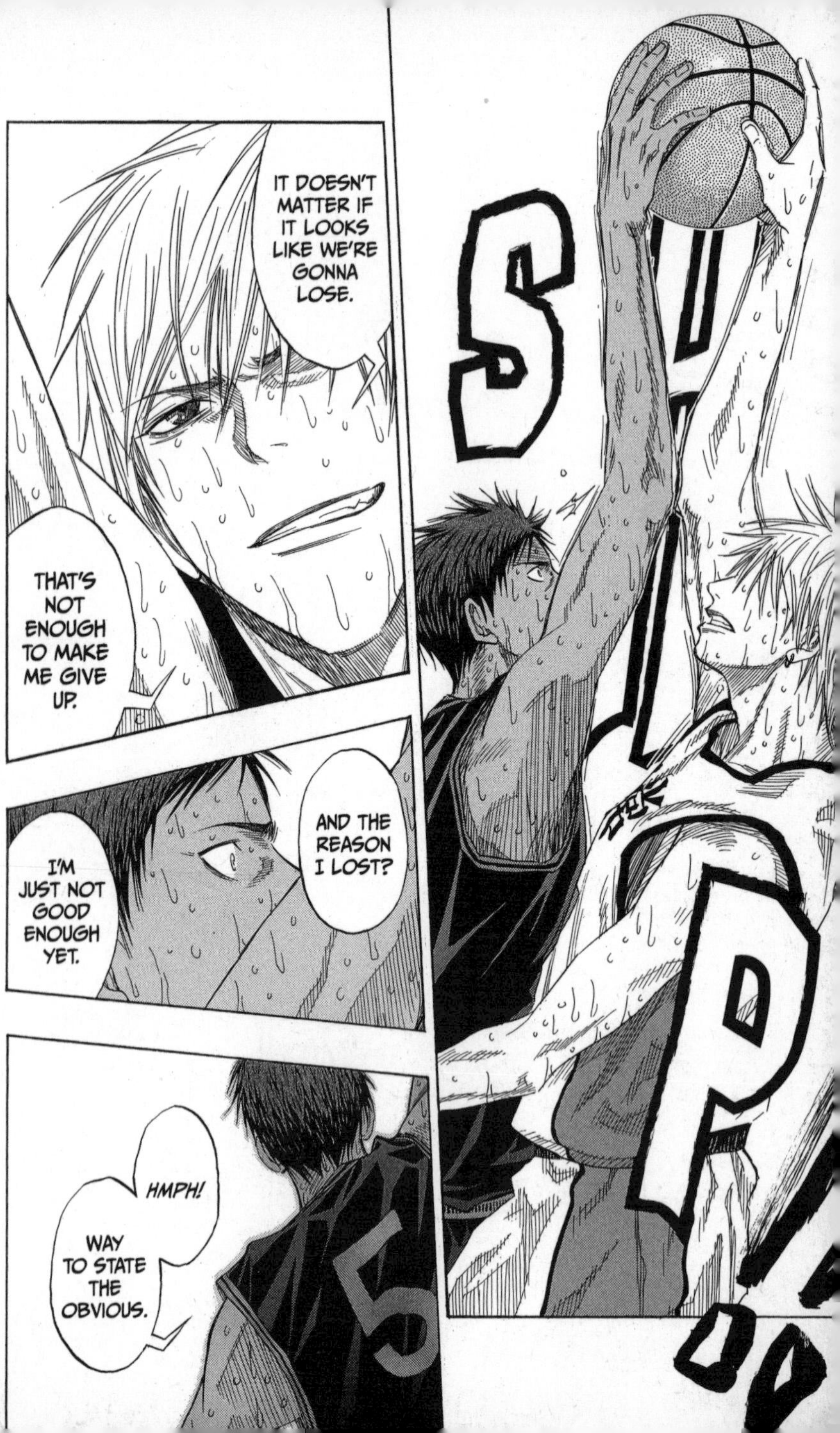
IT DOESN'T MATTER IF IT LOOKS LIKE WE'RE GONNA LOSE.
THAT'S NOT ENOUGH TO MAKE ME GIVE UP.
AND THE REASON I LOST?
I'M JUST NOT GOOD ENOUGH YET.
HMPH!
WAY TO STATE THE OBVIOUS.

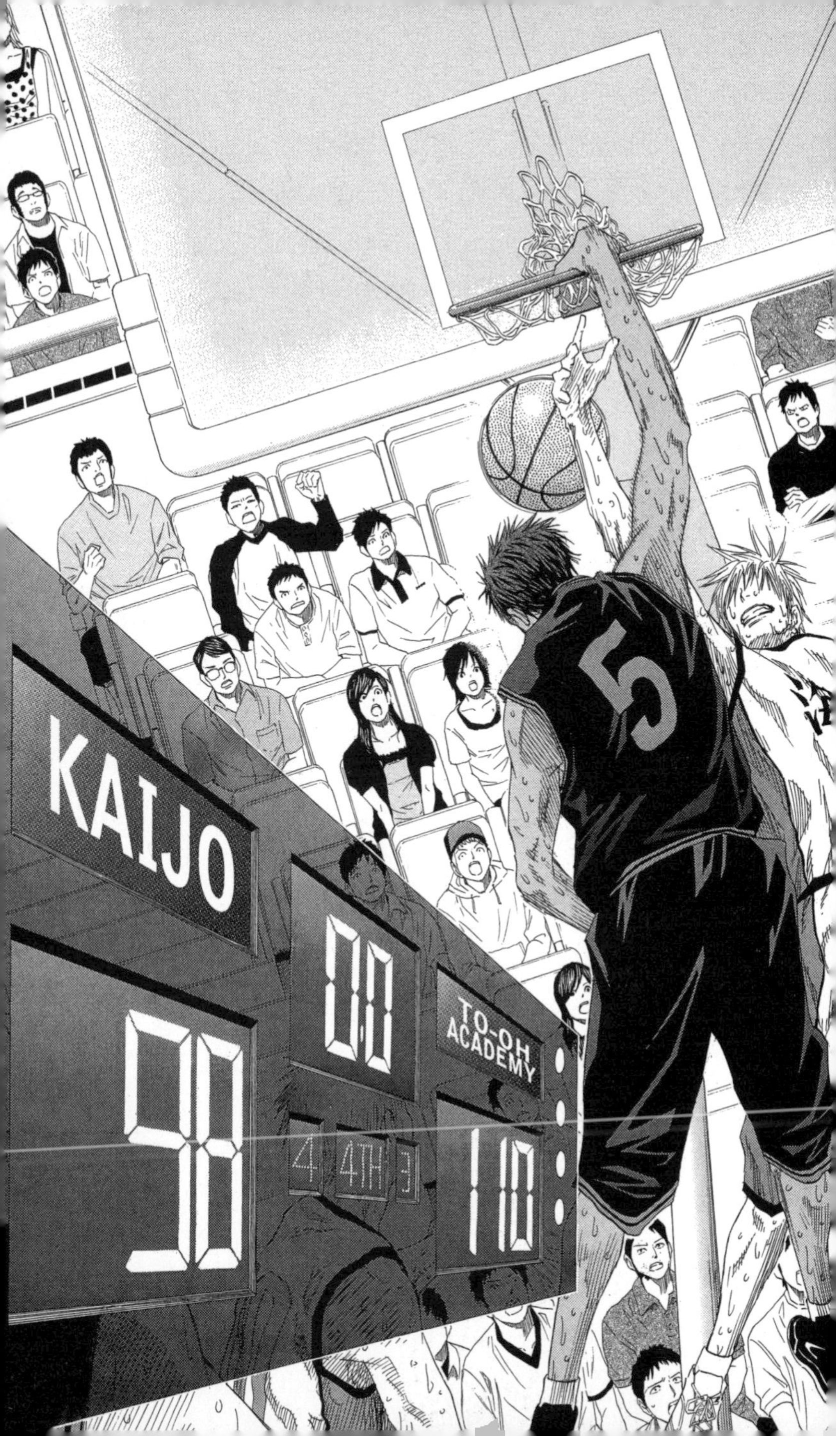
KAIJO
98
0.0
4TH
TO-OH ACADEMY
110

KUROKO'S BASKETBALL BLOOPERS

TAKE 4

HE'S REALLY FOCUSED NOW!
INSTEAD OF TRYING TO READ HIS MAN'S MOVES, HE'S GETTING READY TO NULLIFY HIS OPPONENT'S ATTACK!!
KAGAMI-KUN...
HOW DO YOU KNOW SUCH ADVANCED JAPANESE VOCABULARY WHEN YOU'VE BEEN OVERSEAS FOR SO LONG?
NULLIFY?
NOW'S NOT THE TIME TO...
HEY, STOP READ-ING MY MIND!!
I CAN'T HELP IT EVERY NOW AND THEN.
YOU ADMIT IT?!

73RD QUARTER: GET PAYBACK

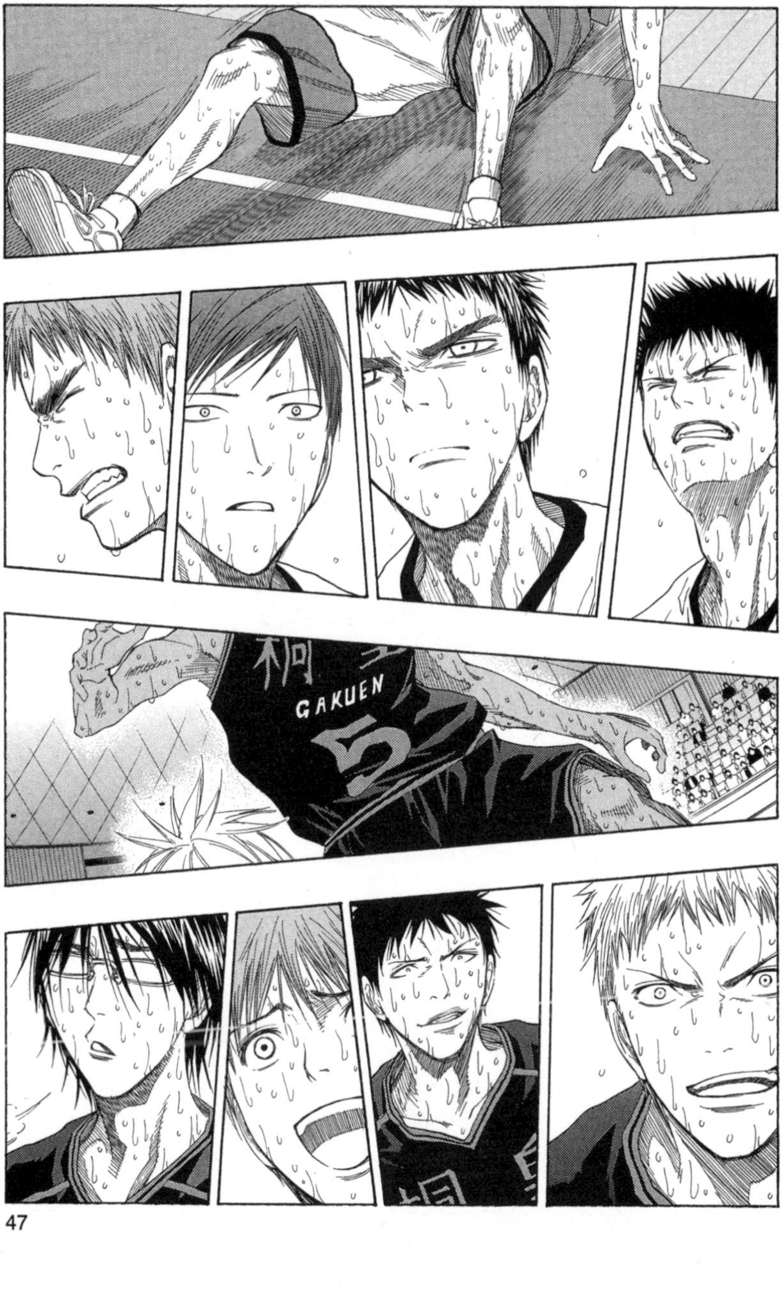
GAKUEN

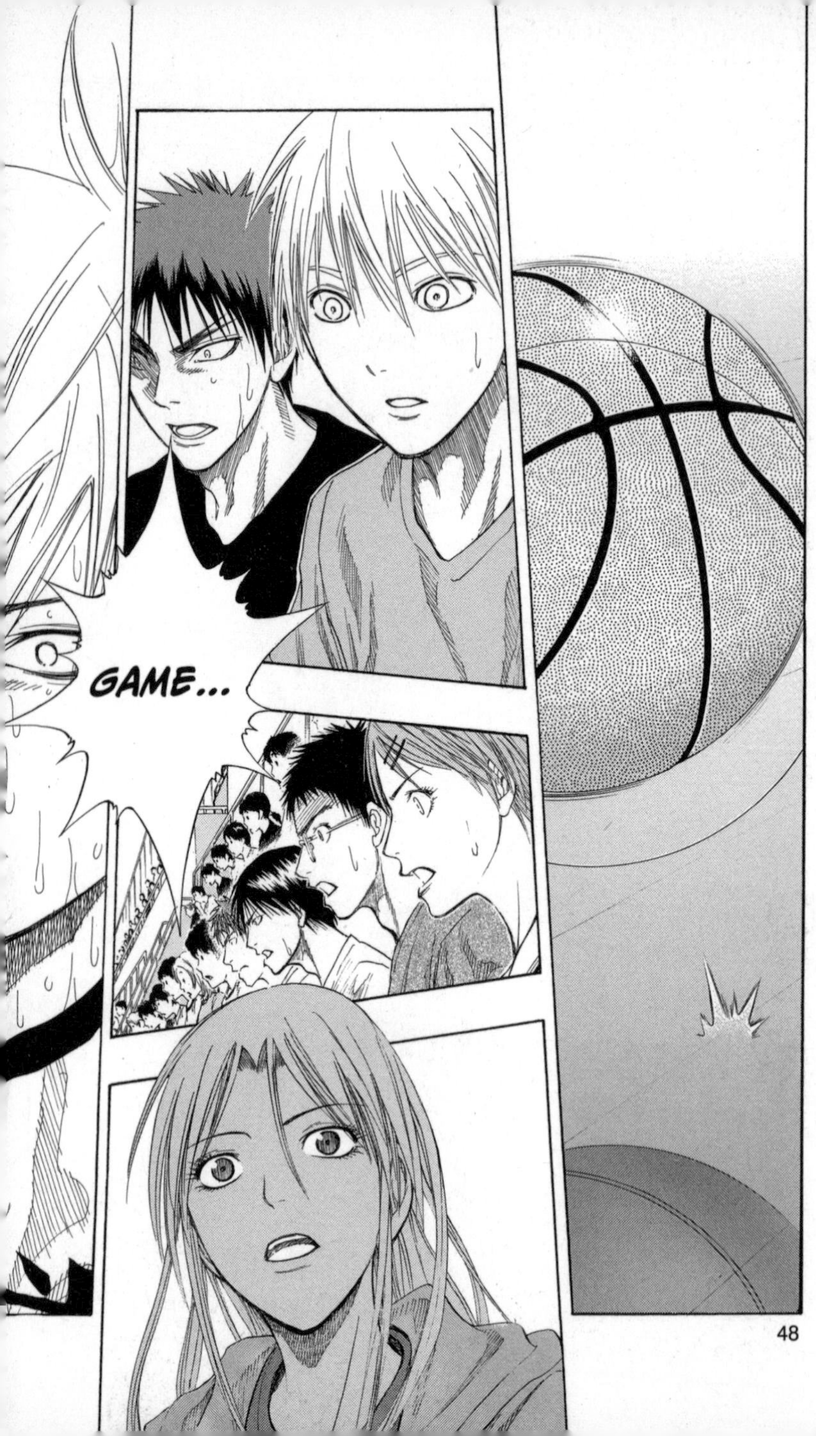
GAME...

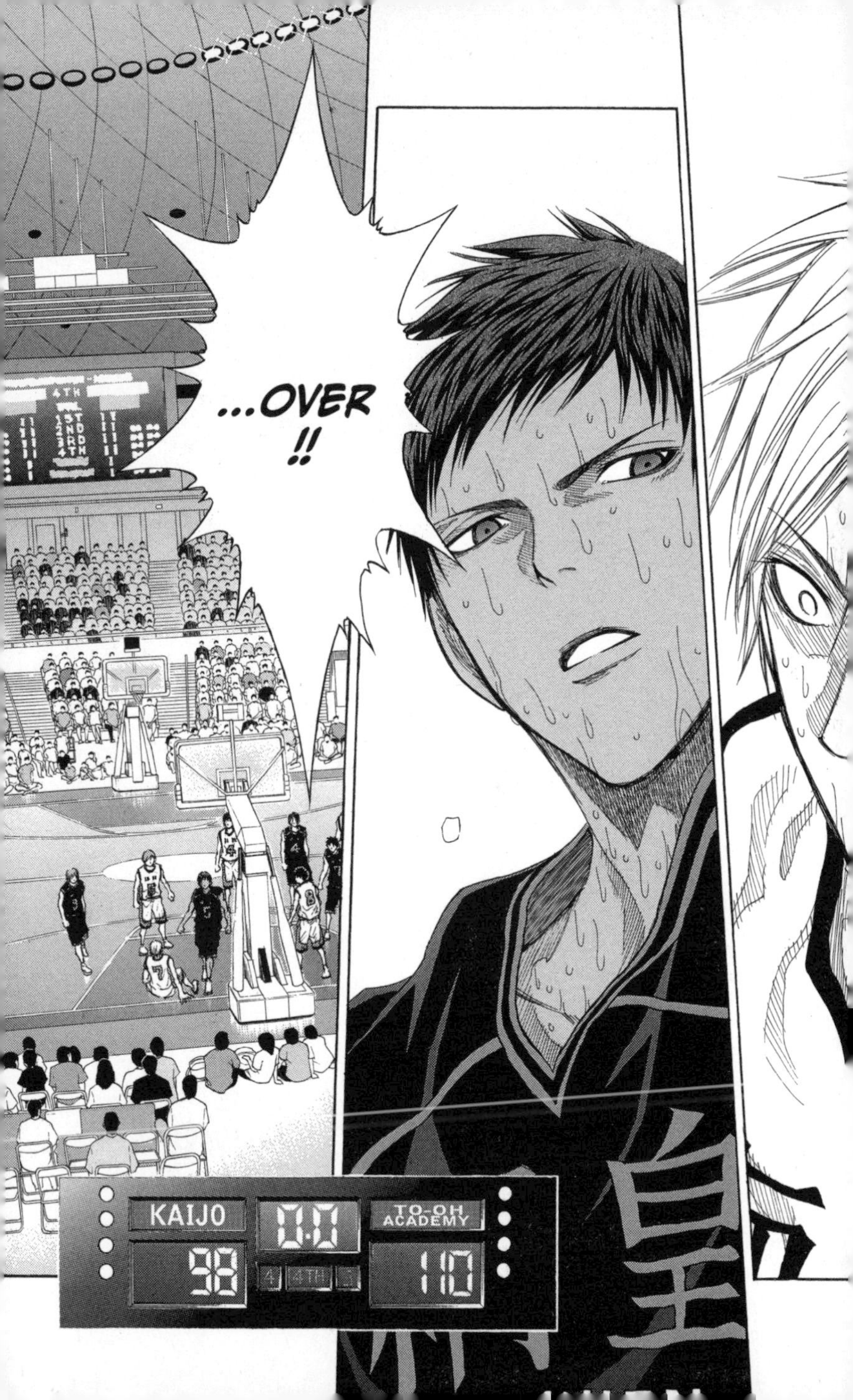
...OVER !!
KAIJO
0.0
TO-OH ACADEMY
98
4TH
110

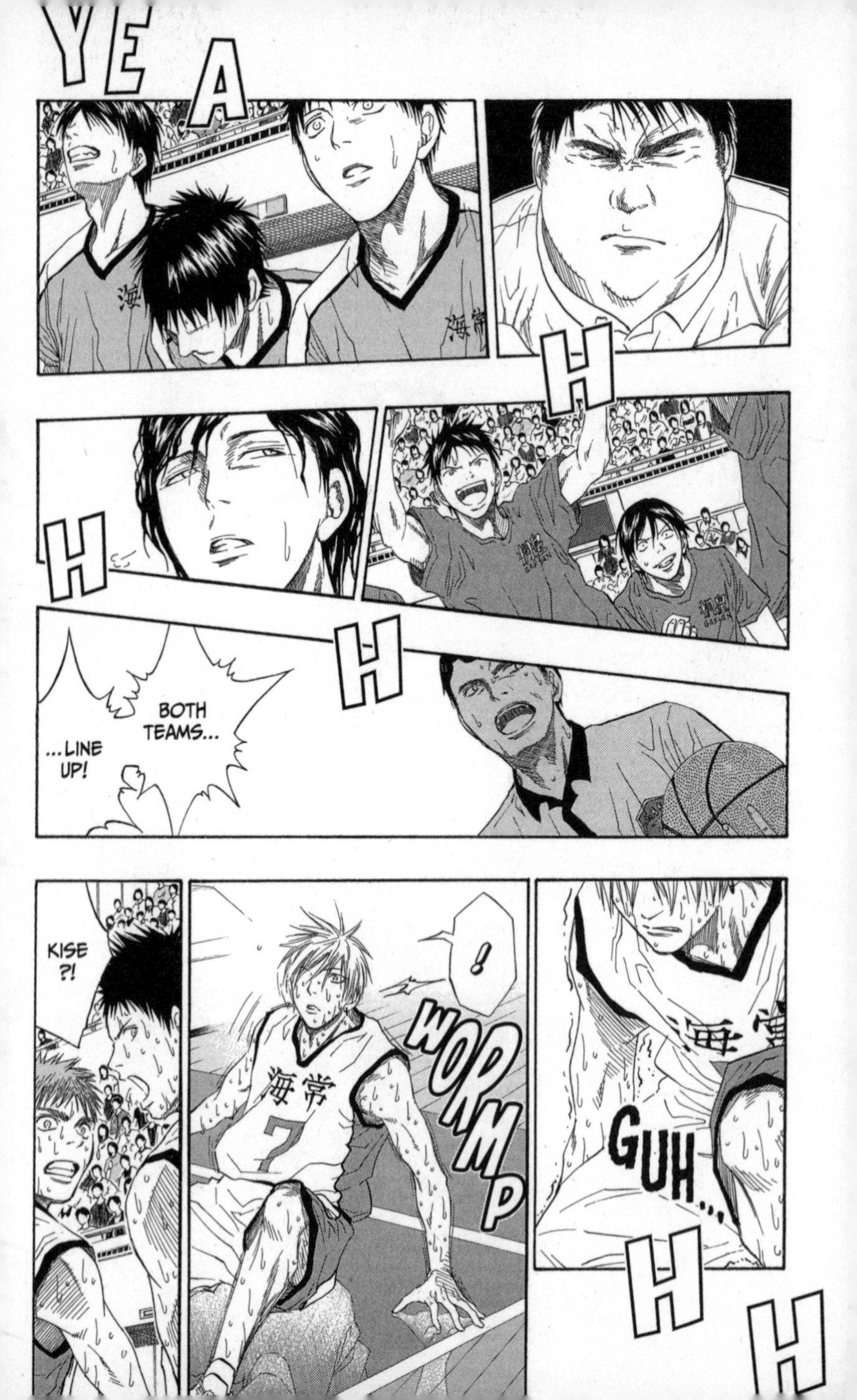
YEAHHHHH
BOTH TEAMS...
...LINE UP!
GUH...
!
WOMP
KISE ?!

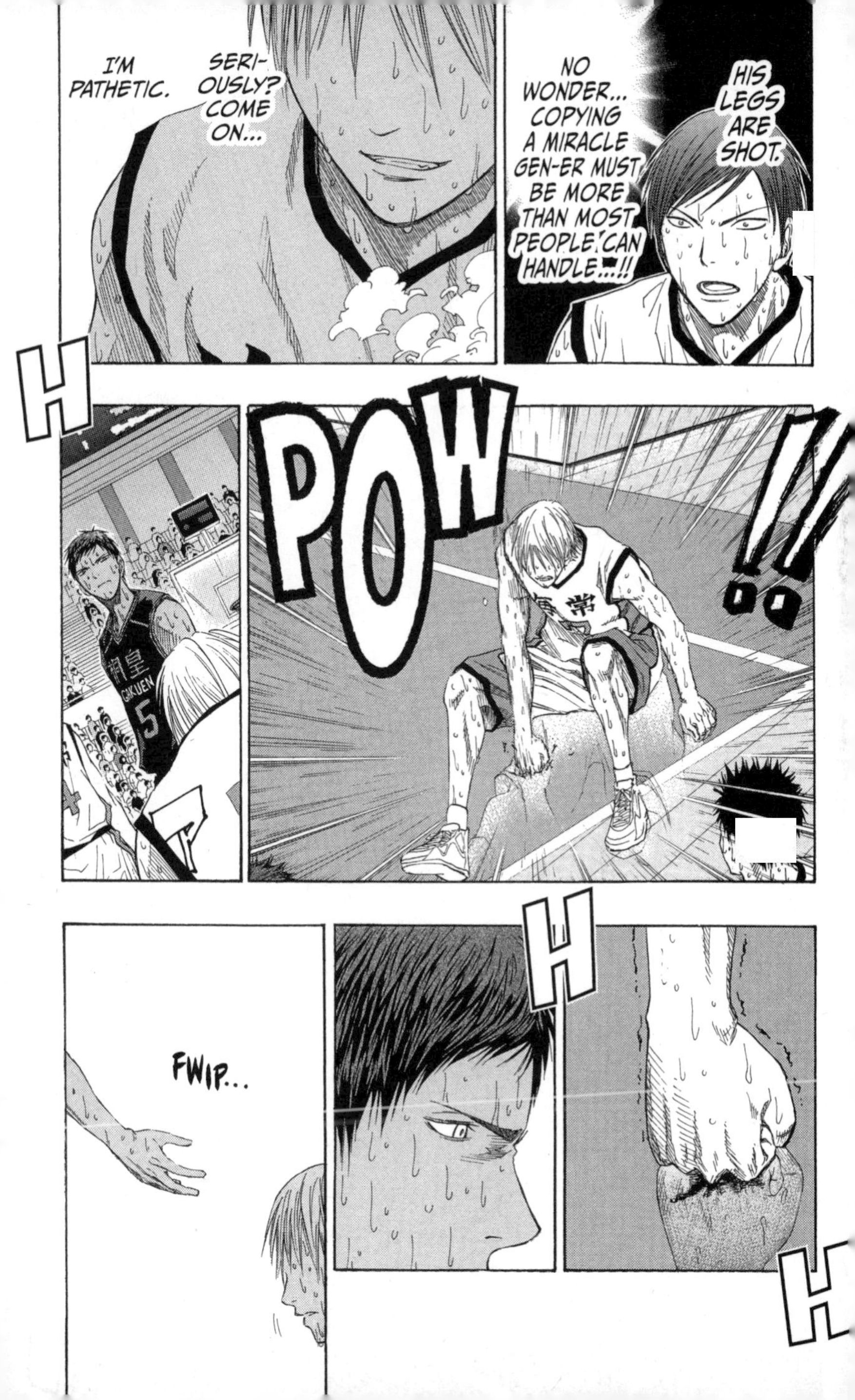

HIS LEGS ARE SHOT.
NO WONDER... COPYING A MIRACLE GEN-ER MUST BE MORE THAN MOST PEOPLE CAN HANDLE...!!
SERI-OUSLY? COME ON...
I'M PATHETIC.
H
POW!!
H
H
FWIP...

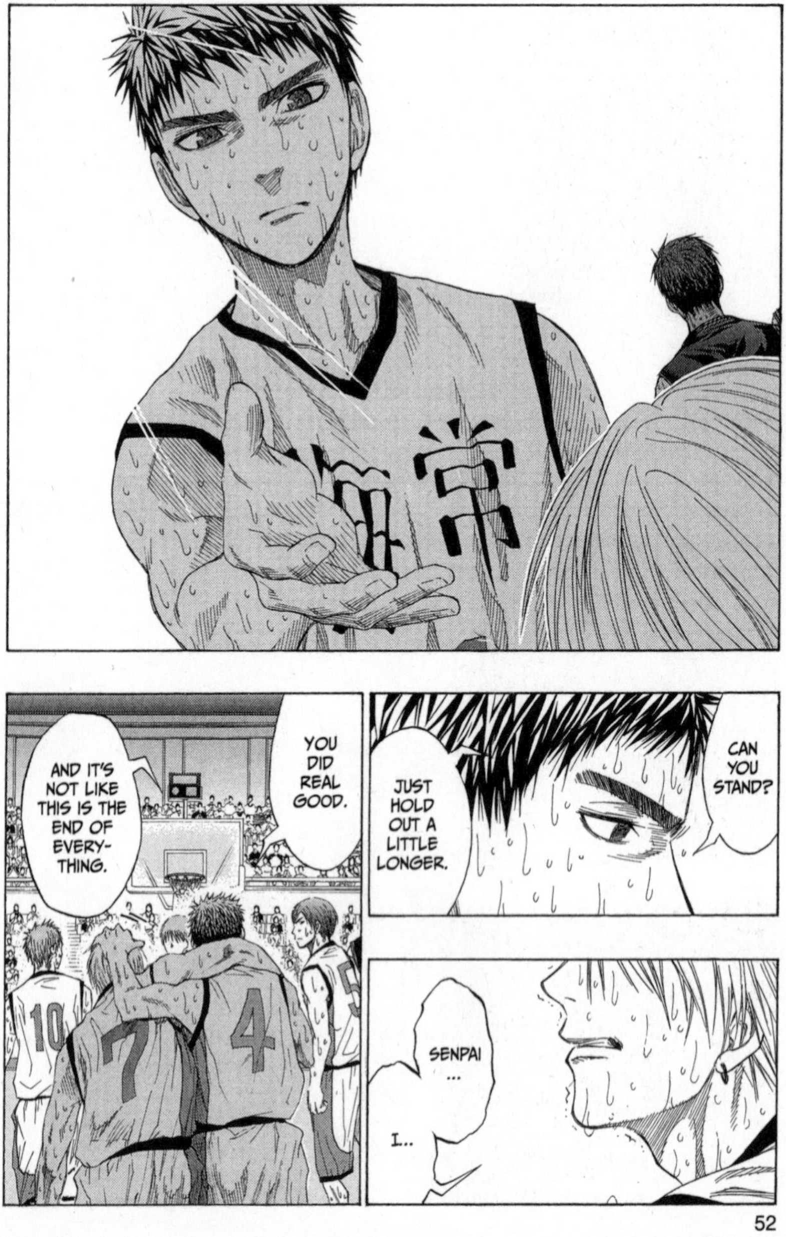
CAN YOU STAND?
JUST HOLD OUT A LITTLE LONGER.
SENPAI ...
I..
YOU DID REAL GOOD.
AND IT'S NOT LIKE THIS IS THE END OF EVERY-THING.

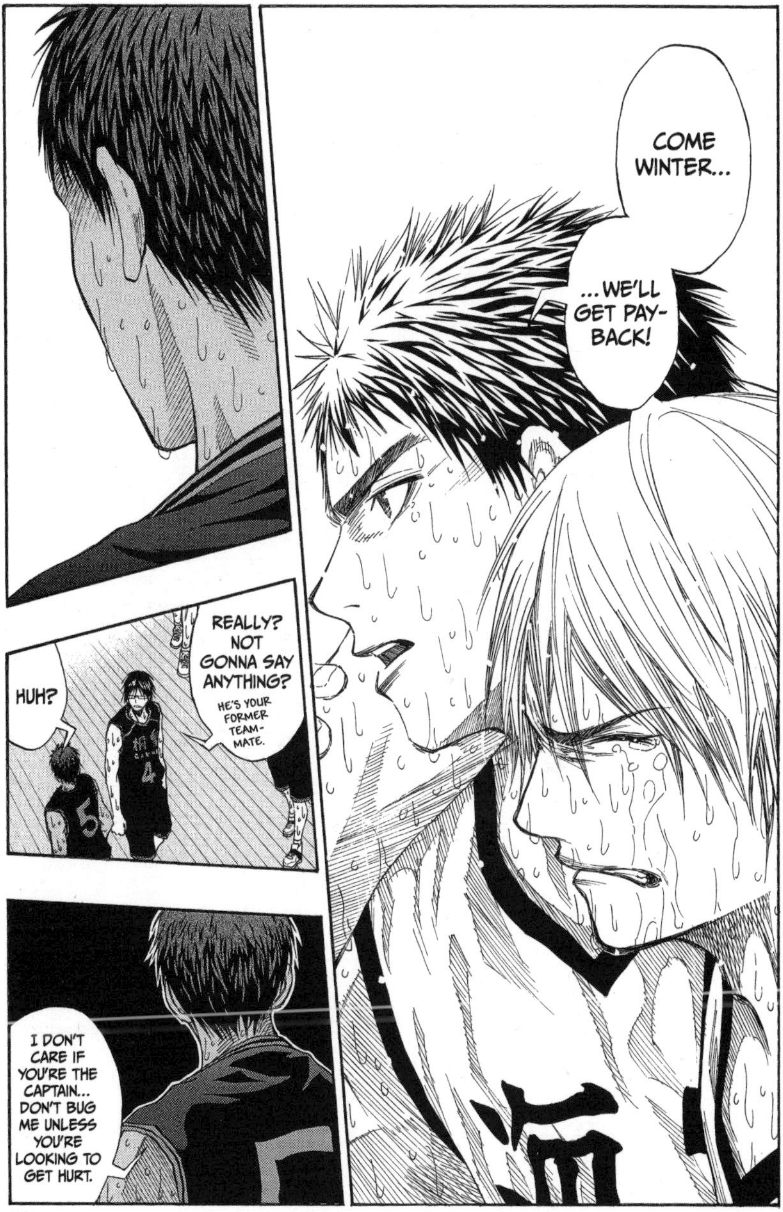
COME WINTER...
...WE'LL GET PAY-BACK!
REALLY? NOT GONNA SAY ANYTHING?
HE'S YOUR FORMER TEAM-MATE.
HUH?
I DON'T CARE IF YOU'RE THE CAPTAIN... DON'T BUG ME UNLESS YOU'RE LOOKING TO GET HURT.

YOU WANNA KNOW WHAT A WINNER SHOULD SAY TO A LOSER?

NOTHING.

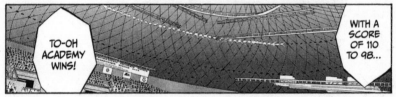

WITH A SCORE OF 110 TO 98...

TO-OH ACADEMY WINS!

LINE UP!!

THANK YOU FOR THE GAME!

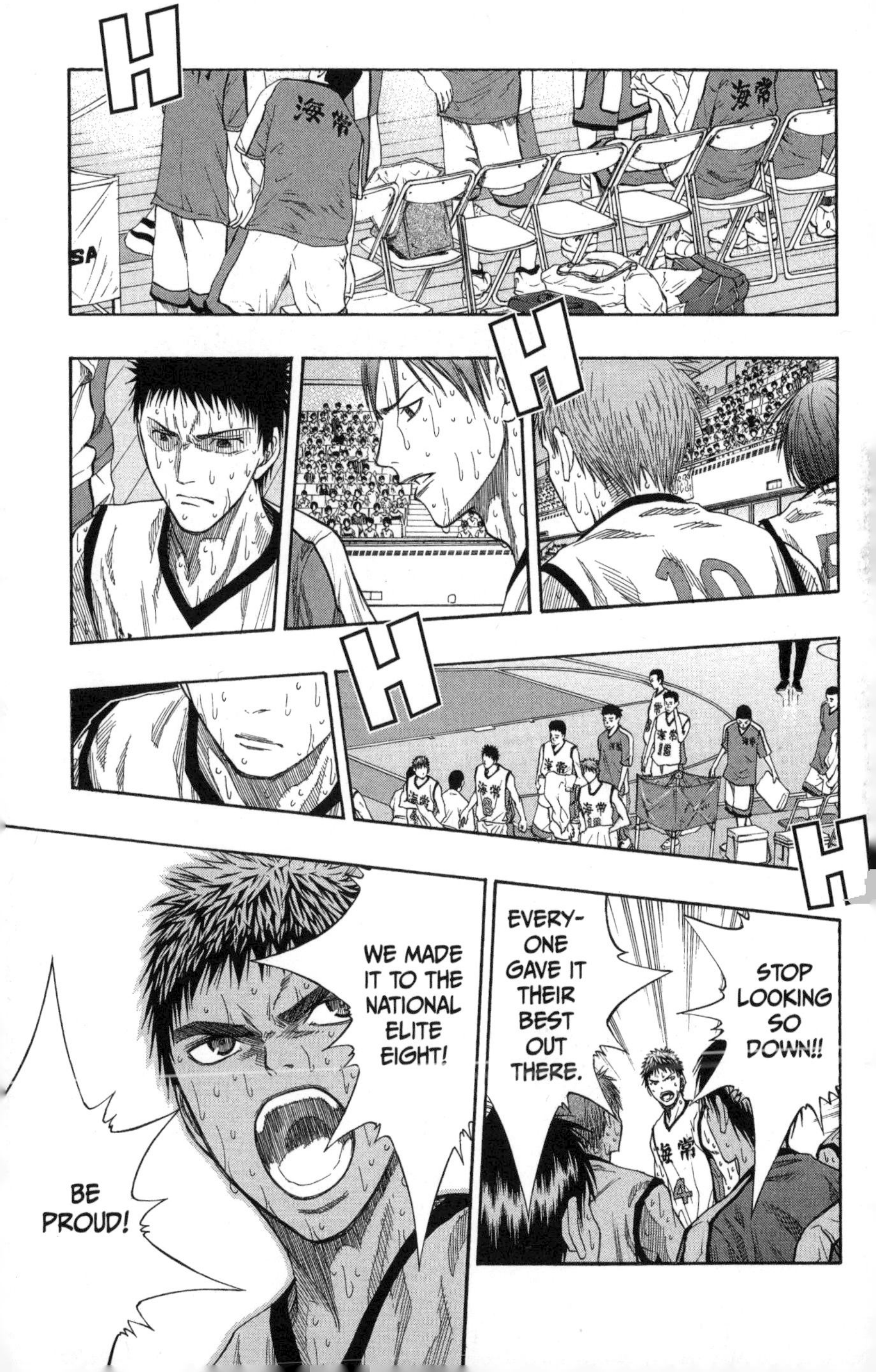
H
H
H
H
STOP LOOKING SO DOWN!!
EVERY-ONE GAVE IT THEIR BEST OUT THERE.
WE MADE IT TO THE NATIONAL ELITE EIGHT!
BE PROUD!

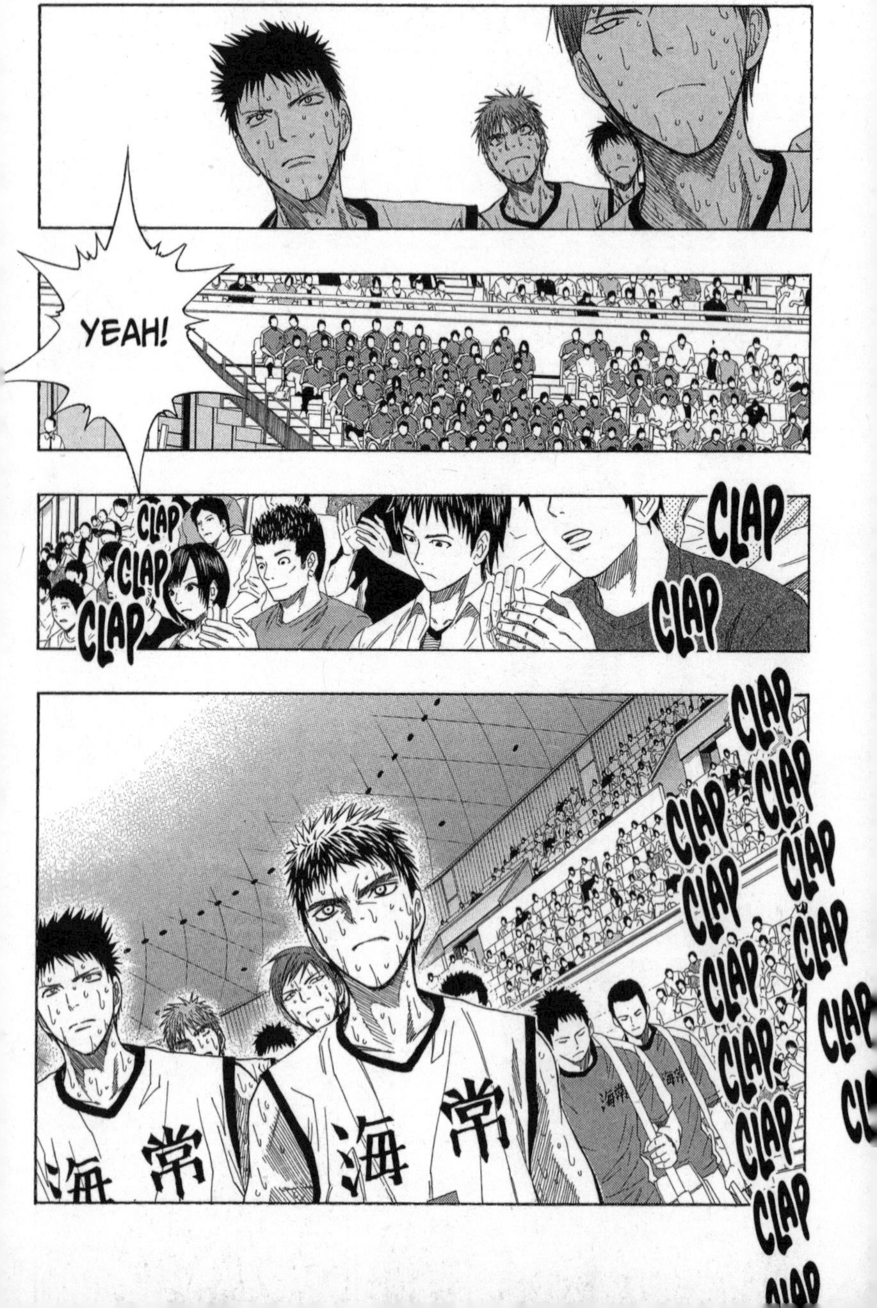
YEAH!
CLAP
CLAP
CLAP
CLAP
CLAP
CLAP
CLAP
CLAP
CLAP
CLAP
CLAP
CLAP
CLAP
CLAP
CLAP
CLAP
CLAP
海常
海常
海常

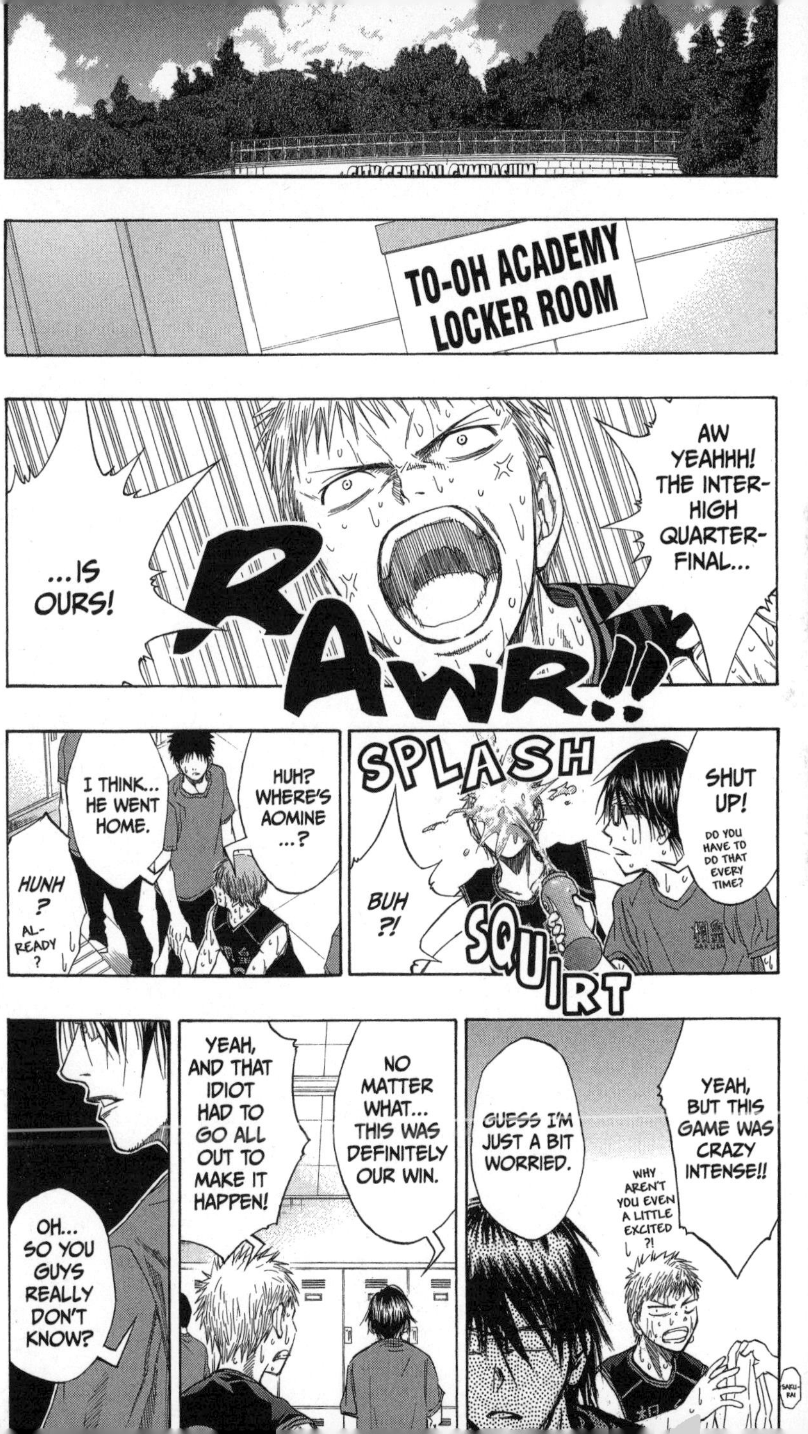
TO-OH ACADEMY LOCKER ROOM
AW YEAHHH! THE INTER-HIGH QUARTER-FINAL...
RAWR!!
...IS OURS!
SHUT UP!
DO YOU HAVE TO DO THAT EVERY TIME?
SPLASH
SQUIRT
BUH ?!
HUH? WHERE'S AOMINE ...?
I THINK... HE WENT HOME.
HUNH ? AL-READY ?
YEAH, BUT THIS GAME WAS CRAZY INTENSE!!
WHY AREN'T YOU EVEN A LITTLE EXCITED ?!
GUESS I'M JUST A BIT WORRIED.
SAKU-RAI
NO MATTER WHAT... THIS WAS DEFINITELY OUR WIN.
YEAH, AND THAT IDIOT HAD TO GO ALL OUT TO MAKE IT HAPPEN!
OH... SO YOU GUYS REALLY DON'T KNOW?

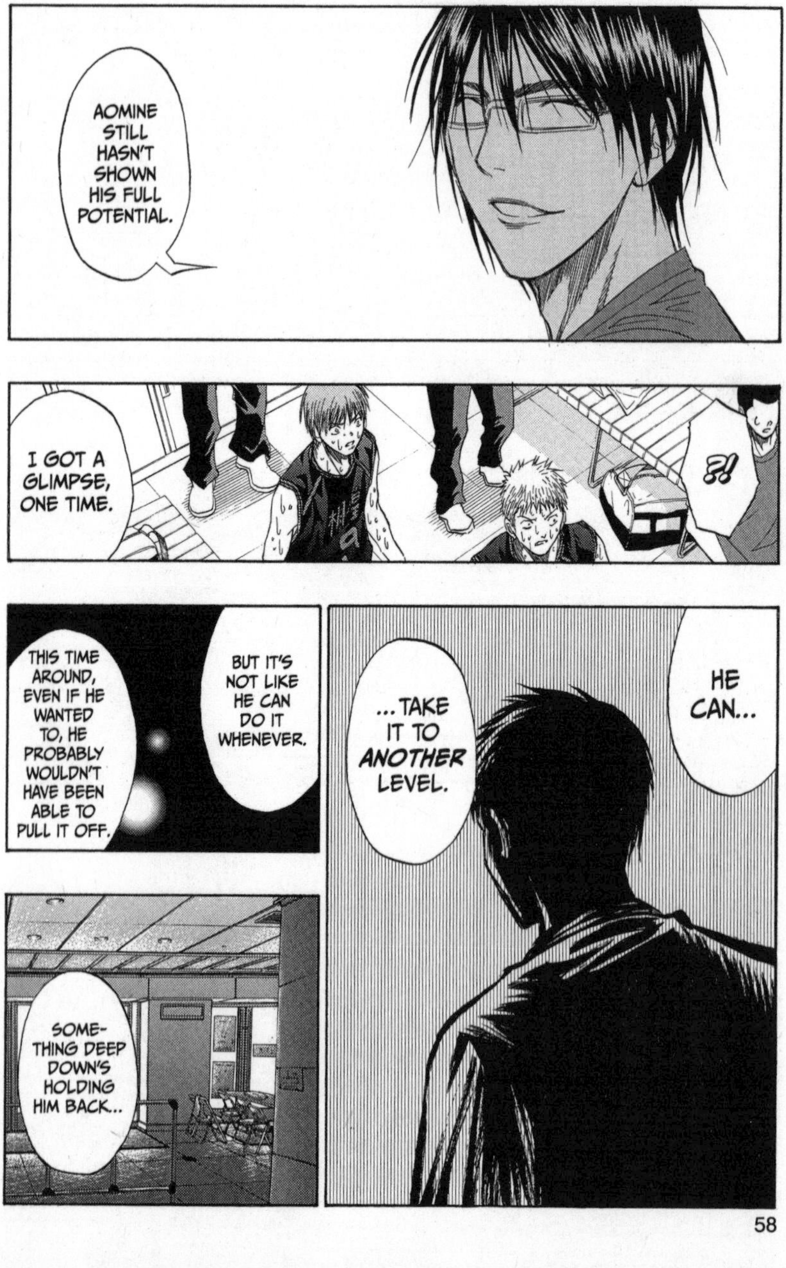
AOMINE STILL HASN'T SHOWN HIS FULL POTENTIAL.
?!
I GOT A GLIMPSE, ONE TIME.
HE CAN...
...TAKE IT TO ANOTHER LEVEL.
BUT IT'S NOT LIKE HE CAN DO IT WHENEVER.
THIS TIME AROUND, EVEN IF HE WANTED TO, HE PROBABLY WOULDN'T HAVE BEEN ABLE TO PULL IT OFF.
SOME-THING DEEP DOWN'S HOLDING HIM BACK..

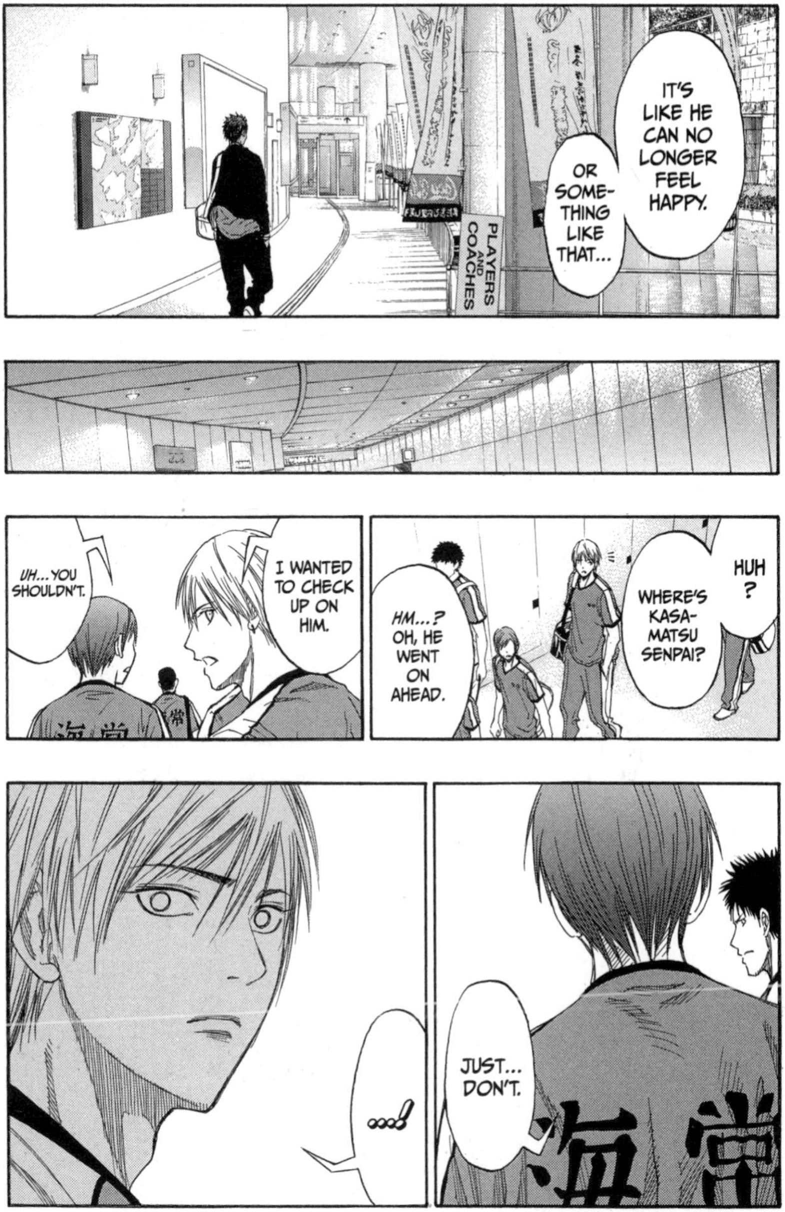
PLAYERS AND COACHES
IT'S LIKE HE CAN NO LONGER FEEL HAPPY.
OR SOMETHING LIKE THAT...
HUH?
WHERE'S KASAMATSU SENPAI?
HM...? OH, HE WENT ON AHEAD.
I WANTED TO CHECK UP ON HIM.
UH...YOU SHOULDN'T.
JUST... DON'T.
...!

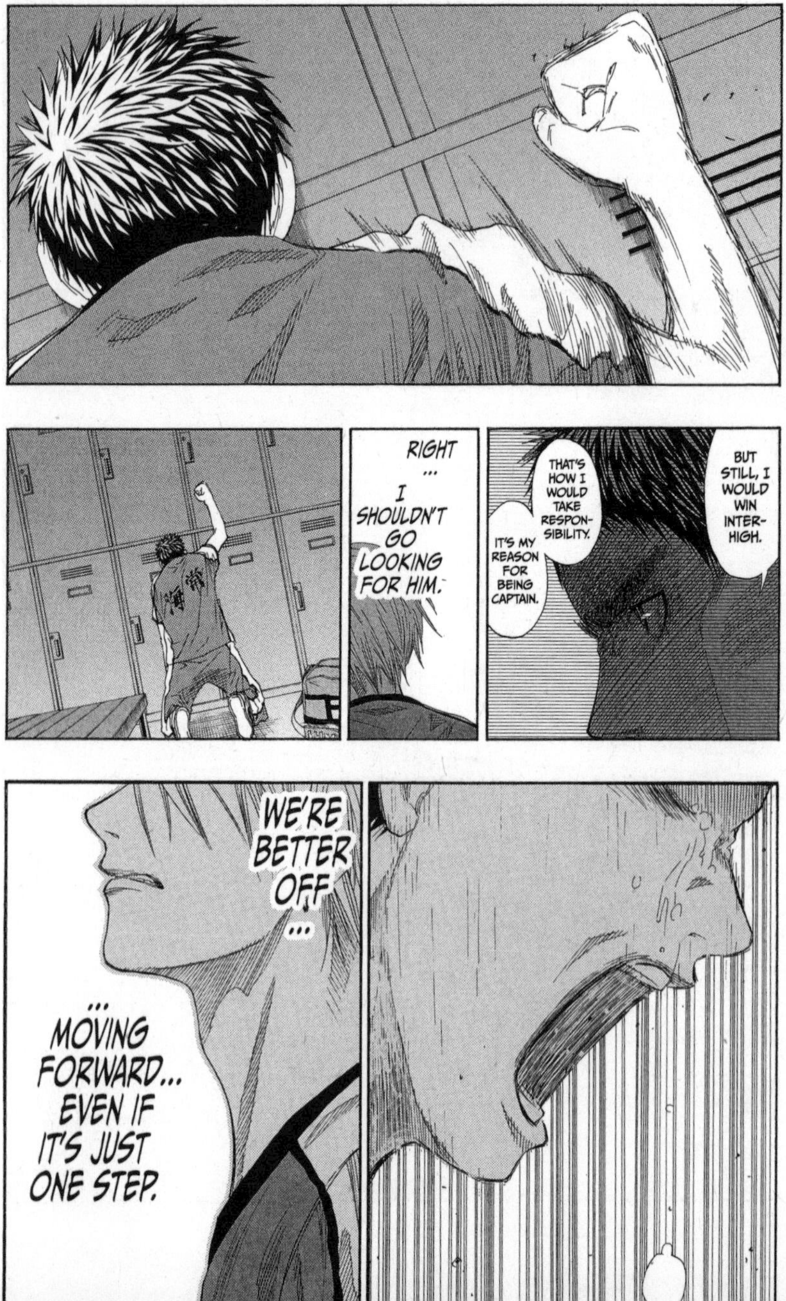
BUT STILL, I WOULD WIN INTER-HIGH.
THAT'S HOW I WOULD TAKE RESPON-SIBILITY.
IT'S MY REASON FOR BEING CAPTAIN.
RIGHT... I SHOULDN'T GO LOOKING FOR HIM.
WE'RE BETTER OFF...
...MOVING FORWARD... EVEN IF IT'S JUST ONE STEP.

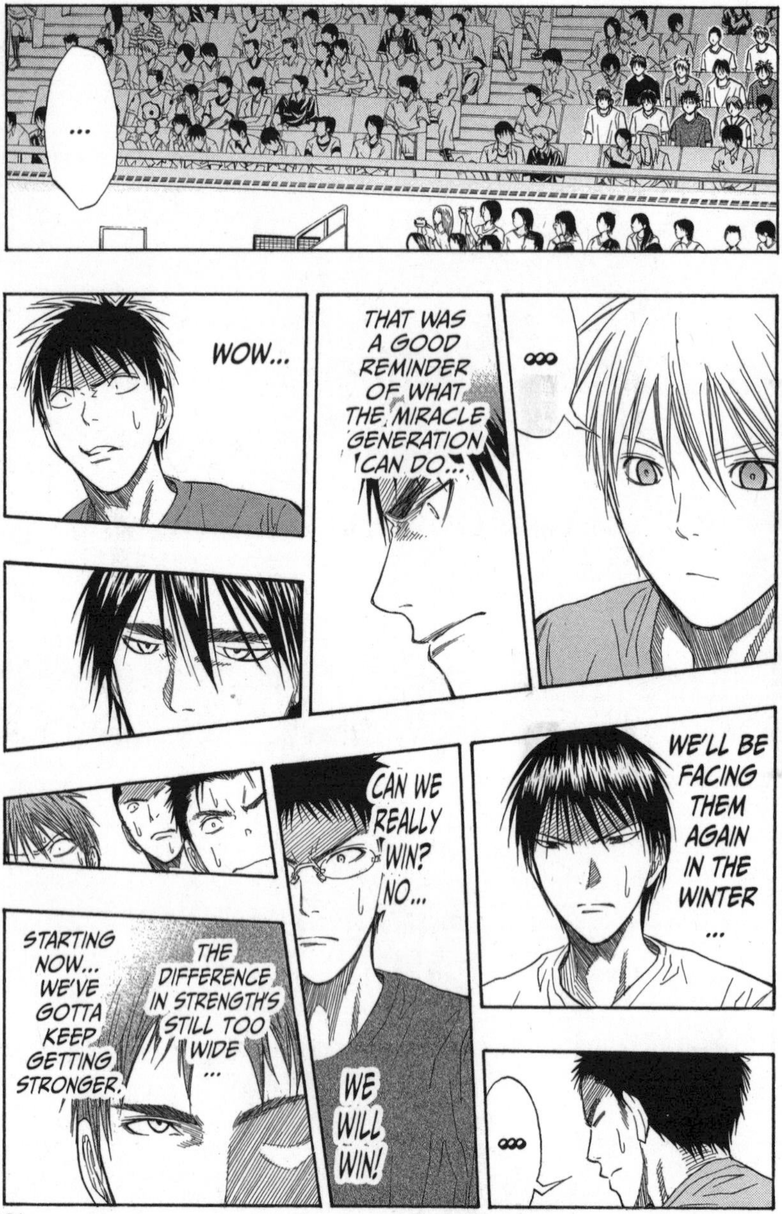
...
...
THAT WAS A GOOD REMINDER OF WHAT THE MIRACLE GENERATION CAN DO...
WOW...
WE'LL BE FACING THEM AGAIN IN THE WINTER ...
CAN WE REALLY WIN? NO...
...
WE WILL WIN!
THE DIFFERENCE IN STRENGTH'S STILL TOO WIDE ...
STARTING NOW... WE'VE GOTTA KEEP GETTING STRONGER.

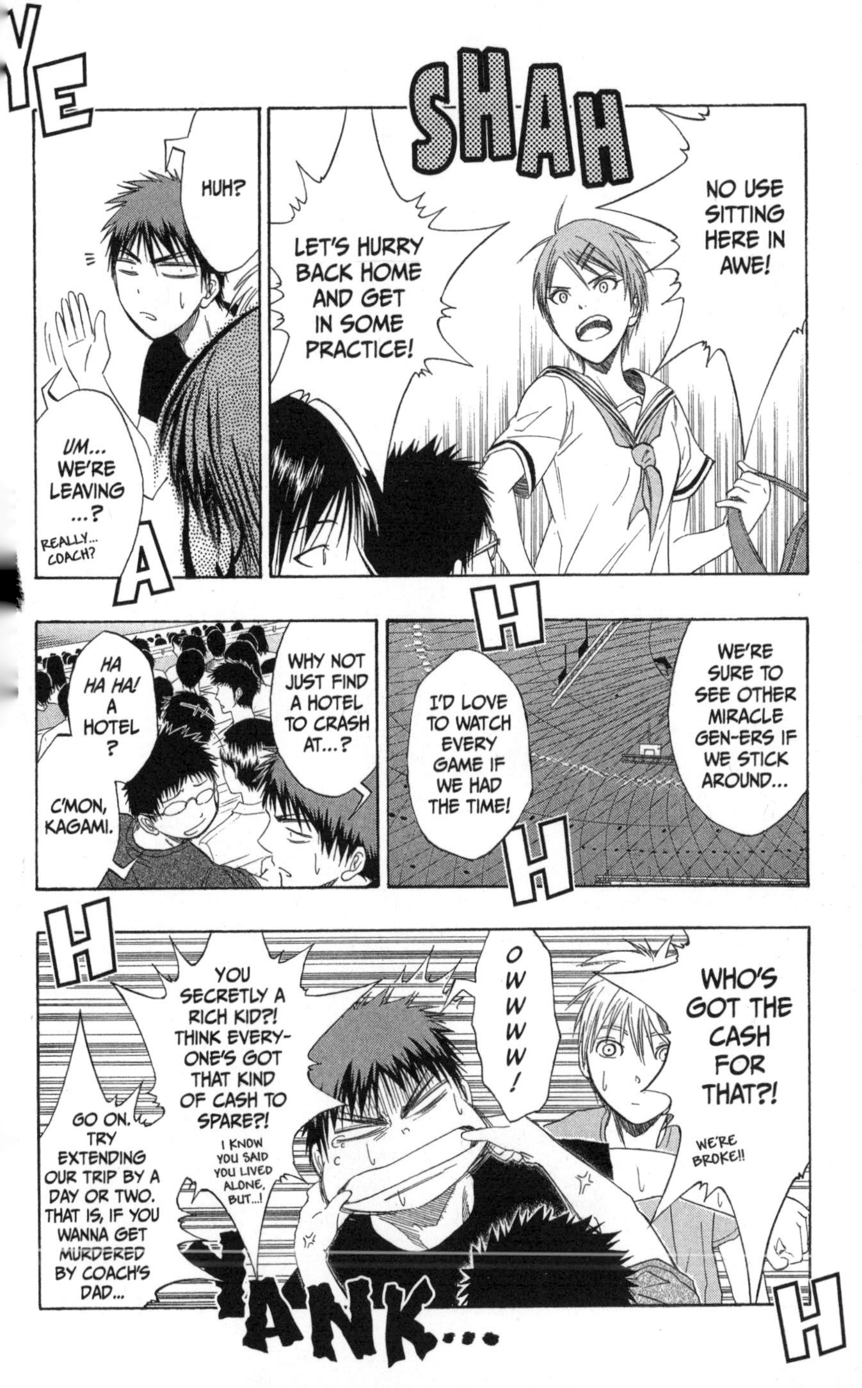
SHAH
NO USE SITTING HERE IN AWE!
LET'S HURRY BACK HOME AND GET IN SOME PRACTICE!
HUH?
UM... WE'RE LEAVING ...?
REALLY... COACH?
YEAHHHH
WE'RE SURE TO SEE OTHER MIRACLE GEN-ERS IF WE STICK AROUND...
I'D LOVE TO WATCH EVERY GAME IF WE HAD THE TIME!
WHY NOT JUST FIND A HOTEL TO CRASH AT...?
HA HA HA! A HOTEL?
C'MON, KAGAMI.
WHO'S GOT THE CASH FOR THAT?!
WE'RE BROKE!!
OWWWW!
YOU SECRETLY A RICH KID?! THINK EVERY-ONE'S GOT THAT KIND OF CASH TO SPARE?!
I KNOW YOU SAID YOU LIVED ALONE, BUT...!
GO ON. TRY EXTENDING OUR TRIP BY A DAY OR TWO. THAT IS, IF YOU WANNA GET MURDERED BY COACH'S DAD...
YANK...

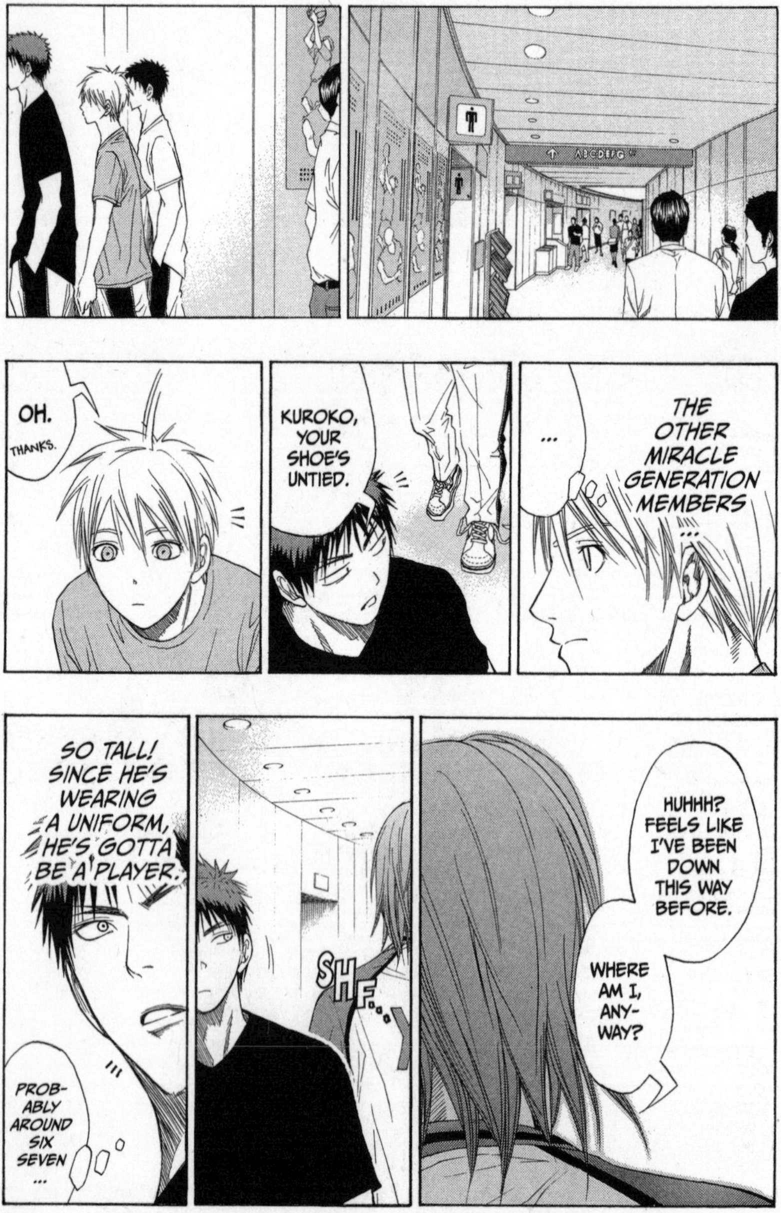

ABCDEFG
THE OTHER MIRACLE GENERATION MEMBERS ...
...
KUROKO, YOUR SHOE'S UNTIED.
OH.
THANKS.
HUHHH? FEELS LIKE I'VE BEEN DOWN THIS WAY BEFORE.
WHERE AM I, ANY-WAY?
SHF...
SO TALL! SINCE HE'S WEARING A UNIFORM, HE'S GOTTA BE A PLAYER.
PROB-ABLY AROUND SIX SEVEN ...

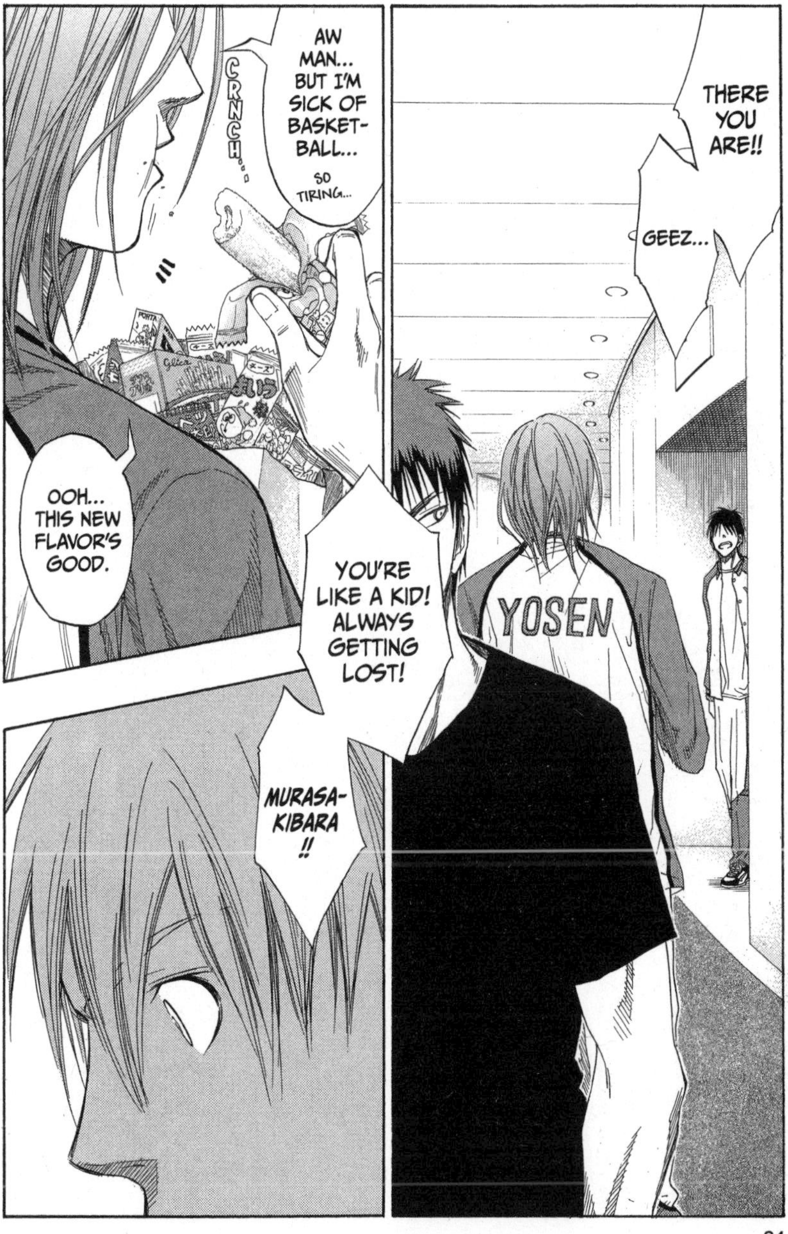
THERE YOU ARE!!
GEEZ...
YOU'RE LIKE A KID! ALWAYS GETTING LOST!
MURASA-KIBARA!!
AW MAN... BUT I'M SICK OF BASKET-BALL...
SO TIRING...
CRNCH..
OOH... THIS NEW FLAVOR'S GOOD.

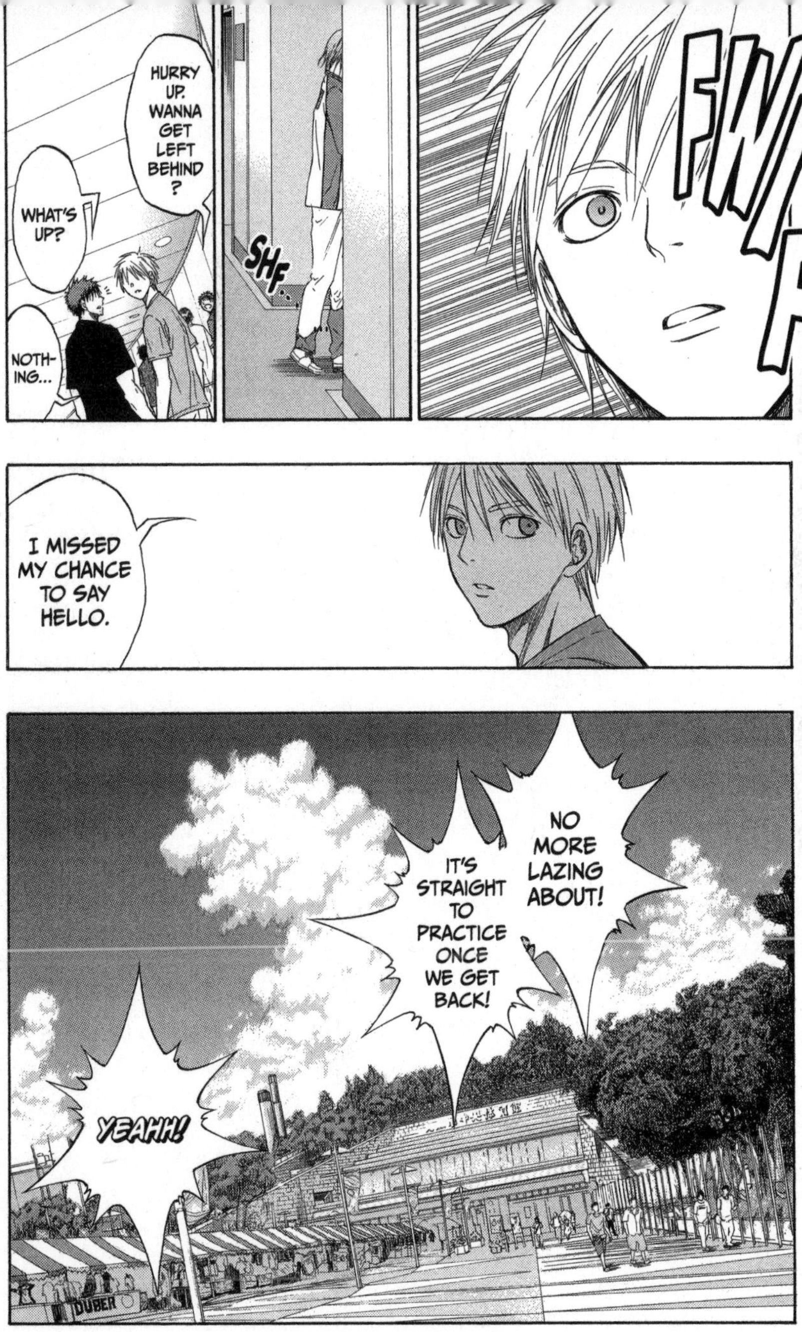
FWIP
SHF...
HURRY UP. WANNA GET LEFT BEHIND?
WHAT'S UP?
NOTHING...
I MISSED MY CHANCE TO SAY HELLO.
NO MORE LAZING ABOUT!
IT'S STRAIGHT TO PRACTICE ONCE WE GET BACK!
YEAHH!
DUBER

KUROKO'S BASKETBALL BLOOPERS

TAKE 8

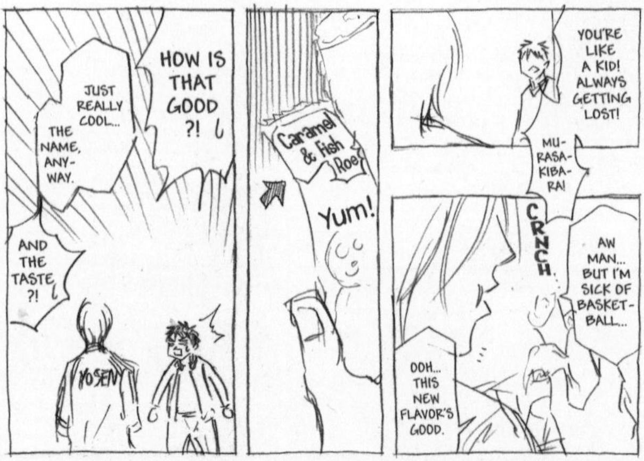

YOU'RE LIKE A KID! ALWAYS GETTING LOST!
MU-RASA-KIBA-RA!
CRNCH..
AW MAN... BUT I'M SICK OF BASKET-BALL...
OOH... THIS NEW FLAVOR'S GOOD.
Caramel & Fish Roe
Yum!
HOW IS THAT GOOD ?!
JUST REALLY COOL...
THE NAME, ANY-WAY.
AND THE TASTE ?!
YOSEN

74TH QUARTER: I ADOPTED HIM

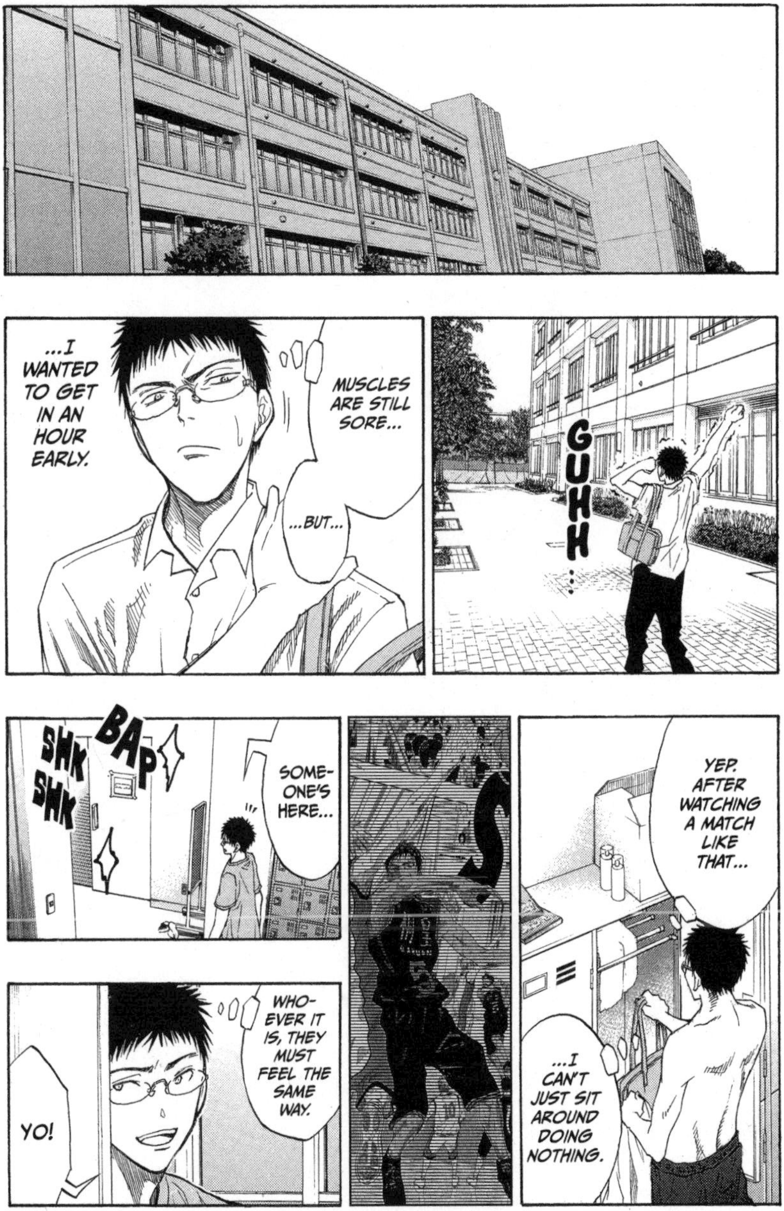
GUHH...
MUSCLES ARE STILL SORE...
...BUT...
...I WANTED TO GET IN AN HOUR EARLY.
YEP. AFTER WATCHING A MATCH LIKE THAT...
...I CAN'T JUST SIT AROUND DOING NOTHING.
BAP
SHK SHK
SOME-ONE'S HERE...
WHO-EVER IT IS, THEY MUST FEEL THE SAME WAY.
YO!

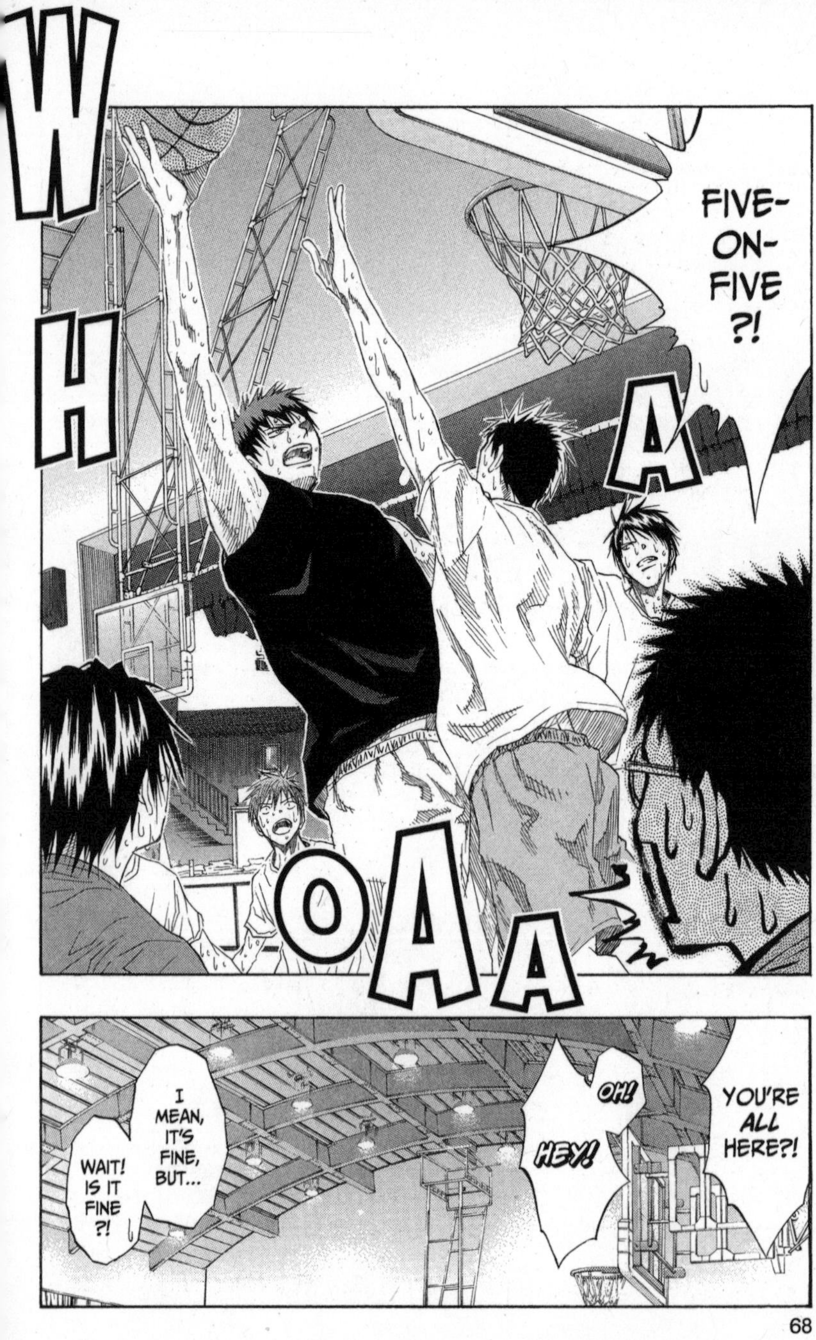
FIVE-ON-FIVE?!
W
H
A
OAA
YOU'RE ALL HERE?!
OH! HEY!
I MEAN, IT'S FINE, BUT...
WAIT! IS IT FINE?!

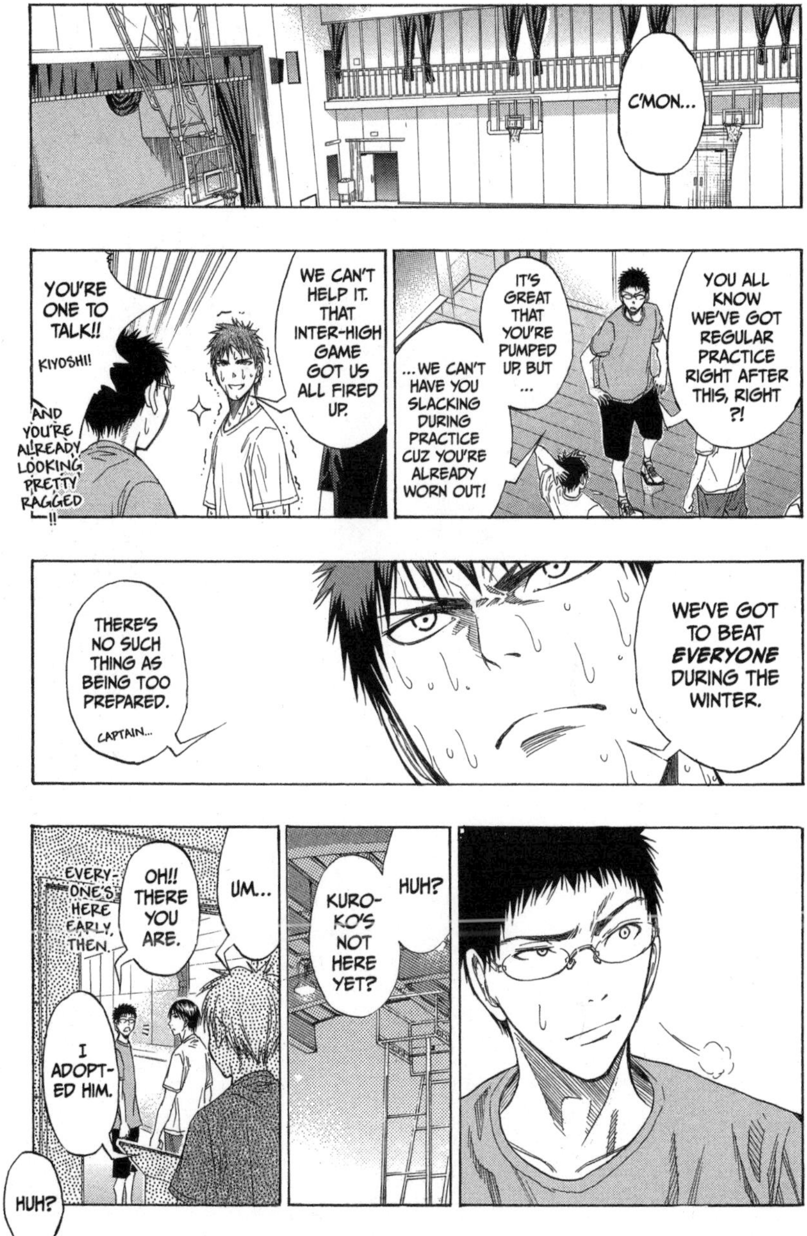
C'MON...
YOU ALL KNOW WE'VE GOT REGULAR PRACTICE RIGHT AFTER THIS, RIGHT?!
IT'S GREAT THAT YOU'RE PUMPED UP, BUT ...
...WE CAN'T HAVE YOU SLACKING DURING PRACTICE CUZ YOU'RE ALREADY WORN OUT!
WE CAN'T HELP IT. THAT INTER-HIGH GAME GOT US ALL FIRED UP.
YOU'RE ONE TO TALK!!
KIYOSHI!
AND YOU'RE ALREADY LOOKING PRETTY RAGGED!!
WE'VE GOT TO BEAT *EVERYONE* DURING THE WINTER.
THERE'S NO SUCH THING AS BEING TOO PREPARED.
CAPTAIN...
HUH?
KURO-KO'S NOT HERE YET?
UM...
OH!! THERE YOU ARE.
EVERY-ONE'S HERE EARLY, THEN.
I ADOPT-ED HIM.
HUH?

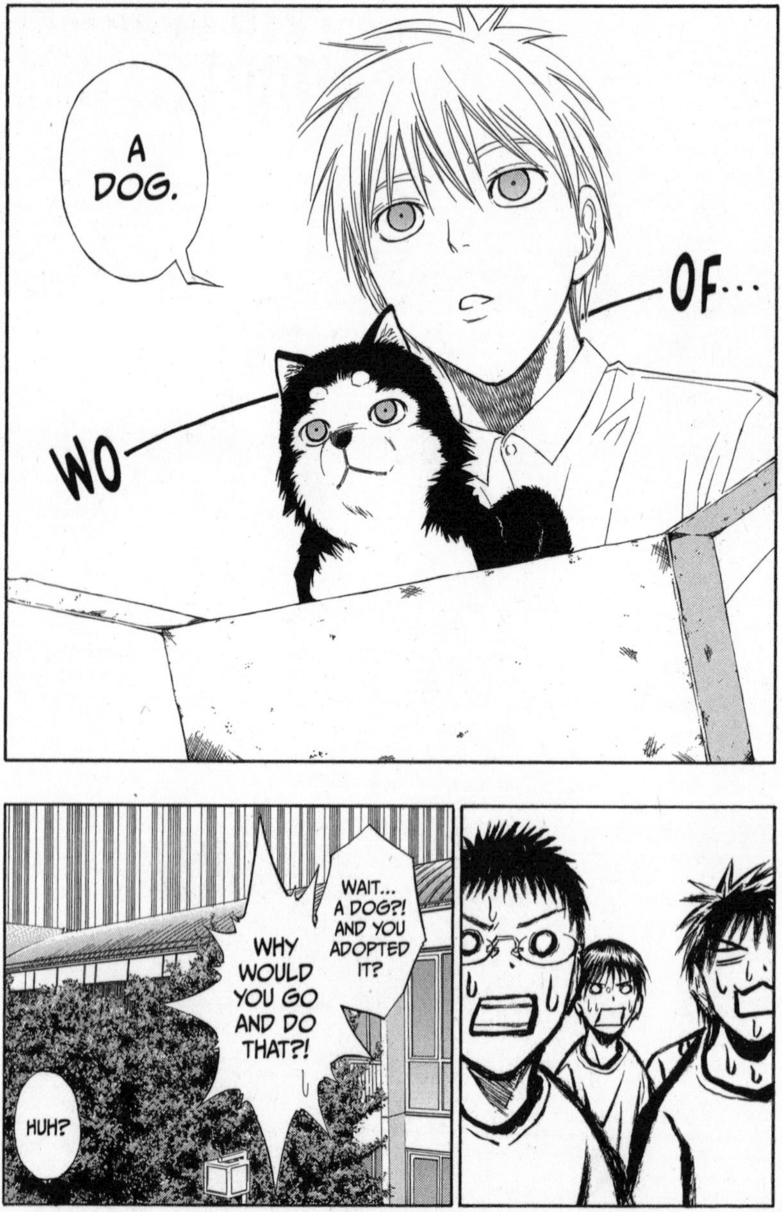
A DOG.
WO—OF...
WAIT... A DOG?! AND YOU ADOPTED IT?
WHY WOULD YOU GO AND DO THAT?!
HUH?

74TH QUARTER: I ADOPTED HIM

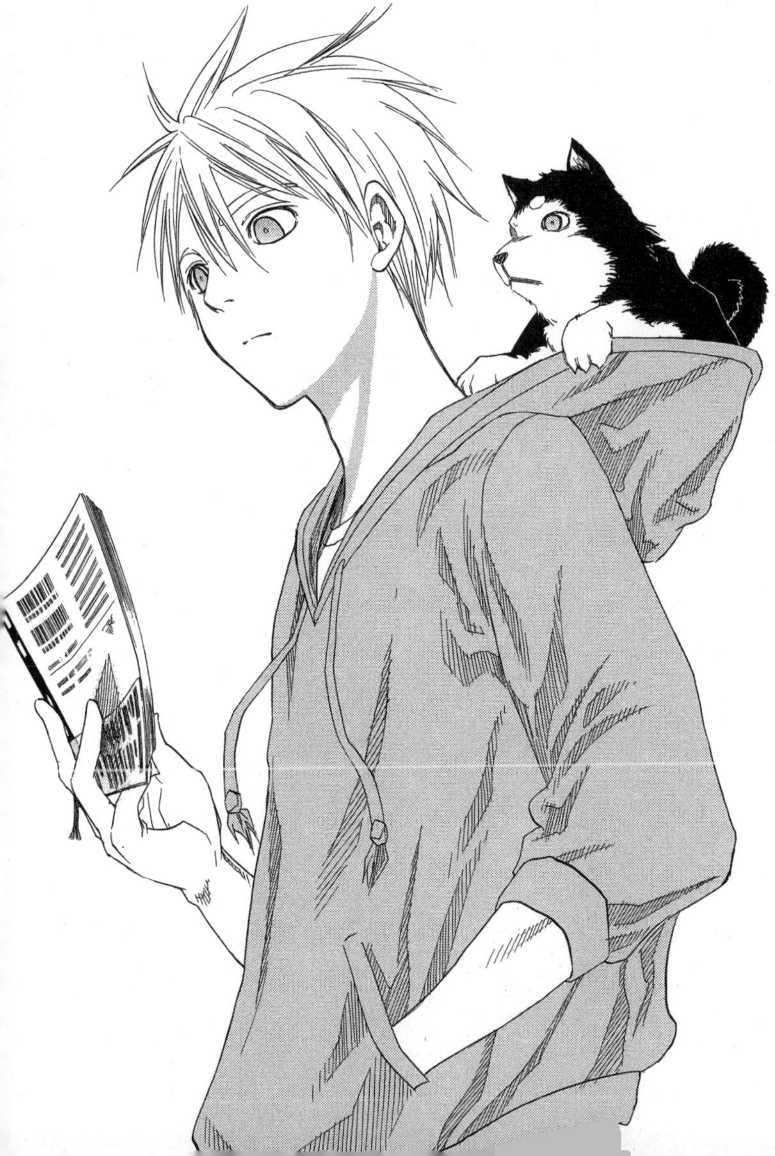

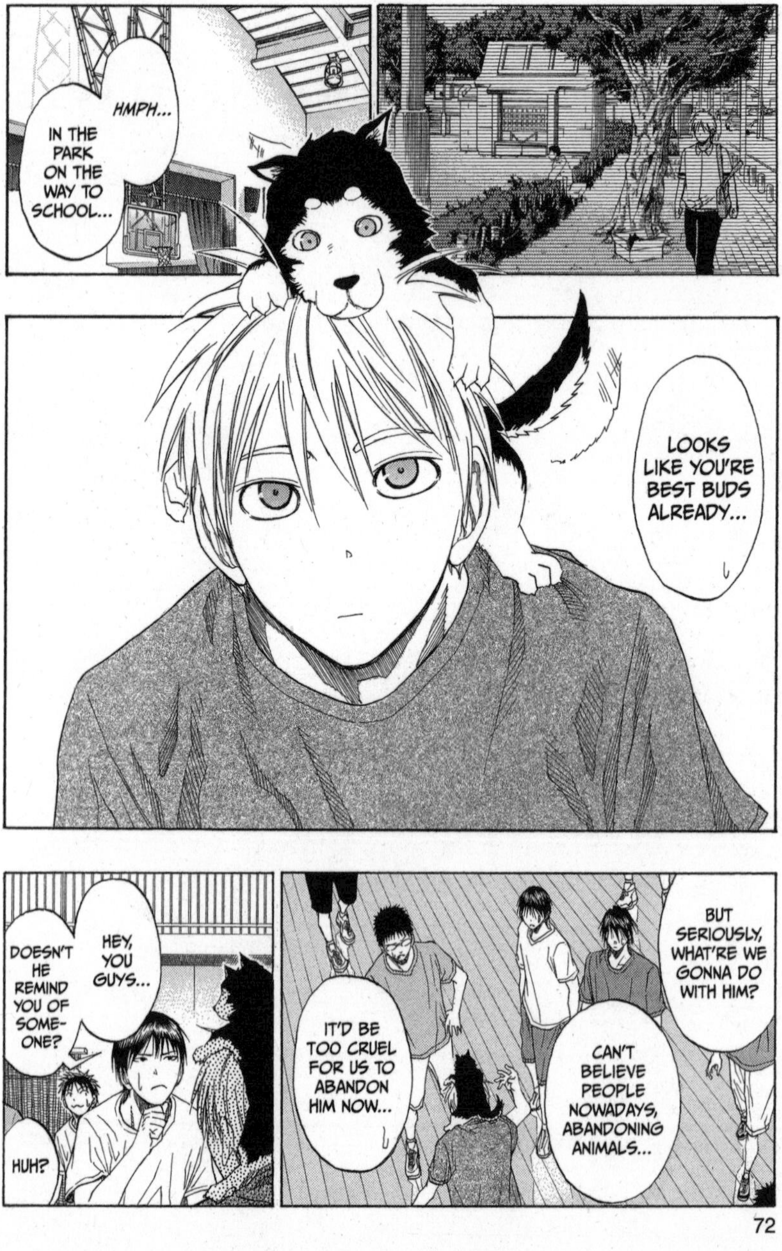
HMPH...
IN THE PARK ON THE WAY TO SCHOOL...
LOOKS LIKE YOU'RE BEST BUDS ALREADY...
BUT SERIOUSLY, WHAT'RE WE GONNA DO WITH HIM?
CAN'T BELIEVE PEOPLE NOWADAYS, ABANDONING ANIMALS...
IT'D BE TOO CRUEL FOR US TO ABANDON HIM NOW...
HEY, YOU GUYS...
DOESN'T HE REMIND YOU OF SOME-ONE?
HUH?

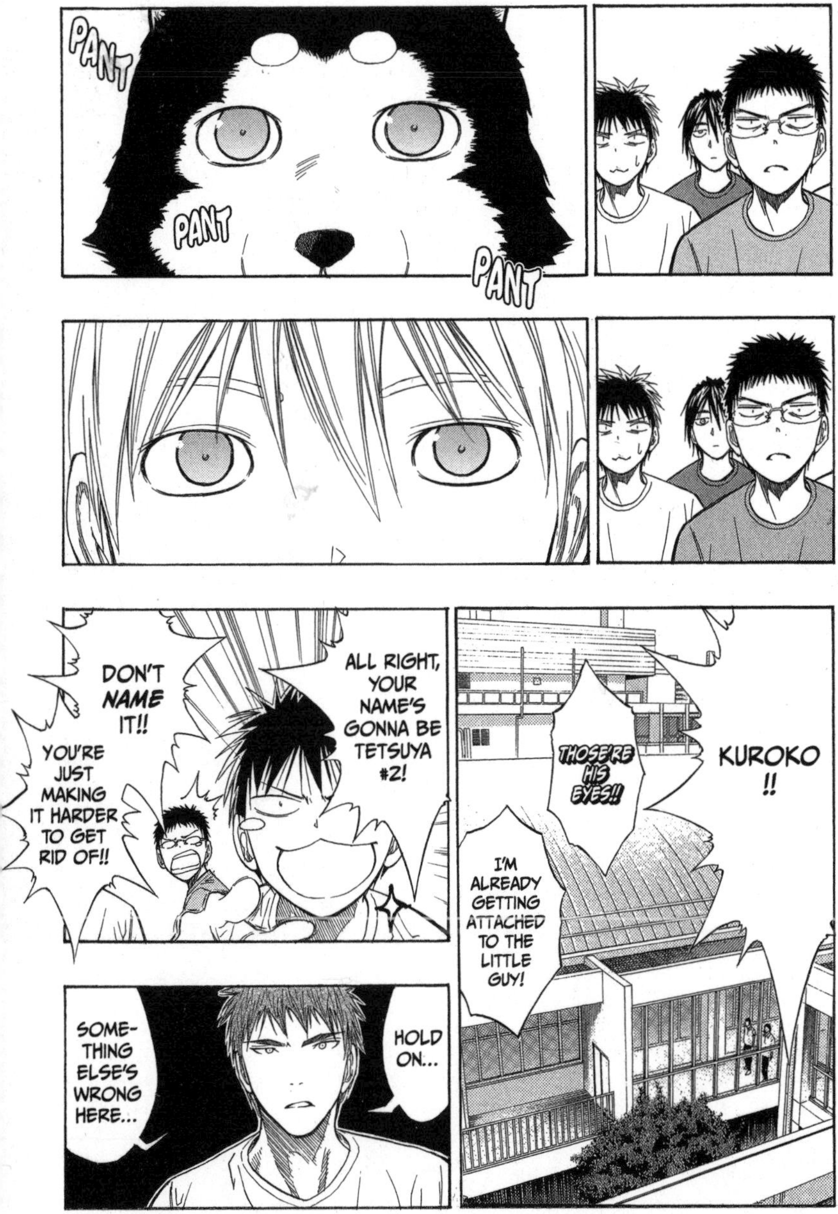
PANT
PANT
PANT
KUROKO !!
THOSE'RE HIS EYES!!
I'M ALREADY GETTING ATTACHED TO THE LITTLE GUY!
ALL RIGHT, YOUR NAME'S GONNA BE TETSUYA #2!
DON'T *NAME* IT!!
YOU'RE JUST MAKING IT HARDER TO GET RID OF!!
HOLD ON...
SOME-THING ELSE'S WRONG HERE...

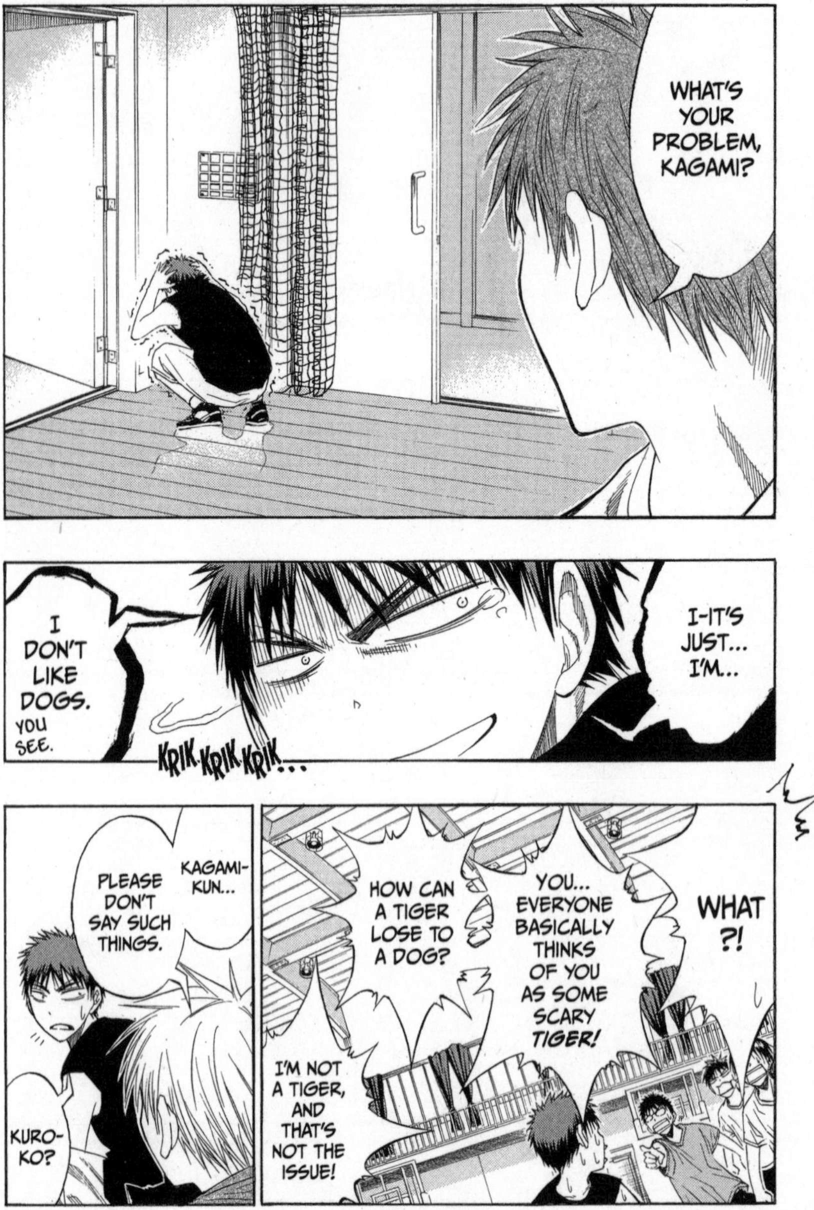
WHAT'S YOUR PROBLEM, KAGAMI?
I-IT'S JUST... I'M...
I DON'T LIKE DOGS.
YOU SEE.
KRIK KRIK KRIK...
WHAT?!
YOU... EVERYONE BASICALLY THINKS OF YOU AS SOME SCARY TIGER!
HOW CAN A TIGER LOSE TO A DOG?
I'M NOT A TIGER, AND THAT'S NOT THE ISSUE!
KAGAMI-KUN...
PLEASE DON'T SAY SUCH THINGS.
KURO-KO?

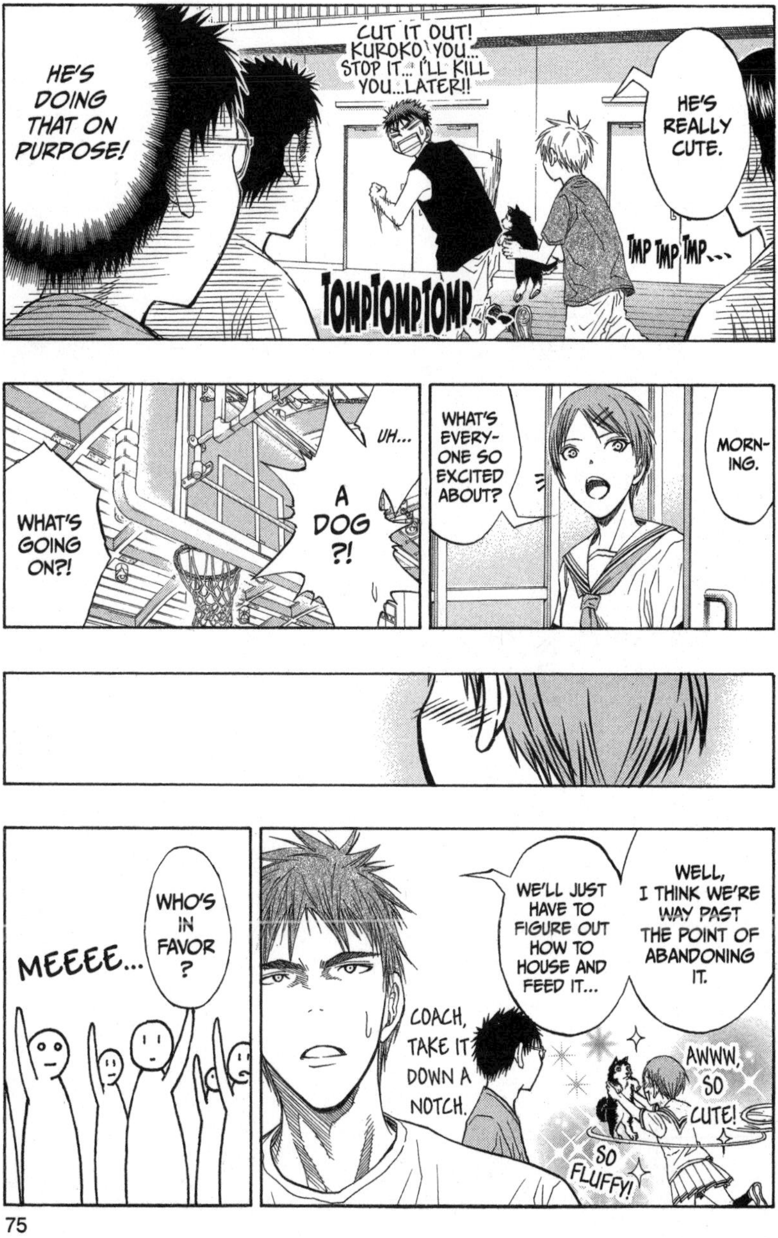
HE'S REALLY CUTE.
TMP TMP TMP...
CUT IT OUT! KUROKO, YOU... STOP IT... I'LL KILL YOU...LATER!!
TOMPTOMPTOMP
HE'S DOING THAT ON PURPOSE!
MORNING.
WHAT'S EVERYONE SO EXCITED ABOUT?
UH...
A DOG ?!
WHAT'S GOING ON?!
WELL, I THINK WE'RE WAY PAST THE POINT OF ABANDONING IT.
WE'LL JUST HAVE TO FIGURE OUT HOW TO HOUSE AND FEED IT...
AWWW, SO CUTE!
SO FLUFFY!
COACH, TAKE IT DOWN A NOTCH.
WHO'S IN FAVOR ?
MEEEE...

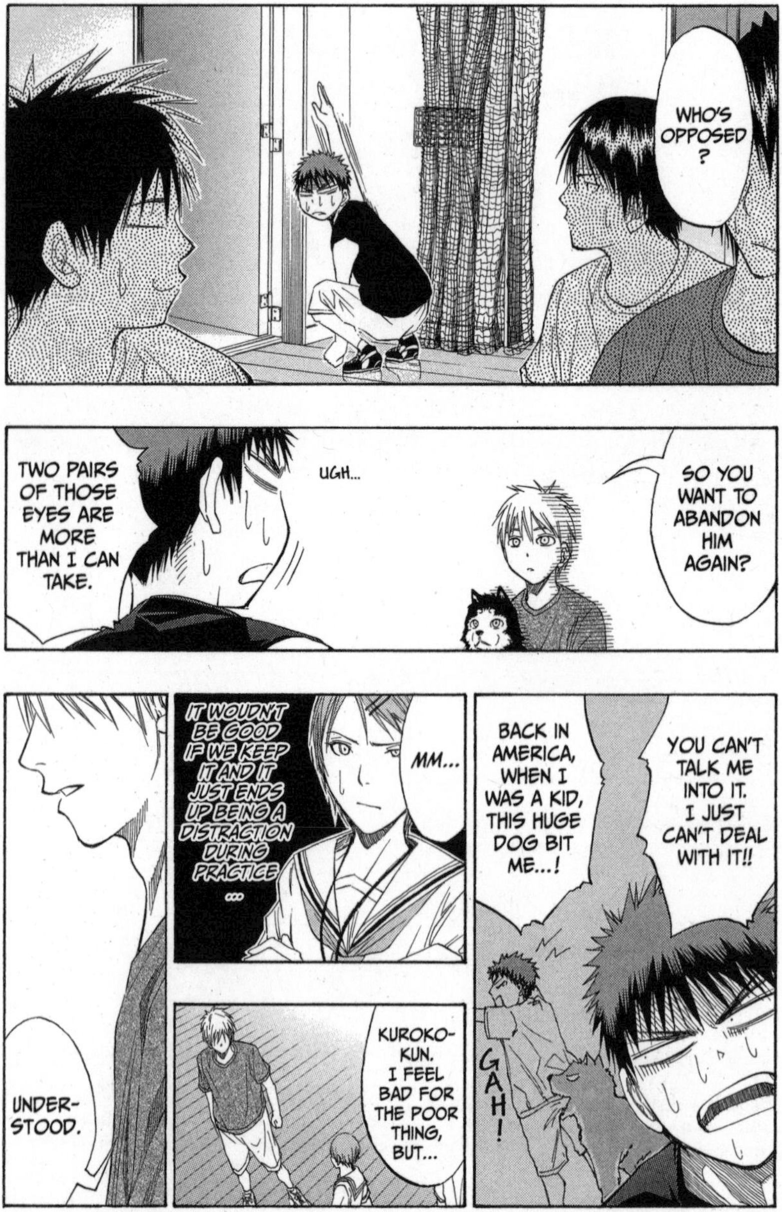
WHO'S OPPOSED?
SO YOU WANT TO ABANDON HIM AGAIN?
UGH...
TWO PAIRS OF THOSE EYES ARE MORE THAN I CAN TAKE.
YOU CAN'T TALK ME INTO IT. I JUST CAN'T DEAL WITH IT!!
BACK IN AMERICA, WHEN I WAS A KID, THIS HUGE DOG BIT ME...!
GAH!
MM...
IT WOUDN'T BE GOOD IF WE KEEP IT AND IT JUST ENDS UP BEING A DISTRACTION DURING PRACTICE...
KUROKO-KUN. I FEEL BAD FOR THE POOR THING, BUT...
UNDER-STOOD.

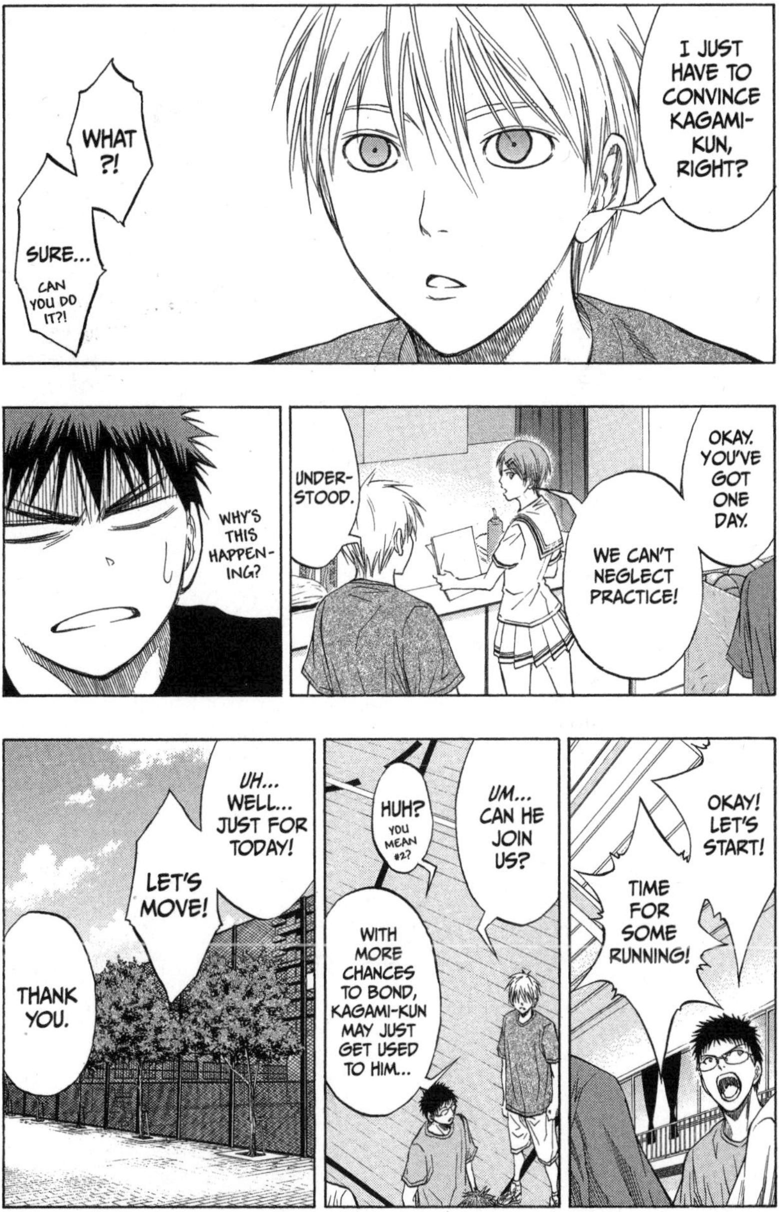
I JUST HAVE TO CONVINCE KAGAMI-KUN, RIGHT?
WHAT?!
SURE...
CAN YOU DO IT?!
OKAY. YOU'VE GOT ONE DAY.
WE CAN'T NEGLECT PRACTICE!
UNDERSTOOD.
WHY'S THIS HAPPENING?
OKAY! LET'S START!
TIME FOR SOME RUNNING!
UM... CAN HE JOIN US?
HUH?
YOU MEAN #2?
WITH MORE CHANCES TO BOND, KAGAMI-KUN MAY JUST GET USED TO HIM...
UH... WELL... JUST FOR TODAY!
LET'S MOVE!
THANK YOU.

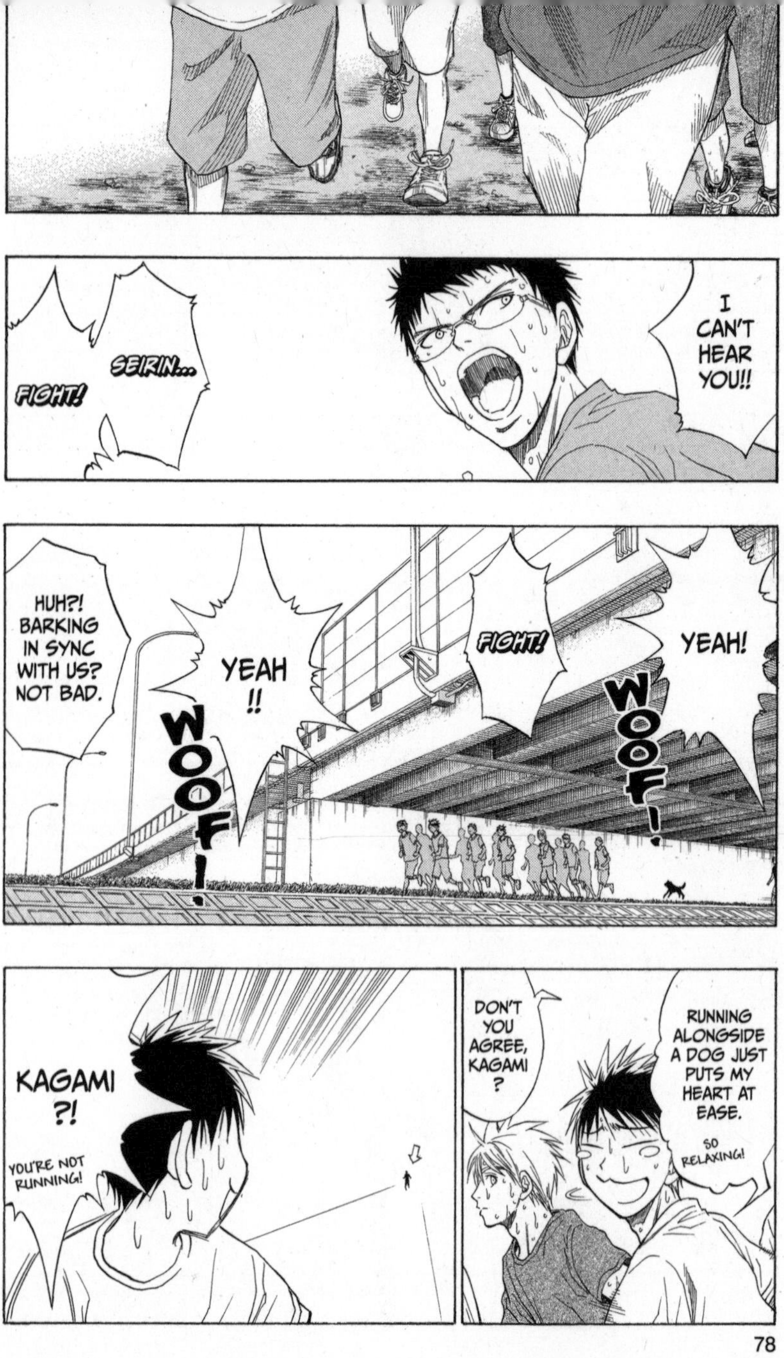
I CAN'T HEAR YOU!!
SEIRIN...
FIGHT!
YEAH!
FIGHT!
WOOF!
YEAH !!
WOOF!
HUH?! BARKING IN SYNC WITH US? NOT BAD.
RUNNING ALONGSIDE A DOG JUST PUTS MY HEART AT EASE.
SO RELAXING!
DON'T YOU AGREE, KAGAMI?
KAGAMI ?!
YOU'RE NOT RUNNING!

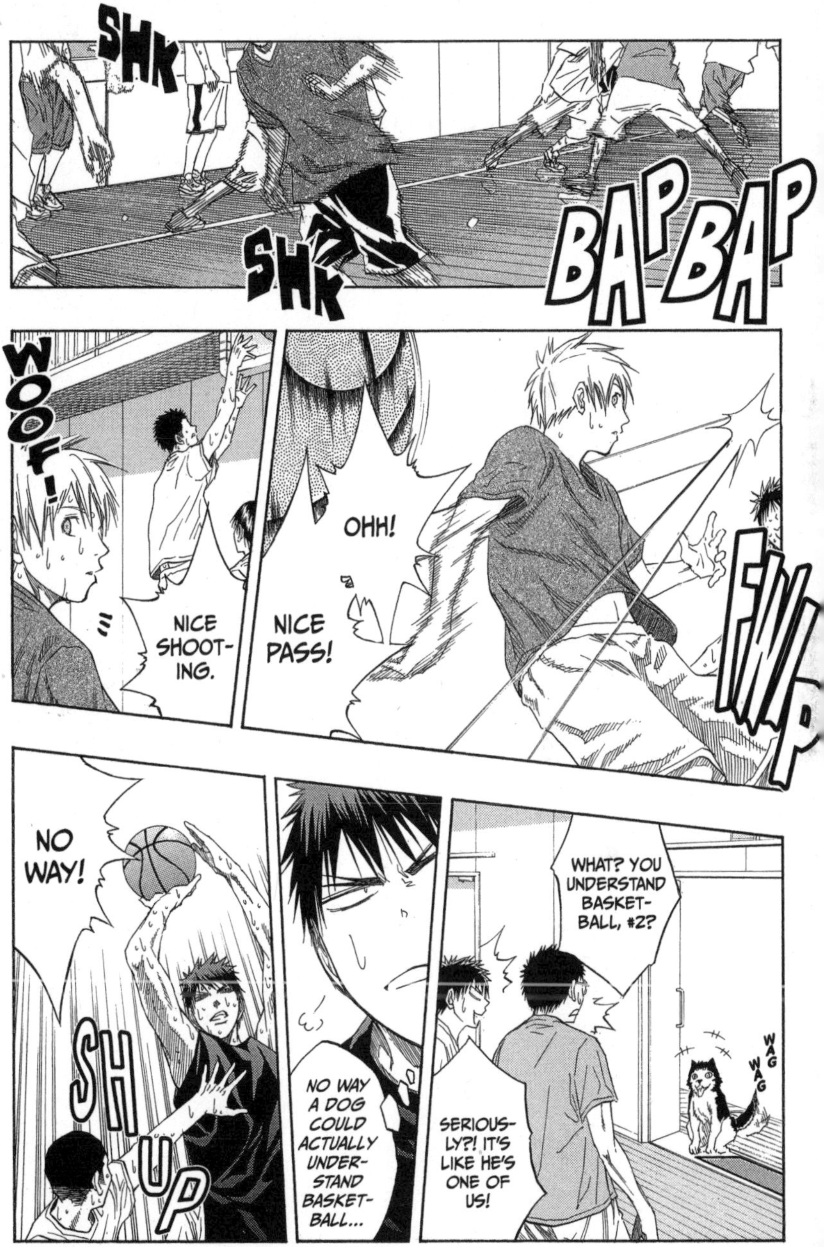
BAP BAP
SHK
SHK
FWIP
OHH!
NICE PASS!
WOOF!
NICE SHOOT-ING.
WHAT? YOU UNDERSTAND BASKET-BALL, #2?
WAG WAG
SERIOUS-LY?! IT'S LIKE HE'S ONE OF US!
NO WAY A DOG COULD ACTUALLY UNDER-STAND BASKET-BALL...
NO WAY!
SHUP

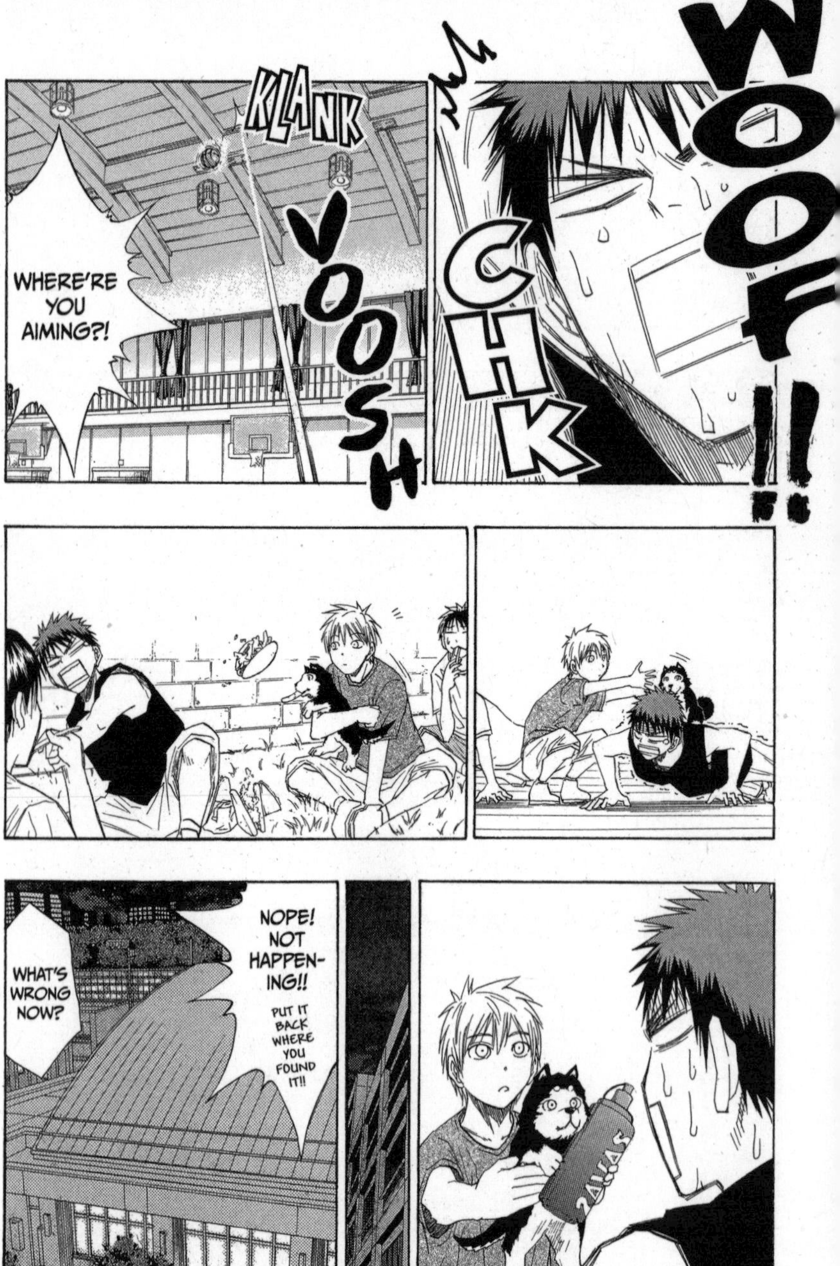
WOOF!!!!
CHK
KLANK
VOOSH
WHERE'RE YOU AIMING?!
NOPE! NOT HAPPENING!!
PUT IT BACK WHERE YOU FOUND IT!!
WHAT'S WRONG NOW?

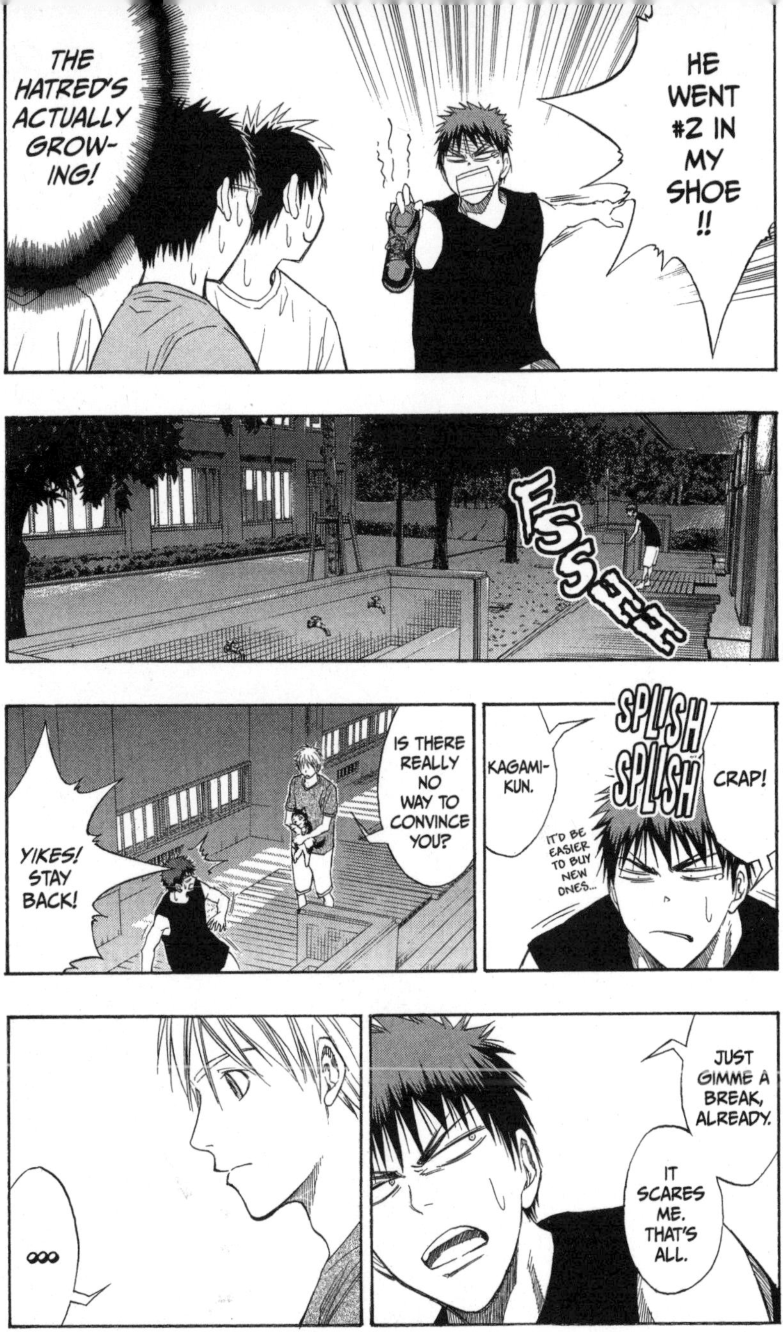
HE WENT #2 IN MY SHOE!!
THE HATRED'S ACTUALLY GROWING!
FSSHHH
SPLISH SPLISH
CRAP!
KAGAMI-KUN.
IT'D BE EASIER TO BUY NEW ONES...
IS THERE REALLY NO WAY TO CONVINCE YOU?
YIKES! STAY BACK!
JUST GIMME A BREAK, ALREADY.
IT SCARES ME. THAT'S ALL.
...

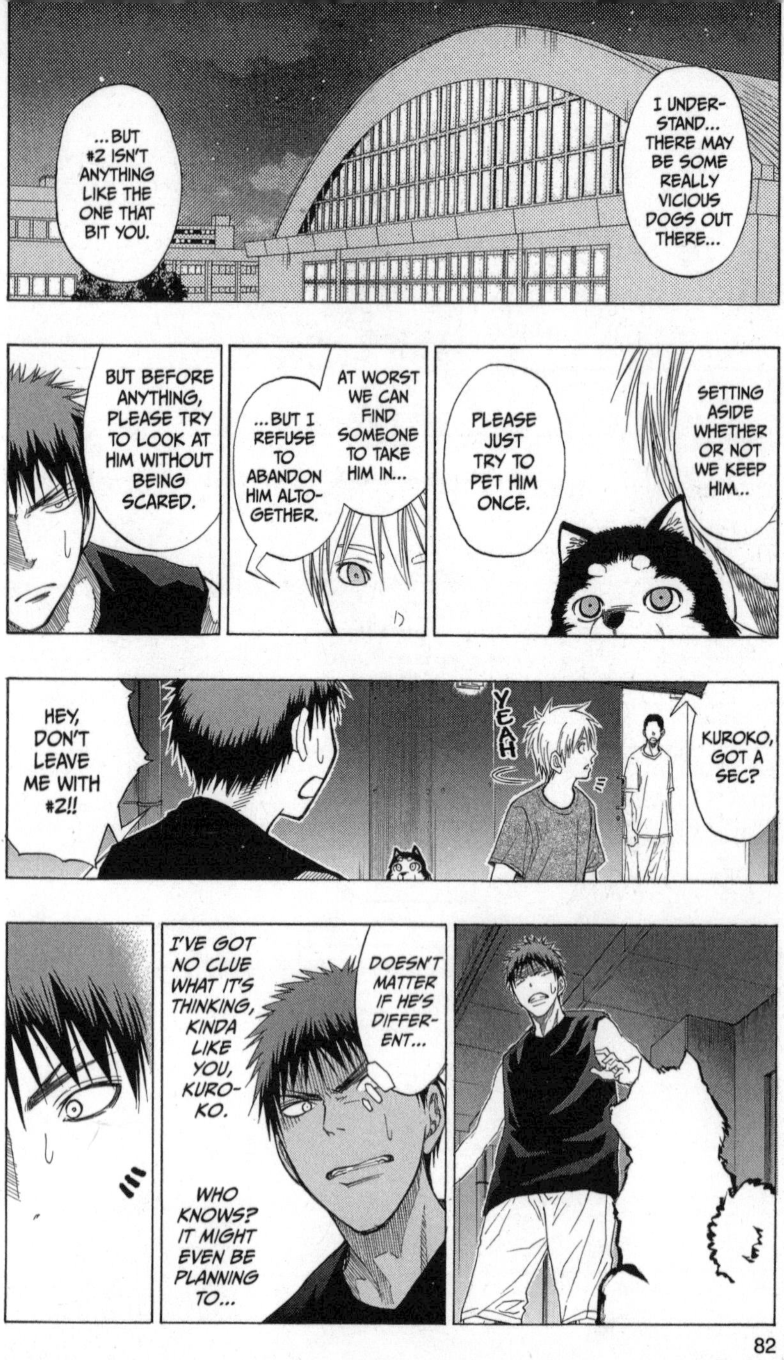
I UNDER-STAND... THERE MAY BE SOME REALLY VICIOUS DOGS OUT THERE...
...BUT #2 ISN'T ANYTHING LIKE THE ONE THAT BIT YOU.
SETTING ASIDE WHETHER OR NOT WE KEEP HIM...
PLEASE JUST TRY TO PET HIM ONCE.
AT WORST WE CAN FIND SOMEONE TO TAKE HIM IN...
...BUT I REFUSE TO ABANDON HIM ALTO-GETHER.
BUT BEFORE ANYTHING, PLEASE TRY TO LOOK AT HIM WITHOUT BEING SCARED.
KUROKO, GOT A SEC?
YEAH
HEY, DON'T LEAVE ME WITH #2!!
DOESN'T MATTER IF HE'S DIFFER-ENT...
I'VE GOT NO CLUE WHAT IT'S THINKING, KINDA LIKE YOU, KURO-KO.
WHO KNOWS? IT MIGHT EVEN BE PLANNING TO...

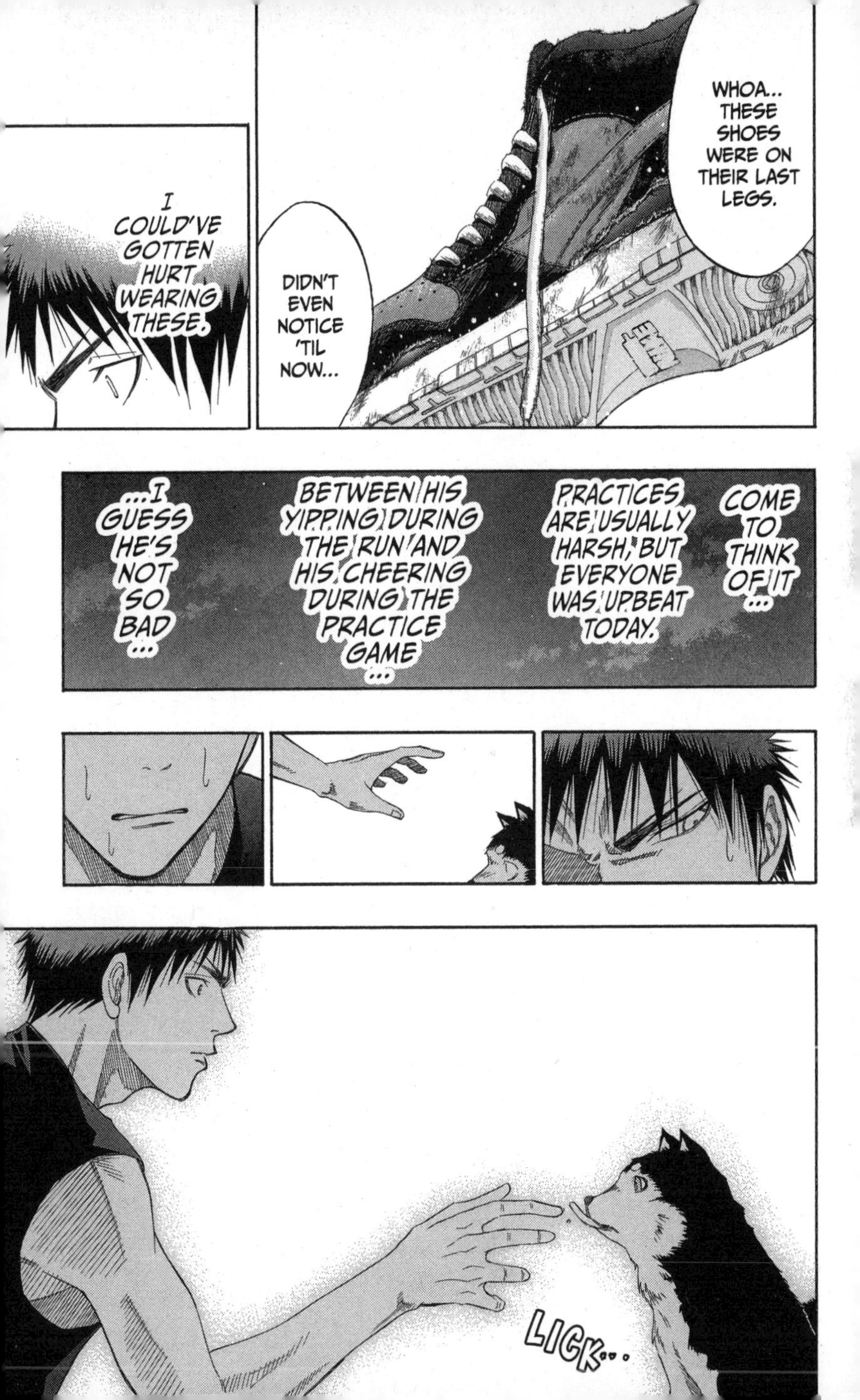
WHOA... THESE SHOES WERE ON THEIR LAST LEGS.
DIDN'T EVEN NOTICE 'TIL NOW...
I COULD'VE GOTTEN HURT WEARING THESE.
COME TO THINK OF IT...
PRACTICES ARE USUALLY HARSH, BUT EVERYONE WAS UPBEAT TODAY.
BETWEEN HIS YIPPING DURING THE RUN AND HIS CHEERING DURING THE PRACTICE GAME...
...I GUESS HE'S NOT SO BAD...
LICK...

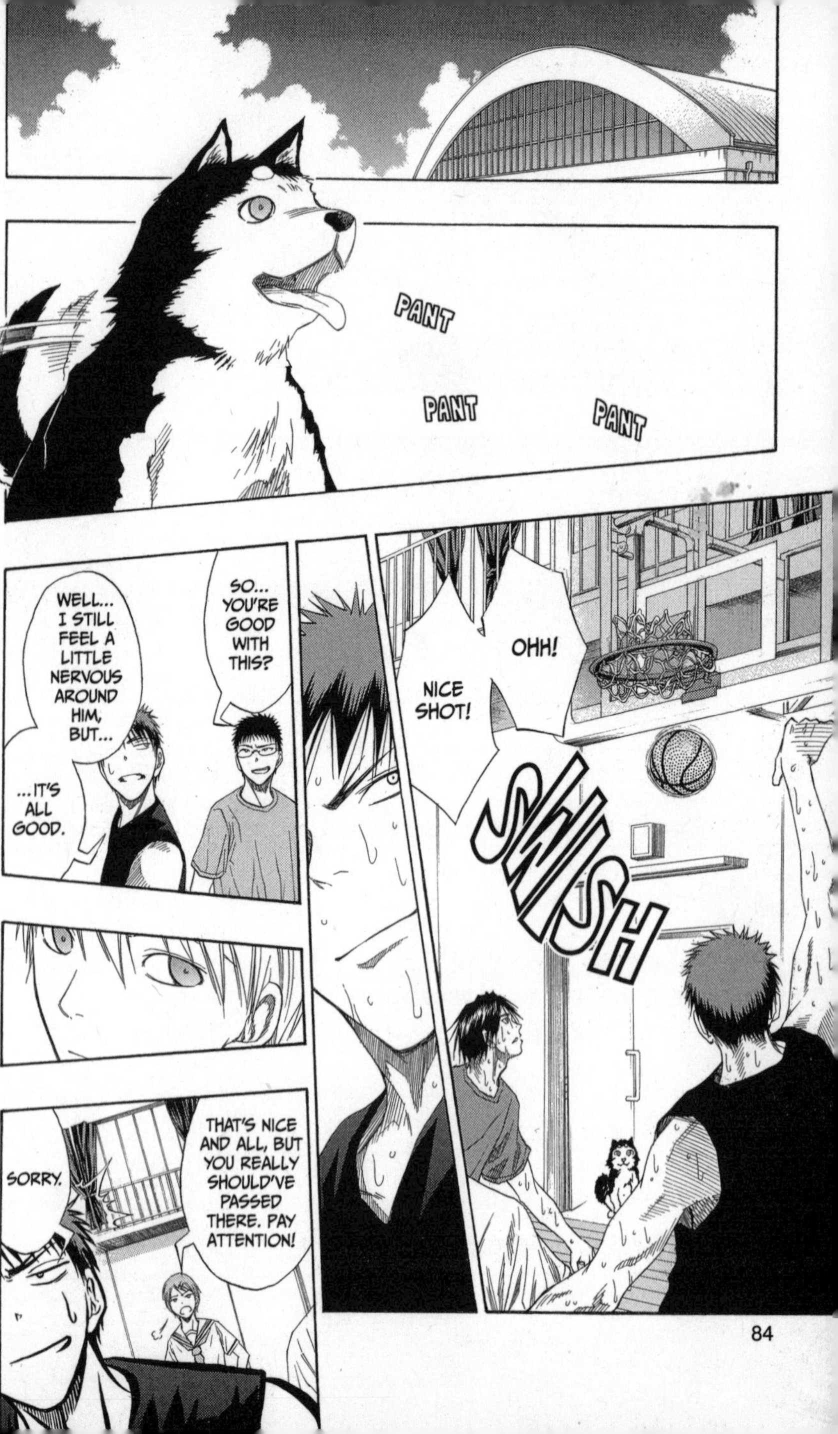
PANT
PANT
PANT
OHH!
NICE SHOT!
SWISH
SO... YOU'RE GOOD WITH THIS?
WELL... I STILL FEEL A LITTLE NERVOUS AROUND HIM, BUT...
...IT'S ALL GOOD.
THAT'S NICE AND ALL, BUT YOU REALLY SHOULD'VE PASSED THERE. PAY ATTENTION!
SORRY.

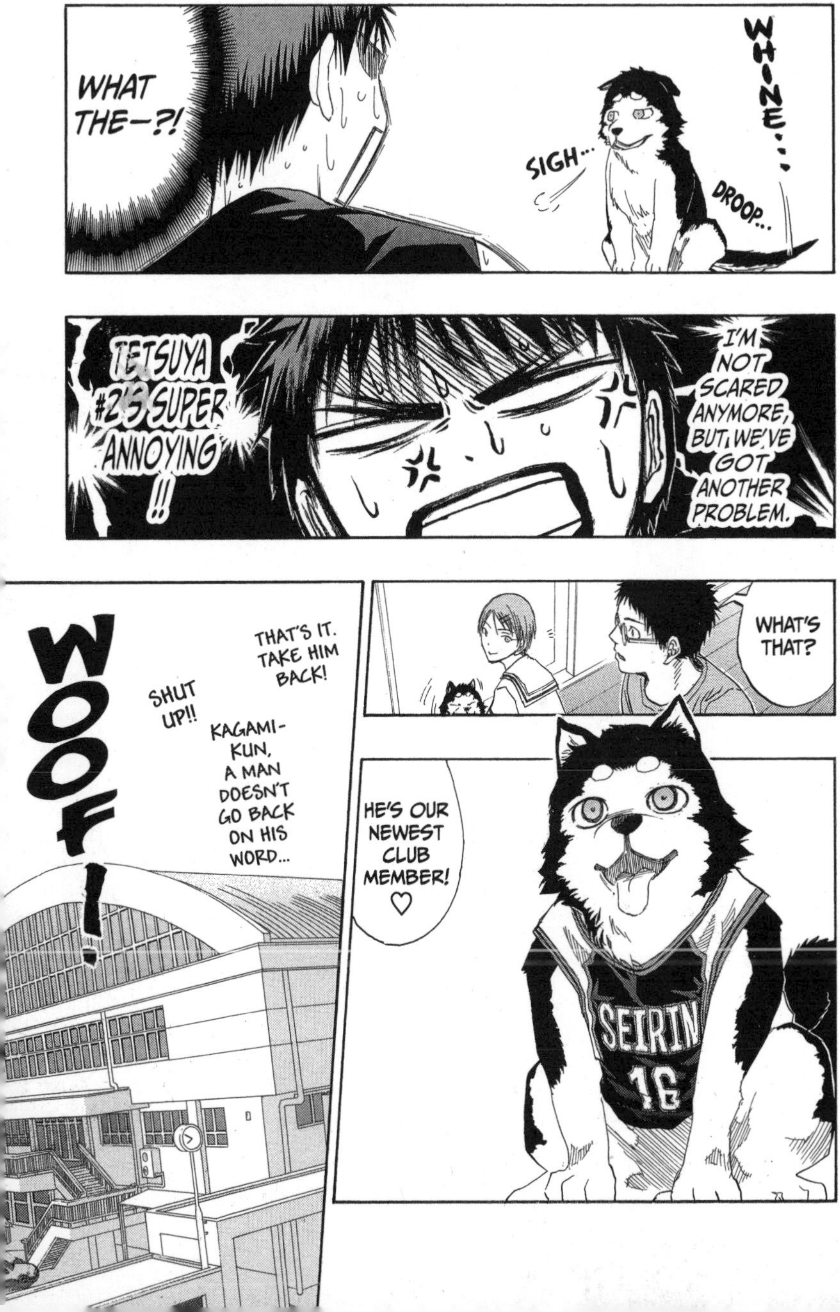
WHINE...
DROOP...
SIGH...
WHAT THE—?!
I'M NOT SCARED ANYMORE, BUT WE'VE GOT ANOTHER PROBLEM.
TETSUYA #2'S SUPER ANNOYING!!
WHAT'S THAT?
HE'S OUR NEWEST CLUB MEMBER! ♡
SEIRIN 16
THAT'S IT. TAKE HIM BACK!
SHUT UP!!
KAGAMI-KUN, A MAN DOESN'T GO BACK ON HIS WORD...
WOOF!

KUROKO'S BASKETBALL BLOOPERS

TAKE 6

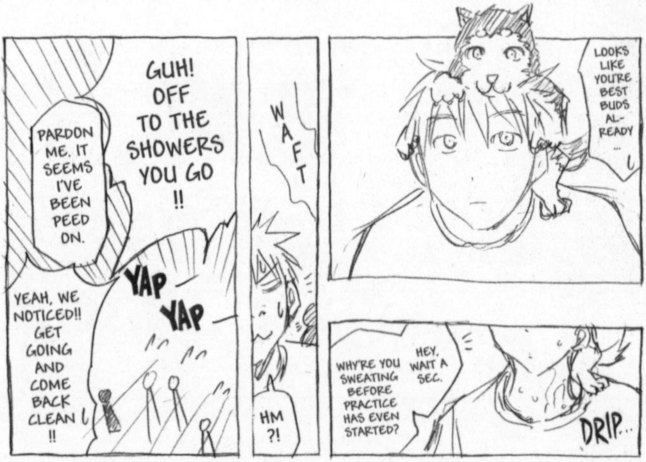
LOOKS LIKE YOU'RE BEST BUDS AL-READY ...
HEY, WAIT A SEC.
WHY'RE YOU SWEATING BEFORE PRACTICE HAS EVEN STARTED?
DRIP...
WAFT
HM ?!
GUH! OFF TO THE SHOWERS YOU GO !!
PARDON ME. IT SEEMS I'VE BEEN PEED ON.
YAP YAP
YEAH, WE NOTICED!! GET GOING AND COME BACK CLEAN !!

75TH QUARTER: NEVER EXPECTED TO MEET YOU HERE

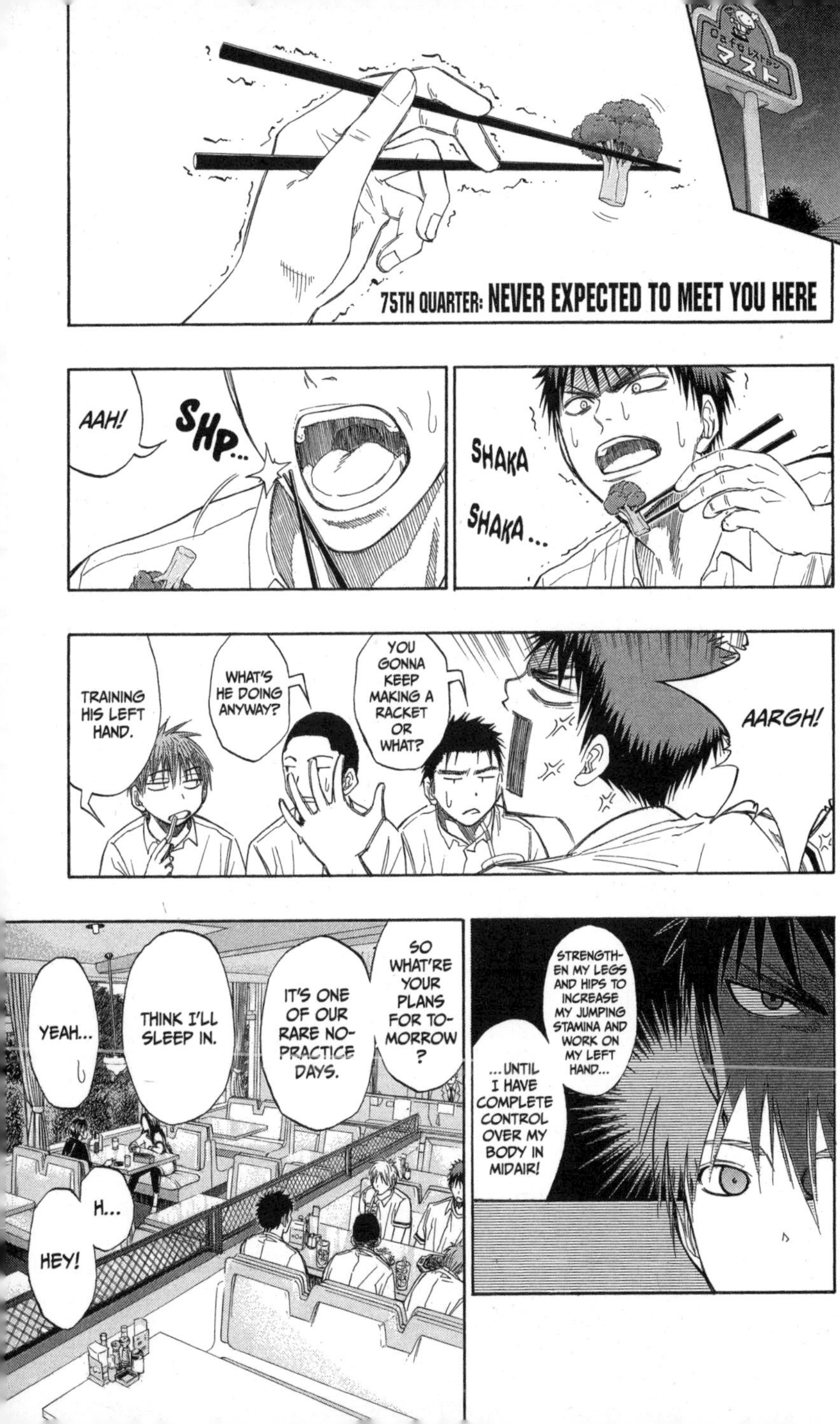
SHAKA
SHAKA...
AAH!
SHP...
AARGH!
YOU GONNA KEEP MAKING A RACKET OR WHAT?
WHAT'S HE DOING ANYWAY?
TRAINING HIS LEFT HAND.
STRENGTH-EN MY LEGS AND HIPS TO INCREASE MY JUMPING STAMINA AND WORK ON MY LEFT HAND...
...UNTIL I HAVE COMPLETE CONTROL OVER MY BODY IN MIDAIR!
SO WHAT'RE YOUR PLANS FOR TO-MORROW?
IT'S ONE OF OUR RARE NO-PRACTICE DAYS.
THINK I'LL SLEEP IN.
YEAH...
H...
HEY!

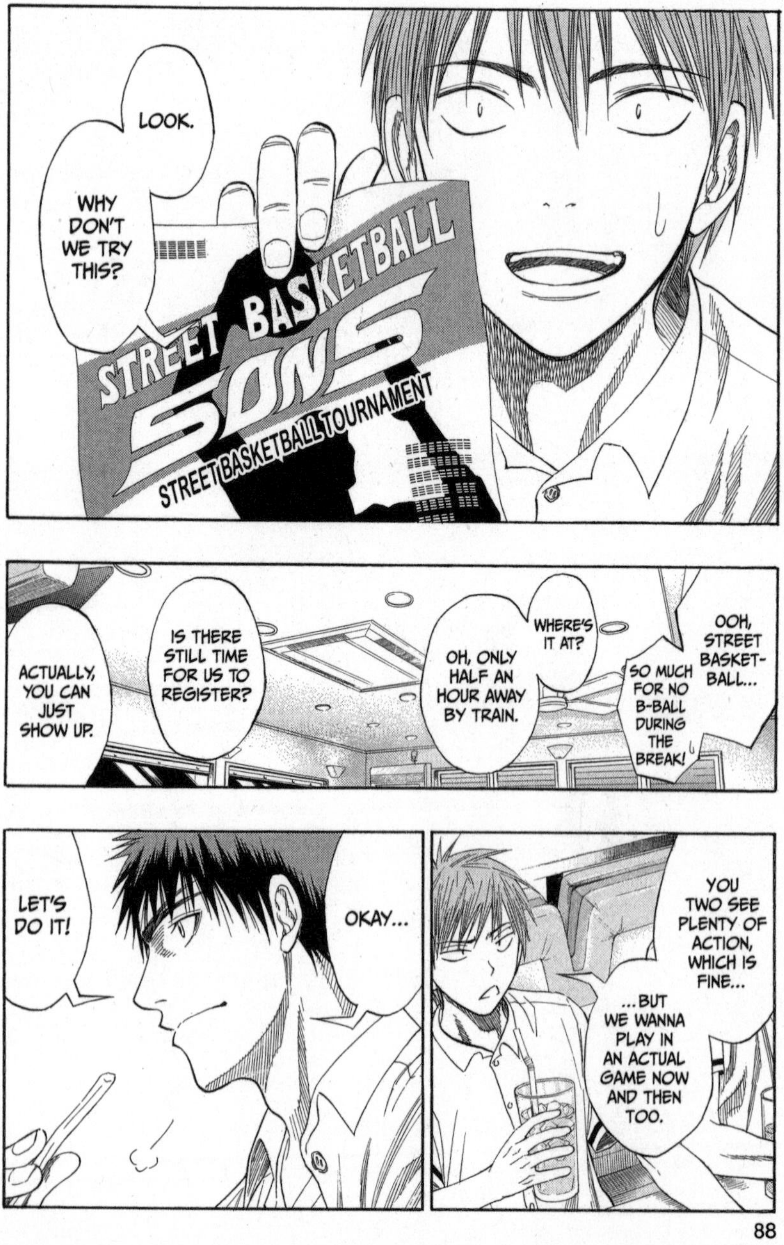
LOOK.
WHY DON'T WE TRY THIS?
STREET BASKETBALL
SONS
STREET BASKETBALL TOURNAMENT
OOH, STREET BASKET-BALL...
SO MUCH FOR NO B-BALL DURING THE BREAK!
WHERE'S IT AT?
OH, ONLY HALF AN HOUR AWAY BY TRAIN.
IS THERE STILL TIME FOR US TO REGISTER?
ACTUALLY, YOU CAN JUST SHOW UP.
YOU TWO SEE PLENTY OF ACTION, WHICH IS FINE...
...BUT WE WANNA PLAY IN AN ACTUAL GAME NOW AND THEN TOO.
OKAY...
LET'S DO IT!

75TH QUARTER:
NEVER EXPECTED TO MEET YOU HERE

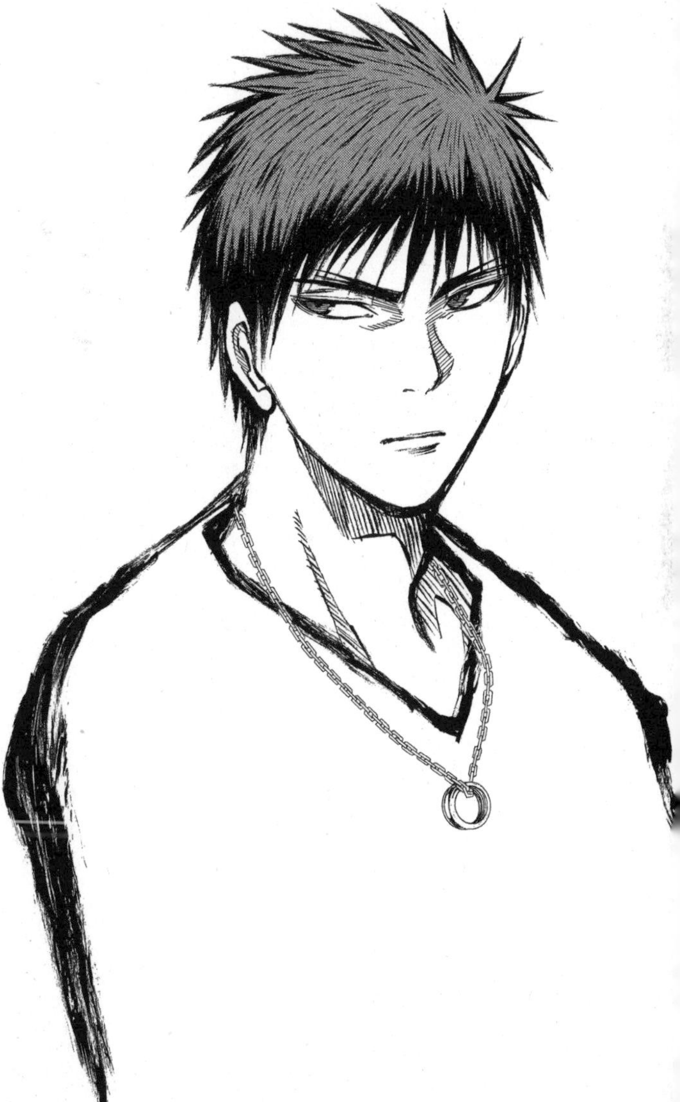

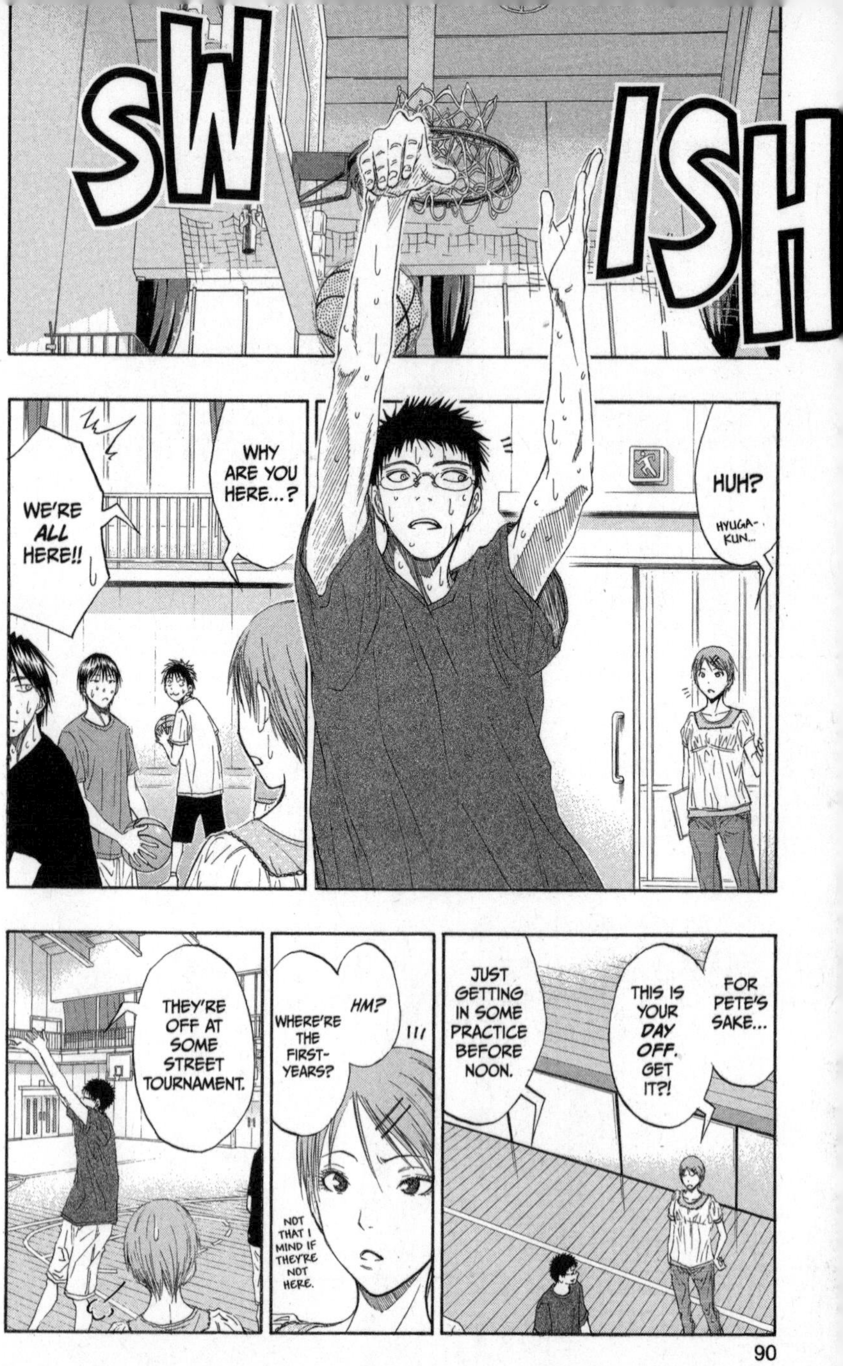
SWISH
HUH?
HYUGA-KUN...
WHY ARE YOU HERE...?
WE'RE ALL HERE!!
FOR PETE'S SAKE...
THIS IS YOUR DAY OFF. GET IT?!
JUST GETTING IN SOME PRACTICE BEFORE NOON.
HM?
WHERE'RE THE FIRST-YEARS?
NOT THAT I MIND IF THEY'RE NOT HERE.
THEY'RE OFF AT SOME STREET TOURNAMENT.

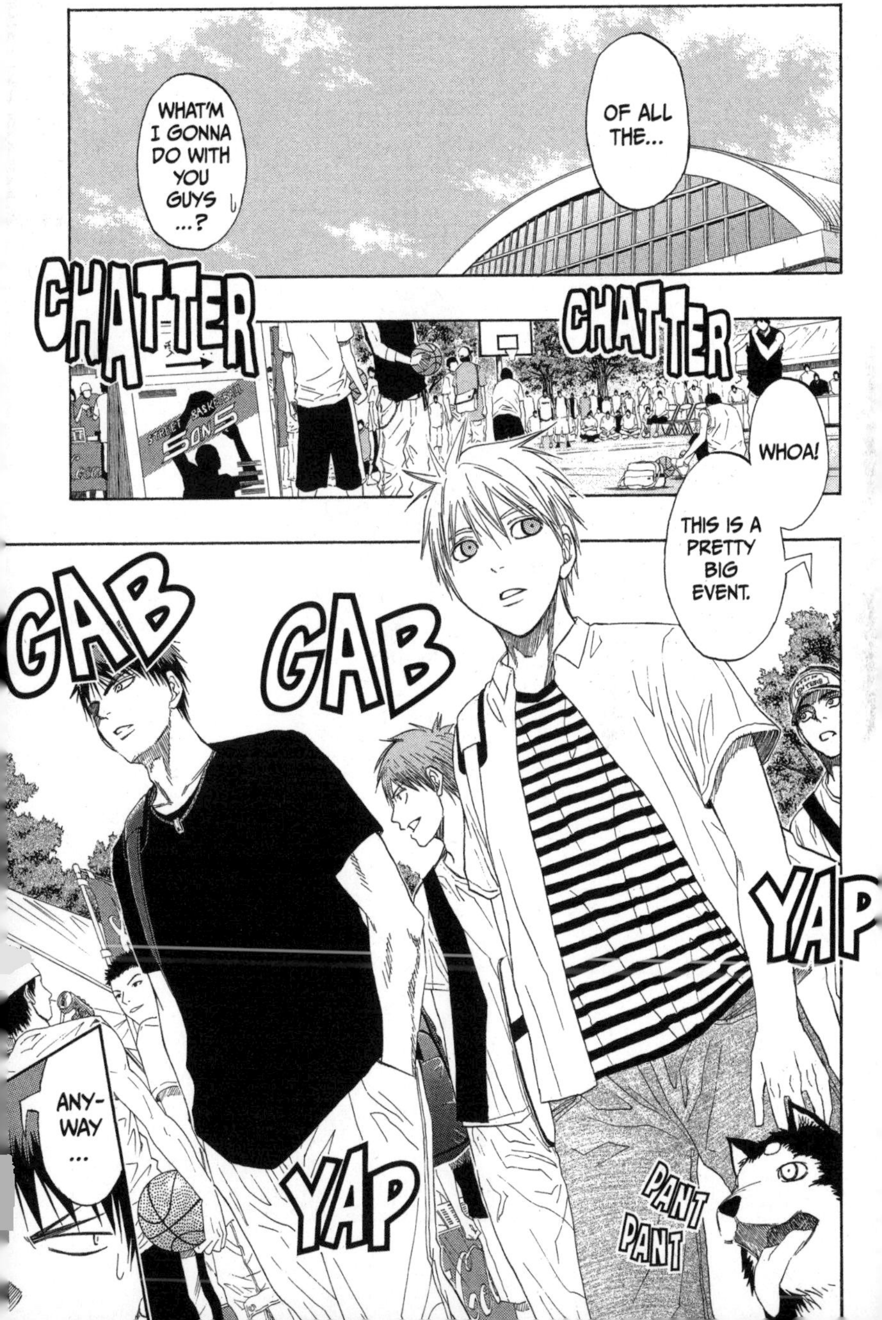
OF ALL THE...
WHAT'M I GONNA DO WITH YOU GUYS ...?
CHATTER
CHATTER
STREET BASKETBALL
5ON5
WHOA!
THIS IS A PRETTY BIG EVENT.
GAB
GAB
YAP
YAP
ANY-WAY ...
PANT
PANT

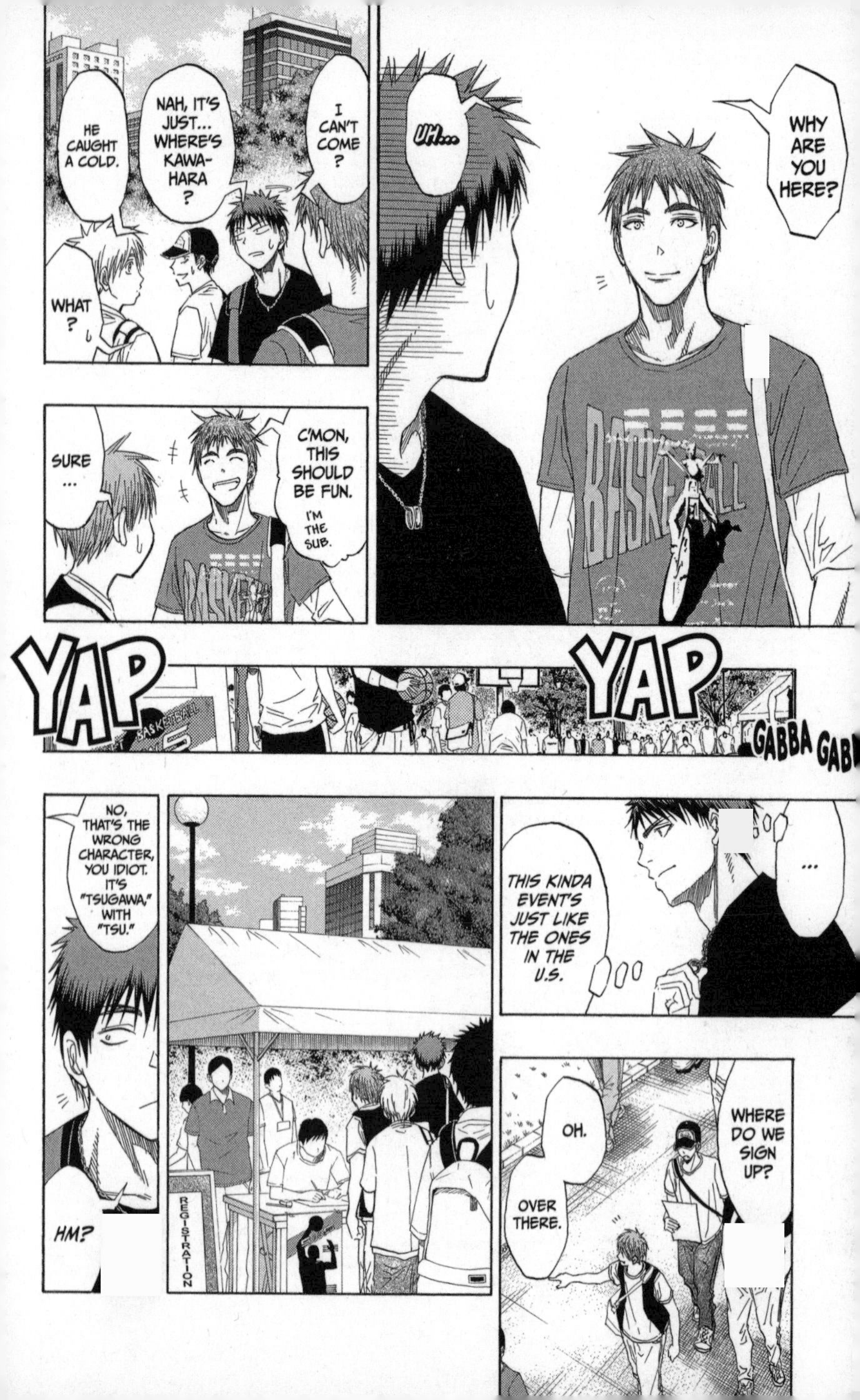
WHY ARE YOU HERE?
UH...
I CAN'T COME?
NAH, IT'S JUST... WHERE'S KAWAHARA?
HE CAUGHT A COLD.
WHAT?
C'MON, THIS SHOULD BE FUN.
I'M THE SUB.
SURE...
GABBA GAB
YAP
YAP
...
THIS KINDA EVENT'S JUST LIKE THE ONES IN THE U.S.
WHERE DO WE SIGN UP?
OH.
OVER THERE.
REGISTRATION
NO, THAT'S THE WRONG CHARACTER, YOU IDIOT. IT'S "TSUGAWA," WITH "TSU."
HM?

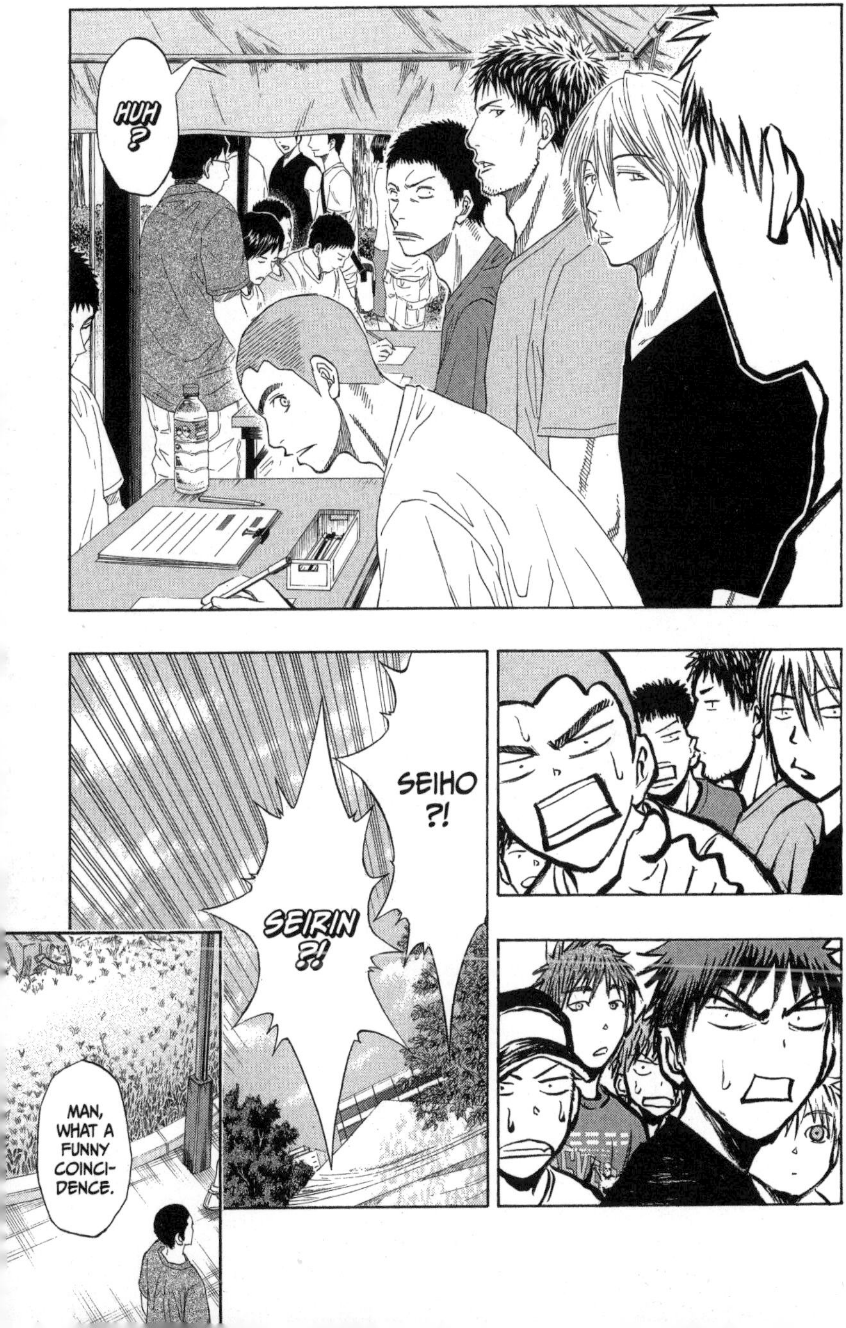
HUH?
SEIHO?!
SEIRIN?!
MAN, WHAT A FUNNY COINCIDENCE.

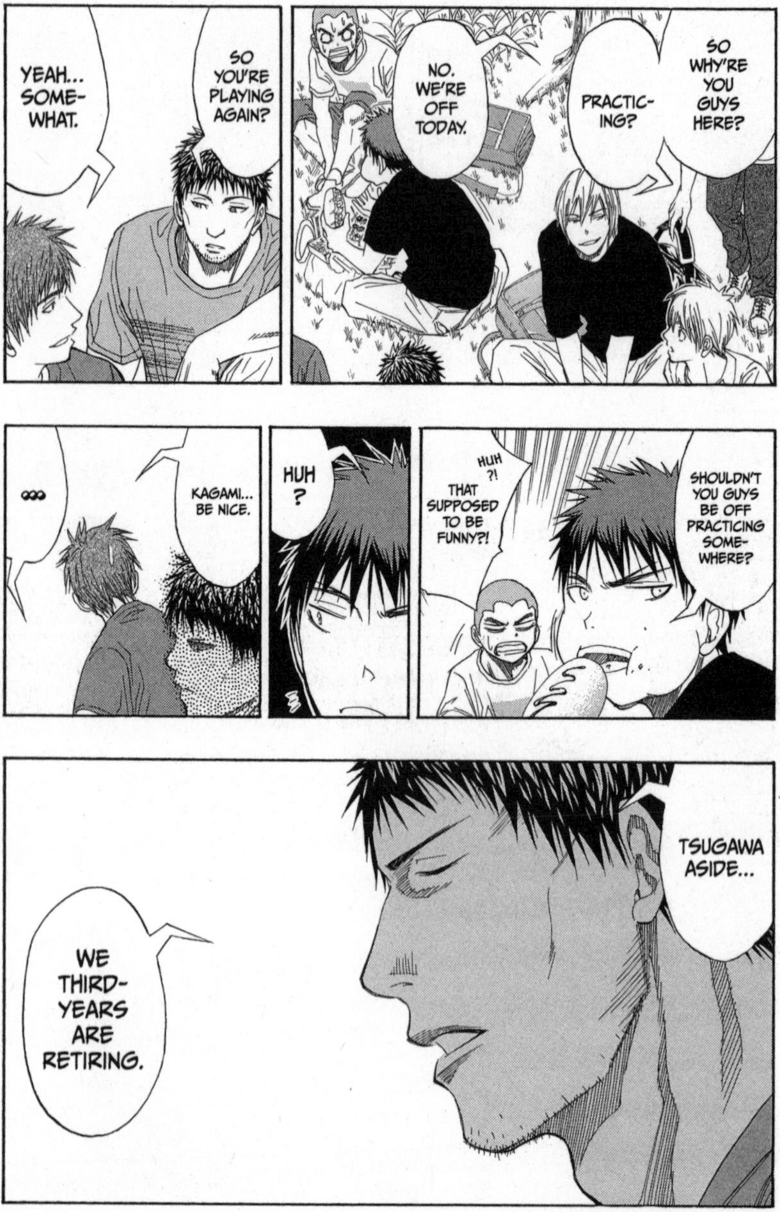

SO WHY'RE YOU GUYS HERE?
PRACTIC-ING?
NO. WE'RE OFF TODAY.
SO YOU'RE PLAYING AGAIN?
YEAH... SOME-WHAT.
SHOULDN'T YOU GUYS BE OFF PRACTICING SOME-WHERE?
HUH ?!
THAT SUPPOSED TO BE FUNNY?!
HUH ?
KAGAMI... BE NICE.
...
TSUGAWA ASIDE...
WE THIRD-YEARS ARE RETIRING.

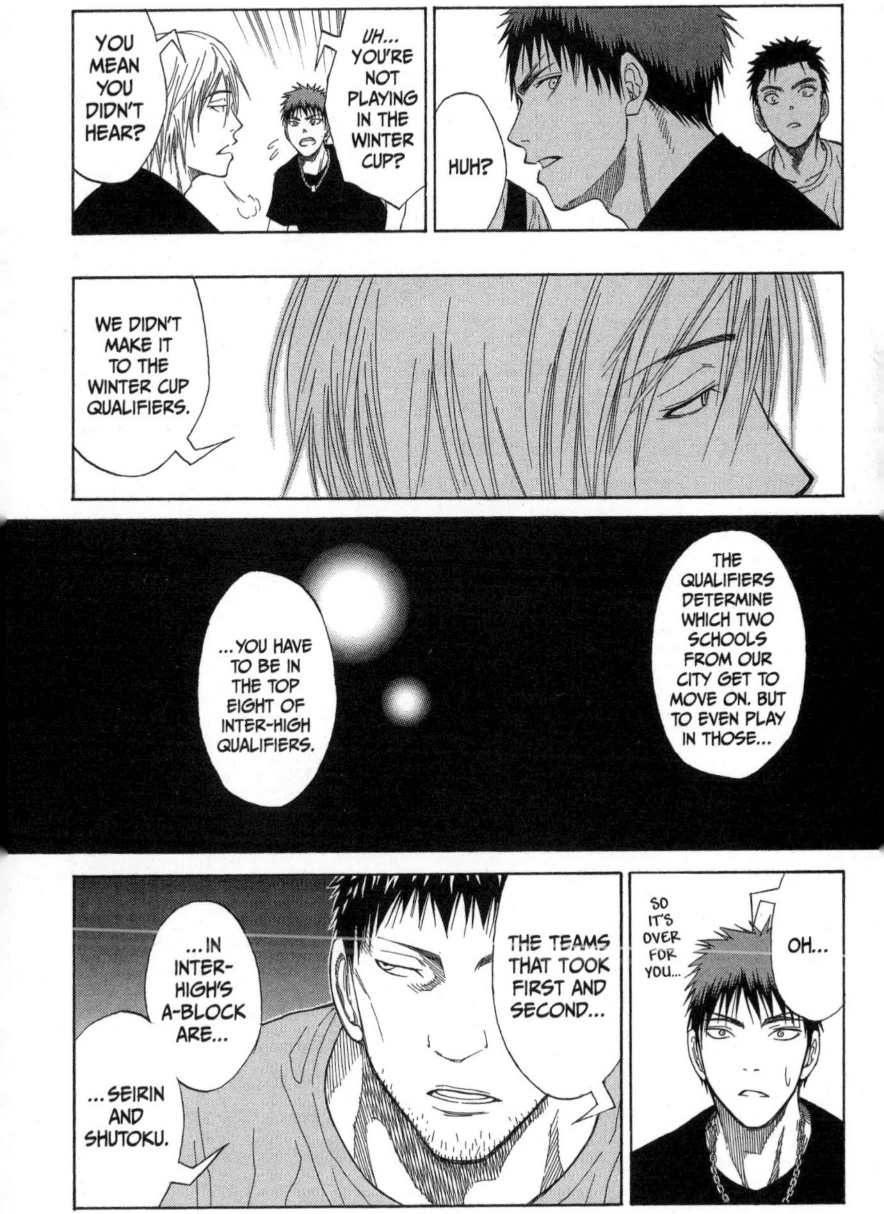
HUH?
UH... YOU'RE NOT PLAYING IN THE WINTER CUP?
YOU MEAN YOU DIDN'T HEAR?
WE DIDN'T MAKE IT TO THE WINTER CUP QUALIFIERS.
THE QUALIFIERS DETERMINE WHICH TWO SCHOOLS FROM OUR CITY GET TO MOVE ON. BUT TO EVEN PLAY IN THOSE...
...YOU HAVE TO BE IN THE TOP EIGHT OF INTER-HIGH QUALIFIERS.
OH...
SO IT'S OVER FOR YOU...
THE TEAMS THAT TOOK FIRST AND SECOND...
...IN INTER-HIGH'S A-BLOCK ARE...
...SEIRIN AND SHUTOKU.

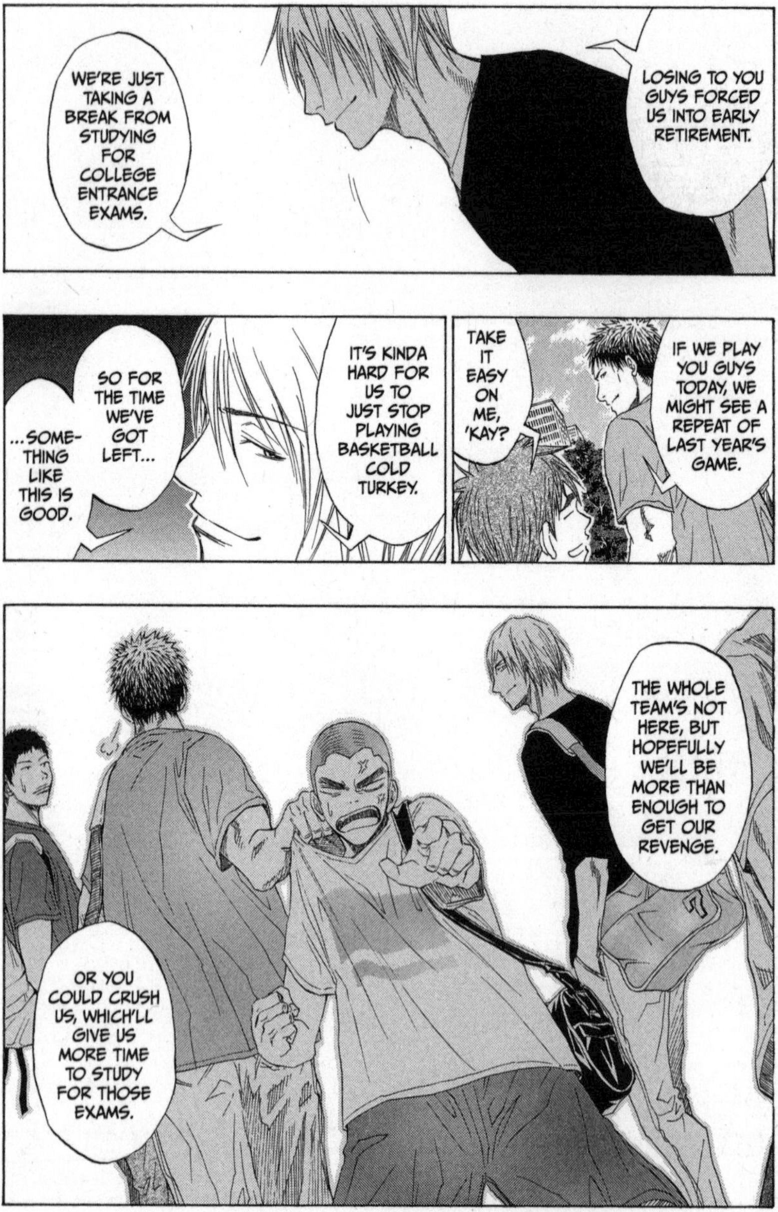
LOSING TO YOU GUYS FORCED US INTO EARLY RETIREMENT.
WE'RE JUST TAKING A BREAK FROM STUDYING FOR COLLEGE ENTRANCE EXAMS.
IF WE PLAY YOU GUYS TODAY, WE MIGHT SEE A REPEAT OF LAST YEAR'S GAME.
TAKE IT EASY ON ME, 'KAY?
IT'S KINDA HARD FOR US TO JUST STOP PLAYING BASKETBALL COLD TURKEY.
SO FOR THE TIME WE'VE GOT LEFT...
...SOME-THING LIKE THIS IS GOOD.
THE WHOLE TEAM'S NOT HERE, BUT HOPEFULLY WE'LL BE MORE THAN ENOUGH TO GET OUR REVENGE.
OR YOU COULD CRUSH US, WHICH'LL GIVE US MORE TIME TO STUDY FOR THOSE EXAMS.

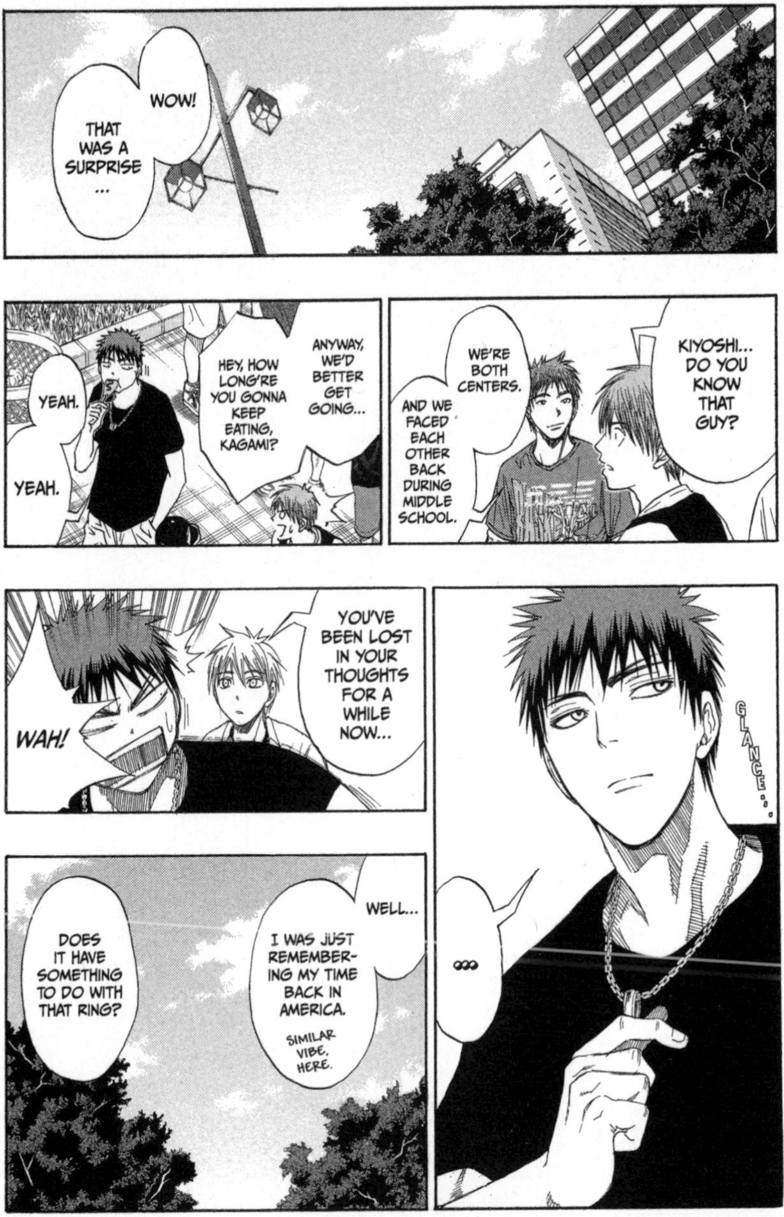
WOW!
THAT WAS A SURPRISE ...
KIYOSHI... DO YOU KNOW THAT GUY?
WE'RE BOTH CENTERS.
AND WE FACED EACH OTHER BACK DURING MIDDLE SCHOOL.
ANYWAY, WE'D BETTER GET GOING...
HEY, HOW LONG'RE YOU GONNA KEEP EATING, KAGAMI?
YEAH.
YEAH.
GLANCE...
...
YOU'VE BEEN LOST IN YOUR THOUGHTS FOR A WHILE NOW...
WAH!
WELL...
I WAS JUST REMEMBERING MY TIME BACK IN AMERICA.
SIMILAR VIBE, HERE.
DOES IT HAVE SOMETHING TO DO WITH THAT RING?

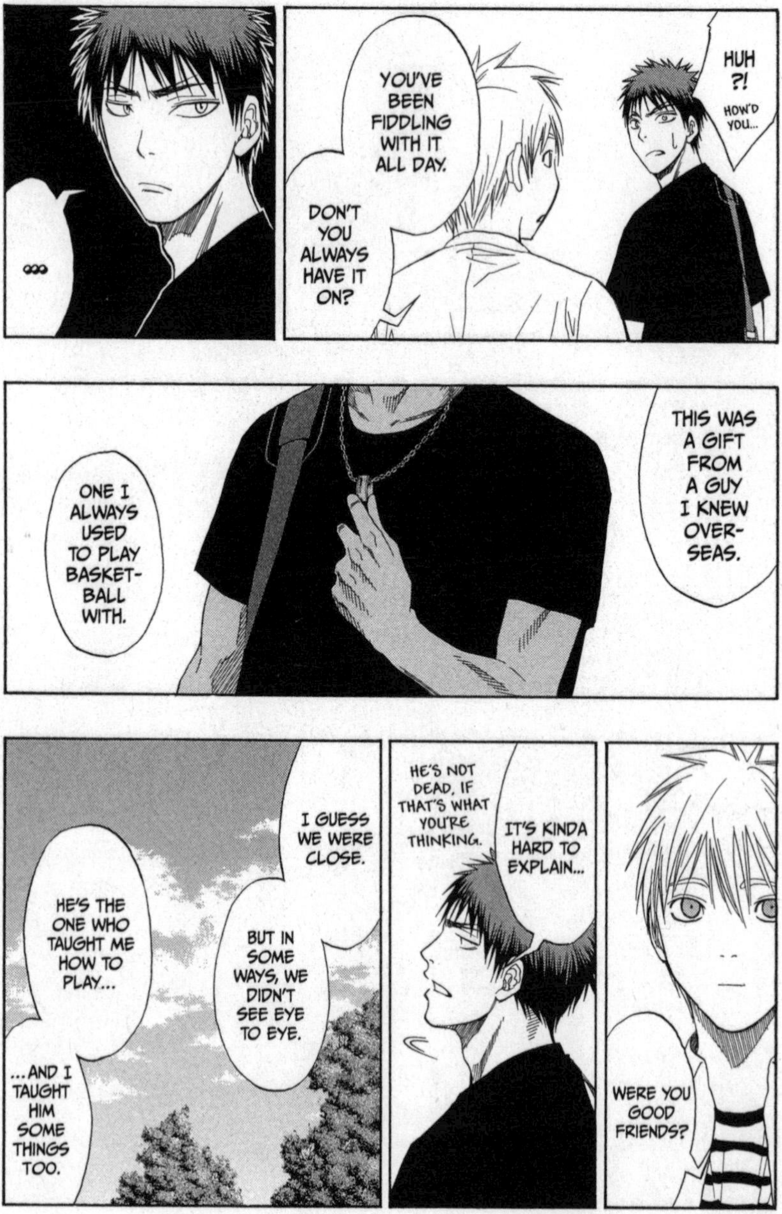
HUH ?!
HOW'D YOU...
YOU'VE BEEN FIDDLING WITH IT ALL DAY.
DON'T YOU ALWAYS HAVE IT ON?
...
THIS WAS A GIFT FROM A GUY I KNEW OVERSEAS.
ONE I ALWAYS USED TO PLAY BASKETBALL WITH.
WERE YOU GOOD FRIENDS?
IT'S KINDA HARD TO EXPLAIN...
HE'S NOT DEAD, IF THAT'S WHAT YOU'RE THINKING.
I GUESS WE WERE CLOSE.
BUT IN SOME WAYS, WE DIDN'T SEE EYE TO EYE.
HE'S THE ONE WHO TAUGHT ME HOW TO PLAY...
...AND I TAUGHT HIM SOME THINGS TOO.

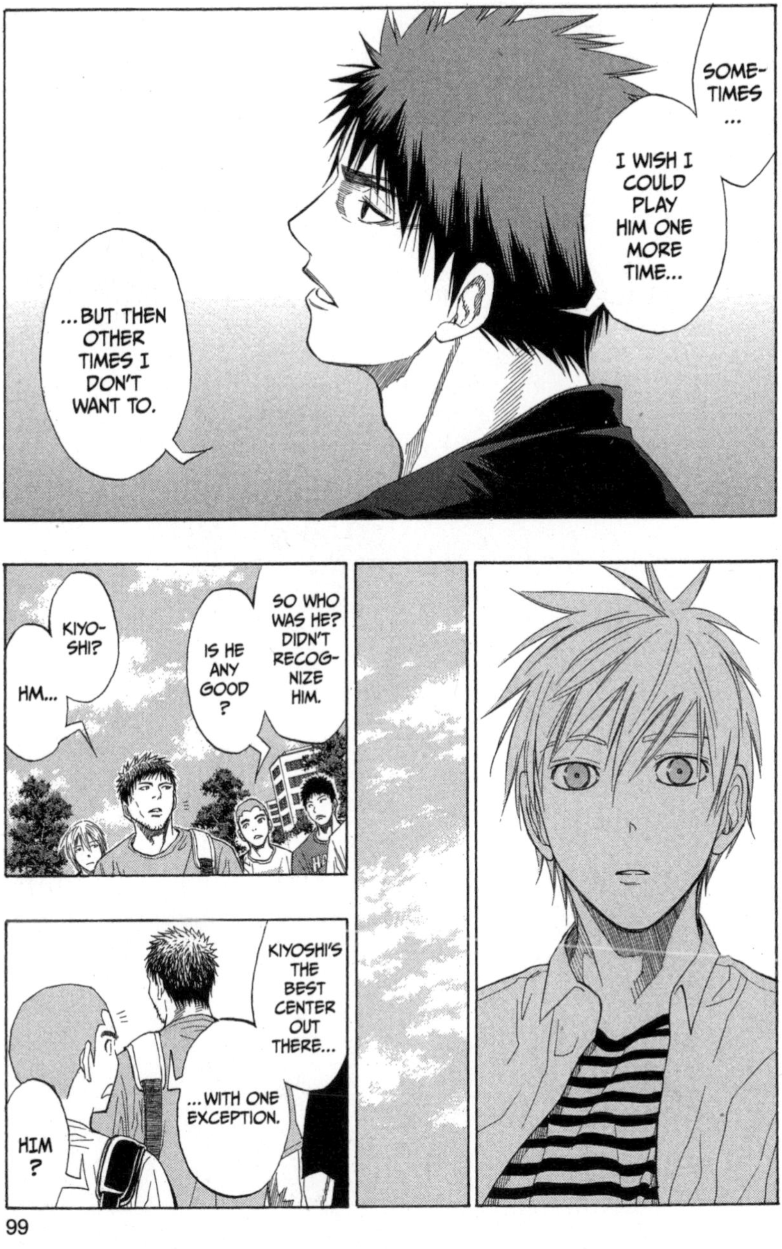
SOME-TIMES ...
I WISH I COULD PLAY HIM ONE MORE TIME...
...BUT THEN OTHER TIMES I DON'T WANT TO.
SO WHO WAS HE? DIDN'T RECOG-NIZE HIM.
IS HE ANY GOOD ?
KIYO-SHI?
HM...
KIYOSHI'S THE BEST CENTER OUT THERE...
...WITH ONE EXCEPTION.
HIM ?

THE MIRACLE GENERATION'S CENTER...

ATSUSHI MURASAKI-BARA.

...YOSEN HIGH.

HE'S AT...

WHAT SCHOOL DOES HE GO TO NOW?

...

HRM...

YOSEN?

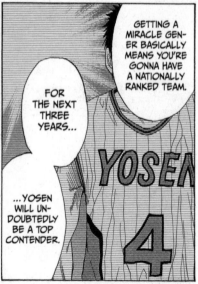

GETTING A MIRACLE GEN-ER BASICALLY MEANS YOU'RE GONNA HAVE A NATIONALLY RANKED TEAM.

FOR THE NEXT THREE YEARS...

...YOSEN WILL UN-DOUBTEDLY BE A TOP CONTENDER.

YOSEN

4

HUH?

I SAW A GUY WITH A YOSEN BAG EARLIER!

FOR REAL!

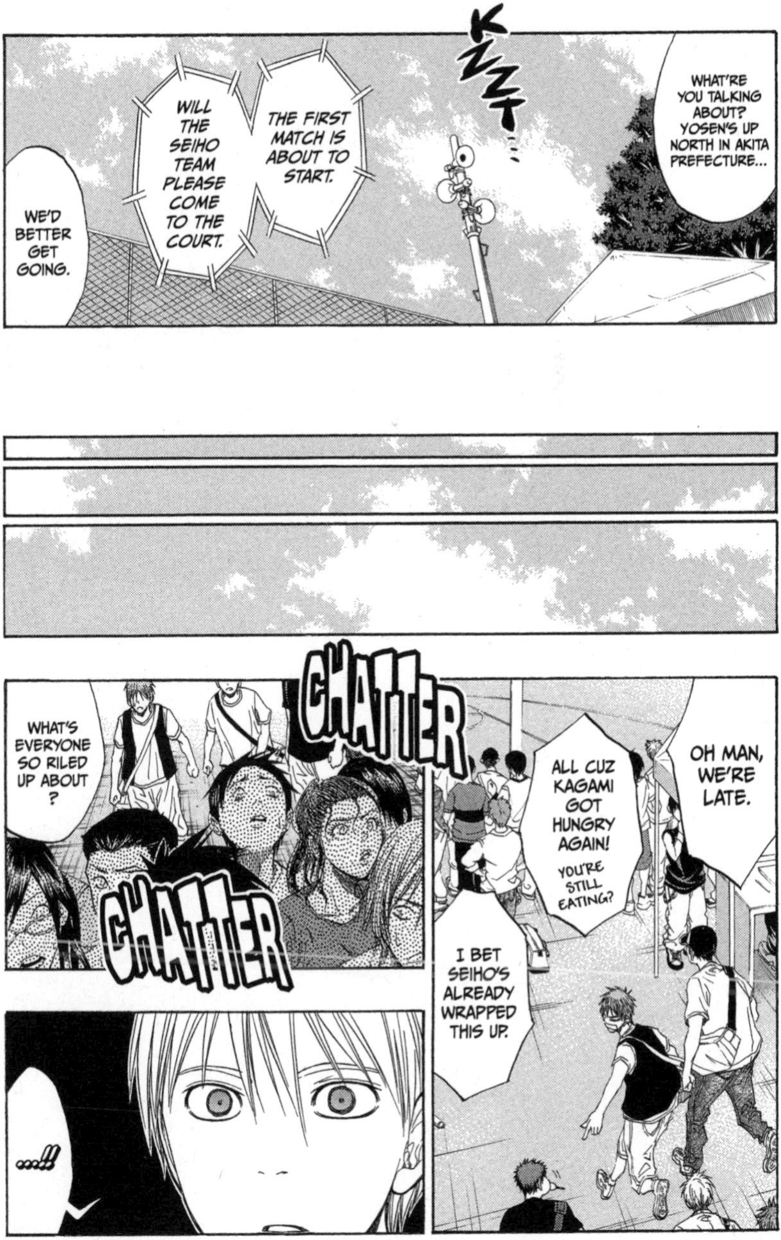
WHAT'RE YOU TALKING ABOUT? YOSEN'S UP NORTH IN AKITA PREFECTURE...
KZZT
THE FIRST MATCH IS ABOUT TO START.
WILL THE SEIHO TEAM PLEASE COME TO THE COURT.
WE'D BETTER GET GOING.
OH MAN, WE'RE LATE.
ALL CUZ KAGAMI GOT HUNGRY AGAIN!
YOU'RE STILL EATING?
I BET SEIHO'S ALREADY WRAPPED THIS UP.
CHATTER
WHAT'S EVERYONE SO RILED UP ABOUT?
CHATTER
...!!

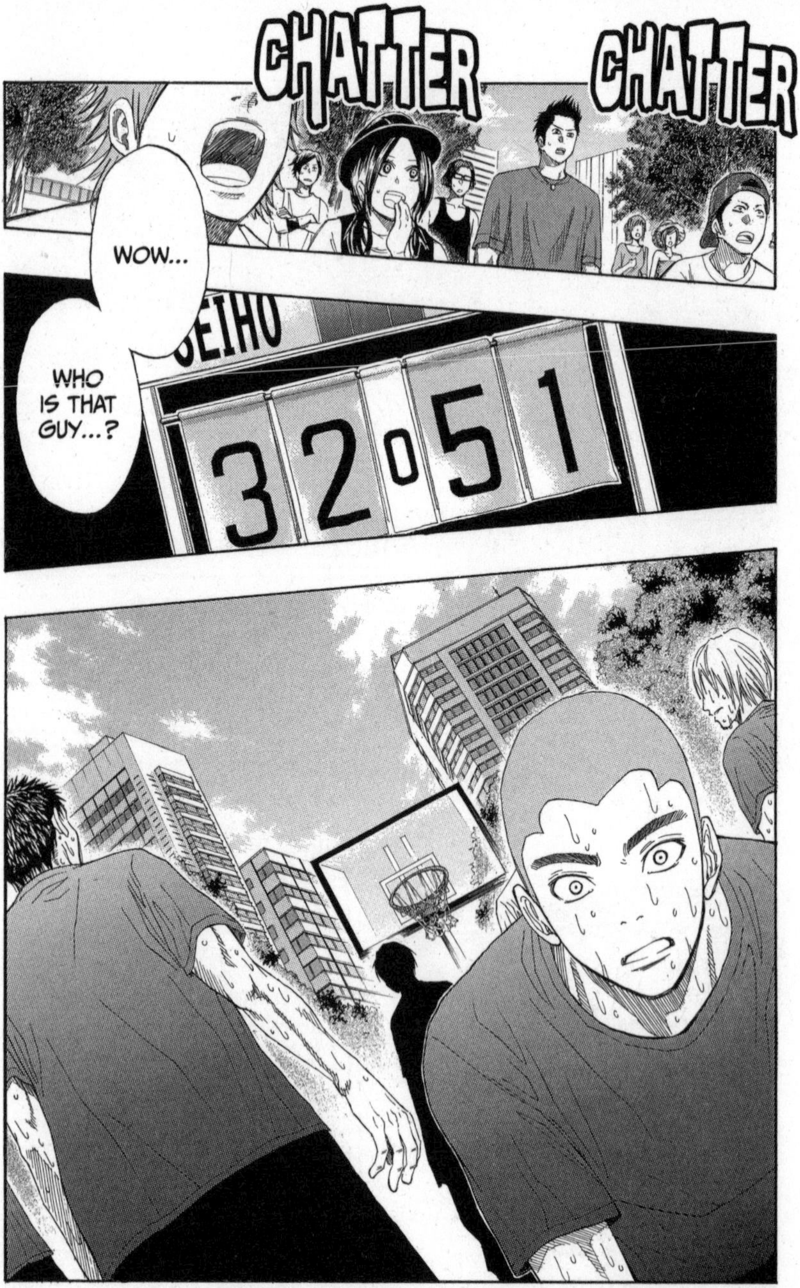
CHATTER
CHATTER
WOW...
WHO IS THAT GUY...?
32 51

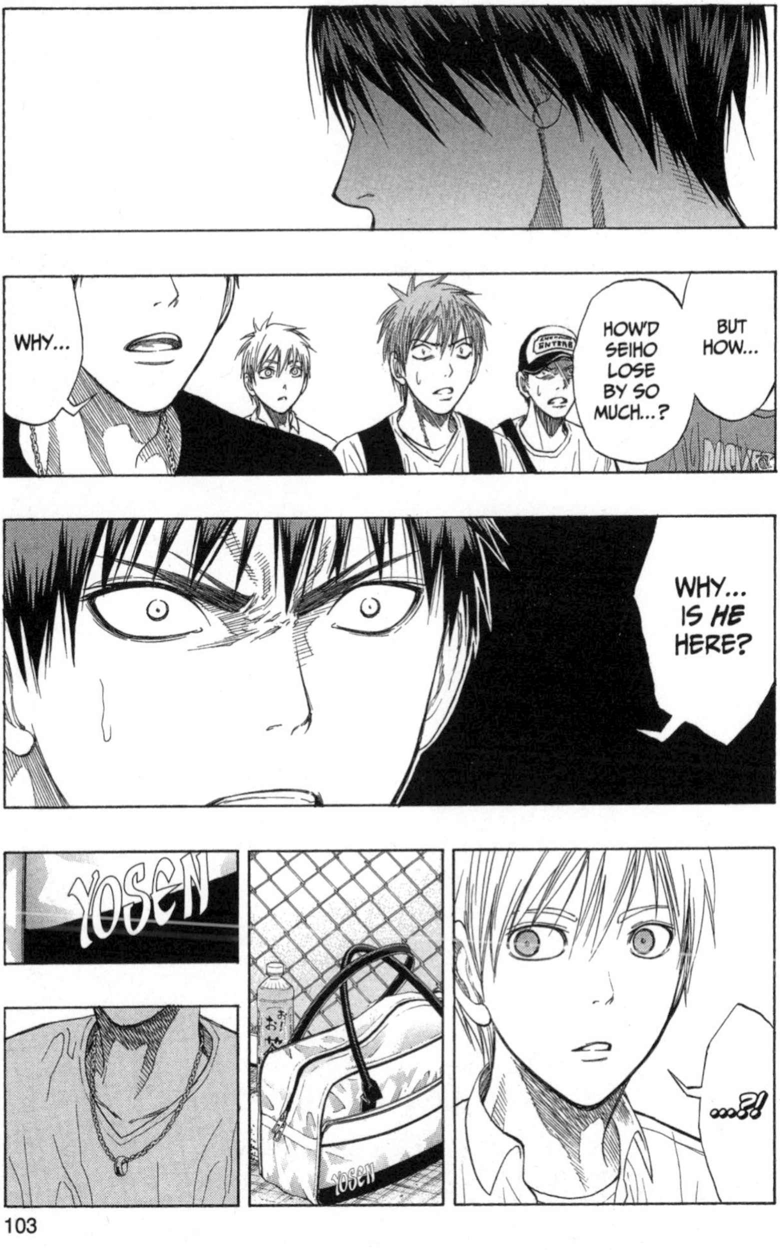
BUT HOW...
HOW'D SEIHO LOSE BY SO MUCH...?
WHY...
WHY... IS HE HERE?
...?!
YOSEN
YOSEN

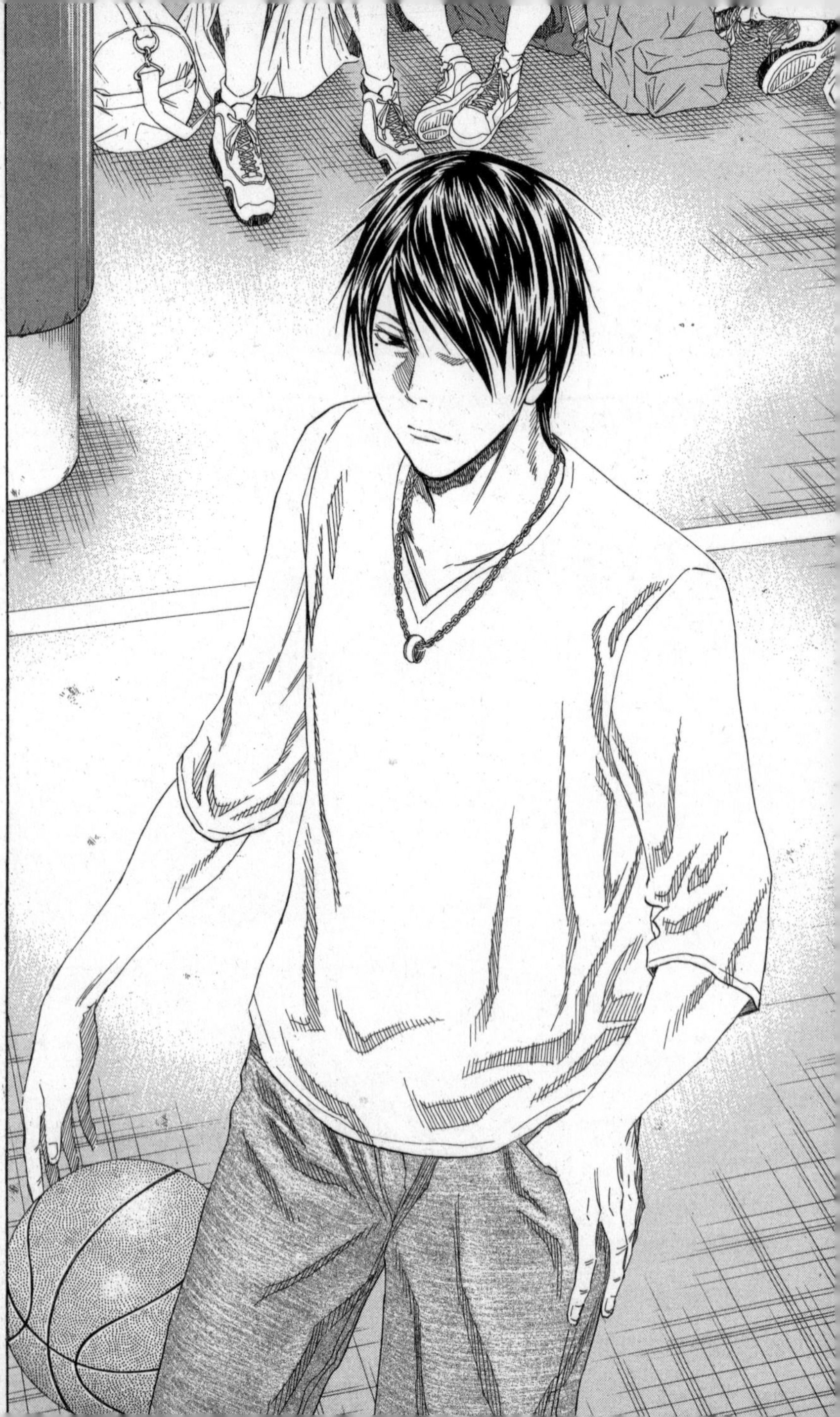

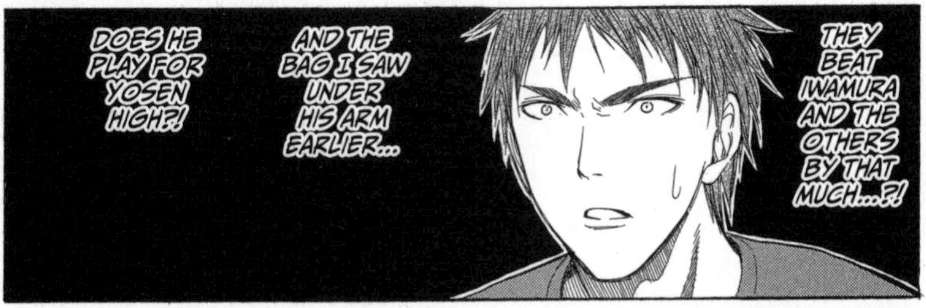
THEY BEAT IWAMURA AND THE OTHERS BY THAT MUCH...?!
AND THE BAG I SAW UNDER HIS ARM EARLIER...
DOES HE PLAY FOR YOSEN HIGH?!
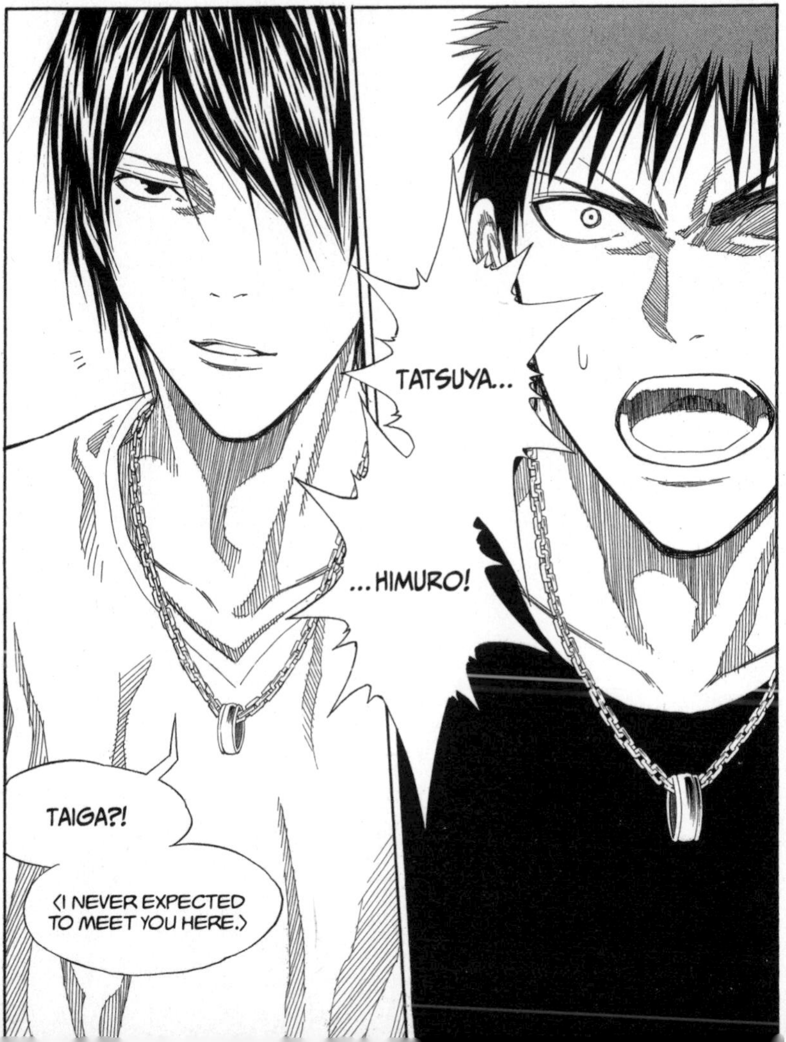
TATSUYA...
...HIMURO!
TAIGA?!
〈I NEVER EXPECTED TO MEET YOU HERE.〉

KUROKO'S BASKETBALL BLOOPERS
TAKE 18

SHAKA
SHAKA
SHp
AH!
PLOp
HOW'D THAT HAPPEN ?!
SHUT UP!
PFFT...
DON'T MOVE, KAGAMI! LEMME GET A PIC!!
BWA HA HA!

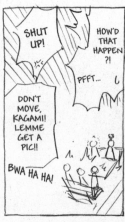

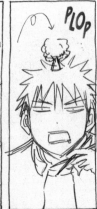

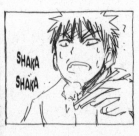

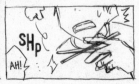

76TH QUARTER: LIKE A BIG BROTHER

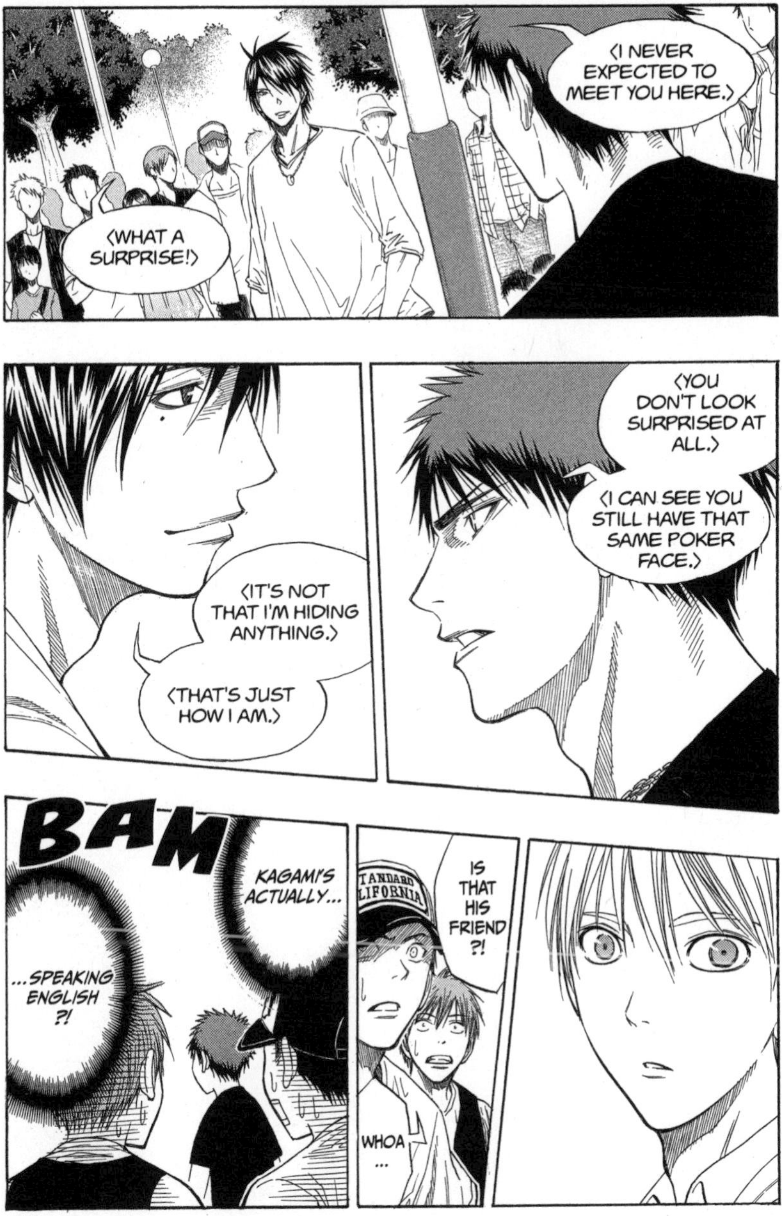
⟨I NEVER EXPECTED TO MEET YOU HERE.⟩
⟨WHAT A SURPRISE!⟩
⟨YOU DON'T LOOK SURPRISED AT ALL.⟩
⟨I CAN SEE YOU STILL HAVE THAT SAME POKER FACE.⟩
⟨IT'S NOT THAT I'M HIDING ANYTHING.⟩
⟨THAT'S JUST HOW I AM.⟩
IS THAT HIS FRIEND ?!
TANDARD LIFORNIA
WHOA ...
BAM
KAGAMI'S ACTUALLY...
...SPEAKING ENGLISH ?!

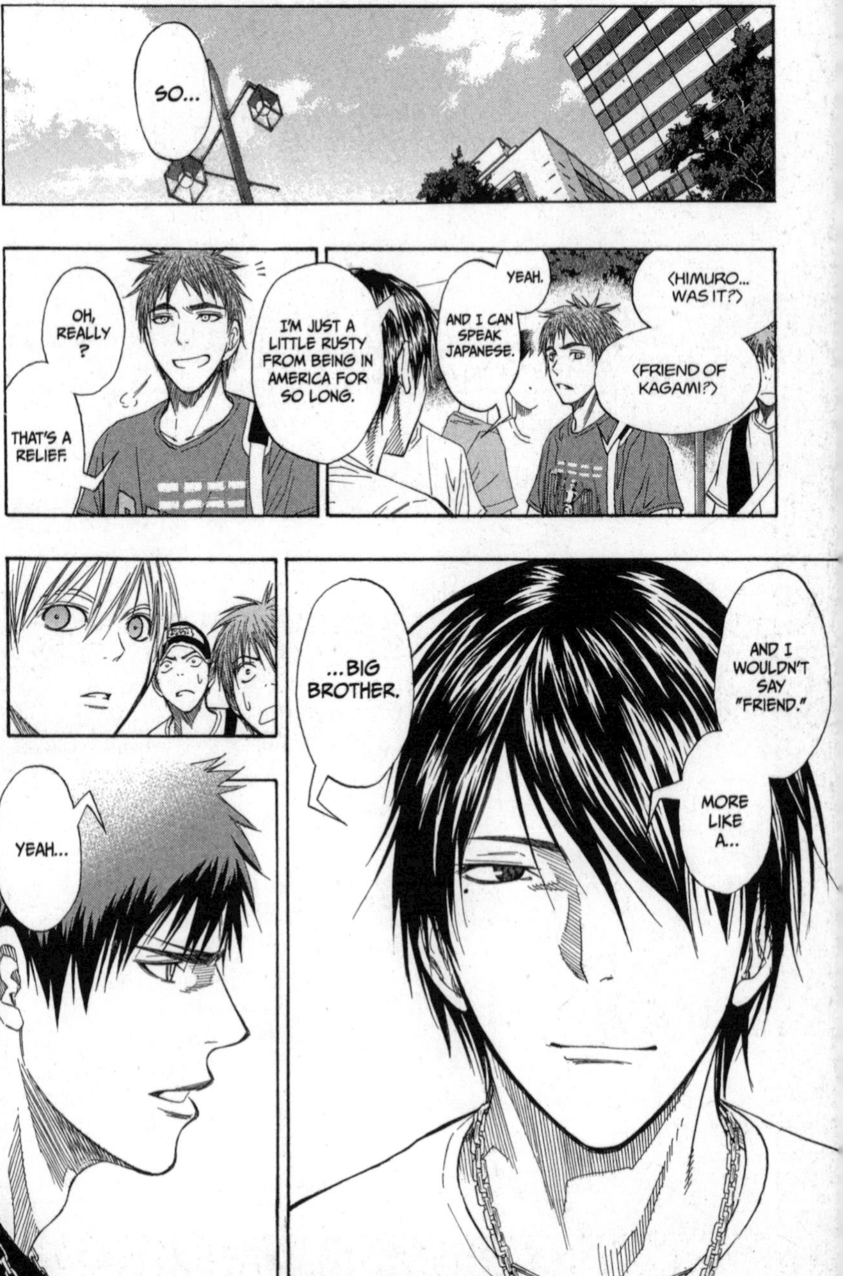
SO...
<HIMURO... WAS IT?>
<FRIEND OF KAGAMI?>
YEAH.
AND I CAN SPEAK JAPANESE.
I'M JUST A LITTLE RUSTY FROM BEING IN AMERICA FOR SO LONG.
OH, REALLY?
THAT'S A RELIEF.
AND I WOULDN'T SAY "FRIEND."
MORE LIKE A...
...BIG BROTHER.
YEAH...

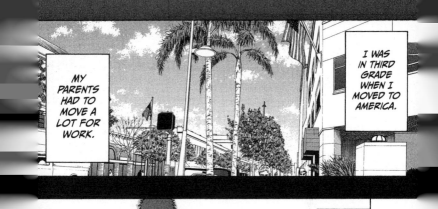

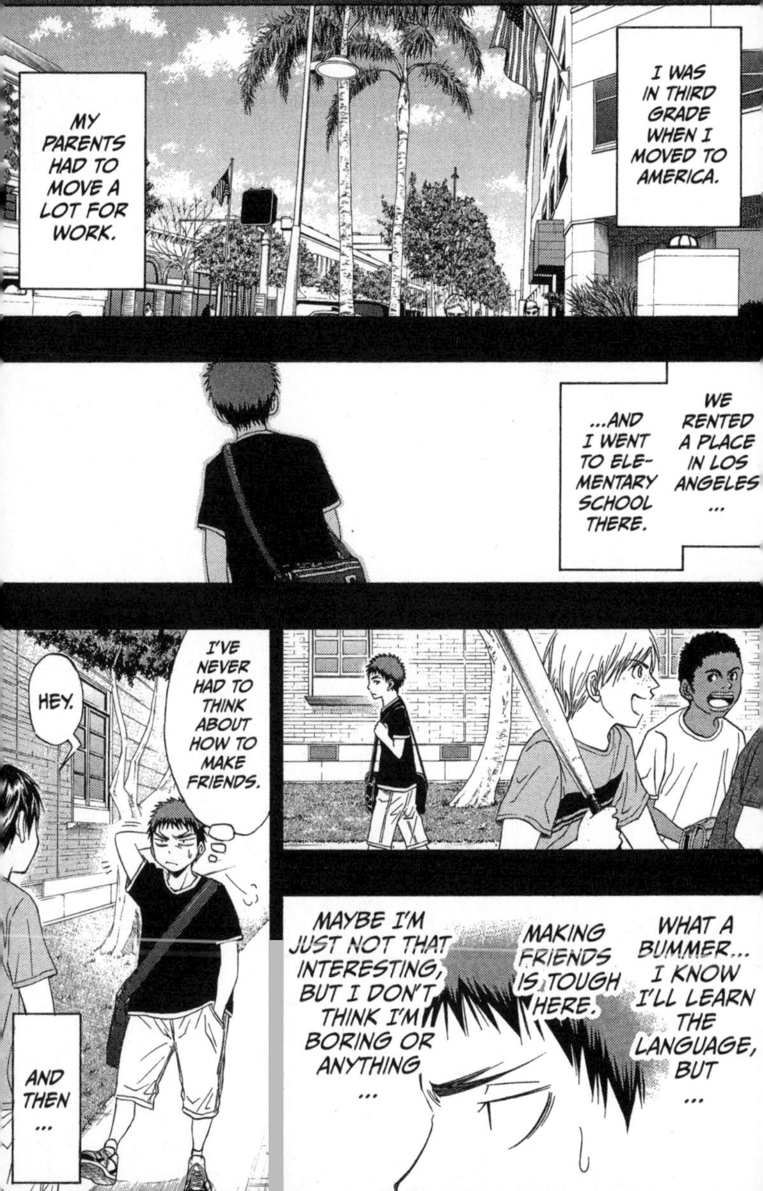
I WAS IN THIRD GRADE WHEN I MOVED TO AMERICA.
MY PARENTS HAD TO MOVE A LOT FOR WORK.
WE RENTED A PLACE IN LOS ANGELES...
...AND I WENT TO ELE-MENTARY SCHOOL THERE.
WHAT A BUMMER... I KNOW I'LL LEARN THE LANGUAGE, BUT...
MAKING FRIENDS IS TOUGH HERE.
MAYBE I'M JUST NOT THAT INTERESTING, BUT I DON'T THINK I'M BORING OR ANYTHING...
I'VE NEVER HAD TO THINK ABOUT HOW TO MAKE FRIENDS.
HEY.
AND THEN...

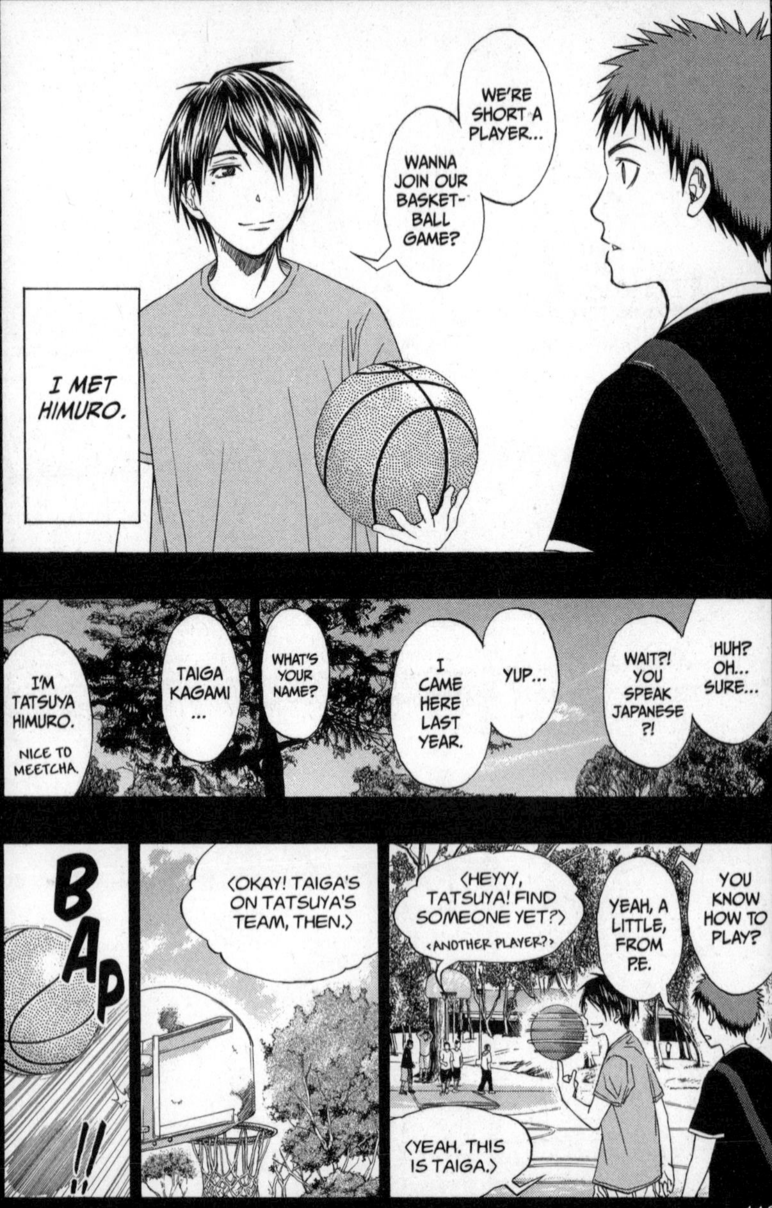
WE'RE SHORT A PLAYER...
WANNA JOIN OUR BASKET-BALL GAME?
I MET HIMURO.
HUH? OH... SURE...
WAIT?! YOU SPEAK JAPANESE?!
YUP...
I CAME HERE LAST YEAR.
WHAT'S YOUR NAME?
TAIGA KAGAMI ...
I'M TATSUYA HIMURO.
NICE TO MEETCHA.
YOU KNOW HOW TO PLAY?
YEAH, A LITTLE, FROM P.E.
〈HEYYY, TATSUYA! FIND SOMEONE YET?〉
〈ANOTHER PLAYER?〉
〈YEAH. THIS IS TAIGA.〉
〈OKAY! TAIGA'S ON TATSUYA'S TEAM, THEN.〉
BAP
!!

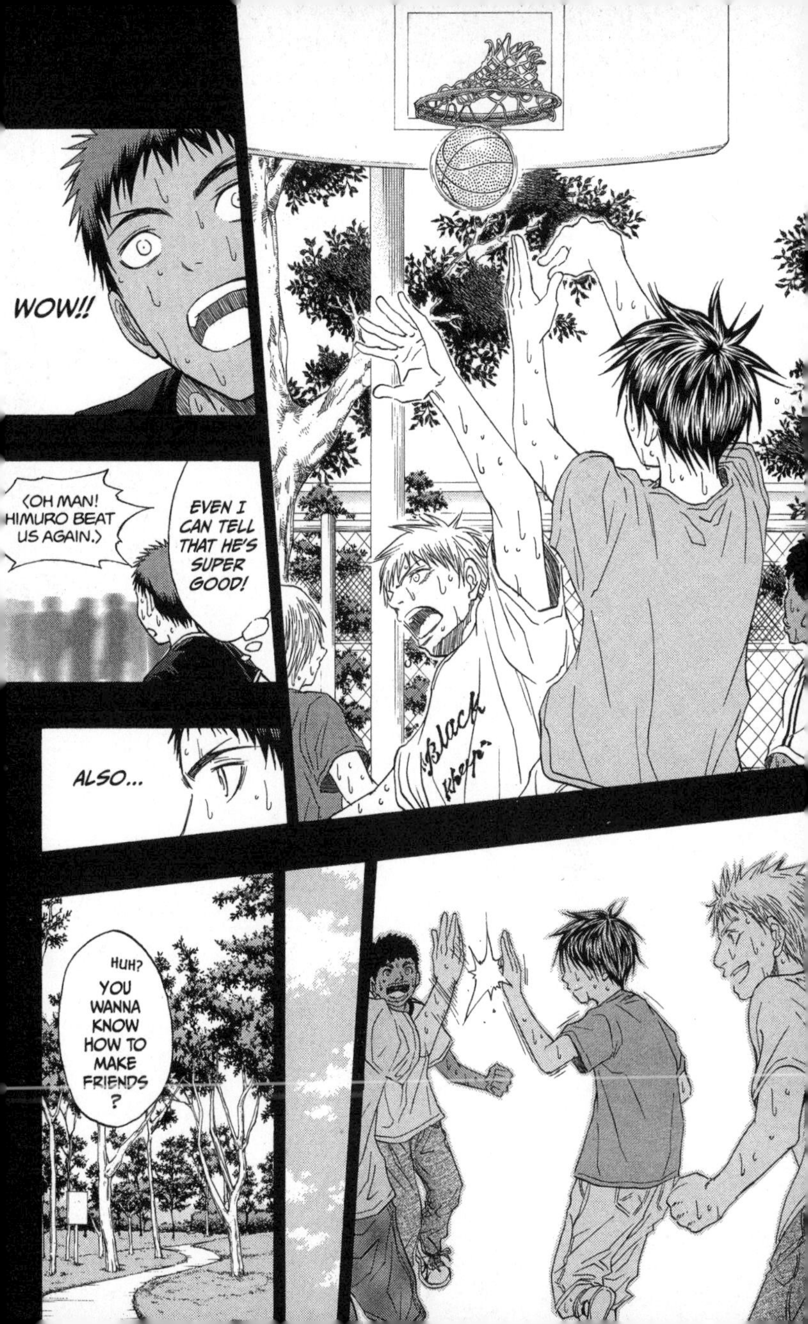
WOW!!
EVEN I CAN TELL THAT HE'S SUPER GOOD!
〈OH MAN! HIMURO BEAT US AGAIN.〉
ALSO...
HUH? YOU WANNA KNOW HOW TO MAKE FRIENDS?

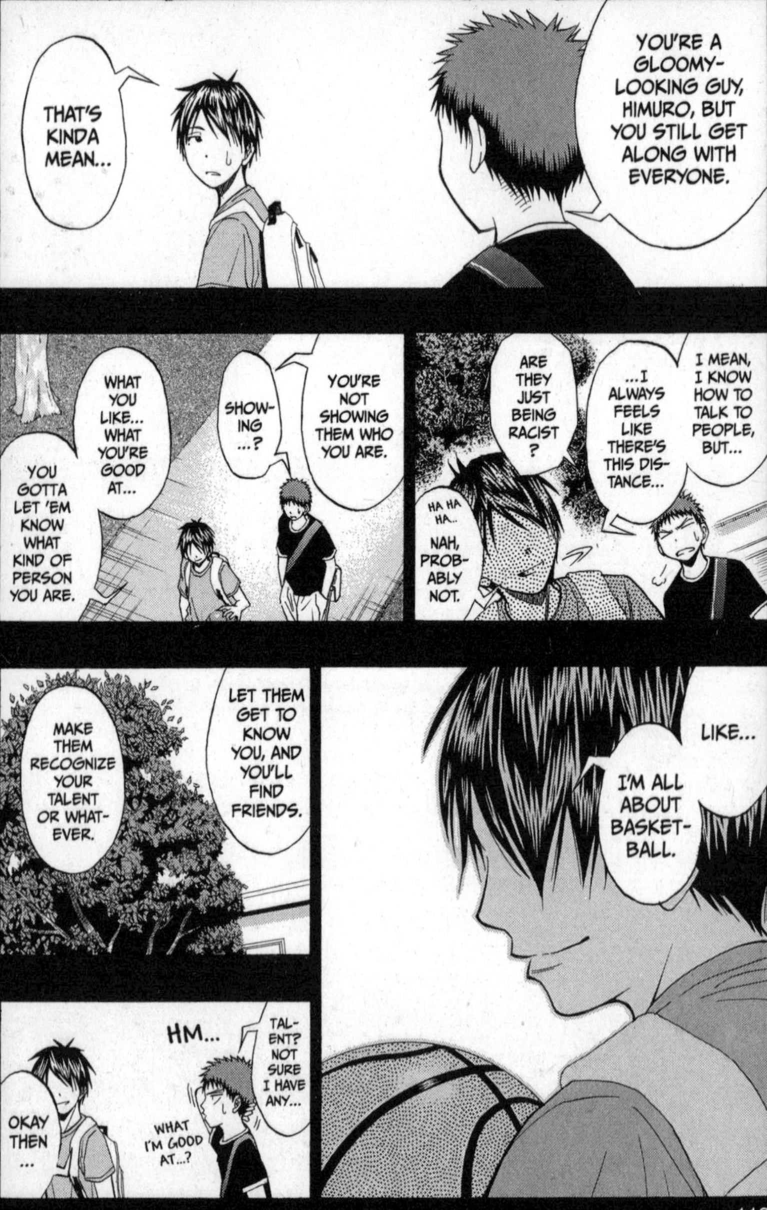
YOU'RE A GLOOMY-LOOKING GUY, HIMURO, BUT YOU STILL GET ALONG WITH EVERYONE.
THAT'S KINDA MEAN...
I MEAN, I KNOW HOW TO TALK TO PEOPLE, BUT...
...I ALWAYS FEELS LIKE THERE'S THIS DISTANCE...
ARE THEY JUST BEING RACIST?
HA HA HA..
NAH, PROBABLY NOT.
YOU'RE NOT SHOWING THEM WHO YOU ARE.
SHOWING...?
WHAT YOU LIKE... WHAT YOU'RE GOOD AT...
YOU GOTTA LET 'EM KNOW WHAT KIND OF PERSON YOU ARE.
LIKE...
I'M ALL ABOUT BASKETBALL.
LET THEM GET TO KNOW YOU, AND YOU'LL FIND FRIENDS.
MAKE THEM RECOGNIZE YOUR TALENT OR WHATEVER.
TALENT? NOT SURE I HAVE ANY...
HM...
WHAT I'M GOOD AT...?
OKAY THEN ...

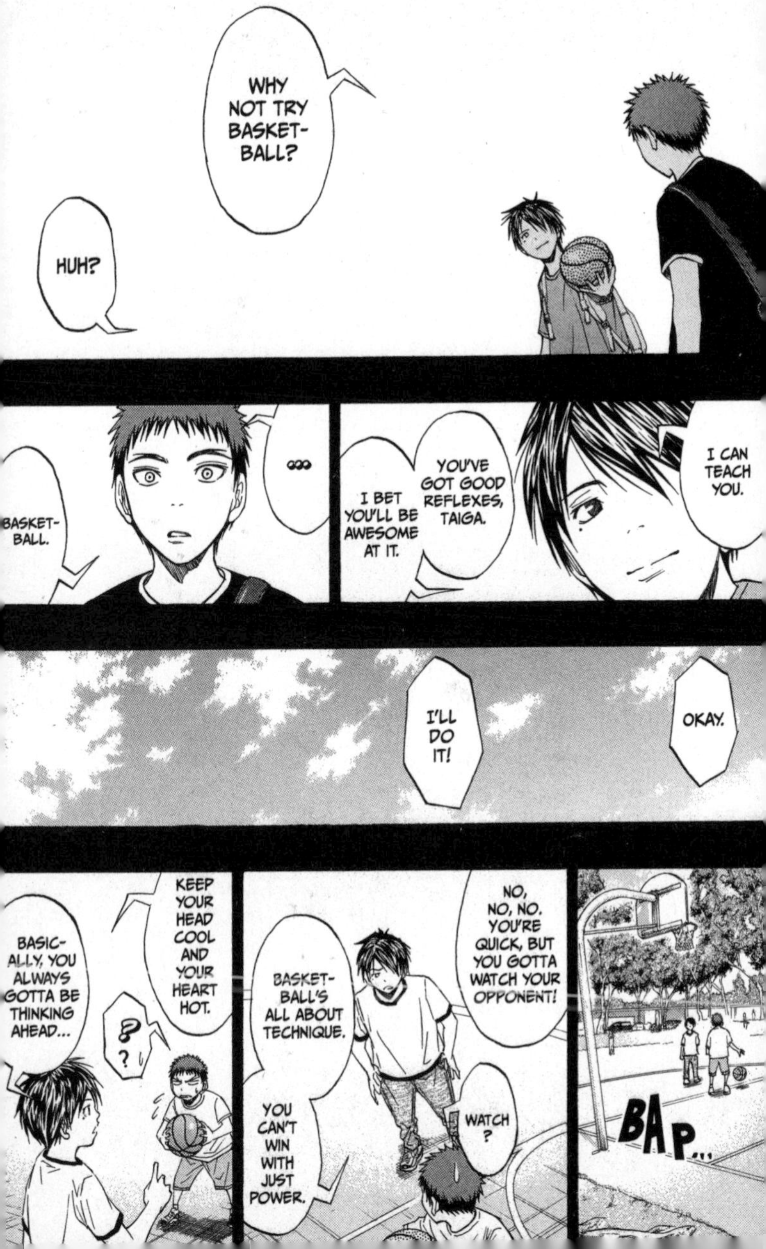
WHY NOT TRY BASKET-BALL?
HUH?
I CAN TEACH YOU.
YOU'VE GOT GOOD REFLEXES, TAIGA.
I BET YOU'LL BE AWESOME AT IT.
...
BASKET-BALL.
OKAY.
I'LL DO IT!
BAP...
NO, NO, NO. YOU'RE QUICK, BUT YOU GOTTA WATCH YOUR OPPONENT!
WATCH?
BASKET-BALL'S ALL ABOUT TECHNIQUE.
YOU CAN'T WIN WITH JUST POWER.
KEEP YOUR HEAD COOL AND YOUR HEART HOT.
BASIC-ALLY, YOU ALWAYS GOTTA BE THINKING AHEAD...
? ?

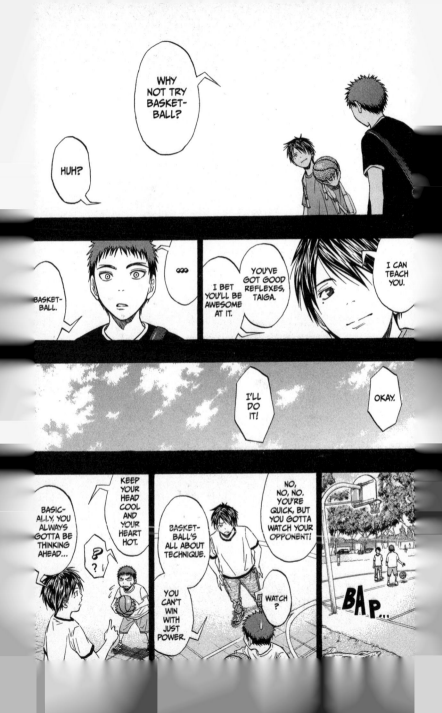

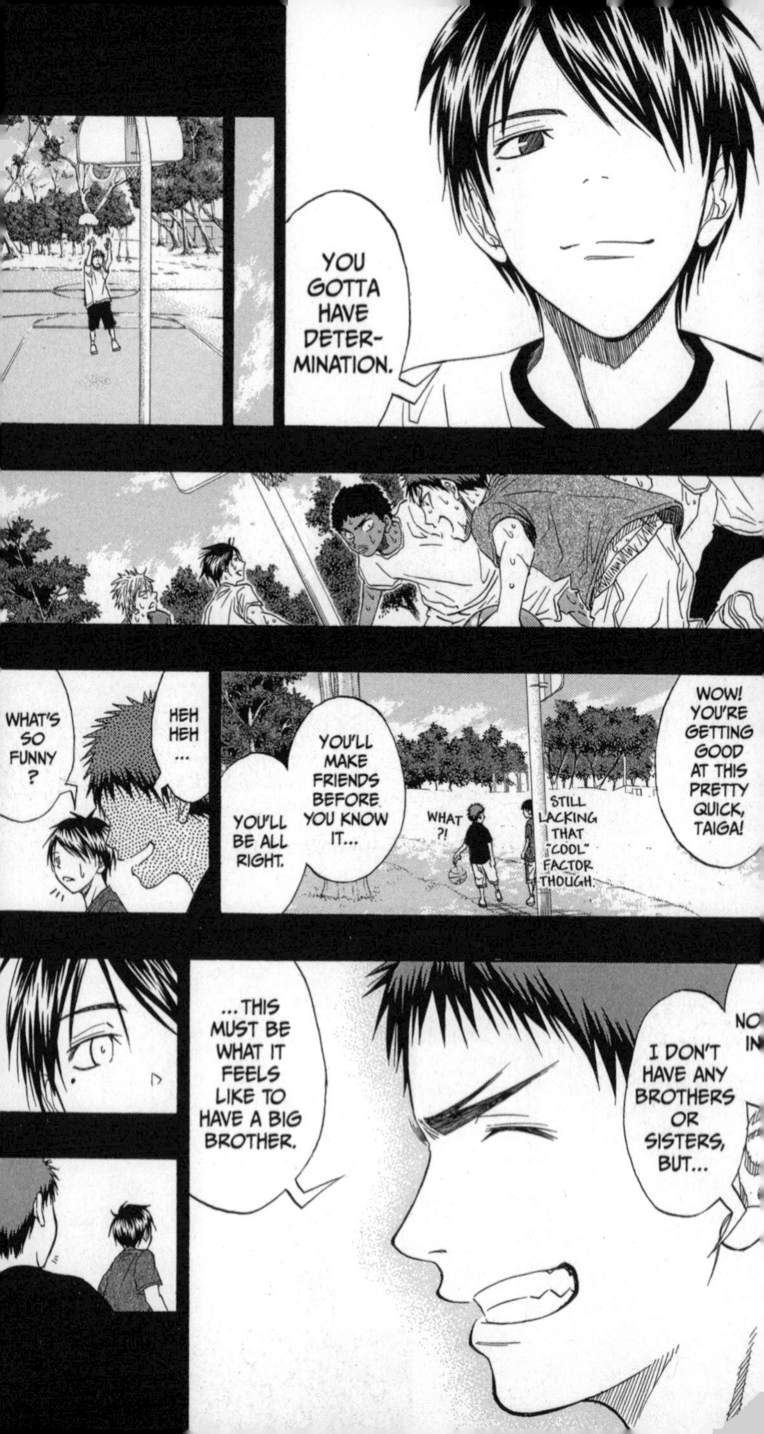
YOU GOTTA HAVE DETER-MINATION.
WOW! YOU'RE GETTING GOOD AT THIS PRETTY QUICK, TAIGA!
STILL LACKING THAT "COOL" FACTOR THOUGH.
WHAT ?!
YOU'LL MAKE FRIENDS BEFORE YOU KNOW IT...
YOU'LL BE ALL RIGHT.
HEH HEH ...
WHAT'S SO FUNNY ?
I DON'T HAVE ANY BROTHERS OR SISTERS, BUT...
...THIS MUST BE WHAT IT FEELS LIKE TO HAVE A BIG BROTHER.

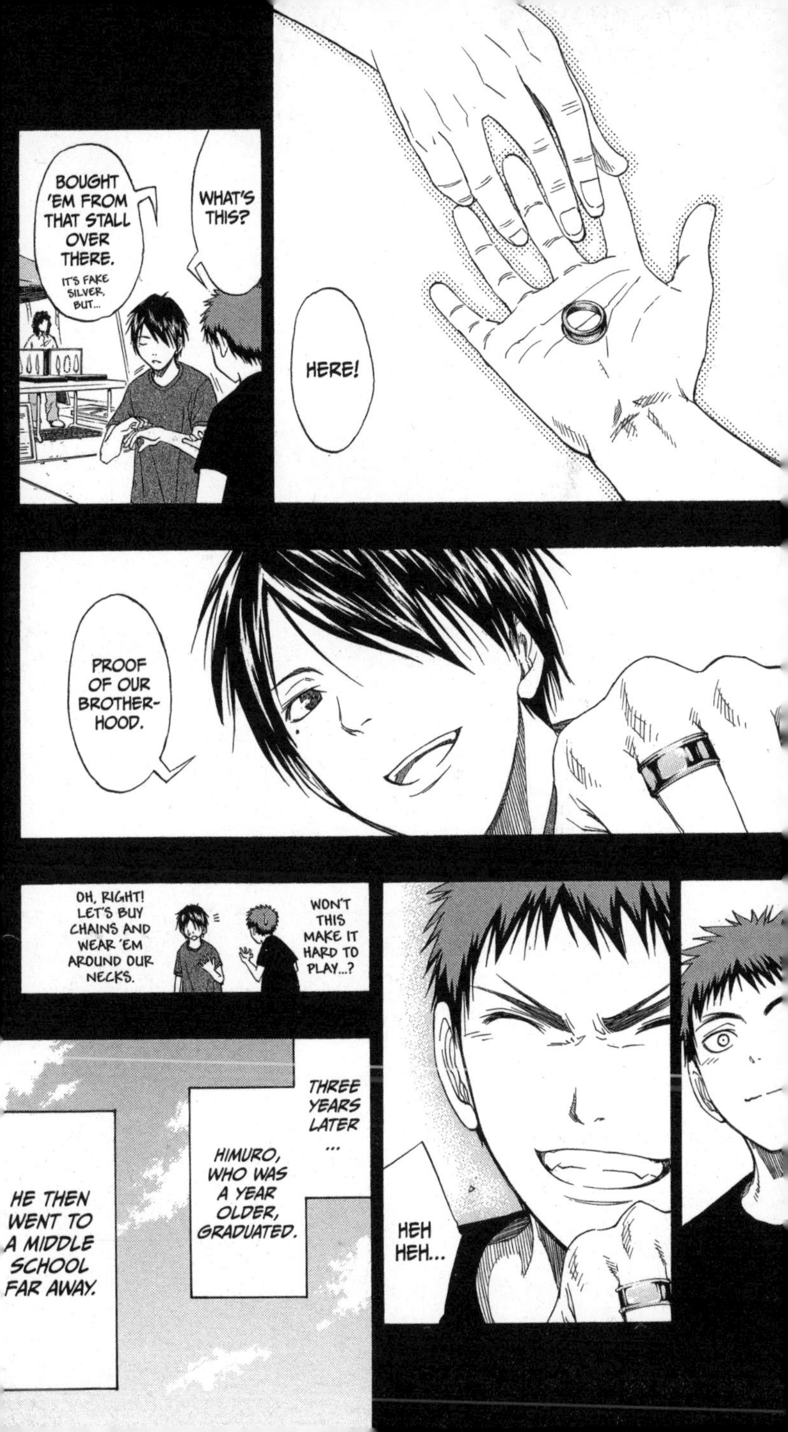
HERE!
WHAT'S THIS?
BOUGHT 'EM FROM THAT STALL OVER THERE.
IT'S FAKE SILVER, BUT...
PROOF OF OUR BROTHERHOOD.
HEH HEH...
WON'T THIS MAKE IT HARD TO PLAY...?
OH, RIGHT! LET'S BUY CHAINS AND WEAR 'EM AROUND OUR NECKS.
THREE YEARS LATER...
HIMURO, WHO WAS A YEAR OLDER, GRADUATED.
HE THEN WENT TO A MIDDLE SCHOOL FAR AWAY.

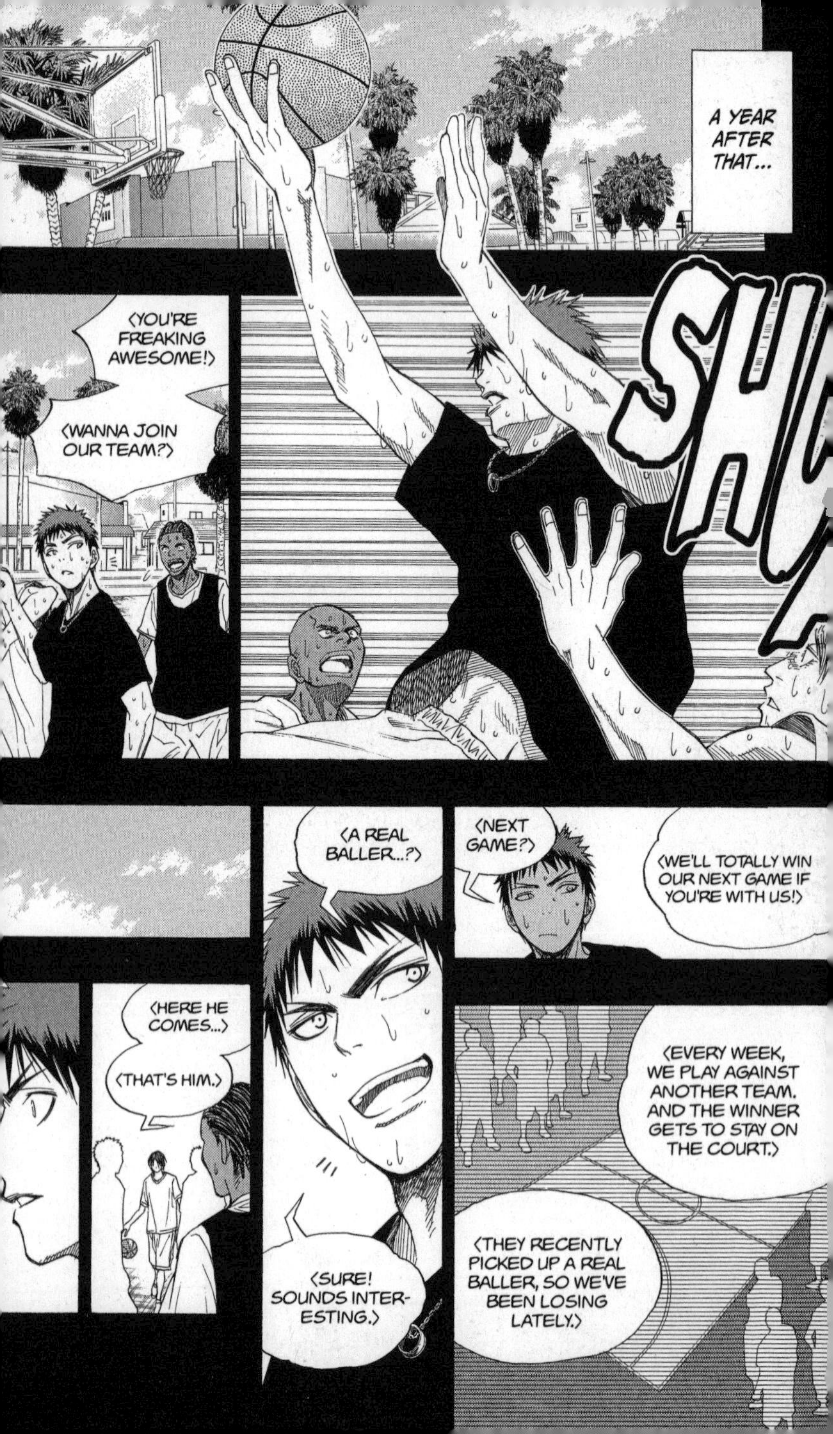
A YEAR AFTER THAT...
SH
〈YOU'RE FREAKING AWESOME!〉
〈WANNA JOIN OUR TEAM?〉
〈WE'LL TOTALLY WIN OUR NEXT GAME IF YOU'RE WITH US!〉
〈NEXT GAME?〉
〈EVERY WEEK, WE PLAY AGAINST ANOTHER TEAM. AND THE WINNER GETS TO STAY ON THE COURT.〉
〈THEY RECENTLY PICKED UP A REAL BALLER, SO WE'VE BEEN LOSING LATELY.〉
〈A REAL BALLER...?〉
〈SURE! SOUNDS INTER-ESTING.〉
〈HERE HE COMES...〉
〈THAT'S HIM.〉

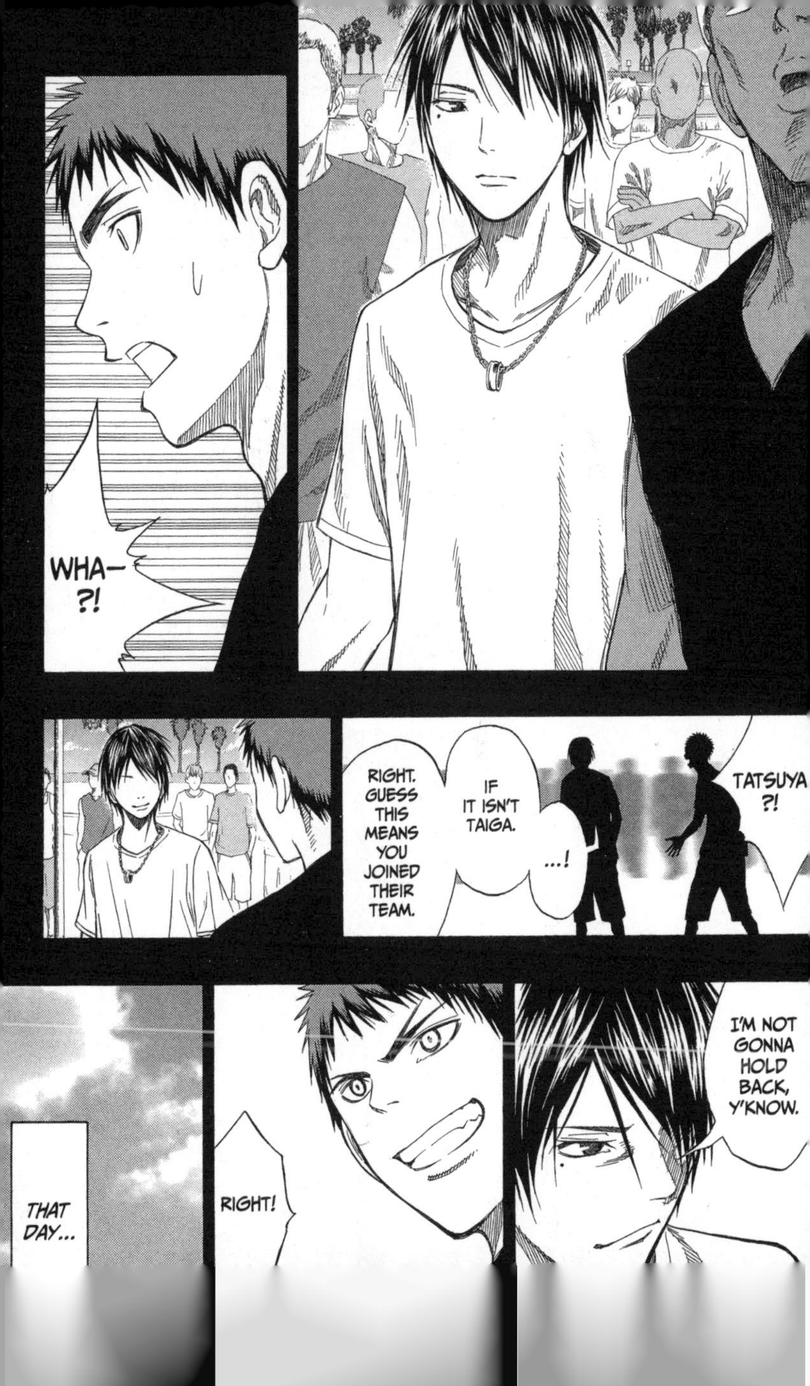
WHA— ?!
TATSUYA ?!
...!
IF IT ISN'T TAIGA.
RIGHT. GUESS THIS MEANS YOU JOINED THEIR TEAM.
I'M NOT GONNA HOLD BACK, Y'KNOW.
RIGHT!
THAT DAY...

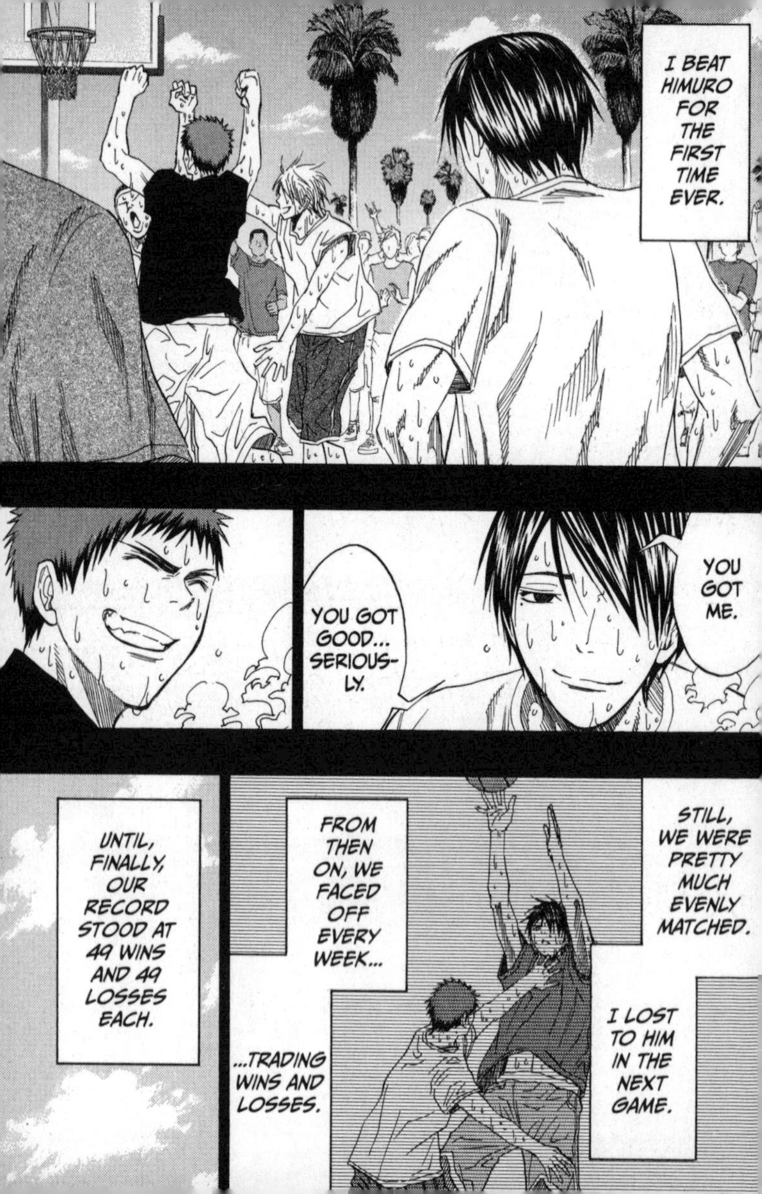
I BEAT HIMURO FOR THE FIRST TIME EVER.
YOU GOT ME.
YOU GOT GOOD... SERIOUS-LY.
STILL, WE WERE PRETTY MUCH EVENLY MATCHED.
I LOST TO HIM IN THE NEXT GAME.
FROM THEN ON, WE FACED OFF EVERY WEEK...
...TRADING WINS AND LOSSES.
UNTIL, FINALLY, OUR RECORD STOOD AT 49 WINS AND 49 LOSSES EACH.

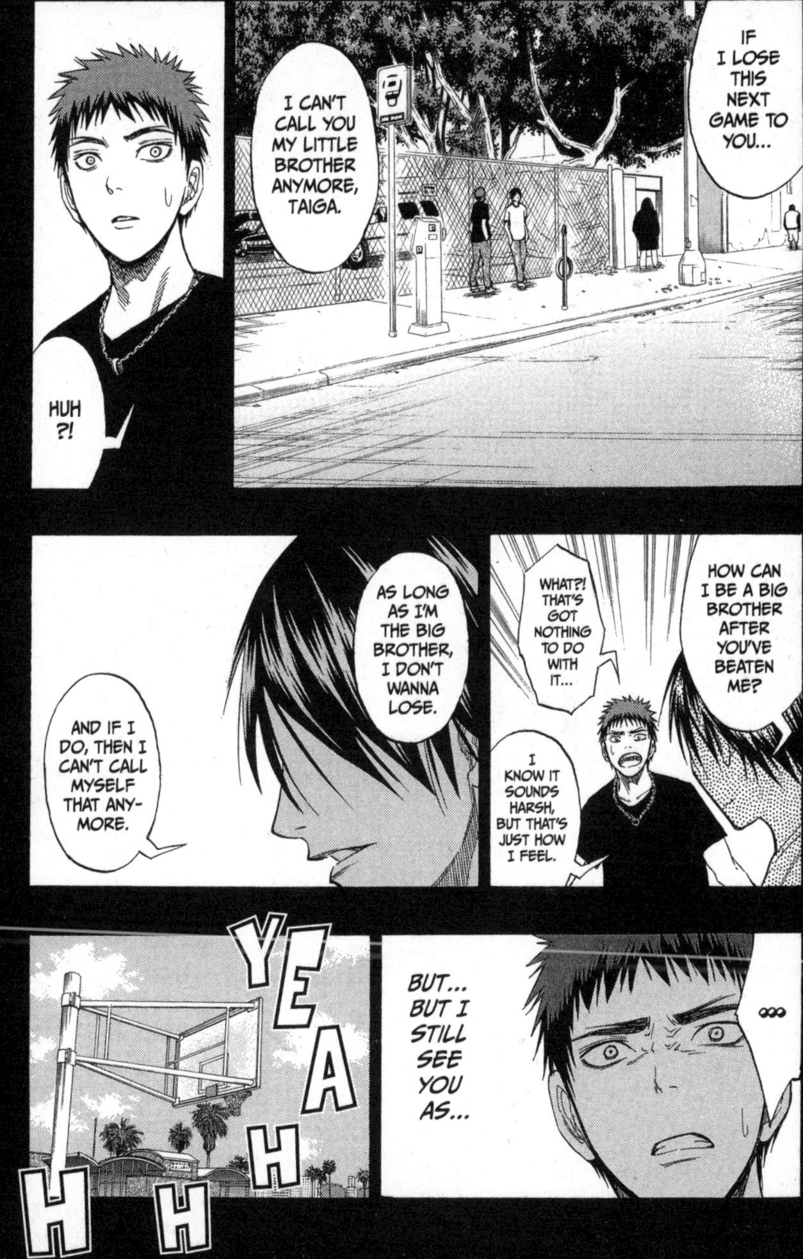
IF I LOSE THIS NEXT GAME TO YOU...
I CAN'T CALL YOU MY LITTLE BROTHER ANYMORE, TAIGA.
HUH ?!
HOW CAN I BE A BIG BROTHER AFTER YOU'VE BEATEN ME?
WHAT?! THAT'S GOT NOTHING TO DO WITH IT...
I KNOW IT SOUNDS HARSH, BUT THAT'S JUST HOW I FEEL.
AS LONG AS I'M THE BIG BROTHER, I DON'T WANNA LOSE.
AND IF I DO, THEN I CAN'T CALL MYSELF THAT ANY-MORE.
...
BUT... BUT I STILL SEE YOU AS...
YEAHHH

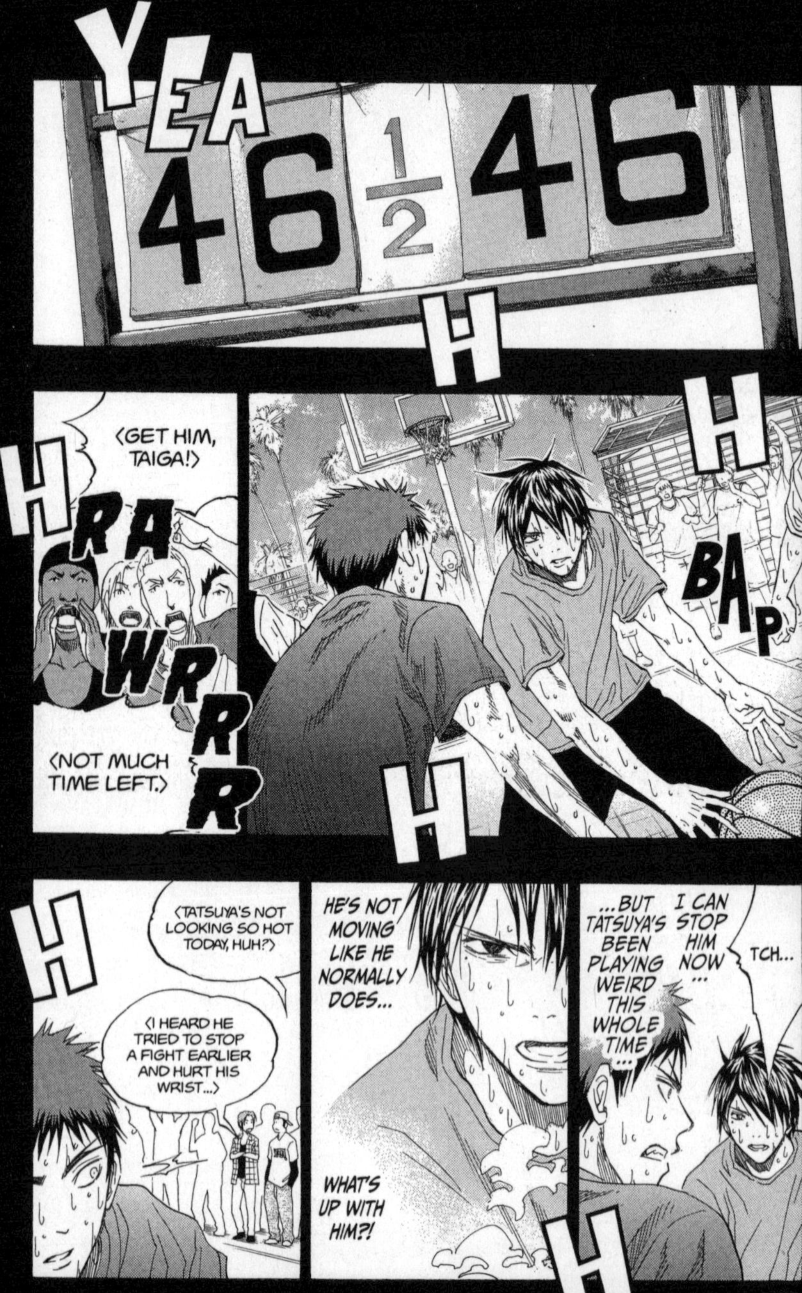
YEAHHHHHH
46 1/2 46
BAP
〈GET HIM, TAIGA!〉
RAWRRR
〈NOT MUCH TIME LEFT.〉
TCH...
I CAN STOP HIM NOW...
...BUT TATSUYA'S BEEN PLAYING WEIRD THIS WHOLE TIME...
HE'S NOT MOVING LIKE HE NORMALLY DOES...
WHAT'S UP WITH HIM?!
〈TATSUYA'S NOT LOOKING SO HOT TODAY, HUH?〉
〈I HEARD HE TRIED TO STOP A FIGHT EARLIER AND HURT HIS WRIST...〉

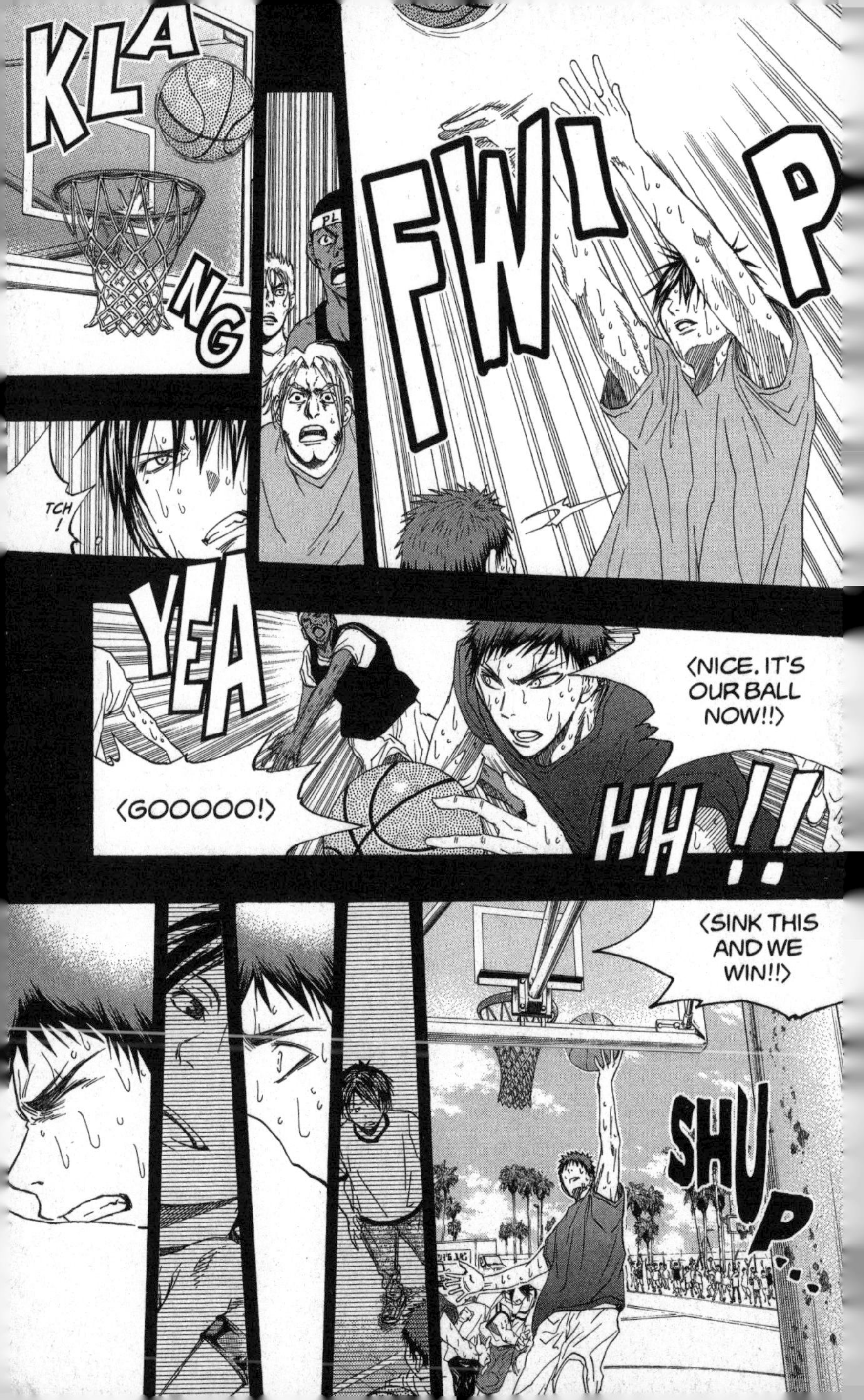
FWIP
KLANG
TCH!
⟨NICE. IT'S OUR BALL NOW!!⟩
YEAHH!!
⟨GOOOOO!⟩
⟨SINK THIS AND WE WIN!!⟩
SHUP..

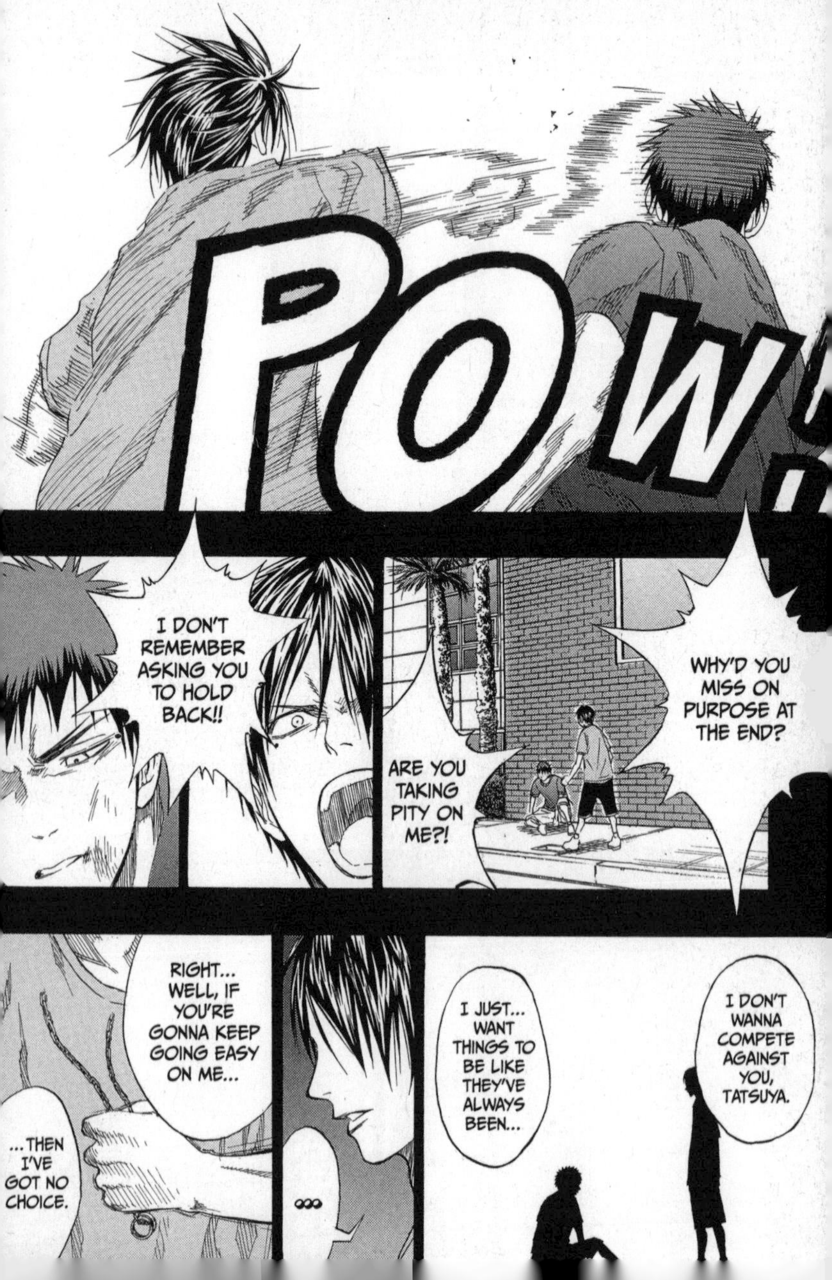
POW!!
WHY'D YOU MISS ON PURPOSE AT THE END?
ARE YOU TAKING PITY ON ME?!
I DON'T REMEMBER ASKING YOU TO HOLD BACK!!
I DON'T WANNA COMPETE AGAINST YOU, TATSUYA.
I JUST... WANT THINGS TO BE LIKE THEY'VE ALWAYS BEEN...
...
RIGHT... WELL, IF YOU'RE GONNA KEEP GOING EASY ON ME...
...THEN I'VE GOT NO CHOICE.

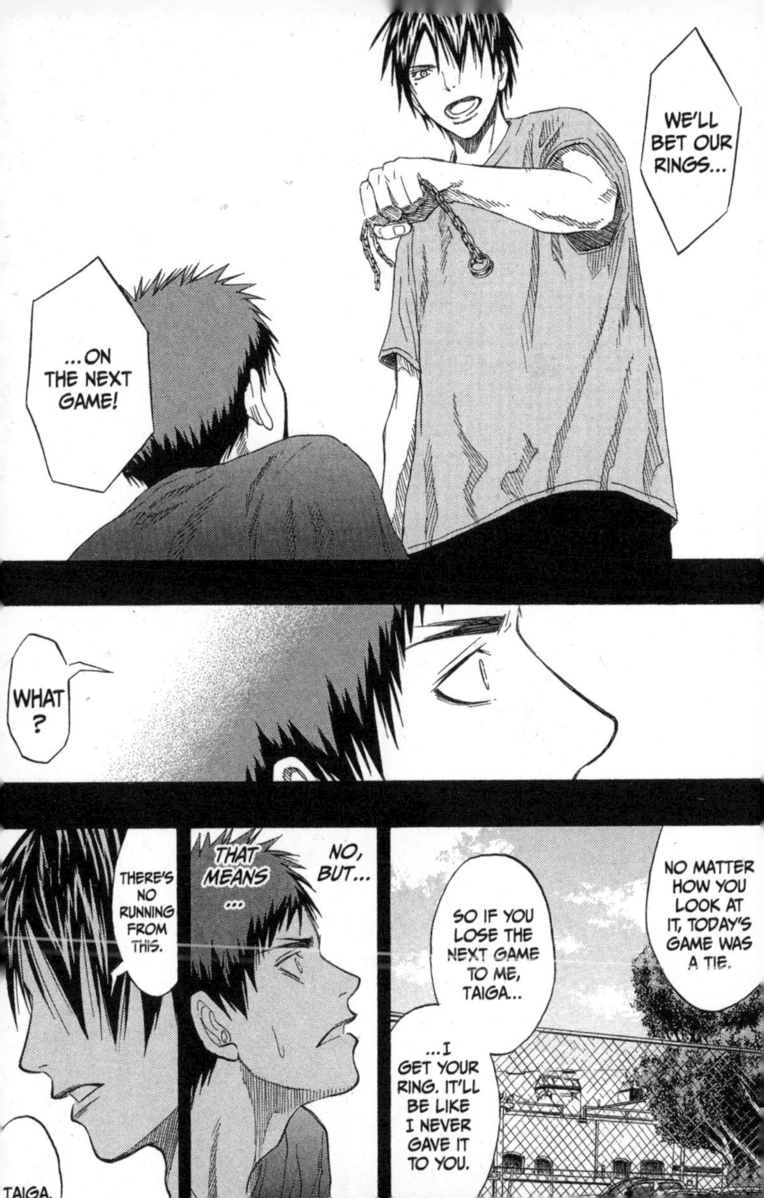
WE'LL BET OUR RINGS...
...ON THE NEXT GAME!
WHAT?
NO MATTER HOW YOU LOOK AT IT, TODAY'S GAME WAS A TIE.
SO IF YOU LOSE THE NEXT GAME TO ME, TAIGA...
...I GET YOUR RING. IT'LL BE LIKE I NEVER GAVE IT TO YOU.
NO, BUT...
THAT MEANS ...
THERE'S NO RUNNING FROM THIS.
TAIGA.

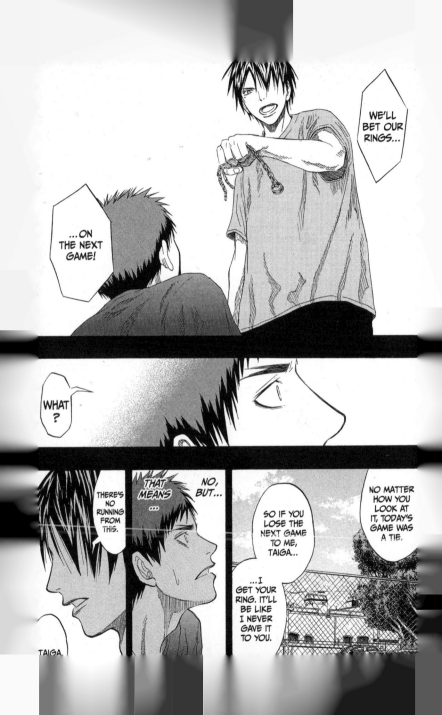

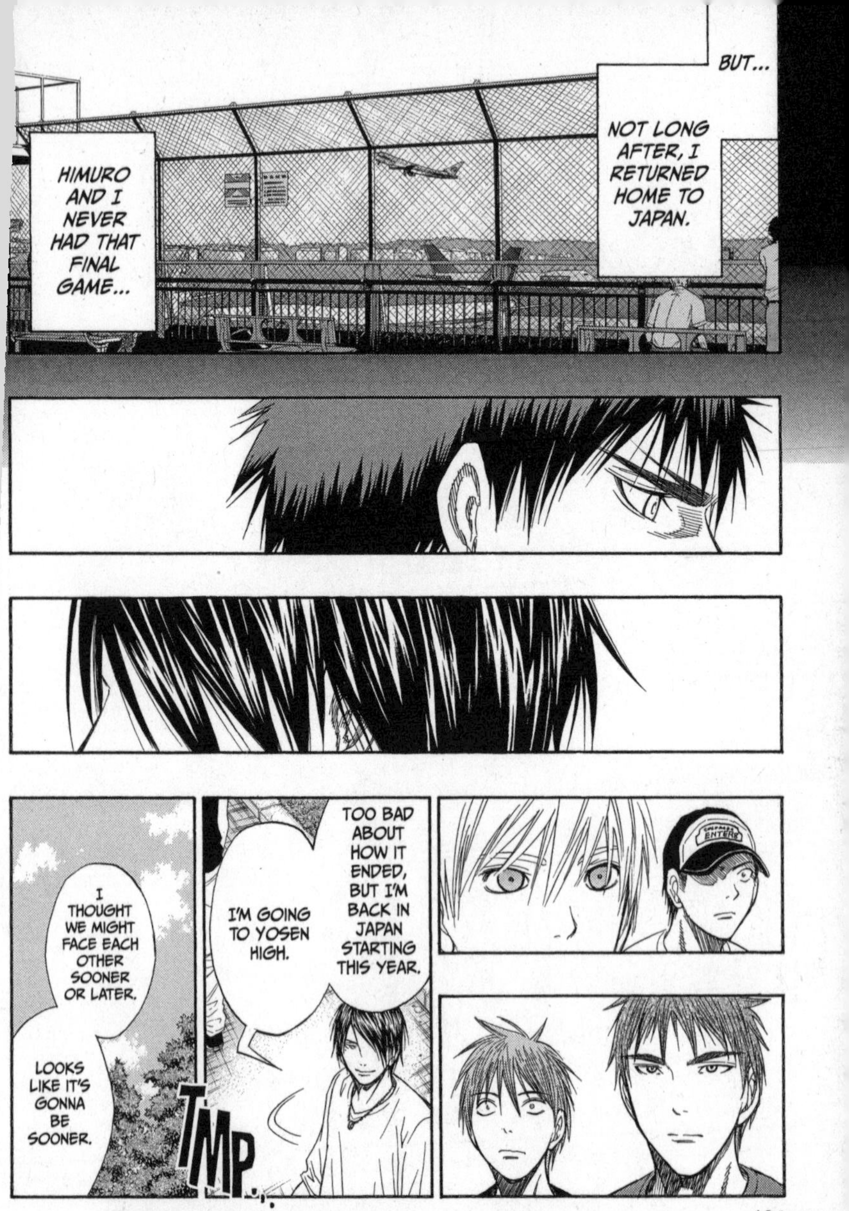
BUT...
NOT LONG AFTER, I RETURNED HOME TO JAPAN.
HIMURO AND I NEVER HAD THAT FINAL GAME...
TOO BAD ABOUT HOW IT ENDED, BUT I'M BACK IN JAPAN STARTING THIS YEAR.
I'M GOING TO YOSEN HIGH.
TMP...
I THOUGHT WE MIGHT FACE EACH OTHER SOONER OR LATER.
LOOKS LIKE IT'S GONNA BE SOONER.

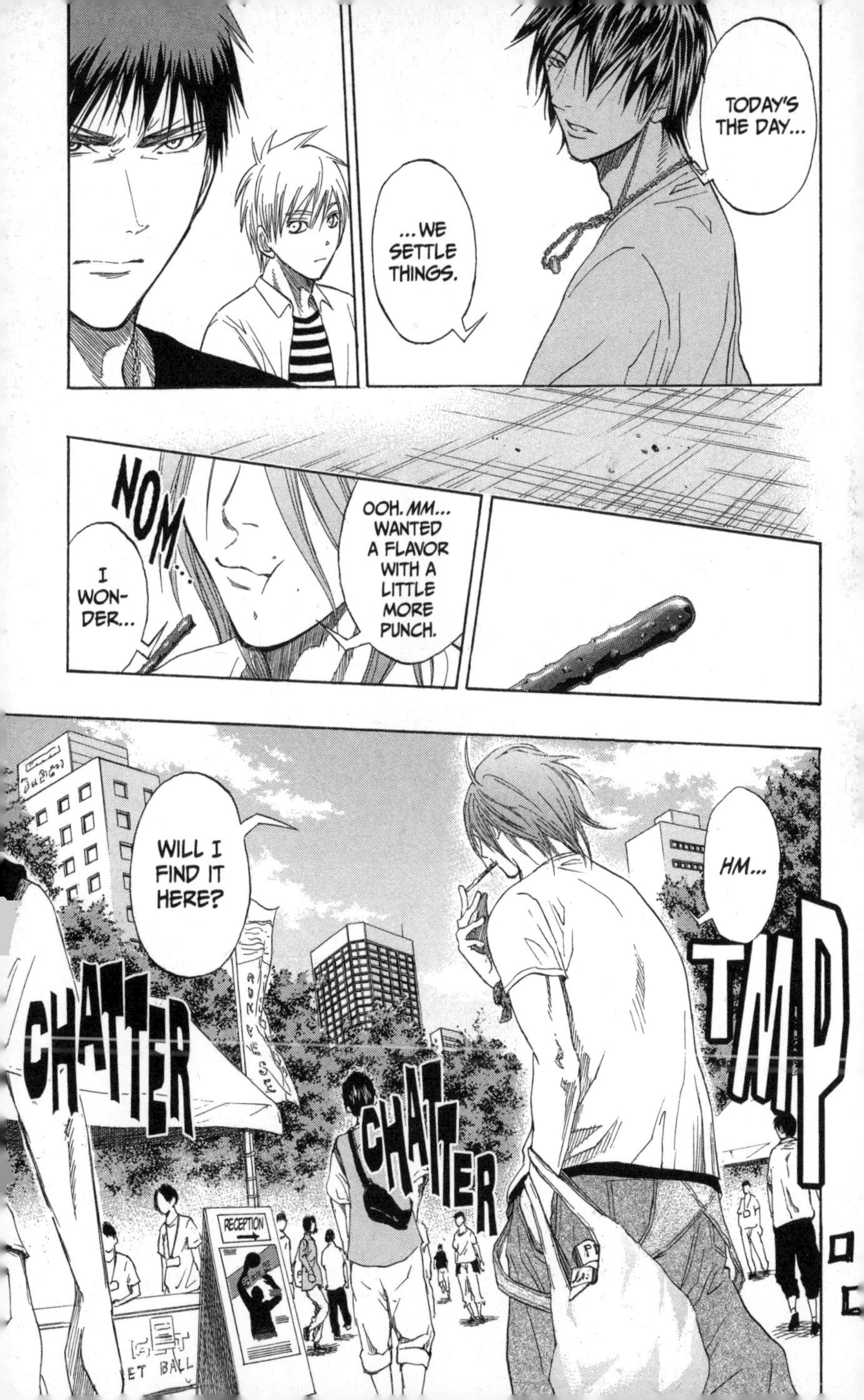
TODAY'S THE DAY...
...WE SETTLE THINGS.
OOH. *MM*... WANTED A FLAVOR WITH A LITTLE MORE PUNCH.
NOM...
I WON-DER...
TMP
HM...
WILL I FIND IT HERE?
CHATTER
CHATTER
RECEPTION
ET BALL

KUROKO'S BASKETBALL BLOOPERS
TAKE 6

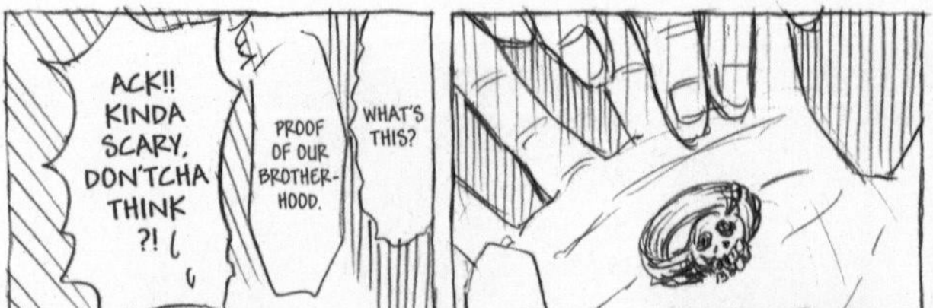
HERE!
DOOM...
WHAT'S THIS?
PROOF OF OUR BROTHER-HOOD.
ACK!! KINDA SCARY, DON'TCHA THINK ?!
GASP!
REALLY ?
YOU'VE GOT... WEIRD TASTE, TATSUYA.

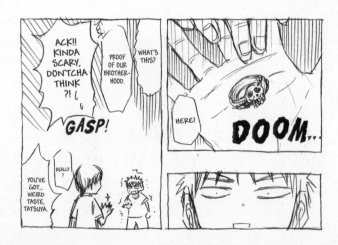

77TH QUARTER: I'M DETERMINED

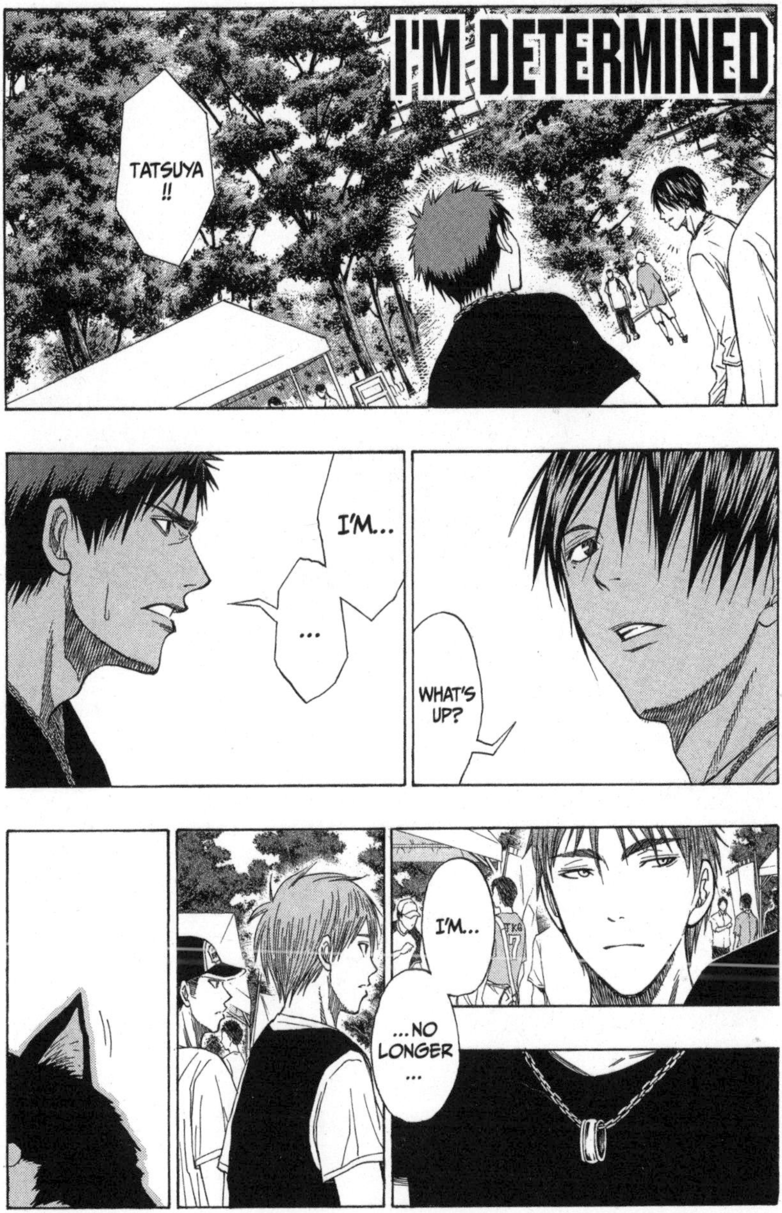
TATSUYA!!
WHAT'S UP?
I'M...
...
I'M...
...NO LONGER...

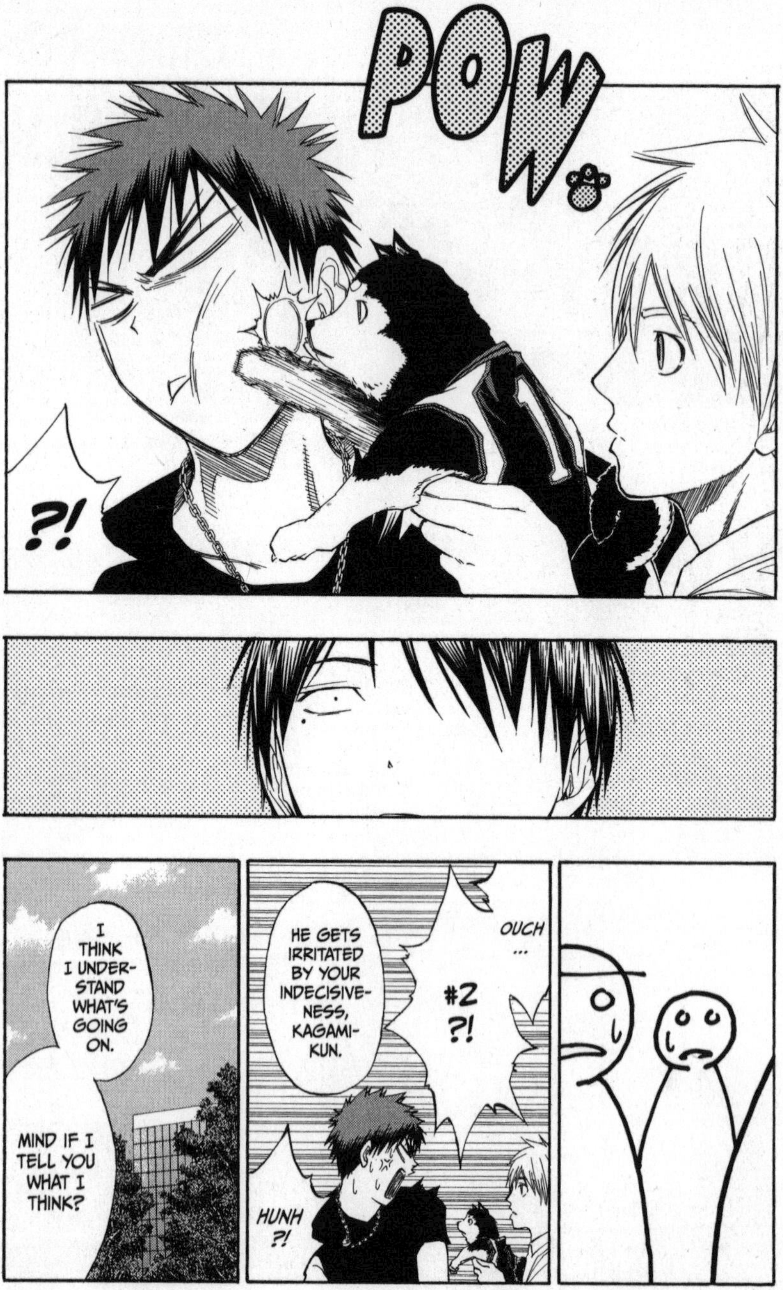
POW
?!
OUCH ...
#2 ?!
HE GETS IRRITATED BY YOUR INDECISIVENESS, KAGAMI-KUN.
HUNH ?!
I THINK I UNDERSTAND WHAT'S GOING ON.
MIND IF I TELL YOU WHAT I THINK?

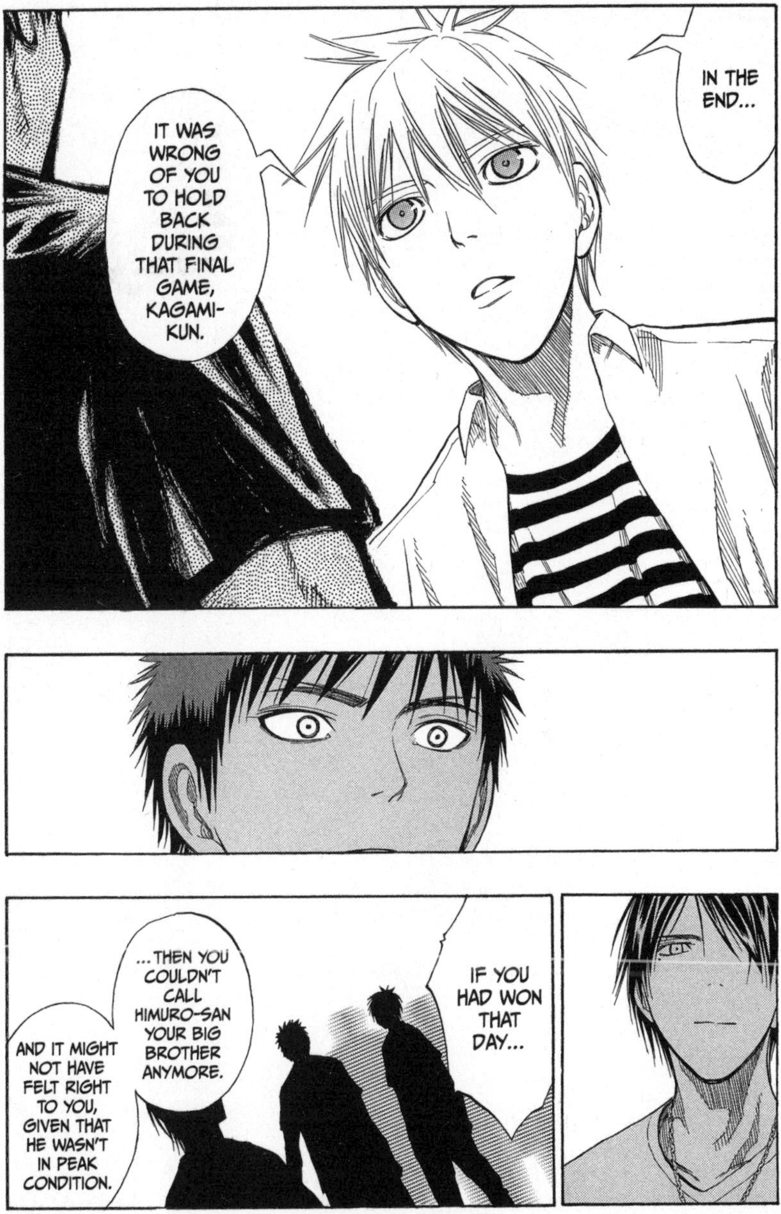
IN THE END...
IT WAS WRONG OF YOU TO HOLD BACK DURING THAT FINAL GAME, KAGAMI-KUN.
IF YOU HAD WON THAT DAY...
...THEN YOU COULDN'T CALL HIMURO-SAN YOUR BIG BROTHER ANYMORE.
AND IT MIGHT NOT HAVE FELT RIGHT TO YOU, GIVEN THAT HE WASN'T IN PEAK CONDITION.

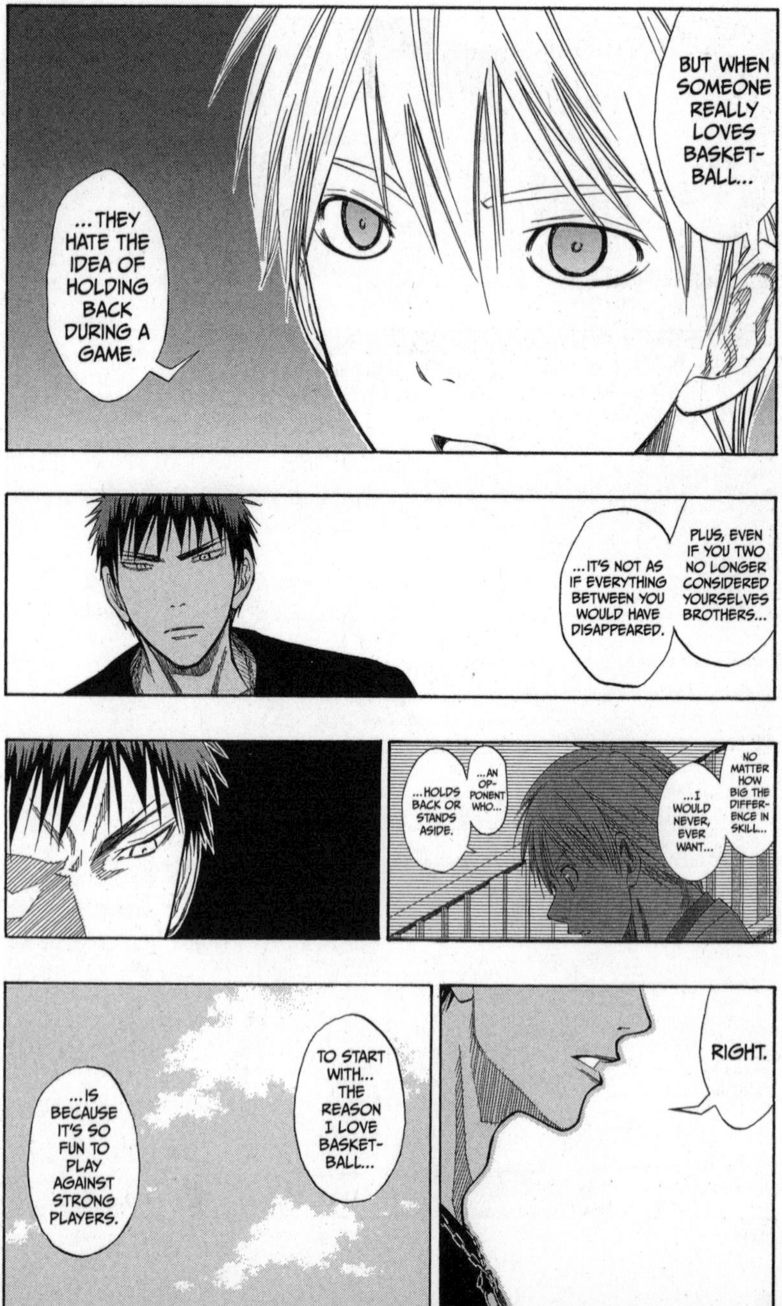
BUT WHEN SOMEONE REALLY LOVES BASKET-BALL...
...THEY HATE THE IDEA OF HOLDING BACK DURING A GAME.
PLUS, EVEN IF YOU TWO NO LONGER CONSIDERED YOURSELVES BROTHERS...
...IT'S NOT AS IF EVERYTHING BETWEEN YOU WOULD HAVE DISAPPEARED.
NO MATTER HOW BIG THE DIFFER-ENCE IN SKILL...
...I WOULD NEVER, EVER WANT...
...AN OP-PONENT WHO...
...HOLDS BACK OR STANDS ASIDE.
RIGHT.
TO START WITH... THE REASON I LOVE BASKET-BALL...
...IS BECAUSE IT'S SO FUN TO PLAY AGAINST STRONG PLAYERS.

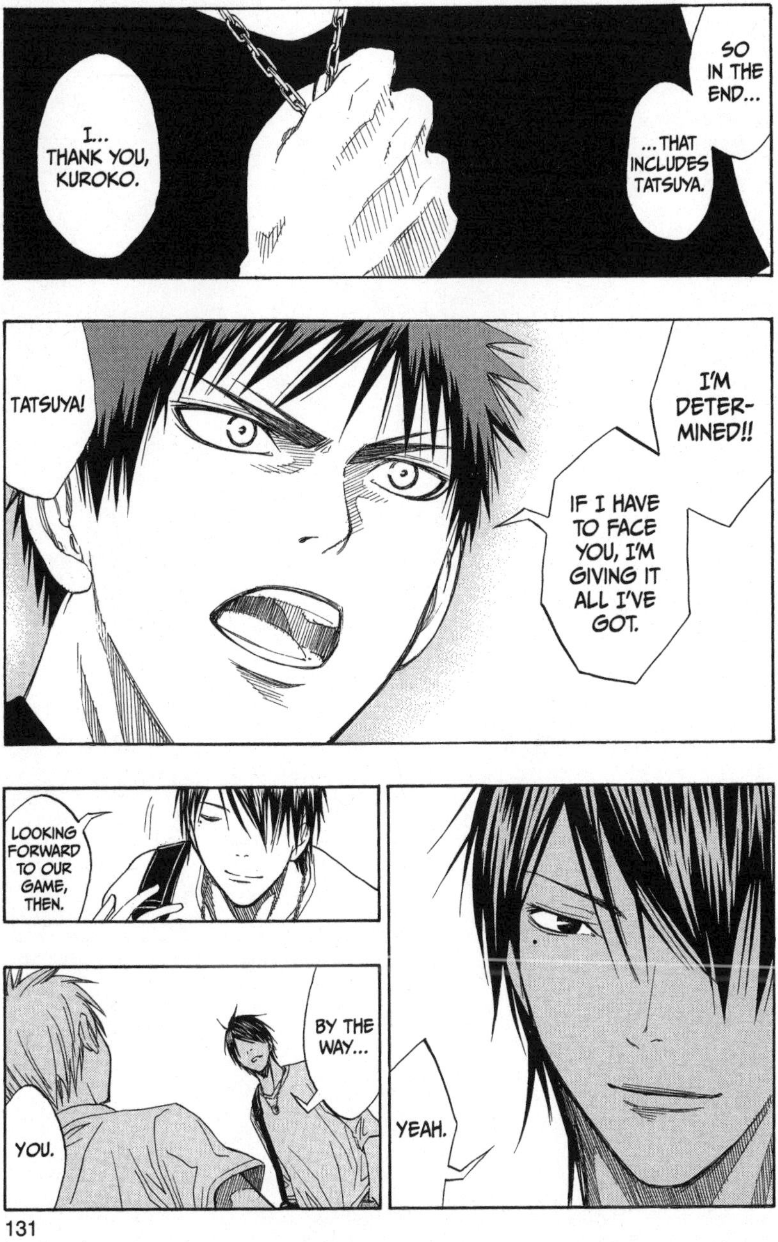
SO IN THE END...
...THAT INCLUDES TATSUYA.
I... THANK YOU, KUROKO.
I'M DETERMINED!!
TATSUYA!
IF I HAVE TO FACE YOU, I'M GIVING IT ALL I'VE GOT.
YEAH.
LOOKING FORWARD TO OUR GAME, THEN.
BY THE WAY...
YOU.

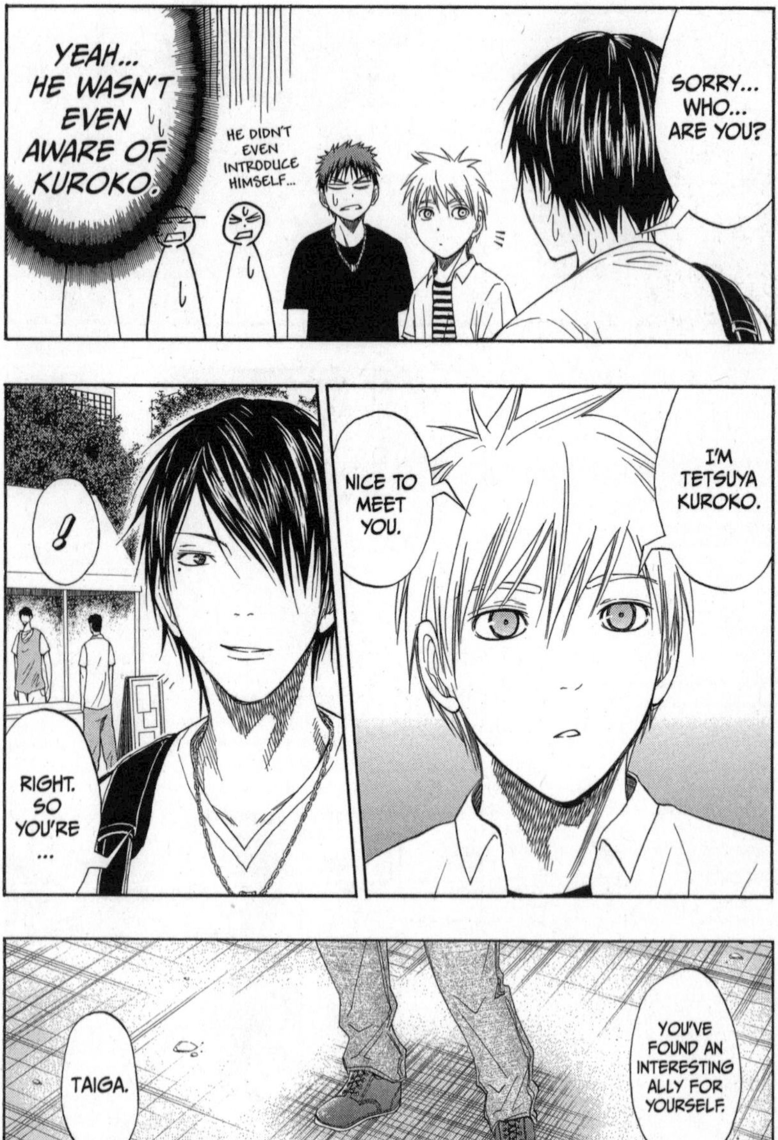
SORRY... WHO... ARE YOU?
HE DIDN'T EVEN INTRODUCE HIMSELF...
YEAH... HE WASN'T EVEN AWARE OF KUROKO.
I'M TETSUYA KUROKO.
NICE TO MEET YOU.
!
RIGHT. SO YOU'RE ...
YOU'VE FOUND AN INTERESTING ALLY FOR YOURSELF.
TAIGA.

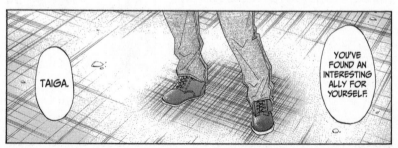

WAIT... TATSUYA!
DO YOU KNOW ABOUT KUROKO ?!
A LITTLE BIT.
THE TEAM I'M ON ALSO HAS AN INTERESTING GUY...
...!
BET YOU'LL RUN INTO HIM AT SOME POINT.
I'LL HAVE TO INTRODUCE YOU.

SIGH...
WHO WOULD HAVE THOUGHT WE'D RUN INTO A BEAST LIKE THAT RIGHT FROM THE START?
THAT WAS A SHOCKER
ARGH!
CRAAP!
WE LOST. THAT'S ALL THERE IS TO IT.
RELAX, TSUGAWA.
STILL, TO THINK THEY HAD A GUY LIKE THAT...
IT'S HARD TO BELIEVE, BUT HE MAY ACTUALLY BE EQUAL TO THE MIRACLE GENERATION.
WHAT?
SHF...
THAT GUY. HE'S ...?!
BUT WHY'S HE HERE?! INTER-HIGH ONLY JUST ENDED...

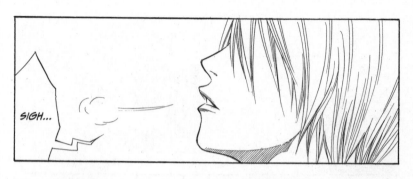

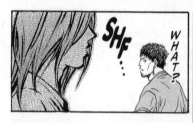

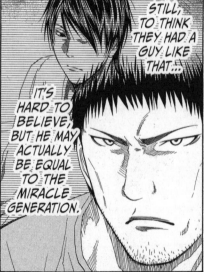

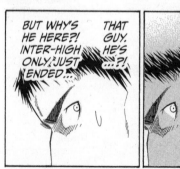

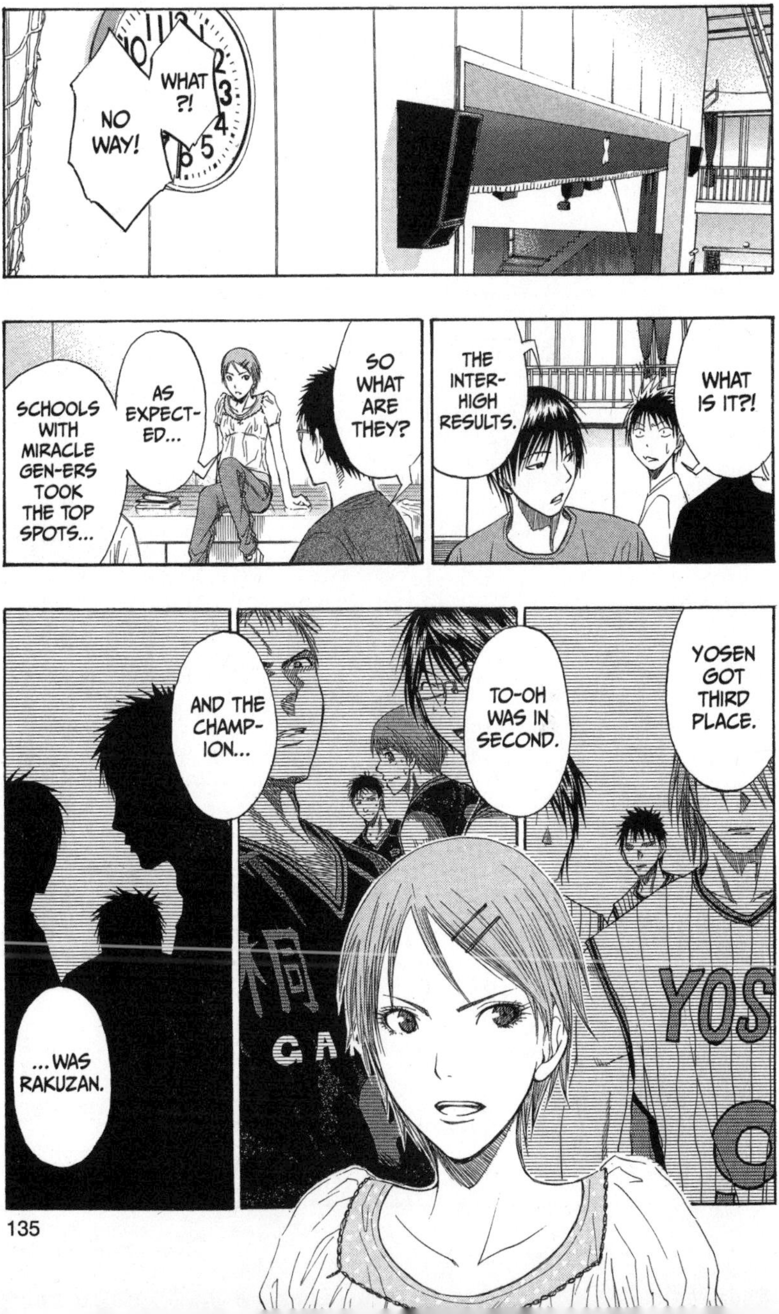
WHAT?!
NO WAY!
WHAT IS IT?!
THE INTER-HIGH RESULTS.
SO WHAT ARE THEY?
AS EXPECTED...
SCHOOLS WITH MIRACLE GEN-ERS TOOK THE TOP SPOTS...
YOSEN GOT THIRD PLACE.
YOS
TO-OH WAS IN SECOND.
AND THE CHAMPION...
...WAS RAKUZAN.

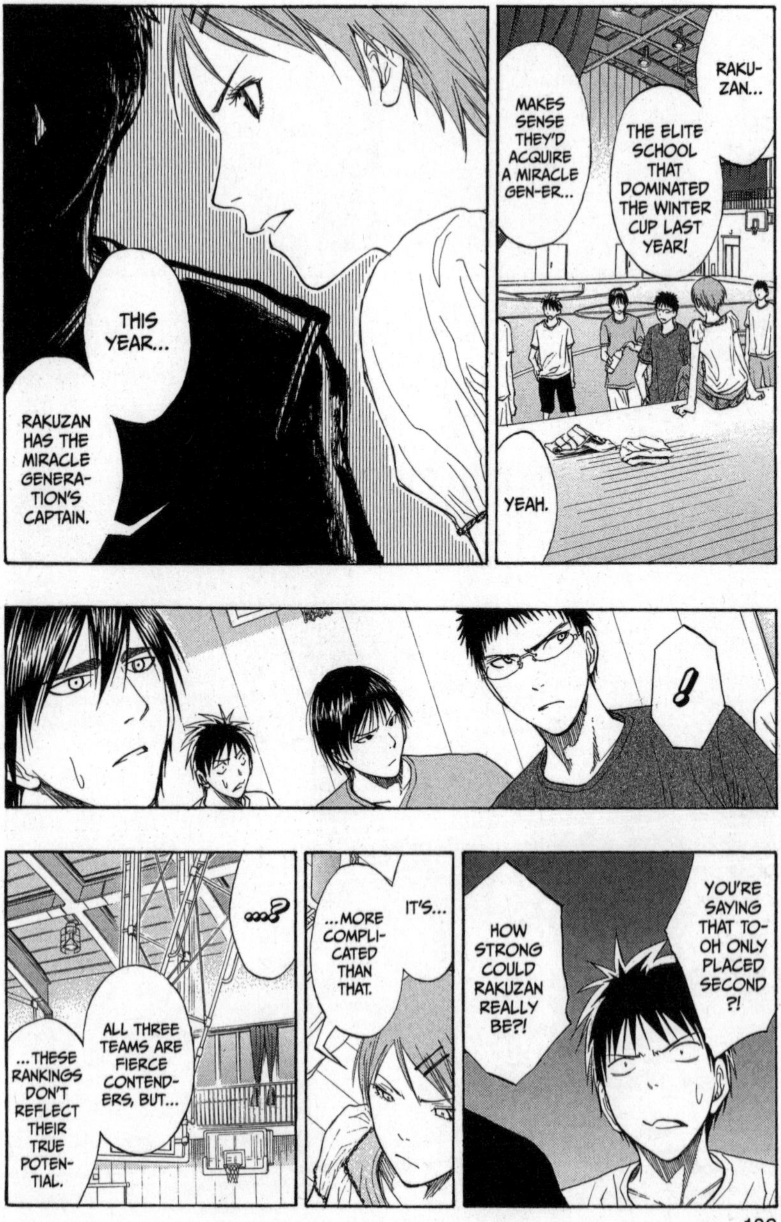
RAKU-ZAN...
THE ELITE SCHOOL THAT DOMINATED THE WINTER CUP LAST YEAR!
MAKES SENSE THEY'D ACQUIRE A MIRACLE GEN-ER...
YEAH.
THIS YEAR...
RAKUZAN HAS THE MIRACLE GENERA-TION'S CAPTAIN.
!
YOU'RE SAYING THAT TO-OH ONLY PLACED SECOND?!
HOW STRONG COULD RAKUZAN REALLY BE?!
IT'S...
...MORE COMPLI-CATED THAN THAT.
...?
ALL THREE TEAMS ARE FIERCE CONTEND-ERS, BUT...
...THESE RANKINGS DON'T REFLECT THEIR TRUE POTEN-TIAL.

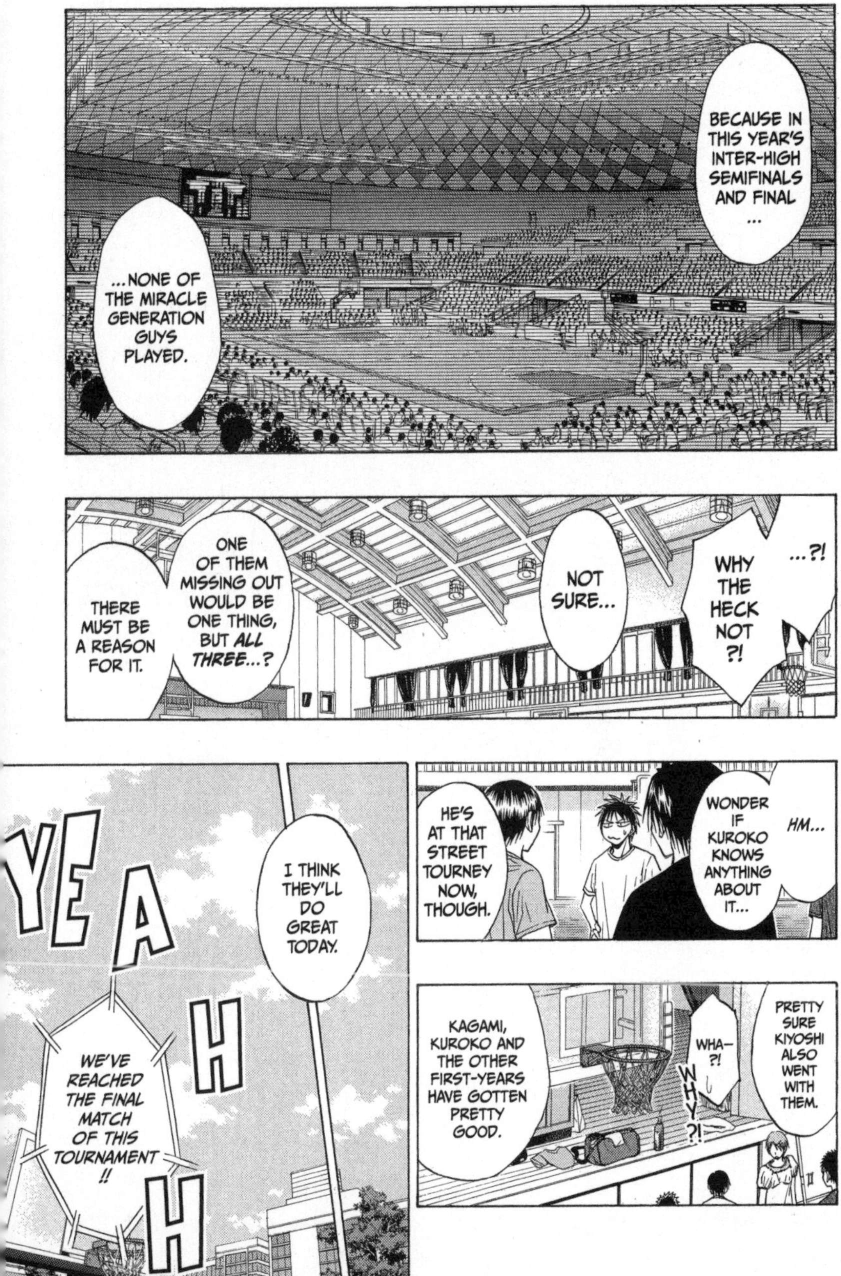
BECAUSE IN THIS YEAR'S INTER-HIGH SEMIFINALS AND FINAL ...
...NONE OF THE MIRACLE GENERATION GUYS PLAYED.
...?!
WHY THE HECK NOT ?!
NOT SURE...
ONE OF THEM MISSING OUT WOULD BE ONE THING, BUT ALL THREE...?
THERE MUST BE A REASON FOR IT.
HM...
WONDER IF KUROKO KNOWS ANYTHING ABOUT IT...
HE'S AT THAT STREET TOURNEY NOW, THOUGH.
PRETTY SURE KIYOSHI ALSO WENT WITH THEM.
WHA- ?!
WHY ?!
KAGAMI, KUROKO AND THE OTHER FIRST-YEARS HAVE GOTTEN PRETTY GOOD.
I THINK THEY'LL DO GREAT TODAY.
YEAHHH
WE'VE REACHED THE FINAL MATCH OF THIS TOURNAMENT !!

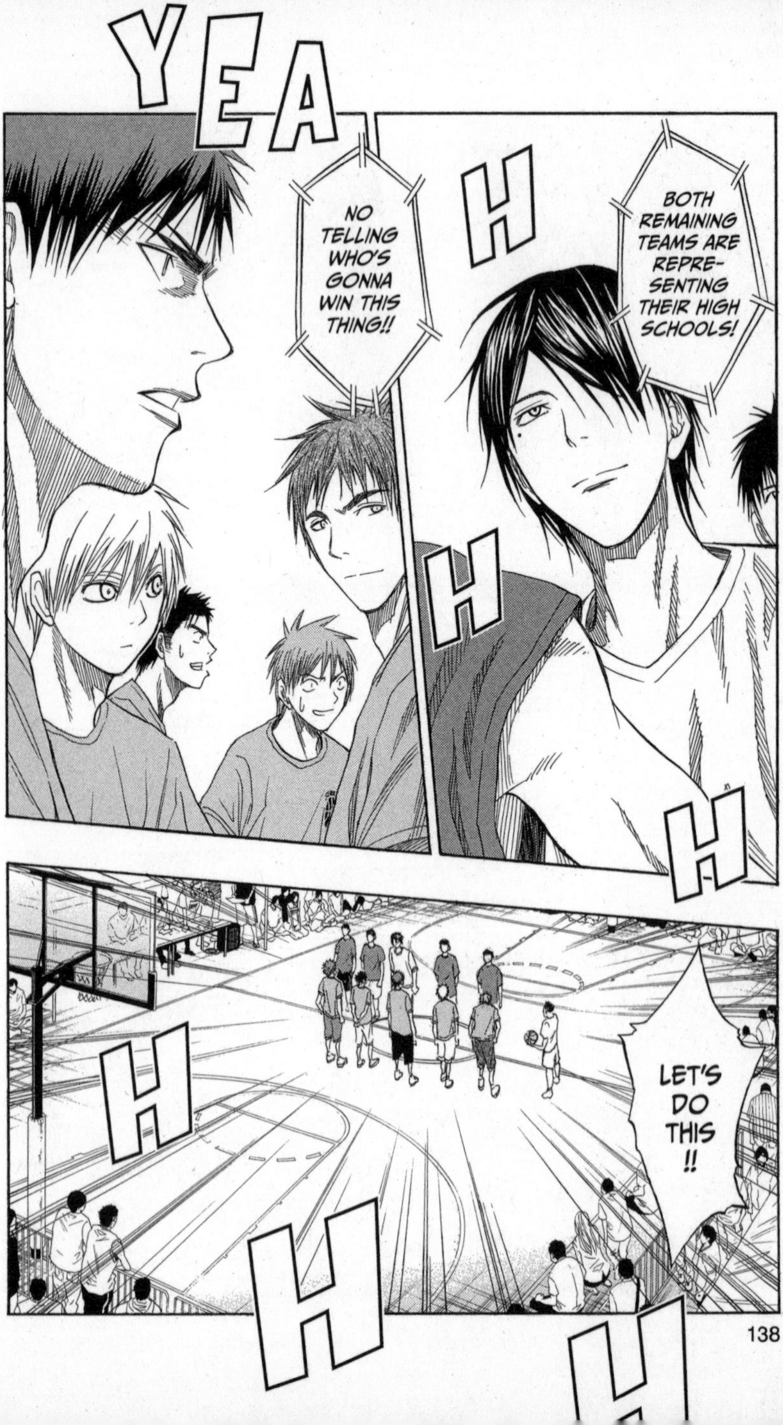
YEAHHHHHH
BOTH REMAINING TEAMS ARE REPRESENTING THEIR HIGH SCHOOLS!
NO TELLING WHO'S GONNA WIN THIS THING!!
LET'S DO THIS!!

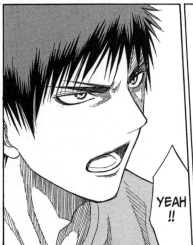

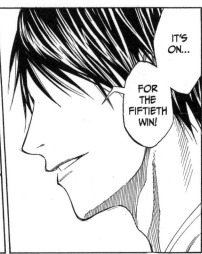

IT'S ON...
FOR THE FIFTIETH WIN!
YEAH!!
NOT THAT THIS IS GONNA BE EASY FOR ME.
I'M JUST FILLING IN FOR ONE OF THE REGULARS ON THIS IMPROMPTU TEAM.
WELL... WHATEVER.
KAGAMI-KUN... THERE'S SOMETHING BOTHERING ME FROM OUR TALK EARLIER...
HUH?
YOU WERE EVENLY MATCHED IN MIDDLE SCHOOL, RIGHT?
YEAH.
NOW DON'T GET MAD AT ME. YOU'RE STRONG, KAGAMI-KUN, BUT...
BUT WHAT?!
TELL ME HOW YOU REALLY FEEL!!

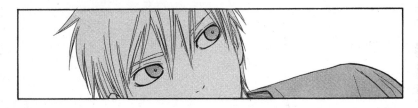

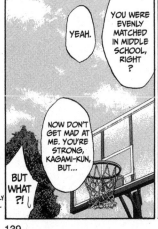

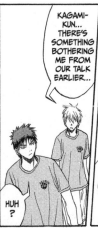

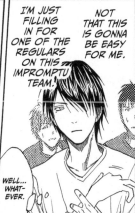

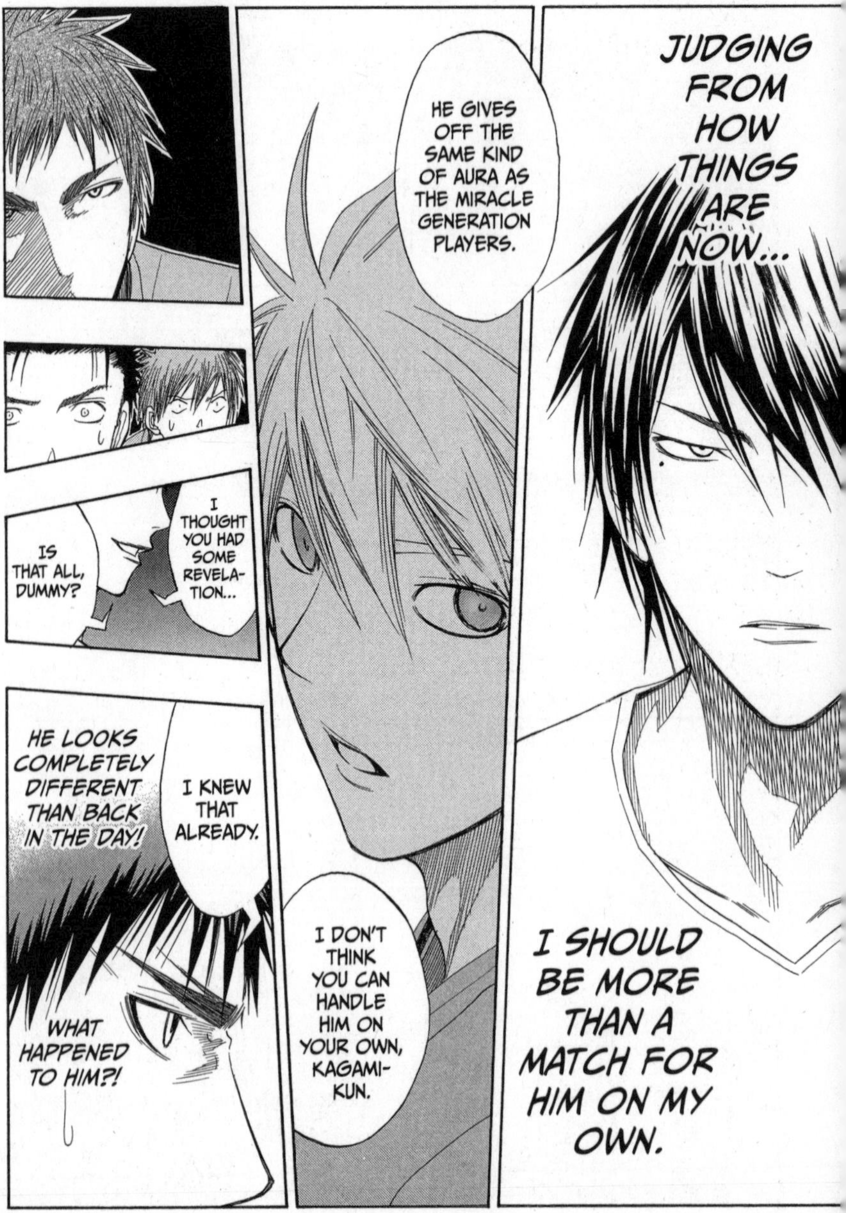
JUDGING FROM HOW THINGS ARE NOW...
I SHOULD BE MORE THAN A MATCH FOR HIM ON MY OWN.
HE GIVES OFF THE SAME KIND OF AURA AS THE MIRACLE GENERATION PLAYERS.
I DON'T THINK YOU CAN HANDLE HIM ON YOUR OWN, KAGAMI-KUN.
I THOUGHT YOU HAD SOME REVELA-TION...
IS THAT ALL, DUMMY?
I KNEW THAT ALREADY.
HE LOOKS COMPLETELY DIFFERENT THAN BACK IN THE DAY!
WHAT HAPPENED TO HIM?!

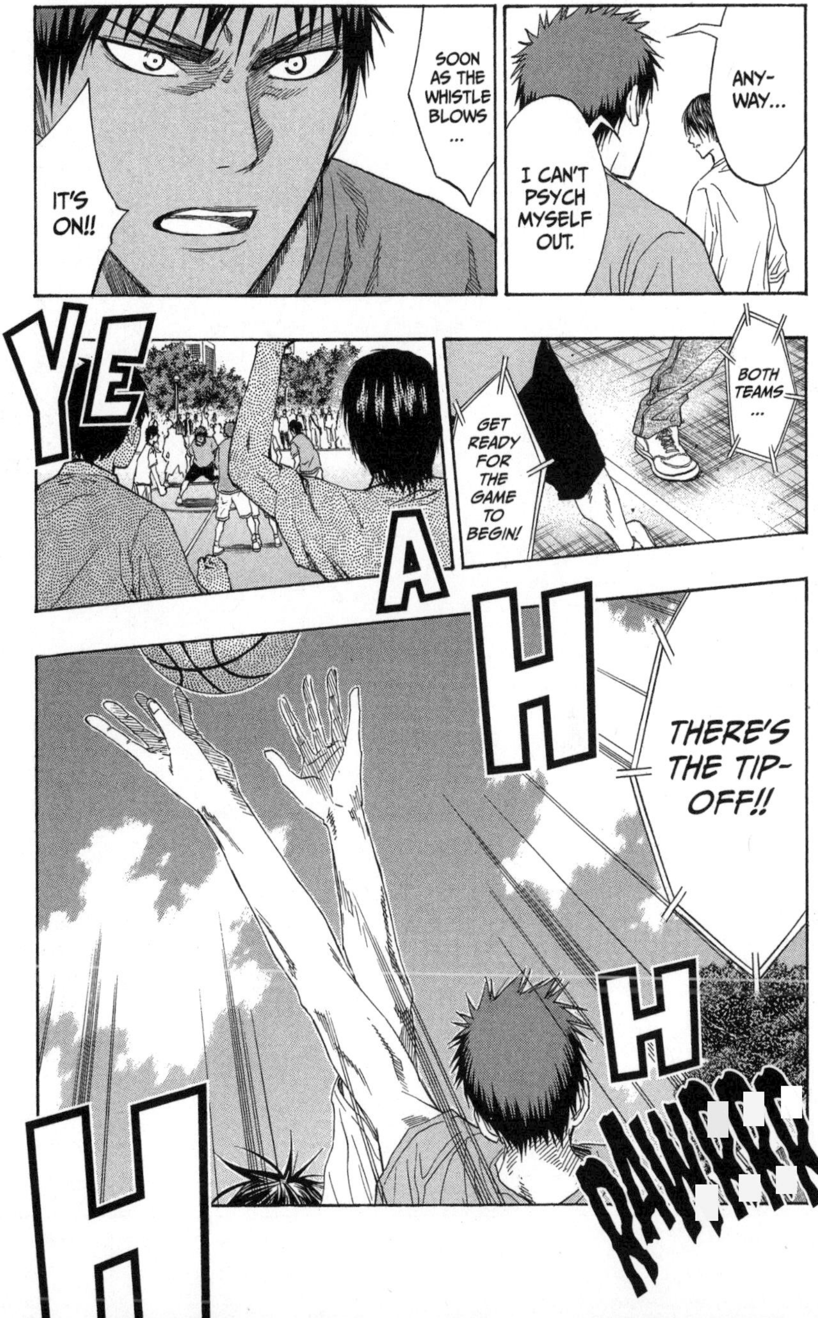
ANY-WAY...
I CAN'T PSYCH MYSELF OUT.
SOON AS THE WHISTLE BLOWS...
IT'S ON!!
BOTH TEAMS...
GET READY FOR THE GAME TO BEGIN!
YEAHHH
THERE'S THE TIP-OFF!!
RAWRRR

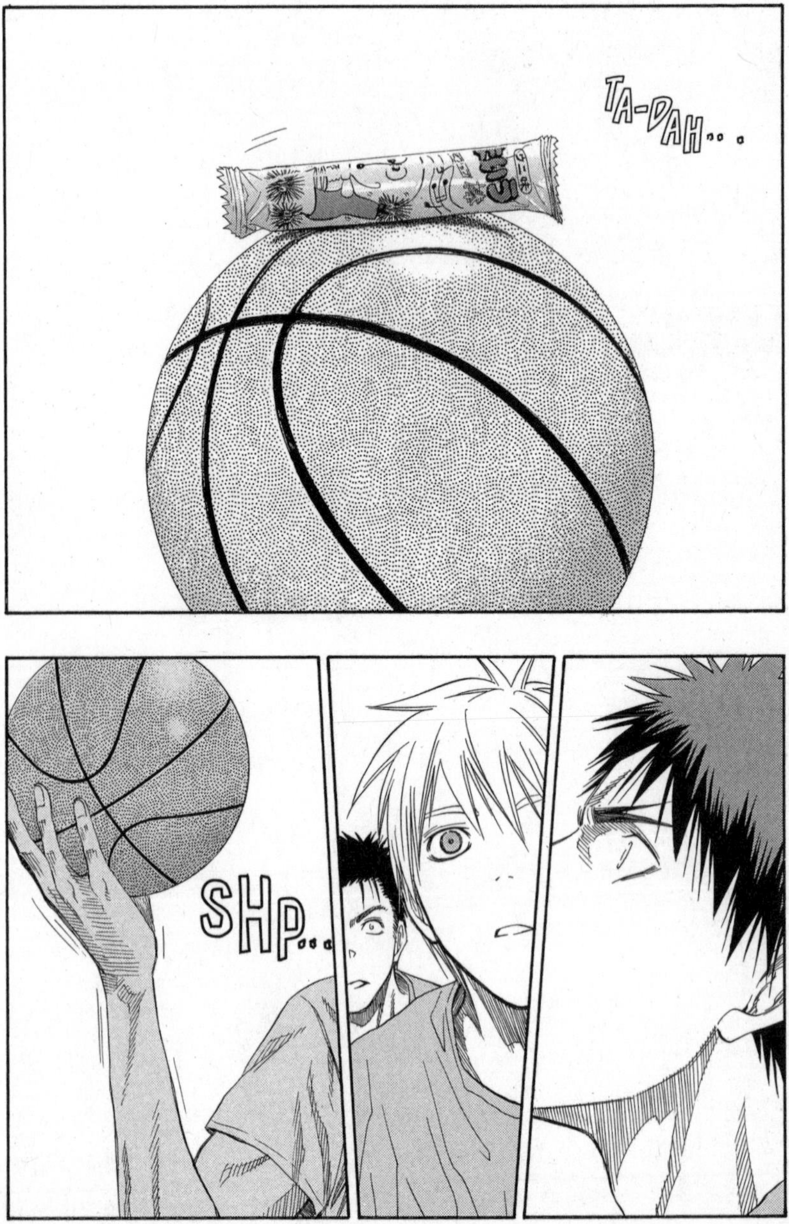
TA-DAH...
SHP...

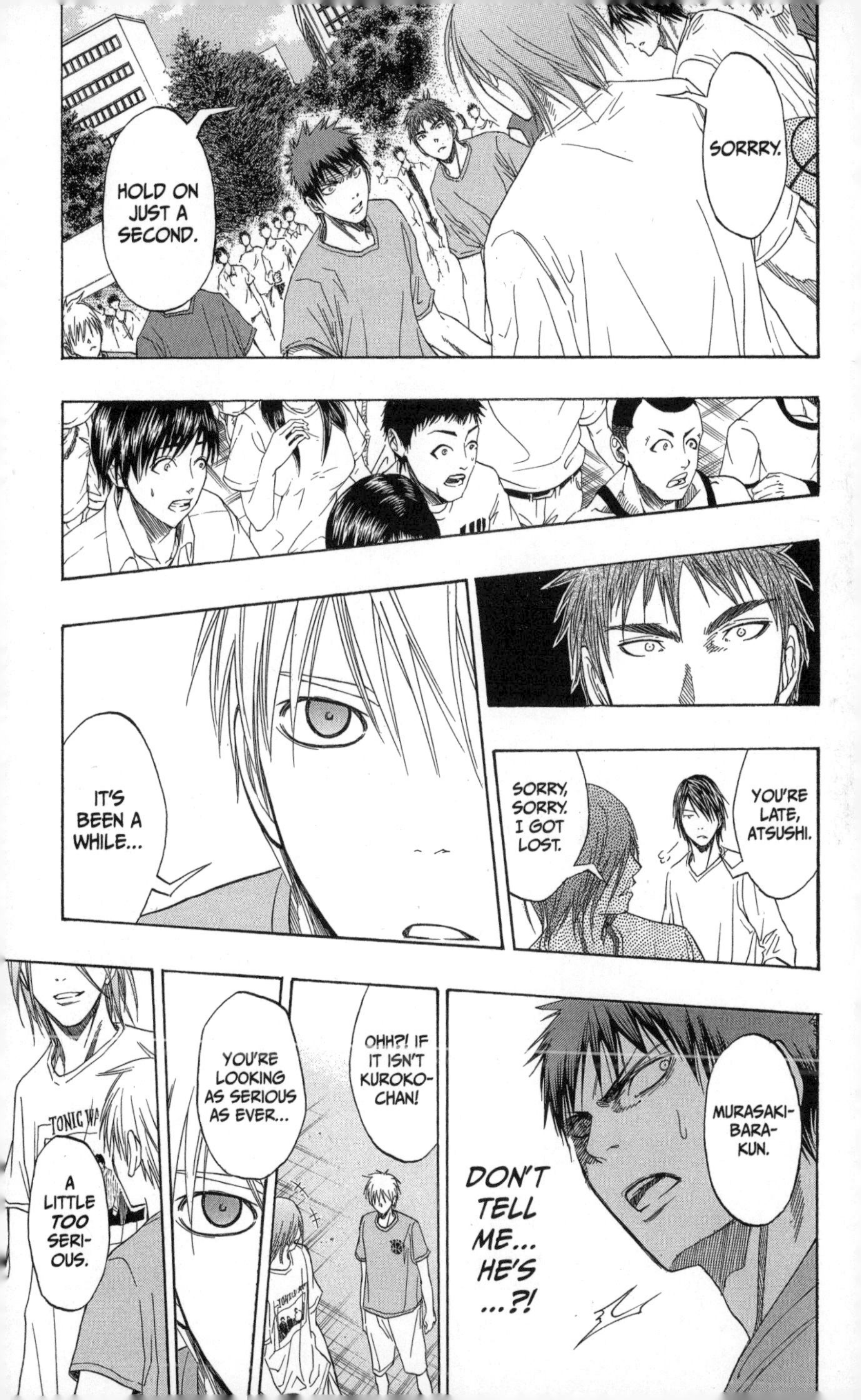
SORRRY.
HOLD ON JUST A SECOND.
YOU'RE LATE, ATSUSHI.
SORRY, SORRY. I GOT LOST.
IT'S BEEN A WHILE...
MURASAKIBARA-KUN.
DON'T TELL ME... HE'S ...?!
OHH?! IF IT ISN'T KUROKO-CHAN!
YOU'RE LOOKING AS SERIOUS AS EVER...
A LITTLE TOO SERIOUS.

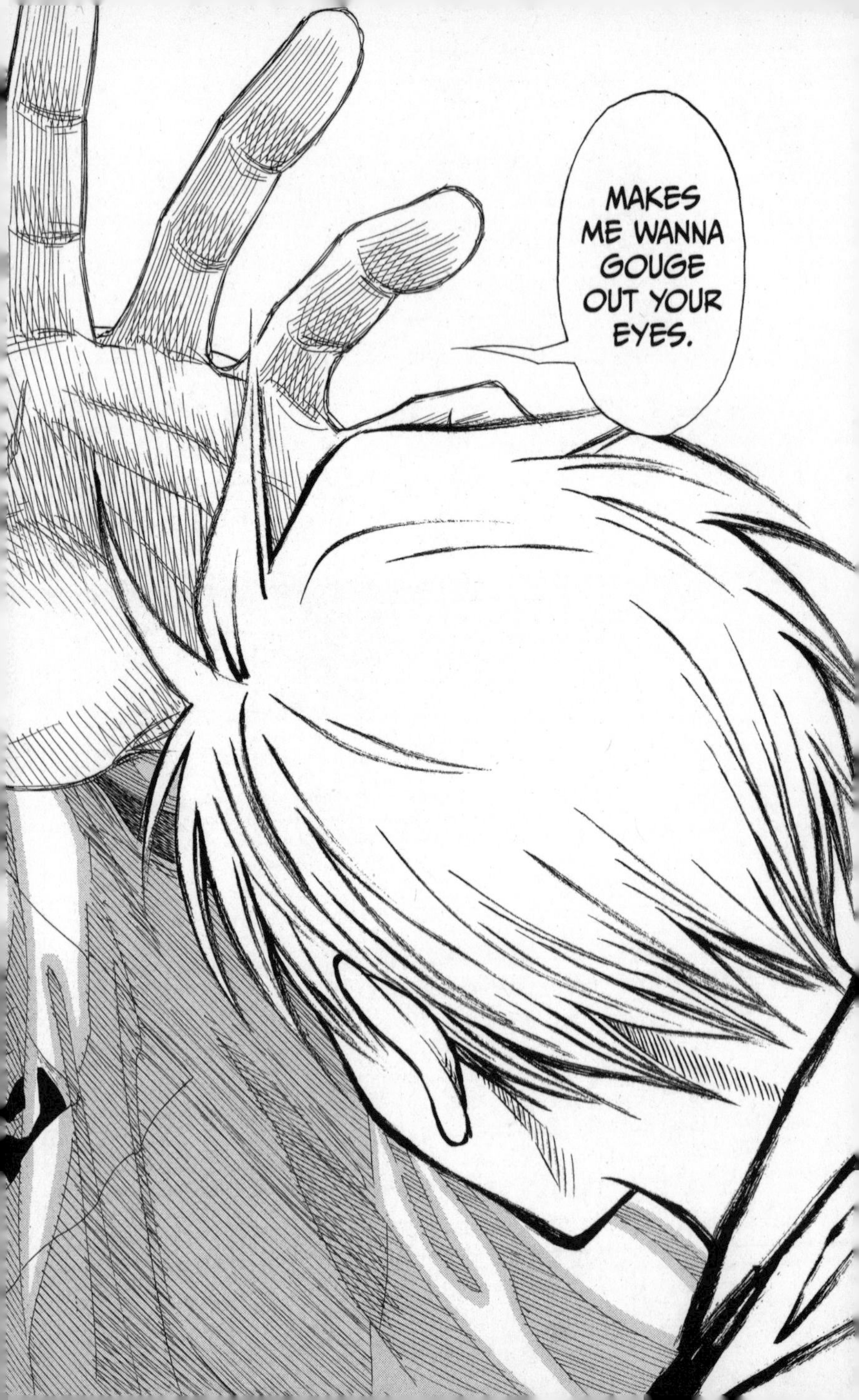
MAKES ME WANNA GOUGE OUT YOUR EYES.

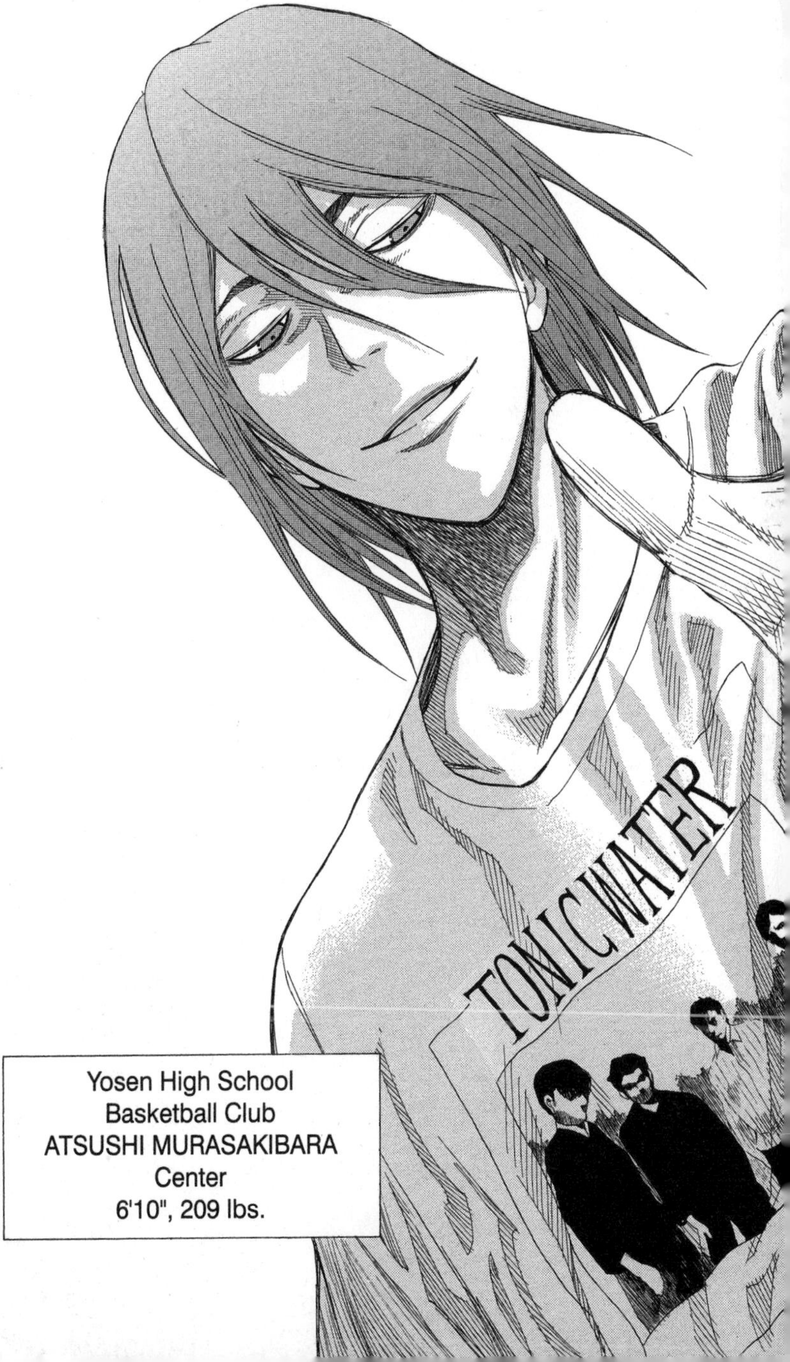
TONIC WATER
Yosen High School
Basketball Club
ATSUSHI MURASAKIBARA
Center
6'10", 209 lbs.

KUROKO'S BASKETBALL BLOOPERS

TAKE 1

TA-DAH...
INSTANT REPLAY
JUMP BALL!!
SHOOP!
FWIP!!
YOU BIG FAT LIAR!!
NO, IT'S TRUE.
YOUR STUPID SNACK COULD NEVER FLY LIKE THAT!!

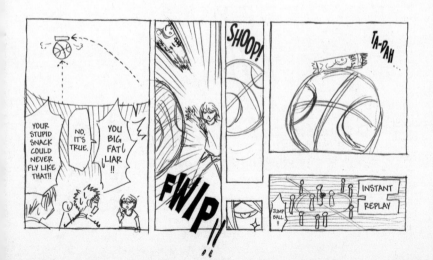

YOU'RE LOOKING AS SERIOUS AS EVER ...

A LITTLE *TOO* SERIOUS.

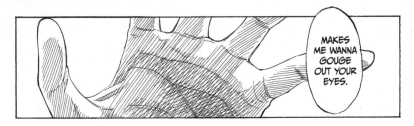

MAKES ME WANNA GOUGE OUT YOUR EYES.

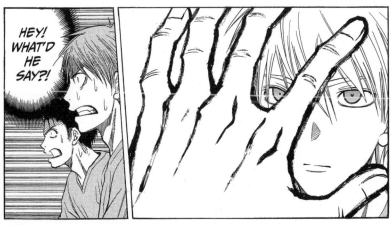

HEY! WHAT'D HE SAY?!

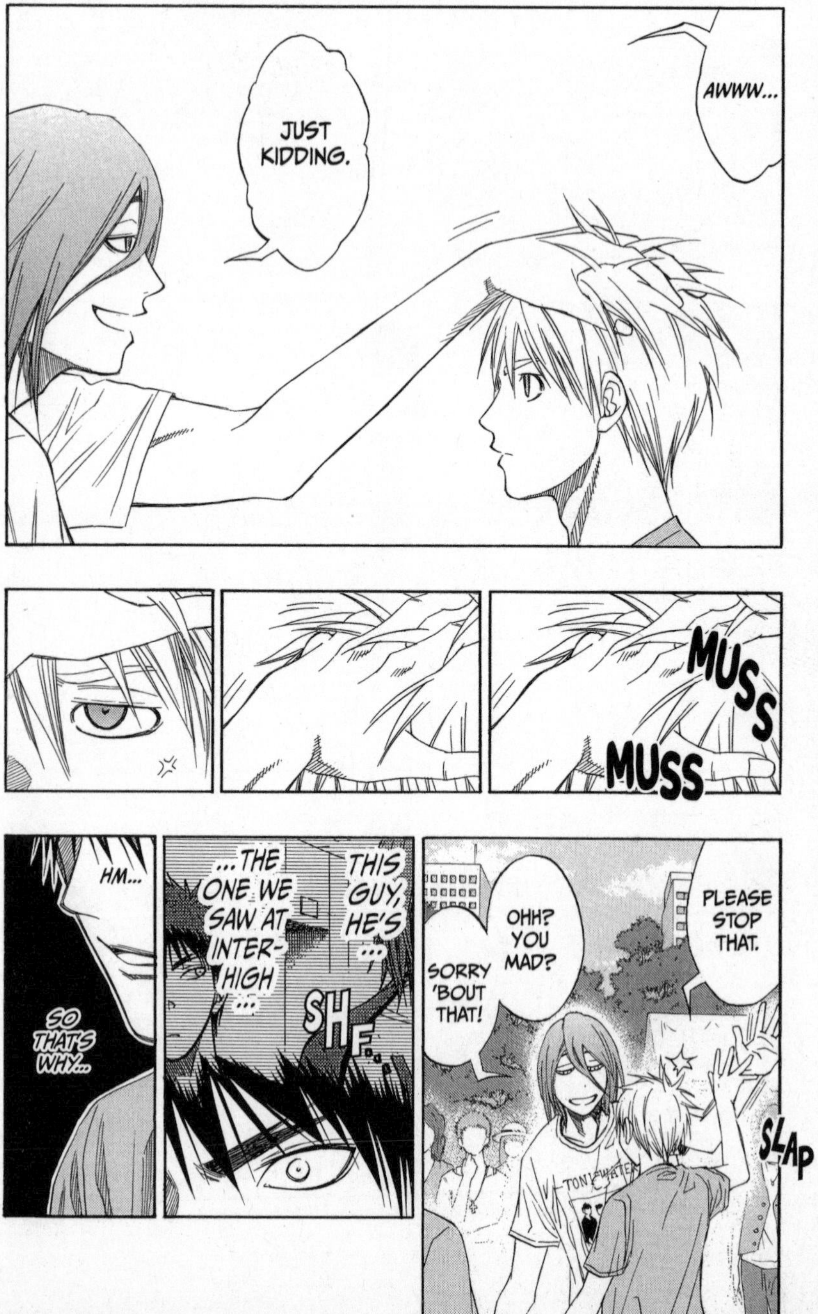
AWWW...
JUST KIDDING.
MUSS
MUSS
PLEASE STOP THAT.
OHH? YOU MAD?
SORRY 'BOUT THAT!
SLAP
THIS GUY, HE'S...
...THE ONE WE SAW AT INTER-HIGH...
SHF
HM...
SO THAT'S WHY...

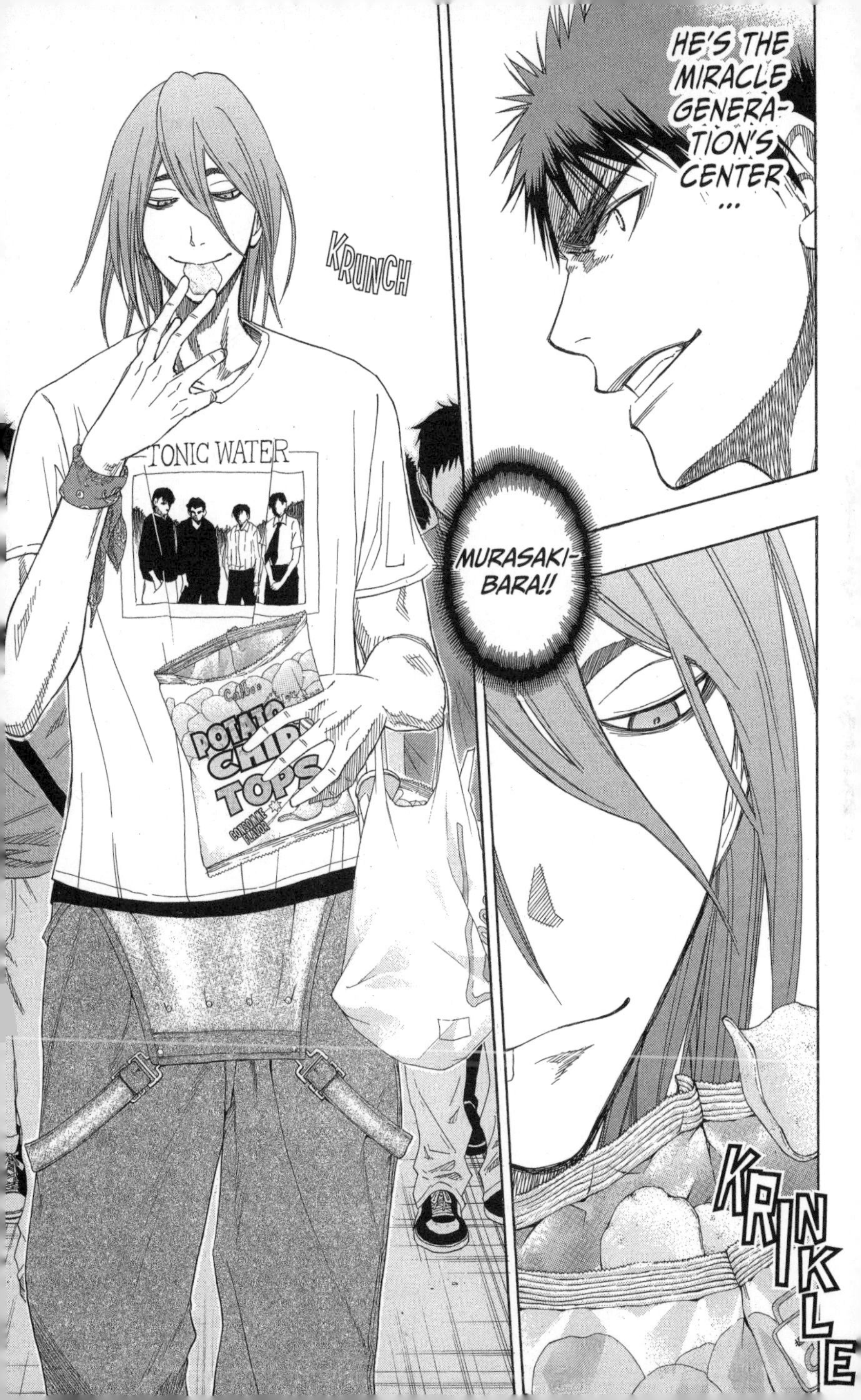
HE'S THE MIRACLE GENERATION'S CENTER...
MURASAKIBARA!!
KRINKLE
KRUNCH
TONIC WATER

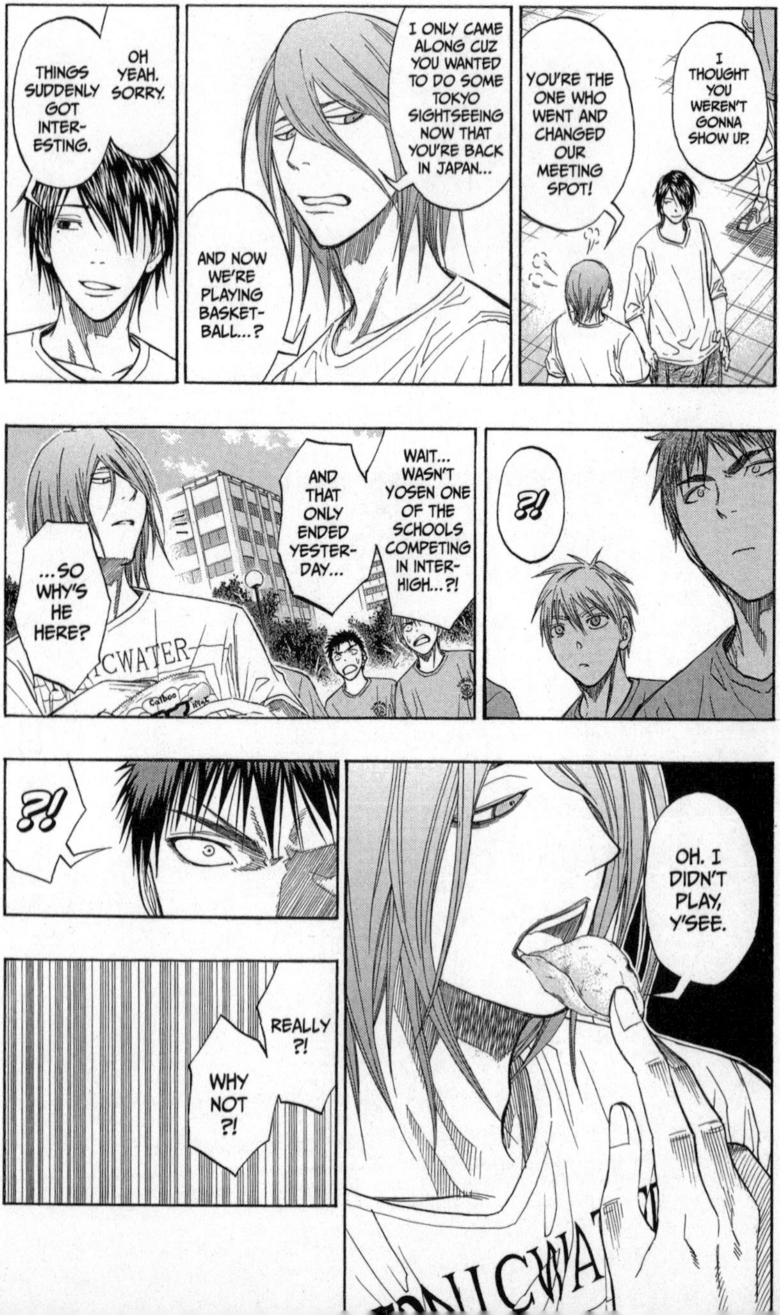
I THOUGHT YOU WEREN'T GONNA SHOW UP.
YOU'RE THE ONE WHO WENT AND CHANGED OUR MEETING SPOT!
I ONLY CAME ALONG CUZ YOU WANTED TO DO SOME TOKYO SIGHTSEEING NOW THAT YOU'RE BACK IN JAPAN...
AND NOW WE'RE PLAYING BASKETBALL...?
OH YEAH. SORRY.
THINGS SUDDENLY GOT INTERESTING.
?!
WAIT... WASN'T YOSEN ONE OF THE SCHOOLS COMPETING IN INTER-HIGH...?!
AND THAT ONLY ENDED YESTERDAY...
...SO WHY'S HE HERE?
OH. I DIDN'T PLAY, Y'SEE.
?!
REALLY?!
WHY NOT?!

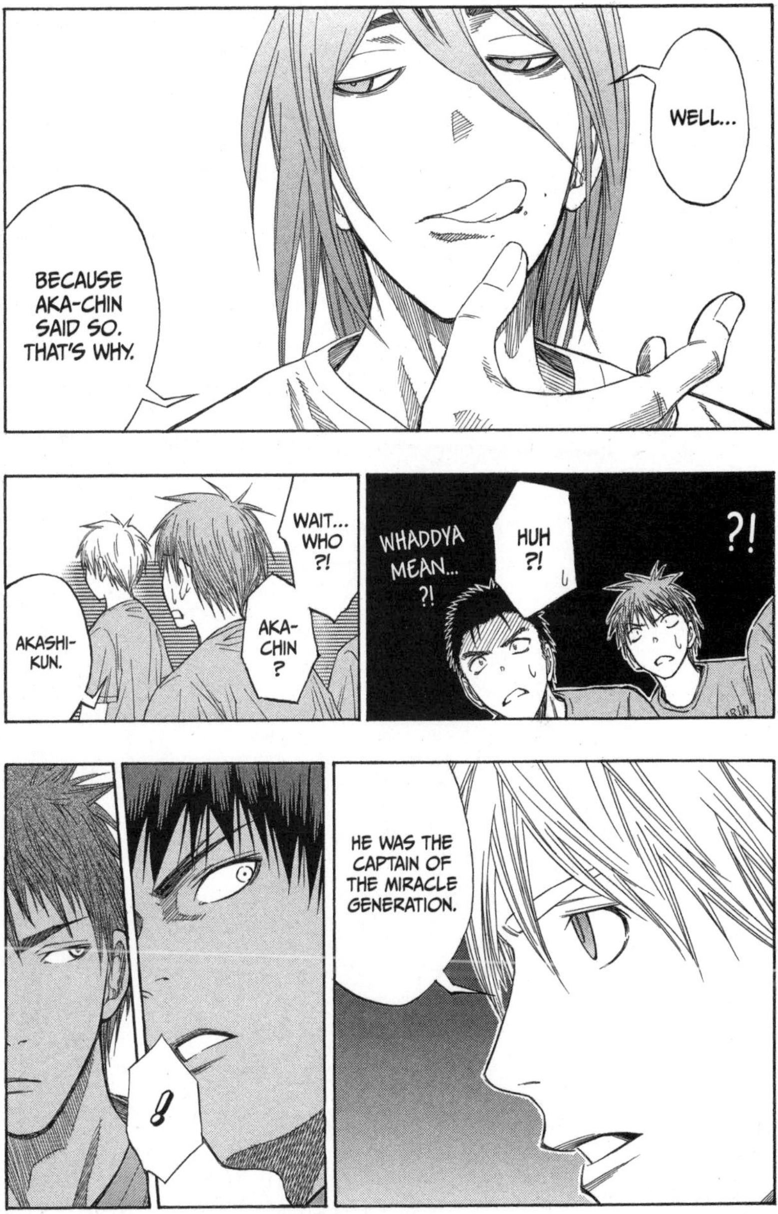
WELL...
BECAUSE AKA-CHIN SAID SO. THAT'S WHY.
?!
HUH ?!
WHADDYA MEAN... ?!
WAIT... WHO ?!
AKA-CHIN ?
AKASHI-KUN.
HE WAS THE CAPTAIN OF THE MIRACLE GENERATION.
!

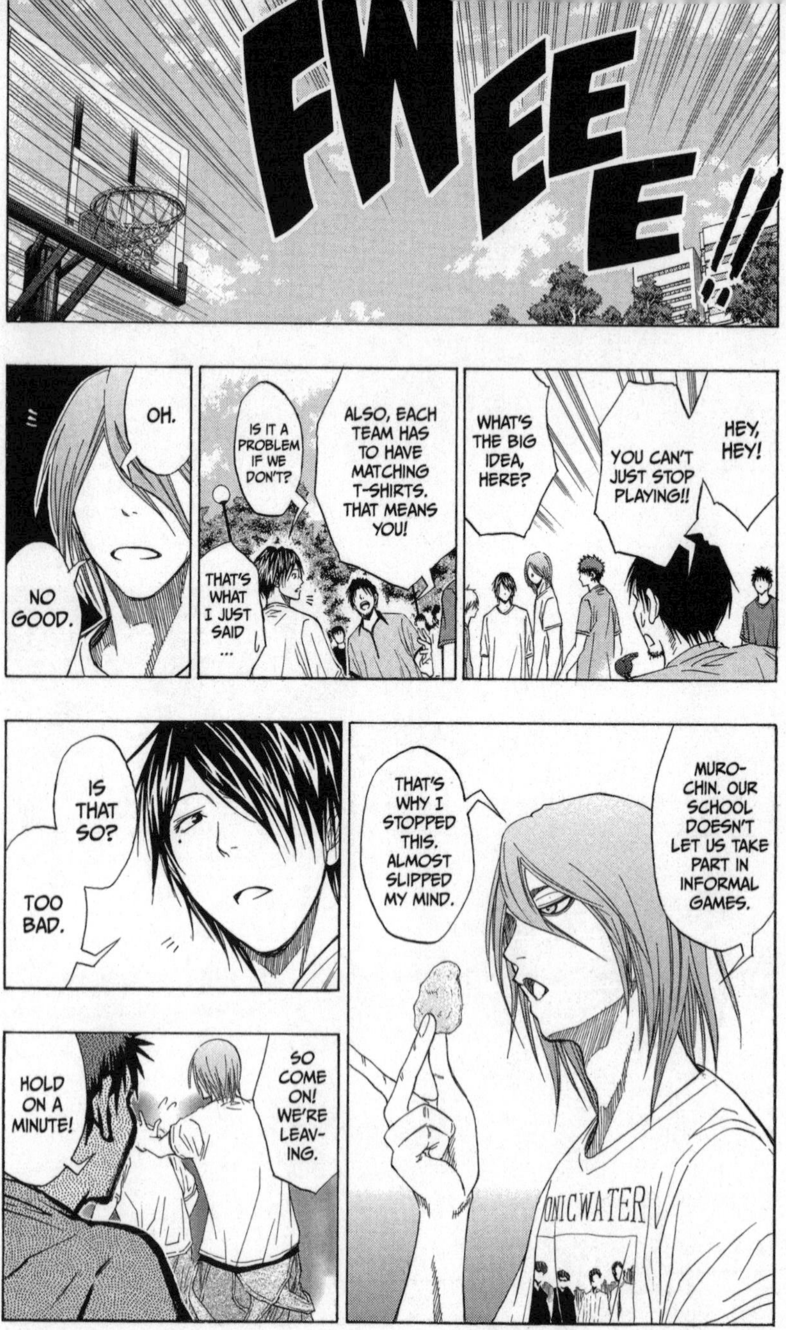
FWEE
E!!
HEY, HEY!
YOU CAN'T JUST STOP PLAYING!!
WHAT'S THE BIG IDEA, HERE?
ALSO, EACH TEAM HAS TO HAVE MATCHING T-SHIRTS. THAT MEANS YOU!
IS IT A PROBLEM IF WE DON'T?
THAT'S WHAT I JUST SAID ...
OH.
NO GOOD.
MURO-CHIN. OUR SCHOOL DOESN'T LET US TAKE PART IN INFORMAL GAMES.
THAT'S WHY I STOPPED THIS. ALMOST SLIPPED MY MIND.
IS THAT SO?
TOO BAD.
SO COME ON! WE'RE LEAVING.
HOLD ON A MINUTE!

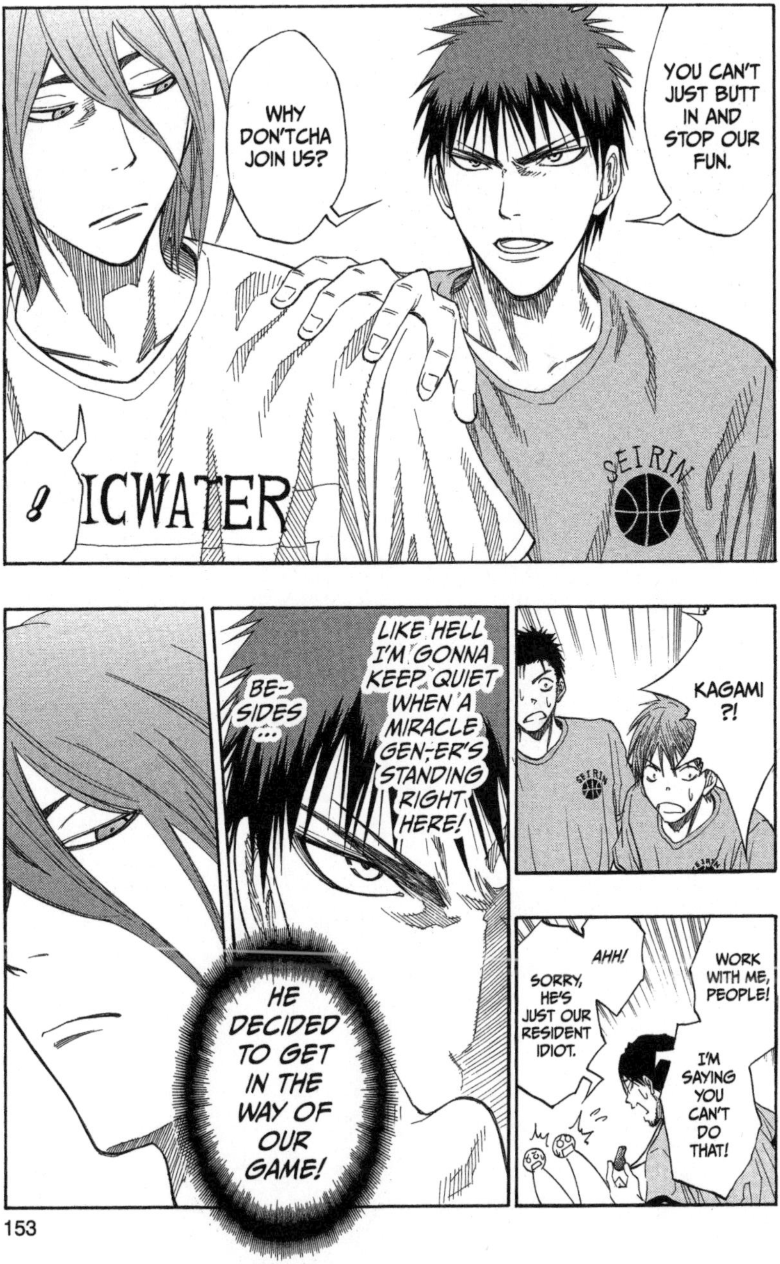
YOU CAN'T JUST BUTT IN AND STOP OUR FUN.
WHY DON'TCHA JOIN US?
!
ICWATER
SEIRIN
KAGAMI ?!
WORK WITH ME, PEOPLE!
AHH!
SORRY, HE'S JUST OUR RESIDENT IDIOT.
I'M SAYING YOU CAN'T DO THAT!
LIKE HELL I'M GONNA KEEP QUIET WHEN A MIRACLE GEN-ER'S STANDING RIGHT HERE!
BE-SIDES...
HE DECIDED TO GET IN THE WAY OF OUR GAME!

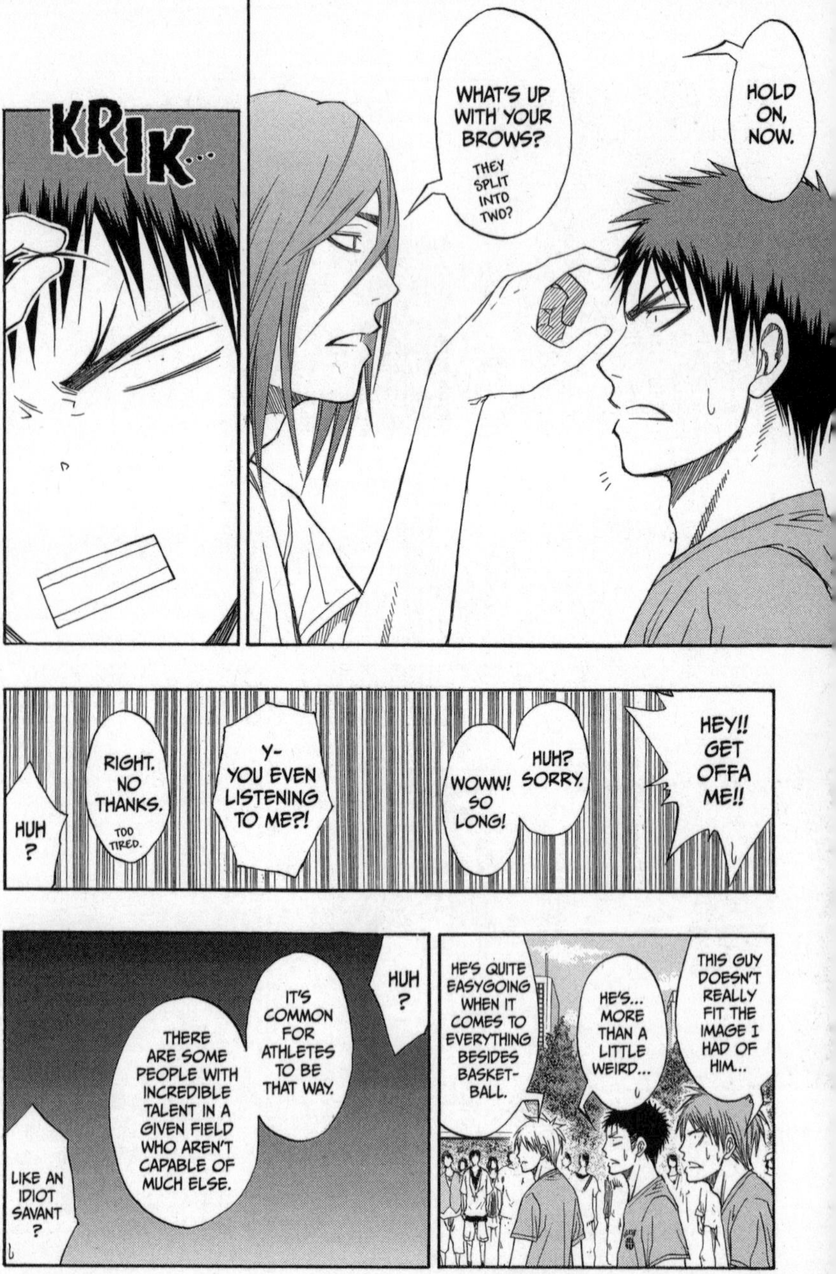
HOLD ON, NOW.
WHAT'S UP WITH YOUR BROWS?
THEY SPLIT INTO TWO?
KRIK...
HEY!! GET OFFA ME!!
HUH? SORRY.
WOWW! SO LONG!
Y- YOU EVEN LISTENING TO ME?!
RIGHT. NO THANKS.
TOO TIRED.
HUH?
THIS GUY DOESN'T REALLY FIT THE IMAGE I HAD OF HIM...
HE'S... MORE THAN A LITTLE WEIRD...
HE'S QUITE EASYGOING WHEN IT COMES TO EVERYTHING BESIDES BASKET-BALL.
HUH?
IT'S COMMON FOR ATHLETES TO BE THAT WAY.
THERE ARE SOME PEOPLE WITH INCREDIBLE TALENT IN A GIVEN FIELD WHO AREN'T CAPABLE OF MUCH ELSE.
LIKE AN IDIOT SAVANT?

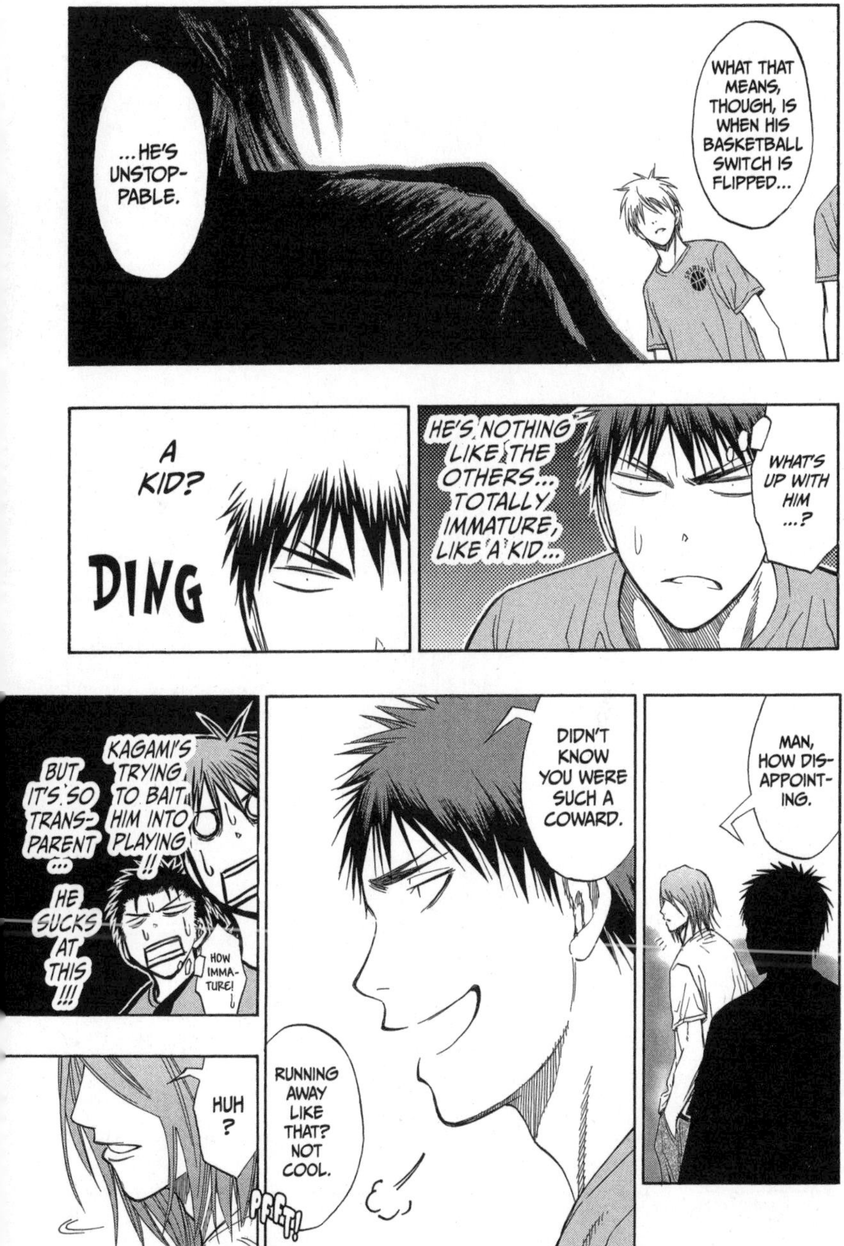
WHAT THAT MEANS, THOUGH, IS WHEN HIS BASKETBALL SWITCH IS FLIPPED...
...HE'S UNSTOP-PABLE.
WHAT'S UP WITH HIM ...?
HE'S NOTHING LIKE THE OTHERS... TOTALLY IMMATURE, LIKE A KID...
A KID?
DING
MAN, HOW DIS-APPOINT-ING.
DIDN'T KNOW YOU WERE SUCH A COWARD.
RUNNING AWAY LIKE THAT? NOT COOL.
KAGAMI'S TRYING TO BAIT HIM INTO PLAYING!!
BUT IT'S SO TRANS-PARENT...
HE SUCKS AT THIS!!!
HOW IMMA-TURE!
HUH?
PFFT!

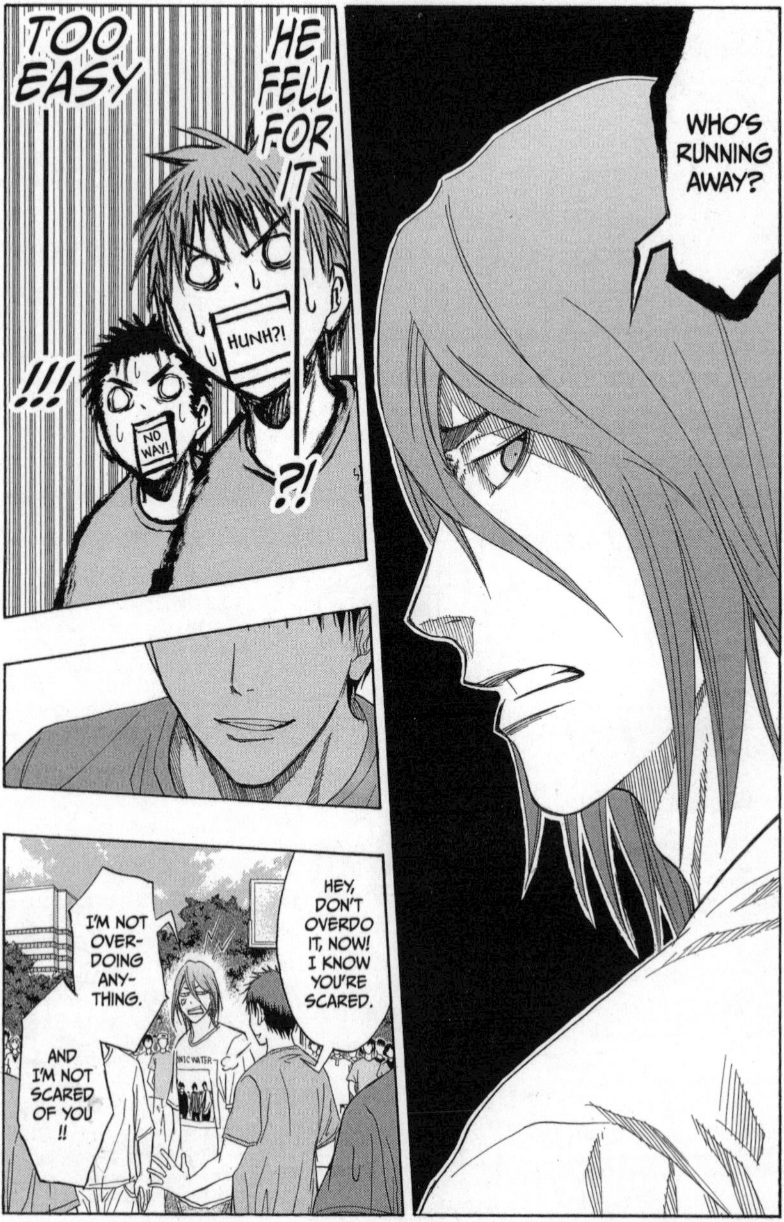
WHO'S RUNNING AWAY?
HE FELL FOR IT ?!
HUNH?!
TOO EASY !!!
NO WAY!
HEY, DON'T OVERDO IT, NOW! I KNOW YOU'RE SCARED.
I'M NOT OVER-DOING ANY-THING.
AND I'M NOT SCARED OF YOU !!

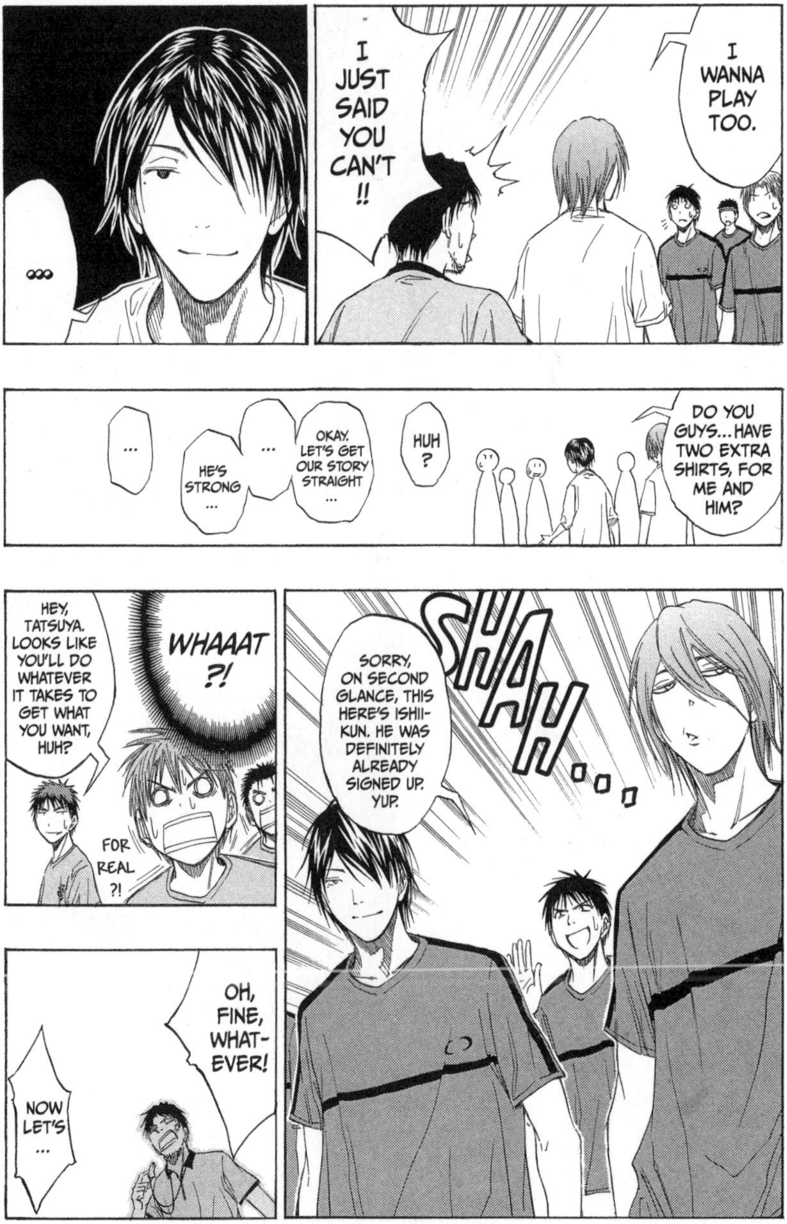
I WANNA PLAY TOO.
I JUST SAID YOU CAN'T!!
...
DO YOU GUYS...HAVE TWO EXTRA SHIRTS, FOR ME AND HIM?
HUH?
OKAY. LET'S GET OUR STORY STRAIGHT...
...
HE'S STRONG...
...
SHAHH...
SORRY, ON SECOND GLANCE, THIS HERE'S ISHII-KUN. HE WAS DEFINITELY ALREADY SIGNED UP. YUP.
WHAAAT?!
HEY, TATSUYA. LOOKS LIKE YOU'LL DO WHATEVER IT TAKES TO GET WHAT YOU WANT, HUH?
FOR REAL?!
OH, FINE, WHATEVER!
NOW LET'S...

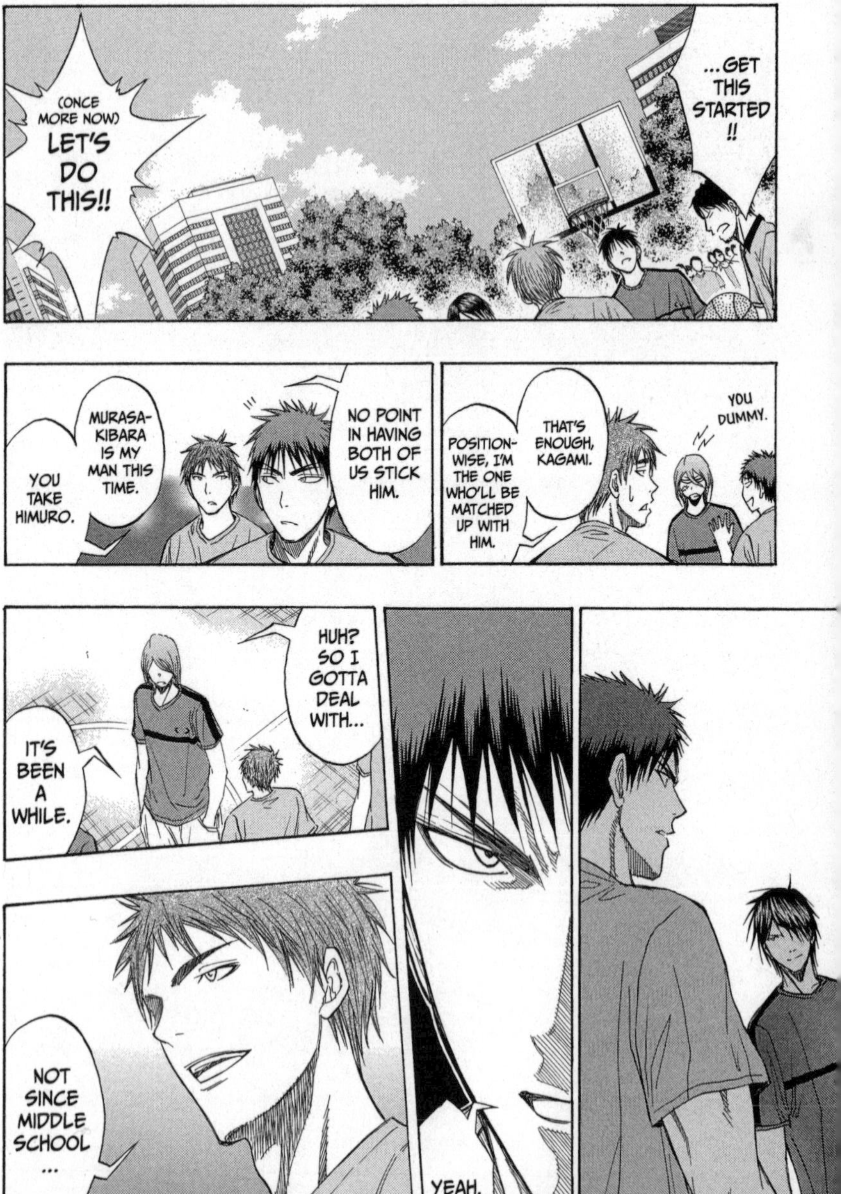
...GET THIS STARTED!!
(ONCE MORE NOW) LET'S DO THIS!!
YOU DUMMY.
THAT'S ENOUGH, KAGAMI.
POSITION-WISE, I'M THE ONE WHO'LL BE MATCHED UP WITH HIM.
NO POINT IN HAVING BOTH OF US STICK HIM.
MURASA-KIBARA IS MY MAN THIS TIME.
YOU TAKE HIMURO.
YEAH.
HUH? SO I GOTTA DEAL WITH...
IT'S BEEN A WHILE.
NOT SINCE MIDDLE SCHOOL...

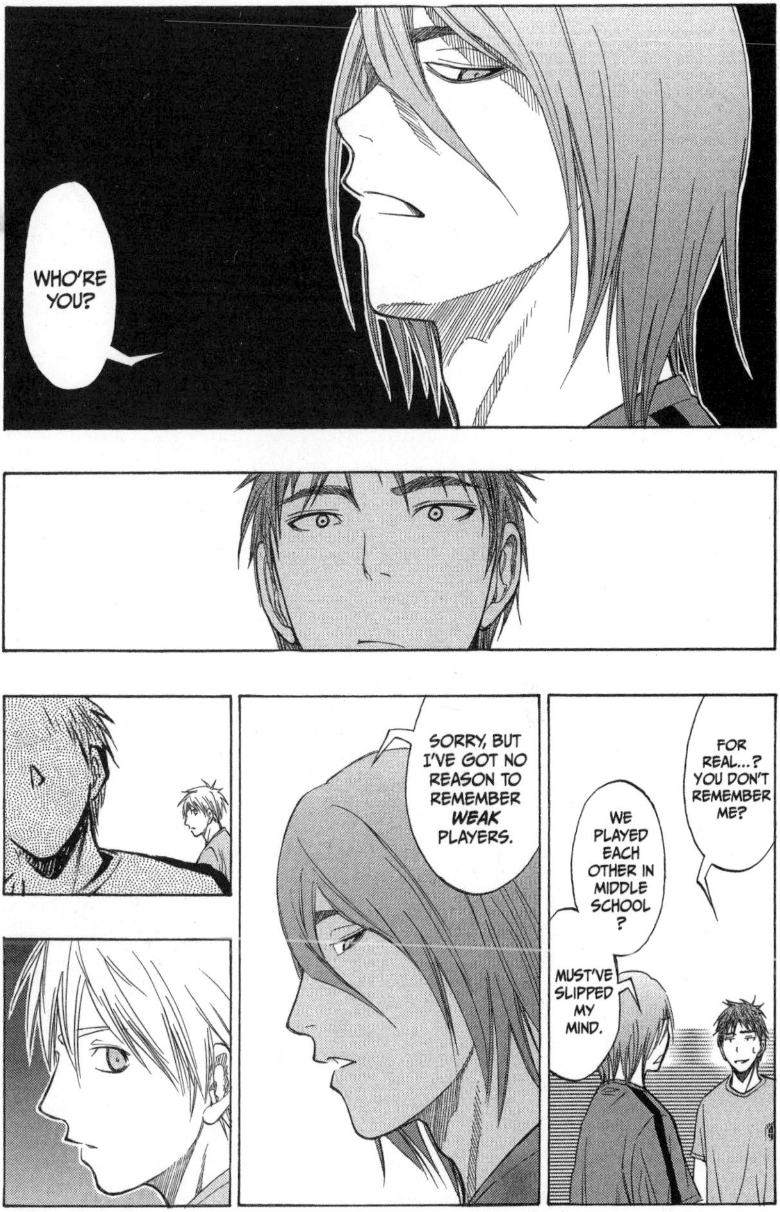
WHO'RE YOU?
FOR REAL...? YOU DON'T REMEMBER ME?
WE PLAYED EACH OTHER IN MIDDLE SCHOOL?
MUST'VE SLIPPED MY MIND.
SORRY, BUT I'VE GOT NO REASON TO REMEMBER ***WEAK*** PLAYERS.

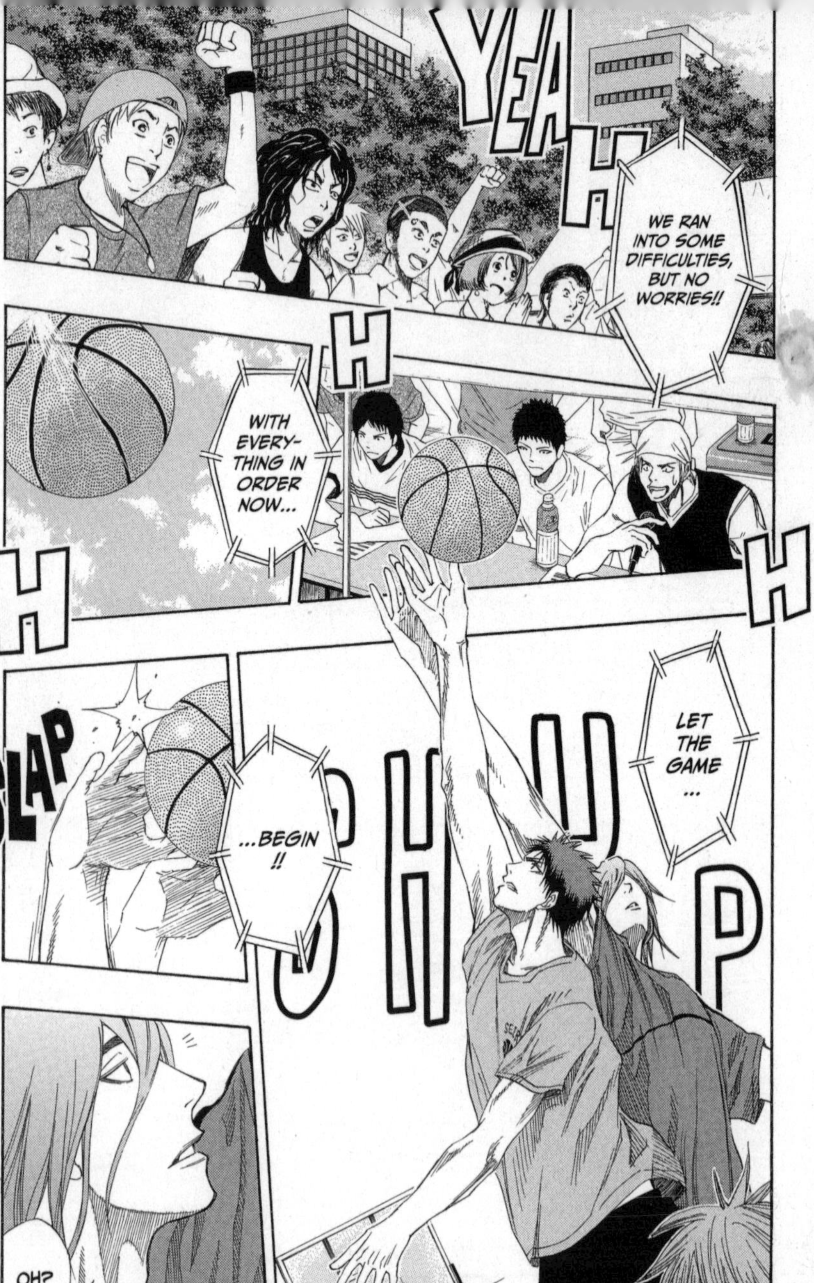
YEAHHHHH
WE RAN INTO SOME DIFFICULTIES, BUT NO WORRIES!!
WITH EVERY-THING IN ORDER NOW...
LET THE GAME...
SHUP
SLAP
...BEGIN!!
OH?

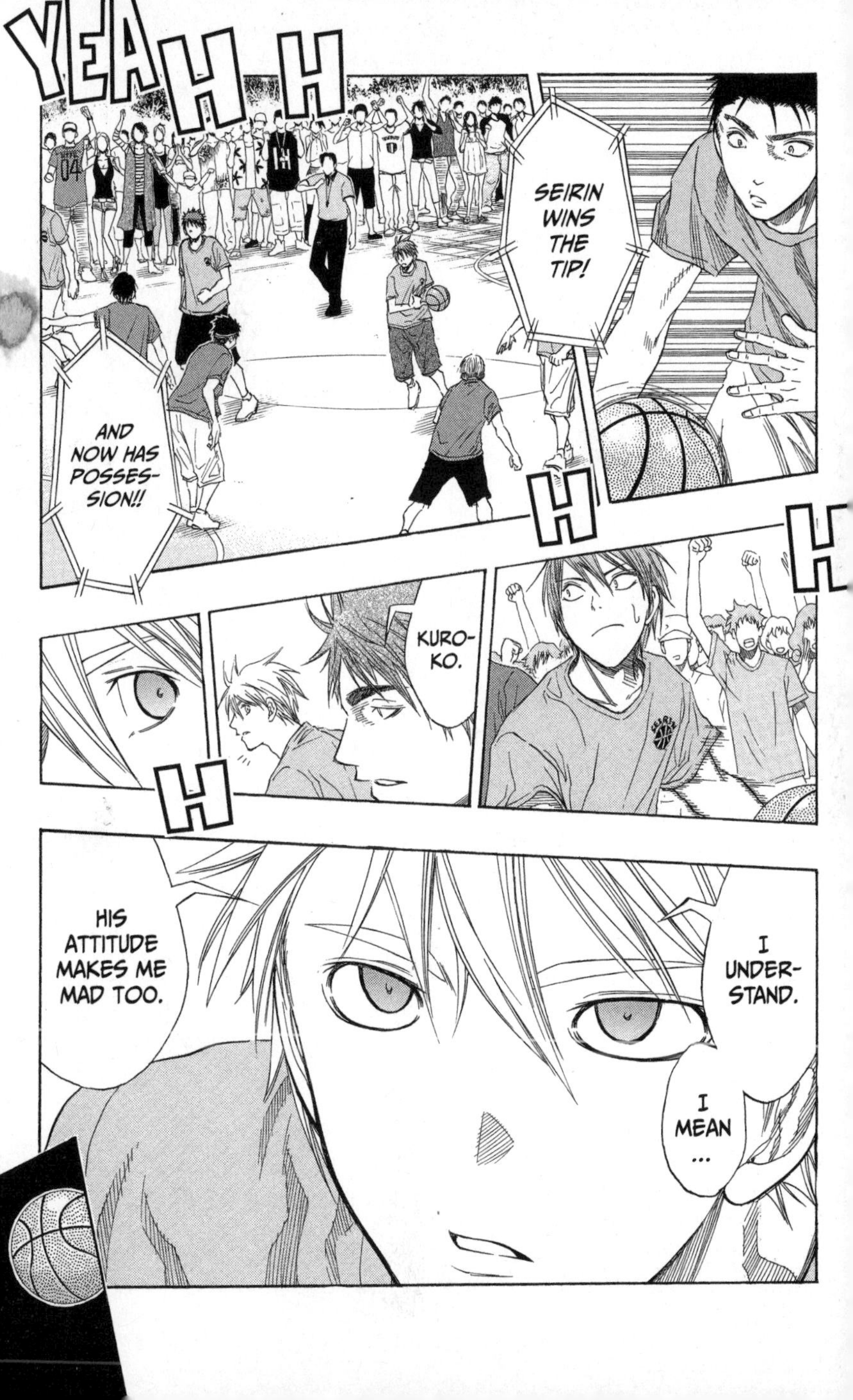
SEIRIN WINS THE TIP!
YEAHHHHH
AND NOW HAS POSSES-SION!!
KURO-KO.
I UNDER-STAND.
I MEAN ...
HIS ATTITUDE MAKES ME MAD TOO.

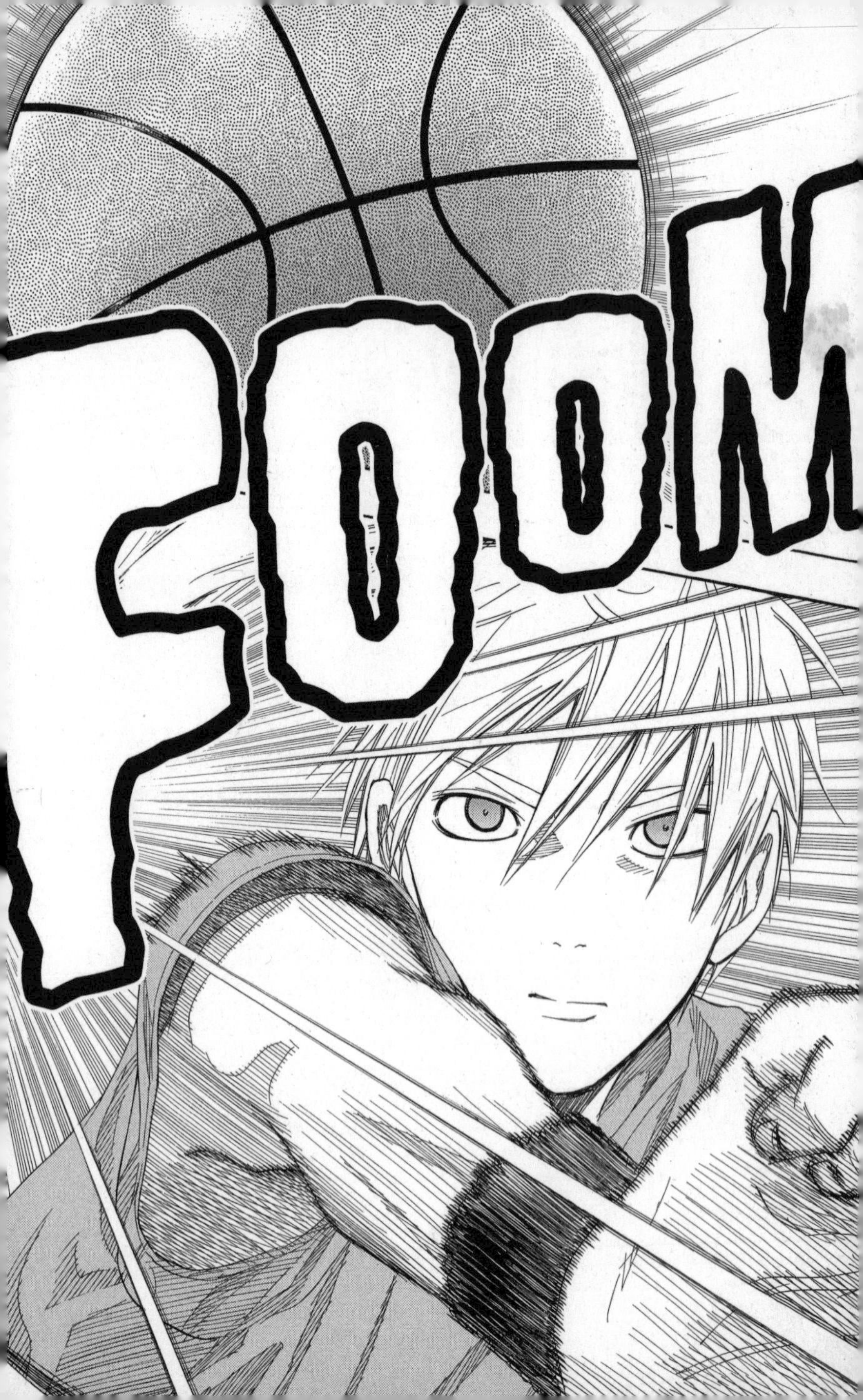
FOOM

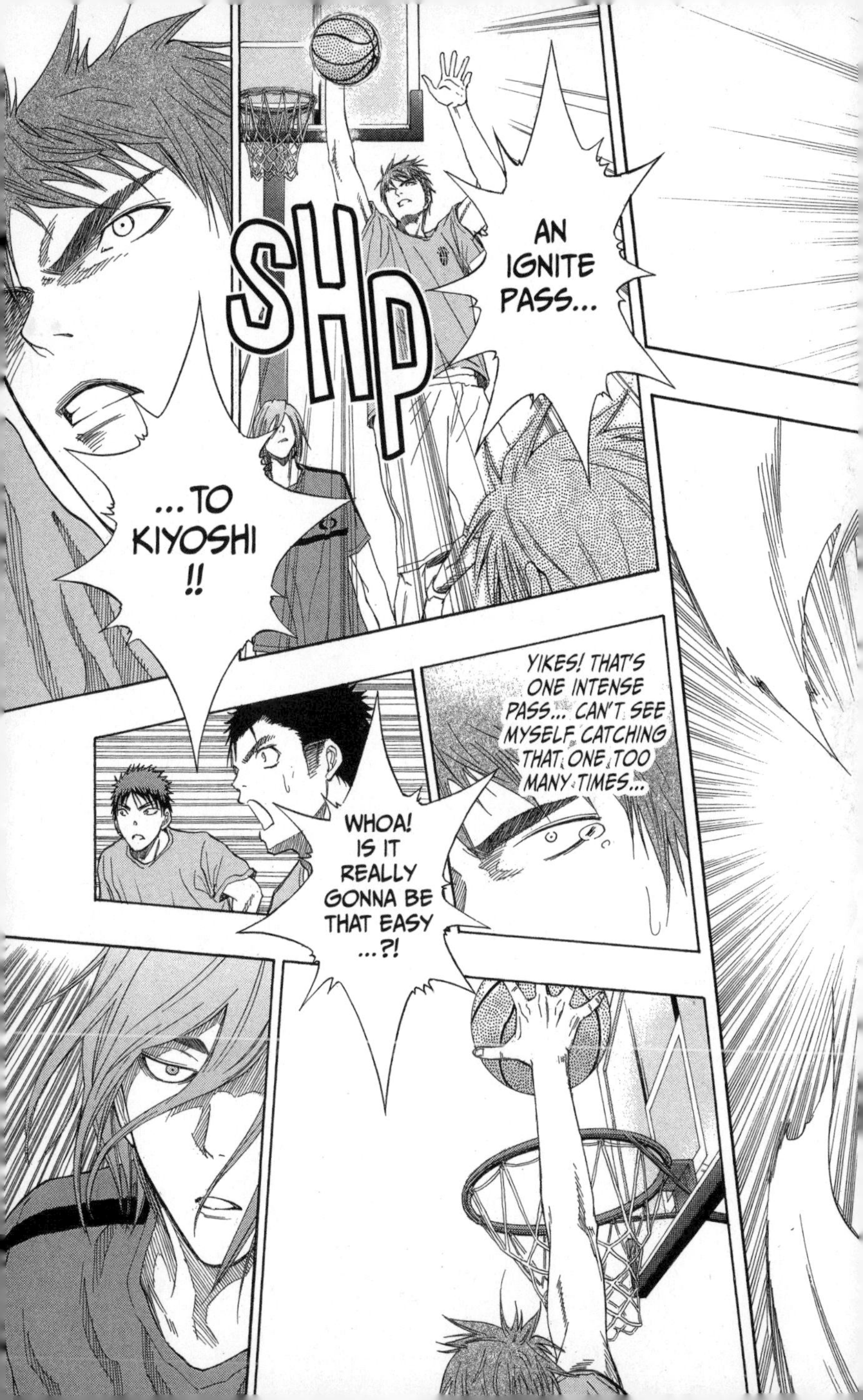
AN IGNITE PASS...
SHP
...TO KIYOSHI!!
YIKES! THAT'S ONE INTENSE PASS... CAN'T SEE MYSELF CATCHING THAT ONE TOO MANY TIMES...
WHOA! IS IT REALLY GONNA BE THAT EASY ...?!

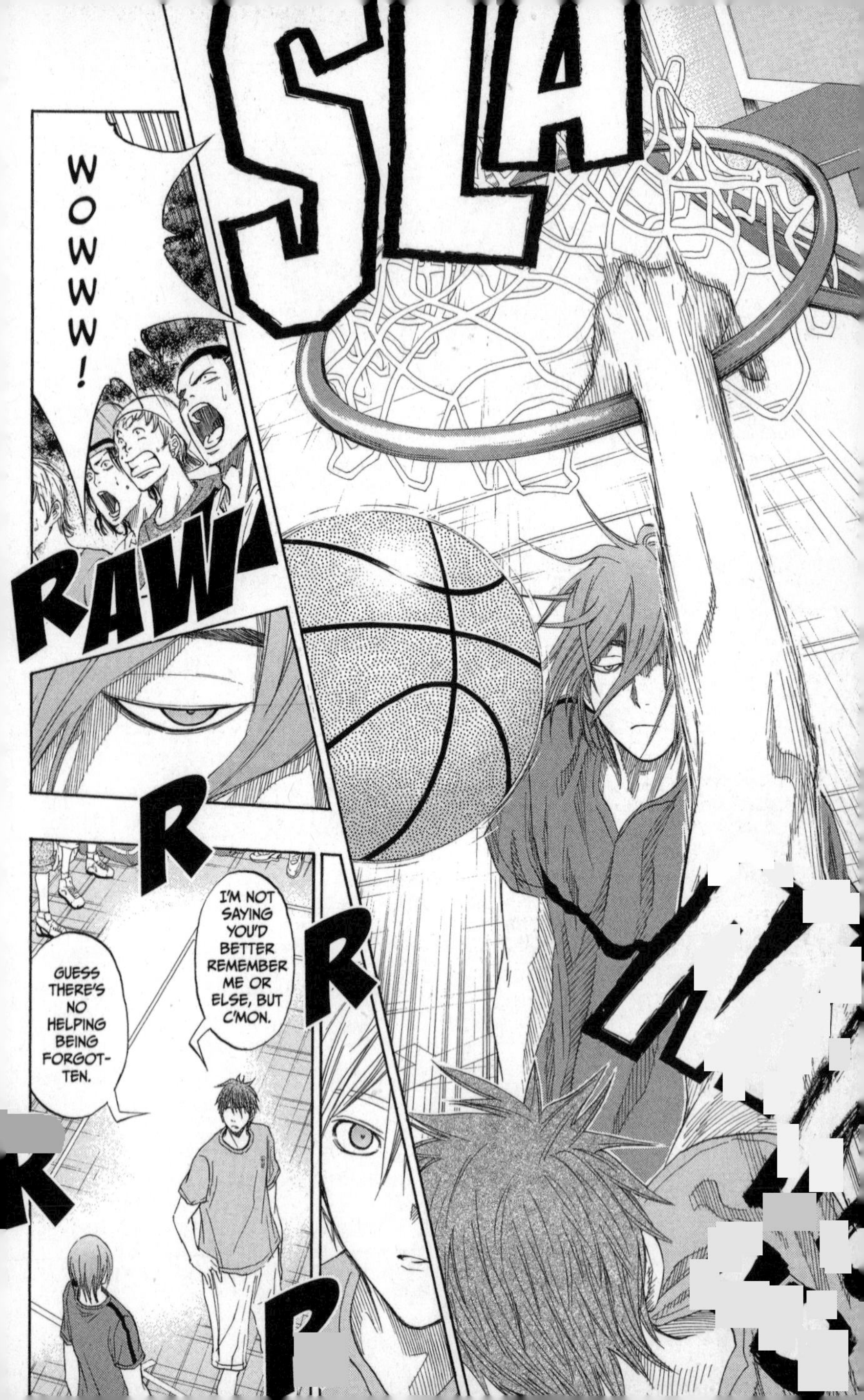
SLA
WOWWWW!
RAW
R
R
I'M NOT SAYING YOU'D BETTER REMEMBER ME OR ELSE, BUT C'MON.
GUESS THERE'S NO HELPING BEING FORGOT-TEN.

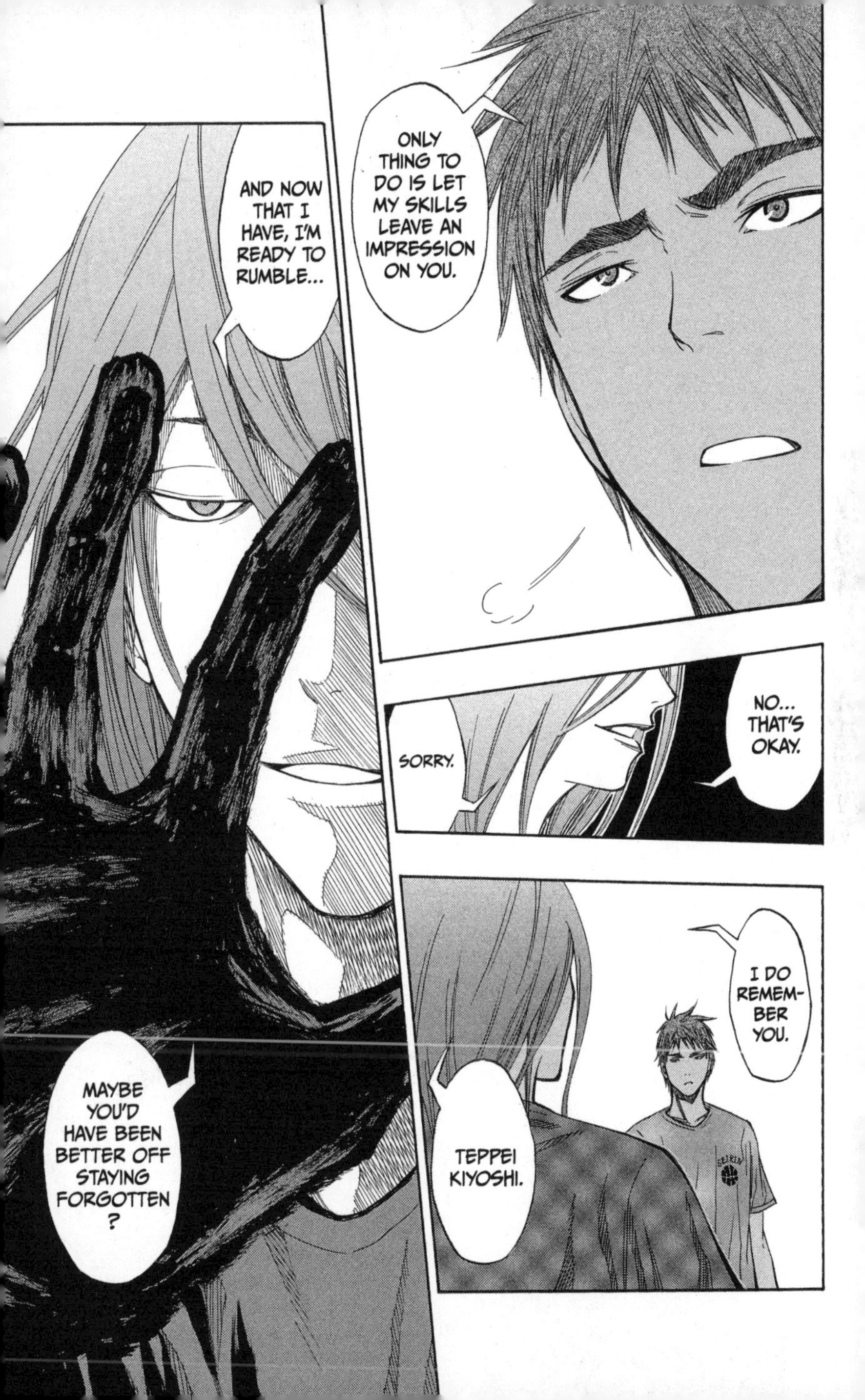
ONLY THING TO DO IS LET MY SKILLS LEAVE AN IMPRESSION ON YOU.
NO... THAT'S OKAY.
SORRY.
I DO REMEM-BER YOU.
TEPPEI KIYOSHI.
AND NOW THAT I HAVE, I'M READY TO RUMBLE...
MAYBE YOU'D HAVE BEEN BETTER OFF STAYING FORGOTTEN ?

KUROKO'S BASKETBALL BLOOPERS

TAKE 5

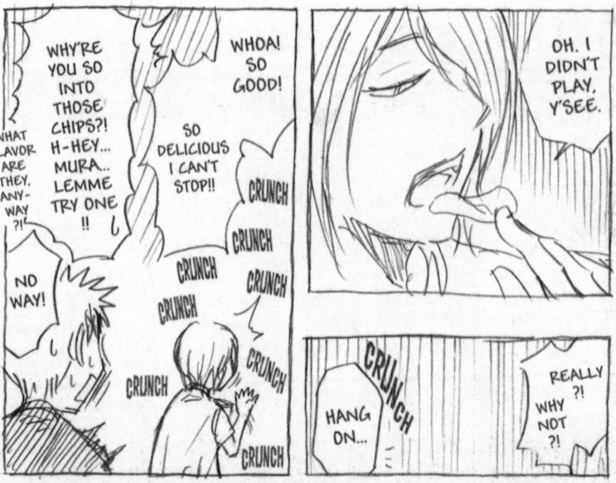
OH. I DIDN'T PLAY, Y'SEE.
REALLY?! WHY NOT?!
CRUNCH
HANG ON...
WHOA! SO GOOD!
WHY'RE YOU SO INTO THOSE CHIPS?! H-HEY... MURA... LEMME TRY ONE!!
SO DELICIOUS I CAN'T STOP!!
WHAT FLAVOR ARE THEY, ANY-WAY?!
CRUNCH
CRUNCH
CRUNCH
CRUNCH
CRUNCH
NO WAY!
CRUNCH
CRUNCH
CRUNCH

79TH QUARTER: AT THE WINTER CUP

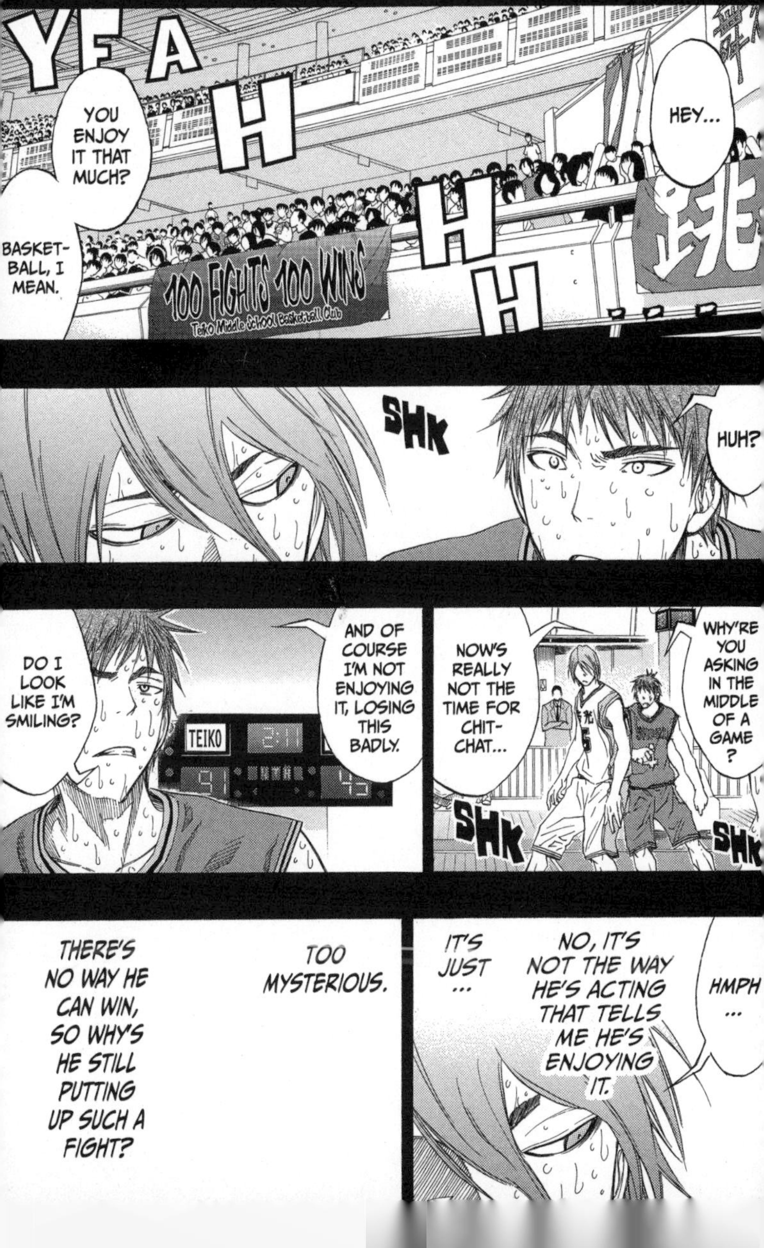
YEAHHH
100 FIGHTS 100 WINS
Teiko Middle School Basketball Club
HEY...
YOU ENJOY IT THAT MUCH?
BASKETBALL, I MEAN.
SHK
HUH?
WHY'RE YOU ASKING IN THE MIDDLE OF A GAME?
NOW'S REALLY NOT THE TIME FOR CHIT-CHAT...
SHK
SHK
AND OF COURSE I'M NOT ENJOYING IT, LOSING THIS BADLY.
DO I LOOK LIKE I'M SMILING?
TEIKO 2:11
91 43
HMPH...
NO, IT'S NOT THE WAY HE'S ACTING THAT TELLS ME HE'S ENJOYING IT.
IT'S JUST...
TOO MYSTERIOUS.
THERE'S NO WAY HE CAN WIN, SO WHY'S HE STILL PUTTING UP SUCH A FIGHT?

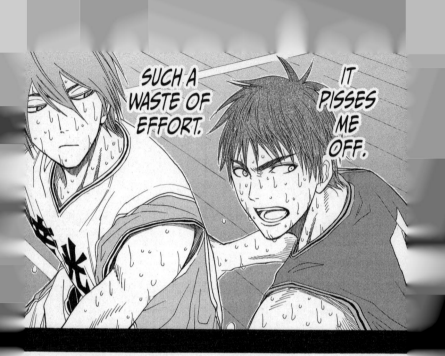

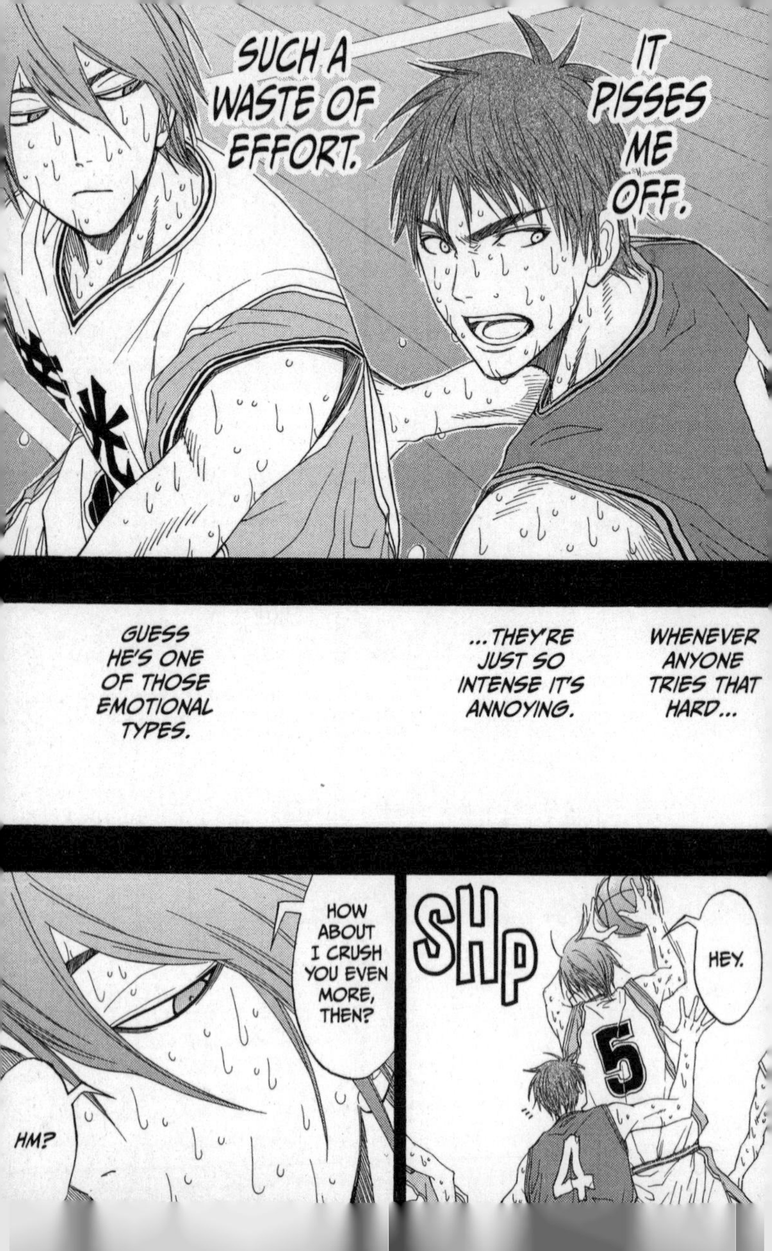
IT PISSES ME OFF.
SUCH A WASTE OF EFFORT.
WHENEVER ANYONE TRIES THAT HARD...
...THEY'RE JUST SO INTENSE IT'S ANNOYING.
GUESS HE'S ONE OF THOSE EMOTIONAL TYPES.
HEY.
SHP
HOW ABOUT I CRUSH YOU EVEN MORE, THEN?
HM?

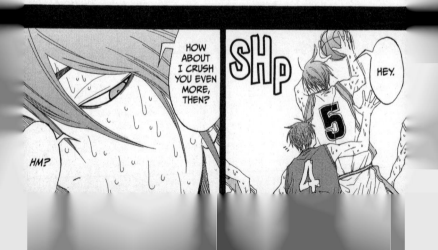

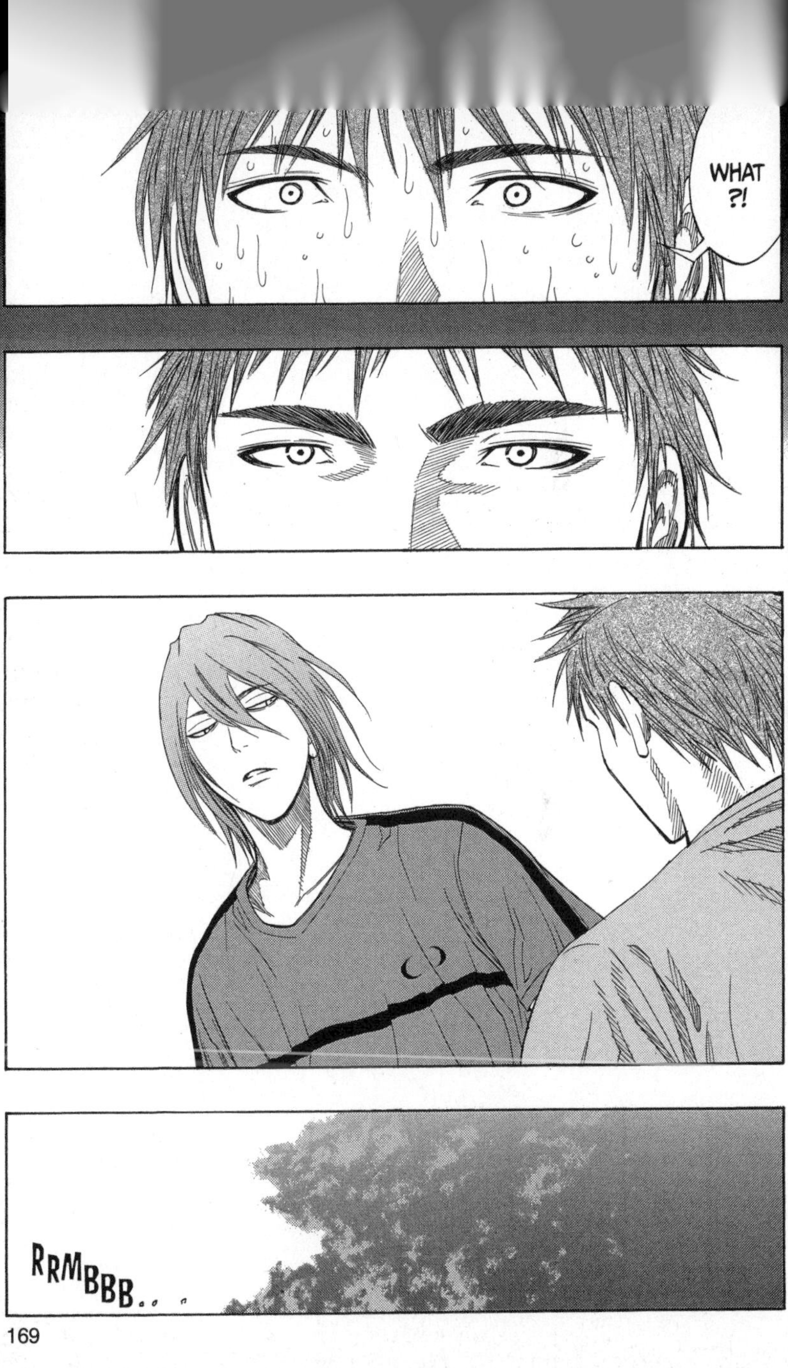
WHAT ?!
RRMBBB...

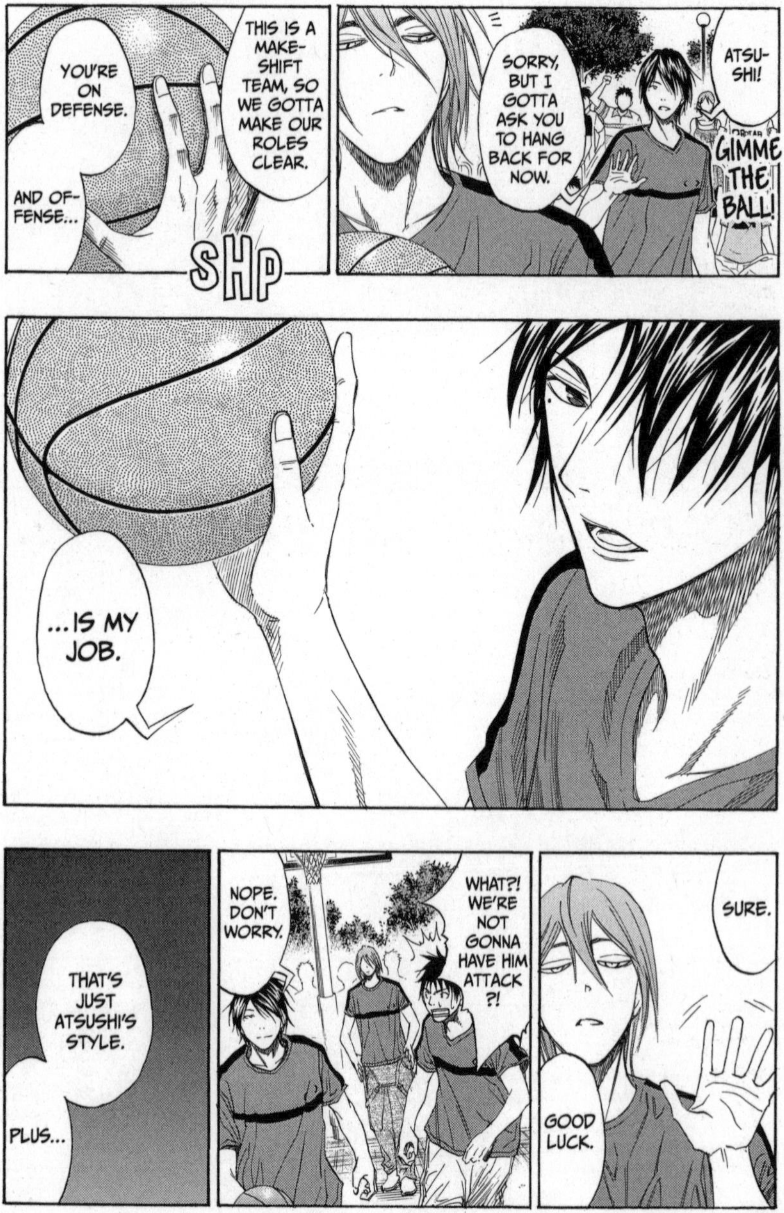
ATSU-SHI!
GIMME THE BALL!
SORRY, BUT I GOTTA ASK YOU TO HANG BACK FOR NOW.
THIS IS A MAKE-SHIFT TEAM, SO WE GOTTA MAKE OUR ROLES CLEAR.
YOU'RE ON DEFENSE.
AND OF-FENSE...
SHP
...IS MY JOB.
SURE.
GOOD LUCK.
WHAT?! WE'RE NOT GONNA HAVE HIM ATTACK ?!
NOPE. DON'T WORRY.
THAT'S JUST ATSUSHI'S STYLE.
PLUS...

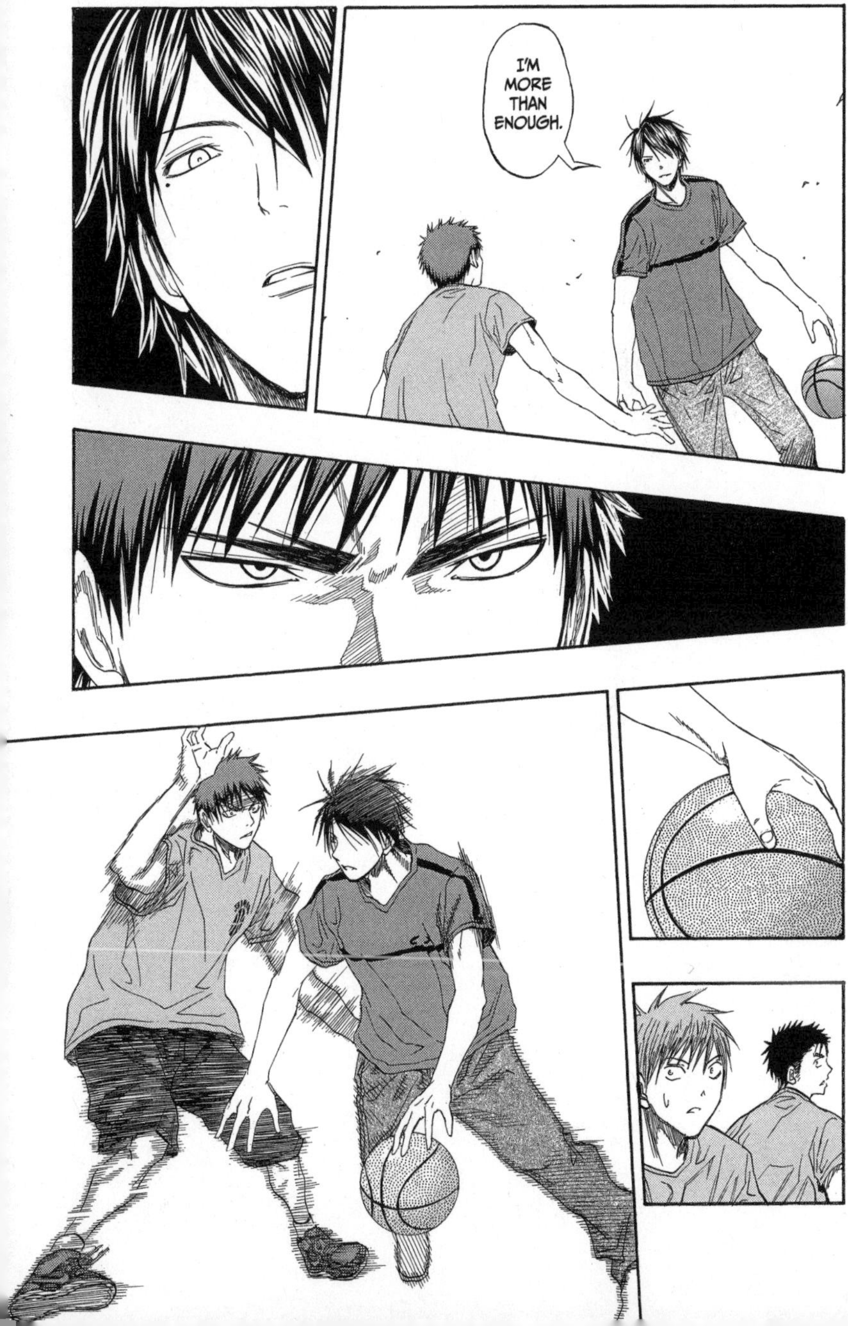
I'M MORE THAN ENOUGH.

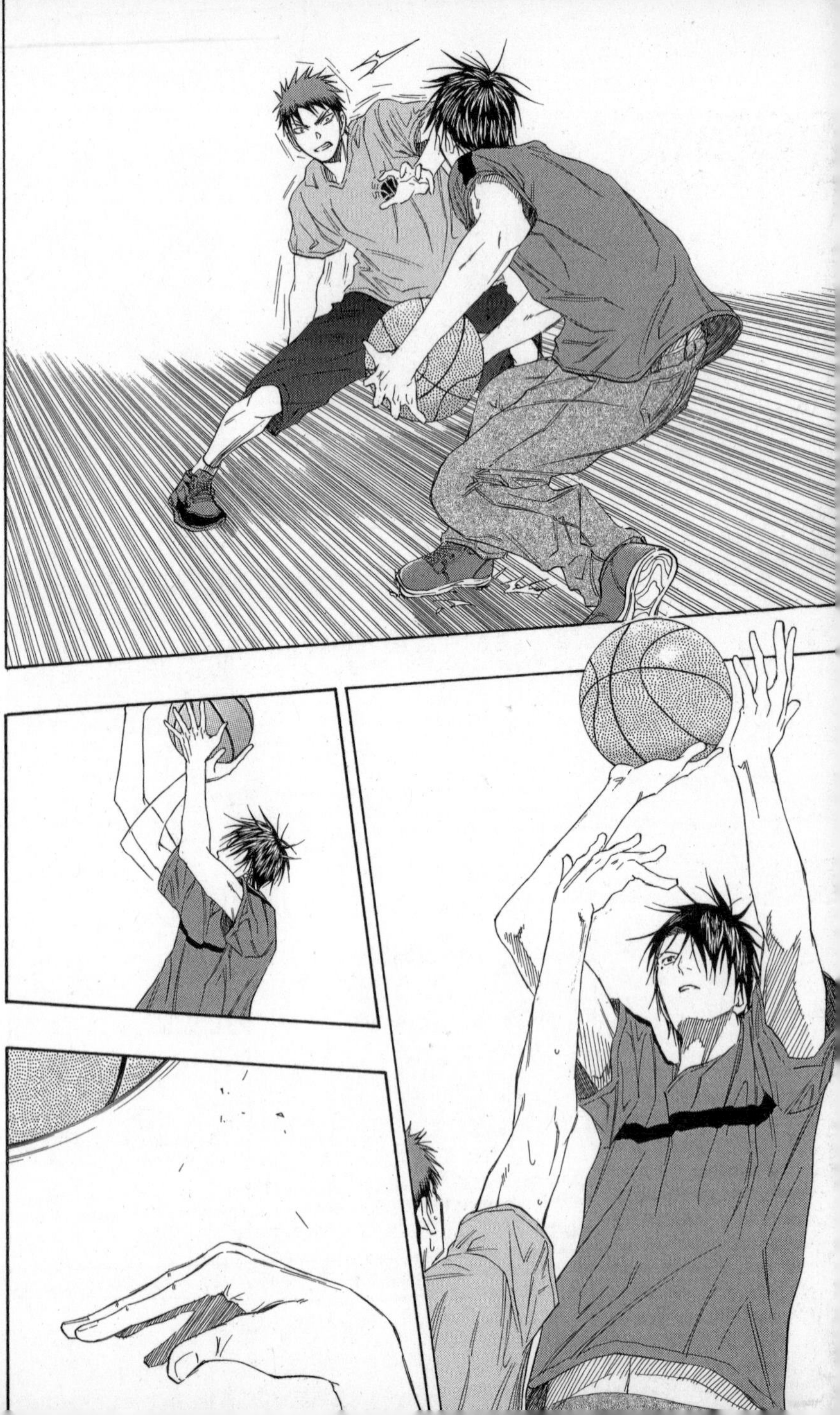

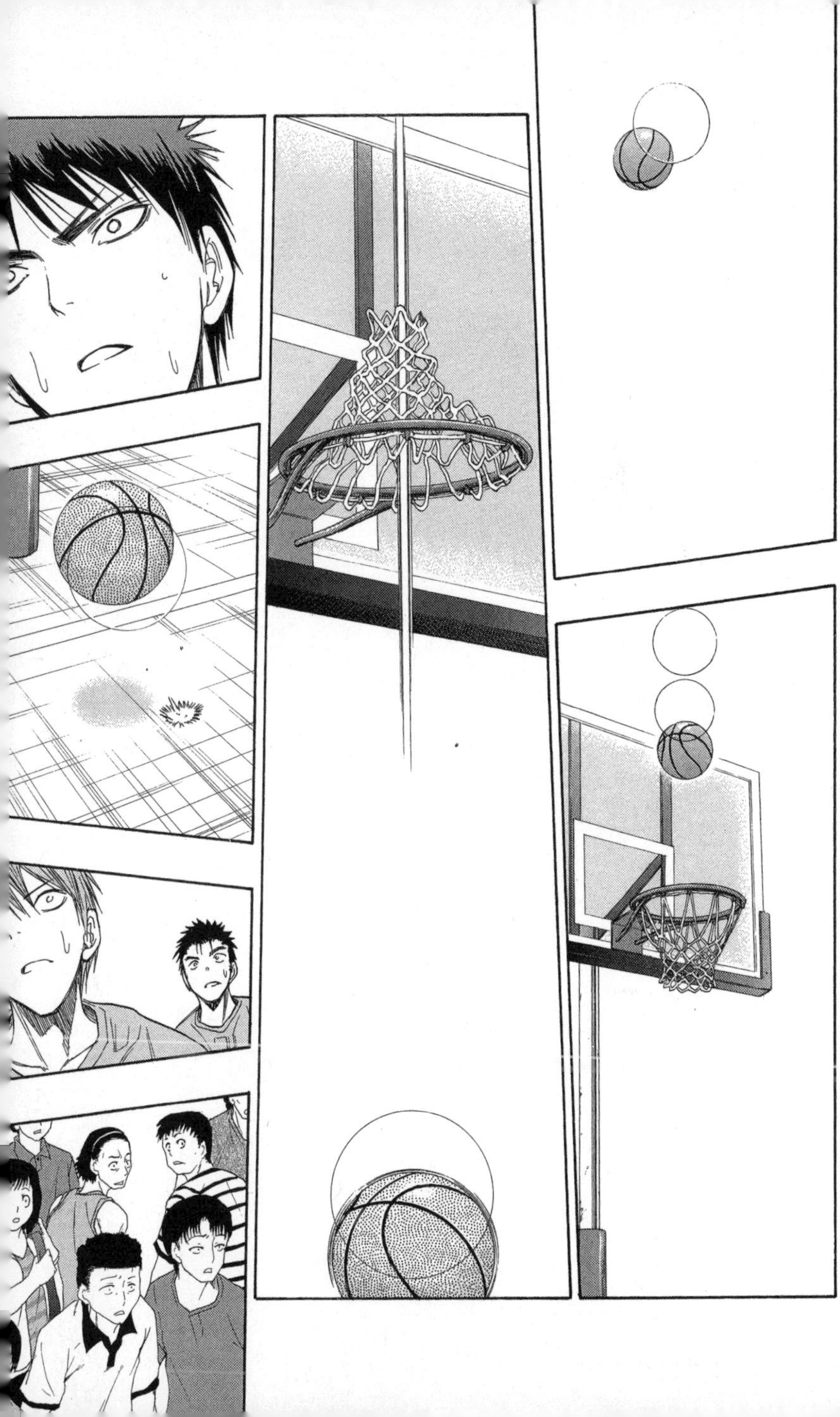

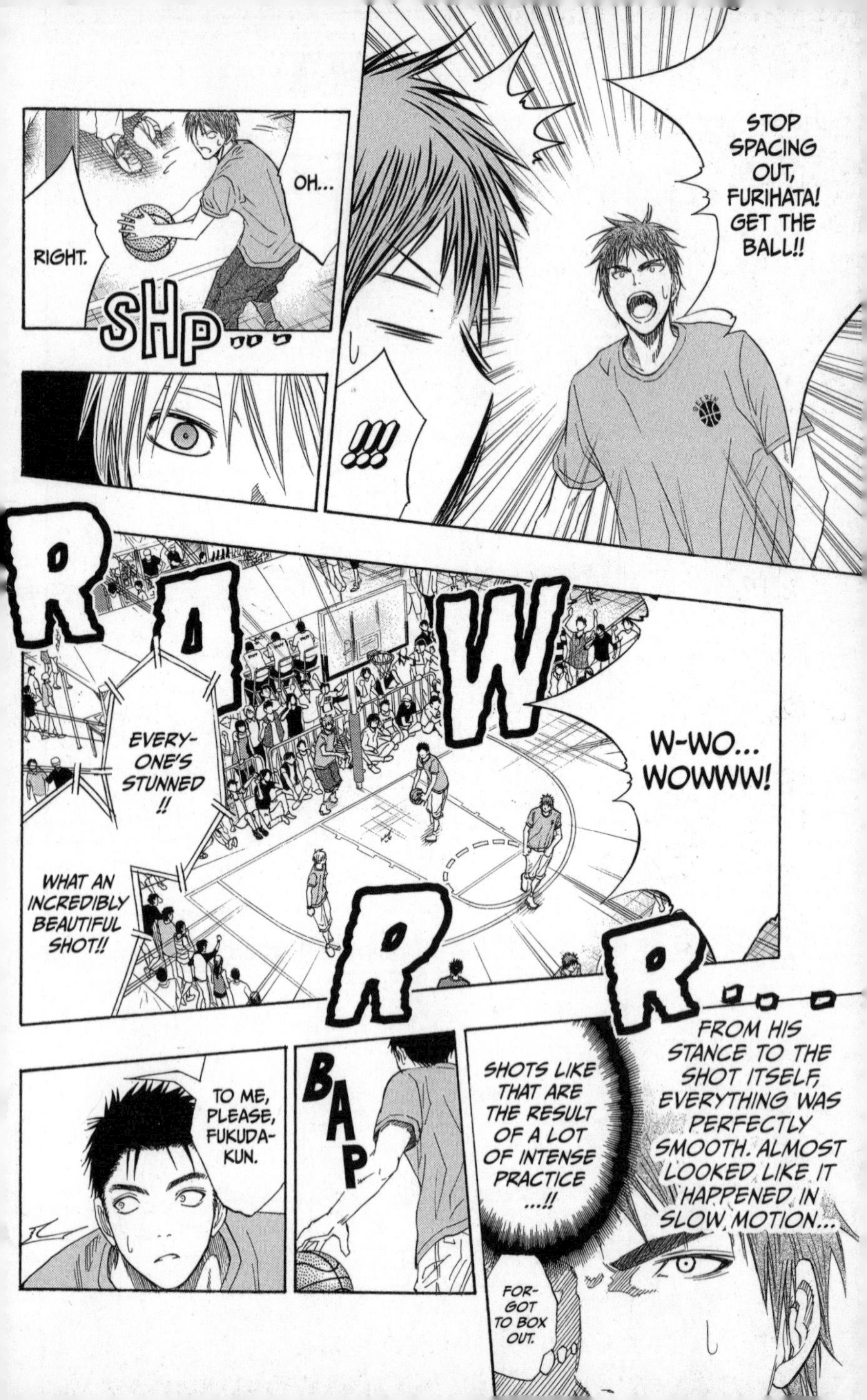
STOP SPACING OUT, FURIHATA! GET THE BALL!!
!!!
OH...
RIGHT.
SHP
RAWRR...
W-WO... WOWWW!
EVERY-ONE'S STUNNED!!
WHAT AN INCREDIBLY BEAUTIFUL SHOT!!
FROM HIS STANCE TO THE SHOT ITSELF, EVERYTHING WAS PERFECTLY SMOOTH. ALMOST LOOKED LIKE IT HAPPENED IN SLOW MOTION...
SHOTS LIKE THAT ARE THE RESULT OF A LOT OF INTENSE PRACTICE ...!!
FOR-GOT TO BOX OUT.
BAP
TO ME, PLEASE, FUKUDA-KUN.

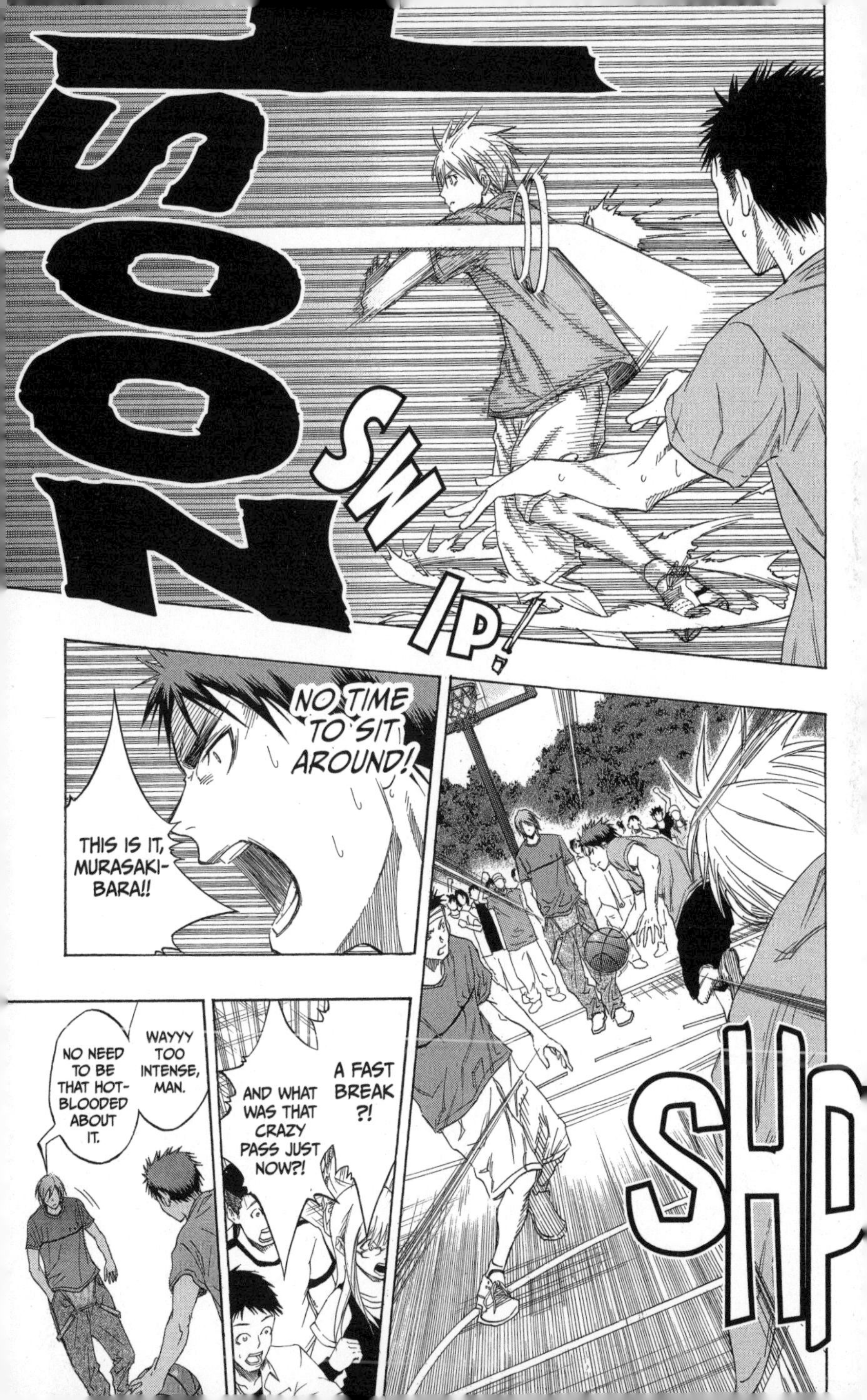
SWIP!
SHP
NO TIME TO SIT AROUND!
THIS IS IT, MURASAKIBARA!!
A FAST BREAK?!
AND WHAT WAS THAT CRAZY PASS JUST NOW?!
WAYYY TOO INTENSE, MAN.
NO NEED TO BE THAT HOT-BLOODED ABOUT IT.

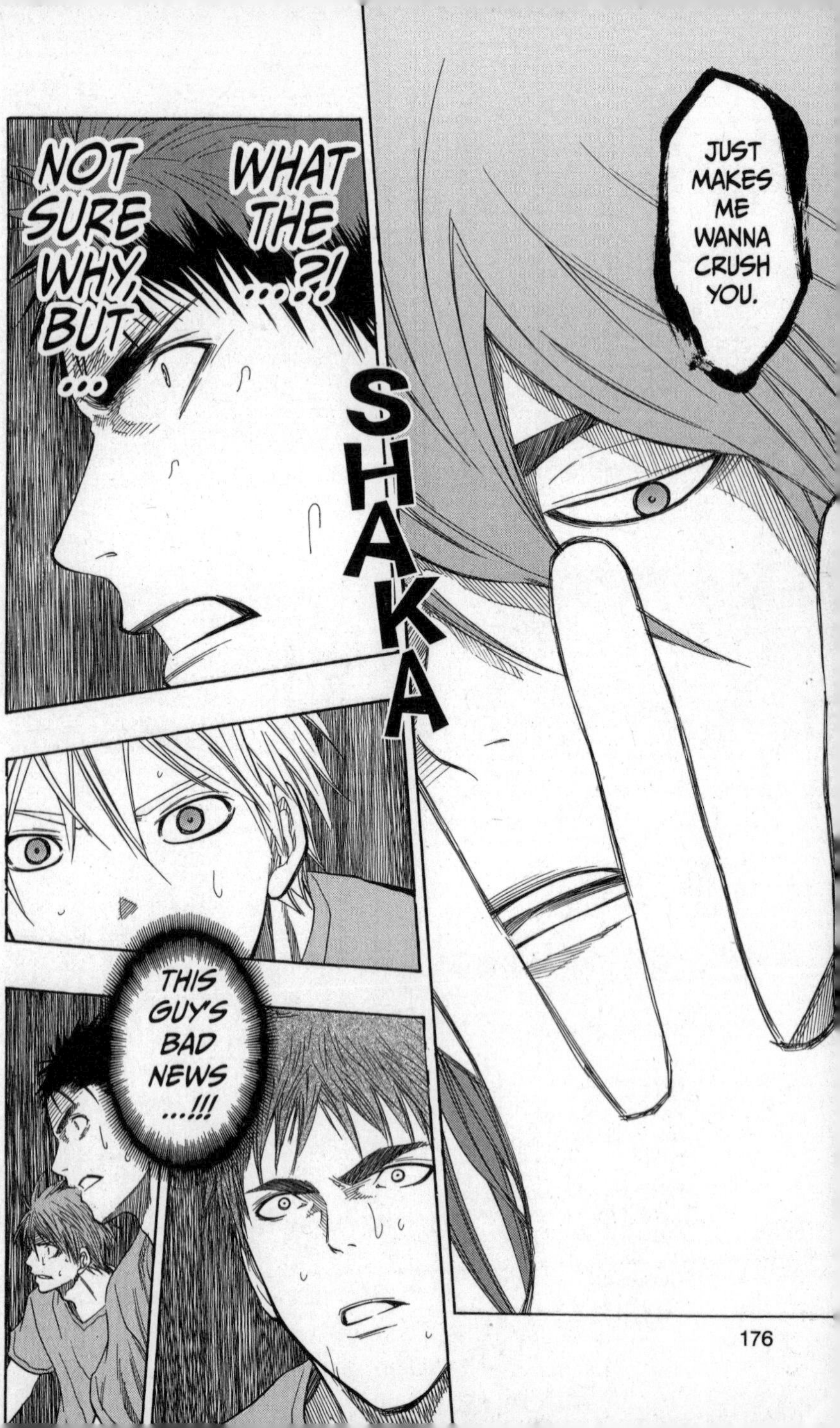
JUST MAKES ME WANNA CRUSH YOU.
SHAKA
WHAT THE ...?!
NOT SURE WHY BUT...
THIS GUY'S BAD NEWS ...!!!

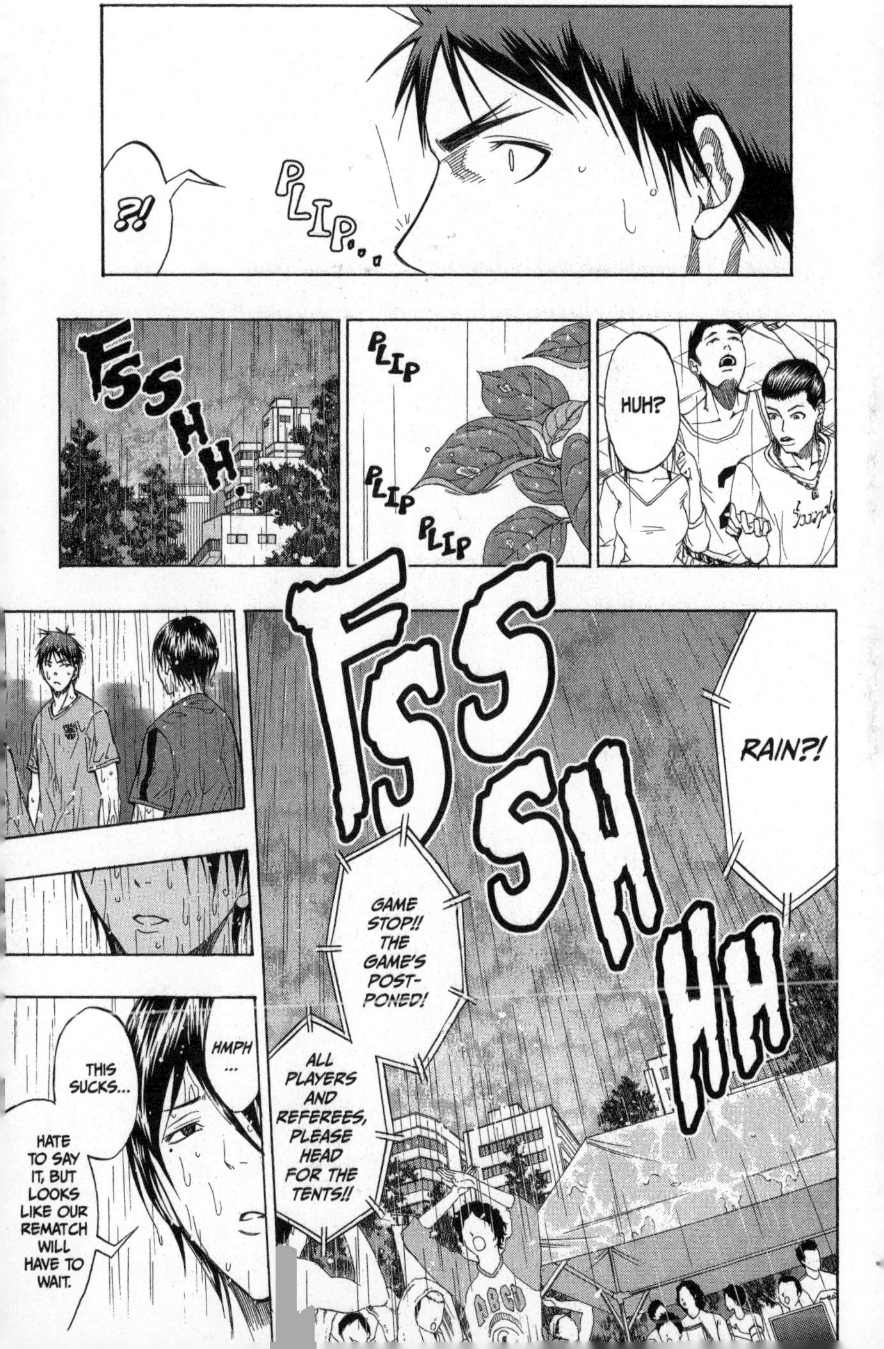

PLIP...
?!
HUH?
PLIP
PLIP
PLIP
FSSHH
RAIN?!
FSSSHAHH
GAME STOP!! THE GAME'S POST-PONED!
ALL PLAYERS AND REFEREES, PLEASE HEAD FOR THE TENTS!!
HMPH...
THIS SUCKS...
HATE TO SAY IT, BUT LOOKS LIKE OUR REMATCH WILL HAVE TO WAIT.

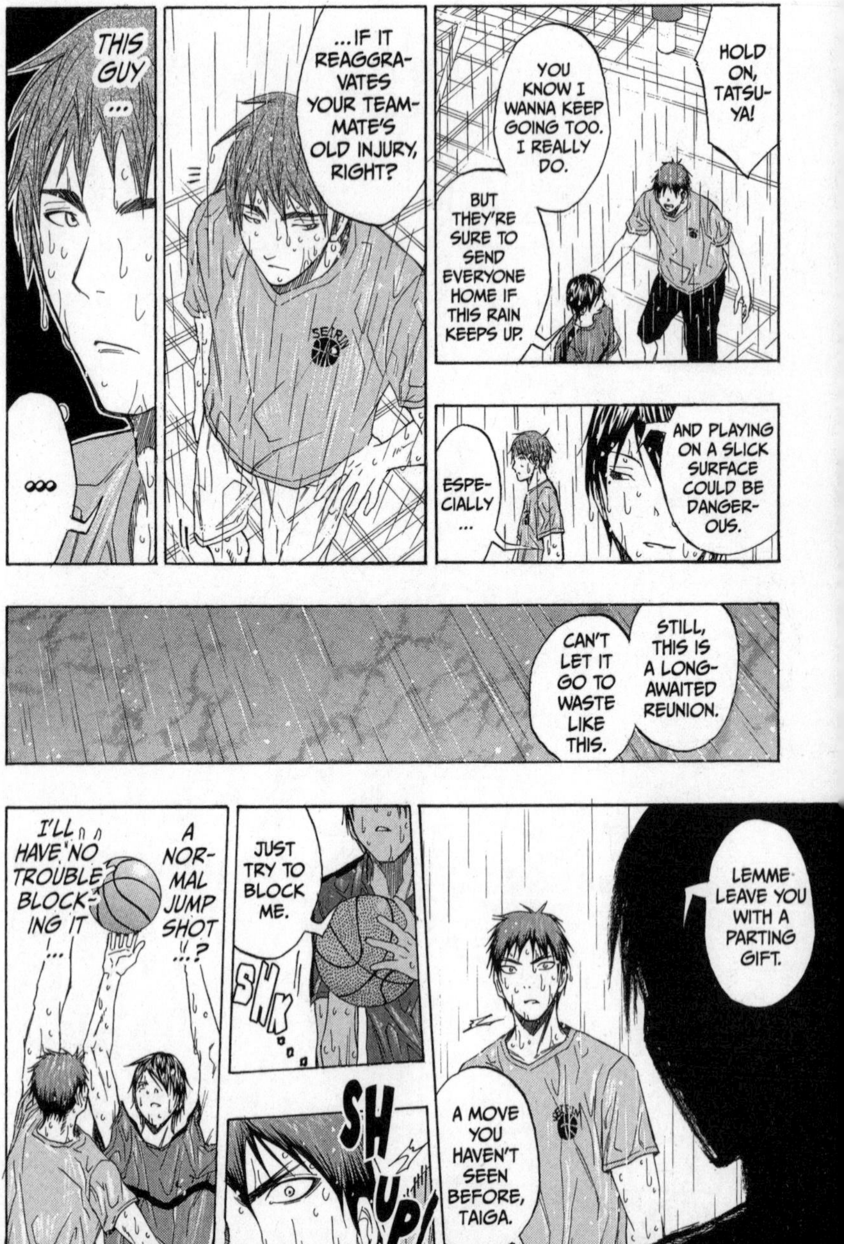
HOLD ON, TATSUYA!
YOU KNOW I WANNA KEEP GOING TOO. I REALLY DO.
BUT THEY'RE SURE TO SEND EVERYONE HOME IF THIS RAIN KEEPS UP.
AND PLAYING ON A SLICK SURFACE COULD BE DANGEROUS.
ESPECIALLY...
...IF IT REAGGRAVATES YOUR TEAMMATE'S OLD INJURY, RIGHT?
THIS GUY...
...
STILL, THIS IS A LONG-AWAITED REUNION.
CAN'T LET IT GO TO WASTE LIKE THIS.
LEMME LEAVE YOU WITH A PARTING GIFT.
A MOVE YOU HAVEN'T SEEN BEFORE, TAIGA.
JUST TRY TO BLOCK ME.
SHK...
SHUP!
A NORMAL JUMP SHOT...?
I'LL HAVE NO TROUBLE BLOCKING IT...

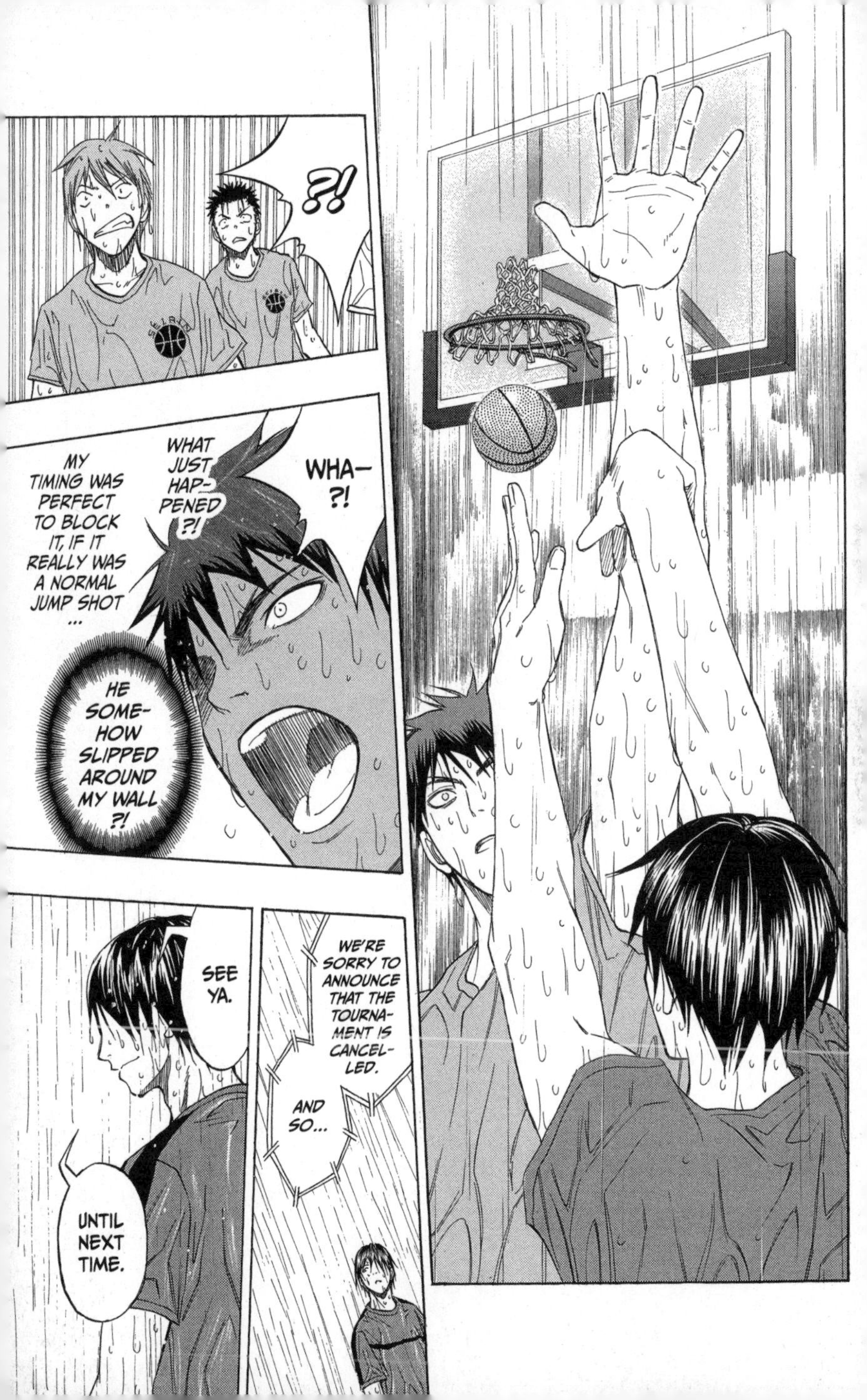
?!
WHA— ?!
WHAT JUST HAPPENED ?!
MY TIMING WAS PERFECT TO BLOCK IT, IF IT REALLY WAS A NORMAL JUMP SHOT ...
HE SOMEHOW SLIPPED AROUND MY WALL ?!
WE'RE SORRY TO ANNOUNCE THAT THE TOURNAMENT IS CANCELLED.
AND SO...
SEE YA.
UNTIL NEXT TIME.

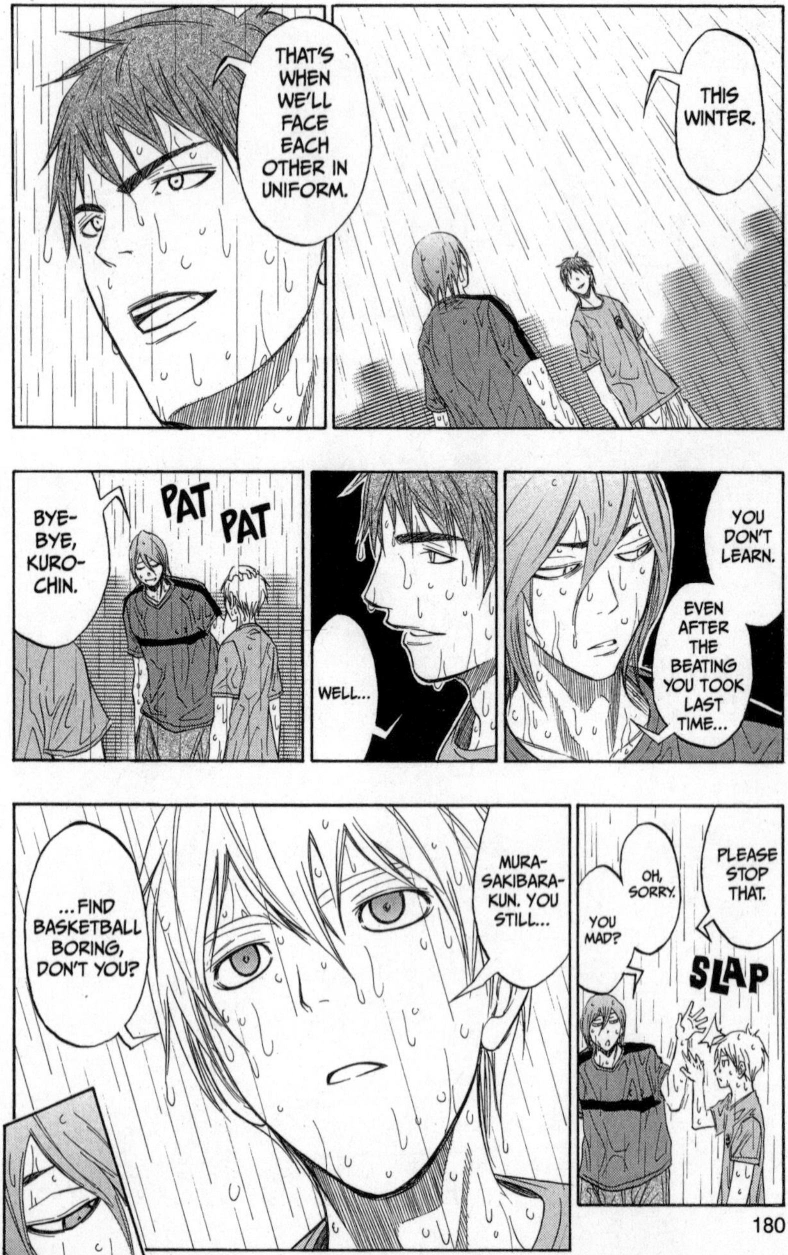
THIS WINTER.
THAT'S WHEN WE'LL FACE EACH OTHER IN UNIFORM.
YOU DON'T LEARN.
EVEN AFTER THE BEATING YOU TOOK LAST TIME...
WELL...
PAT PAT
BYE-BYE, KURO-CHIN.
PLEASE STOP THAT.
OH, SORRY.
YOU MAD?
SLAP
MURA-SAKIBARA-KUN. YOU STILL...
...FIND BASKETBALL BORING, DON'T YOU?

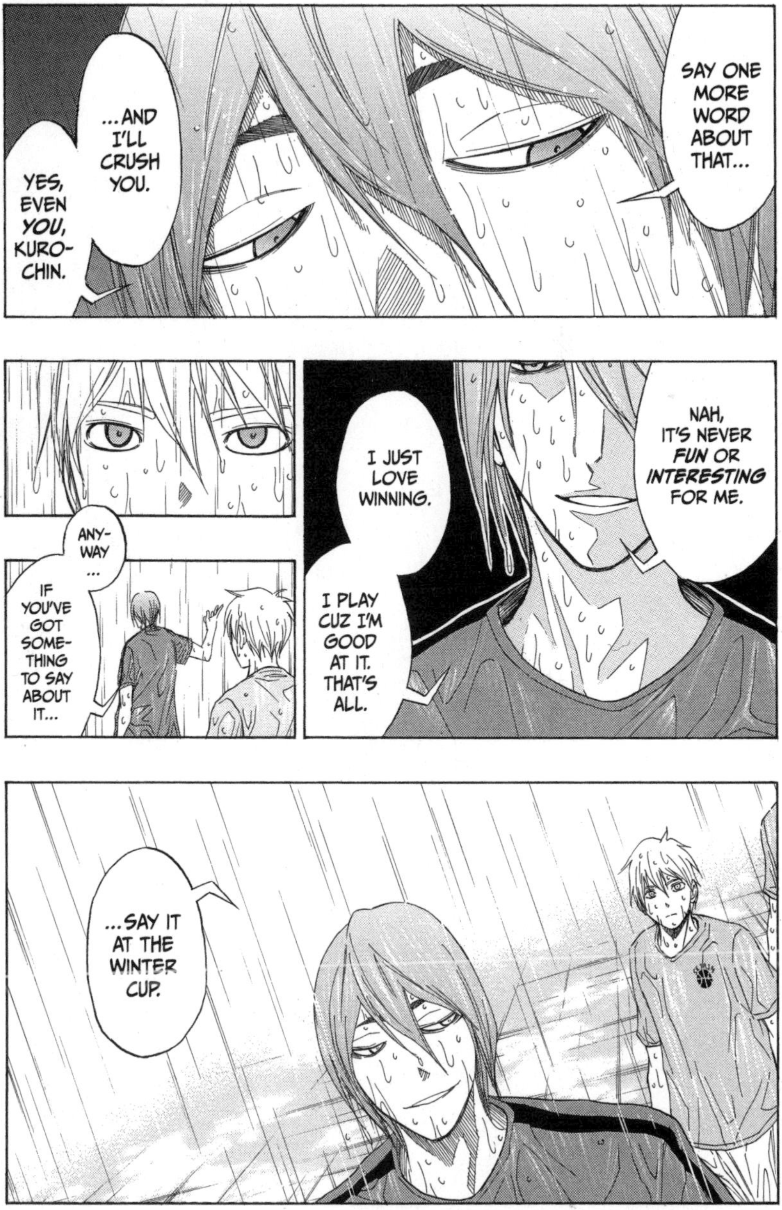
SAY ONE MORE WORD ABOUT THAT...
...AND I'LL CRUSH YOU.
YES, EVEN *YOU*, KURO-CHIN.
NAH, IT'S NEVER *FUN* OR *INTERESTING* FOR ME.
I JUST LOVE WINNING.
I PLAY CUZ I'M GOOD AT IT. THAT'S ALL.
ANYWAY...
IF YOU'VE GOT SOMETHING TO SAY ABOUT IT...
...SAY IT AT THE WINTER CUP.

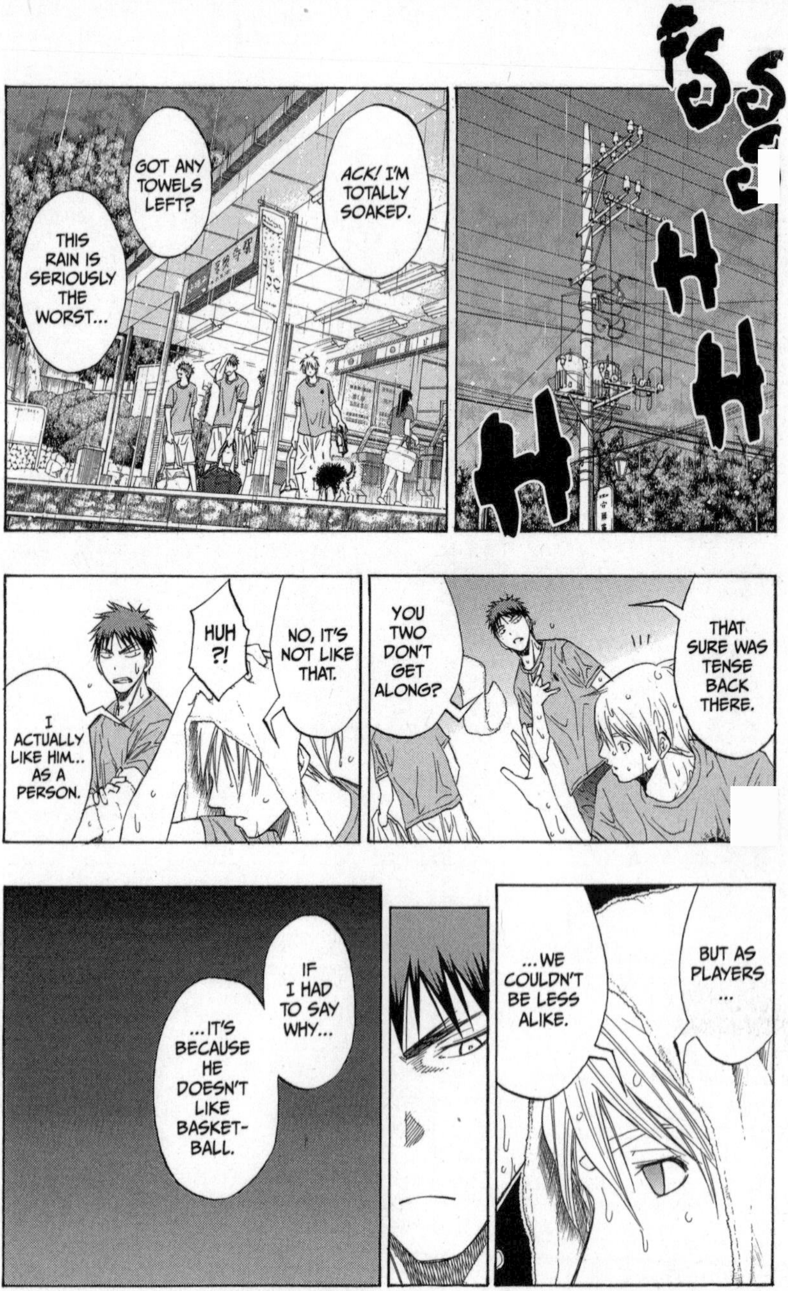
ACK! I'M TOTALLY SOAKED.
GOT ANY TOWELS LEFT?
THIS RAIN IS SERIOUSLY THE WORST...
THAT SURE WAS TENSE BACK THERE.
YOU TWO DON'T GET ALONG?
NO, IT'S NOT LIKE THAT.
HUH ?!
I ACTUALLY LIKE HIM... AS A PERSON.
BUT AS PLAYERS...
...WE COULDN'T BE LESS ALIKE.
IF I HAD TO SAY WHY...
...IT'S BECAUSE HE DOESN'T LIKE BASKET-BALL.

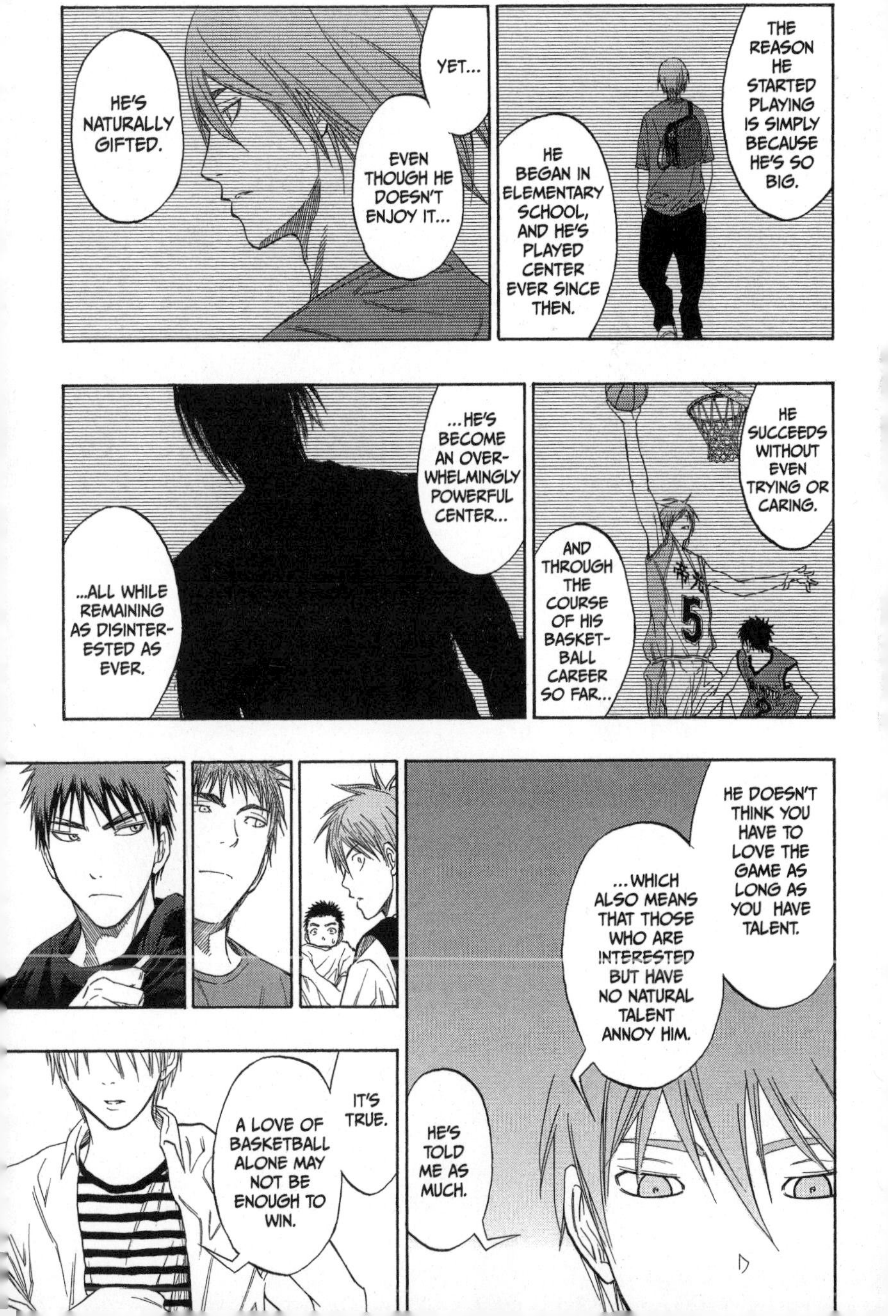
THE REASON HE STARTED PLAYING IS SIMPLY BECAUSE HE'S SO BIG.
HE BEGAN IN ELEMENTARY SCHOOL, AND HE'S PLAYED CENTER EVER SINCE THEN.
YET...
EVEN THOUGH HE DOESN'T ENJOY IT...
HE'S NATURALLY GIFTED.
HE SUCCEEDS WITHOUT EVEN TRYING OR CARING.
AND THROUGH THE COURSE OF HIS BASKETBALL CAREER SO FAR...
...HE'S BECOME AN OVERWHELMINGLY POWERFUL CENTER...
...ALL WHILE REMAINING AS DISINTERESTED AS EVER.
HE DOESN'T THINK YOU HAVE TO LOVE THE GAME AS LONG AS YOU HAVE TALENT.
...WHICH ALSO MEANS THAT THOSE WHO ARE INTERESTED BUT HAVE NO NATURAL TALENT ANNOY HIM.
HE'S TOLD ME AS MUCH.
IT'S TRUE.
A LOVE OF BASKETBALL ALONE MAY NOT BE ENOUGH TO WIN.

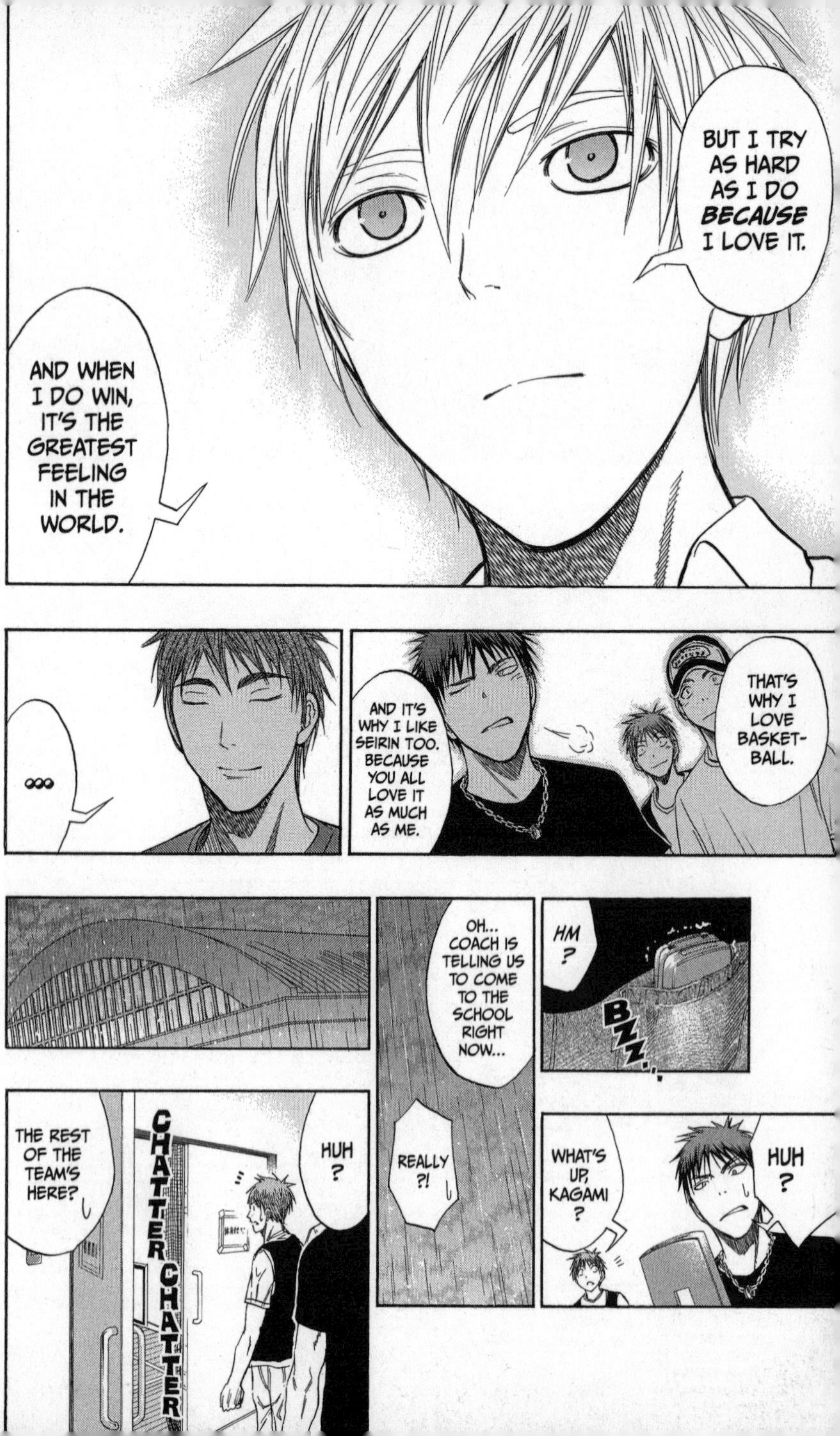
BUT I TRY AS HARD AS I DO *BECAUSE* I LOVE IT.
AND WHEN I DO WIN, IT'S THE GREATEST FEELING IN THE WORLD.
THAT'S WHY I LOVE BASKET-BALL.
AND IT'S WHY I LIKE SEIRIN TOO. BECAUSE YOU ALL LOVE IT AS MUCH AS ME.
...
HM?
BZZ...
HUH?
WHAT'S UP, KAGAMI?
OH... COACH IS TELLING US TO COME TO THE SCHOOL RIGHT NOW...
REALLY?!
HUH?
THE REST OF THE TEAM'S HERE?
CHATTER CHATTER

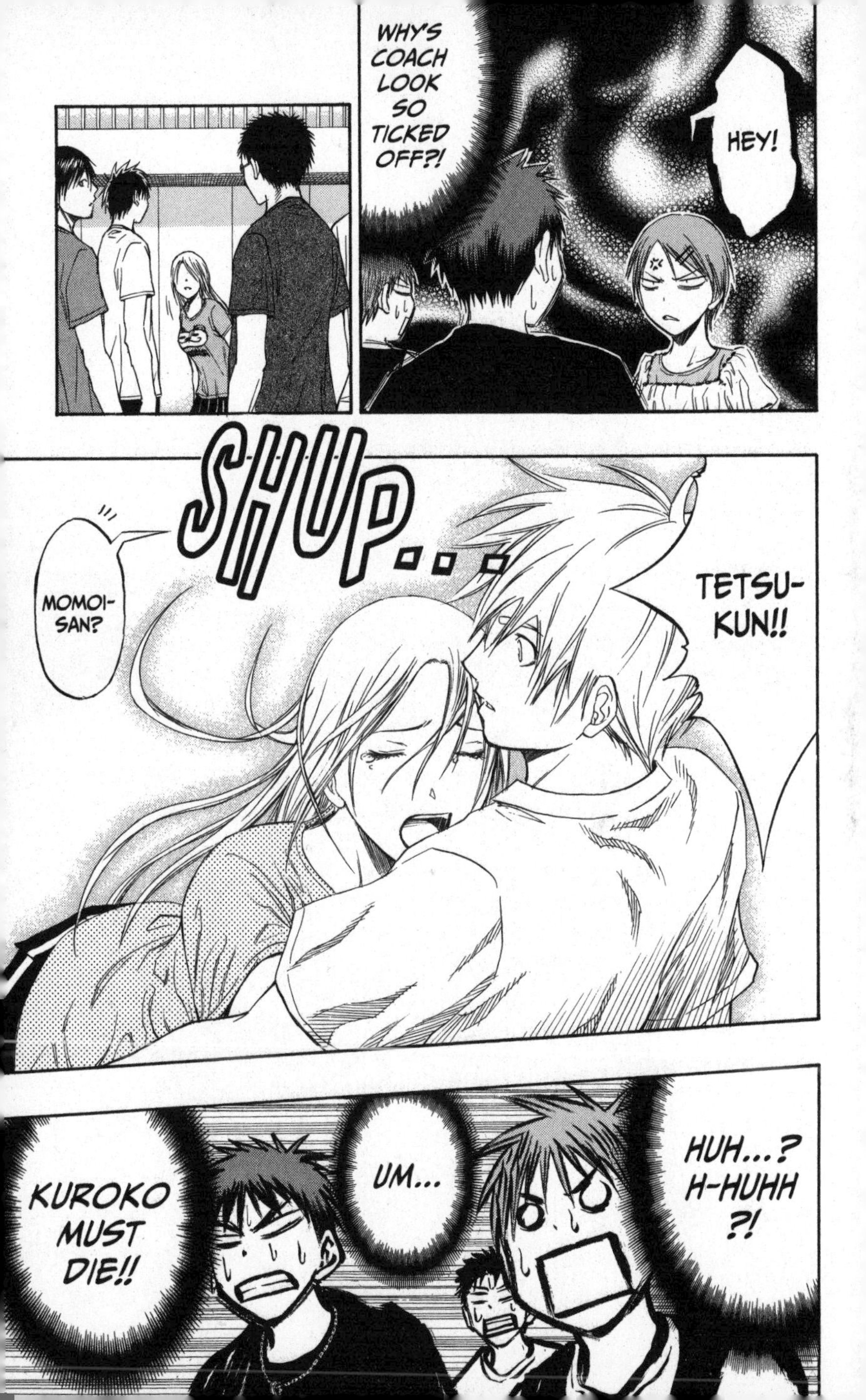
WHY'S COACH LOOK SO TICKED OFF?!
HEY!
SHUP...
TETSU-KUN!!
MOMOI-SAN?
HUH...? H-HUHH?!
UM...
KUROKO MUST DIE!!

KUROKO'S BASKETBALL BLOOPERS

TAKE 3

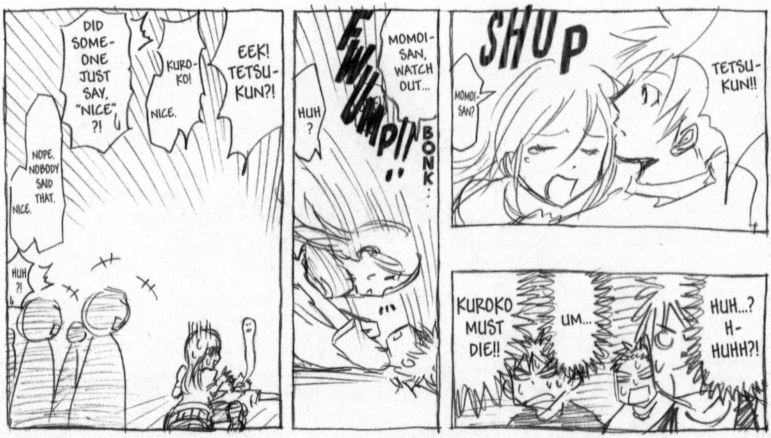
TETSU-KUN!!
SHUP
MOMOI-SAN?
HUH...? H-HUHH?!
UM...
KUROKO MUST DIE!!
MOMOI-SAN, WATCH OUT...
FWUMP!!
HUH?
BONK...
EEK! TETSU-KUN?!
KURO-KO!
NICE.
DID SOME-ONE JUST SAY, "NICE"?!
NOPE. NOBODY SAID THAT.
NICE.
HUH?!

80TH QUARTER:
PLEASE JUST WATCH

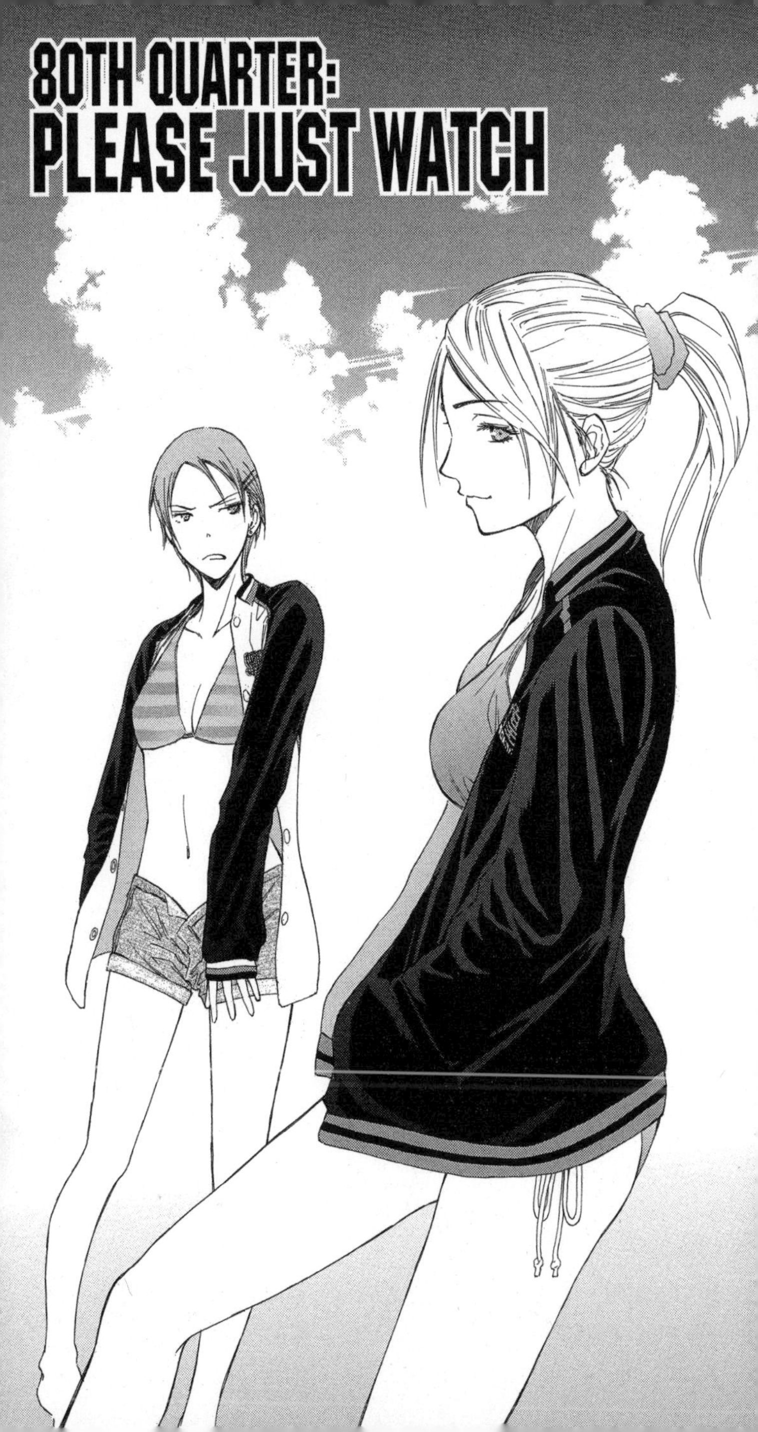

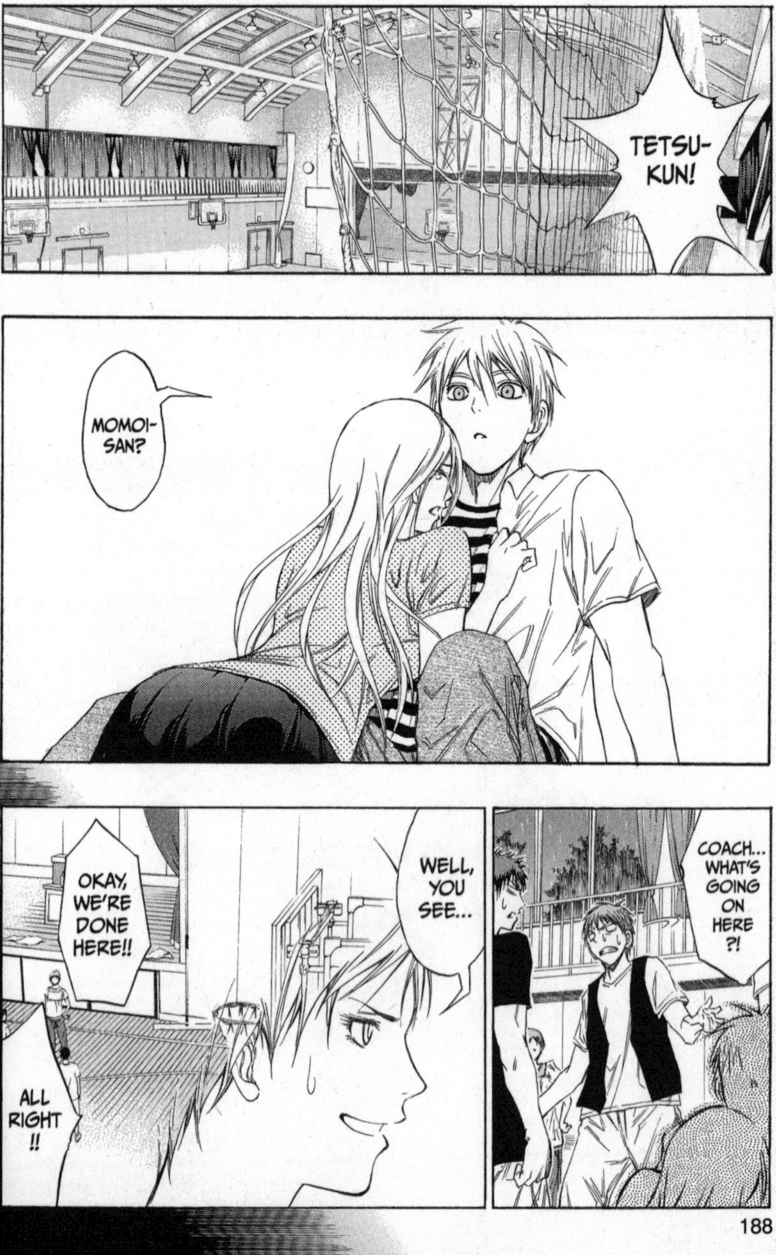

TETSU-KUN!
MOMOI-SAN?
COACH... WHAT'S GOING ON HERE ?!
WELL, YOU SEE...
OKAY, WE'RE DONE HERE!!
ALL RIGHT !!

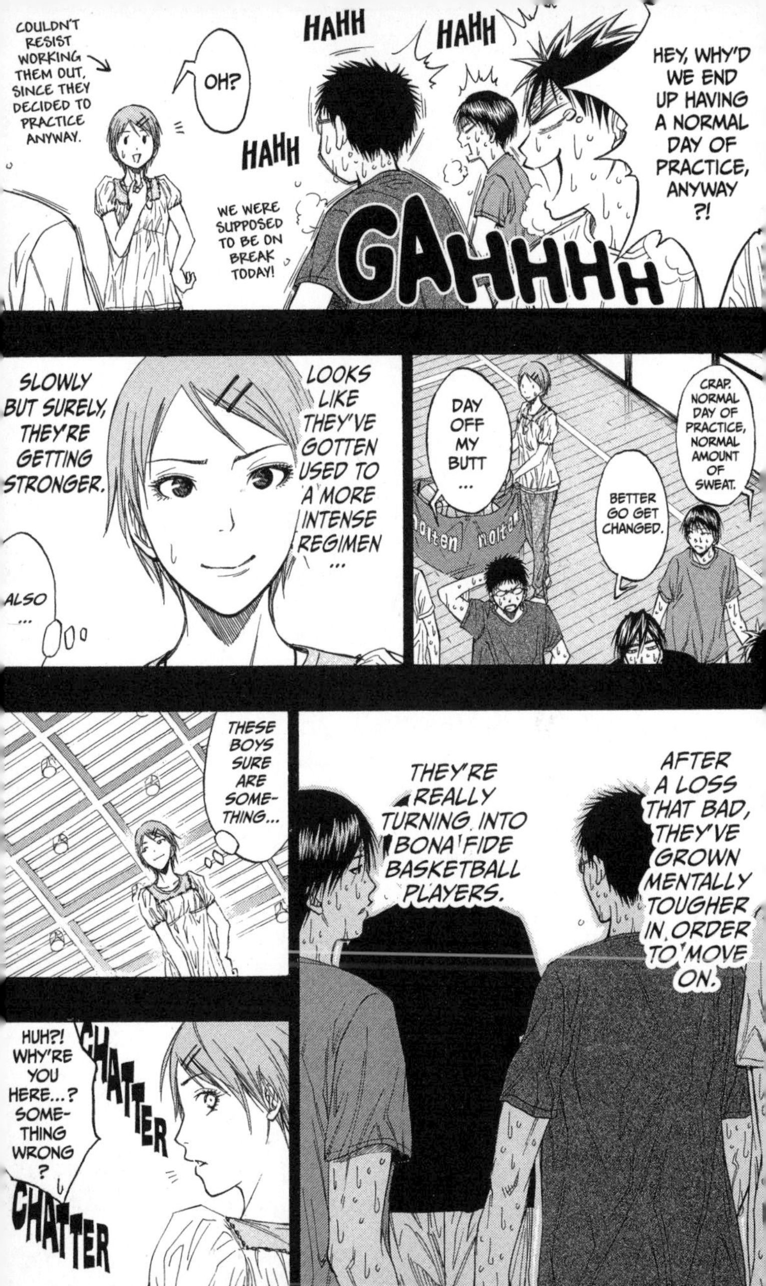
HEY, WHY'D WE END UP HAVING A NORMAL DAY OF PRACTICE, ANYWAY ?!
HAHH
HAHH
GAHHHH
HAHH
WE WERE SUPPOSED TO BE ON BREAK TODAY!
OH?
COULDN'T RESIST WORKING THEM OUT, SINCE THEY DECIDED TO PRACTICE ANYWAY.
CRAP. NORMAL DAY OF PRACTICE, NORMAL AMOUNT OF SWEAT.
BETTER GO GET CHANGED.
DAY OFF MY BUTT...
LOOKS LIKE THEY'VE GOTTEN USED TO A MORE INTENSE REGIMEN...
SLOWLY BUT SURELY, THEY'RE GETTING STRONGER.
ALSO...
AFTER A LOSS THAT BAD, THEY'VE GROWN MENTALLY TOUGHER IN ORDER TO MOVE ON.
THEY'RE REALLY TURNING INTO BONA FIDE BASKETBALL PLAYERS.
THESE BOYS SURE ARE SOMETHING...
CHATTER
HUH?! WHY'RE YOU HERE...? SOMETHING WRONG ?
CHATTER

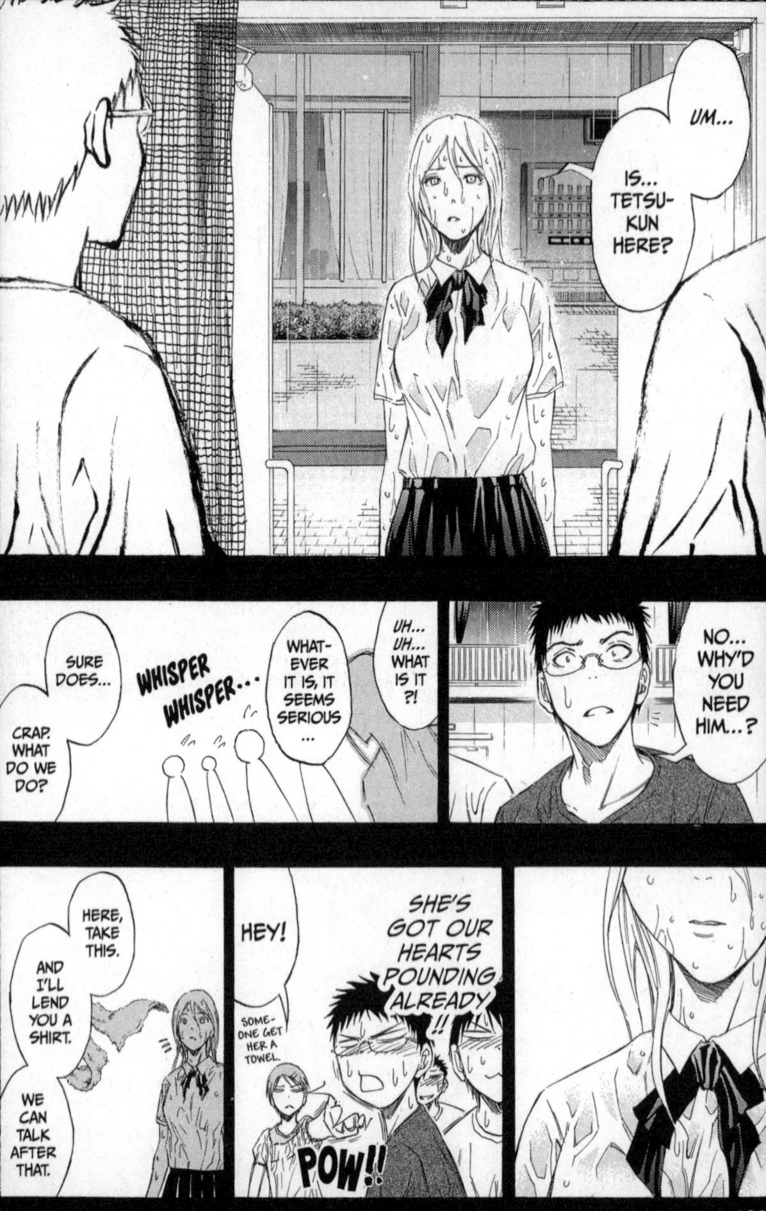
UM...
IS... TETSU-KUN HERE?
NO... WHY'D YOU NEED HIM...?
UH... UH... WHAT IS IT?!
WHAT-EVER IT IS, IT SEEMS SERIOUS...
WHISPER WHISPER...
SURE DOES...
CRAP. WHAT DO WE DO?
SHE'S GOT OUR HEARTS POUNDING ALREADY!!
HEY!
SOME-ONE GET HER A TOWEL.
POW!!
HERE, TAKE THIS.
AND I'LL LEND YOU A SHIRT.
WE CAN TALK AFTER THAT.

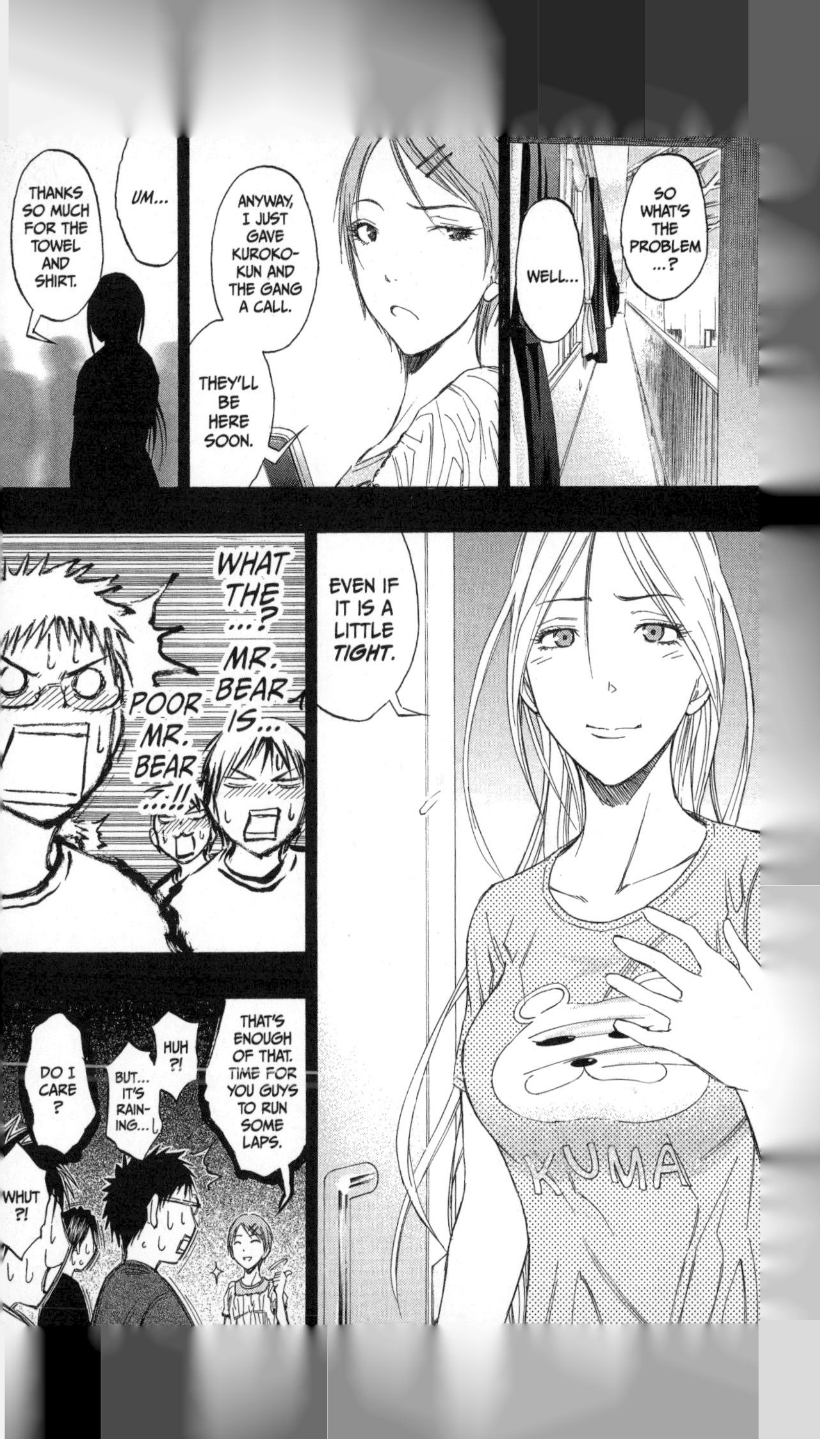
SO WHAT'S THE PROBLEM ...?
WELL...
ANYWAY, I JUST GAVE KUROKO-KUN AND THE GANG A CALL.
THEY'LL BE HERE SOON.
UM...
THANKS SO MUCH FOR THE TOWEL AND SHIRT.
EVEN IF IT IS A LITTLE TIGHT.
KUMA
WHAT THE ...? MR. BEAR IS...
POOR MR. BEAR ...!!
THAT'S ENOUGH OF THAT. TIME FOR YOU GUYS TO RUN SOME LAPS.
HUH ?!
BUT... IT'S RAIN-ING...
DO I CARE ?
WHUT ?!

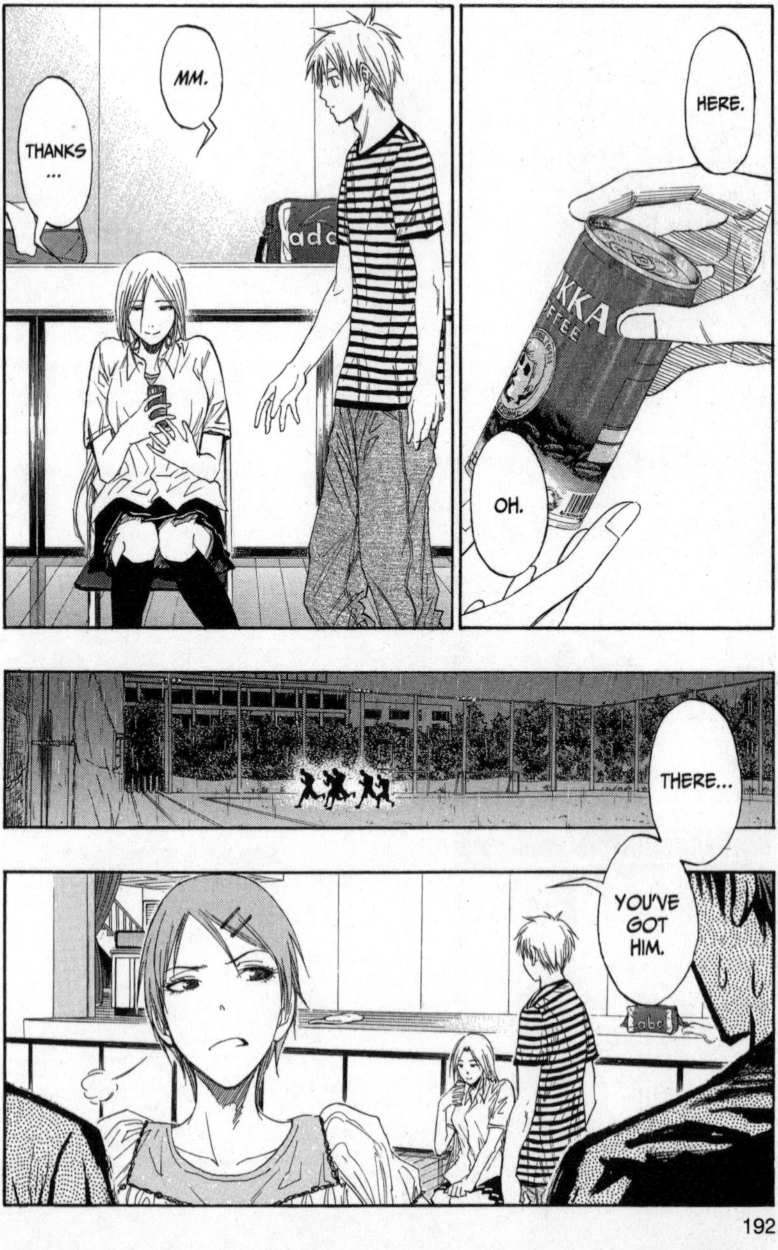
HERE.
OH.
MM.
THANKS ...
THERE...
YOU'VE GOT HIM.

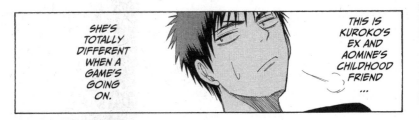

THIS IS KUROKO'S EX AND AOMINE'S CHILDHOOD FRIEND...
SHE'S TOTALLY DIFFERENT WHEN A GAME'S GOING ON.
TELL ME...
WHAT'S WRONG, MOMOI-SAN?
...
WHAT DO I DO, TETSU-KUN?
WAHHHHHHH
I THINK THAT...
SNIFFLE...
...AOMINE-KUN HATES ME!!

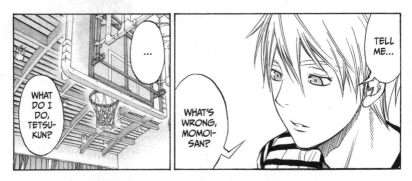

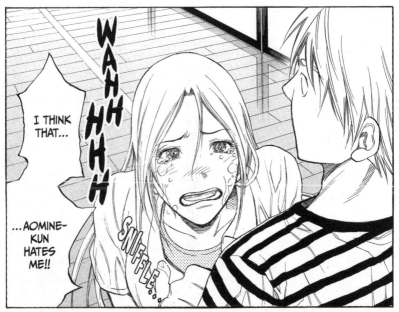

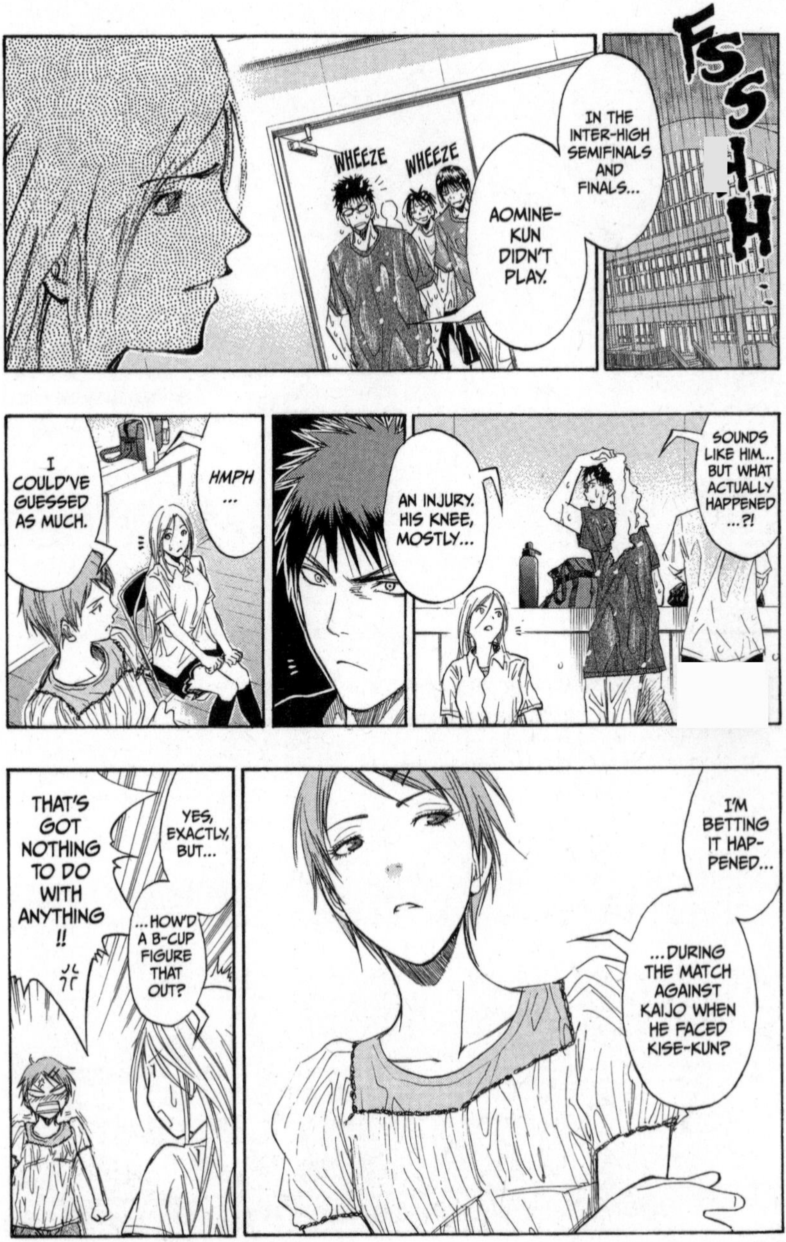
FSSHH...
WHEEZE
WHEEZE
IN THE INTER-HIGH SEMIFINALS AND FINALS...
AOMINE-KUN DIDN'T PLAY.
SOUNDS LIKE HIM... BUT WHAT ACTUALLY HAPPENED...?!
AN INJURY. HIS KNEE, MOSTLY...
HMPH...
I COULD'VE GUESSED AS MUCH.
I'M BETTING IT HAPPENED...
...DURING THE MATCH AGAINST KAIJO WHEN HE FACED KISE-KUN?
YES, EXACTLY, BUT...
...HOW'D A B-CUP FIGURE THAT OUT?
THAT'S GOT NOTHING TO DO WITH ANYTHING!!

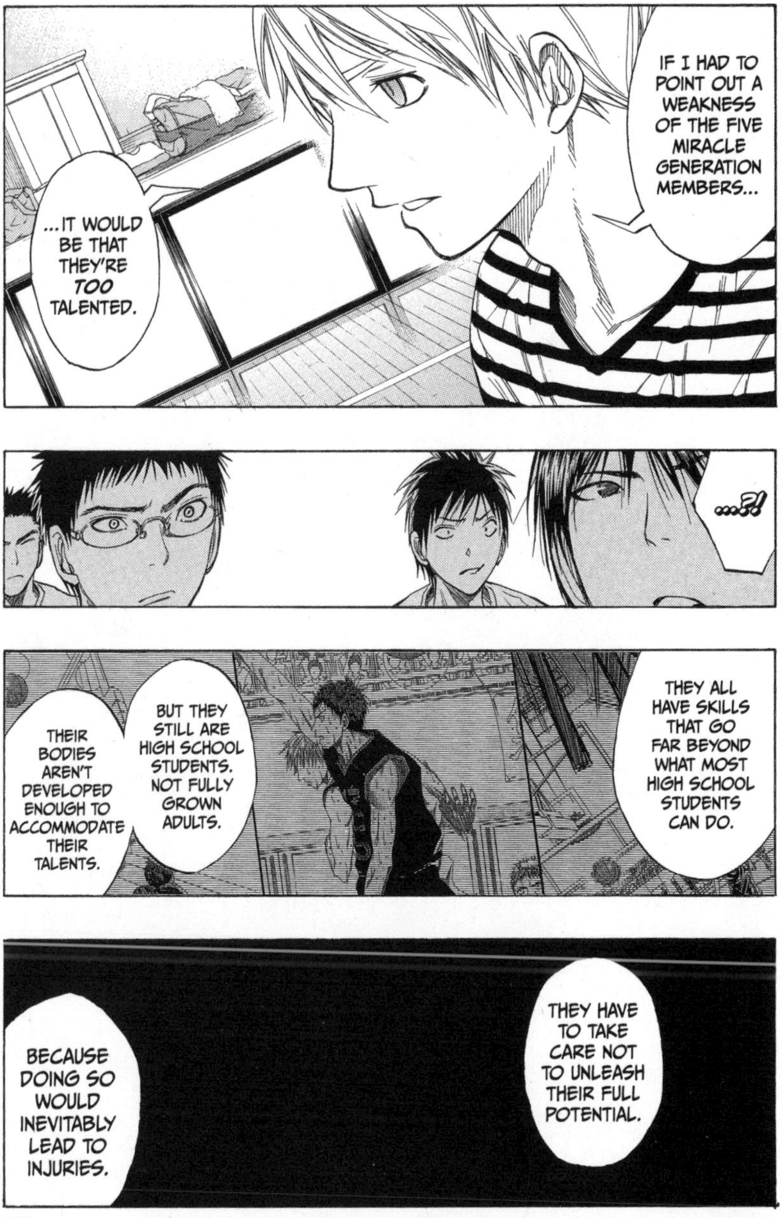
IF I HAD TO POINT OUT A WEAKNESS OF THE FIVE MIRACLE GENERATION MEMBERS...
...IT WOULD BE THAT THEY'RE *TOO* TALENTED.
...?!
THEY ALL HAVE SKILLS THAT GO FAR BEYOND WHAT MOST HIGH SCHOOL STUDENTS CAN DO.
BUT THEY STILL ARE HIGH SCHOOL STUDENTS. NOT FULLY GROWN ADULTS.
THEIR BODIES AREN'T DEVELOPED ENOUGH TO ACCOMMODATE THEIR TALENTS.
THEY HAVE TO TAKE CARE NOT TO UNLEASH THEIR FULL POTENTIAL.
BECAUSE DOING SO WOULD INEVITABLY LEAD TO INJURIES.

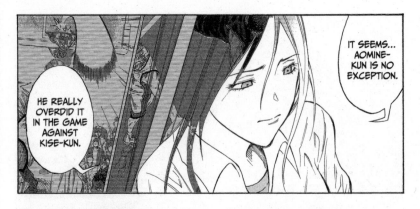

IT SEEMS... AOMINE-KUN IS NO EXCEPTION.
HE REALLY OVERDID IT IN THE GAME AGAINST KISE-KUN.
I REALIZED THAT AND TOLD THE COACH.
I BEGGED HIM NOT TO LET AOMINE-KUN PLAY.
AOMINE-KUN WENT ABSOLUTELY WILD, BUT THE COACH WOULDN'T GIVE IN TO HIM.
HE HAD HIM FORCIBLY REMOVED FROM THE LINEUP HALFWAY THROUGH THE GAME.
THEN HE FOUND OUT IT WAS MY DOING...
WHO TOLD YOU TO MESS WITH ME? DAMN YOU, SATSUKI!
YOU THINK THAT WAS ENOUGH TO GET ME HURT?
STOP BUTTING IN WHERE YOU DON'T BELONG!!

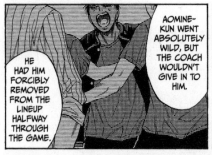

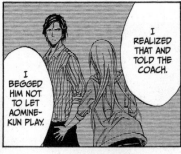

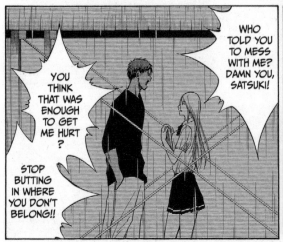

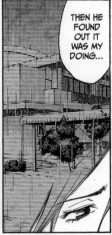

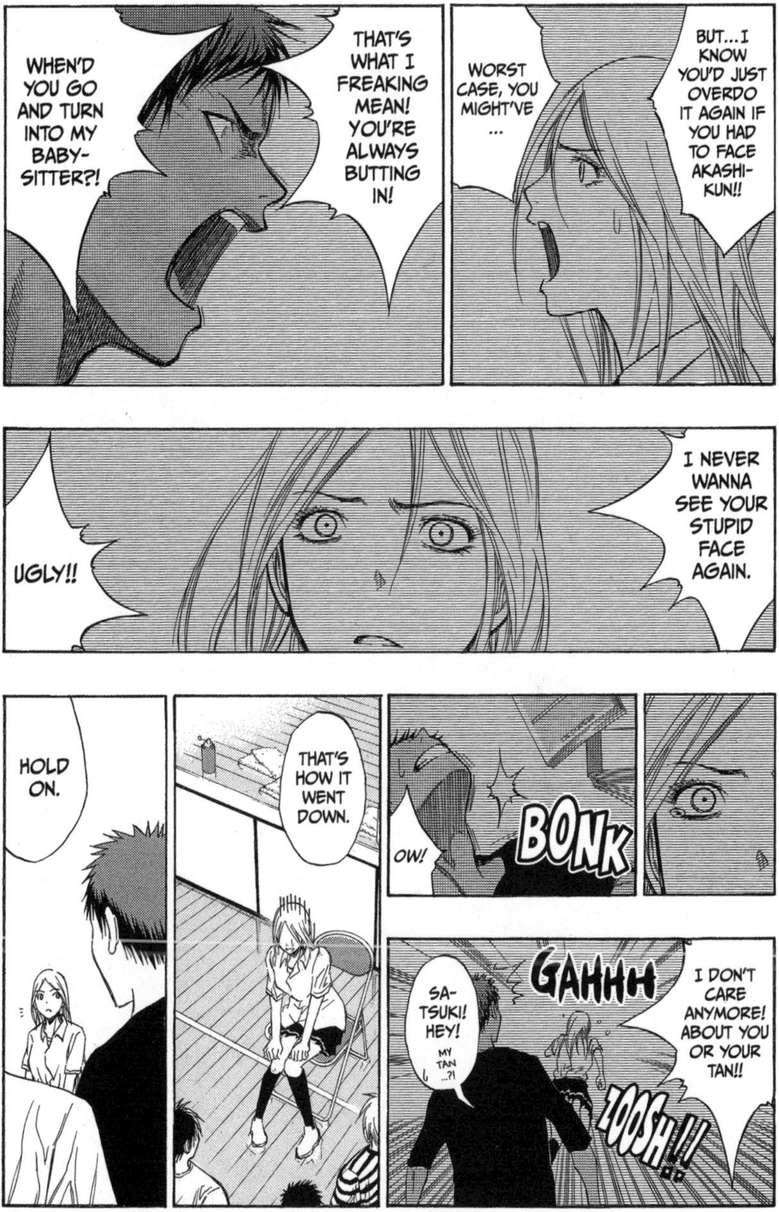
BUT...I KNOW YOU'D JUST OVERDO IT AGAIN IF YOU HAD TO FACE AKASHI-KUN!!
WORST CASE, YOU MIGHT'VE ...
THAT'S WHAT I FREAKING MEAN! YOU'RE ALWAYS BUTTING IN!
WHEN'D YOU GO AND TURN INTO MY BABY-SITTER?!
I NEVER WANNA SEE YOUR STUPID FACE AGAIN.
UGLY!!
BONK
OW!
I DON'T CARE ANYMORE! ABOUT YOU OR YOUR TAN!!
GAHHH
ZOOSH!!
SA-TSUKI! HEY!
MY TAN ...?!
THAT'S HOW IT WENT DOWN.
HOLD ON.

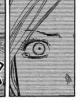

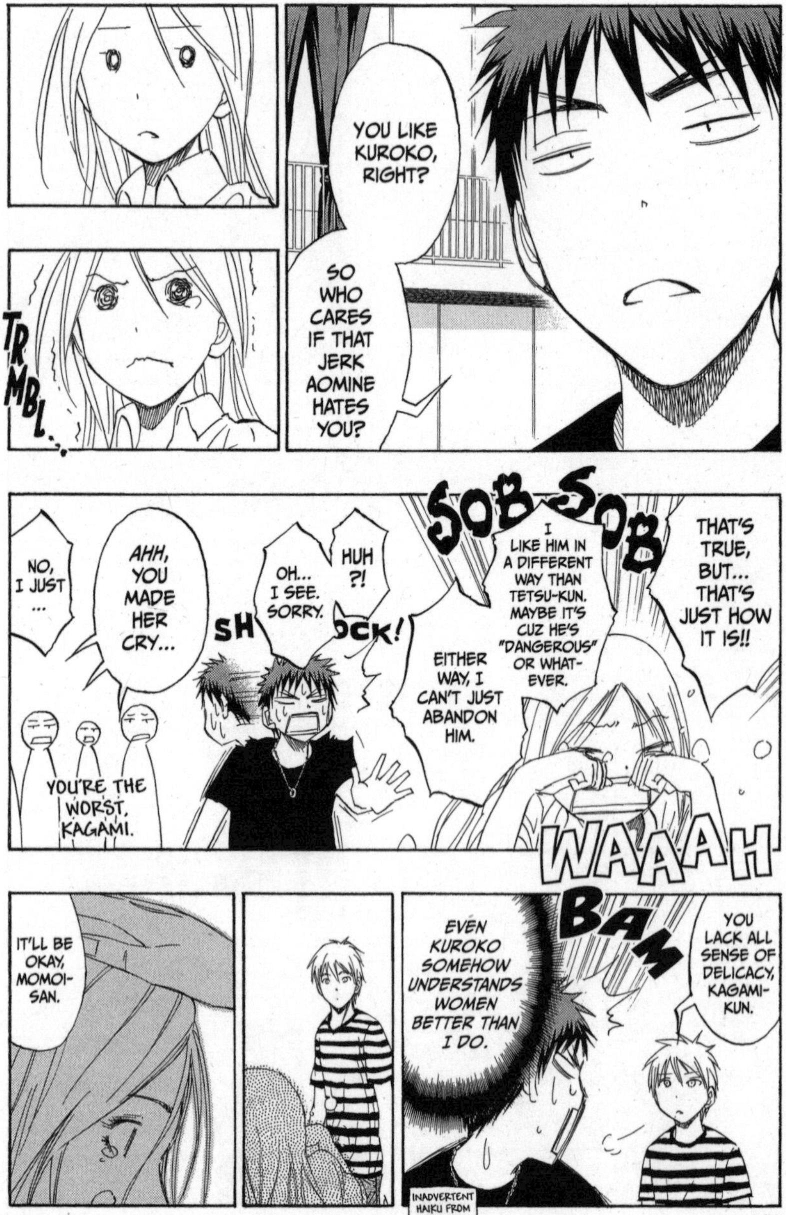
YOU LIKE KUROKO, RIGHT?
SO WHO CARES IF THAT JERK AOMINE HATES YOU?
TRMBL...
THAT'S TRUE, BUT... THAT'S JUST HOW IT IS!!
SOB SOB
I LIKE HIM IN A DIFFERENT WAY THAN TETSU-KUN. MAYBE IT'S CUZ HE'S "DANGEROUS" OR WHATEVER.
EITHER WAY, I CAN'T JUST ABANDON HIM.
WAAAH
HUH ?!
SHOCK!
OH... I SEE. SORRY.
AHH, YOU MADE HER CRY...
NO, I JUST ...
YOU'RE THE WORST, KAGAMI.
BAM
YOU LACK ALL SENSE OF DELICACY, KAGAMI-KUN.
EVEN KUROKO SOMEHOW UNDERSTANDS WOMEN BETTER THAN I DO.
INADVERTENT HAIKU FROM KAGAMI
IT'LL BE OKAY, MOMOI-SAN.

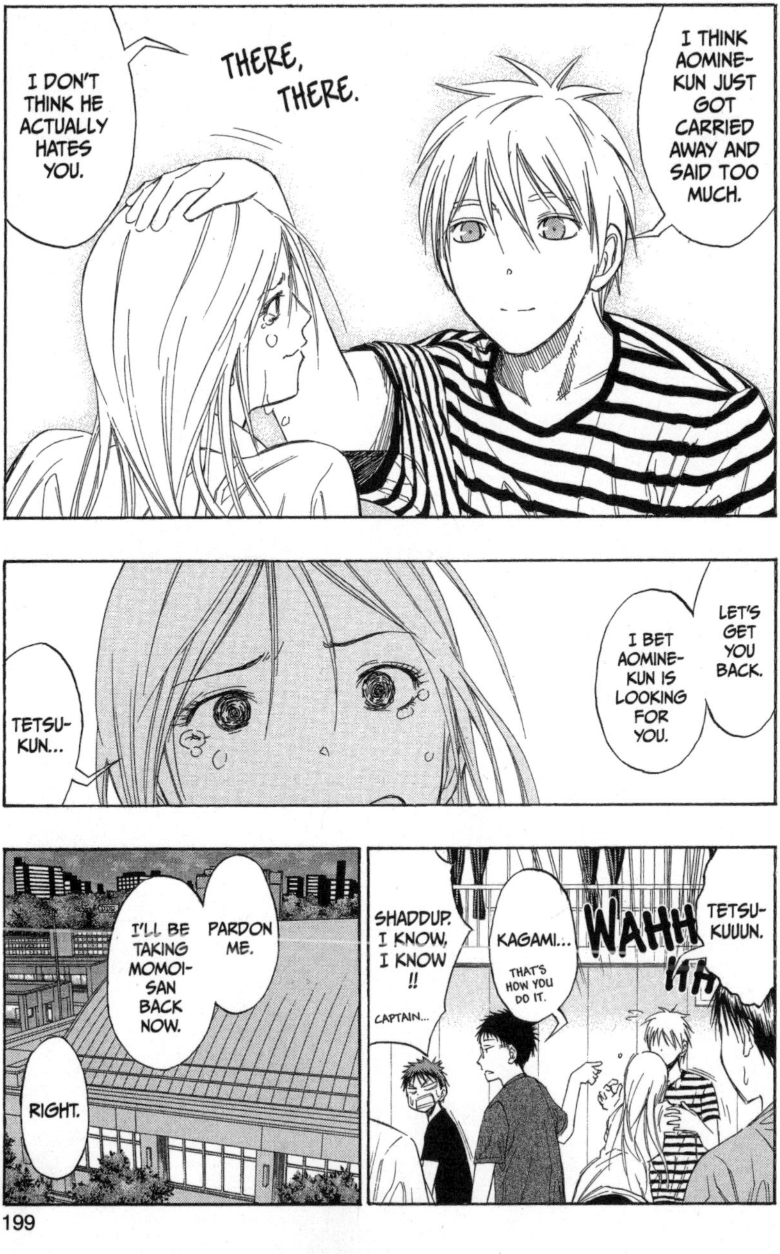
I THINK AOMINE-KUN JUST GOT CARRIED AWAY AND SAID TOO MUCH.
THERE, THERE.
I DON'T THINK HE ACTUALLY HATES YOU.
LET'S GET YOU BACK.
I BET AOMINE-KUN IS LOOKING FOR YOU.
TETSU-KUN...
TETSU-KUUUN.
WAHH HH
KAGAMI...
THAT'S HOW YOU DO IT.
SHADDUP. I KNOW, I KNOW !!
CAPTAIN...
PARDON ME.
I'LL BE TAKING MOMOI-SAN BACK NOW.
RIGHT.

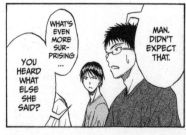

MAN. DIDN'T EXPECT THAT.
WHAT'S EVEN MORE SUR-PRISING...
YOU HEARD WHAT ELSE SHE SAID?
ALSO, MOMOI-SAN...
NOW WE KNOW WHY AOMINE DIDN'T PARTICIPATE AT THE END OF INTER-HIGH, BUT...
...WHAT ABOUT THE OTHER TWO?
I CAN'T BE SURE, BUT I DO HAVE A THEORY...
I THINK IT'S BECAUSE THEY DIDN'T HAVE ANY MORE REASON TO PLAY.
MU-KUN... I MEAN, MURASAKIBARA-KUN DOESN'T LISTEN TO ANYONE EXCEPT AKASHI-KUN.
AND HE FLAT-OUT REFUSES TO FACE AKASHI-KUN ON THE COURT.
THAT'S PROBABLY WHY HE DIDN'T PLAY IN THE SEMIFINAL MATCH BETWEEN RAKUZAN AND YOSEN.
WHAT ABOUT THIS AKASHI, THEN...?
HE...
...HAS NO INTEREST IN WINNING.
HUH?!

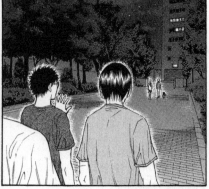

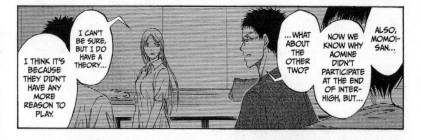

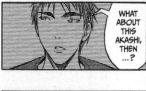

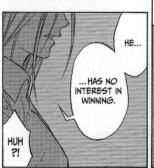

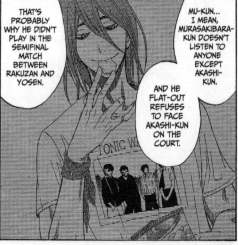

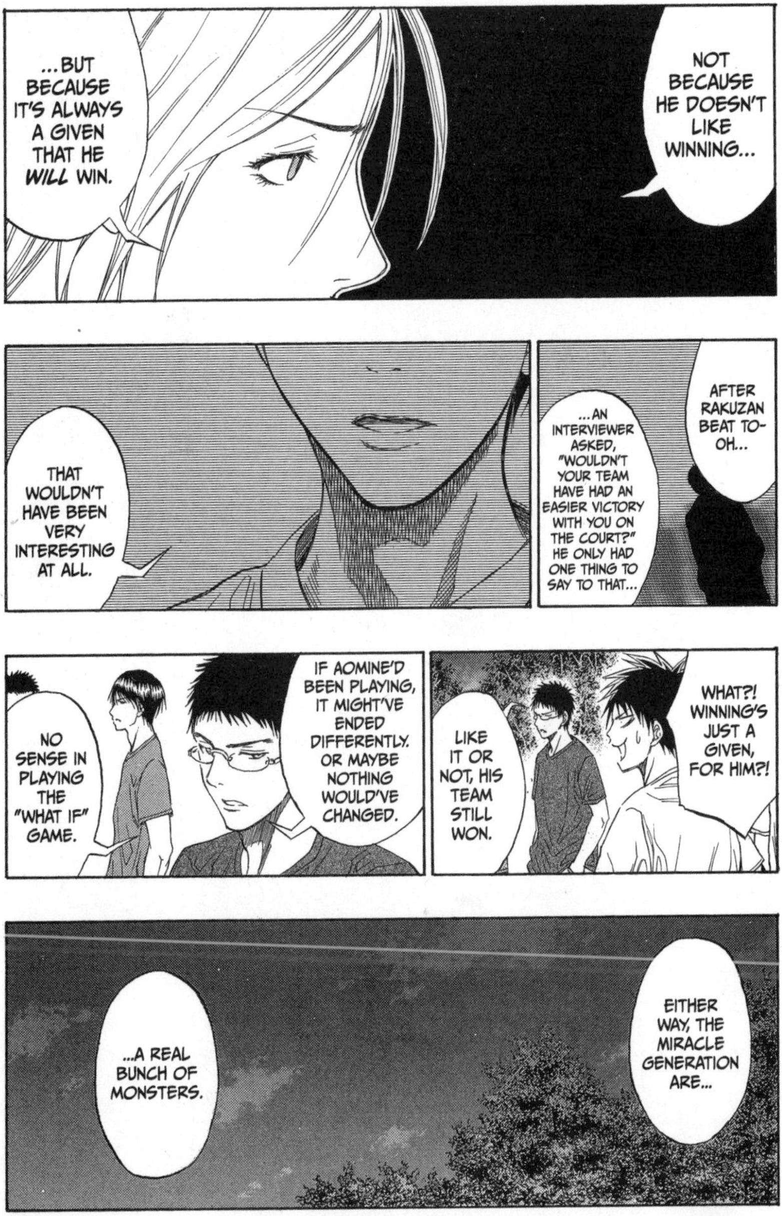
NOT BECAUSE HE DOESN'T LIKE WINNING...
...BUT BECAUSE IT'S ALWAYS A GIVEN THAT HE *WILL* WIN.
AFTER RAKUZAN BEAT TO-OH...
...AN INTERVIEWER ASKED, "WOULDN'T YOUR TEAM HAVE HAD AN EASIER VICTORY WITH YOU ON THE COURT?" HE ONLY HAD ONE THING TO SAY TO THAT...
THAT WOULDN'T HAVE BEEN VERY INTERESTING AT ALL.
WHAT?! WINNING'S JUST A GIVEN, FOR HIM?!
LIKE IT OR NOT, HIS TEAM STILL WON.
IF AOMINE'D BEEN PLAYING, IT MIGHT'VE ENDED DIFFERENTLY. OR MAYBE NOTHING WOULD'VE CHANGED.
NO SENSE IN PLAYING THE "WHAT IF" GAME.
EITHER WAY, THE MIRACLE GENERATION ARE...
...A REAL BUNCH OF MONSTERS.

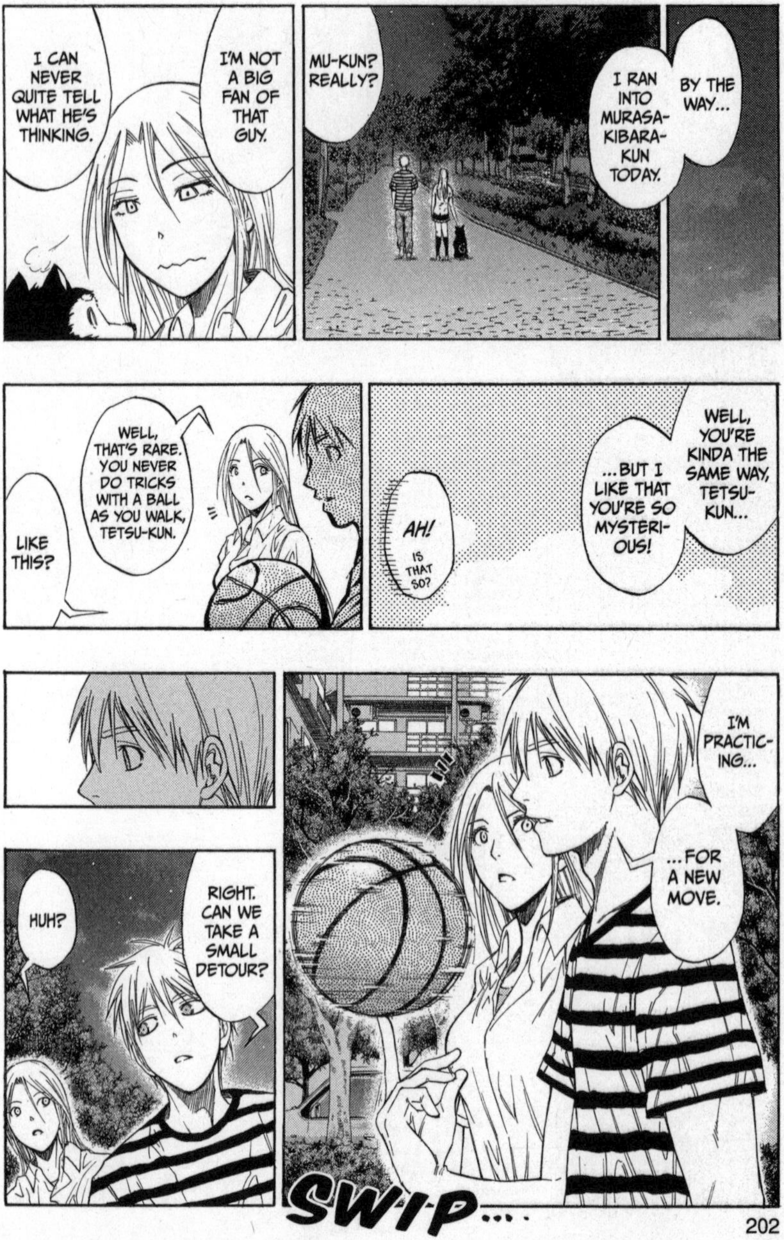
BY THE WAY...
I RAN INTO MURASAKIBARA-KUN TODAY.
MU-KUN? REALLY?
I'M NOT A BIG FAN OF THAT GUY.
I CAN NEVER QUITE TELL WHAT HE'S THINKING.
WELL, YOU'RE KINDA THE SAME WAY, TETSU-KUN...
...BUT I LIKE THAT YOU'RE SO MYSTERIOUS!
AH! IS THAT SO?
WELL, THAT'S RARE. YOU NEVER DO TRICKS WITH A BALL AS YOU WALK, TETSU-KUN.
LIKE THIS?
I'M PRACTICING...
...FOR A NEW MOVE.
SWIP...
RIGHT. CAN WE TAKE A SMALL DETOUR?
HUH?

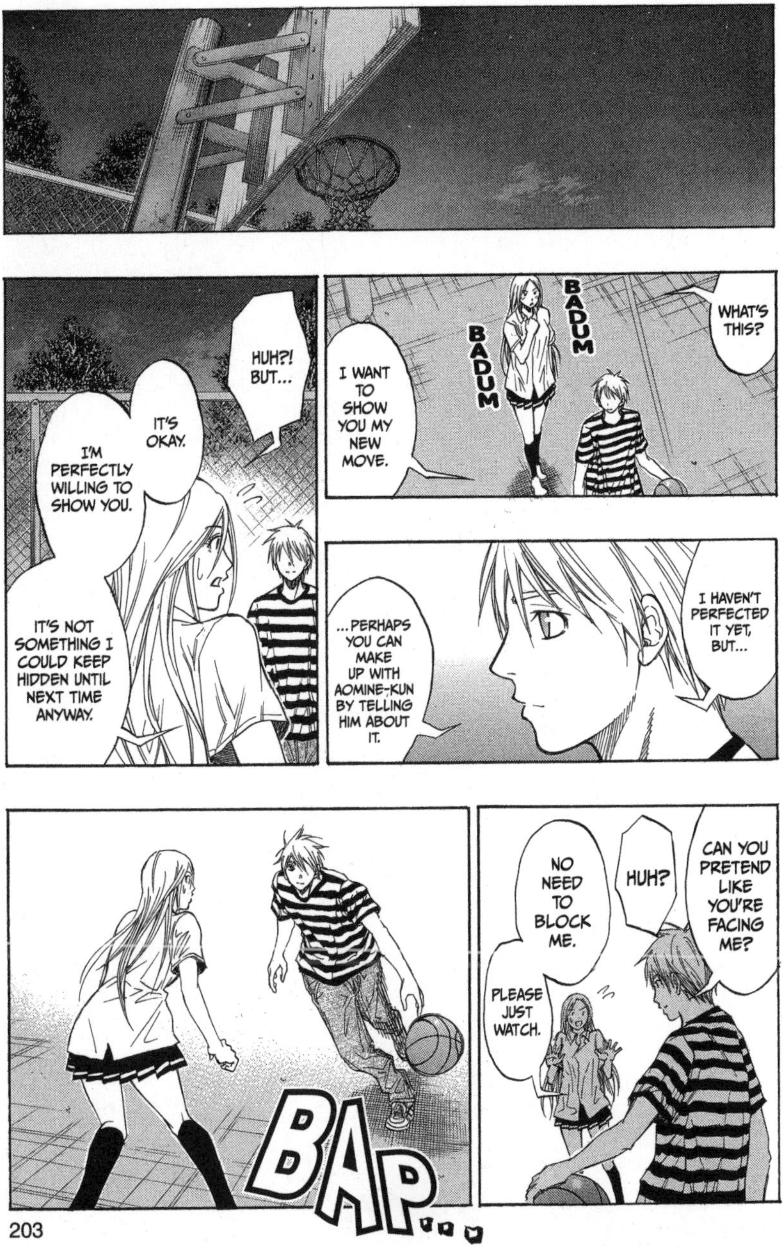
WHAT'S THIS?
BADUM
BADUM
BADUM
I WANT TO SHOW YOU MY NEW MOVE.
I HAVEN'T PERFECTED IT YET, BUT...
...PERHAPS YOU CAN MAKE UP WITH AOMINE-KUN BY TELLING HIM ABOUT IT.
HUH?! BUT...
IT'S OKAY.
I'M PERFECTLY WILLING TO SHOW YOU.
IT'S NOT SOMETHING I COULD KEEP HIDDEN UNTIL NEXT TIME ANYWAY.
CAN YOU PRETEND LIKE YOU'RE FACING ME?
HUH?
NO NEED TO BLOCK ME.
PLEASE JUST WATCH.
BAP...

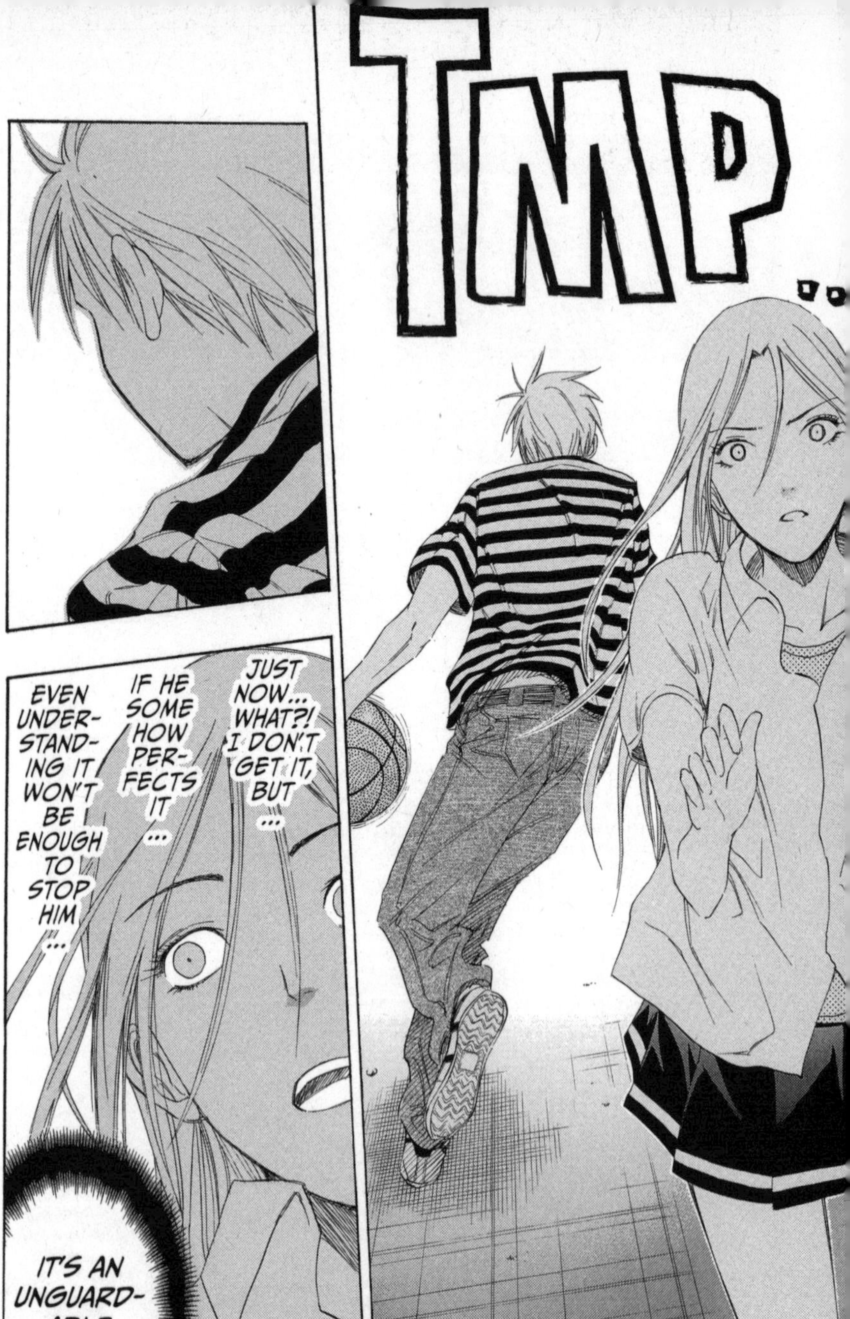
TMP...
JUST NOW... WHAT?! I DON'T GET IT, BUT ...
IF HE SOMEHOW PERFECTS IT ...
EVEN UNDERSTANDING IT WON'T BE ENOUGH TO STOP HIM ...
IT'S AN UNGUARDABLE DRIVE!

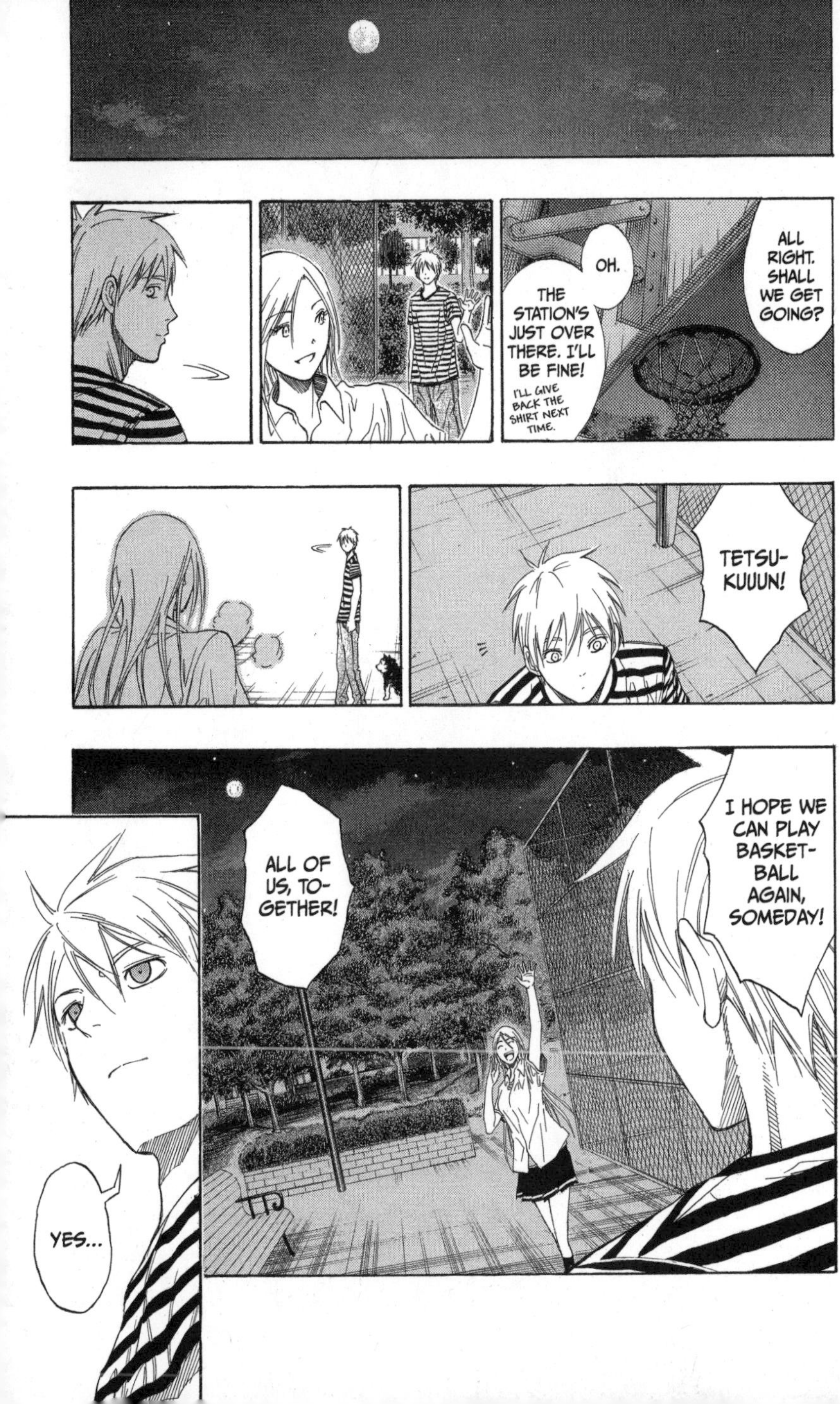
ALL RIGHT. SHALL WE GET GOING?
OH.
THE STATION'S JUST OVER THERE. I'LL BE FINE!
I'LL GIVE BACK THE SHIRT NEXT TIME.
TETSU-KUUUN!
I HOPE WE CAN PLAY BASKET-BALL AGAIN, SOMEDAY!
ALL OF US, TO-GETHER!
YES...

Kuroko's
BASKETBALL

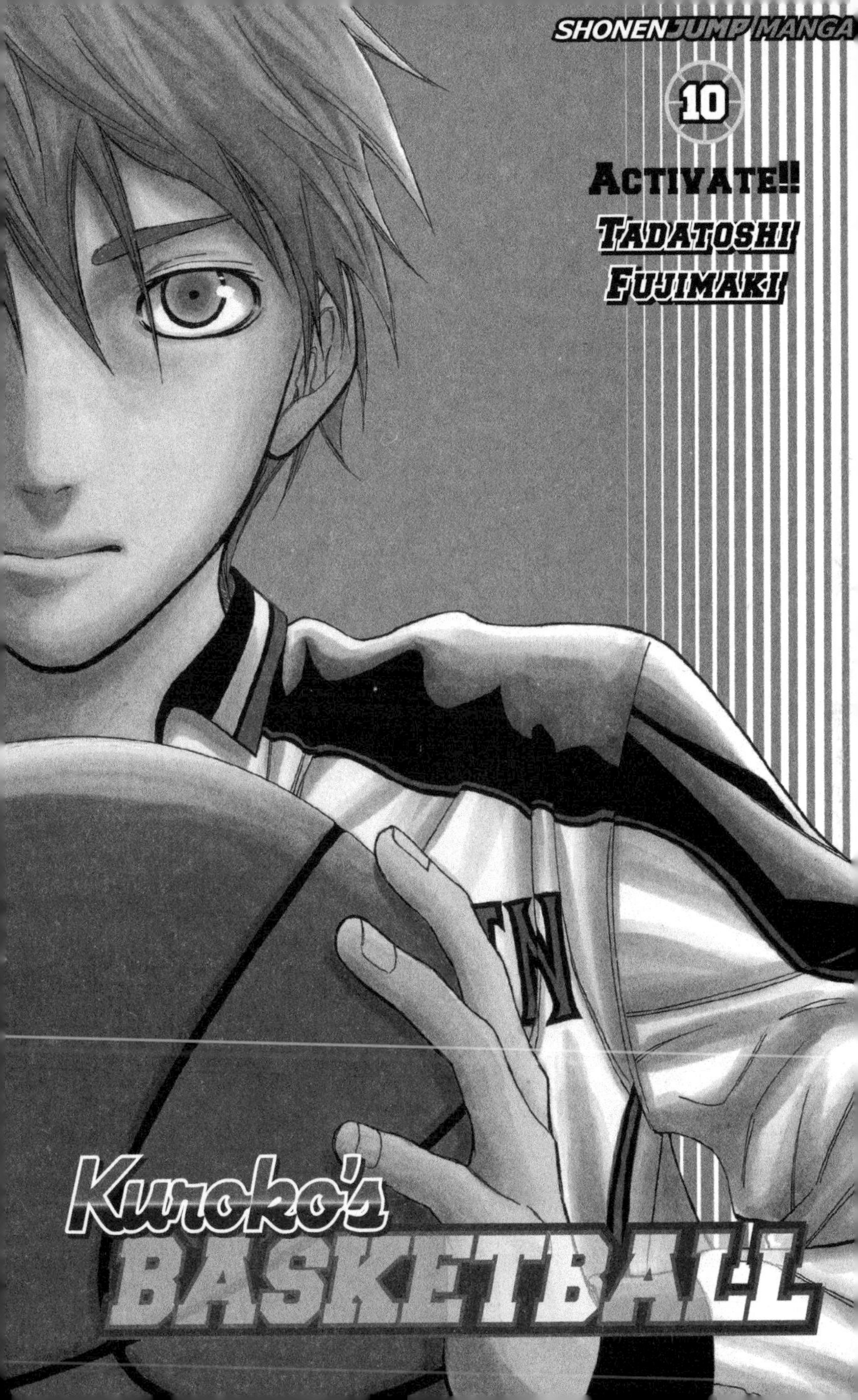
SHONEN JUMP MANGA
10
ACTIVATE!!
TADATOSHI FUJIMAKI
Kuroko's
BASKETBALL

TADATOSHI FUJIMAKI

There's this one soba restaurant I tend to visit after finishing up with work. One day, after I was done eating, this grim old man suddenly said to me, "You...really like soba, don't you? I can tell from how you eat it."

I *do* like it, but...hard to believe I looked *that* happy eating it. Who was he, anyway?

—2010

81ST QUARTER: ACTIVATE!!

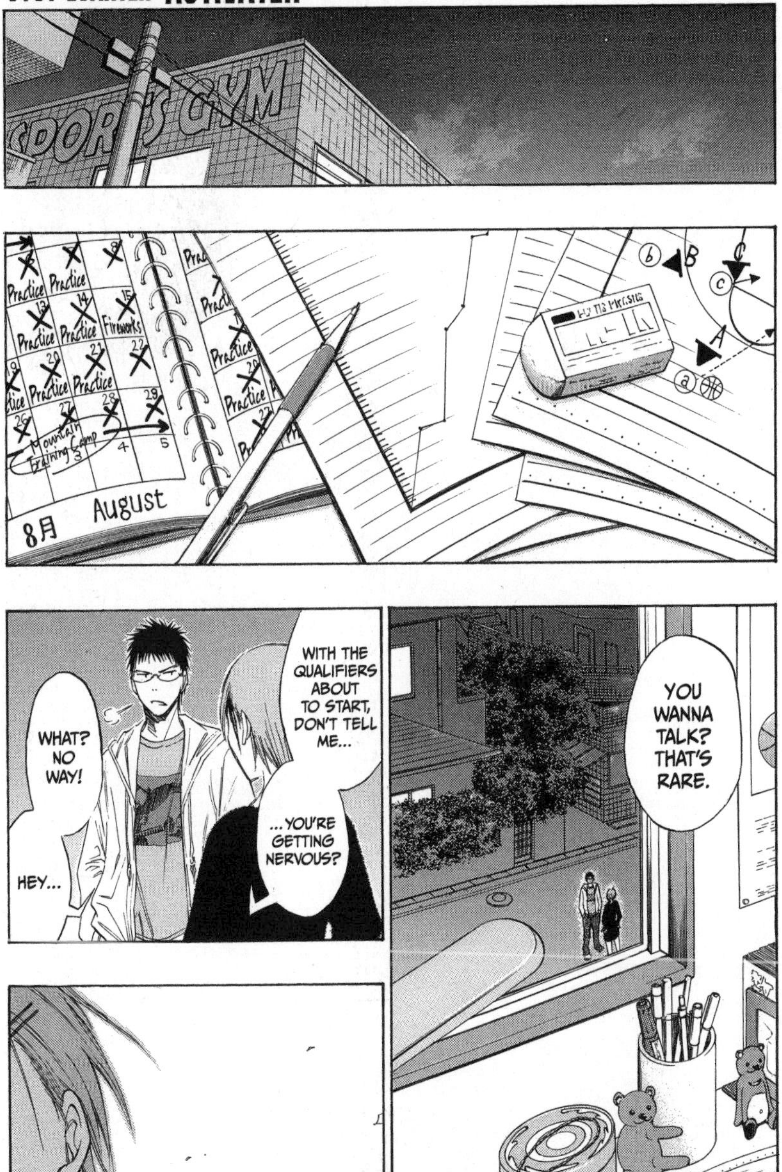
Practice
Fireworks
Mountain Training Camp
August
8月
YOU WANNA TALK? THAT'S RARE.
WITH THE QUALIFIERS ABOUT TO START, DON'T TELL ME...
...YOU'RE GETTING NERVOUS?
WHAT? NO WAY!
HEY...

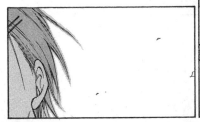

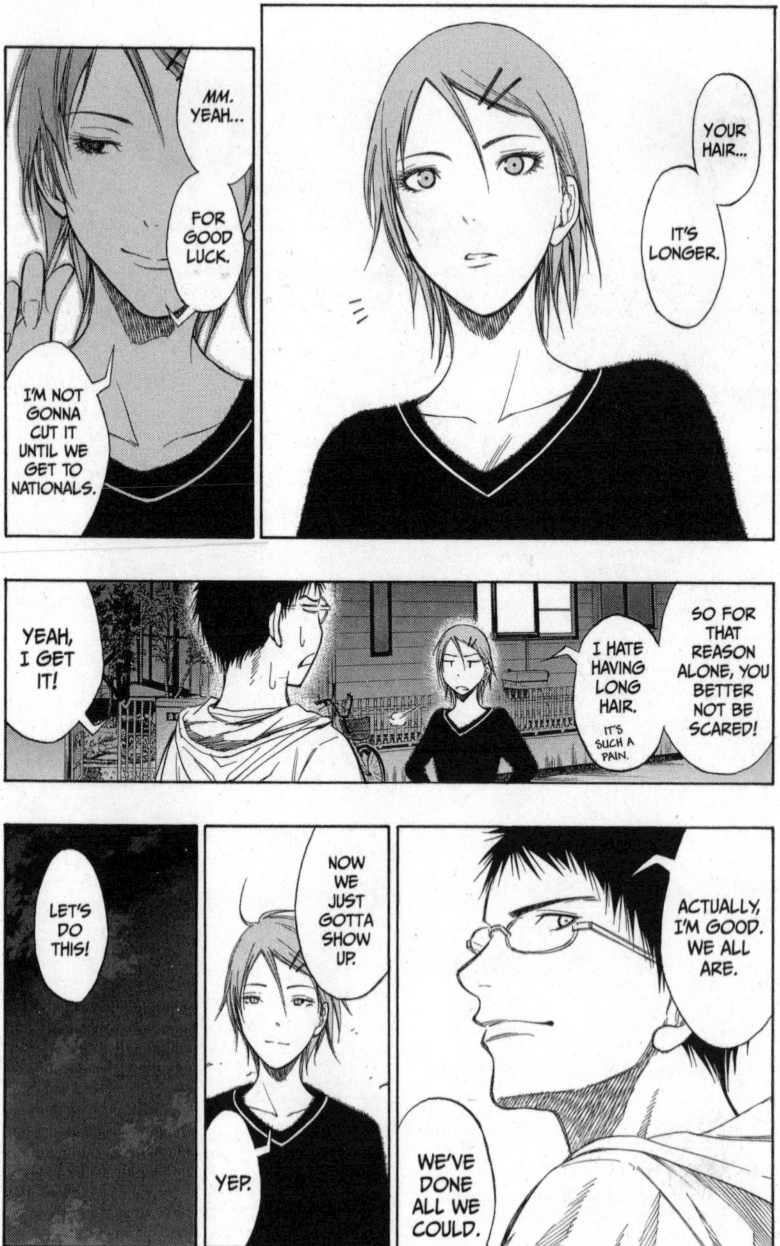
YOUR HAIR...
IT'S LONGER.
MM. YEAH...
FOR GOOD LUCK.
I'M NOT GONNA CUT IT UNTIL WE GET TO NATIONALS.
SO FOR THAT REASON ALONE, YOU BETTER NOT BE SCARED!
I HATE HAVING LONG HAIR.
IT'S SUCH A PAIN.
YEAH, I GET IT!
ACTUALLY, I'M GOOD. WE ALL ARE.
WE'VE DONE ALL WE COULD.
NOW WE JUST GOTTA SHOW UP.
YEP.
LET'S DO THIS!

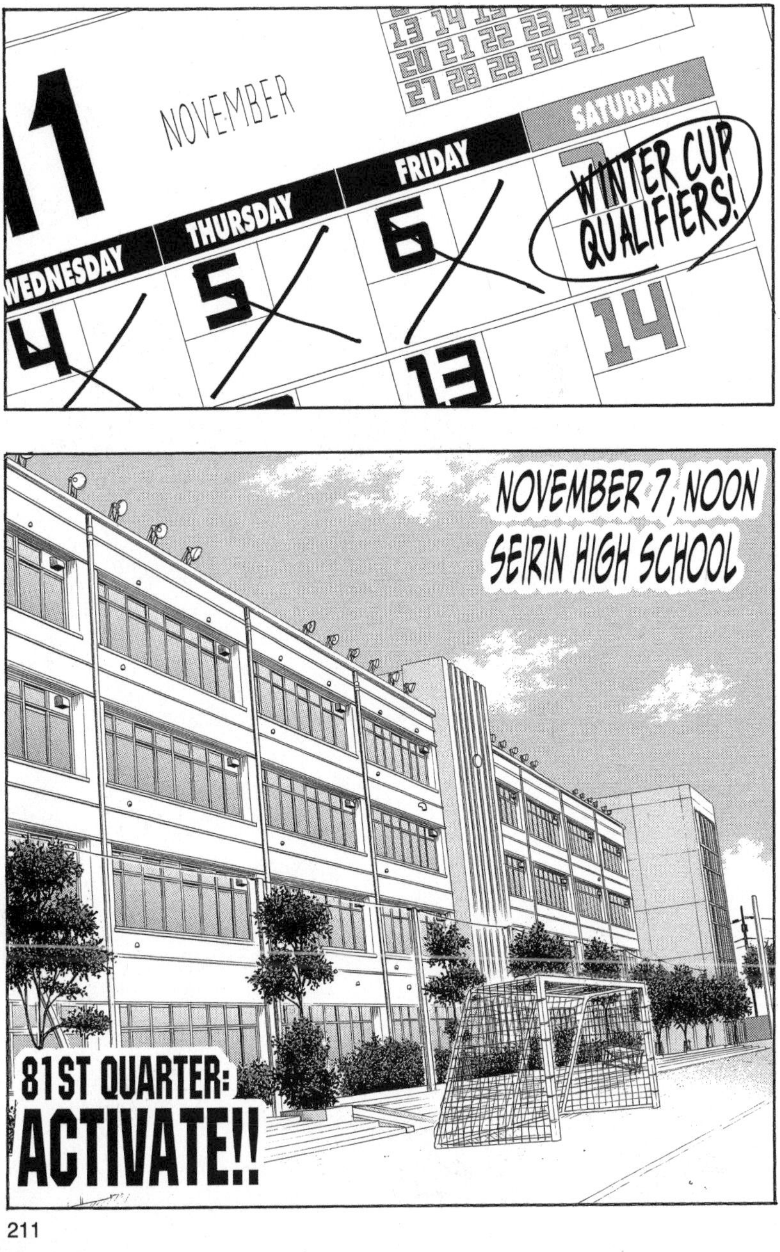
NOVEMBER
SATURDAY
FRIDAY
THURSDAY
WEDNESDAY
WINTER CUP QUALIFIERS!
NOVEMBER 7, NOON
SEIRIN HIGH SCHOOL
81ST QUARTER:
ACTIVATE!!

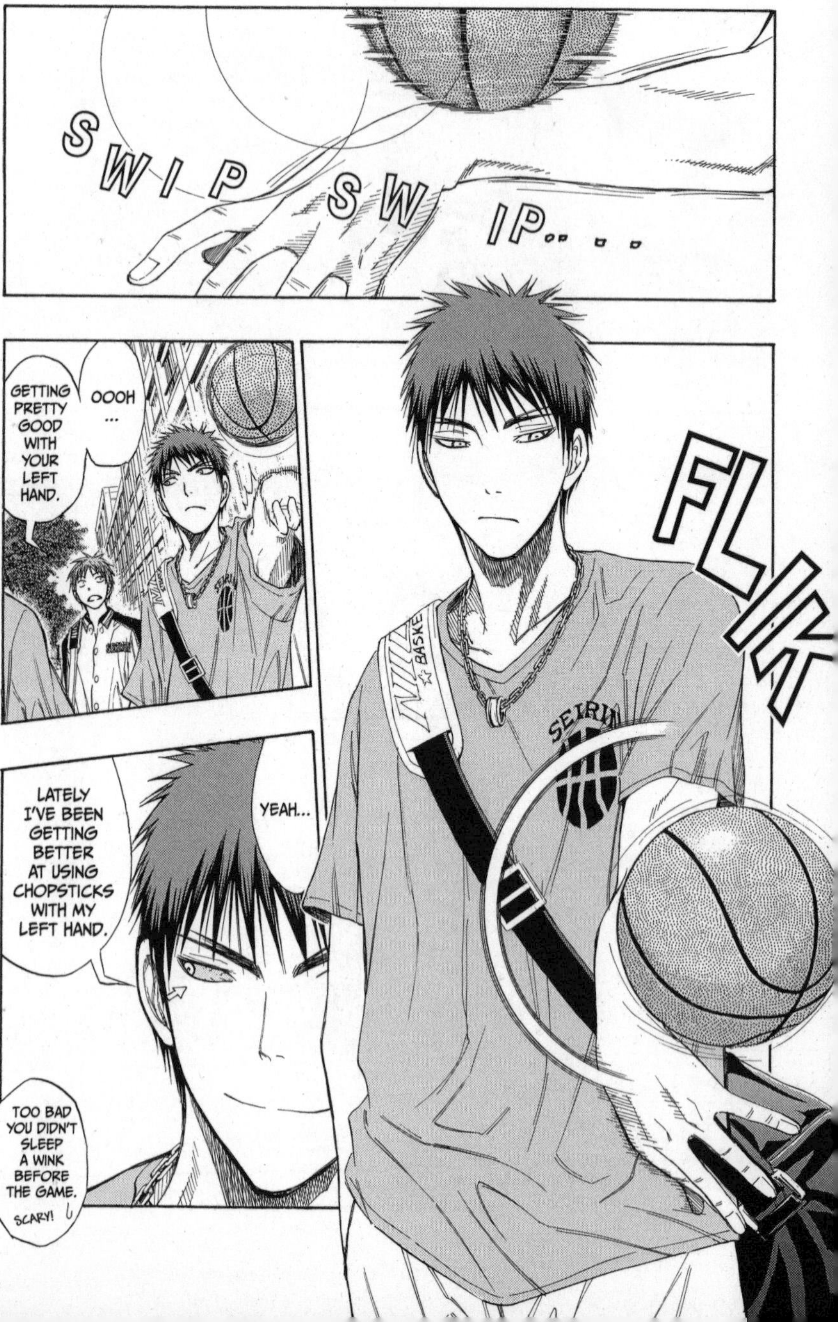
SWIP SWIP...
FLIK
OOOH ...
GETTING PRETTY GOOD WITH YOUR LEFT HAND.
YEAH...
LATELY I'VE BEEN GETTING BETTER AT USING CHOPSTICKS WITH MY LEFT HAND.
TOO BAD YOU DIDN'T SLEEP A WINK BEFORE THE GAME.
SCARY!

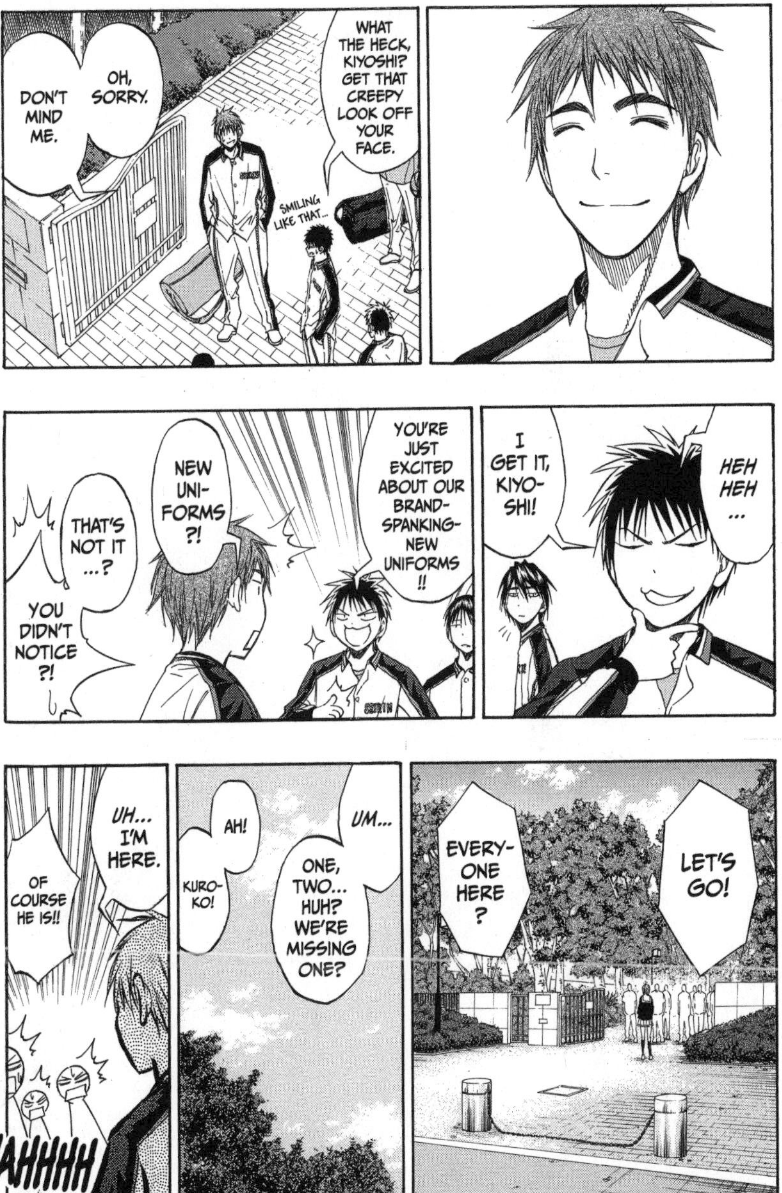
WHAT THE HECK, KIYOSHI? GET THAT CREEPY LOOK OFF YOUR FACE.
SMILING LIKE THAT...
OH, SORRY.
DON'T MIND ME.
HEH HEH ...
I GET IT, KIYO-SHI!
YOU'RE JUST EXCITED ABOUT OUR BRAND-SPANKING-NEW UNIFORMS !!
NEW UNI-FORMS ?!
THAT'S NOT IT ...?
YOU DIDN'T NOTICE ?!
LET'S GO!
EVERY-ONE HERE ?
UM...
ONE, TWO... HUH? WE'RE MISSING ONE?
AH!
KURO-KO!
UH... I'M HERE.
OF COURSE HE IS!!
WAHHHH

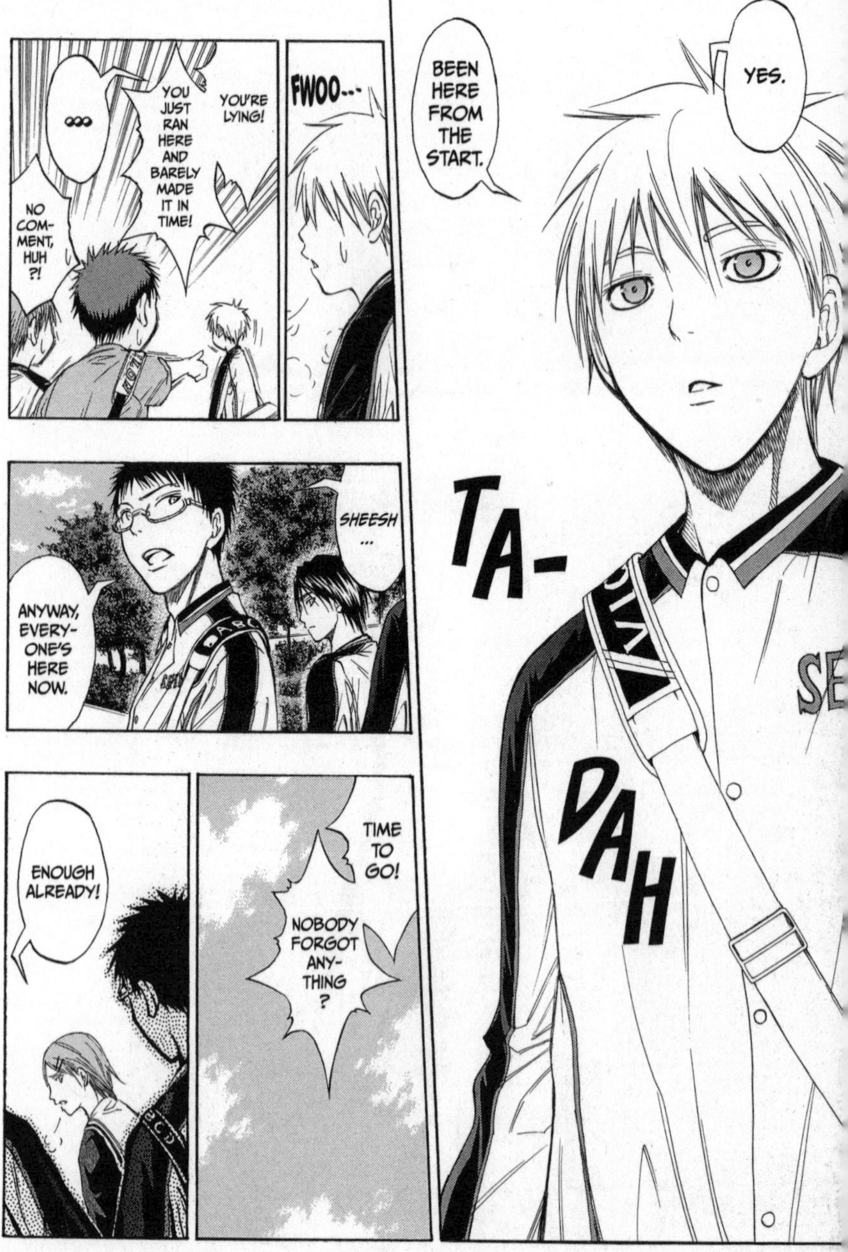
YES.
BEEN HERE FROM THE START.
TA-DAH
FWOO...
YOU'RE LYING!
YOU JUST RAN HERE AND BARELY MADE IT IN TIME!
...
NO COMMENT, HUH?!
SHEESH...
ANYWAY, EVERYONE'S HERE NOW.
TIME TO GO!
NOBODY FORGOT ANYTHING?
ENOUGH ALREADY!

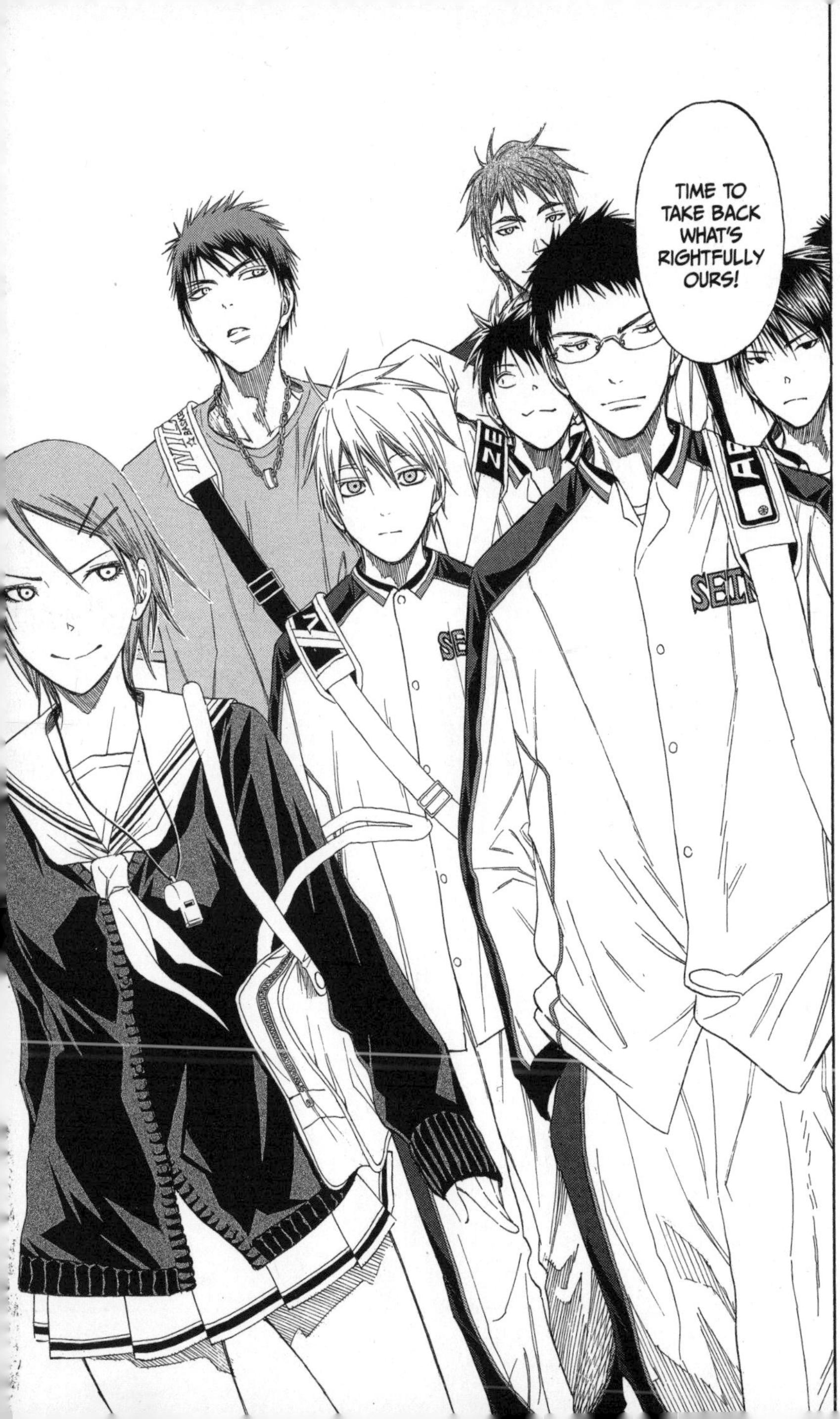
TIME TO TAKE BACK WHAT'S RIGHTFULLY OURS!

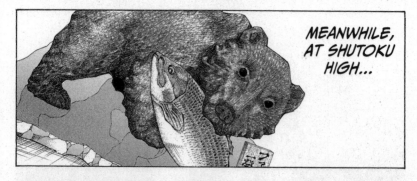

MEANWHILE, AT SHUTOKU HIGH...

RRIP...

SHF...

RIGHT.

HEY, SHIN-CHAN. THE UPPERCLASSMEN ARE WAITING ON US!

BZZZ...

KLIK...

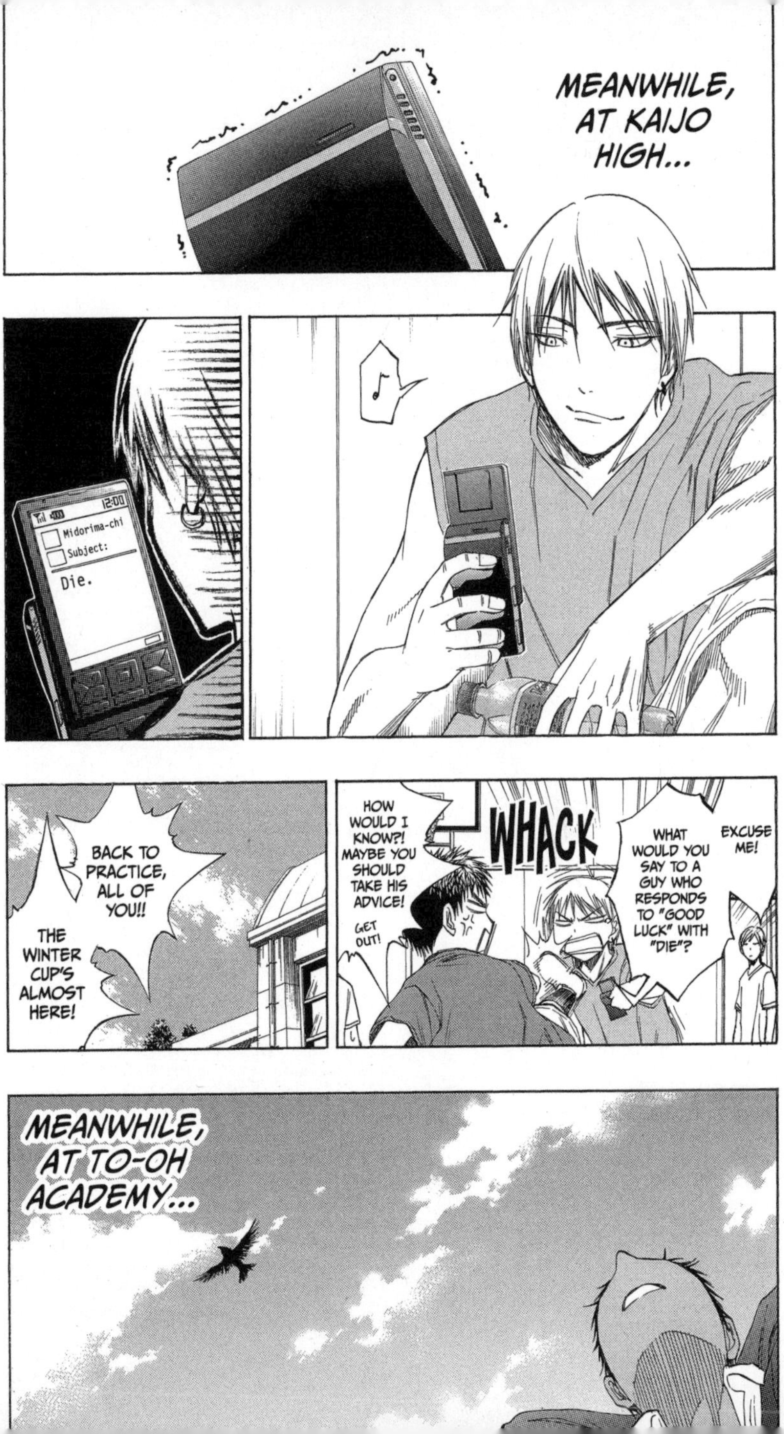
MEANWHILE, AT KAIJO HIGH...
♪
12:00
Midorima-chi
Subject:
Die.
EXCUSE ME!
WHAT WOULD YOU SAY TO A GUY WHO RESPONDS TO "GOOD LUCK" WITH "DIE"?
WHACK
HOW WOULD I KNOW?! MAYBE YOU SHOULD TAKE HIS ADVICE!
GET OUT!
BACK TO PRACTICE, ALL OF YOU!!
THE WINTER CUP'S ALMOST HERE!
MEANWHILE, AT TO-OH ACADEMY...

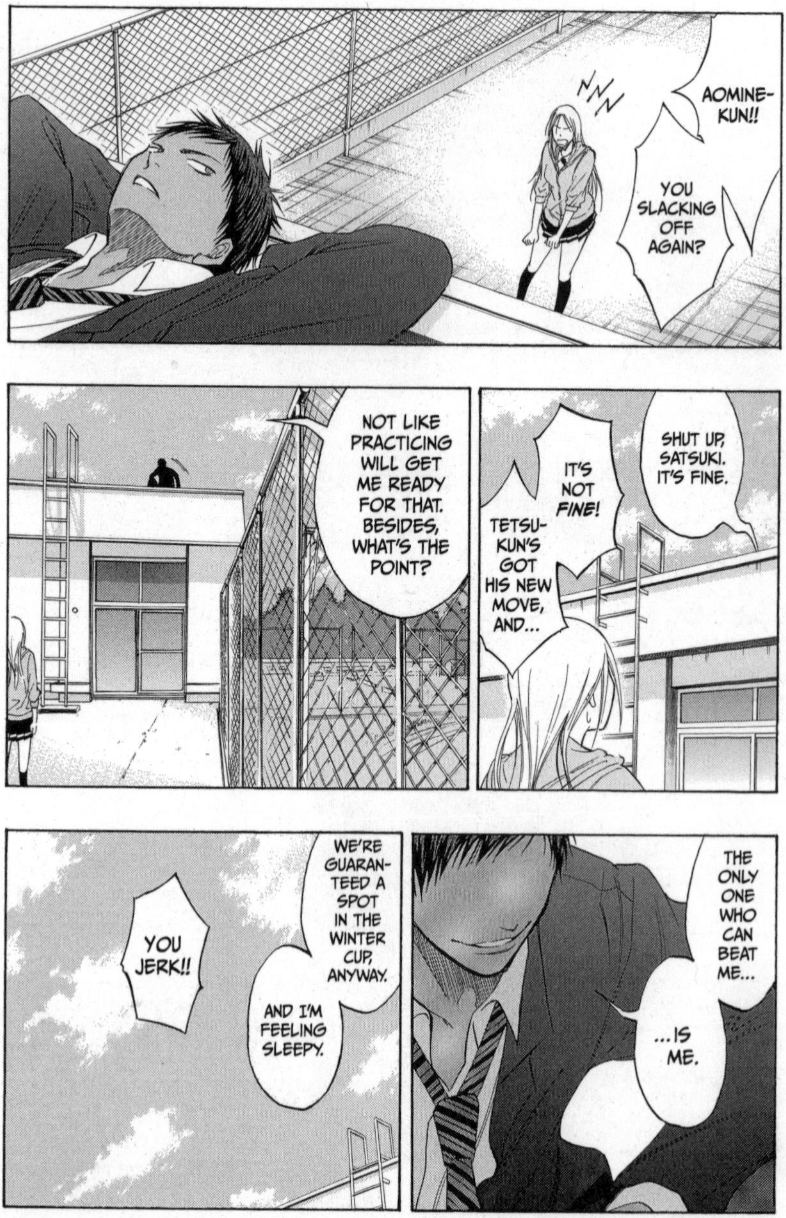
AOMINE-KUN!!
YOU SLACKING OFF AGAIN?
NNN
SHUT UP, SATSUKI. IT'S FINE.
IT'S NOT *FINE*!
TETSU-KUN'S GOT HIS NEW MOVE, AND...
NOT LIKE PRACTICING WILL GET ME READY FOR THAT. BESIDES, WHAT'S THE POINT?
THE ONLY ONE WHO CAN BEAT ME...
...IS ME.
WE'RE GUARANTEED A SPOT IN THE WINTER CUP, ANYWAY.
AND I'M FEELING SLEEPY.
YOU JERK!!

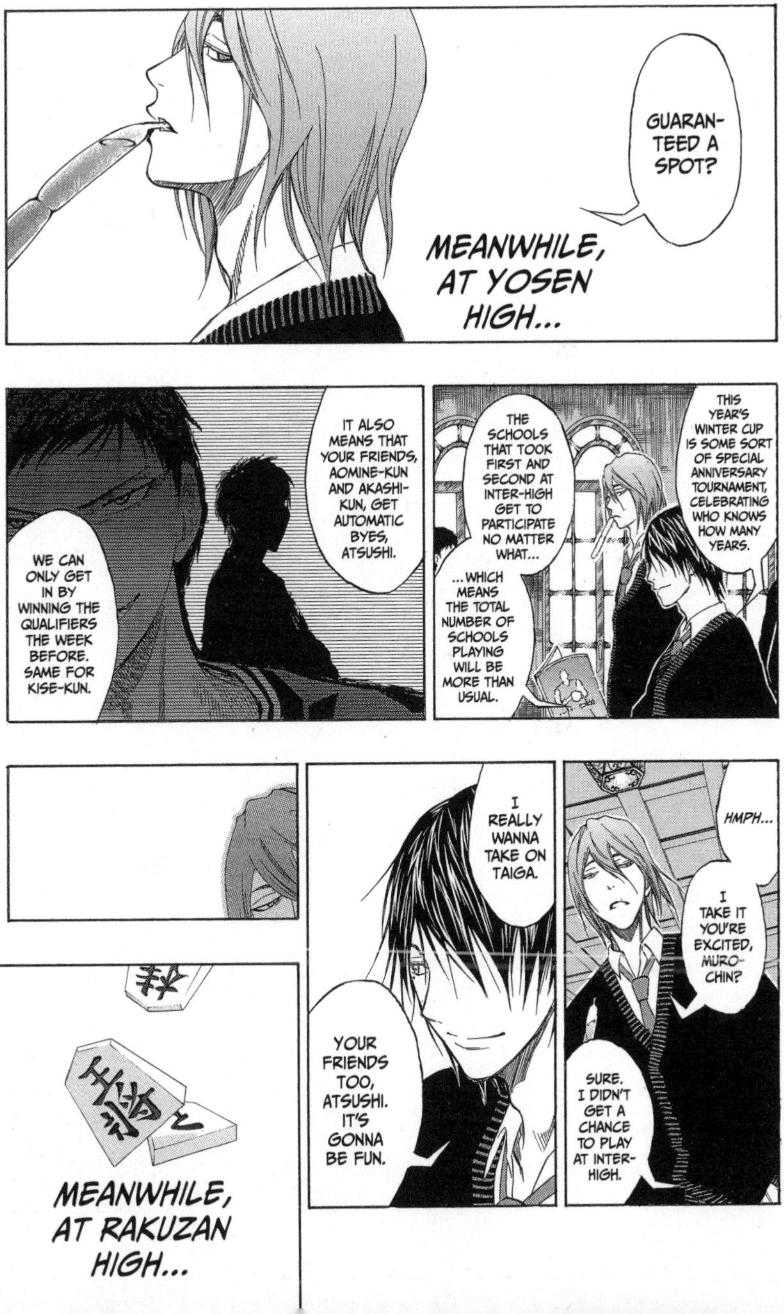
GUARAN-TEED A SPOT?
MEANWHILE, AT YOSEN HIGH...
THIS YEAR'S WINTER CUP IS SOME SORT OF SPECIAL ANNIVERSARY TOURNAMENT, CELEBRATING WHO KNOWS HOW MANY YEARS.
THE SCHOOLS THAT TOOK FIRST AND SECOND AT INTER-HIGH GET TO PARTICIPATE NO MATTER WHAT...
...WHICH MEANS THE TOTAL NUMBER OF SCHOOLS PLAYING WILL BE MORE THAN USUAL.
IT ALSO MEANS THAT YOUR FRIENDS, AOMINE-KUN AND AKASHI-KUN, GET AUTOMATIC BYES, ATSUSHI.
WE CAN ONLY GET IN BY WINNING THE QUALIFIERS THE WEEK BEFORE. SAME FOR KISE-KUN.
HMPH...
I TAKE IT YOU'RE EXCITED, MURO-CHIN?
SURE. I DIDN'T GET A CHANCE TO PLAY AT INTER-HIGH.
I REALLY WANNA TAKE ON TAIGA.
YOUR FRIENDS TOO, ATSUSHI. IT'S GONNA BE FUN.
MEANWHILE, AT RAKUZAN HIGH...

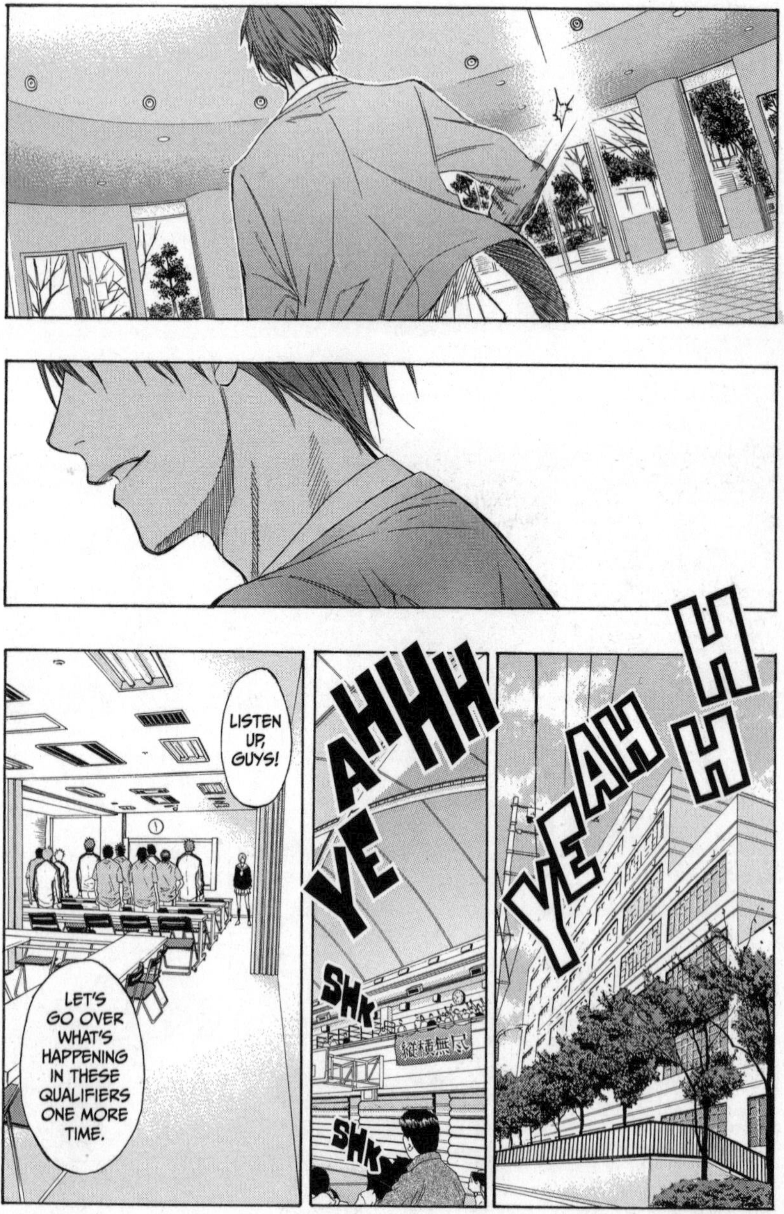
YEAH HHH
YEAHHHH
SHK
縦横無尽
SHK
LISTEN UP, GUYS!
LET'S GO OVER WHAT'S HAPPENING IN THESE QUALIFIERS ONE MORE TIME.

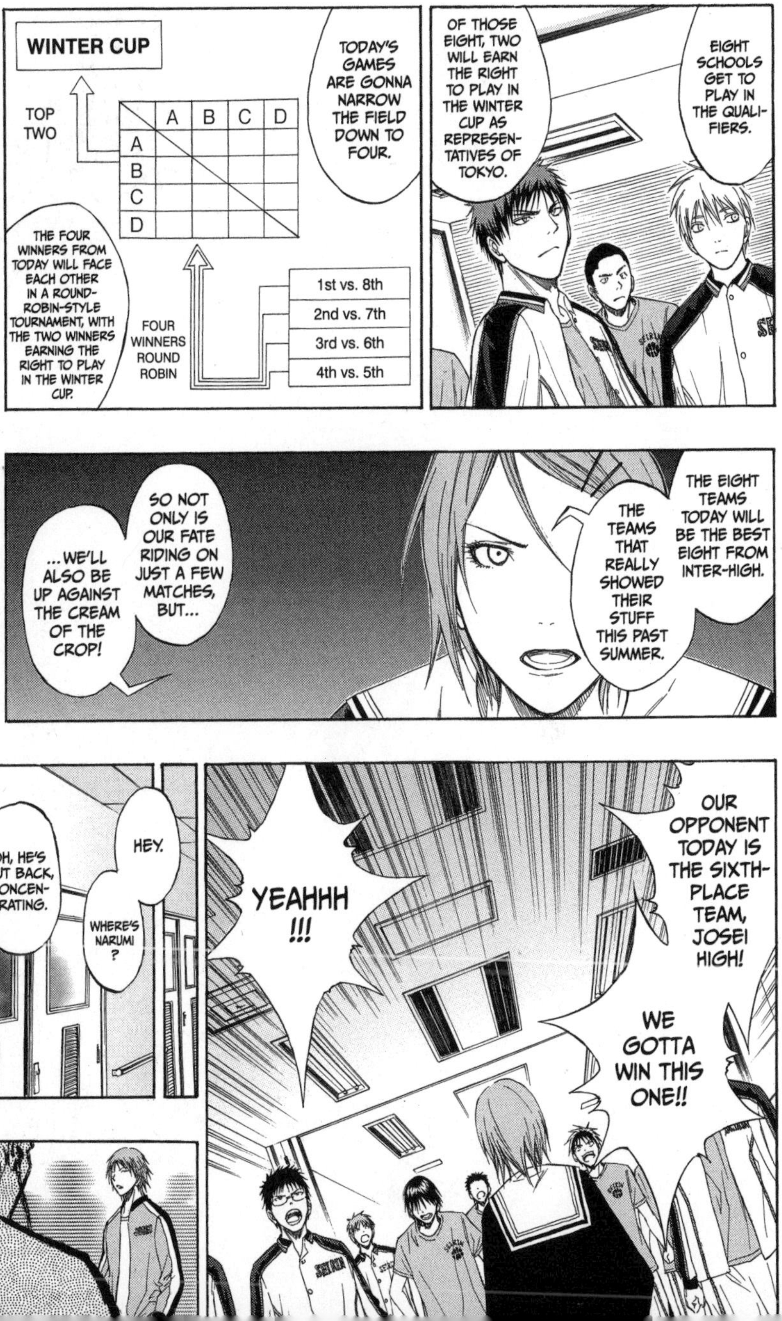
EIGHT SCHOOLS GET TO PLAY IN THE QUALIFIERS.
OF THOSE EIGHT, TWO WILL EARN THE RIGHT TO PLAY IN THE WINTER CUP AS REPRESENTATIVES OF TOKYO.
TODAY'S GAMES ARE GONNA NARROW THE FIELD DOWN TO FOUR.
WINTER CUP
TOP TWO
A B C D
A
B
C
D
FOUR WINNERS ROUND ROBIN
1st vs. 8th
2nd vs. 7th
3rd vs. 6th
4th vs. 5th
THE FOUR WINNERS FROM TODAY WILL FACE EACH OTHER IN A ROUND-ROBIN-STYLE TOURNAMENT, WITH THE TWO WINNERS EARNING THE RIGHT TO PLAY IN THE WINTER CUP.
THE EIGHT TEAMS TODAY WILL BE THE BEST EIGHT FROM INTER-HIGH.
THE TEAMS THAT REALLY SHOWED THEIR STUFF THIS PAST SUMMER.
SO NOT ONLY IS OUR FATE RIDING ON JUST A FEW MATCHES, BUT...
...WE'LL ALSO BE UP AGAINST THE CREAM OF THE CROP!
OUR OPPONENT TODAY IS THE SIXTH-PLACE TEAM, JOSEI HIGH!
WE GOTTA WIN THIS ONE!!
YEAHHH !!!
HEY.
WHERE'S NARUMI ?
OH, HE'S OUT BACK, CONCENTRATING.

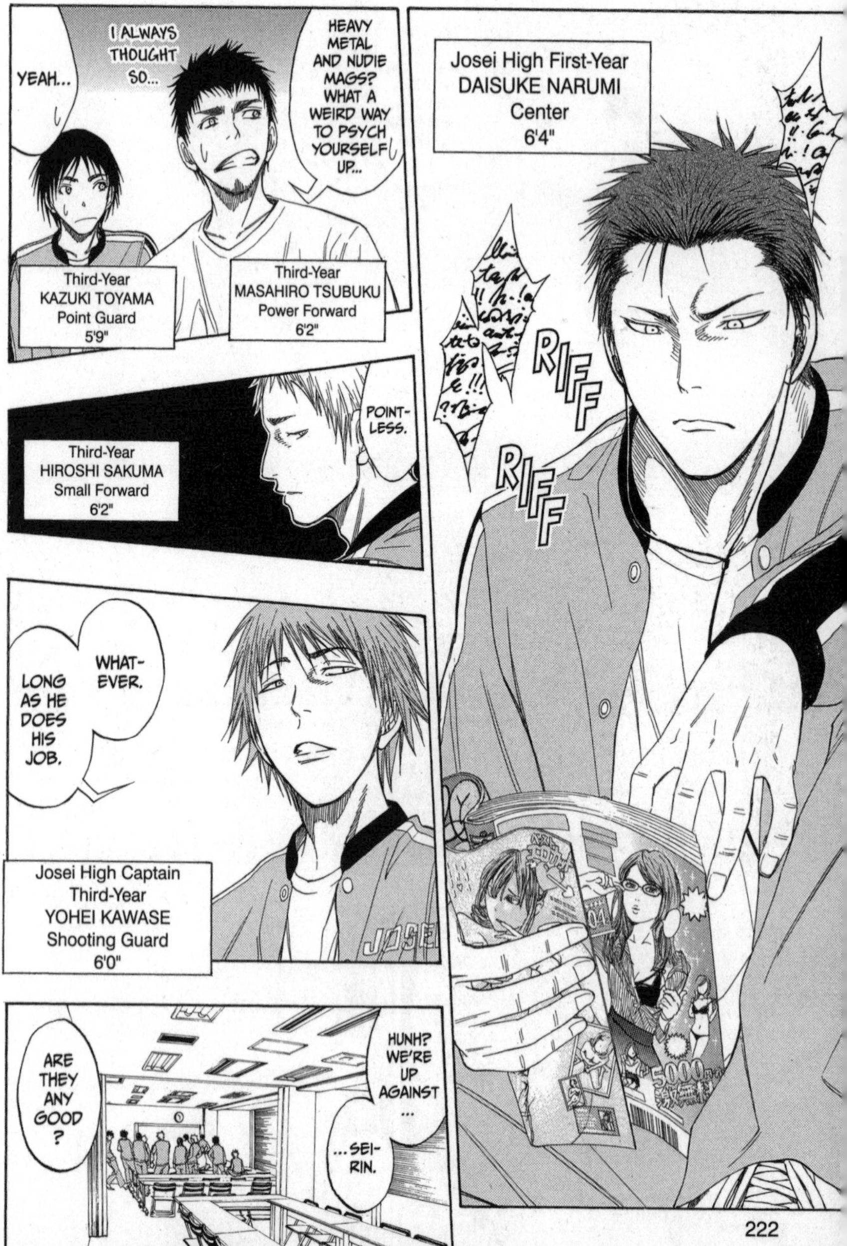
Josei High First-Year
DAISUKE NARUMI
Center
6'4"
RIFF
RIFF
HEAVY METAL AND NUDIE MAGS? WHAT A WEIRD WAY TO PSYCH YOURSELF UP...
I ALWAYS THOUGHT SO...
YEAH...
Third-Year
MASAHIRO TSUBUKU
Power Forward
6'2"
Third-Year
KAZUKI TOYAMA
Point Guard
5'9"
POINT-LESS.
Third-Year
HIROSHI SAKUMA
Small Forward
6'2"
WHAT-EVER.
LONG AS HE DOES HIS JOB.
Josei High Captain
Third-Year
YOHEI KAWASE
Shooting Guard
6'0"
HUNH? WE'RE UP AGAINST ...
...SEI-RIN.
ARE THEY ANY GOOD?

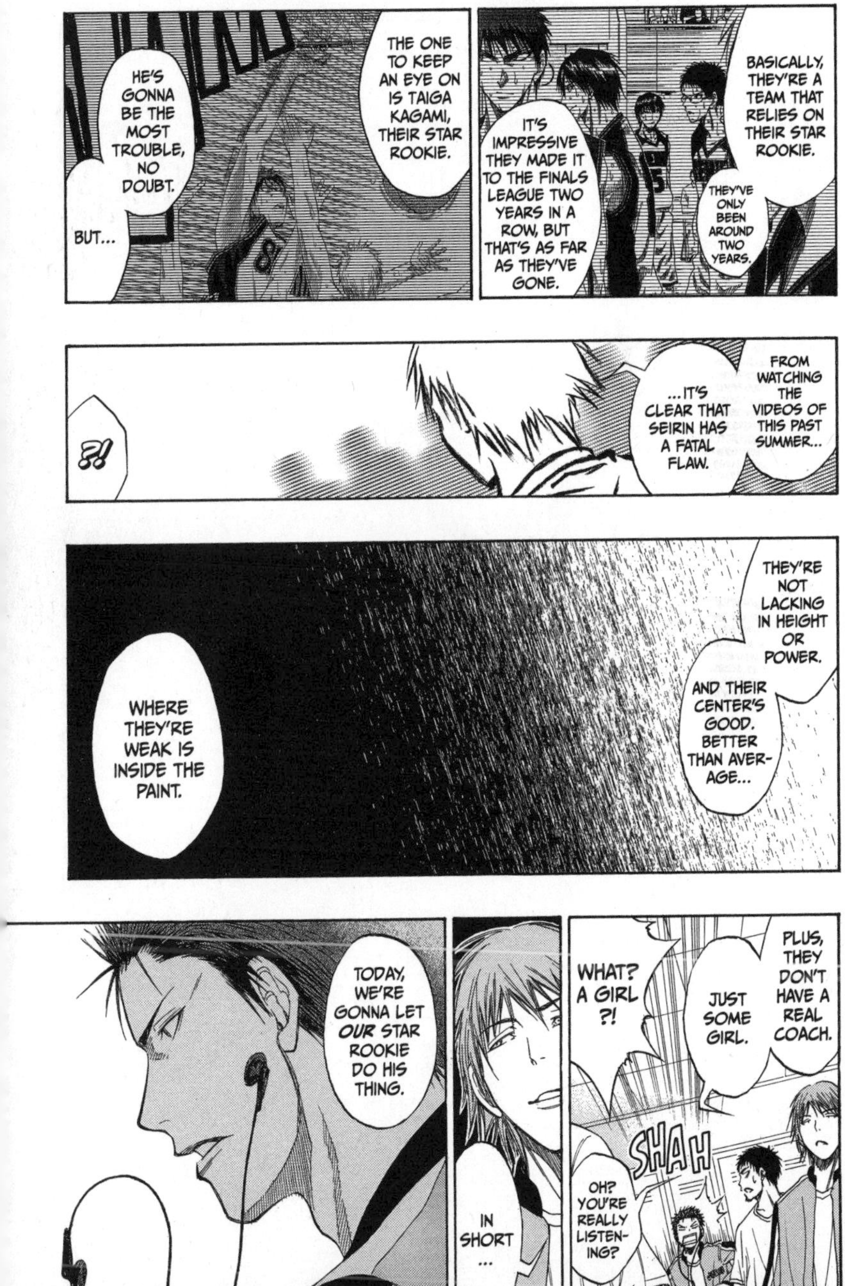
BASICALLY, THEY'RE A TEAM THAT RELIES ON THEIR STAR ROOKIE.
THEY'VE ONLY BEEN AROUND TWO YEARS.
IT'S IMPRESSIVE THEY MADE IT TO THE FINALS LEAGUE TWO YEARS IN A ROW, BUT THAT'S AS FAR AS THEY'VE GONE.
THE ONE TO KEEP AN EYE ON IS TAIGA KAGAMI, THEIR STAR ROOKIE.
HE'S GONNA BE THE MOST TROUBLE, NO DOUBT.
BUT...
FROM WATCHING THE VIDEOS OF THIS PAST SUMMER...
...IT'S CLEAR THAT SEIRIN HAS A FATAL FLAW.
?!
THEY'RE NOT LACKING IN HEIGHT OR POWER.
AND THEIR CENTER'S GOOD. BETTER THAN AVER-AGE...
WHERE THEY'RE WEAK IS INSIDE THE PAINT.
PLUS, THEY DON'T HAVE A REAL COACH.
JUST SOME GIRL.
WHAT? A GIRL?!
SHAH
OH? YOU'RE REALLY LISTEN-ING?
IN SHORT...
TODAY, WE'RE GONNA LET *OUR* STAR ROOKIE DO HIS THING.

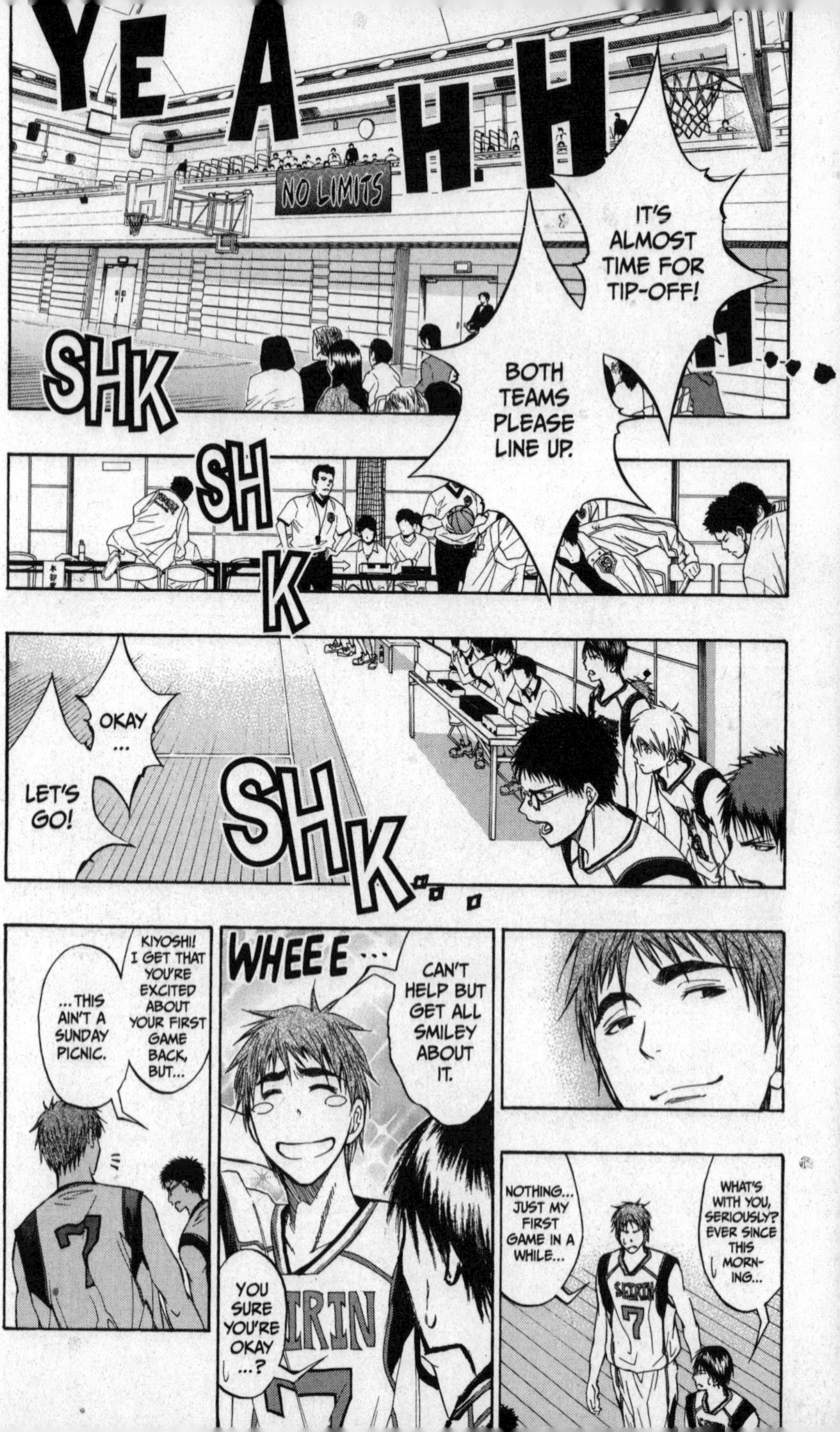
YEAHHH...
IT'S ALMOST TIME FOR TIP-OFF!
BOTH TEAMS PLEASE LINE UP.
SHK
SHK
OKAY... LET'S GO!
SHK...
WHAT'S WITH YOU, SERIOUSLY? EVER SINCE THIS MORNING...
NOTHING... JUST MY FIRST GAME IN A WHILE...
CAN'T HELP BUT GET ALL SMILEY ABOUT IT.
WHEEE...
YOU SURE YOU'RE OKAY...?
KIYOSHI! I GET THAT YOU'RE EXCITED ABOUT YOUR FIRST GAME BACK, BUT...
...THIS AIN'T A SUNDAY PICNIC.

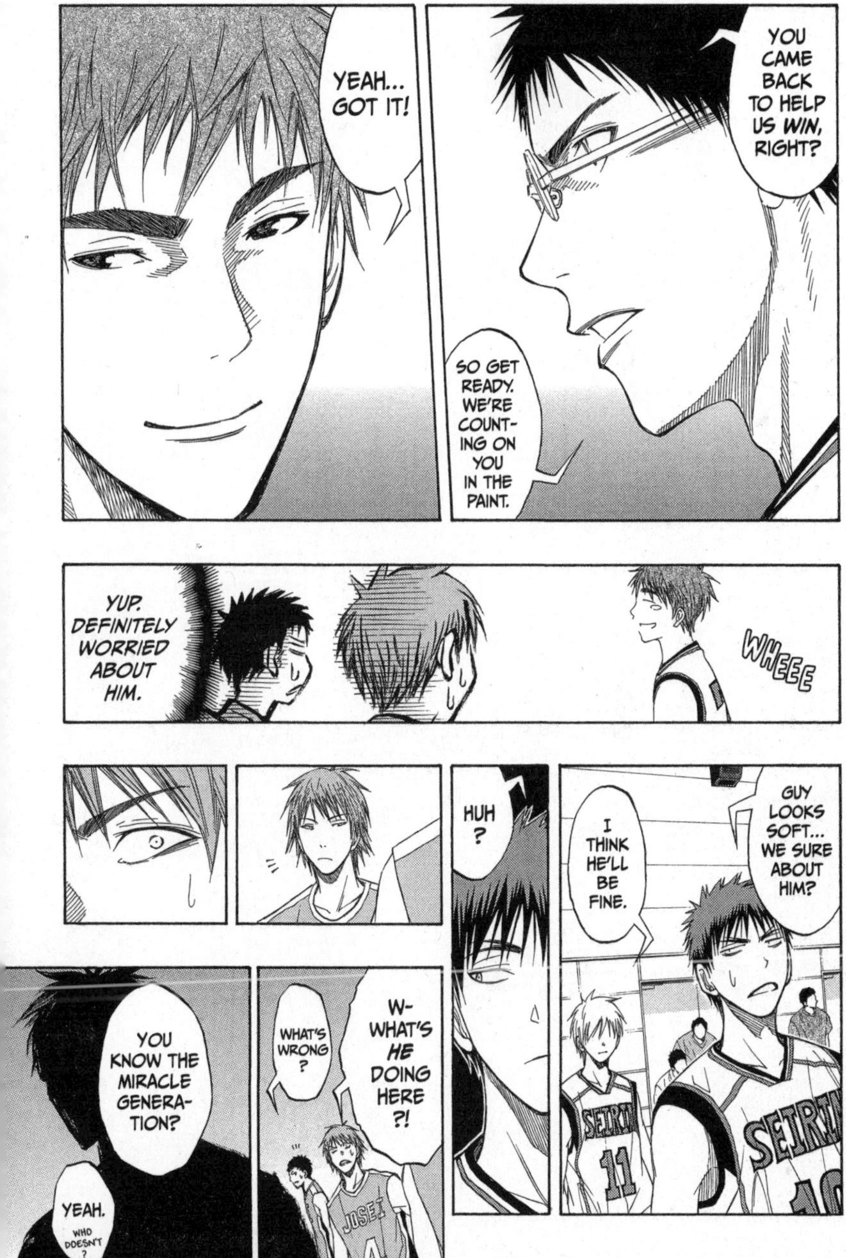
YOU CAME BACK TO HELP US *WIN*, RIGHT?
SO GET READY. WE'RE COUNTING ON YOU IN THE PAINT.
YEAH... GOT IT!
WHEEE
YUP. DEFINITELY WORRIED ABOUT HIM.
GUY LOOKS SOFT... WE SURE ABOUT HIM?
I THINK HE'LL BE FINE.
HUH?
W-WHAT'S *HE* DOING HERE?!
WHAT'S WRONG?
YOU KNOW THE MIRACLE GENERATION?
YEAH.
WHO DOESN'T?

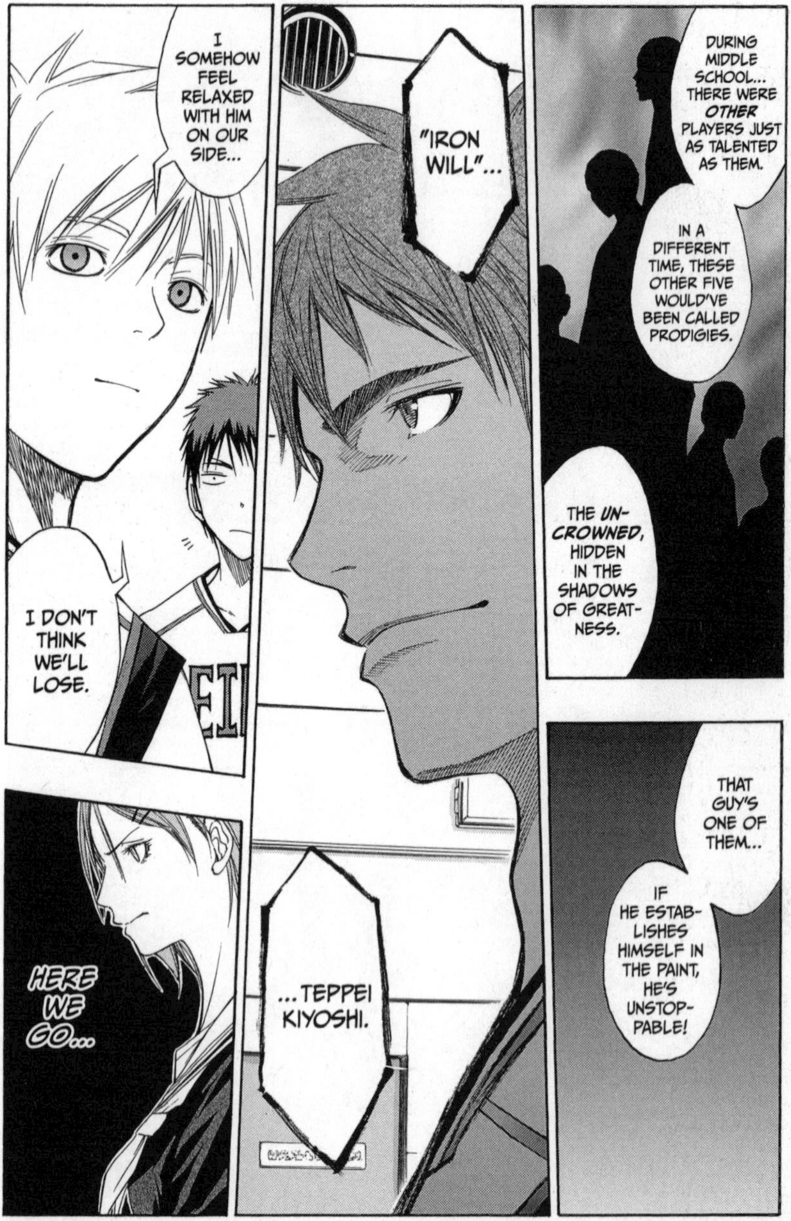
DURING MIDDLE SCHOOL... THERE WERE *OTHER* PLAYERS JUST AS TALENTED AS THEM.
IN A DIFFERENT TIME, THESE OTHER FIVE WOULD'VE BEEN CALLED PRODIGIES.
THE *UNCROWNED*, HIDDEN IN THE SHADOWS OF GREATNESS.
THAT GUY'S ONE OF THEM...
IF HE ESTABLISHES HIMSELF IN THE PAINT, HE'S UNSTOPPABLE!
"IRON WILL"...
...TEPPEI KIYOSHI.
I SOMEHOW FEEL RELAXED WITH HIM ON OUR SIDE...
I DON'T THINK WE'LL LOSE.
HERE WE GO...

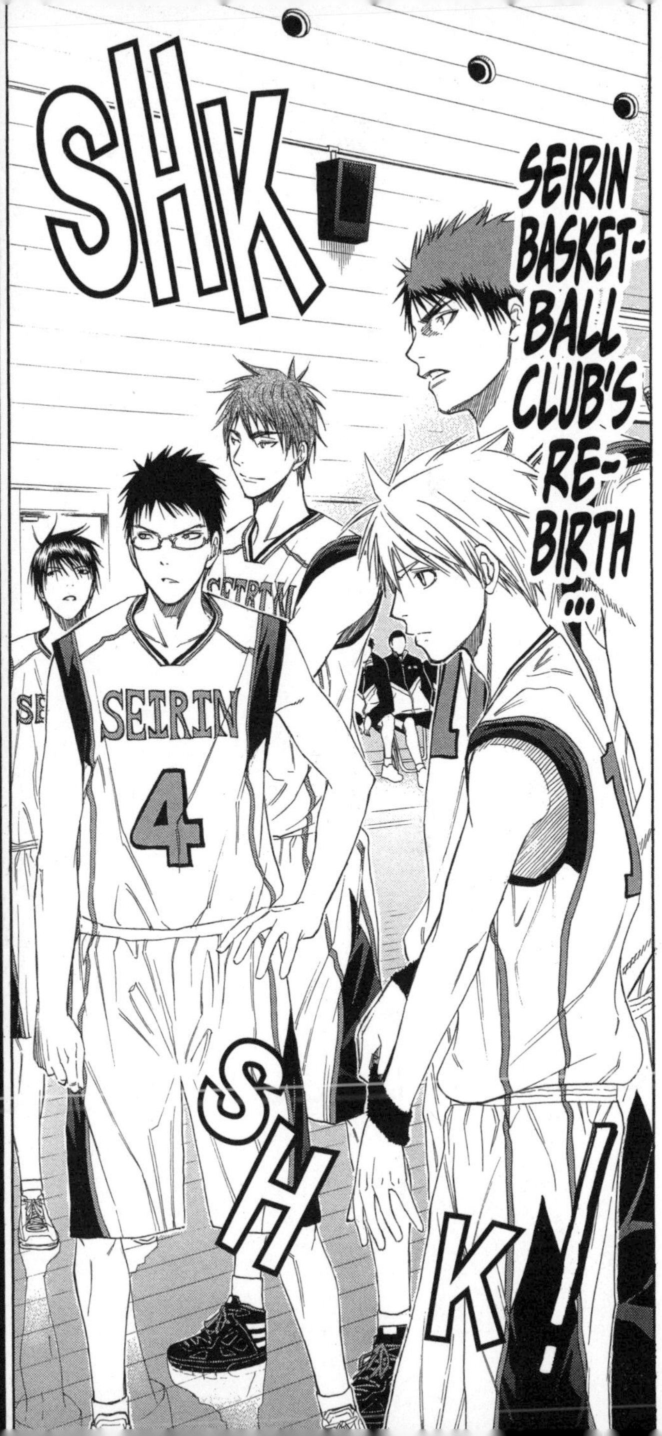
SEIRIN BASKET-BALL CLUB'S RE-BIRTH...
SHK
SHK!

KUROKO'S BASKETBALL BLOOPERS

TAKE 1

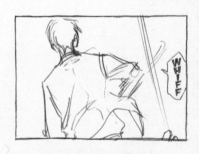

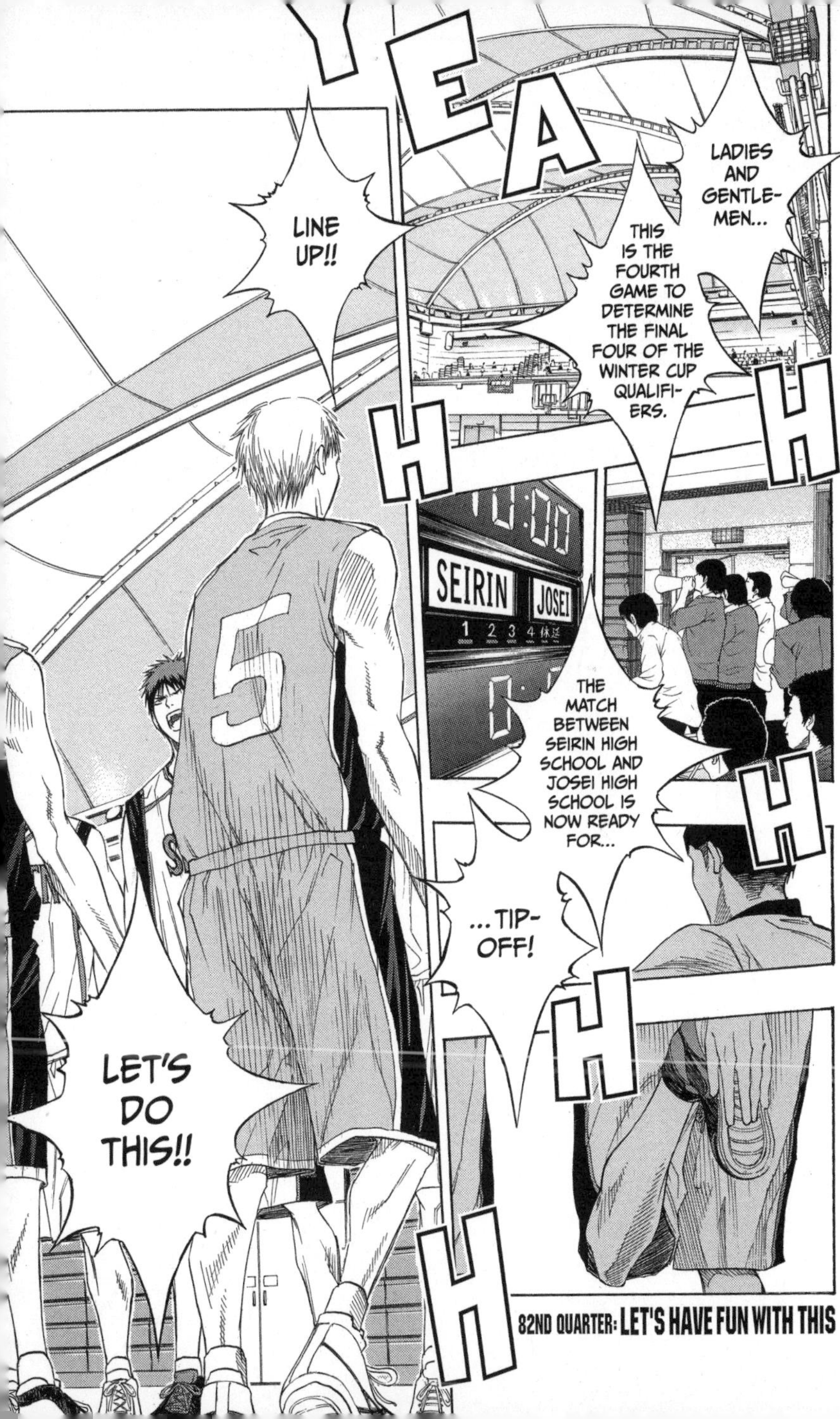
YEAHHHHHH
LADIES AND GENTLE-MEN...
THIS IS THE FOURTH GAME TO DETERMINE THE FINAL FOUR OF THE WINTER CUP QUALIFI-ERS.
SEIRIN
JOSEI
THE MATCH BETWEEN SEIRIN HIGH SCHOOL AND JOSEI HIGH SCHOOL IS NOW READY FOR...
...TIP-OFF!
LINE UP!!
LET'S DO THIS!!

82ND QUARTER: LET'S HAVE FUN WITH THIS

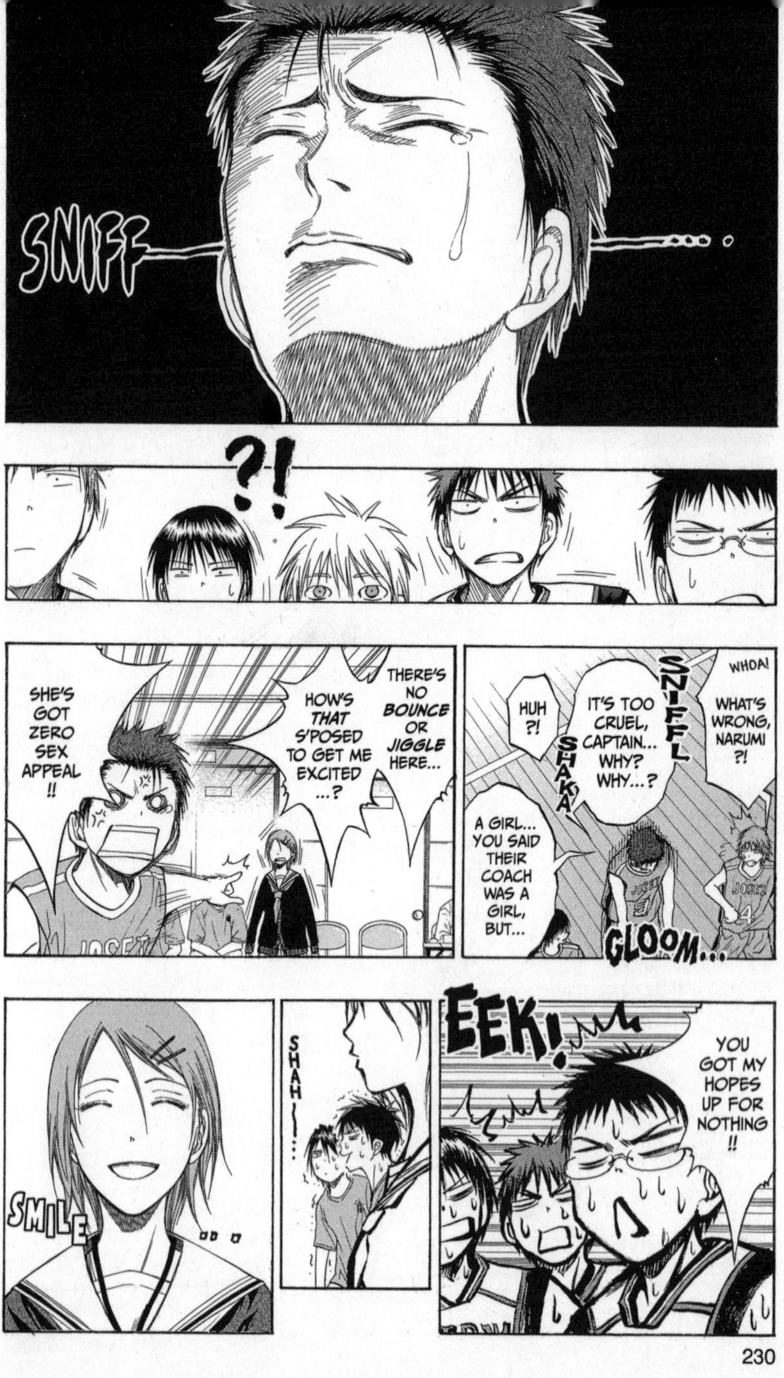
SNIFF
?!
WHOA!
WHAT'S WRONG, NARUMI?!
SNIFFL
IT'S TOO CRUEL, CAPTAIN... WHY? WHY...?
SHAKA
HUH?!
A GIRL... YOU SAID THEIR COACH WAS A GIRL, BUT...
GLOOM...
THERE'S NO BOUNCE OR JIGGLE HERE...
HOW'S THAT S'POSED TO GET ME EXCITED...?
SHE'S GOT ZERO SEX APPEAL!!
EEK!
YOU GOT MY HOPES UP FOR NOTHING!!
SHAH...
SMILE

KILL...
...HIM...
...DEAD!
♡
RRMBBB...
WAHH
GOT IT?!
JOLT!!
YES, MA'AM !!
EVERYONE GOT IT? ONE MORE REASON NOT TO LOSE HERE.
WE'RE DEAD MEAT IF WE LOSE TO THIS GUY...
Y-YEAH.
SHK...
AND HERE'S THE TIP-OFF!
SKF...

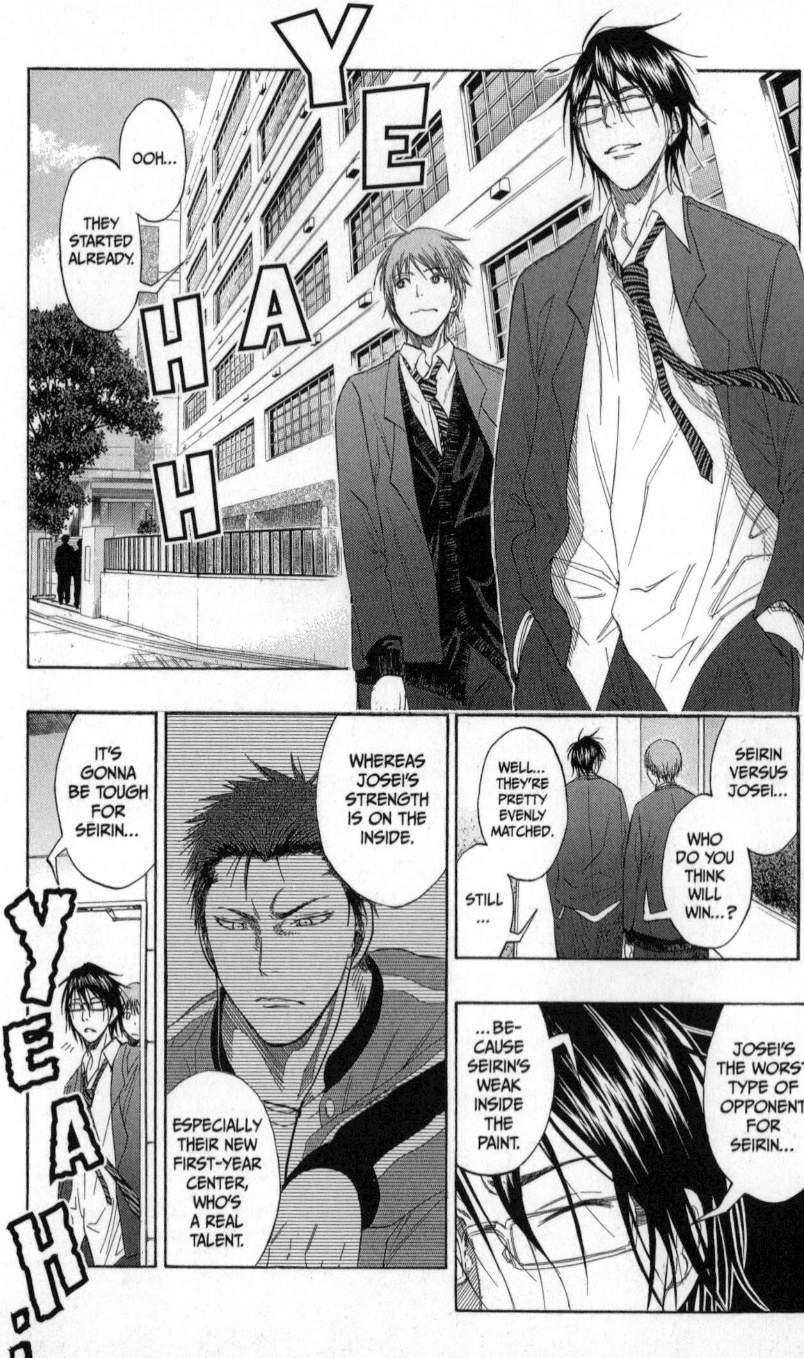
YEAHH
OOH...
THEY STARTED ALREADY.
SEIRIN VERSUS JOSEI...
WHO DO YOU THINK WILL WIN...?
WELL... THEY'RE PRETTY EVENLY MATCHED.
STILL ...
JOSEI'S THE WORST TYPE OF OPPONENT FOR SEIRIN...
...BE-CAUSE SEIRIN'S WEAK INSIDE THE PAINT.
WHEREAS JOSEI'S STRENGTH IS ON THE INSIDE.
ESPECIALLY THEIR NEW FIRST-YEAR CENTER, WHO'S A REAL TALENT.
IT'S GONNA BE TOUGH FOR SEIRIN...
YEAH..!

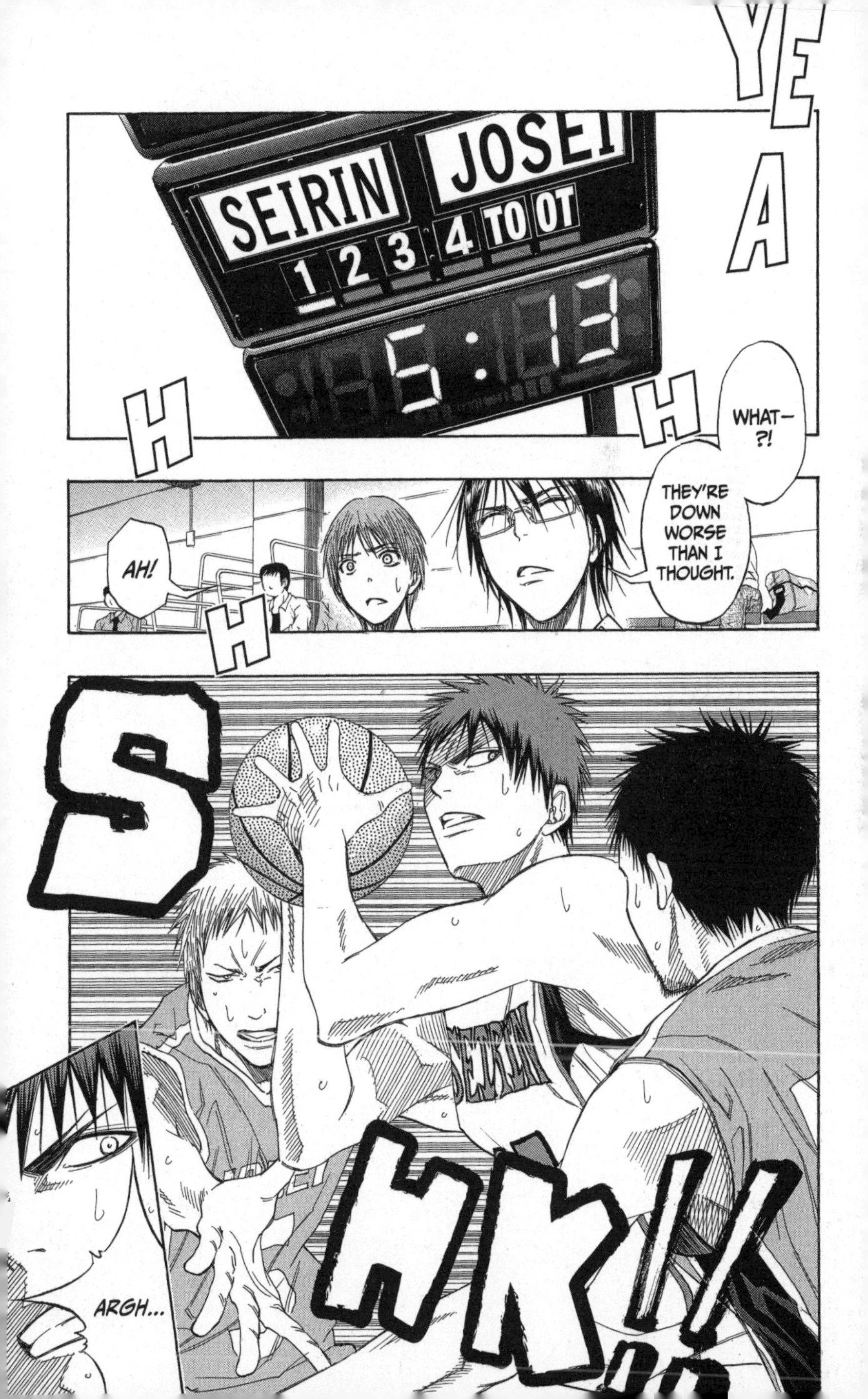
YEAHHH
SEIRIN
JOSEI
1 2 3 4 TO OT
5:13
WHAT—?!
THEY'RE DOWN WORSE THAN I THOUGHT.
AH!
SHKK
ARGH...

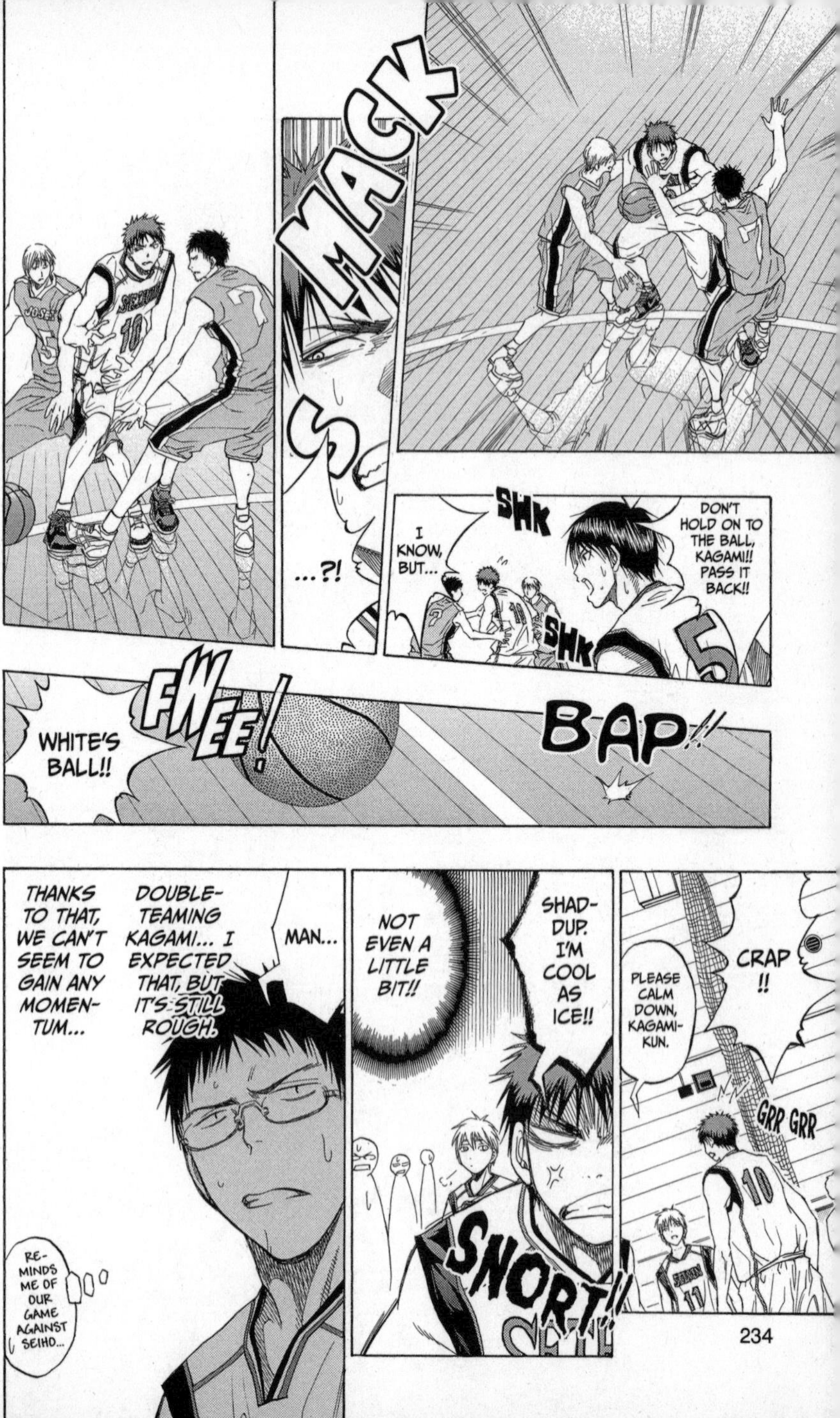
SMACK
DON'T HOLD ON TO THE BALL, KAGAMI!! PASS IT BACK!!
SHK
I KNOW, BUT...
SHK
...?!
BAP!!
FWEE!
WHITE'S BALL!!
CRAP!!
PLEASE CALM DOWN, KAGAMI-KUN.
GRR GRR
SHAD-DUP. I'M COOL AS ICE!!
NOT EVEN A LITTLE BIT!!
SNORT!!
MAN...
DOUBLE-TEAMING KAGAMI... I EXPECTED THAT, BUT IT'S STILL ROUGH.
THANKS TO THAT, WE CAN'T SEEM TO GAIN ANY MOMENTUM...
REMINDS ME OF OUR GAME AGAINST SEIHO...

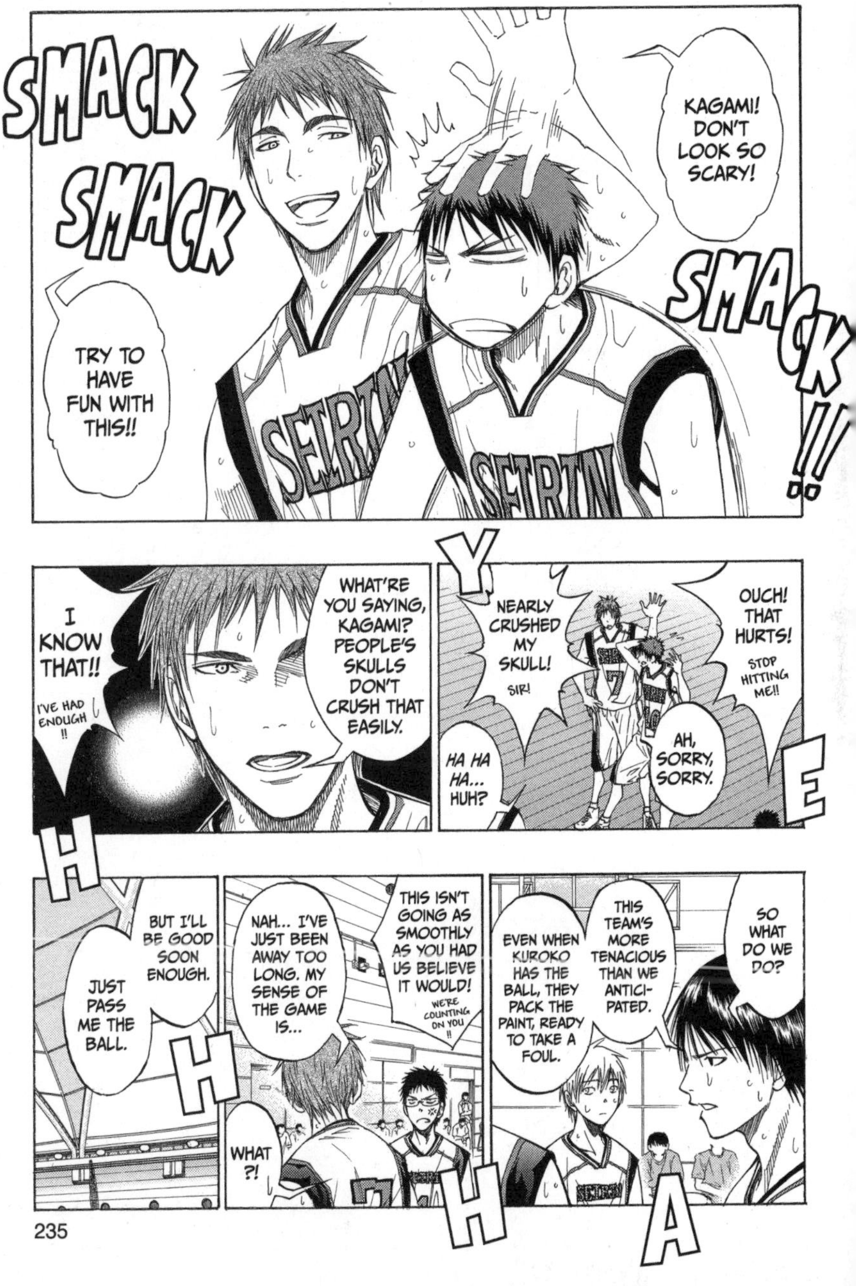

KAGAMI! DON'T LOOK SO SCARY!
SMACK!!
SMACK SMACK
TRY TO HAVE FUN WITH THIS!!
Y
OUCH! THAT HURTS!
STOP HITTING ME!!
AH, SORRY, SORRY.
NEARLY CRUSHED MY SKULL!
SIR!
HA HA HA... HUH?
E
WHAT'RE YOU SAYING, KAGAMI? PEOPLE'S SKULLS DON'T CRUSH THAT EASILY.
I KNOW THAT!!
I'VE HAD ENOUGH!!
H
SO WHAT DO WE DO?
THIS TEAM'S MORE TENACIOUS THAN WE ANTICI-PATED.
EVEN WHEN KUROKO HAS THE BALL, THEY PACK THE PAINT, READY TO TAKE A FOUL.
A
THIS ISN'T GOING AS SMOOTHLY AS YOU HAD US BELIEVE IT WOULD!
WE'RE COUNTING ON YOU!!
NAH... I'VE JUST BEEN AWAY TOO LONG. MY SENSE OF THE GAME IS...
WHAT?!
H
BUT I'LL BE GOOD SOON ENOUGH.
JUST PASS ME THE BALL.
H

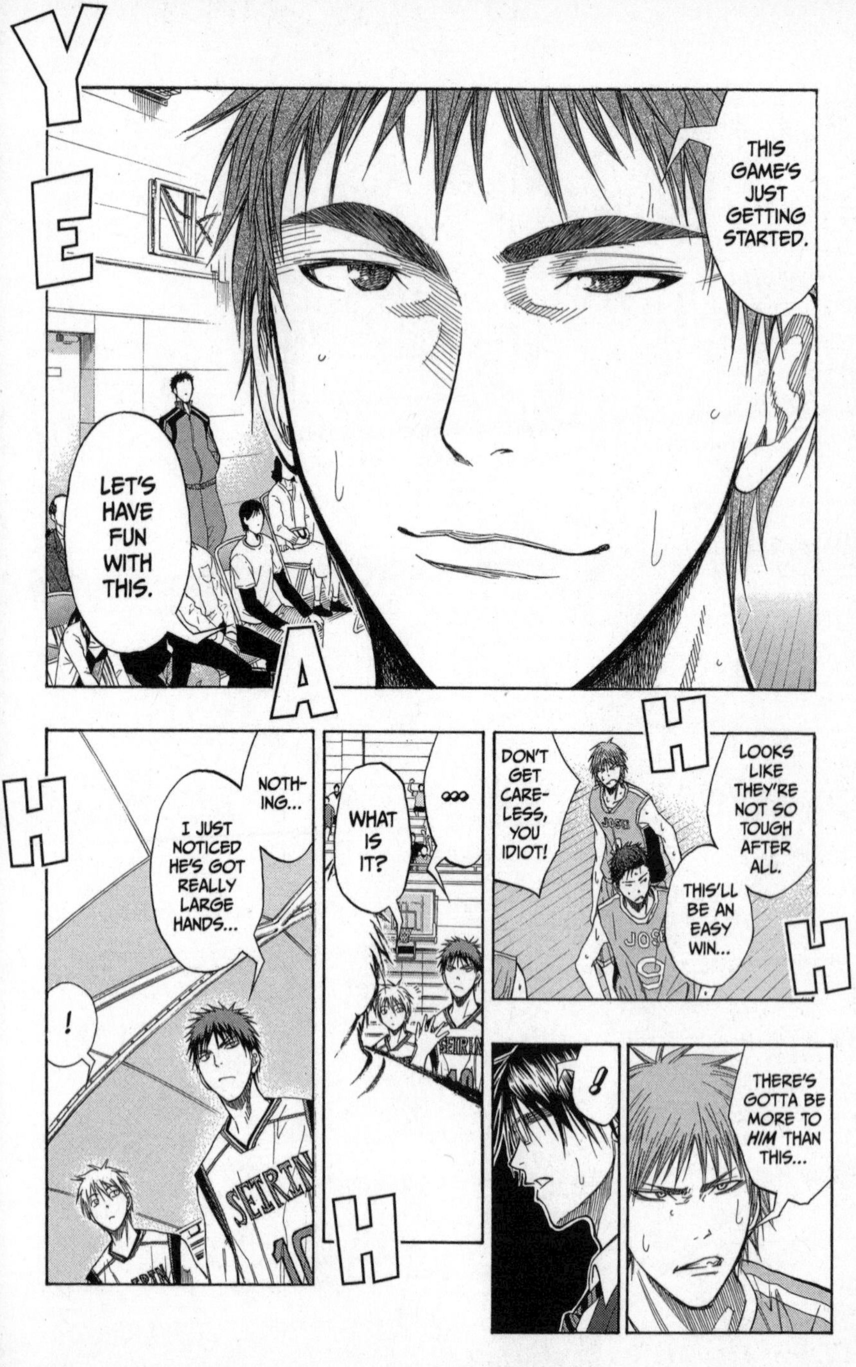
THIS GAME'S JUST GETTING STARTED.
LET'S HAVE FUN WITH THIS.
YEAHHHH
LOOKS LIKE THEY'RE NOT SO TOUGH AFTER ALL.
THIS'LL BE AN EASY WIN...
DON'T GET CARELESS, YOU IDIOT!
THERE'S GOTTA BE MORE TO *HIM* THAN THIS...
!
...
WHAT IS IT?
NOTHING...
I JUST NOTICED HE'S GOT REALLY LARGE HANDS...
!

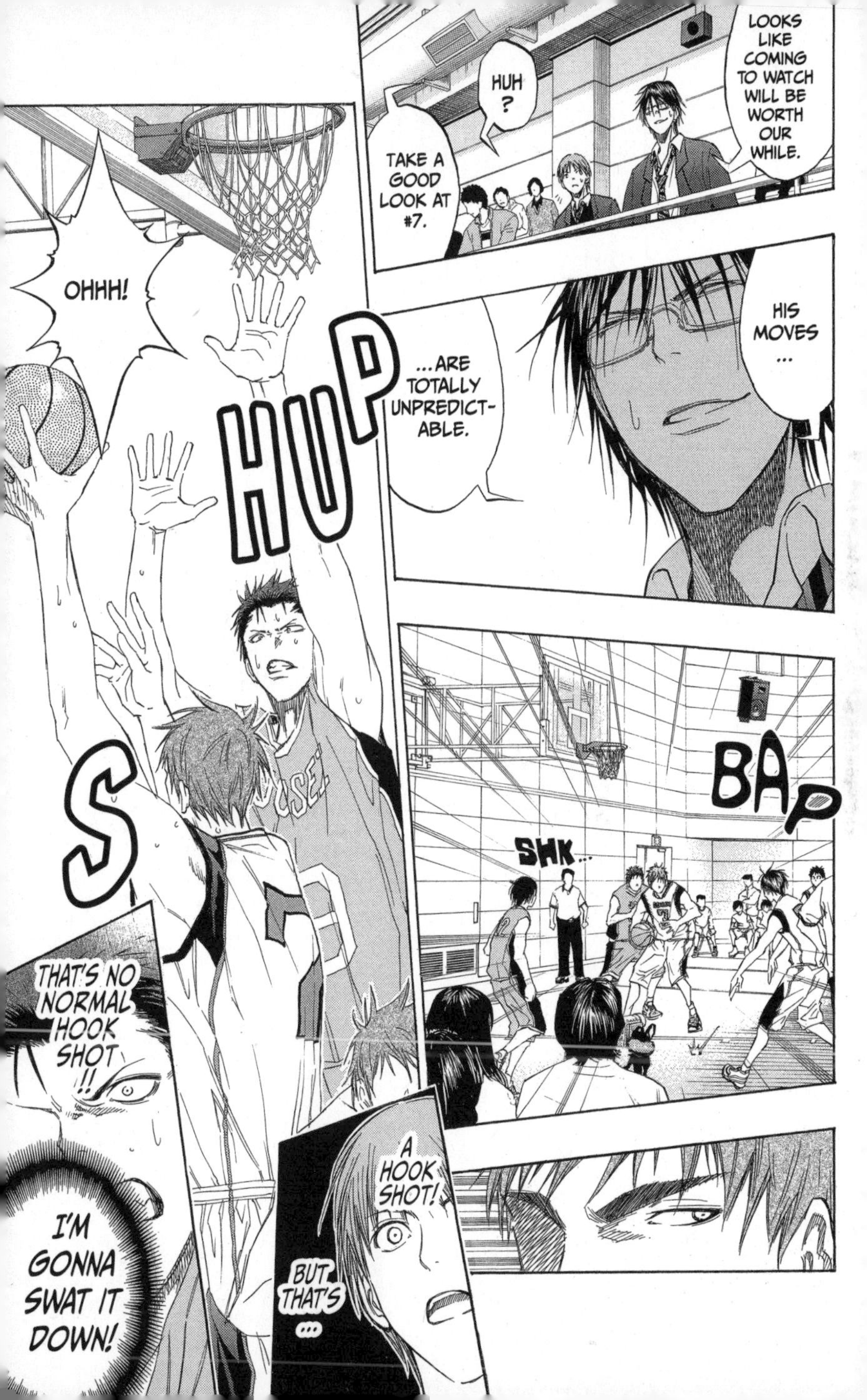
LOOKS LIKE COMING TO WATCH WILL BE WORTH OUR WHILE.
HUH?
TAKE A GOOD LOOK AT #7.
HIS MOVES ...
...ARE TOTALLY UNPREDICT-ABLE.
BAP
SHK...
A HOOK SHOT!
BUT THAT'S ...
OHHH!
HUP
S
THAT'S NO NORMAL HOOK SHOT!!
I'M GONNA SWAT IT DOWN!

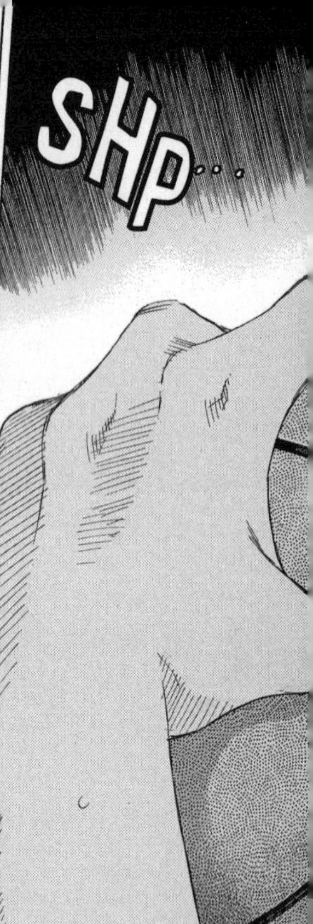
SHP...

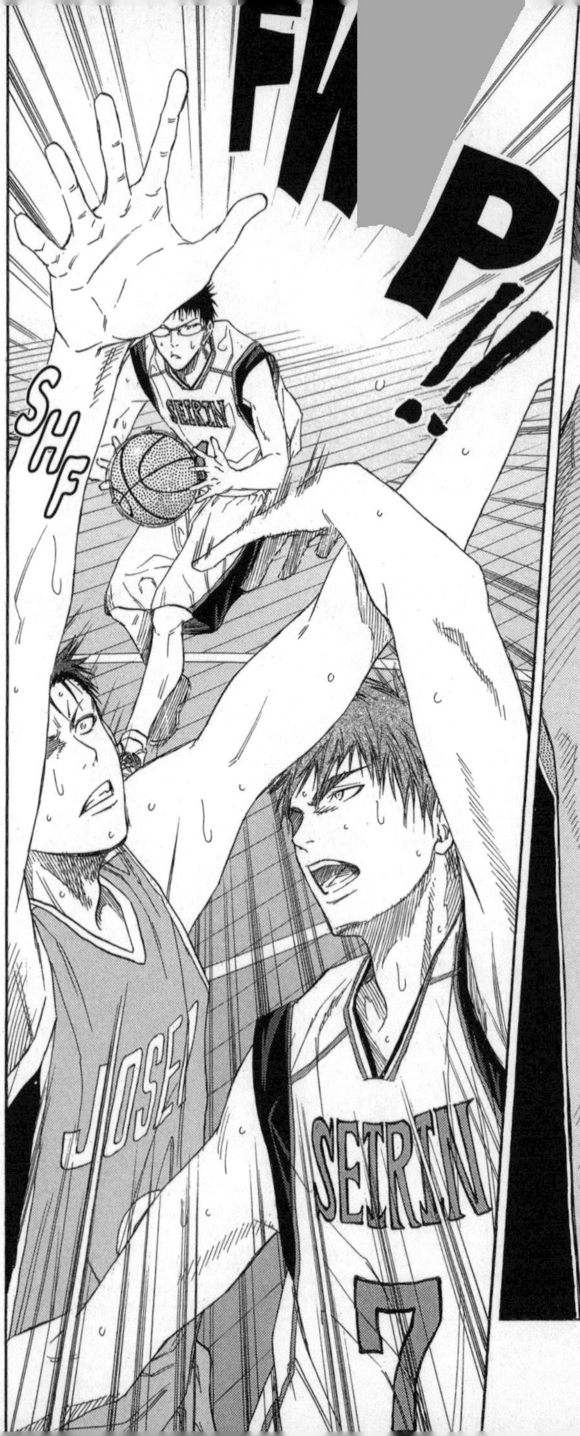
SHF
SEIRIN
JOSEI
SEIRIN
7

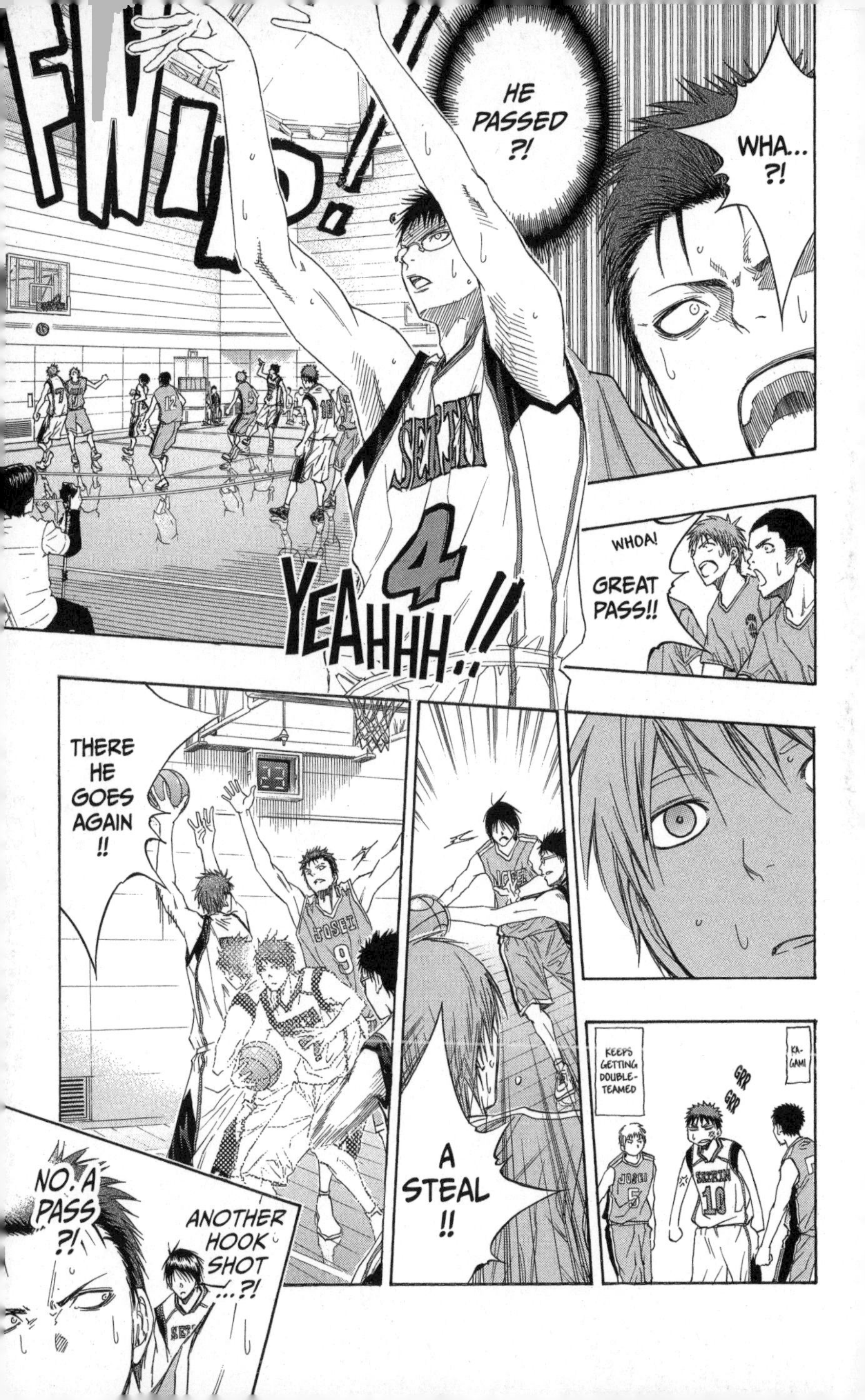
WHA... ?!
HE PASSED ?!
FWOOD!!
YEAHHH!!
WHOA!
GREAT PASS!!
THERE HE GOES AGAIN !!
A STEAL !!
KA-GAMI
KEEPS GETTING DOUBLE-TEAMED
GRR GRR
ANOTHER HOOK SHOT ...?!
NO. A PASS ?!

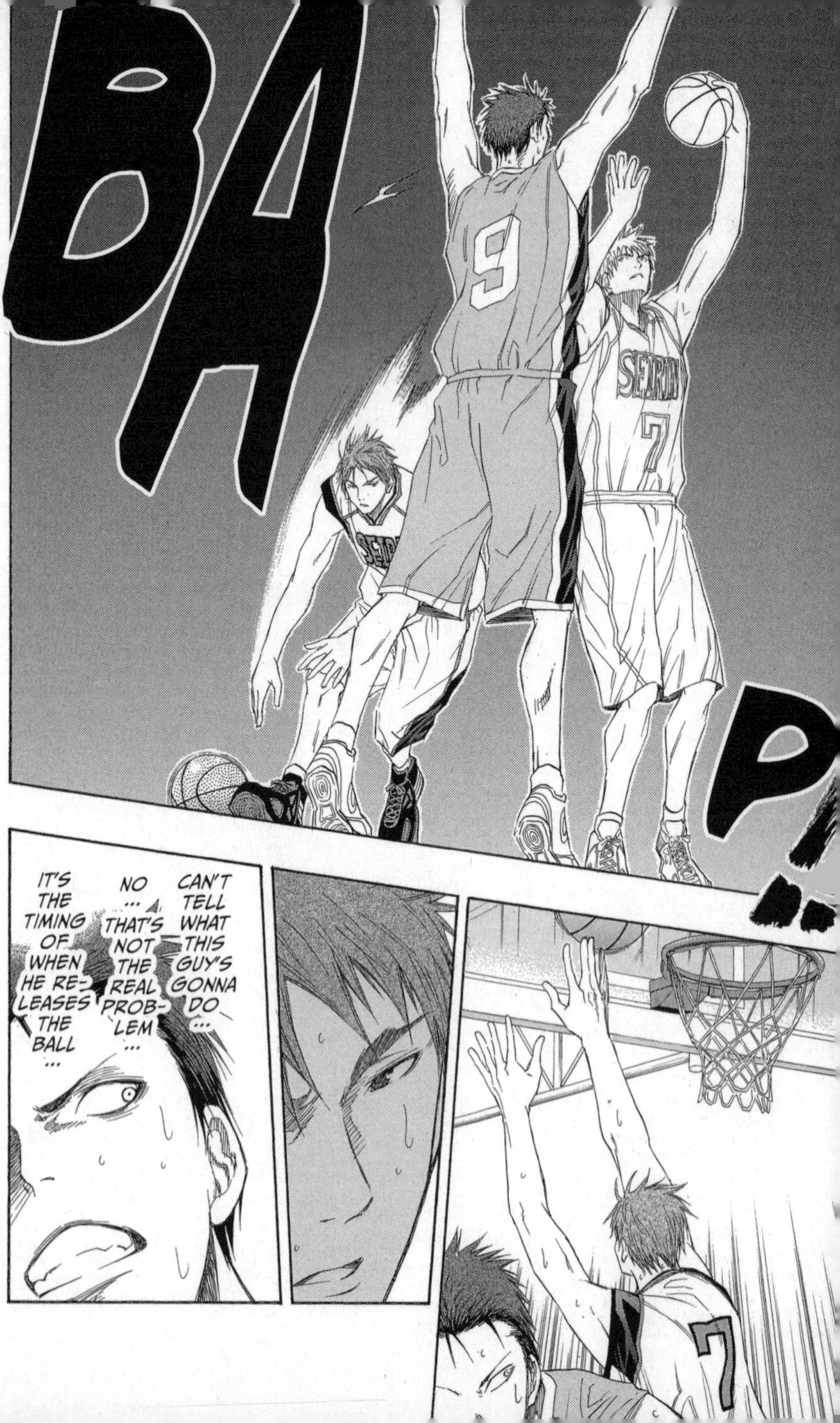
BA
P!!
CAN'T TELL WHAT THIS GUY'S GONNA DO...
NO... THAT'S NOT THE REAL PROBLEM...
IT'S THE TIMING OF WHEN HE RELEASES THE BALL...

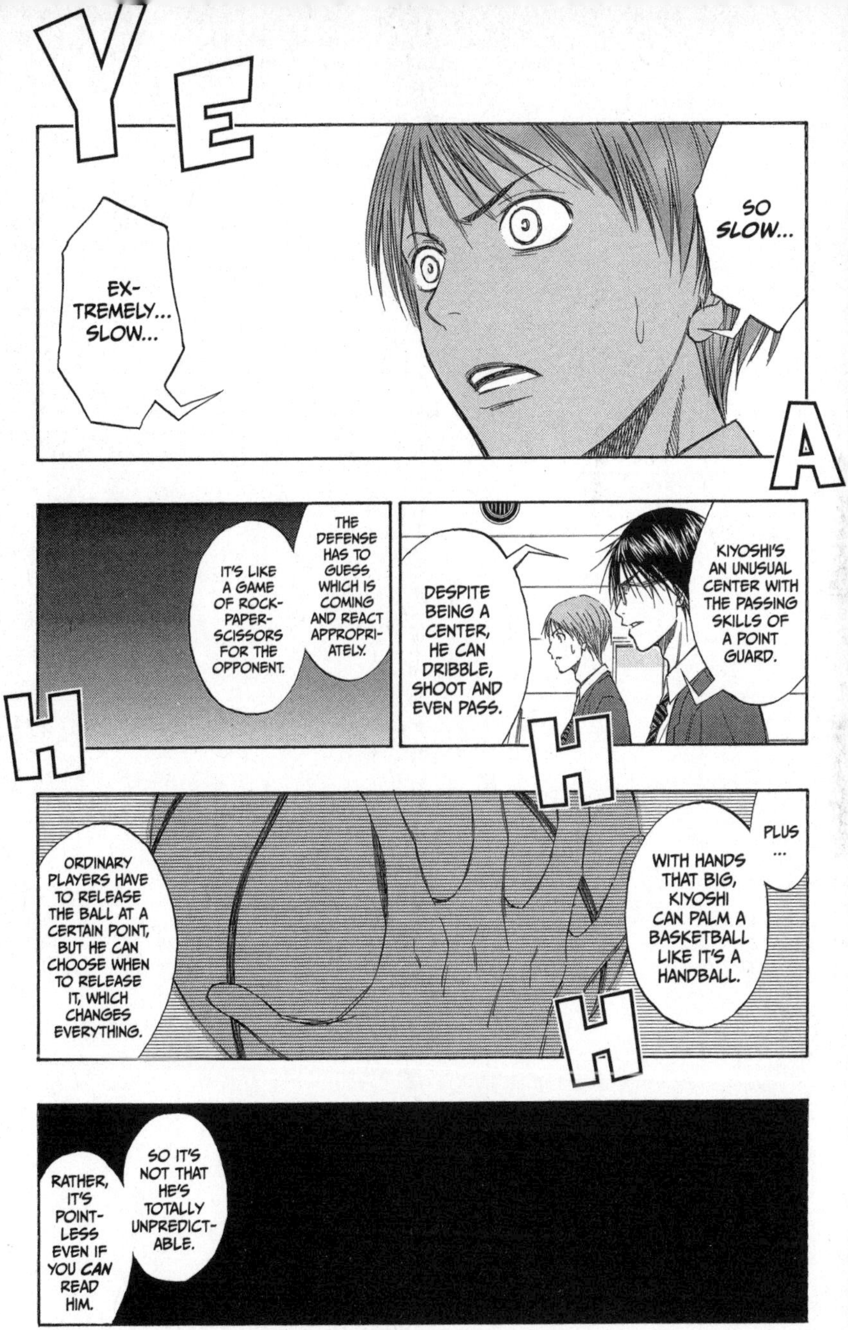
YEAHHH
SO SLOW...
EXTREMELY... SLOW...
KIYOSHI'S AN UNUSUAL CENTER WITH THE PASSING SKILLS OF A POINT GUARD.
DESPITE BEING A CENTER, HE CAN DRIBBLE, SHOOT AND EVEN PASS.
THE DEFENSE HAS TO GUESS WHICH IS COMING AND REACT APPROPRIATELY.
IT'S LIKE A GAME OF ROCK-PAPER-SCISSORS FOR THE OPPONENT.
PLUS...
WITH HANDS THAT BIG, KIYOSHI CAN PALM A BASKETBALL LIKE IT'S A HANDBALL.
ORDINARY PLAYERS HAVE TO RELEASE THE BALL AT A CERTAIN POINT, BUT HE CAN CHOOSE WHEN TO RELEASE IT, WHICH CHANGES EVERYTHING.
SO IT'S NOT THAT HE'S TOTALLY UNPREDICTABLE.
RATHER, IT'S POINTLESS EVEN IF YOU *CAN* READ HIM.

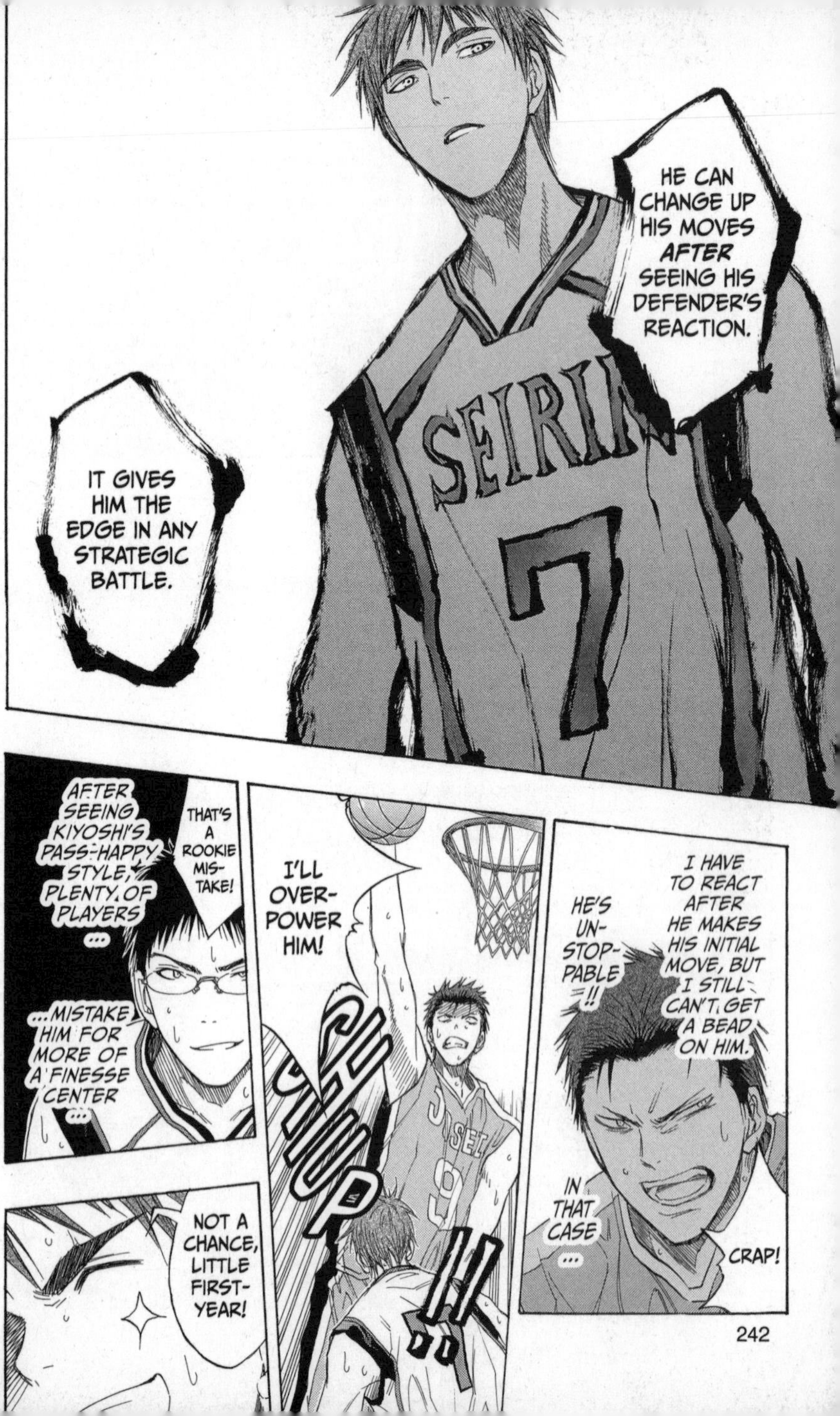
HE CAN CHANGE UP HIS MOVES AFTER SEEING HIS DEFENDER'S REACTION.
IT GIVES HIM THE EDGE IN ANY STRATEGIC BATTLE.
I HAVE TO REACT AFTER HE MAKES HIS INITIAL MOVE, BUT I STILL CAN'T GET A BEAD ON HIM.
HE'S UN-STOP-PABLE!!
CRAP!
IN THAT CASE...
I'LL OVER-POWER HIM!
THAT'S A ROOKIE MIS-TAKE!
AFTER SEEING KIYOSHI'S PASS-HAPPY STYLE, PLENTY OF PLAYERS...
...MISTAKE HIM FOR MORE OF A FINESSE CENTER...
NOT A CHANCE, LITTLE FIRST-YEAR!

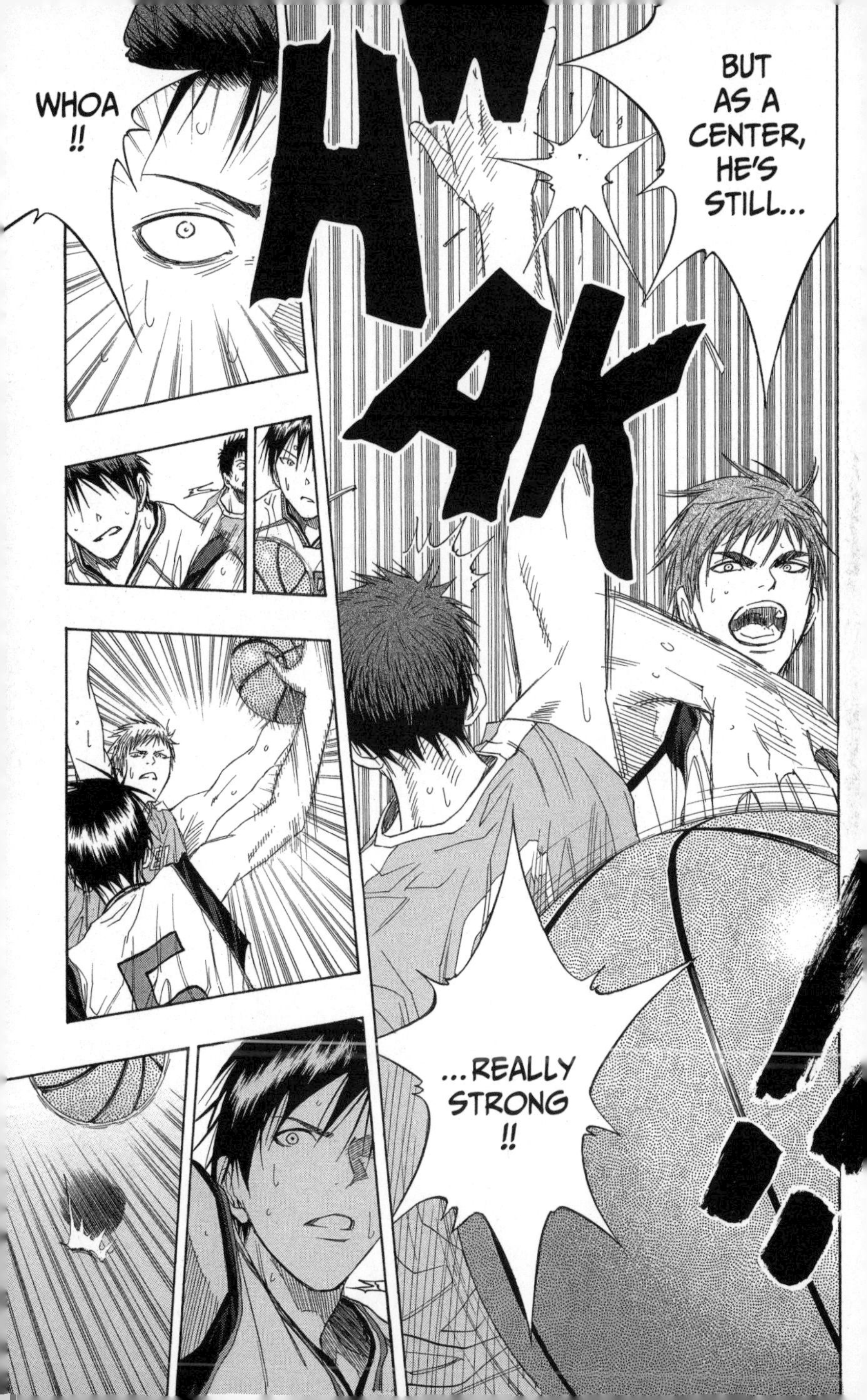
BUT AS A CENTER, HE'S STILL...
WHAK
WHOA !!
...REALLY STRONG !!

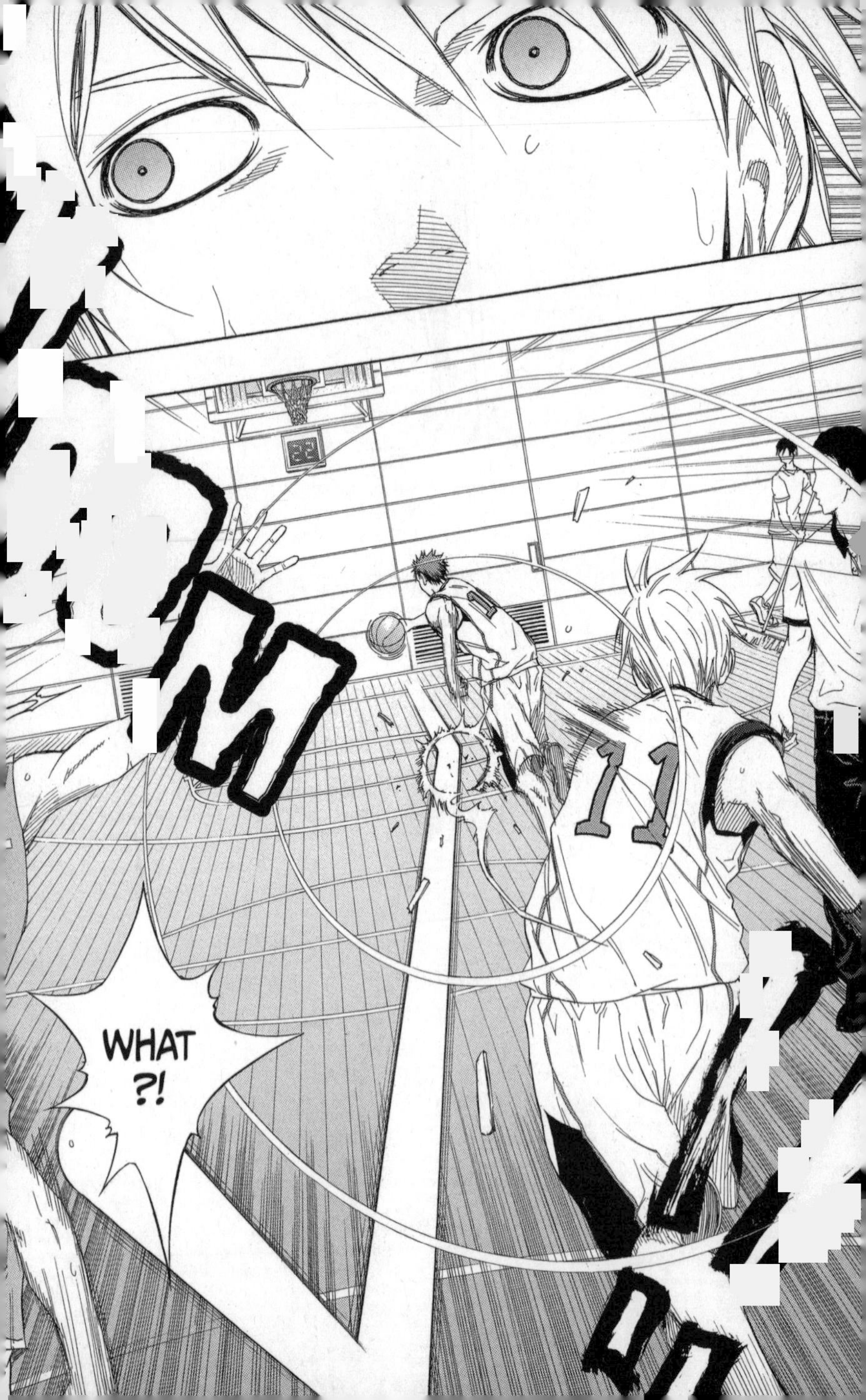
WHAT ?!

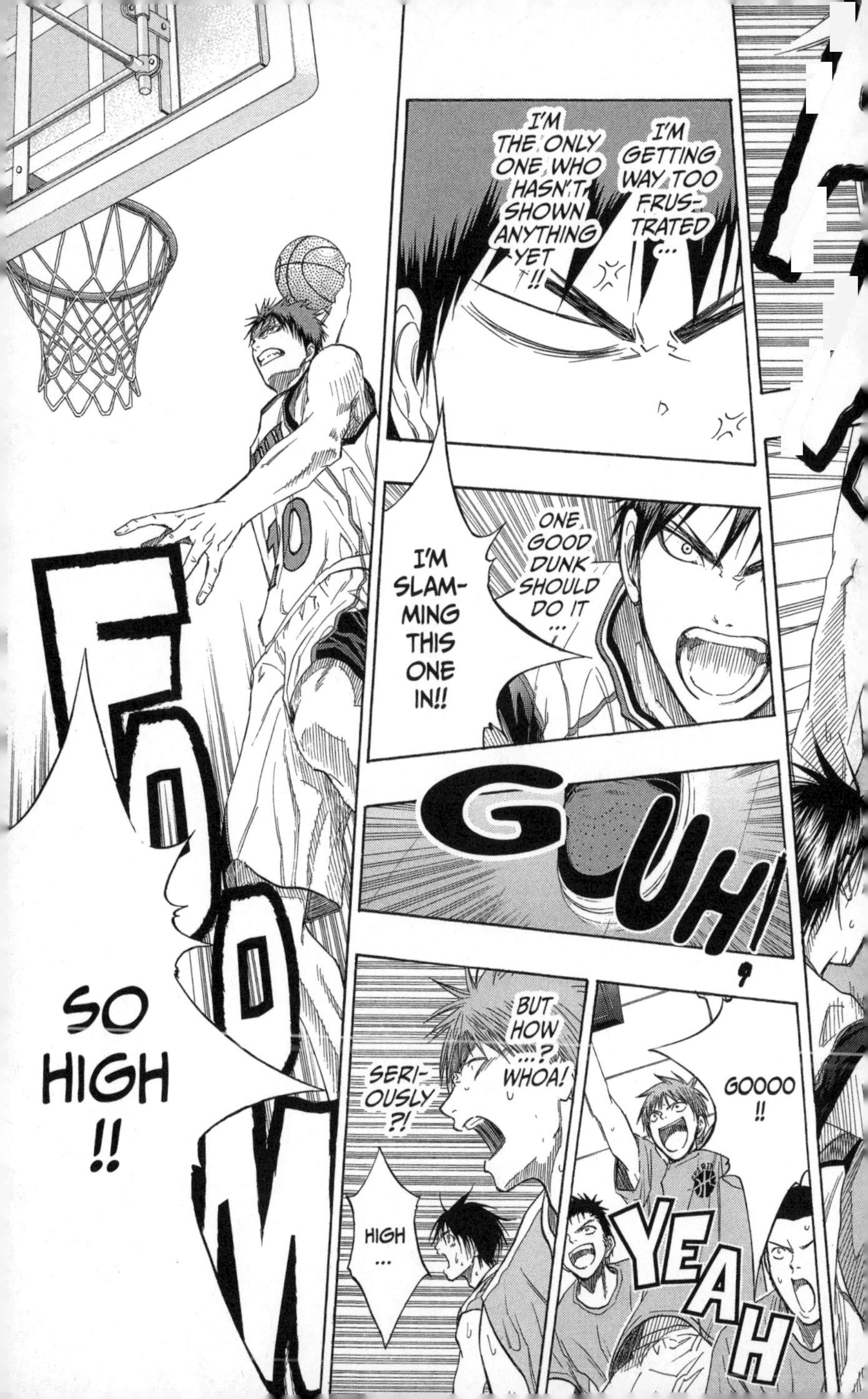
I'M GETTING WAY TOO FRUS-TRATED...
I'M THE ONLY ONE WHO HASN'T SHOWN ANYTHING YET!!
ONE GOOD DUNK SHOULD DO IT...
I'M SLAM-MING THIS ONE IN!!
GUH!
GOOOO!!
YEAH
BUT HOW...? WHOA!
SERI-OUSLY?!
HIGH...
FOOM
SO HIGH!!

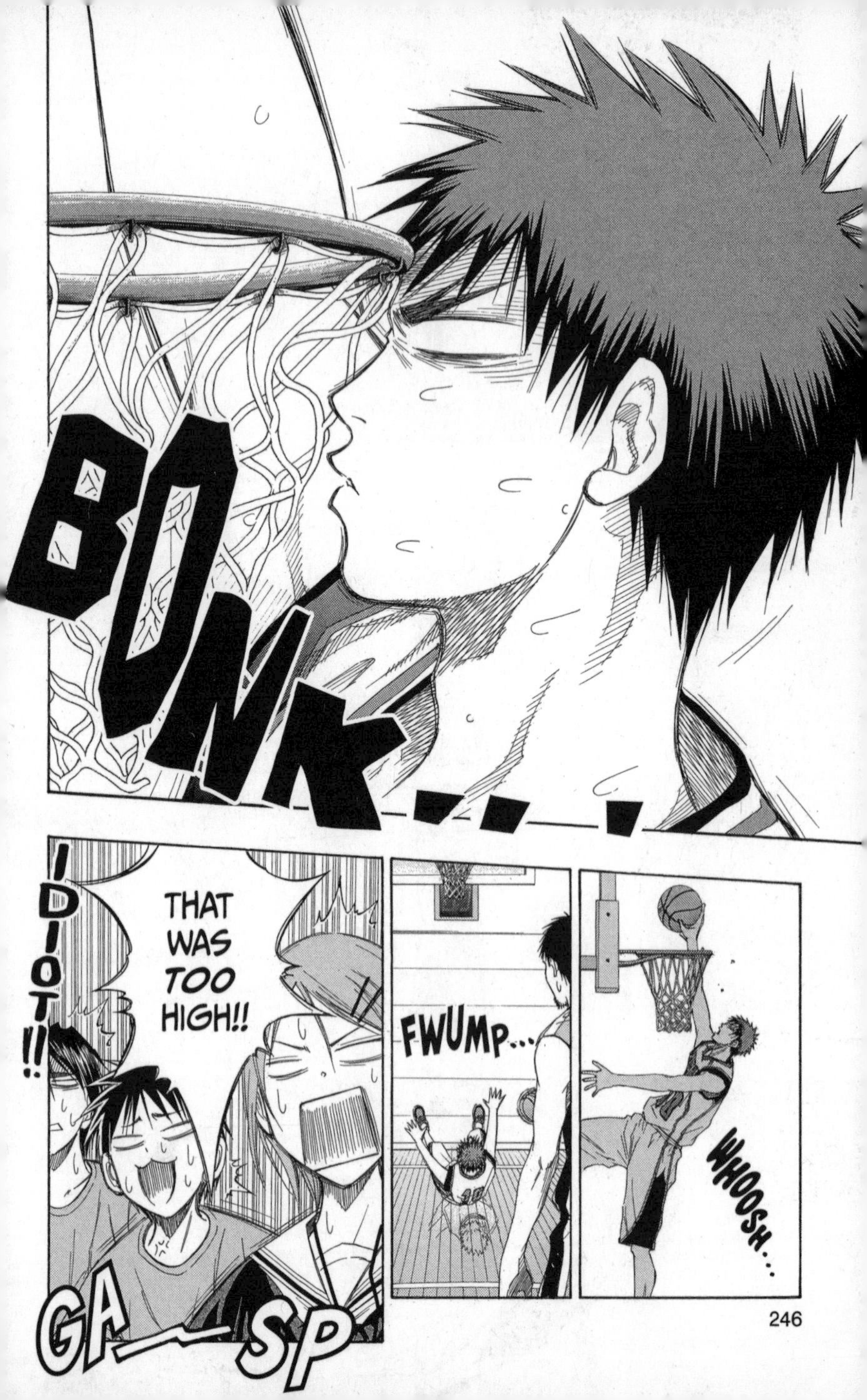
BONK...
WHOOSH...
FWUMP...
THAT WAS TOO HIGH!!
IDIOT!!
GA—SP

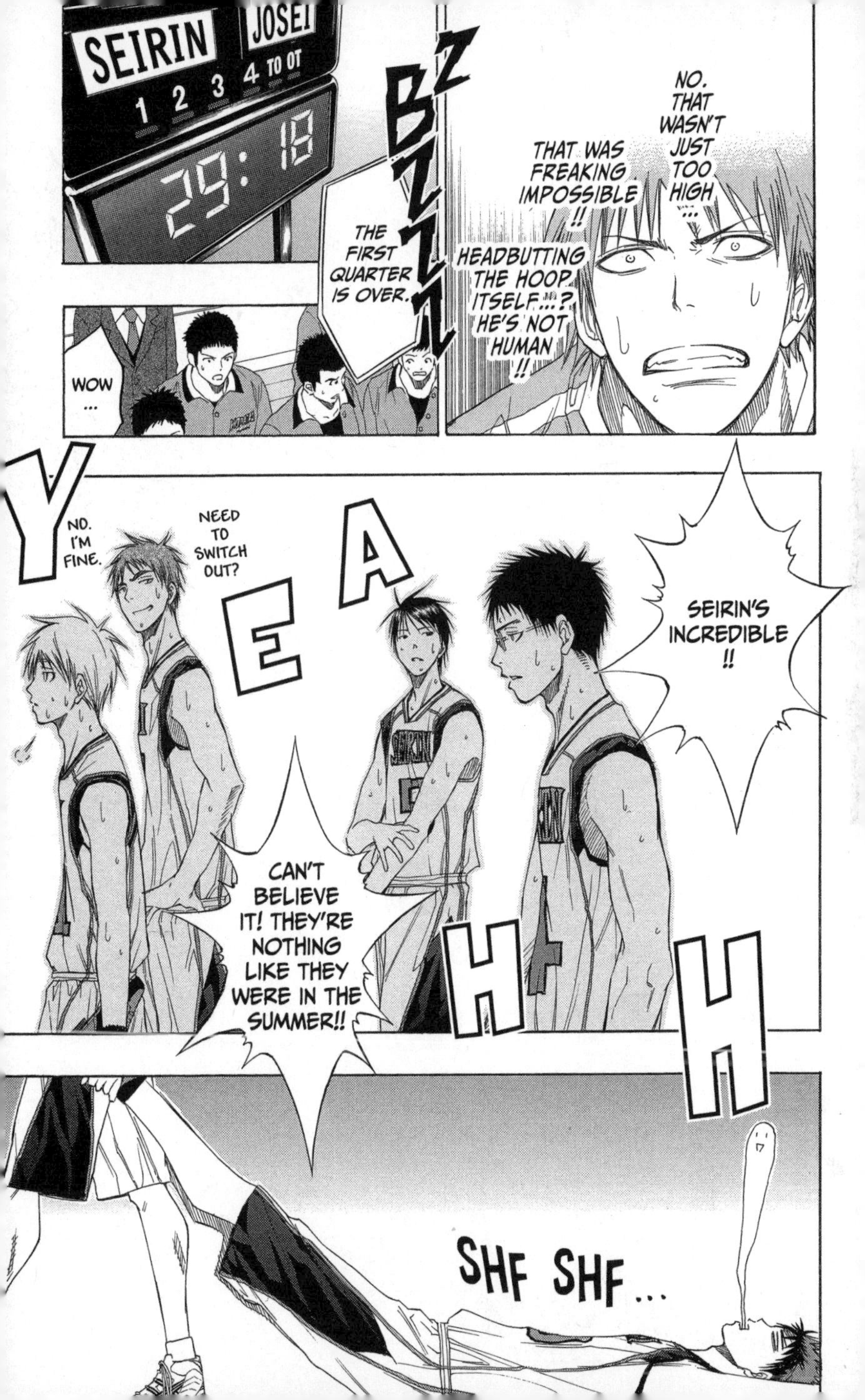
NO. THAT WASN'T JUST TOO HIGH...
THAT WAS FREAKING IMPOSSIBLE!!
HEADBUTTING THE HOOP ITSELF...? HE'S NOT HUMAN!!
BZZZZ
THE FIRST QUARTER IS OVER.
SEIRIN
JOSEI
1 2 3 4 TO OT
29:18
WOW...
YEAHHH
SEIRIN'S INCREDIBLE!!
NEED TO SWITCH OUT?
NO. I'M FINE.
CAN'T BELIEVE IT! THEY'RE NOTHING LIKE THEY WERE IN THE SUMMER!!
SHF SHF...

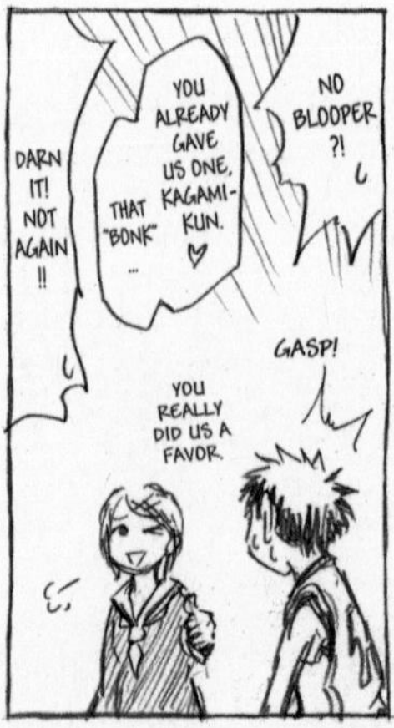
NO BLOOPER?!
YOU ALREADY GAVE US ONE, KAGAMI-KUN. ♥
THAT "BONK"...
DARN IT! NOT AGAIN!!
GASP!
YOU REALLY DID US A FAVOR.

83RD QUARTER: DECLARATION OF WAR

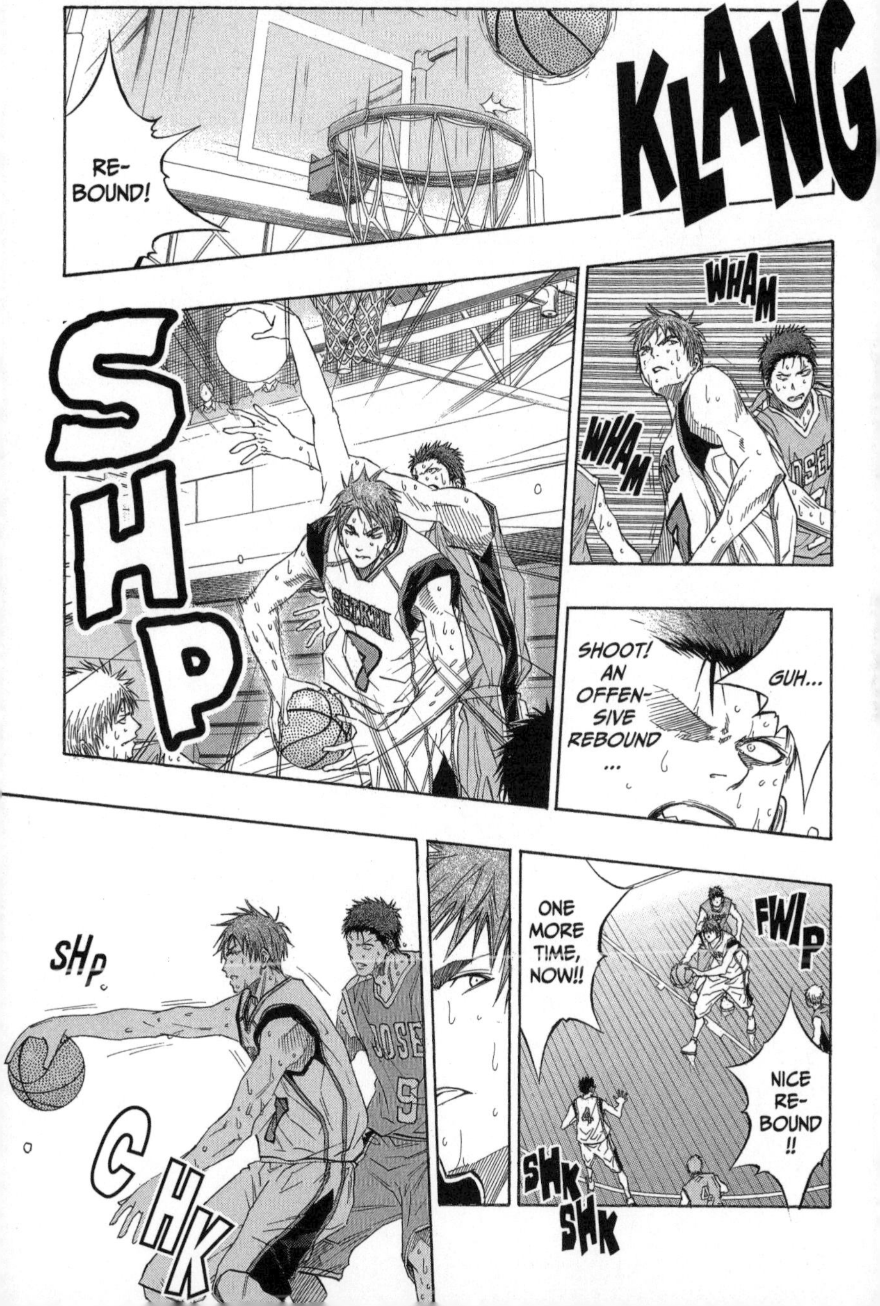
KLANG
RE-BOUND!
WHAM
WHAM
GUH...
SHOOT! AN OFFEN-SIVE REBOUND ...
SHP
FWIP
ONE MORE TIME, NOW!!
NICE RE-BOUND !!
SHK SHK
SHP
CHK

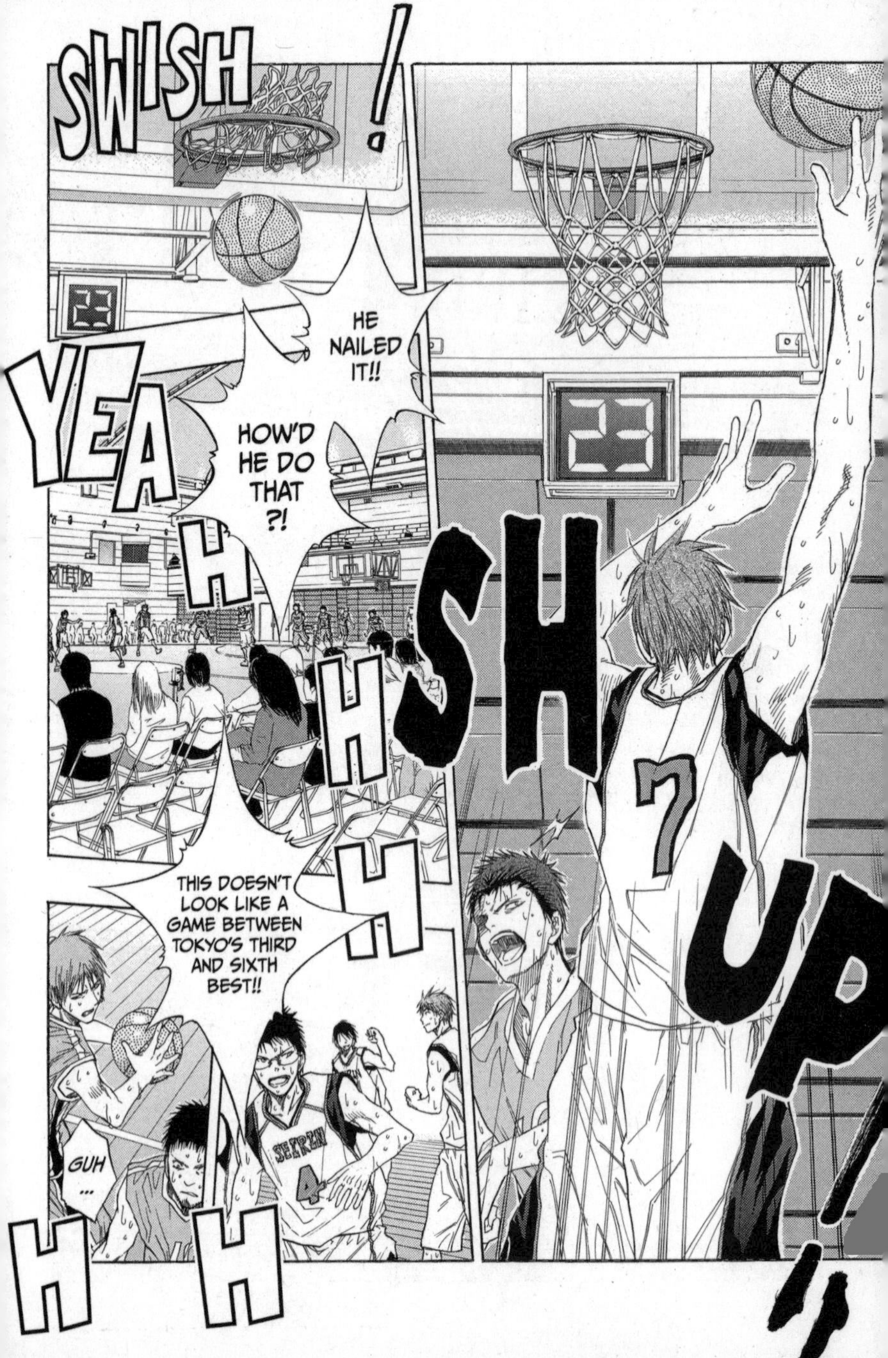
SHUP!!
SWISH!
HE NAILED IT!!
HOW'D HE DO THAT?!
YEAHHHHHH
THIS DOESN'T LOOK LIKE A GAME BETWEEN TOKYO'S THIRD AND SIXTH BEST!!
GUH...

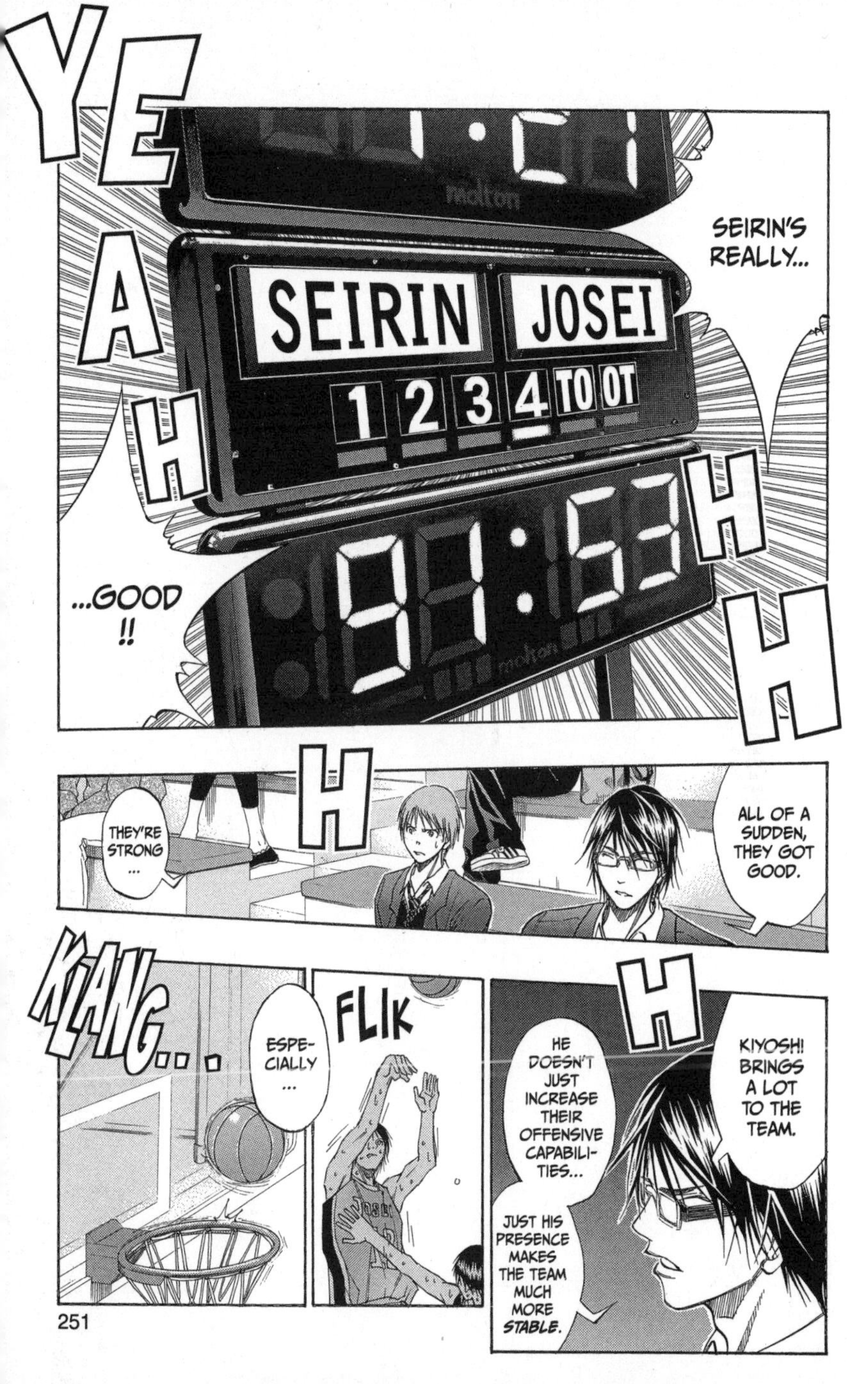
YEAHHHHHH
SEIRIN
JOSEI
1 2 3 4 TO OT
91 : 63
SEIRIN'S REALLY...
...GOOD!!
ALL OF A SUDDEN, THEY GOT GOOD.
THEY'RE STRONG...
KIYOSHI BRINGS A LOT TO THE TEAM.
HE DOESN'T JUST INCREASE THEIR OFFENSIVE CAPABILI-TIES...
JUST HIS PRESENCE MAKES THE TEAM MUCH MORE STABLE.
FLIK
ESPE-CIALLY...
KLANG...

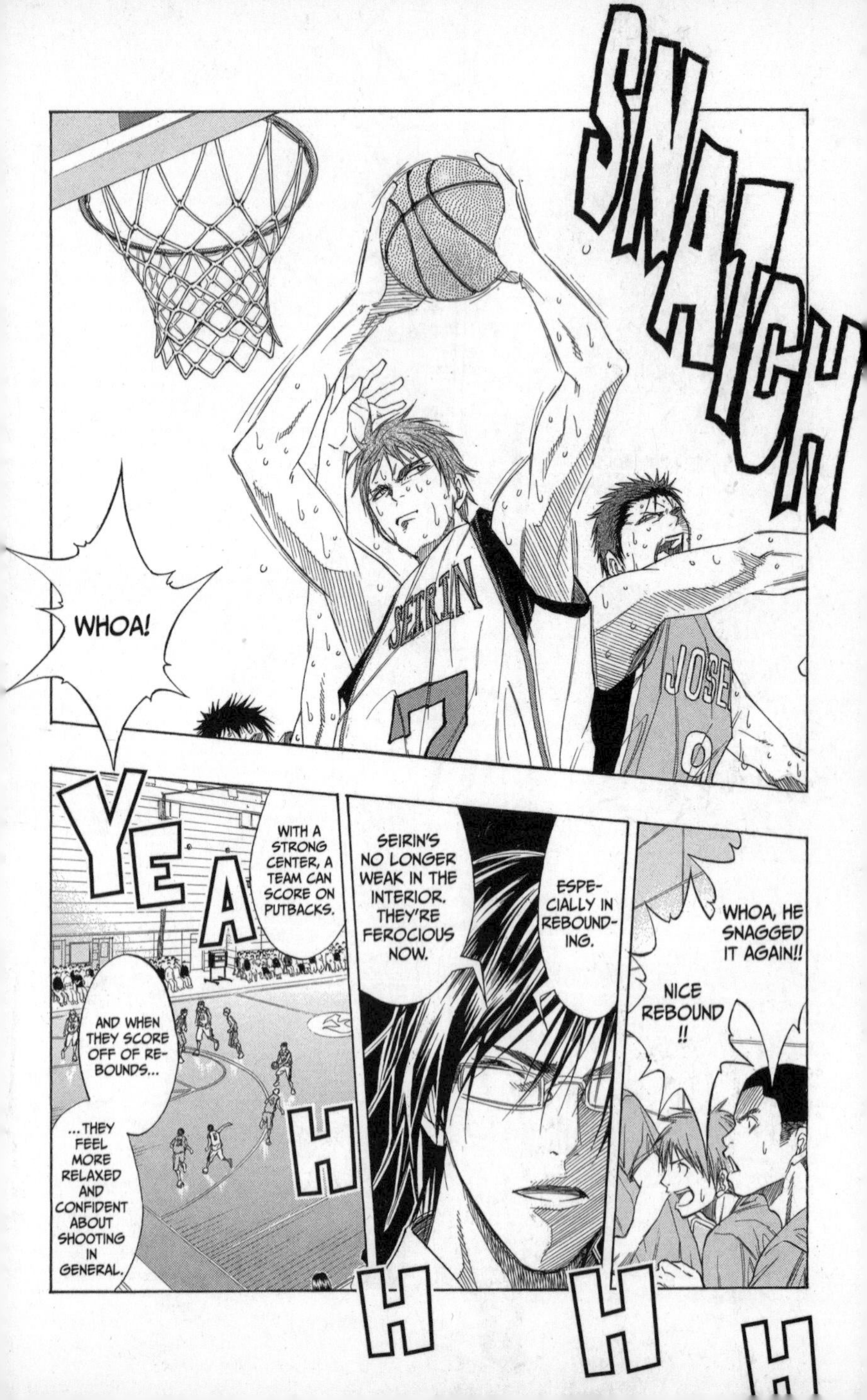
SNATCH
WHOA!
WHOA, HE SNAGGED IT AGAIN!!
NICE REBOUND!!
ESPE-CIALLY IN REBOUND-ING.
SEIRIN'S NO LONGER WEAK IN THE INTERIOR. THEY'RE FEROCIOUS NOW.
YEAHHHHH
WITH A STRONG CENTER, A TEAM CAN SCORE ON PUTBACKS.
AND WHEN THEY SCORE OFF OF RE-BOUNDS...
...THEY FEEL MORE RELAXED AND CONFIDENT ABOUT SHOOTING IN GENERAL.

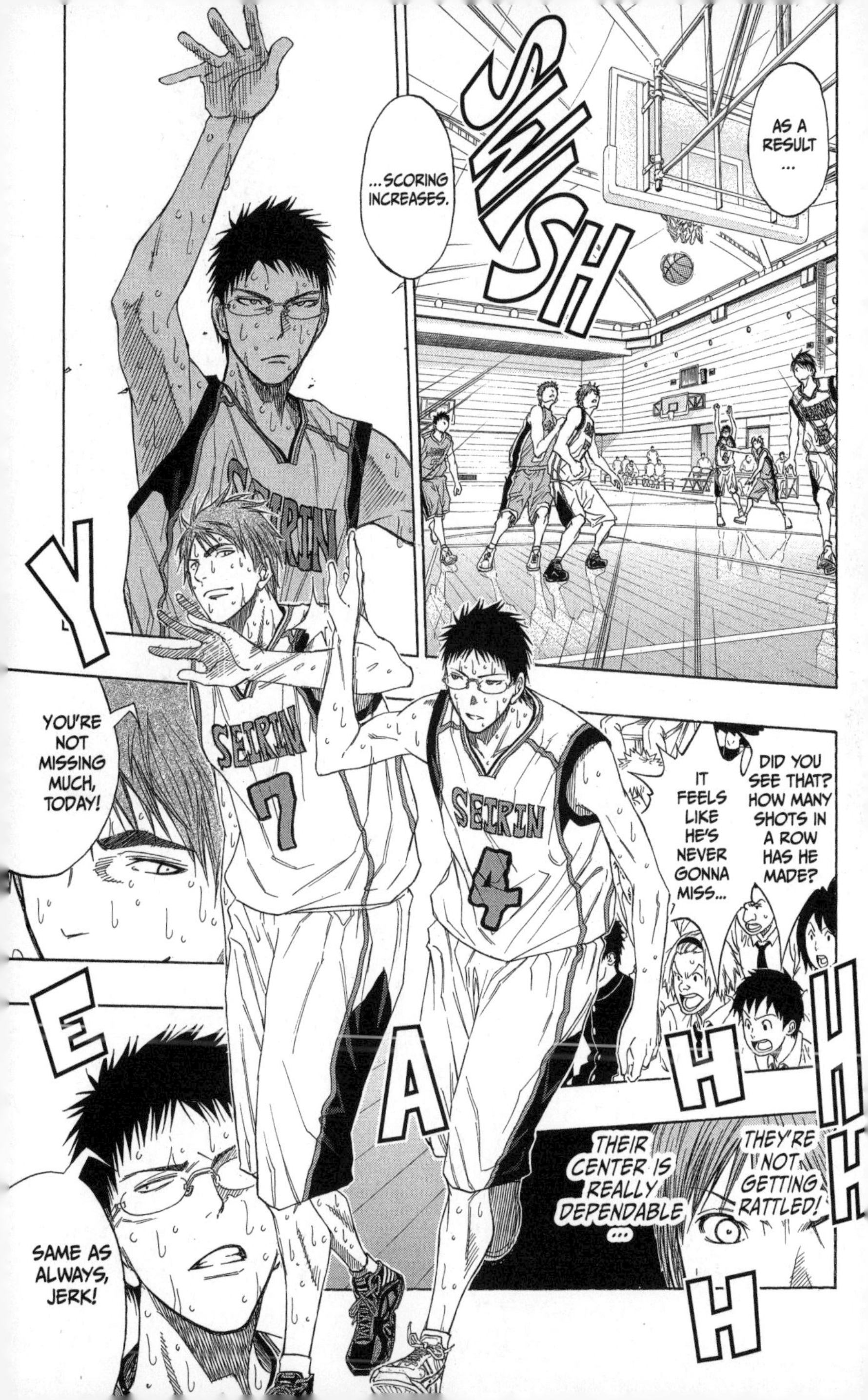
AS A RESULT ...
SWISH
...SCORING INCREASES.
DID YOU SEE THAT? HOW MANY SHOTS IN A ROW HAS HE MADE?
IT FEELS LIKE HE'S NEVER GONNA MISS...
YEAHHHH
THEY'RE NOT GETTING RATTLED!
THEIR CENTER IS REALLY DEPENDABLE ...
YOU'RE NOT MISSING MUCH, TODAY!
SAME AS ALWAYS, JERK!

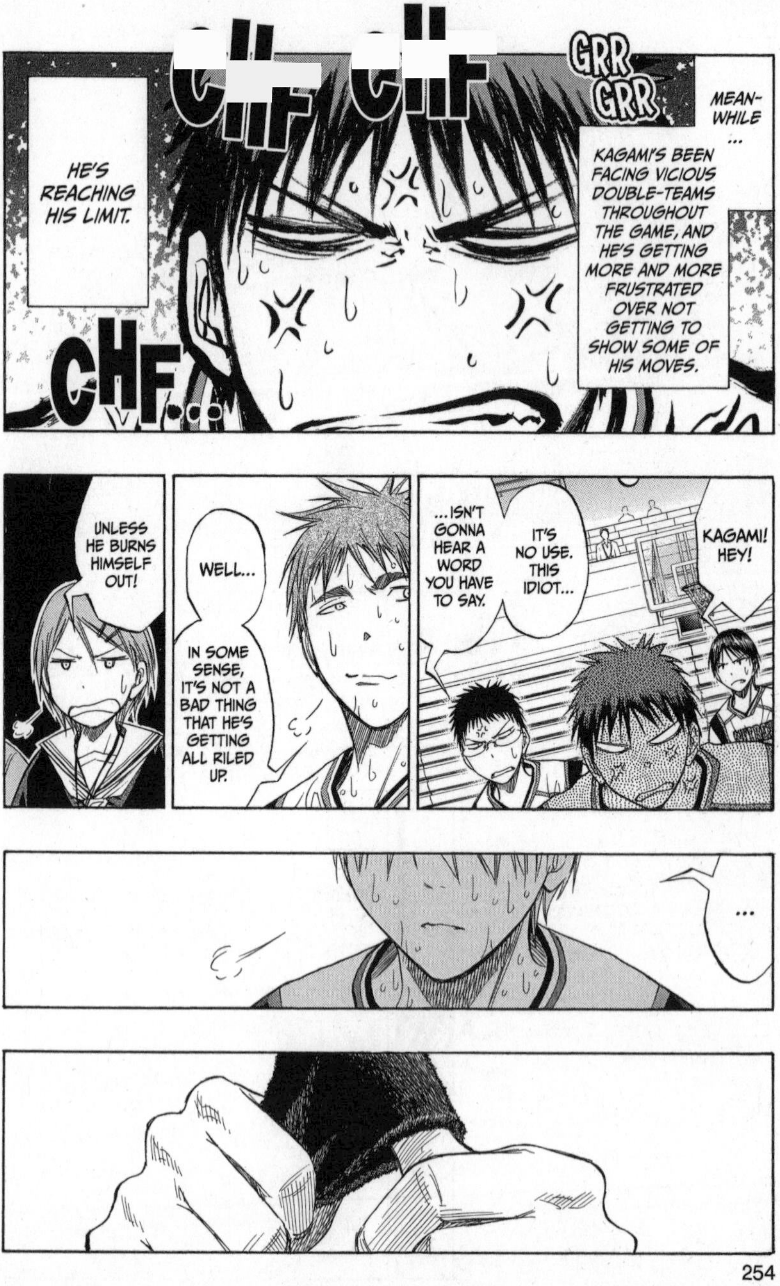
GRR GRR
MEAN-WHILE ...
KAGAMI'S BEEN FACING VICIOUS DOUBLE-TEAMS THROUGHOUT THE GAME, AND HE'S GETTING MORE AND MORE FRUSTRATED OVER NOT GETTING TO SHOW SOME OF HIS MOVES.
CHF CHF
HE'S REACHING HIS LIMIT.
CHF...
KAGAMI! HEY!
IT'S NO USE. THIS IDIOT...
...ISN'T GONNA HEAR A WORD YOU HAVE TO SAY.
WELL...
IN SOME SENSE, IT'S NOT A BAD THING THAT HE'S GETTING ALL RILED UP.
UNLESS HE BURNS HIMSELF OUT!
...

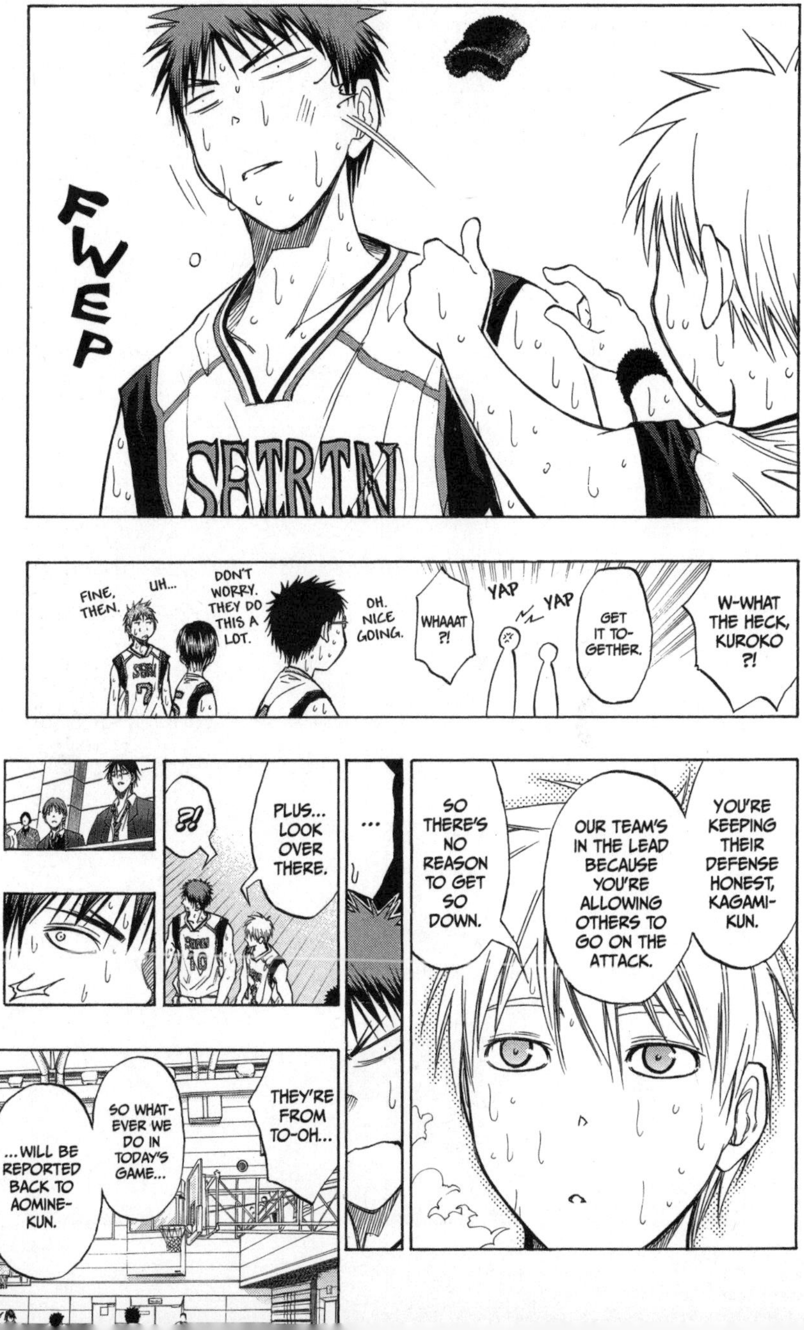
FWEP
W-WHAT THE HECK, KUROKO ?!
GET IT TO-GETHER.
YAP YAP
WHAAAT ?!
OH. NICE GOING.
DON'T WORRY. THEY DO THIS A LOT.
UH...
FINE, THEN.
YOU'RE KEEPING THEIR DEFENSE HONEST, KAGAMI-KUN.
OUR TEAM'S IN THE LEAD BECAUSE YOU'RE ALLOWING OTHERS TO GO ON THE ATTACK.
SO THERE'S NO REASON TO GET SO DOWN.
...
PLUS... LOOK OVER THERE.
?!
THEY'RE FROM TO-OH...
SO WHAT-EVER WE DO IN TODAY'S GAME...
...WILL BE REPORTED BACK TO AOMINE-KUN.

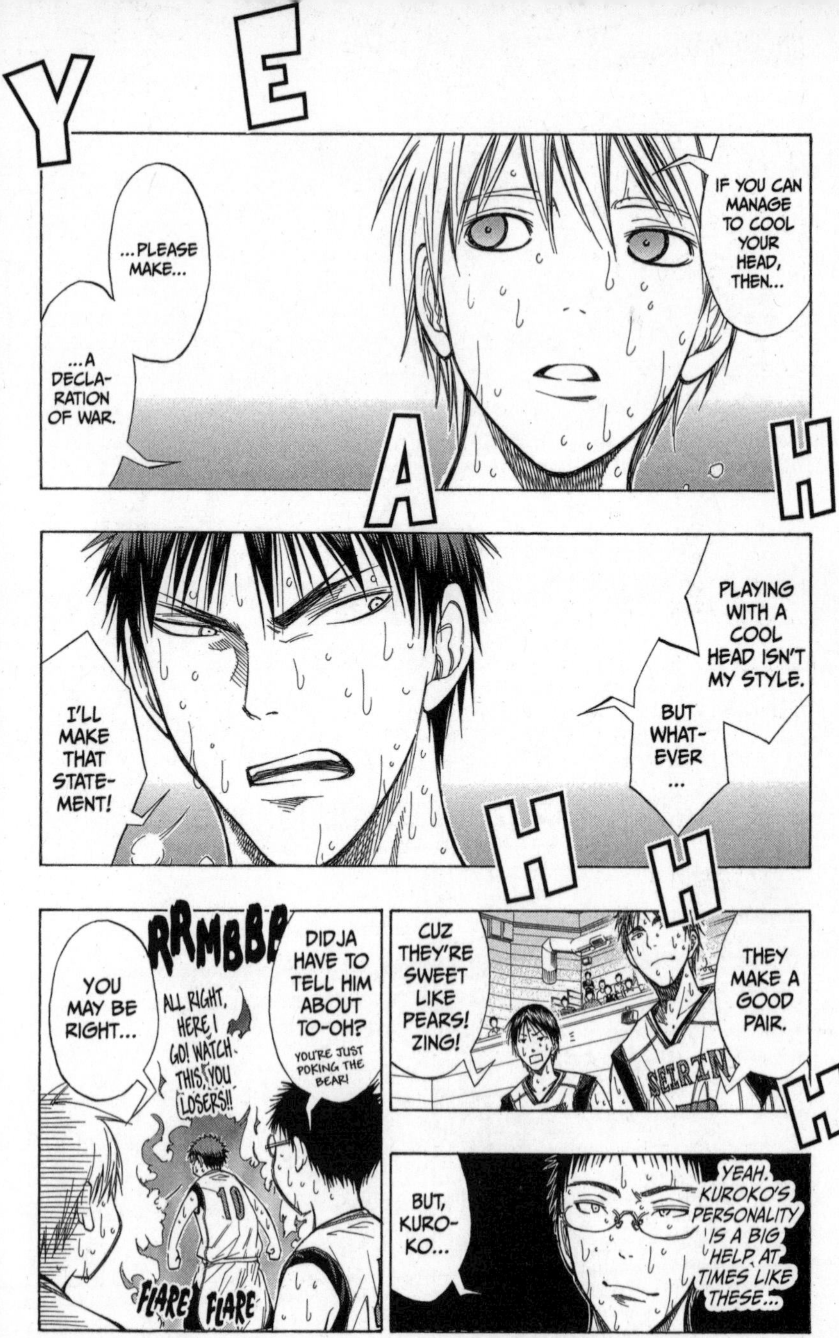
YEAHHHH
IF YOU CAN MANAGE TO COOL YOUR HEAD, THEN...
...PLEASE MAKE...
...A DECLARATION OF WAR.
PLAYING WITH A COOL HEAD ISN'T MY STYLE.
BUT WHATEVER...
I'LL MAKE THAT STATEMENT!
THEY MAKE A GOOD PAIR.
CUZ THEY'RE SWEET LIKE PEARS! ZING!
YEAH. KUROKO'S PERSONALITY IS A BIG HELP AT TIMES LIKE THESE...
BUT, KUROKO...
DIDJA HAVE TO TELL HIM ABOUT TO-OH?
YOU'RE JUST POKING THE BEAR!
RRMBBB
ALL RIGHT, HERE I GO! WATCH THIS, YOU LOSERS!!
YOU MAY BE RIGHT...
FLARE FLARE

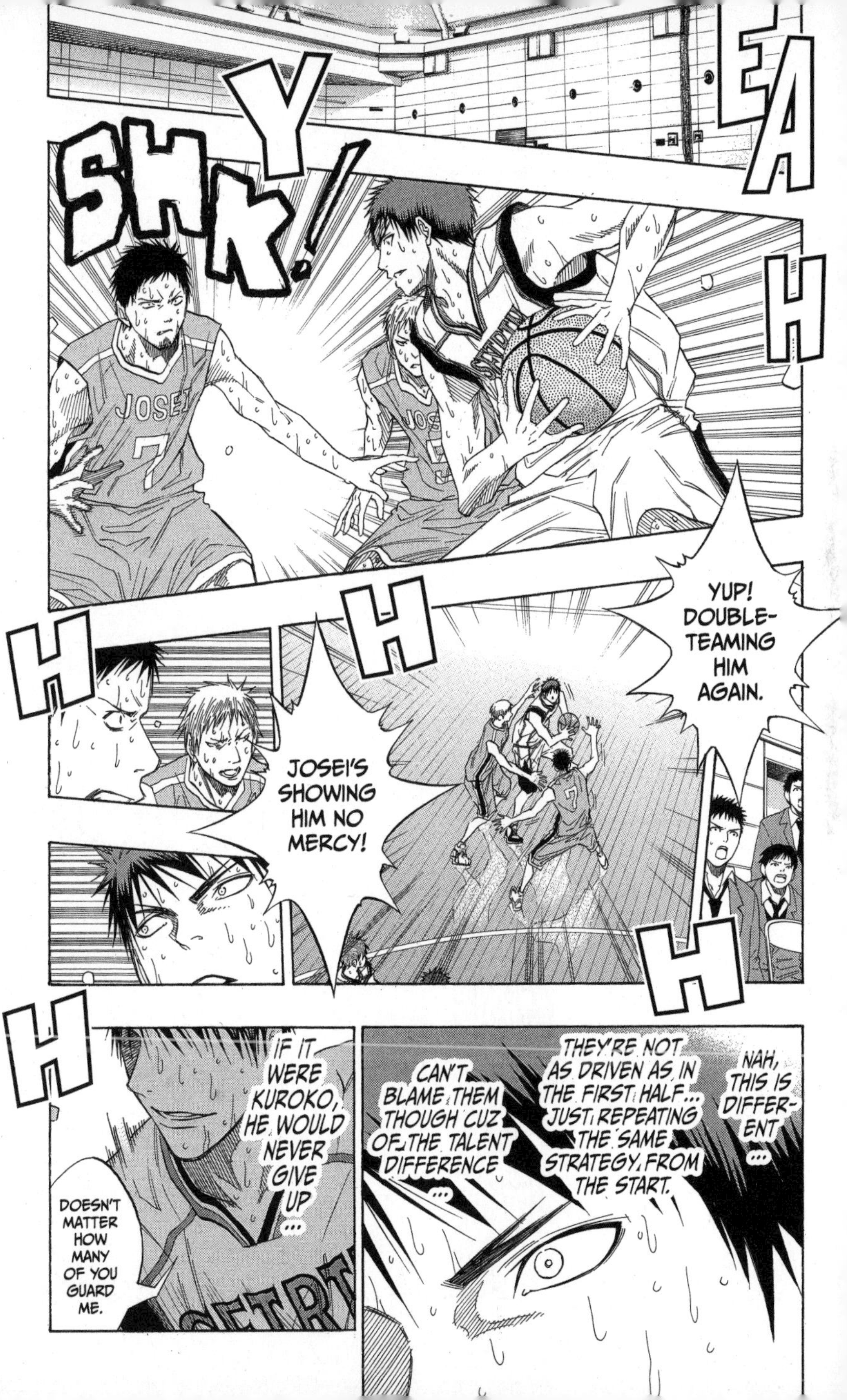

YEAHHHHH
SHK!
YUP! DOUBLE-TEAMING HIM AGAIN.
JOSEI'S SHOWING HIM NO MERCY!
NAH, THIS IS DIFFERENT...
THEY'RE NOT AS DRIVEN AS IN THE FIRST HALF... JUST REPEATING THE SAME STRATEGY FROM THE START.
CAN'T BLAME THEM THOUGH CUZ OF THE TALENT DIFFERENCE...
IF IT WERE KUROKO, HE WOULD NEVER GIVE UP...
DOESN'T MATTER HOW MANY OF YOU GUARD ME.

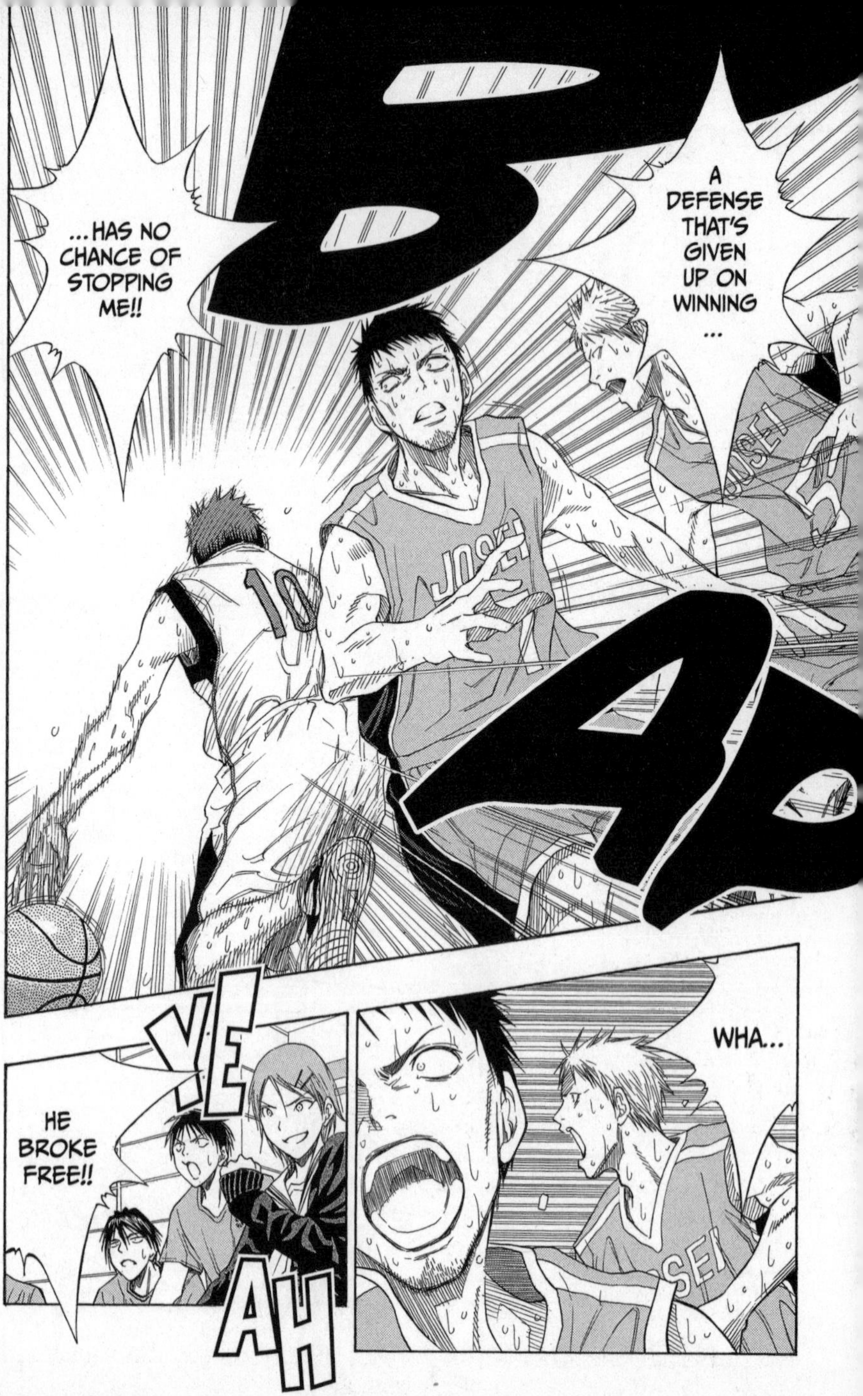
A DEFENSE THAT'S GIVEN UP ON WINNING...
...HAS NO CHANCE OF STOPPING ME!!
WHA...
YE
HE BROKE FREE!!
AH

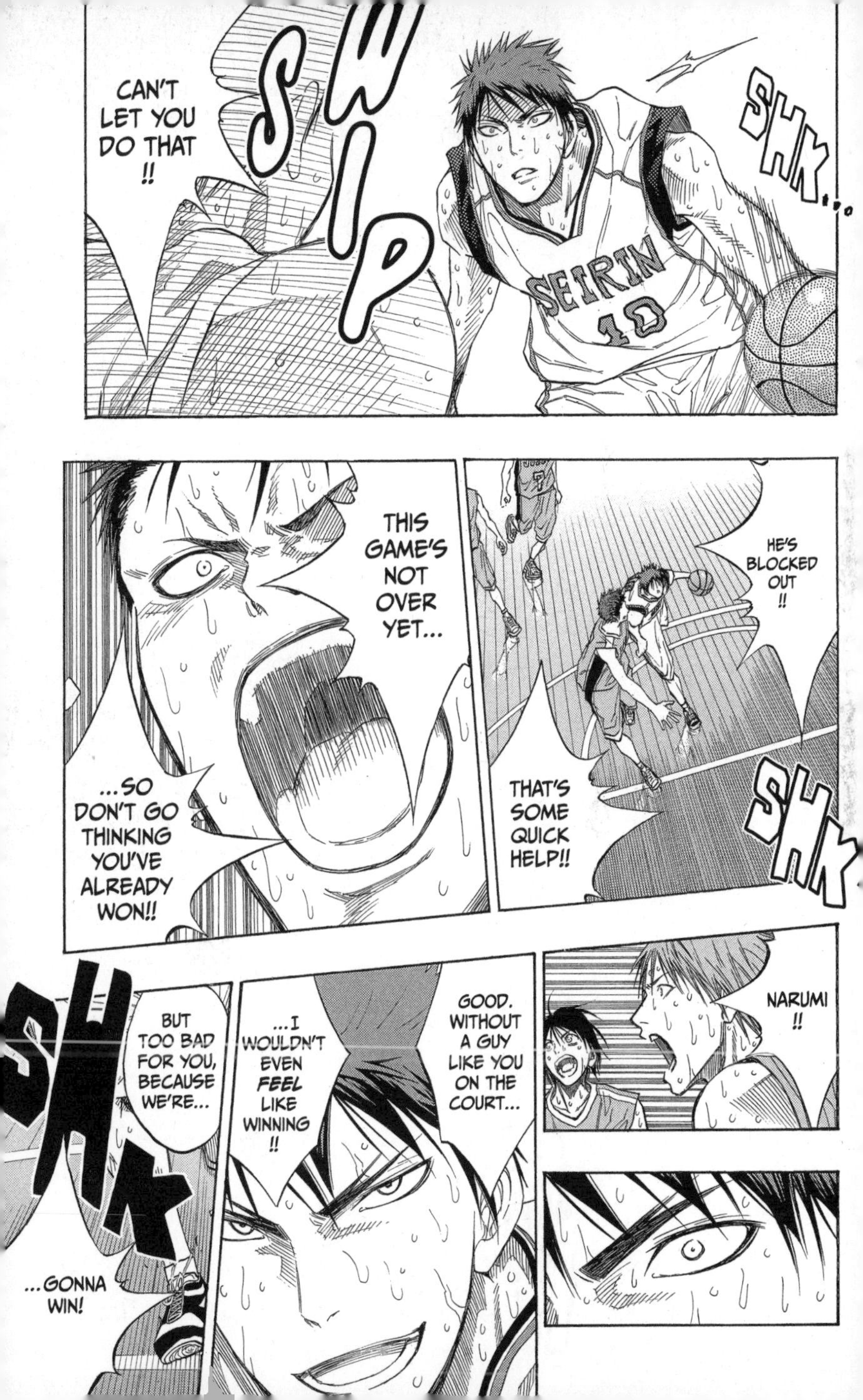
SHK...
SWIP
CAN'T LET YOU DO THAT!!
HE'S BLOCKED OUT!!
SHK
THAT'S SOME QUICK HELP!!
THIS GAME'S NOT OVER YET...
...SO DON'T GO THINKING YOU'VE ALREADY WON!!
NARUMI!!
GOOD. WITHOUT A GUY LIKE YOU ON THE COURT...
...I WOULDN'T EVEN **FEEL** LIKE WINNING!!
SHK
BUT TOO BAD FOR YOU, BECAUSE WE'RE...
...GONNA WIN!

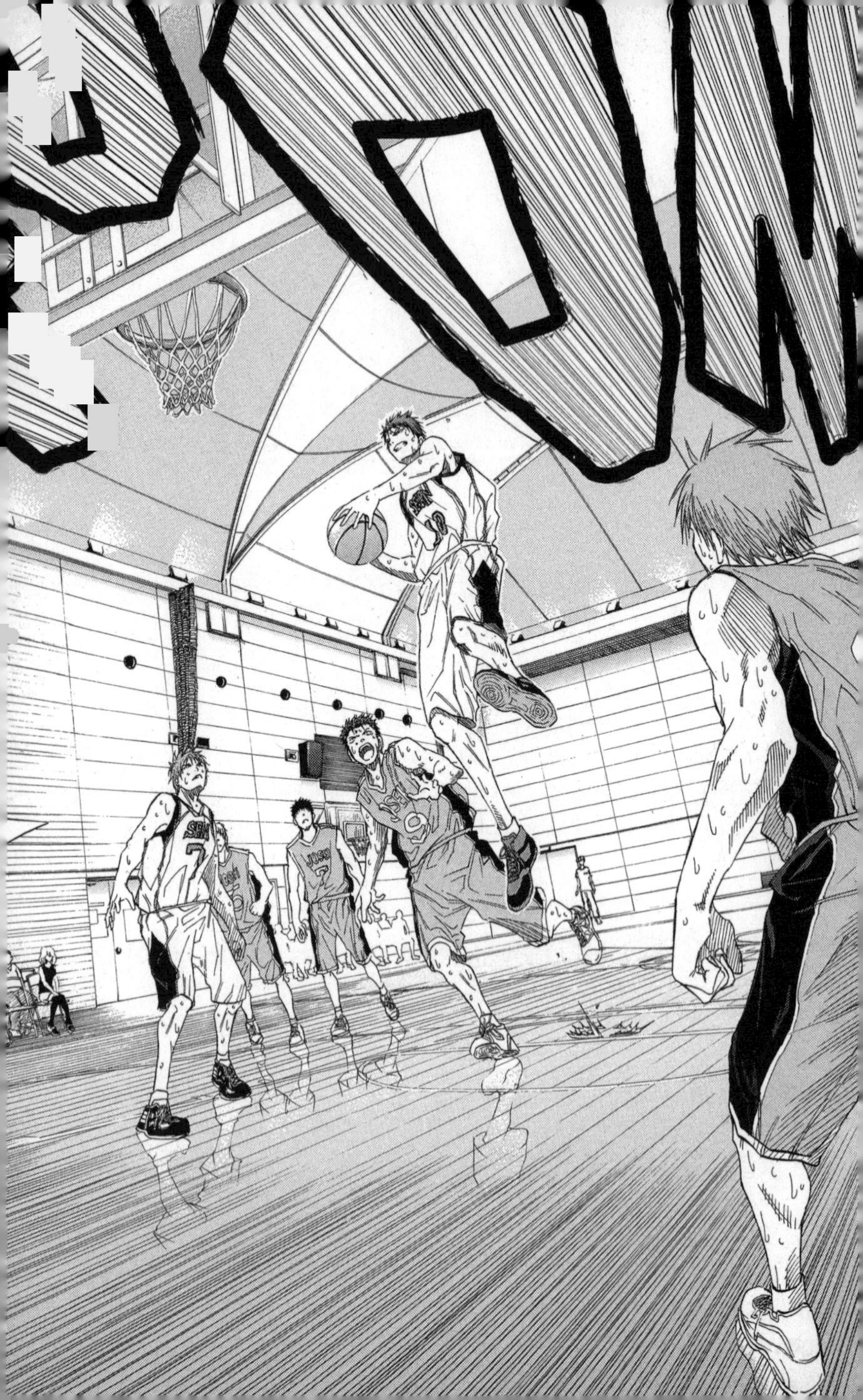

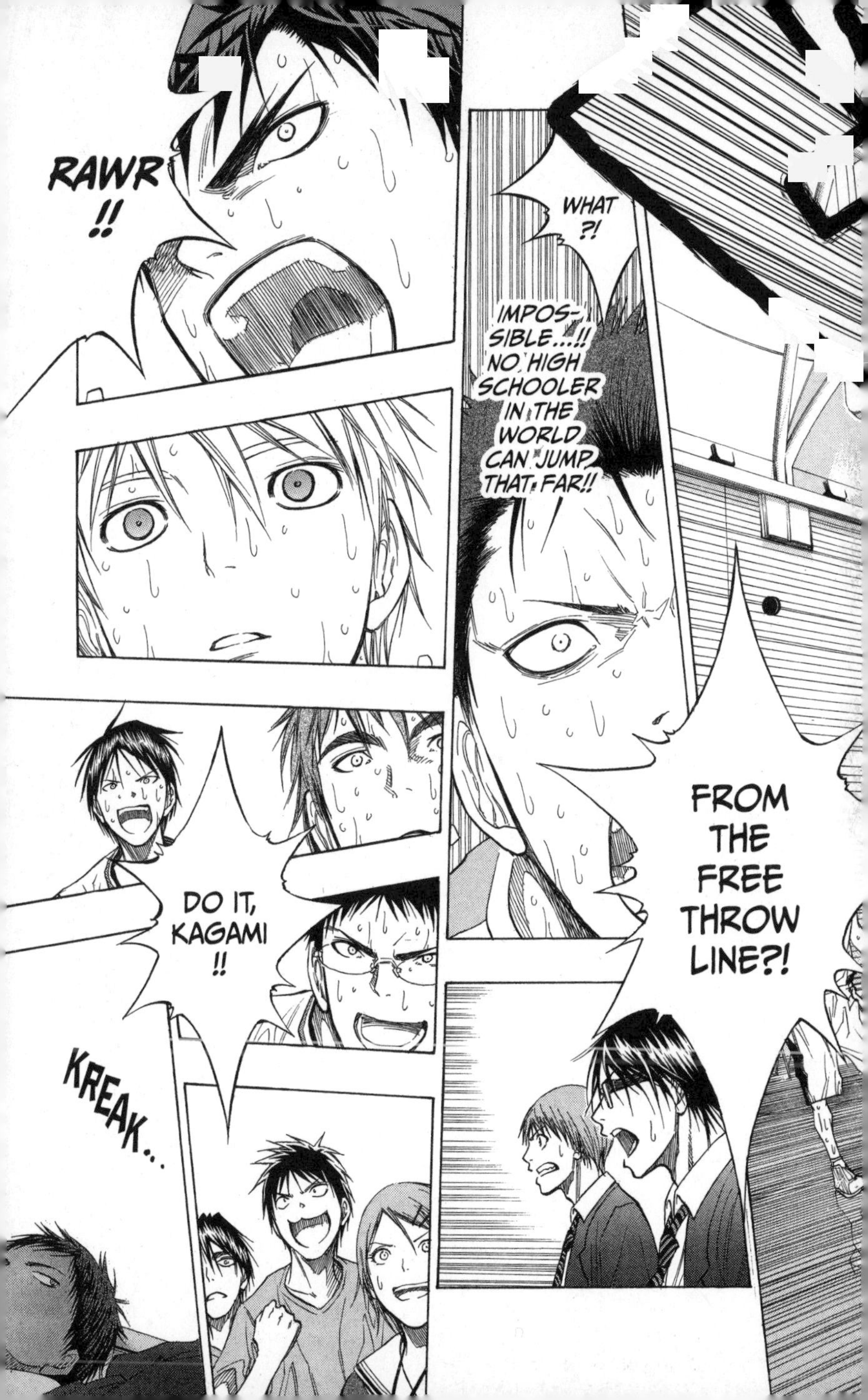
WHAT?!
IMPOSSIBLE...!! NO HIGH SCHOOLER IN THE WORLD CAN JUMP THAT FAR!!
RAWR!!
FROM THE FREE THROW LINE?!
DO IT, KAGAMI!!
KREAK...

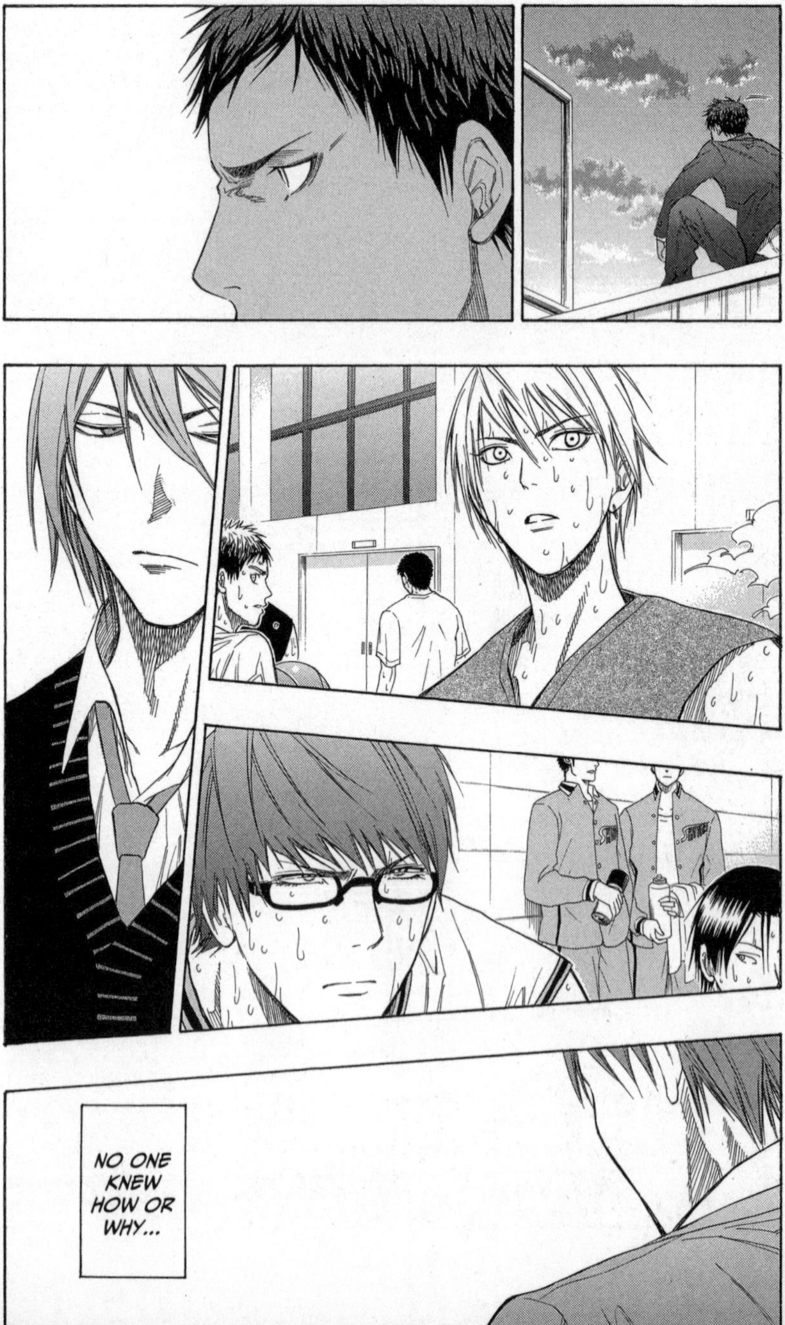
NO ONE KNEW HOW OR WHY...

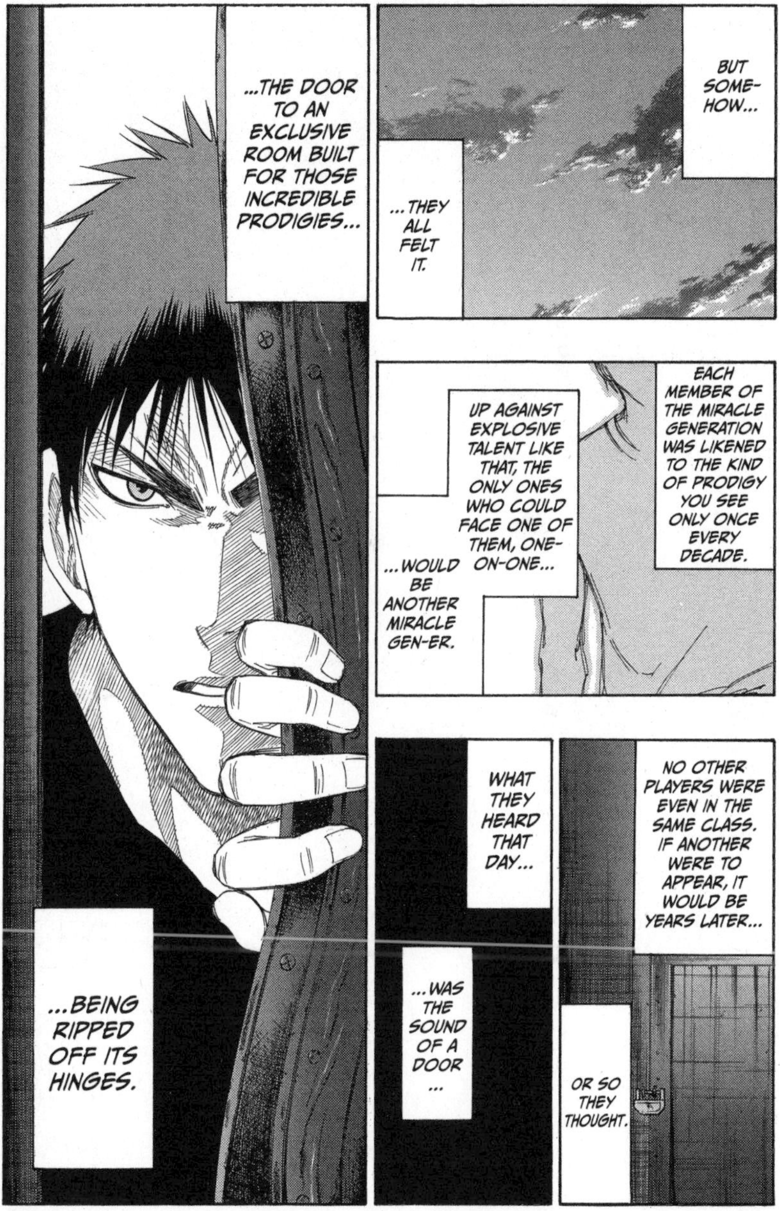
BUT SOMEHOW...
...THEY ALL FELT IT.
EACH MEMBER OF THE MIRACLE GENERATION WAS LIKENED TO THE KIND OF PRODIGY YOU SEE ONLY ONCE EVERY DECADE.
UP AGAINST EXPLOSIVE TALENT LIKE THAT, THE ONLY ONES WHO COULD FACE ONE OF THEM, ONE-ON-ONE...
...WOULD BE ANOTHER MIRACLE GEN-ER.
NO OTHER PLAYERS WERE EVEN IN THE SAME CLASS. IF ANOTHER WERE TO APPEAR, IT WOULD BE YEARS LATER...
OR SO THEY THOUGHT.
WHAT THEY HEARD THAT DAY...
...WAS THE SOUND OF A DOOR ...
...THE DOOR TO AN EXCLUSIVE ROOM BUILT FOR THOSE INCREDIBLE PRODIGIES...
...BEING RIPPED OFF ITS HINGES.

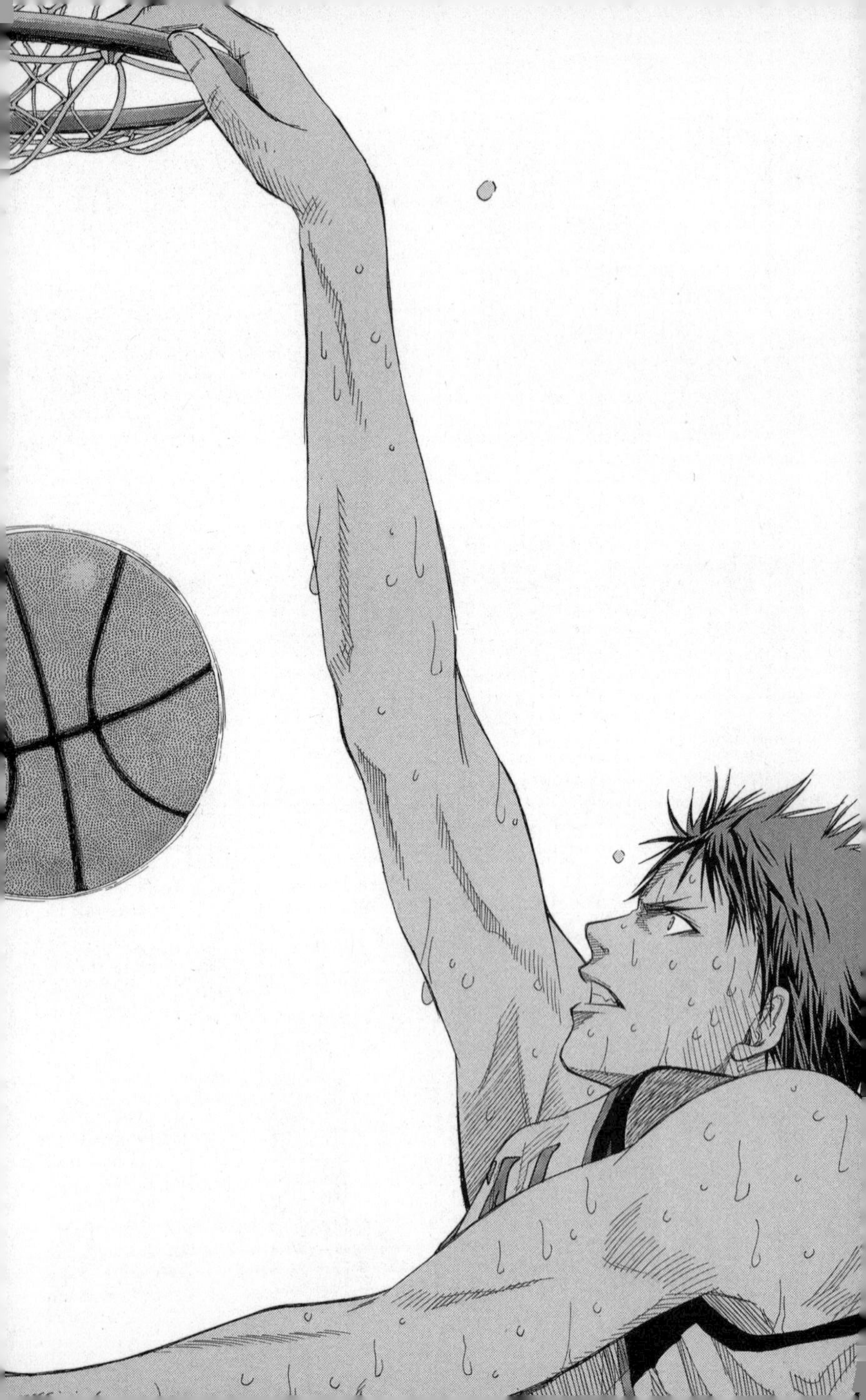

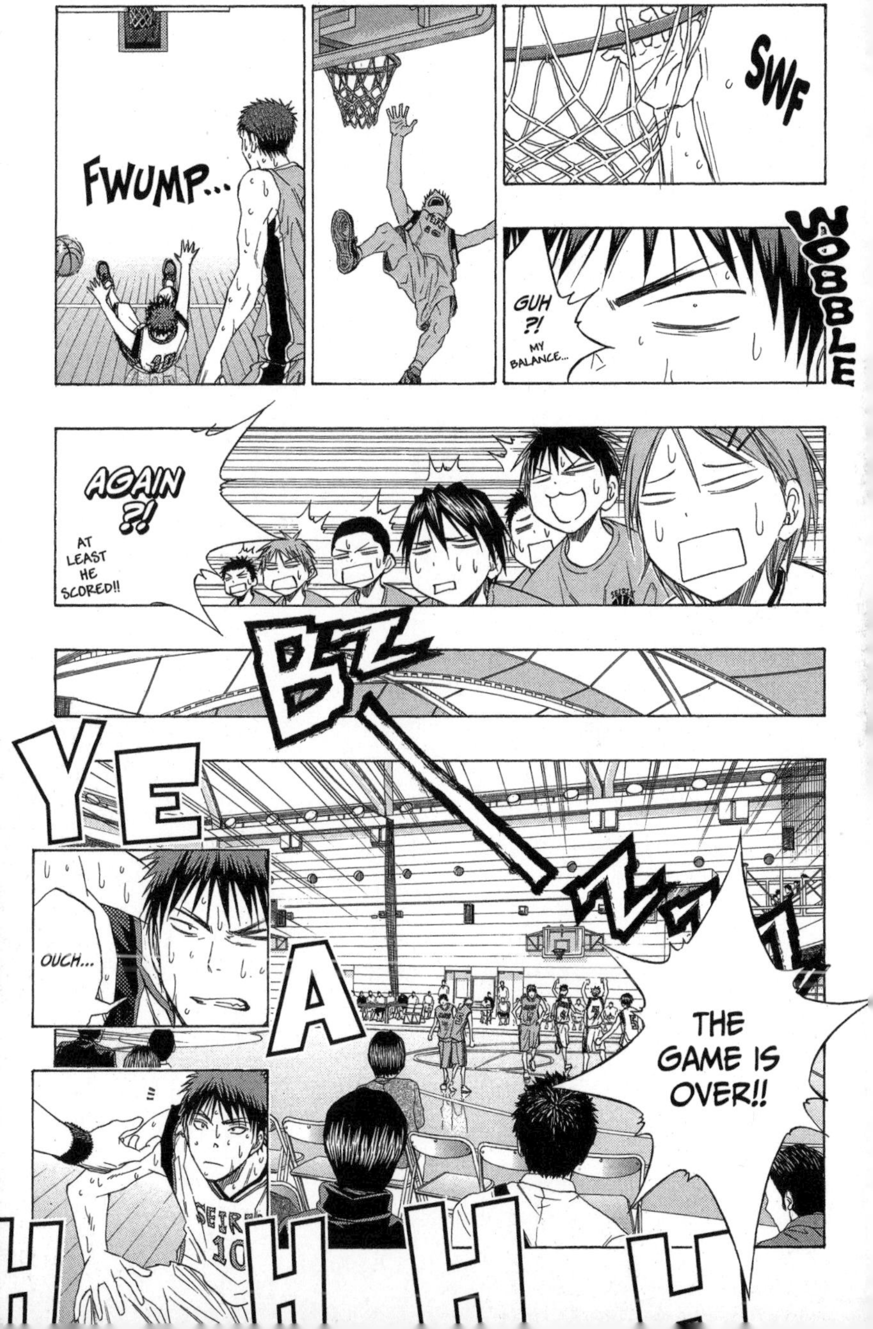
SWF
WOBBLE
GUH ?!
MY BALANCE...
FWUMP...
AGAIN ?!
AT LEAST HE SCORED!!
BZZZT
YEAHHHH
THE GAME IS OVER!!
OUCH...

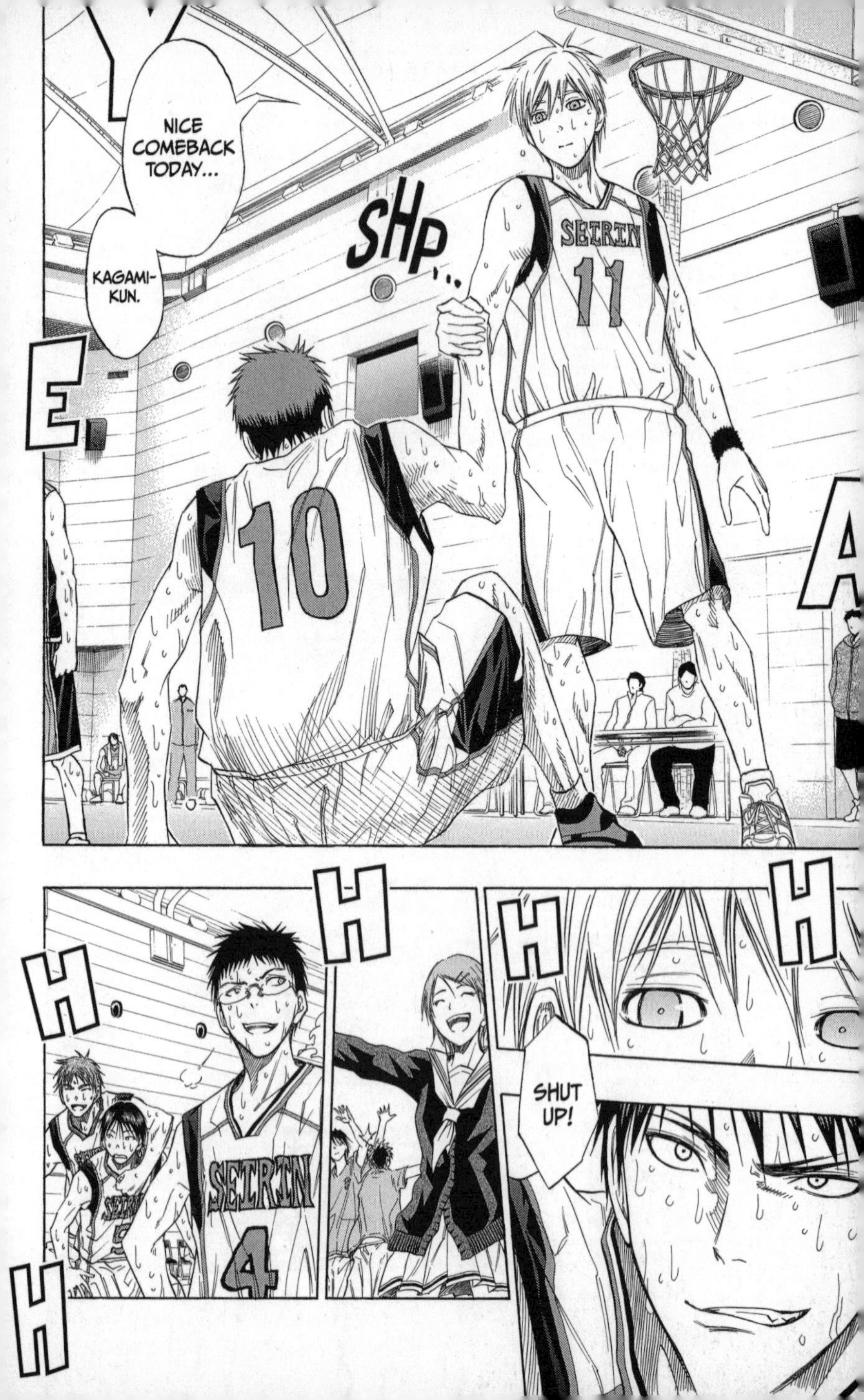

Y
E.
A
NICE COMEBACK TODAY...
KAGAMI-KUN.
SHP...
H
H
SHUT UP!
H
H
H
H

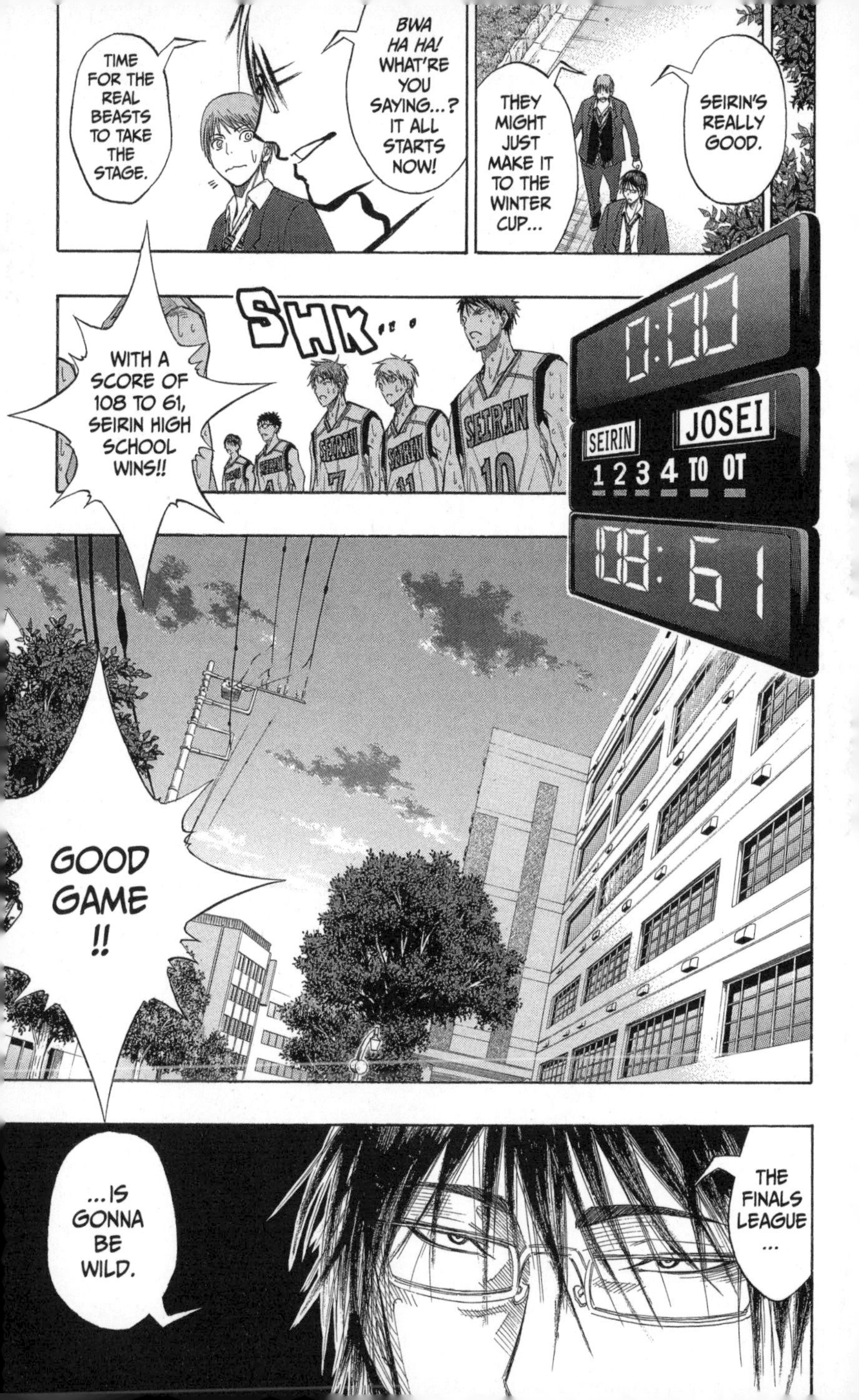
SEIRIN'S REALLY GOOD.
THEY MIGHT JUST MAKE IT TO THE WINTER CUP...
BWA HA HA! WHAT'RE YOU SAYING...? IT ALL STARTS NOW!
TIME FOR THE REAL BEASTS TO TAKE THE STAGE.
0:00
SEIRIN
JOSEI
1 2 3 4 TO OT
108:61
SHK
WITH A SCORE OF 108 TO 61, SEIRIN HIGH SCHOOL WINS!!
GOOD GAME !!
THE FINALS LEAGUE...
...IS GONNA BE WILD.

KUROKO'S BASKETBALL BLOOPERS
TAKE 9

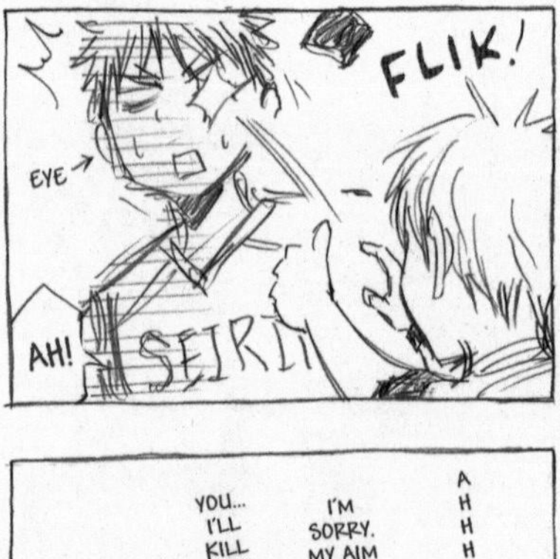
FLIK!
EYE
AH!
AHHHHH!!
I'M SORRY. MY AIM WAS OFF.
YOU... I'LL KILL YOU!!

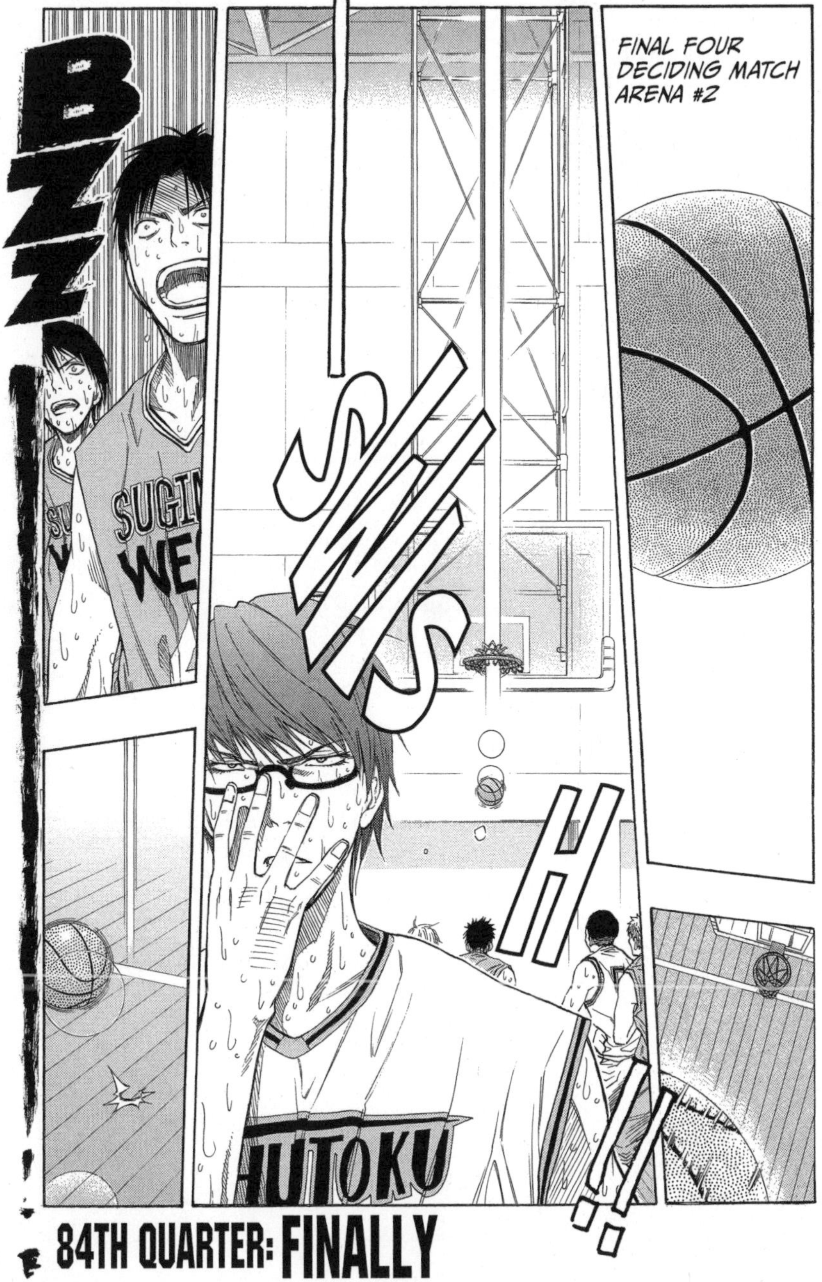
FINAL FOUR
DECIDING MATCH
ARENA #2
SWISH!!
BBZZ

84TH QUARTER: FINALLY

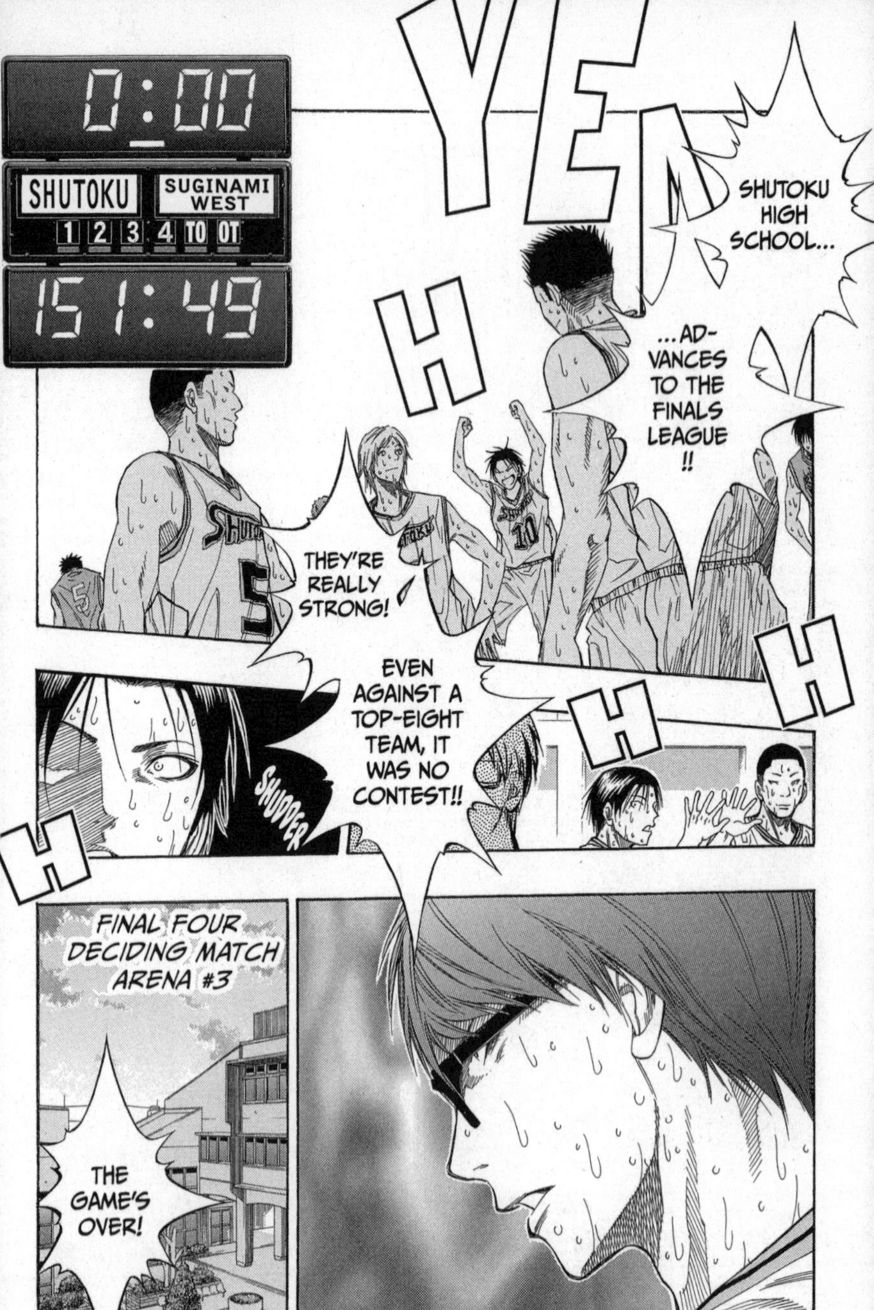
YEAHHHHH
SHUTOKU HIGH SCHOOL...
...AD-VANCES TO THE FINALS LEAGUE!!
0:00
SHUTOKU
SUGINAMI WEST
1 2 3 4 TO OT
151:49
THEY'RE REALLY STRONG!
EVEN AGAINST A TOP-EIGHT TEAM, IT WAS NO CONTEST!!
SHUDDER
FINAL FOUR DECIDING MATCH ARENA #3
THE GAME'S OVER!

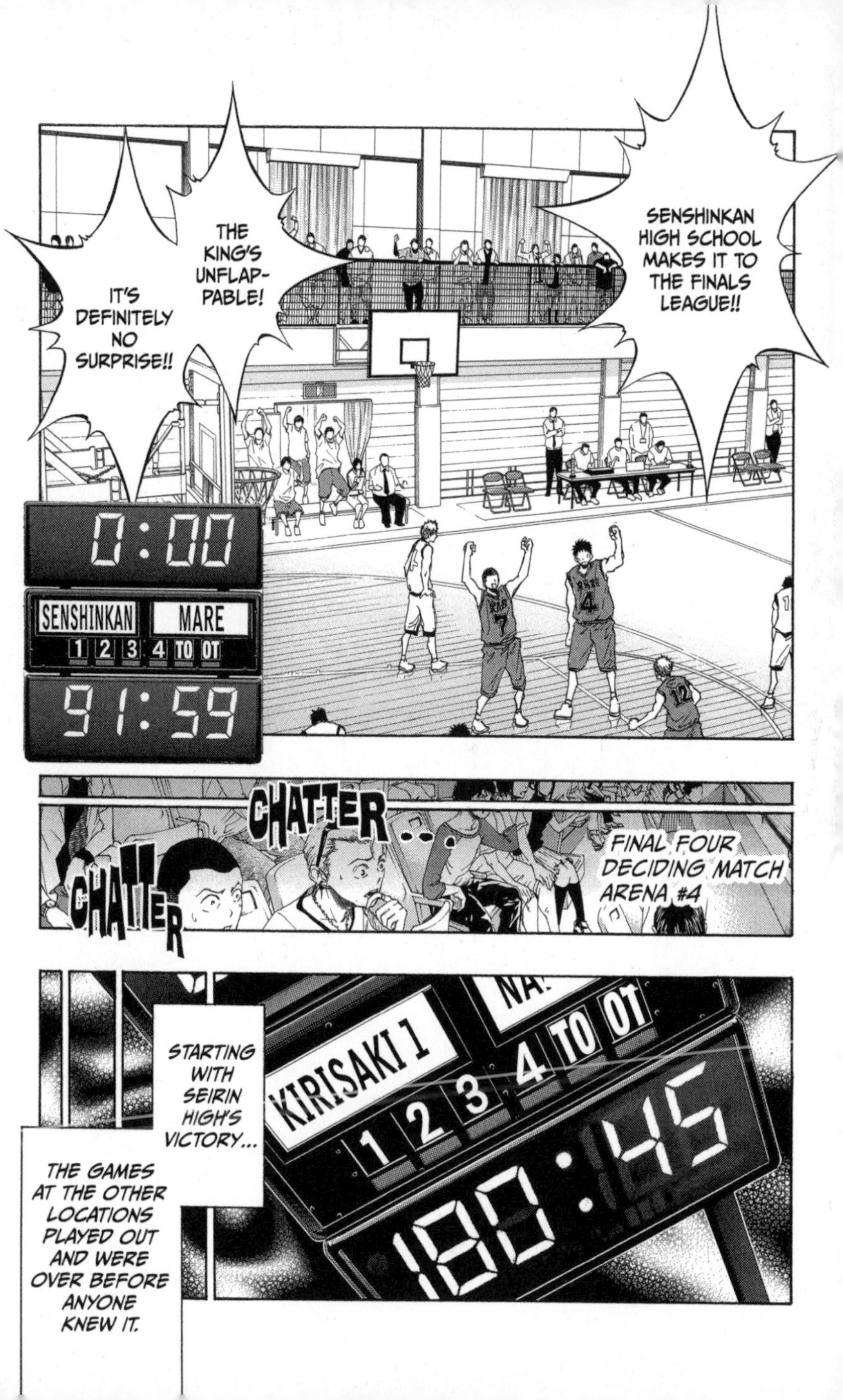
SENSHINKAN HIGH SCHOOL MAKES IT TO THE FINALS LEAGUE!!
THE KING'S UNFLAP-PABLE!
IT'S DEFINITELY NO SURPRISE!!
0:00
SENSHINKAN
MARE
1 2 3 4 TO OT
91:59
FINAL FOUR DECIDING MATCH ARENA #4
CHATTER
CHATTER
STARTING WITH SEIRIN HIGH'S VICTORY...
THE GAMES AT THE OTHER LOCATIONS PLAYED OUT AND WERE OVER BEFORE ANYONE KNEW IT.
KIRISAKI 1
1 2 3 4 TO OT

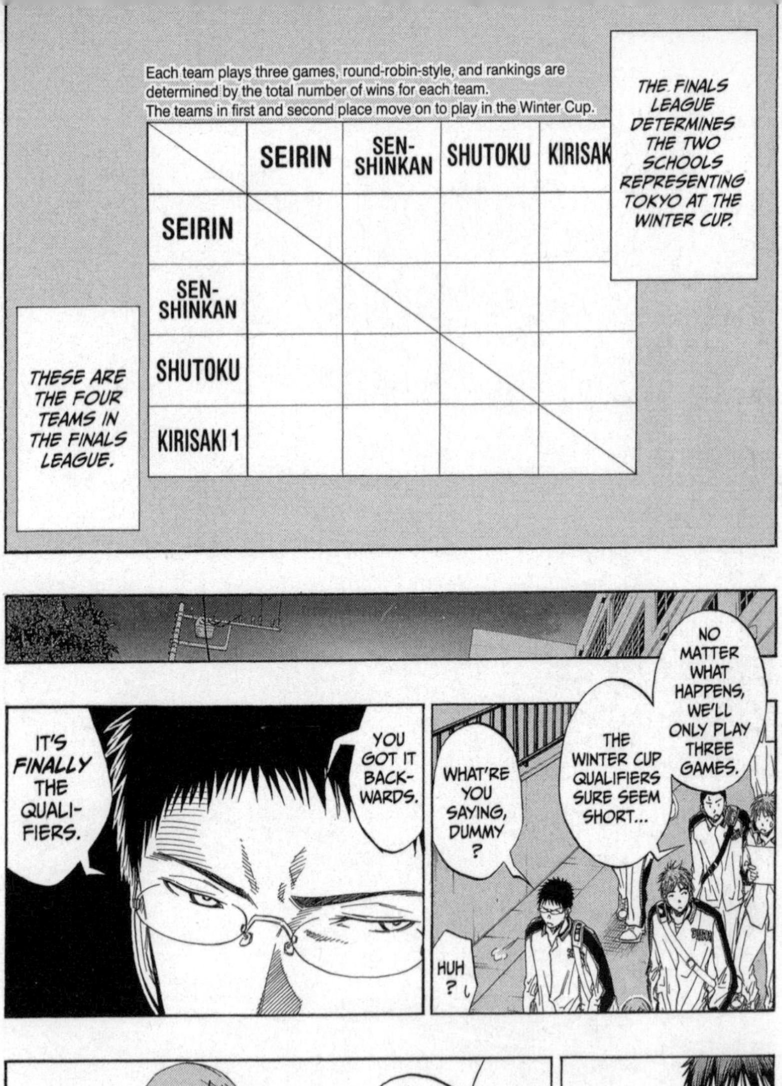

THE FINALS LEAGUE DETERMINES THE TWO SCHOOLS REPRESENTING TOKYO AT THE WINTER CUP.
Each team plays three games, round-robin-style, and rankings are determined by the total number of wins for each team.
The teams in first and second place move on to play in the Winter Cup.

	SEIRIN	SEN-SHINKAN	SHUTOKU	KIRISAK
SEIRIN				
SEN-SHINKAN				
SHUTOKU				
KIRISAKI 1				

THESE ARE THE FOUR TEAMS IN THE FINALS LEAGUE.
NO MATTER WHAT HAPPENS, WE'LL ONLY PLAY THREE GAMES.
THE WINTER CUP QUALIFIERS SURE SEEM SHORT...
WHAT'RE YOU SAYING, DUMMY?
HUH?
YOU GOT IT BACKWARDS.
IT'S FINALLY THE QUALIFIERS.
DID YA FORGET ALREADY?
THE ONLY ONES PLAYING IN THESE QUALIFIERS ARE THE TOP EIGHT FROM OVER 300 TEAMS THAT COMPETED THIS SUMMER.
LOOKING AT IT THAT WAY, THE WINTER CUP QUALIFIERS REALLY BEGAN BACK DURING THE QUALIFIERS FOR INTER-HIGH.

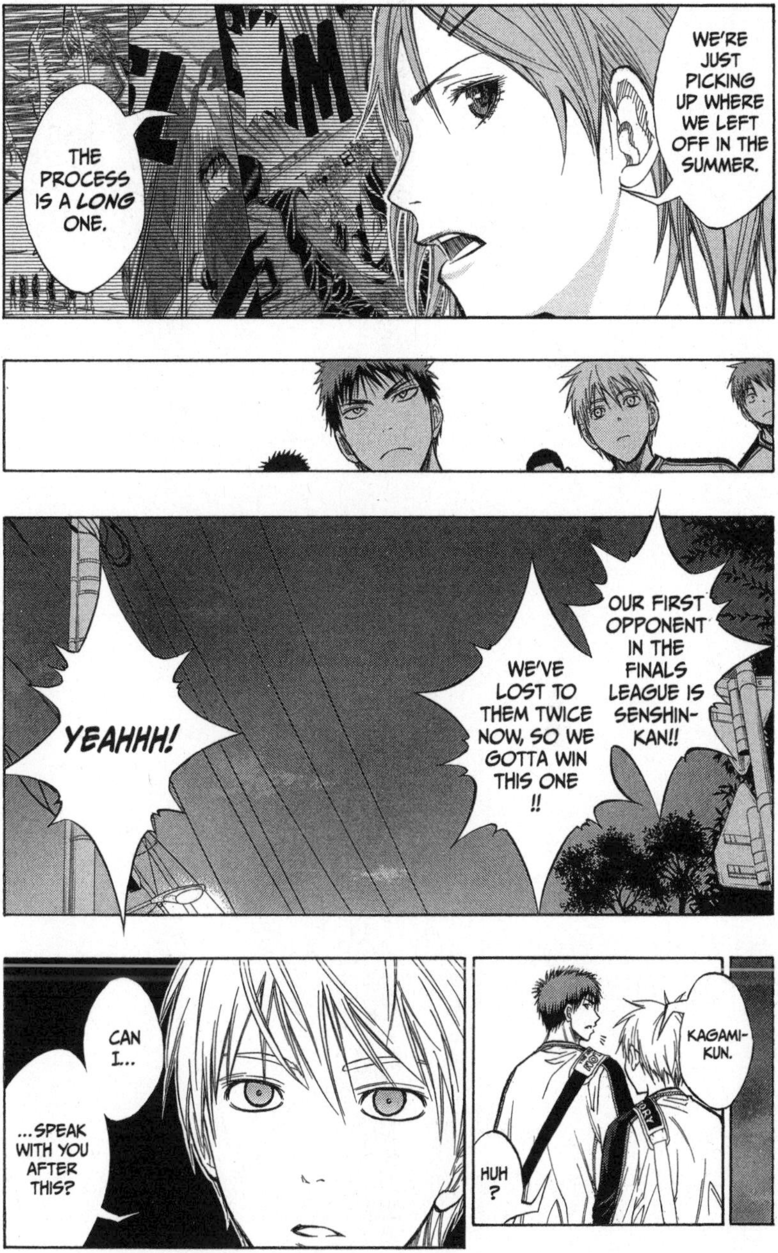
WE'RE JUST PICKING UP WHERE WE LEFT OFF IN THE SUMMER.
THE PROCESS IS A LONG ONE.
OUR FIRST OPPONENT IN THE FINALS LEAGUE IS SENSHIN-KAN!!
WE'VE LOST TO THEM TWICE NOW, SO WE GOTTA WIN THIS ONE !!
YEAHHH!
KAGAMI-KUN.
HUH ?
CAN I...
...SPEAK WITH YOU AFTER THIS?

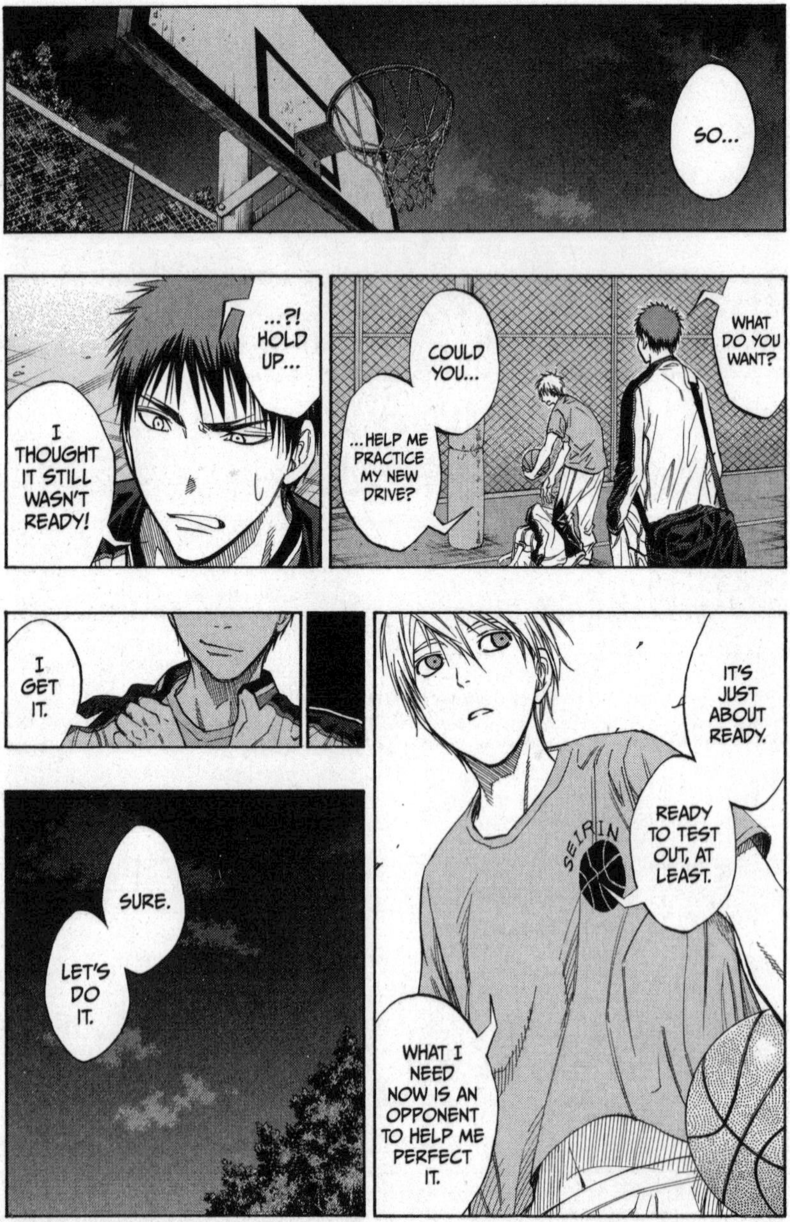
SO...
WHAT DO YOU WANT?
COULD YOU...
...HELP ME PRACTICE MY NEW DRIVE?
...?! HOLD UP...
I THOUGHT IT STILL WASN'T READY!
IT'S JUST ABOUT READY.
READY TO TEST OUT, AT LEAST.
WHAT I NEED NOW IS AN OPPONENT TO HELP ME PERFECT IT.
I GET IT.
SURE.
LET'S DO IT.

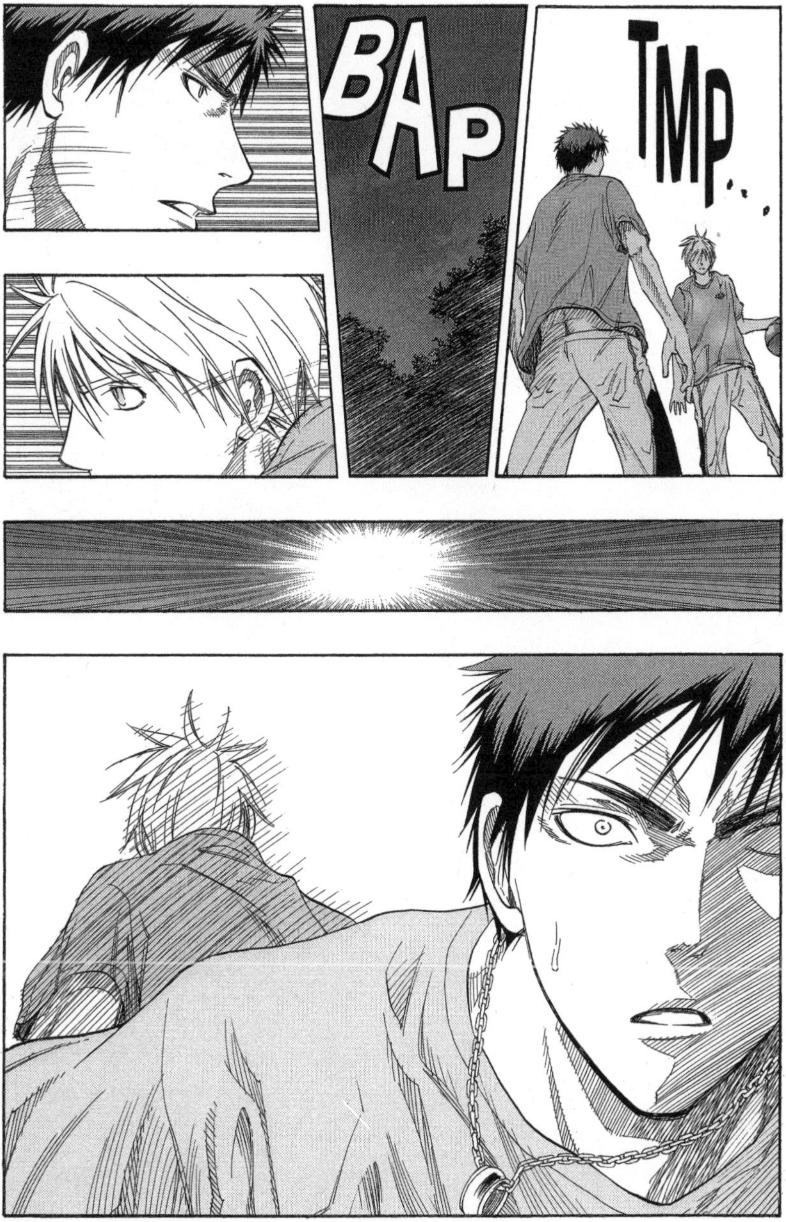
TMP...
BAP

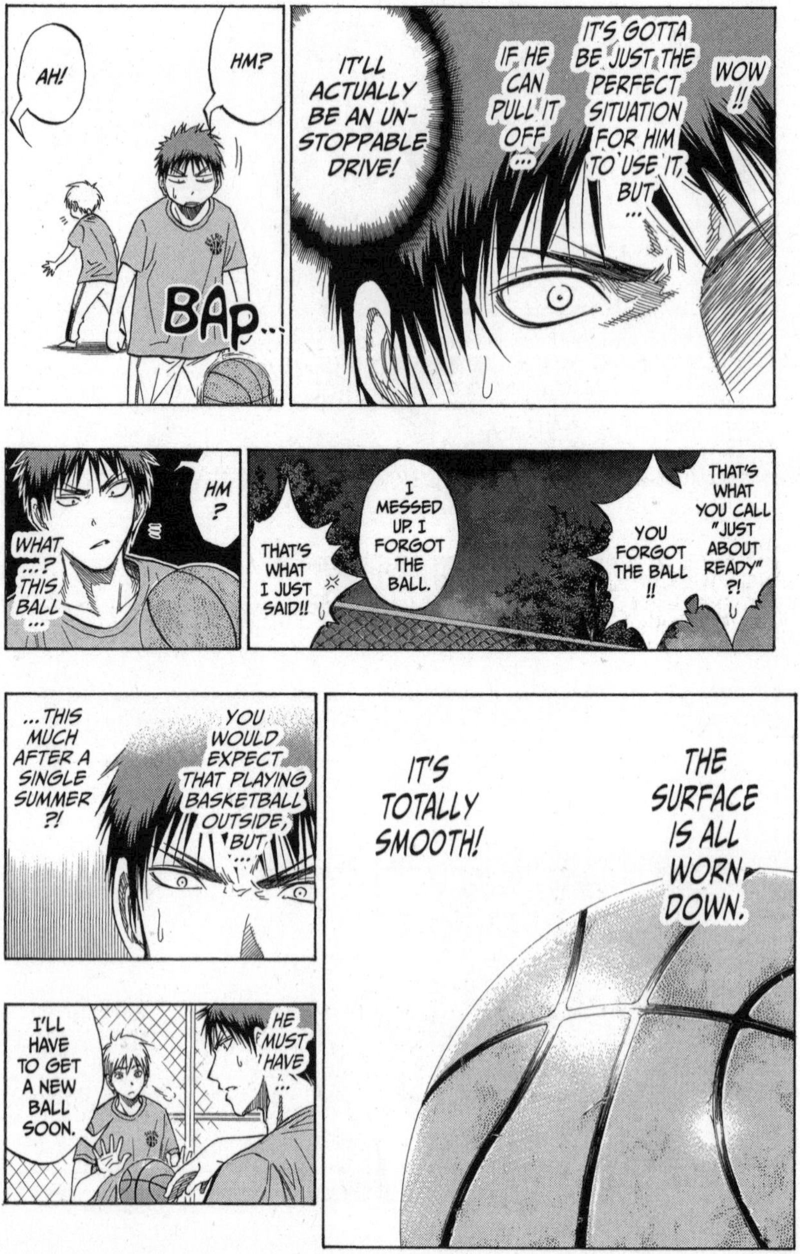
WOW!!
IT'S GOTTA BE JUST THE PERFECT SITUATION FOR HIM TO USE IT, BUT...
IF HE CAN PULL IT OFF...
IT'LL ACTUALLY BE AN UN-STOPPABLE DRIVE!
HM?
AH!
BAP...
THAT'S WHAT YOU CALL "JUST ABOUT READY"?!
YOU FORGOT THE BALL!!
I MESSED UP. I FORGOT THE BALL.
THAT'S WHAT I JUST SAID!!
HM?
WHAT...? THIS BALL...
THE SURFACE IS ALL WORN DOWN.
IT'S TOTALLY SMOOTH!
YOU WOULD EXPECT THAT PLAYING BASKETBALL OUTSIDE, BUT...
...THIS MUCH AFTER A SINGLE SUMMER?!
HE MUST HAVE...
I'LL HAVE TO GET A NEW BALL SOON.

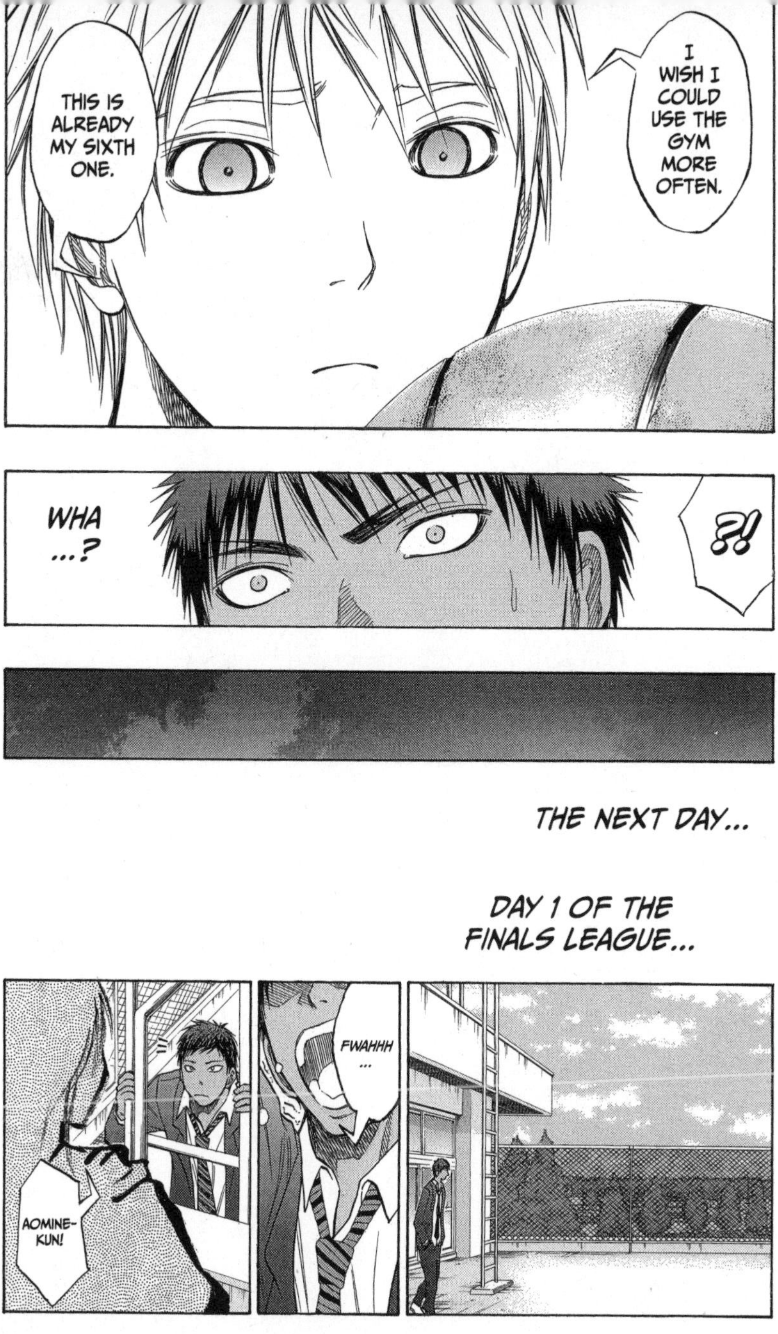
I WISH I COULD USE THE GYM MORE OFTEN.
THIS IS ALREADY MY SIXTH ONE.
?!
WHA ...?
THE NEXT DAY...
DAY 1 OF THE FINALS LEAGUE...
FWAHHH ...
AOMINE-KUN!

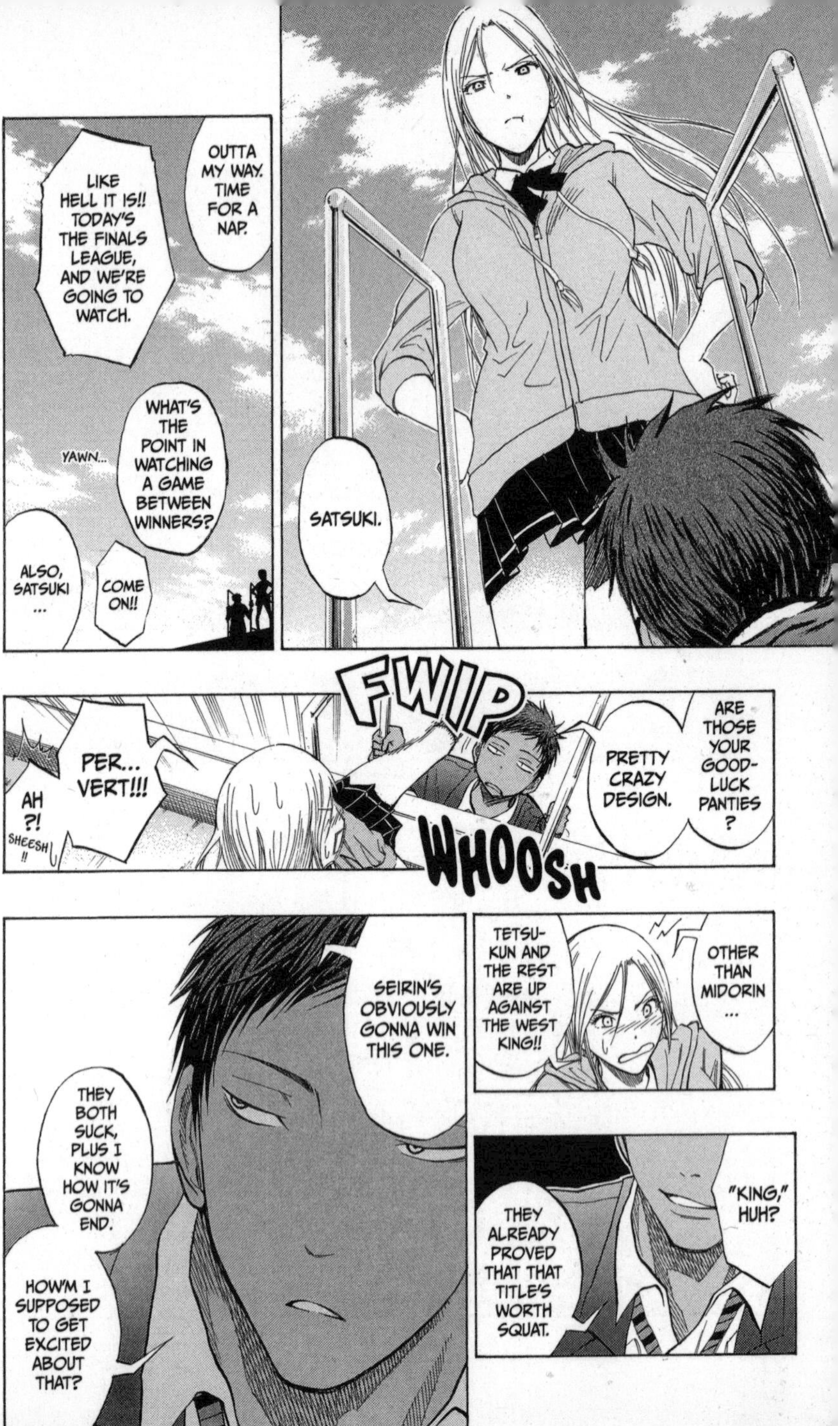
SATSUKI.
OUTTA MY WAY. TIME FOR A NAP.
LIKE HELL IT IS!! TODAY'S THE FINALS LEAGUE, AND WE'RE GOING TO WATCH.
WHAT'S THE POINT IN WATCHING A GAME BETWEEN WINNERS?
YAWN...
COME ON!!
ALSO, SATSUKI ...
ARE THOSE YOUR GOOD-LUCK PANTIES?
PRETTY CRAZY DESIGN.
FWIP
PER... VERT!!!
AH ?!
SHEESH !!
WHOOSH
OTHER THAN MIDORIN ...
TETSU-KUN AND THE REST ARE UP AGAINST THE WEST KING!!
"KING," HUH?
THEY ALREADY PROVED THAT THAT TITLE'S WORTH SQUAT.
SEIRIN'S OBVIOUSLY GONNA WIN THIS ONE.
THEY BOTH SUCK, PLUS I KNOW HOW IT'S GONNA END.
HOW'M I SUPPOSED TO GET EXCITED ABOUT THAT?

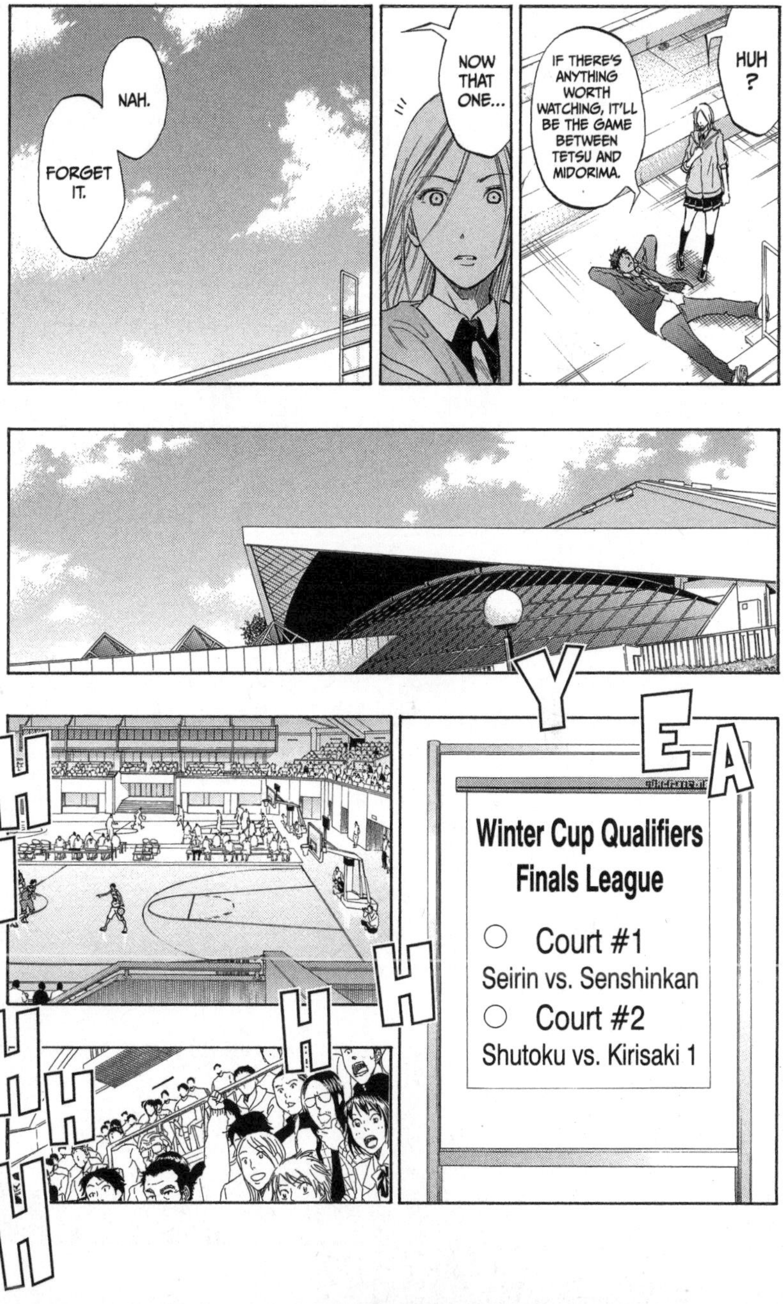
HUH?
IF THERE'S ANYTHING WORTH WATCHING, IT'LL BE THE GAME BETWEEN TETSU AND MIDORIMA.
NOW THAT ONE...
NAH.
FORGET IT.
Winter Cup Qualifiers Finals League
○ Court #1
Seirin vs. Senshinkan
○ Court #2
Shutoku vs. Kirisaki 1
YEAHHHHHHHH

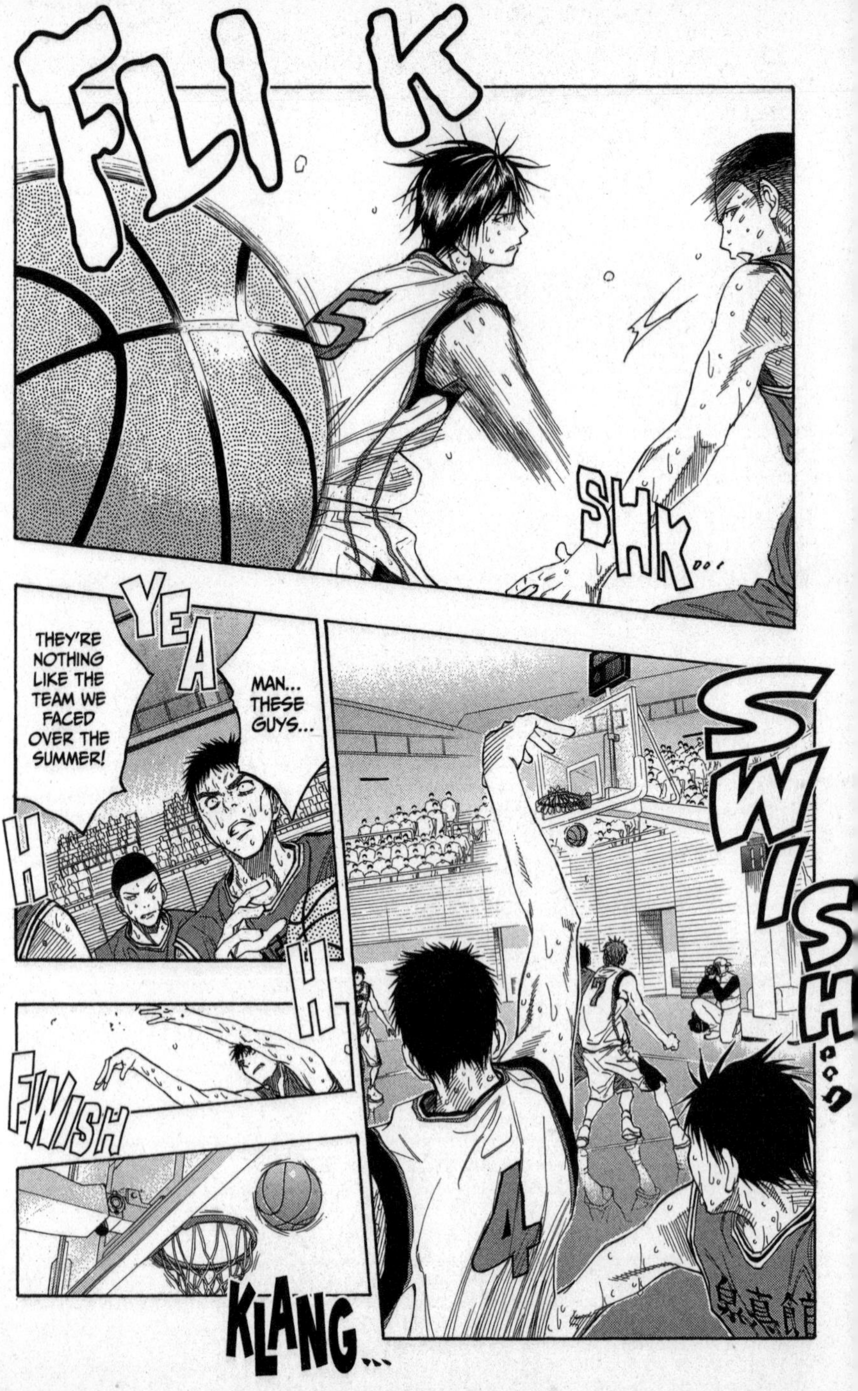
FLI K
SHK...
SWISH...
泉真館
YEA
H
H
MAN... THESE GUYS...
THEY'RE NOTHING LIKE THE TEAM WE FACED OVER THE SUMMER!
FWISH
KLANG...

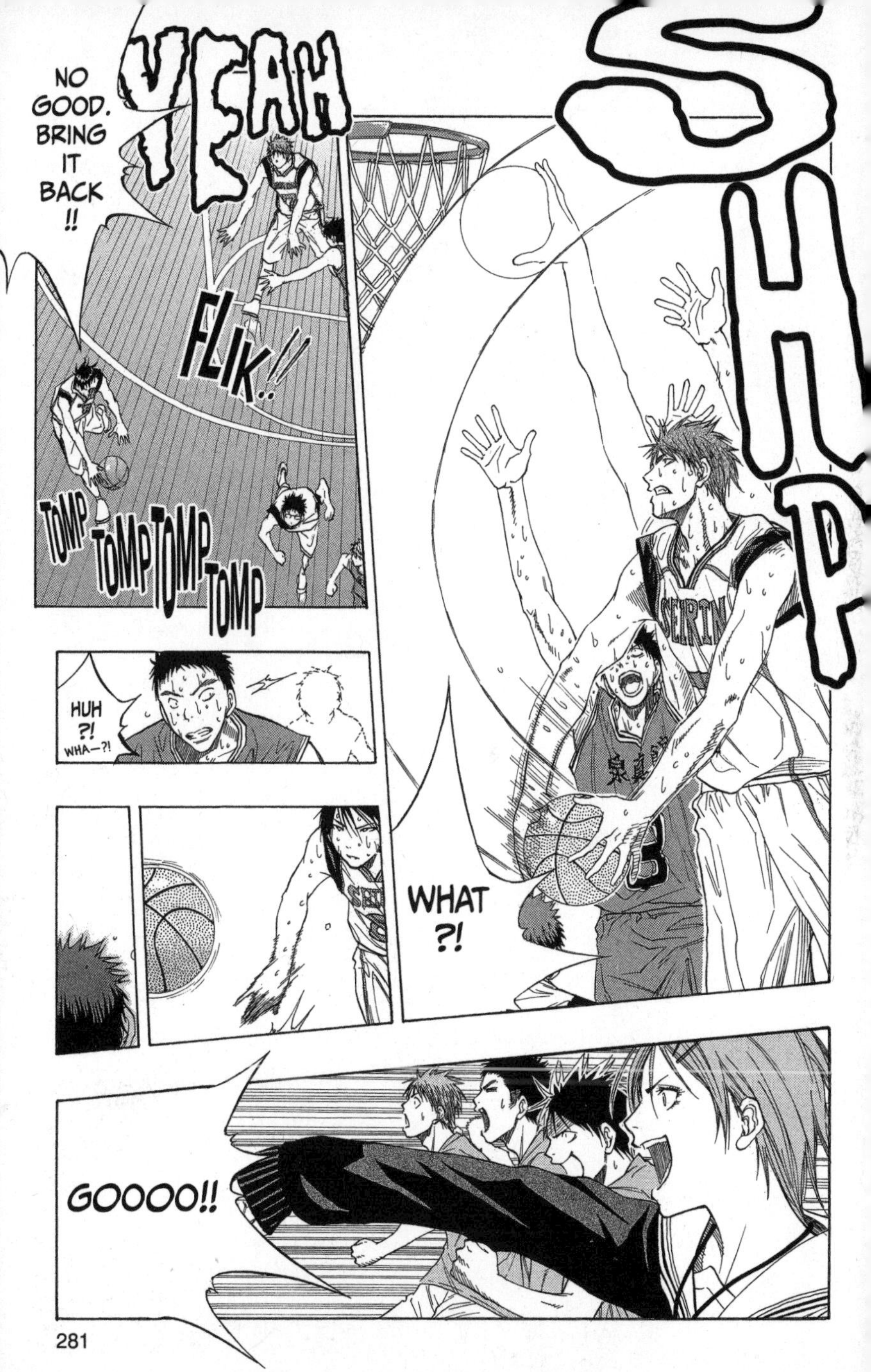
SHP
WHAT ?!
YEAH
NO GOOD. BRING IT BACK !!
FLIK!!
TOMP TOMP TOMP TOMP
HUH ?!
WHA—?!
GOOOO!!

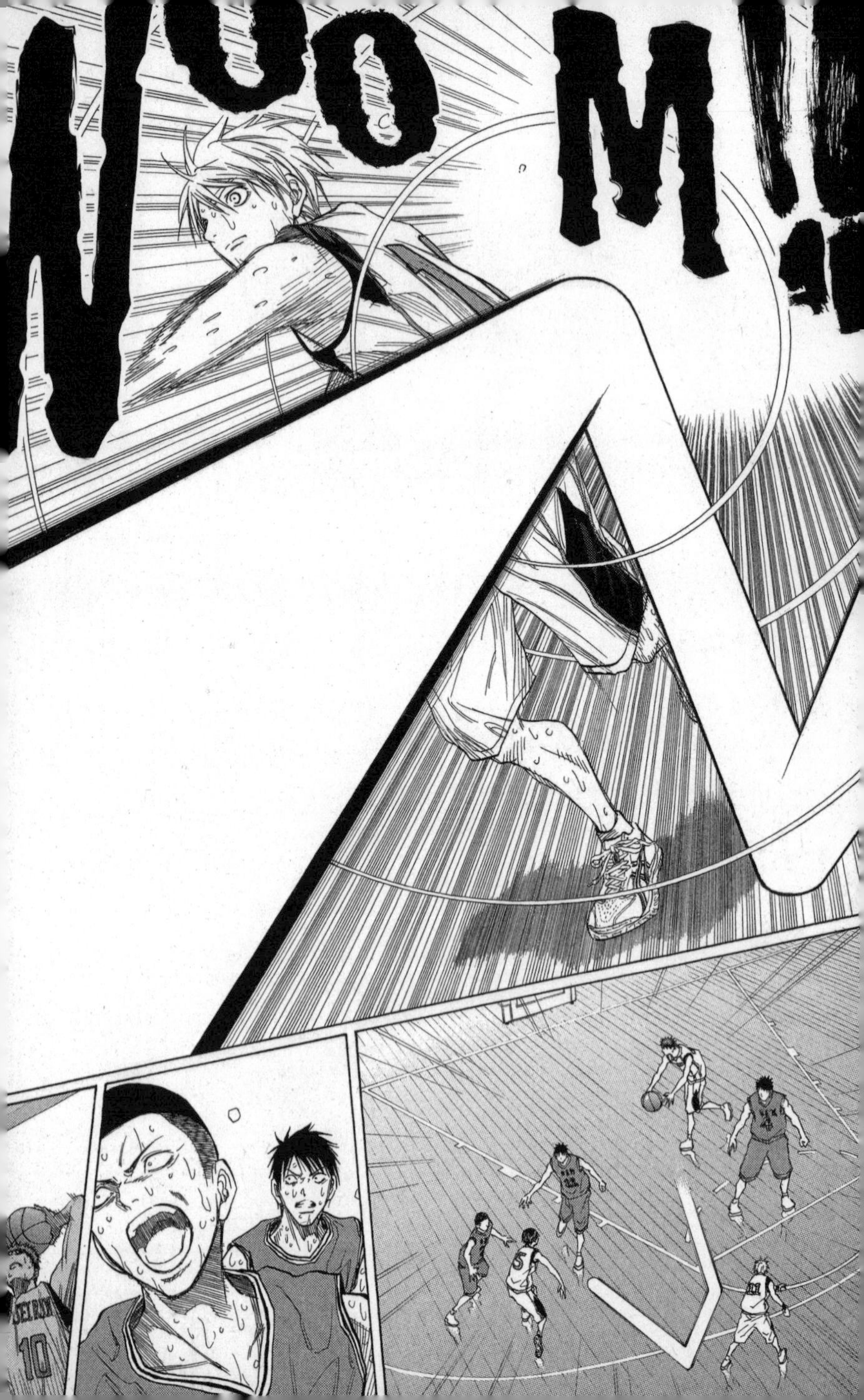
VUOM!!

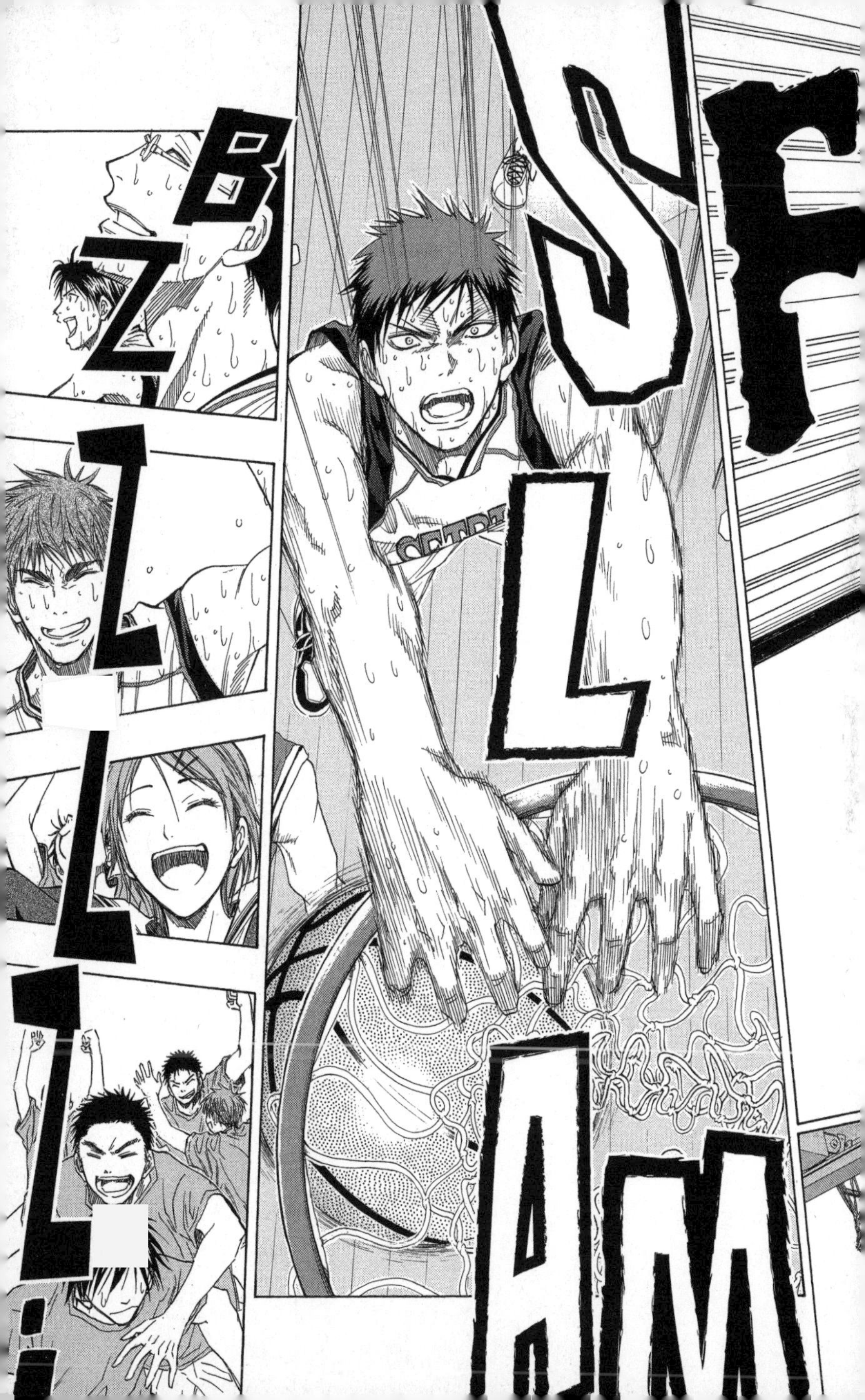
SLAM

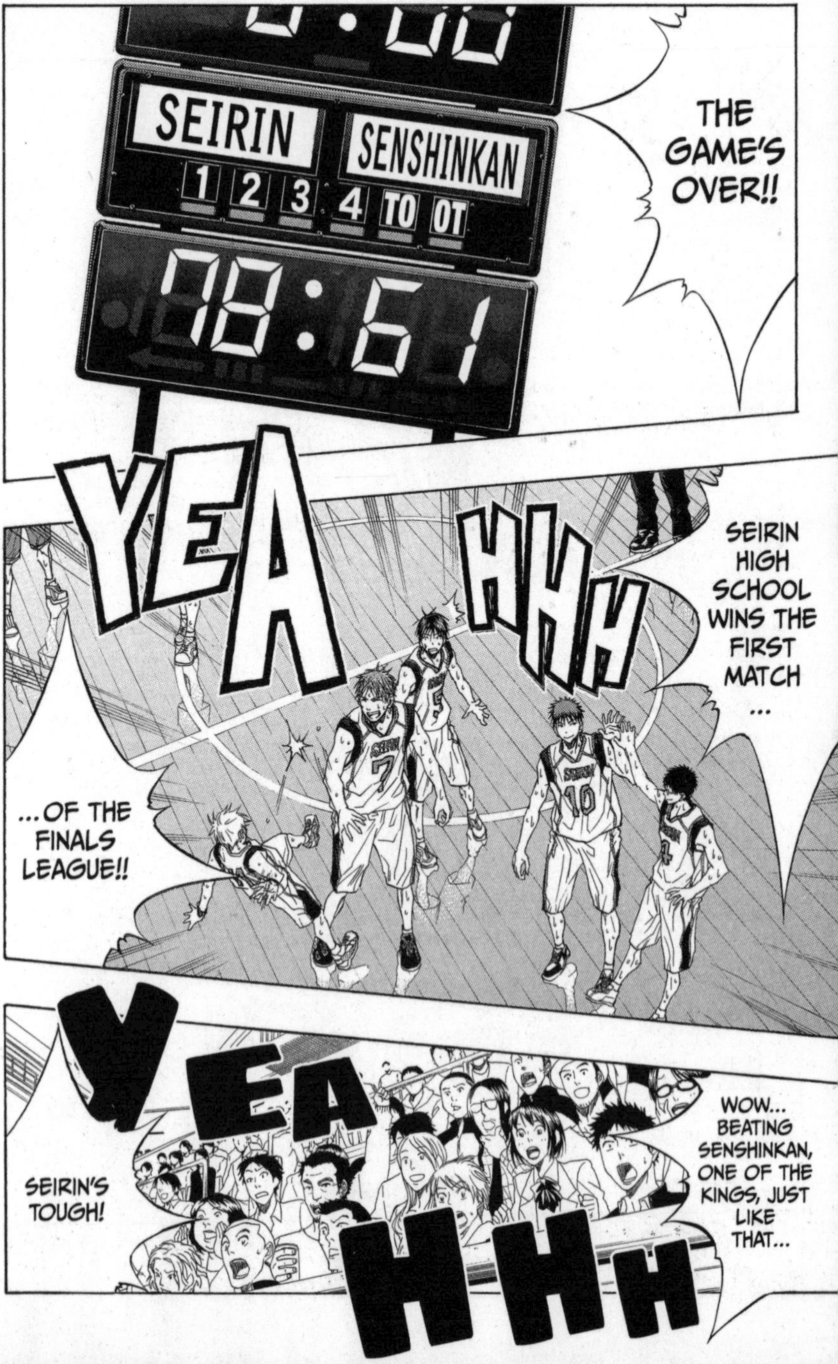
SEIRIN
SENSHINKAN
1 2 3 4 TO OT
78:61
THE GAME'S OVER!!
YEAHHHH
SEIRIN HIGH SCHOOL WINS THE FIRST MATCH ...
...OF THE FINALS LEAGUE!!
YEAHHH
WOW... BEATING SENSHINKAN, ONE OF THE KINGS, JUST LIKE THAT...
SEIRIN'S TOUGH!

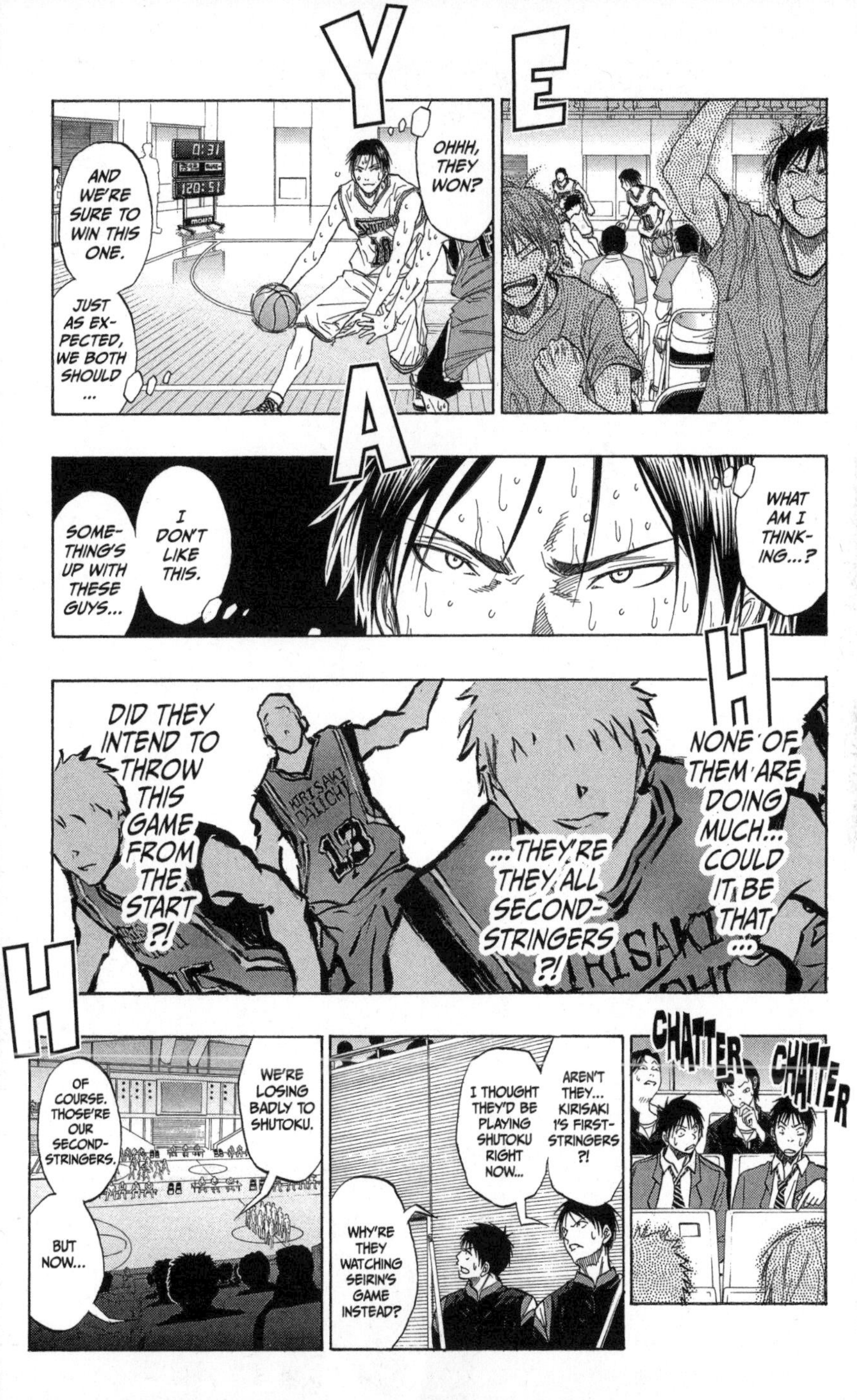
YEAHH
OHHH, THEY WON?
AND WE'RE SURE TO WIN THIS ONE.
JUST AS EXPECTED, WE BOTH SHOULD ...
WHAT AM I THINKING...?
I DON'T LIKE THIS.
SOMETHING'S UP WITH THESE GUYS...
NONE OF THEM ARE DOING MUCH... COULD IT BE THAT...
...THEY'RE THEY ALL SECOND-STRINGERS?!
DID THEY INTEND TO THROW THIS GAME FROM THE START?!
CHATTER CHATTER
AREN'T THEY... KIRISAKI 1'S FIRST-STRINGERS?!
I THOUGHT THEY'D BE PLAYING SHUTOKU RIGHT NOW...
WHY'RE THEY WATCHING SEIRIN'S GAME INSTEAD?
WE'RE LOSING BADLY TO SHUTOKU.
OF COURSE. THOSE'RE OUR SECOND-STRINGERS.
BUT NOW...

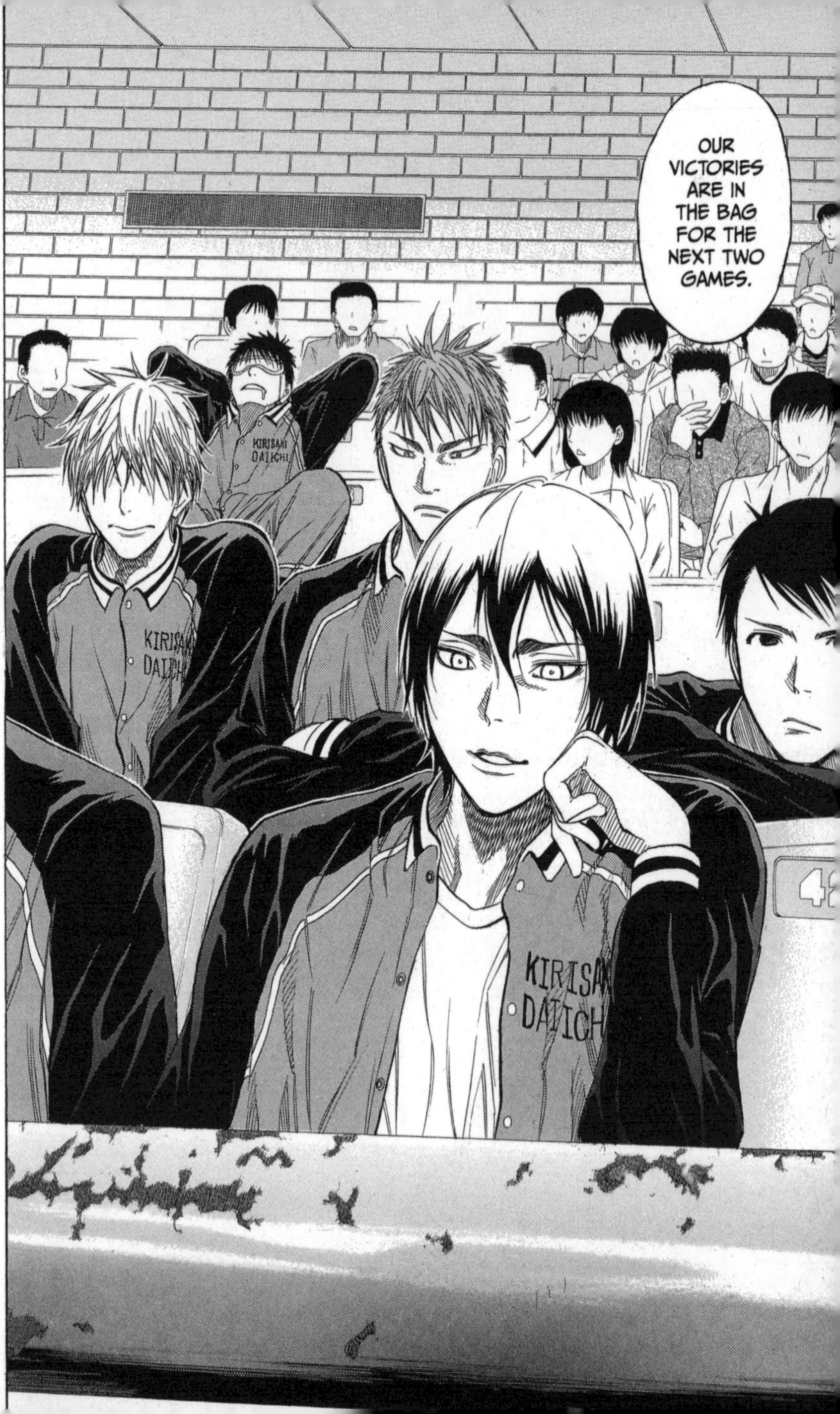
OUR VICTORIES ARE IN THE BAG FOR THE NEXT TWO GAMES.
KIRISAKI DAIICHI
KIRISAKI DAIICH
KIRISAKI DAIICH

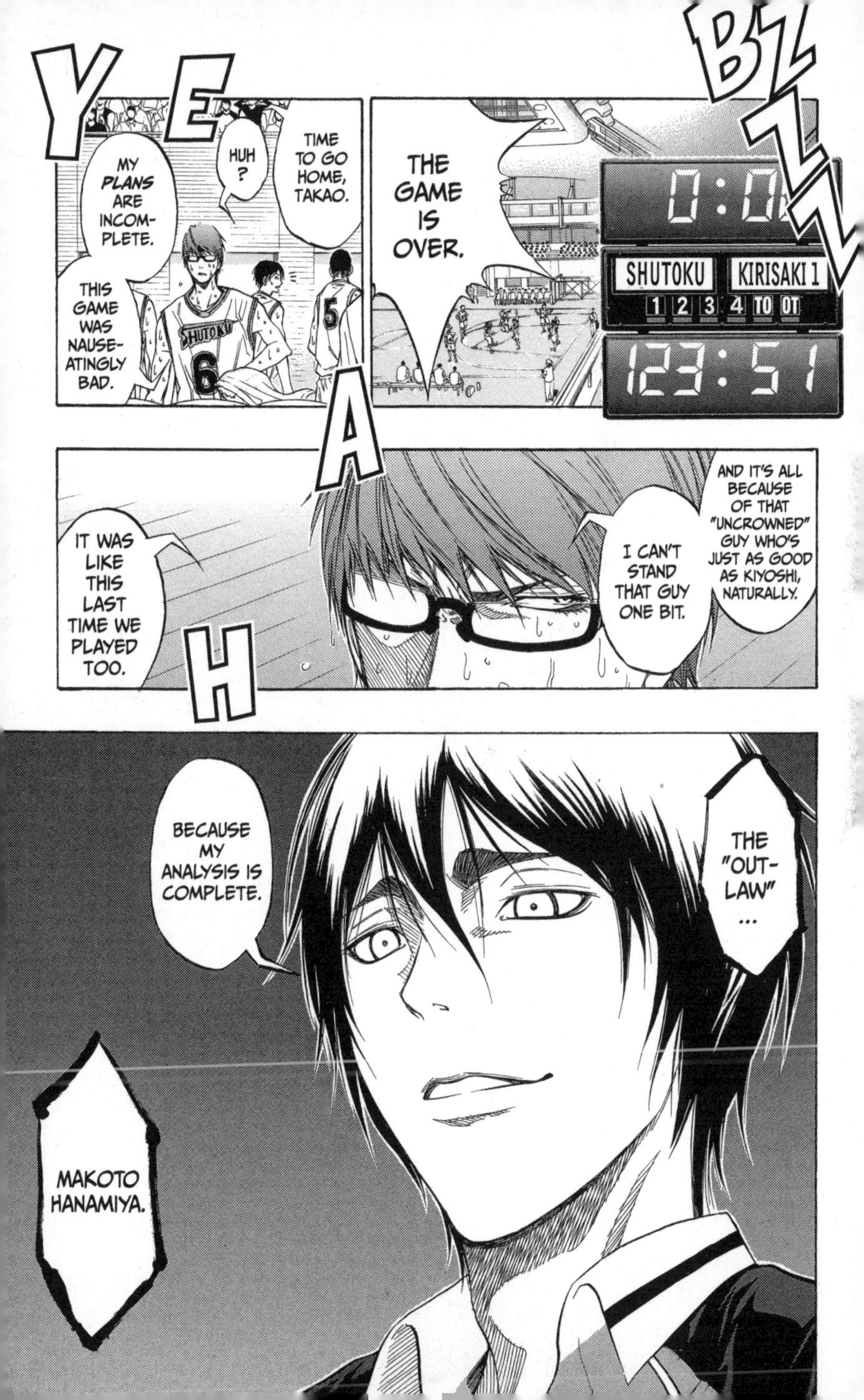
BZZZ
SHUTOKU
KIRISAKI 1
1 2 3 4 TO OT
123 : 51
THE GAME IS OVER.
YEAH
TIME TO GO HOME, TAKAO.
HUH?
MY *PLANS* ARE INCOMPLETE.
THIS GAME WAS NAUSEATINGLY BAD.
AND IT'S ALL BECAUSE OF THAT "UNCROWNED" GUY WHO'S JUST AS GOOD AS KIYOSHI, NATURALLY.
I CAN'T STAND THAT GUY ONE BIT.
IT WAS LIKE THIS LAST TIME WE PLAYED TOO.
THE "OUTLAW"...
BECAUSE MY ANALYSIS IS COMPLETE.
MAKOTO HANAMIYA.

KUROKO'S BASKETBALL BLOOPERS

TAKE 2

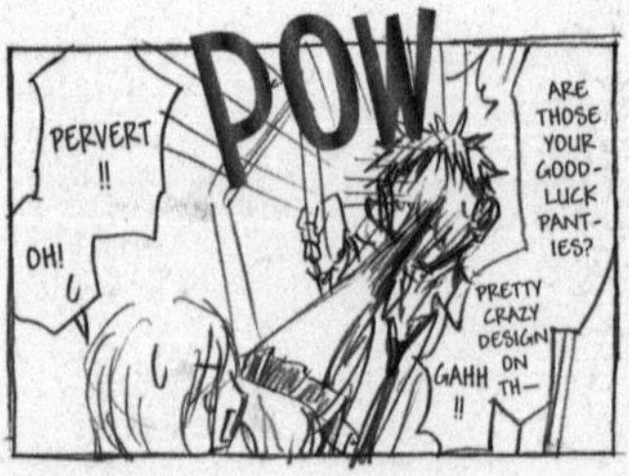
ARE THOSE YOUR GOOD-LUCK PANTIES?
PRETTY CRAZY DESIGN ON TH—
POW
PERVERT!!
GAHH!!
OH!

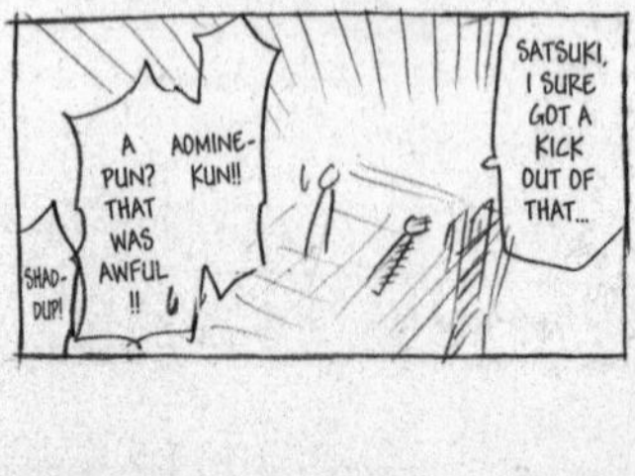
SATSUKI, I SURE GOT A KICK OUT OF THAT...
AOMINE-KUN!!
A PUN? THAT WAS AWFUL!!
SHADDUP!

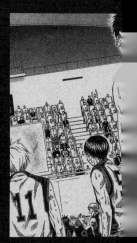

85TH QUARTER:
ONE LOSS IS PLENTY

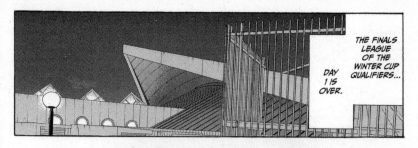

THE FINALS LEAGUE OF THE WINTER CUP QUALIFIERS...
DAY 1 IS OVER.

SEIRIN SHOWED ITSELF TO BE A MASSIVELY IMPROVED TEAM, THANKS TO THE ADDITION OF KIYOSHI AND THEIR EXTENSIVE SUMMER TRAINING.
THOUGH THEY LOST TO THE WEST KING, SENSHINKAN, DURING THE SUMMER, SEIRIN GOT THEIR REVENGE BY BEATING THEM IN THE FIRST GAME OF THE FINALS LEAGUE.
SEIRIN

MEANWHILE, SHUTOKU AND THEIR MIRACLE GENERATION MEMBER SHINTARO MIDORIMA CRUSHED KIRISAKI 1.

HERE ARE THE CURRENT STANDINGS TO DECIDE THE TWO WINTER CUP PARTICI-PANTS...

	SEIRIN	SEN-SHINKAN	SHUTOKU	KIRISAKI 1
SEIRIN		○ 78–61		
SEN-SHINKAN	× 61–78			
SHUTOKU				○ 123–51
KIRISAKI 1			× 51–123	

SEIRIN AND SHUTOKU KICKED OFF THE FESTIVITIES BY WINNING THEIR OPENING GAME.

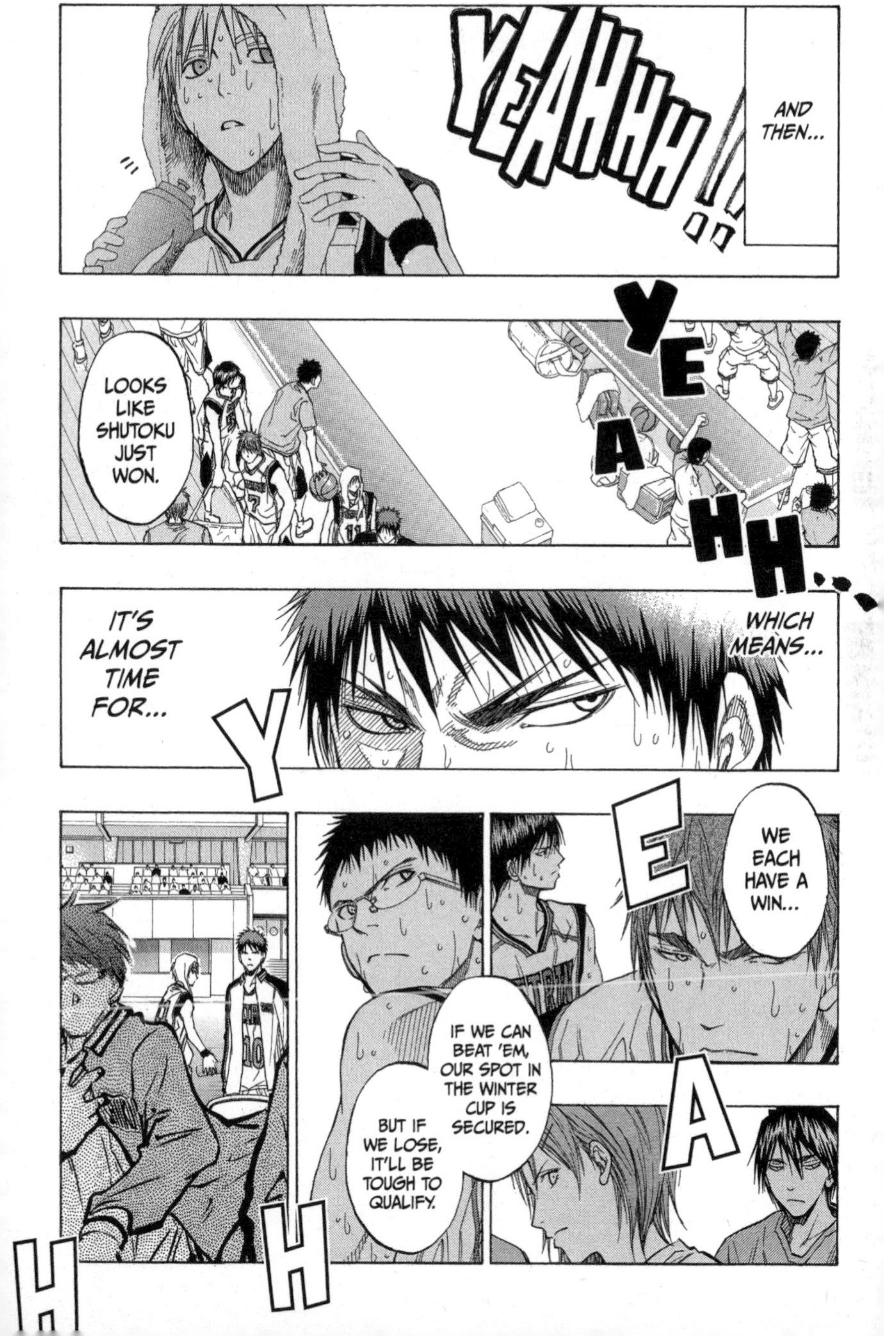
AND THEN...
YEAHHH!!
LOOKS LIKE SHUTOKU JUST WON.
YEAHH...
WHICH MEANS...
IT'S ALMOST TIME FOR...
YEAHH
WE EACH HAVE A WIN...
IF WE CAN BEAT 'EM, OUR SPOT IN THE WINTER CUP IS SECURED.
BUT IF WE LOSE, IT'LL BE TOUGH TO QUALIFY.

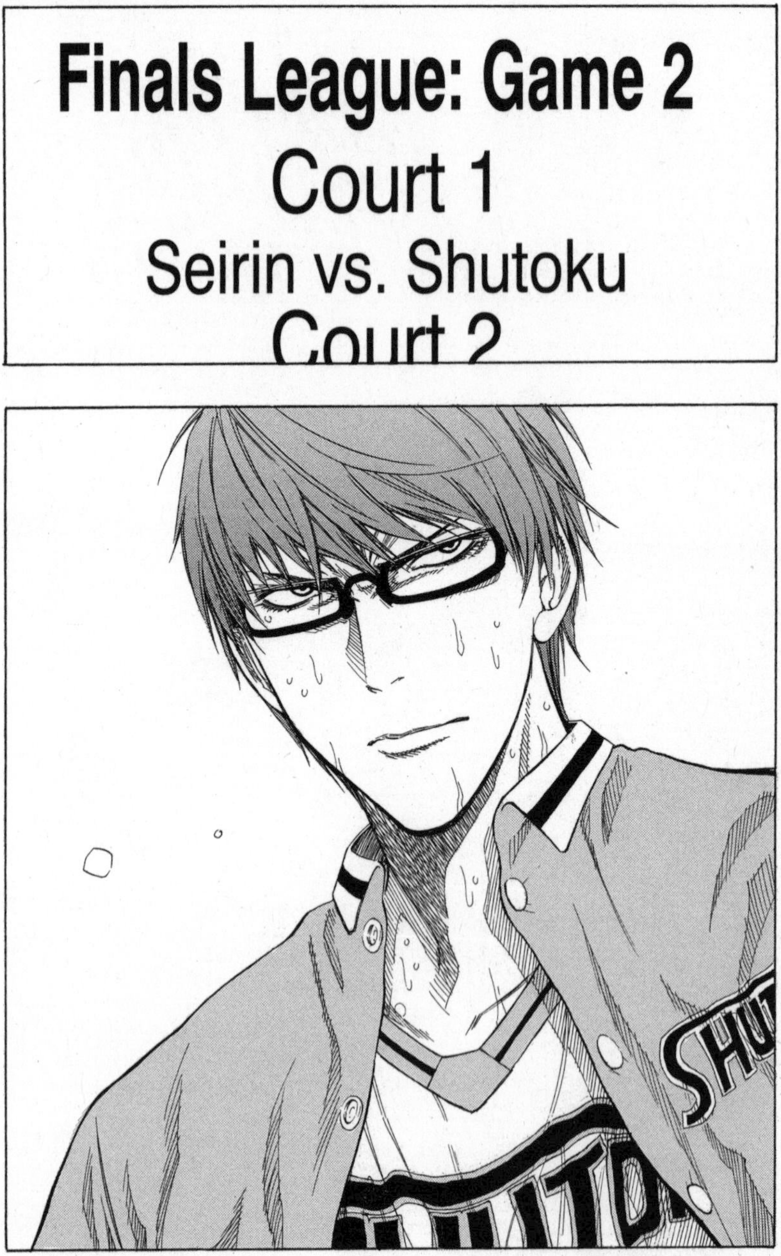
Finals League: Game 2
Court 1
Seirin vs. Shutoku
Court 2

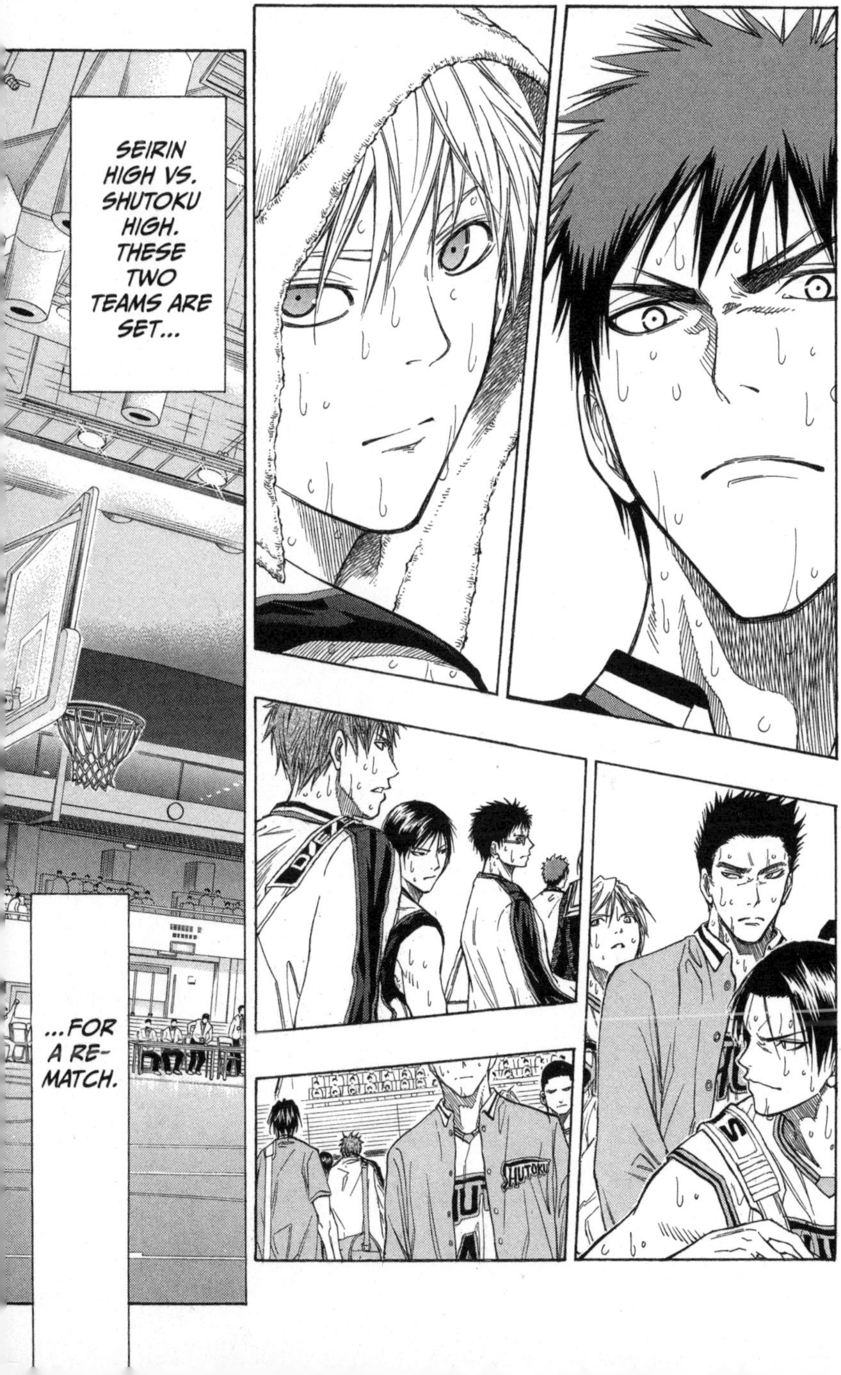
SEIRIN HIGH VS. SHUTOKU HIGH. THESE TWO TEAMS ARE SET...
...FOR A RE-MATCH.
SHUTOKU

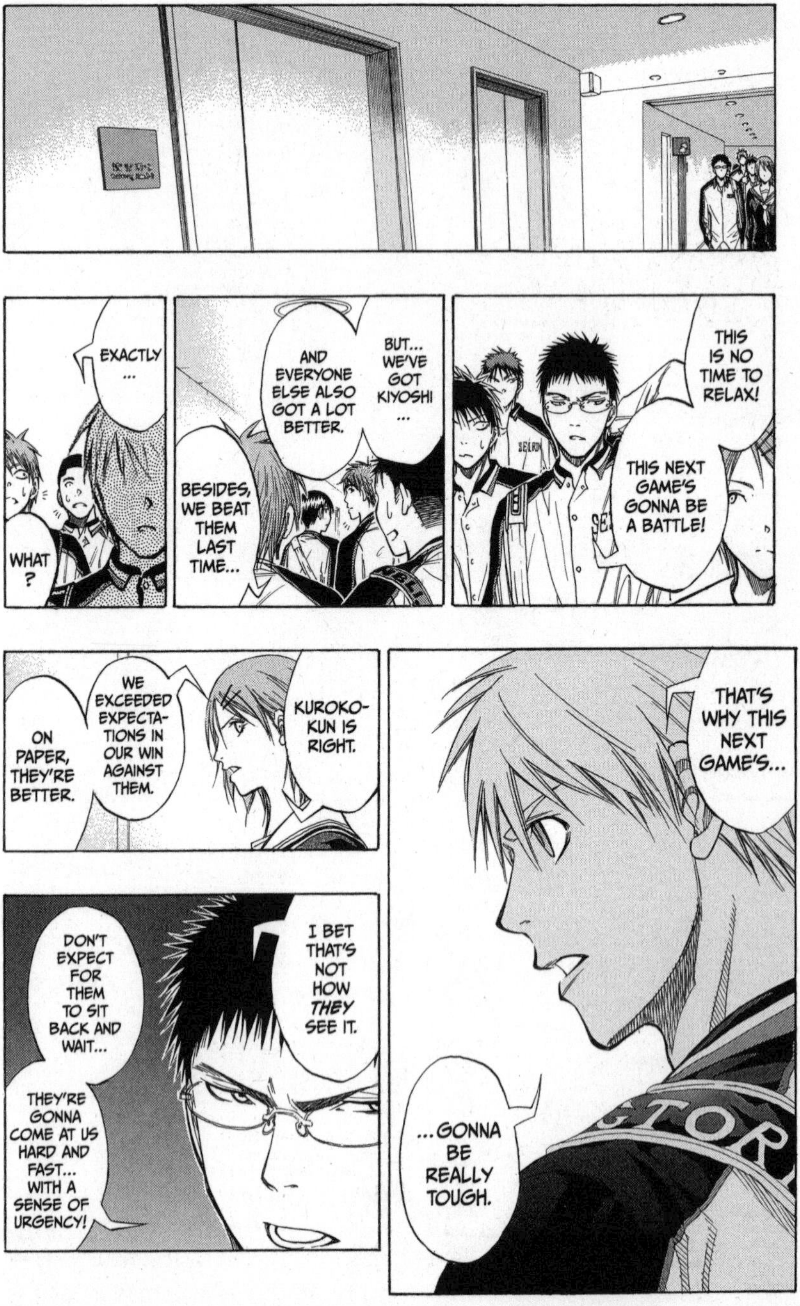
THIS IS NO TIME TO RELAX!
THIS NEXT GAME'S GONNA BE A BATTLE!
BUT... WE'VE GOT KIYOSHI ...
AND EVERYONE ELSE ALSO GOT A LOT BETTER.
BESIDES, WE BEAT THEM LAST TIME...
EXACTLY ...
WHAT ?
THAT'S WHY THIS NEXT GAME'S...
...GONNA BE REALLY TOUGH.
KUROKO-KUN IS RIGHT.
WE EXCEEDED EXPECTATIONS IN OUR WIN AGAINST THEM.
ON PAPER, THEY'RE BETTER.
I BET THAT'S NOT HOW *THEY* SEE IT.
DON'T EXPECT FOR THEM TO SIT BACK AND WAIT...
THEY'RE GONNA COME AT US HARD AND FAST... WITH A SENSE OF URGENCY!

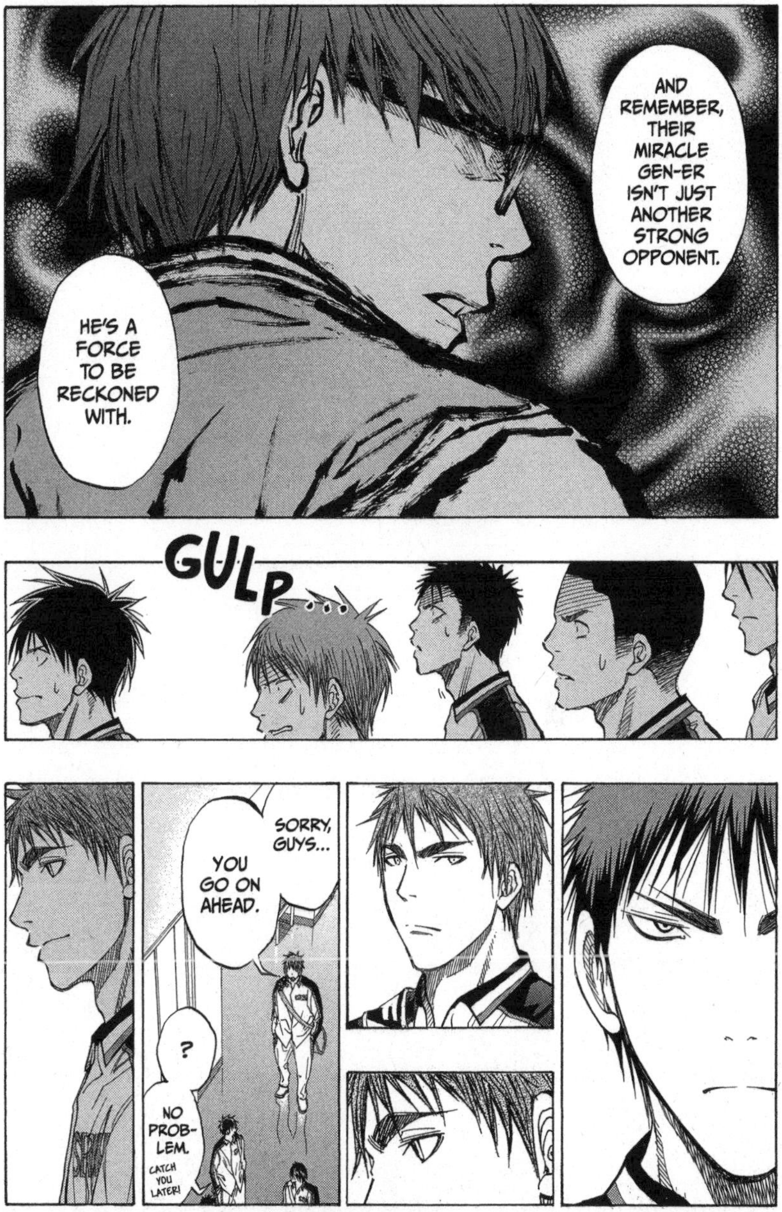
AND REMEMBER, THEIR MIRACLE GEN-ER ISN'T JUST ANOTHER STRONG OPPONENT.
HE'S A FORCE TO BE RECKONED WITH.
GULP
SORRY, GUYS... YOU GO ON AHEAD.
?
NO PROB-LEM.
CATCH YOU LATER!

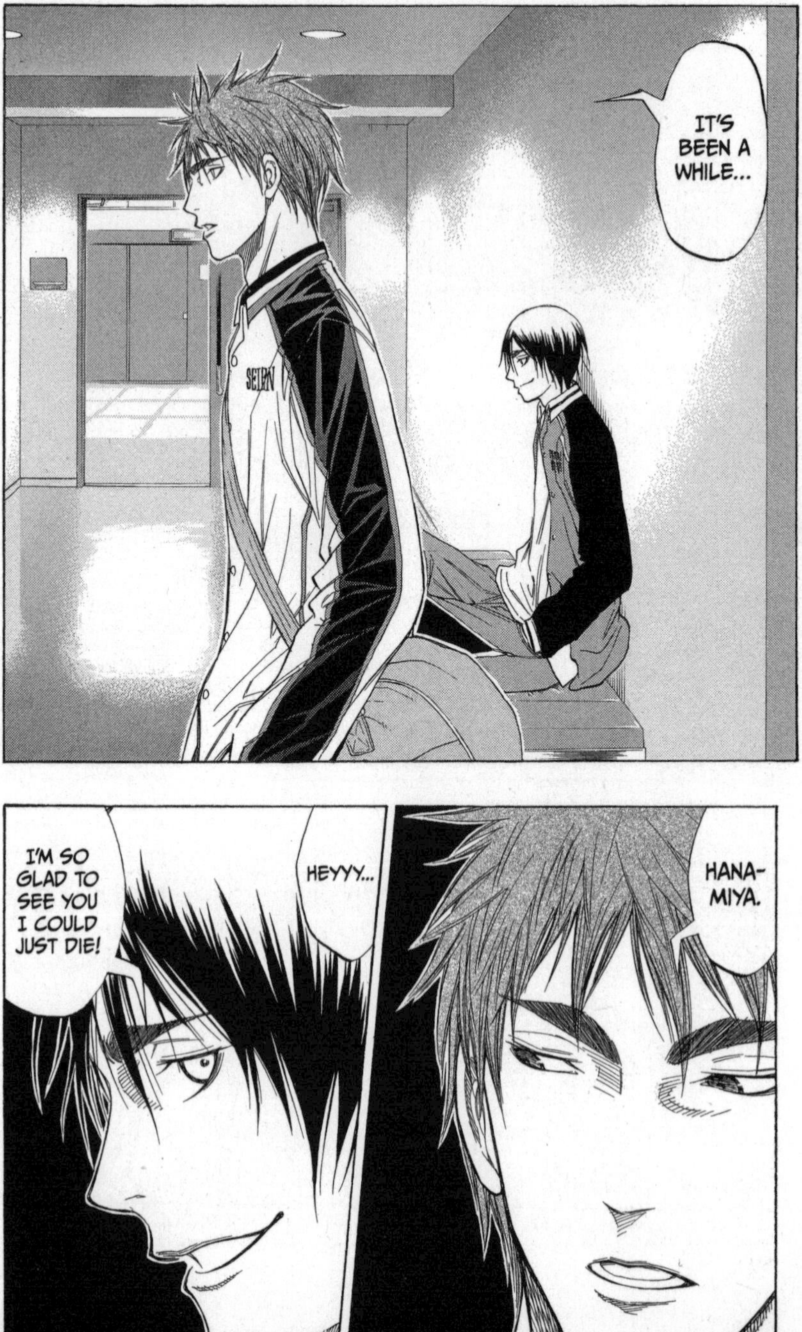
IT'S BEEN A WHILE...
HANA-MIYA.
HEYYY...
I'M SO GLAD TO SEE YOU I COULD JUST DIE!

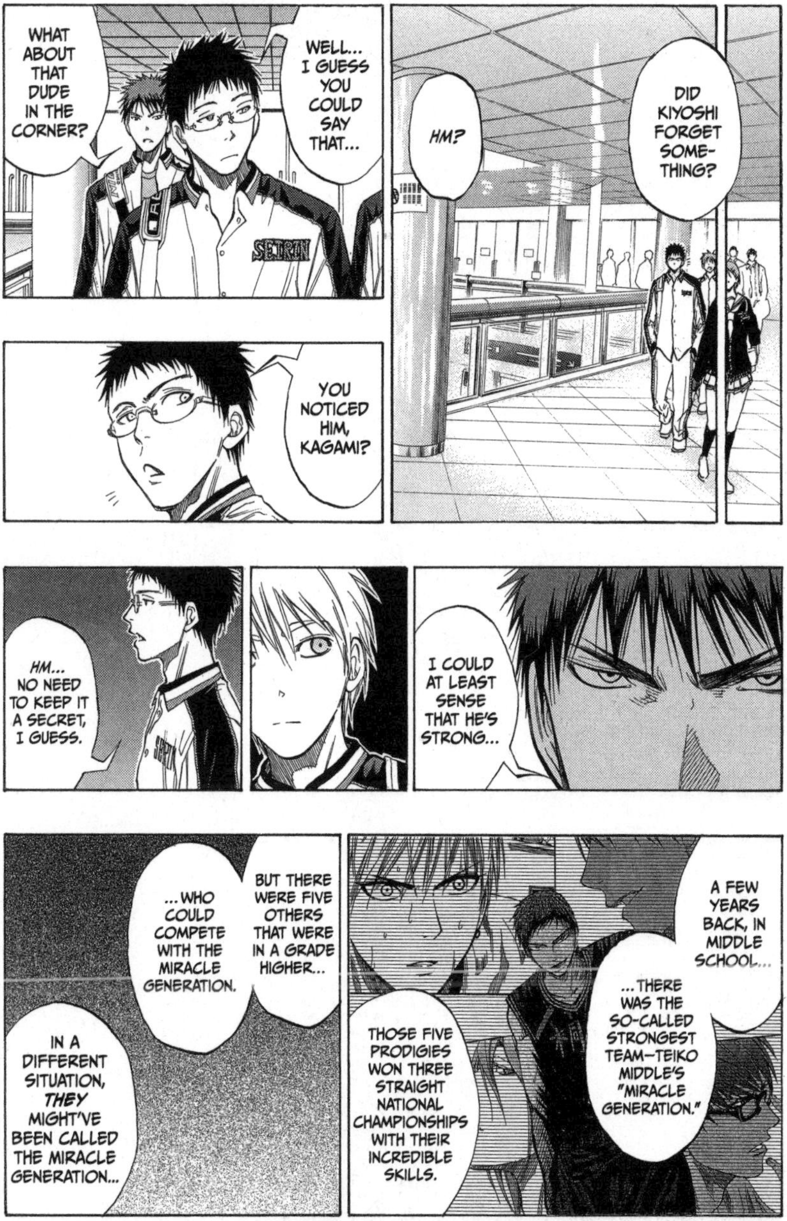
DID KIYOSHI FORGET SOME-THING?
HM?
WELL... I GUESS YOU COULD SAY THAT...
WHAT ABOUT THAT DUDE IN THE CORNER?
YOU NOTICED HIM, KAGAMI?
I COULD AT LEAST SENSE THAT HE'S STRONG...
HM... NO NEED TO KEEP IT A SECRET, I GUESS.
A FEW YEARS BACK, IN MIDDLE SCHOOL...
...THERE WAS THE SO-CALLED STRONGEST TEAM—TEIKO MIDDLE'S "MIRACLE GENERATION."
THOSE FIVE PRODIGIES WON THREE STRAIGHT NATIONAL CHAMPIONSHIPS WITH THEIR INCREDIBLE SKILLS.
BUT THERE WERE FIVE OTHERS THAT WERE IN A GRADE HIGHER...
...WHO COULD COMPETE WITH THE MIRACLE GENERATION.
IN A DIFFERENT SITUATION, *THEY* MIGHT'VE BEEN CALLED THE MIRACLE GENERATION...

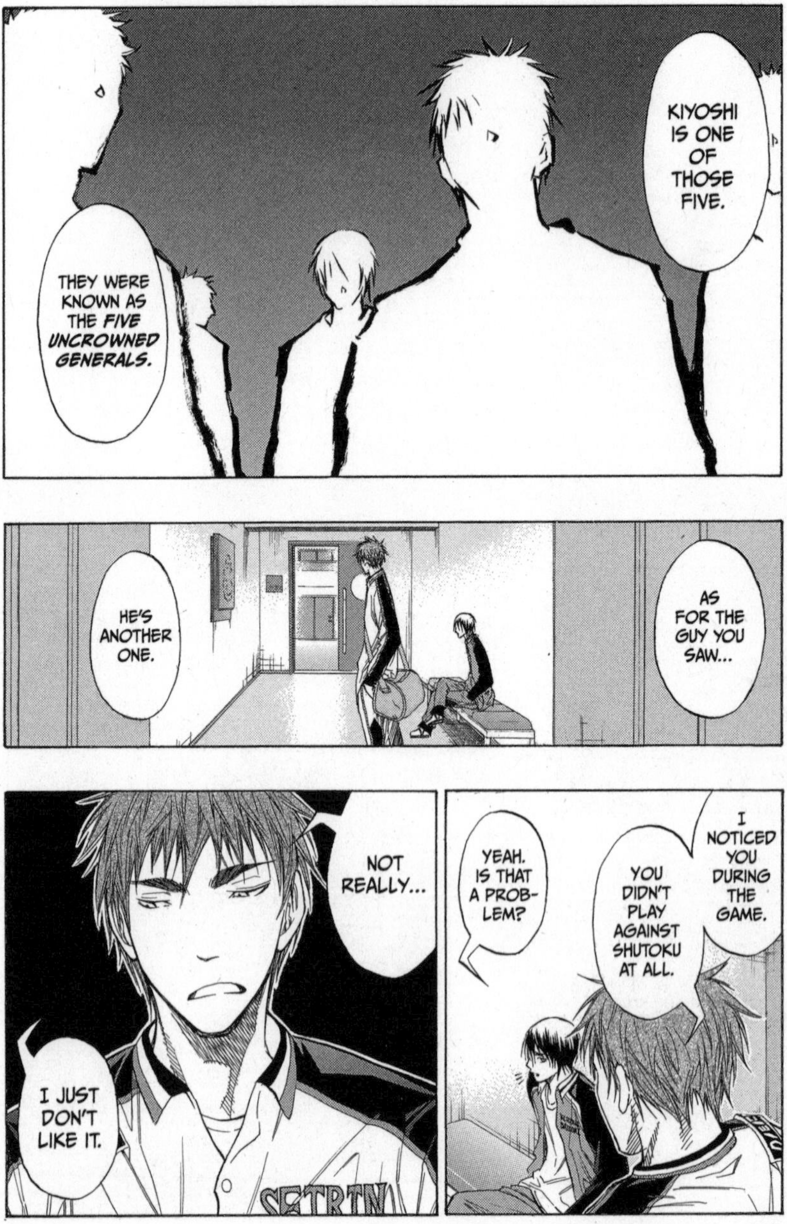

KIYOSHI IS ONE OF THOSE FIVE.
THEY WERE KNOWN AS THE *FIVE UNCROWNED GENERALS.*
AS FOR THE GUY YOU SAW...
HE'S ANOTHER ONE.
I NOTICED YOU DURING THE GAME.
YOU DIDN'T PLAY AGAINST SHUTOKU AT ALL.
YEAH. IS THAT A PROB-LEM?
NOT REALLY...
I JUST DON'T LIKE IT.

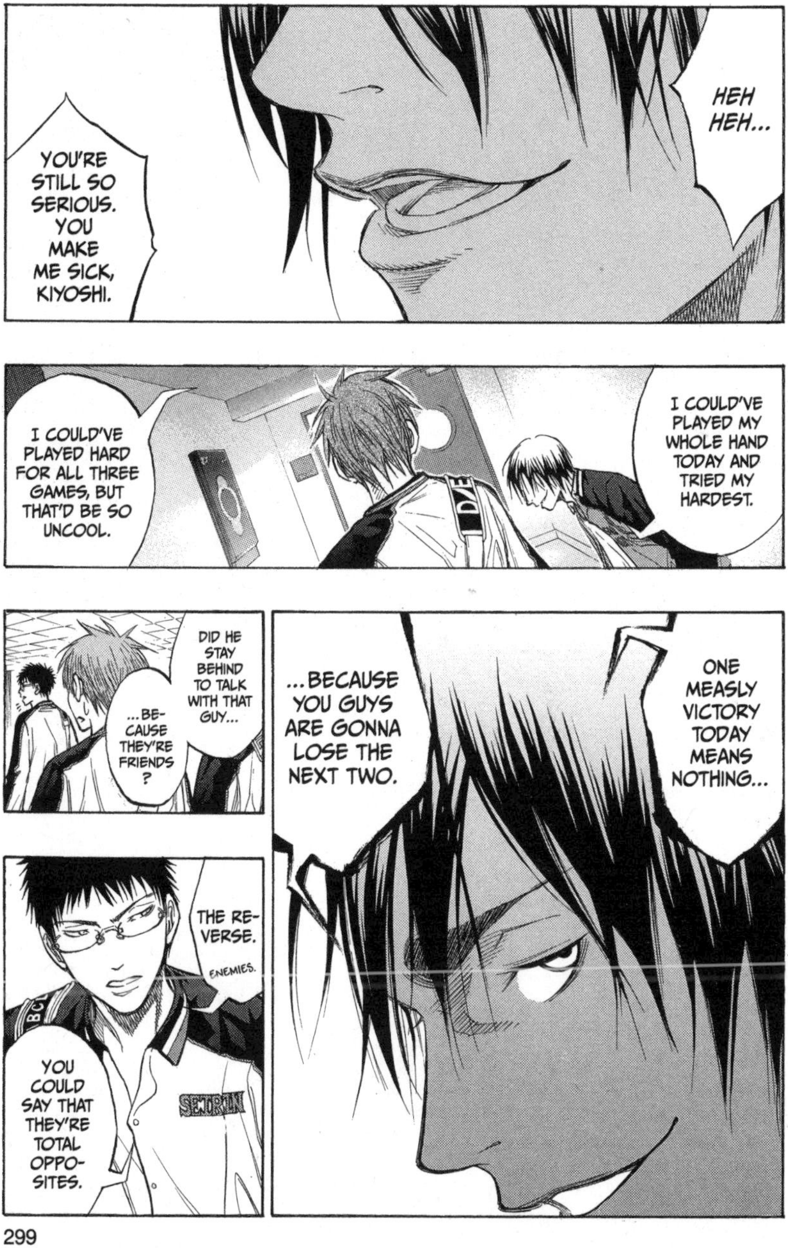
HEH HEH...
YOU'RE STILL SO SERIOUS. YOU MAKE ME SICK, KIYOSHI.
I COULD'VE PLAYED MY WHOLE HAND TODAY AND TRIED MY HARDEST.
I COULD'VE PLAYED HARD FOR ALL THREE GAMES, BUT THAT'D BE SO UNCOOL.
ONE MEASLY VICTORY TODAY MEANS NOTHING...
...BECAUSE YOU GUYS ARE GONNA LOSE THE NEXT TWO.
DID HE STAY BEHIND TO TALK WITH THAT GUY...
...BE-CAUSE THEY'RE FRIENDS?
THE RE-VERSE.
ENEMIES.
YOU COULD SAY THAT THEY'RE TOTAL OPPO-SITES.
SEIRIN

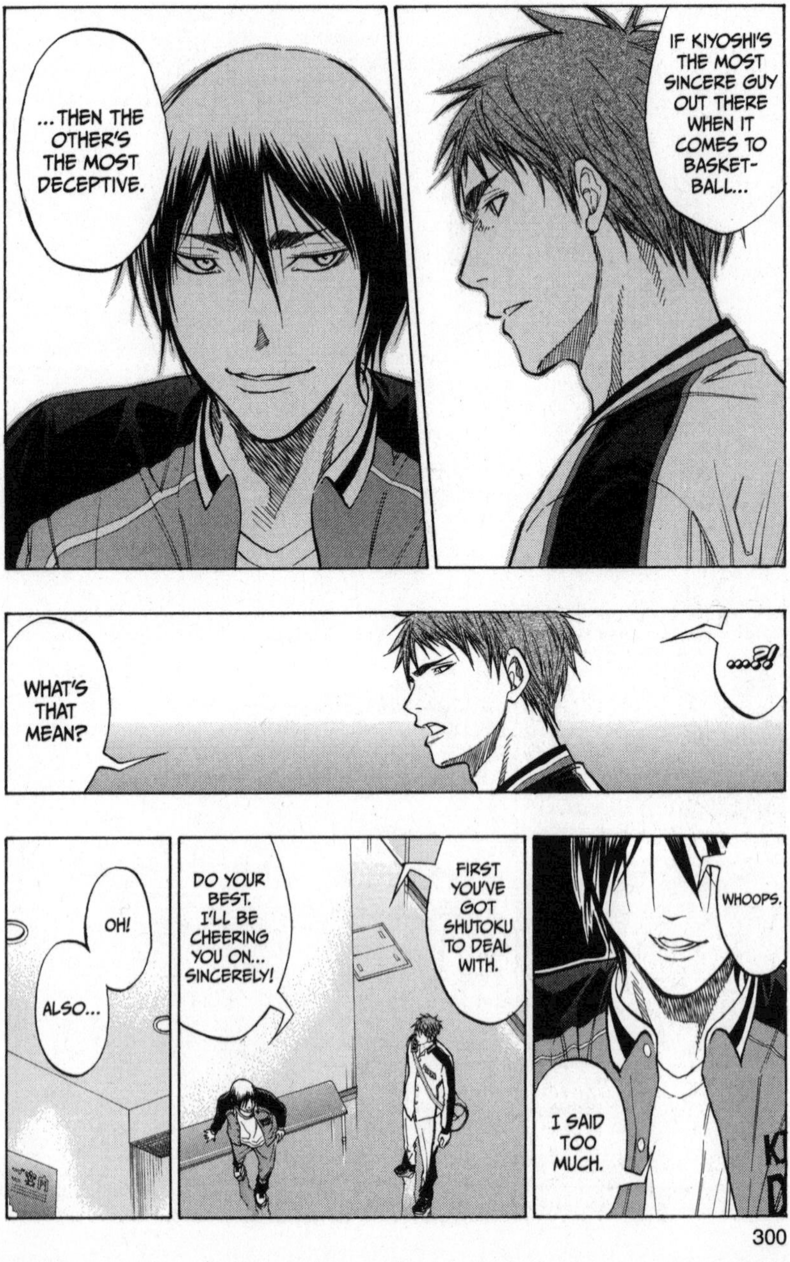
IF KIYOSHI'S THE MOST SINCERE GUY OUT THERE WHEN IT COMES TO BASKET-BALL...
...THEN THE OTHER'S THE MOST DECEPTIVE.
...?!
WHAT'S THAT MEAN?
WHOOPS.
I SAID TOO MUCH.
FIRST YOU'VE GOT SHUTOKU TO DEAL WITH.
DO YOUR BEST. I'LL BE CHEERING YOU ON... SINCERELY!
OH!
ALSO...

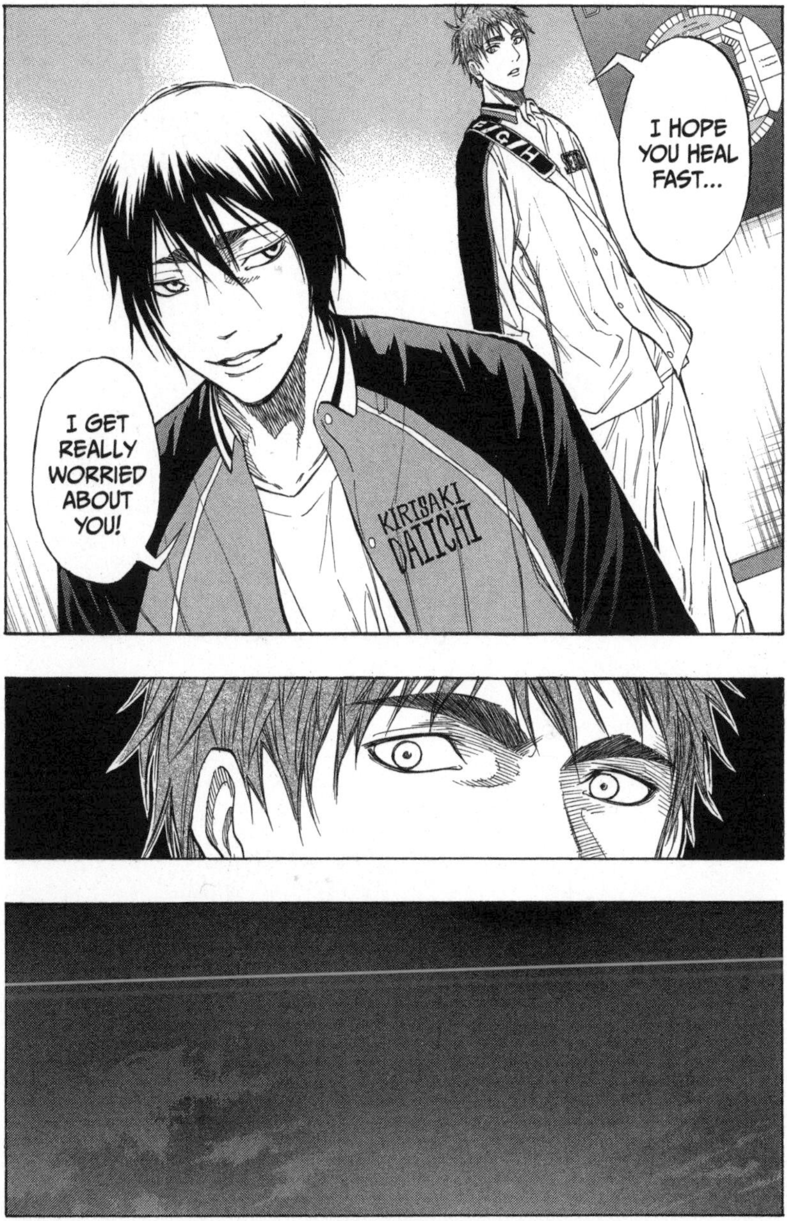
I HOPE YOU HEAL FAST...
I GET REALLY WORRIED ABOUT YOU!
KIRISAKI DAIICHI

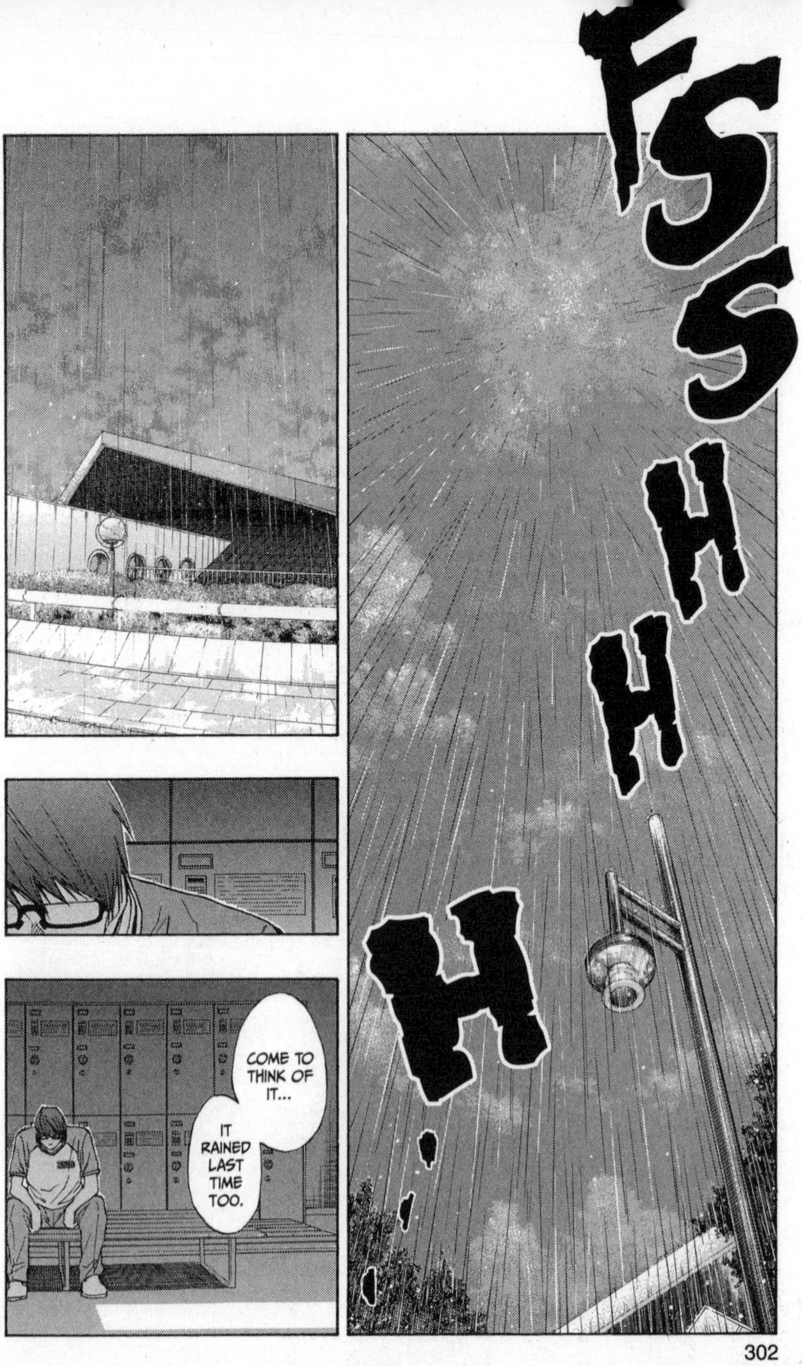
FSSHHH...
COME TO THINK OF IT...
IT RAINED LAST TIME TOO.

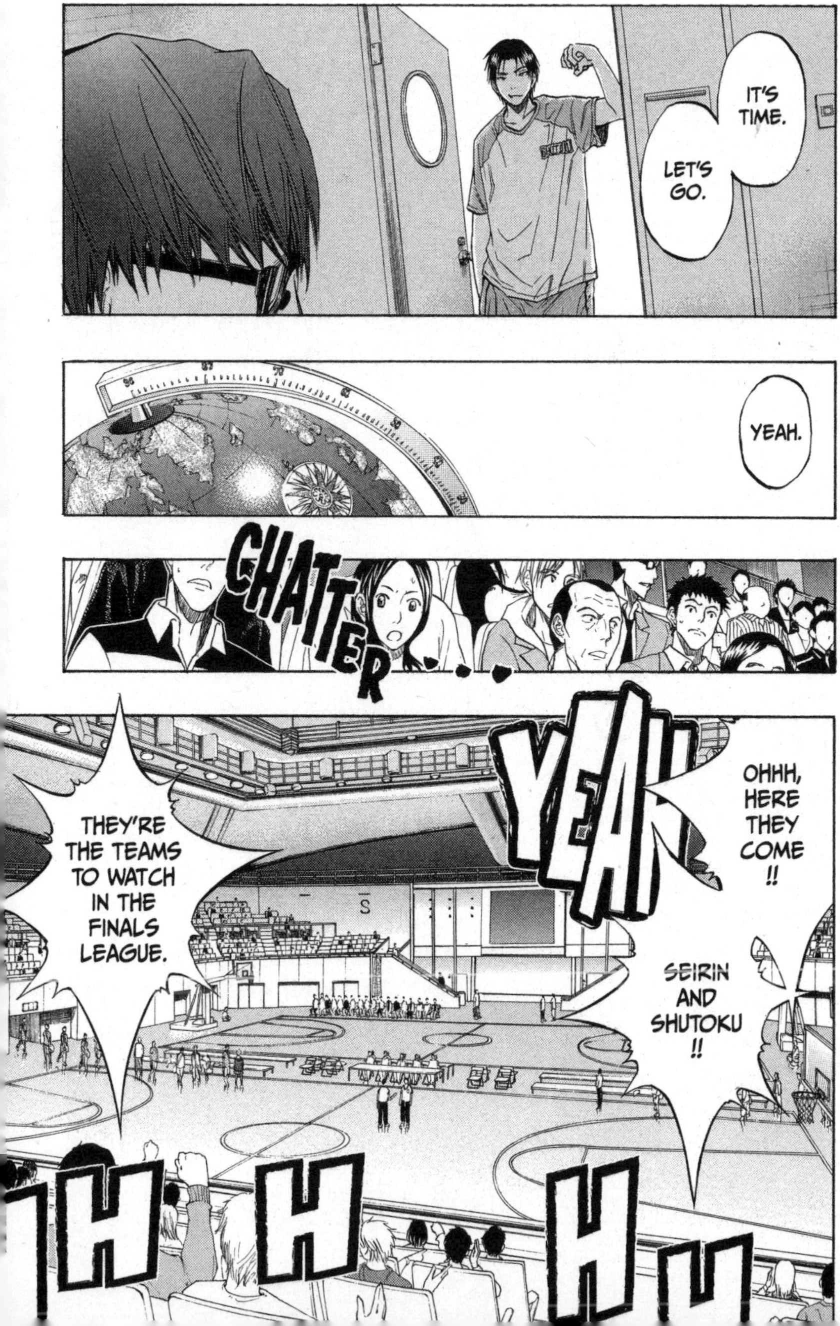
IT'S TIME.
LET'S GO.
YEAH.
CHATTER...
YEAH
HHHH
OHHH, HERE THEY COME!!
SEIRIN AND SHUTOKU!!
THEY'RE THE TEAMS TO WATCH IN THE FINALS LEAGUE.

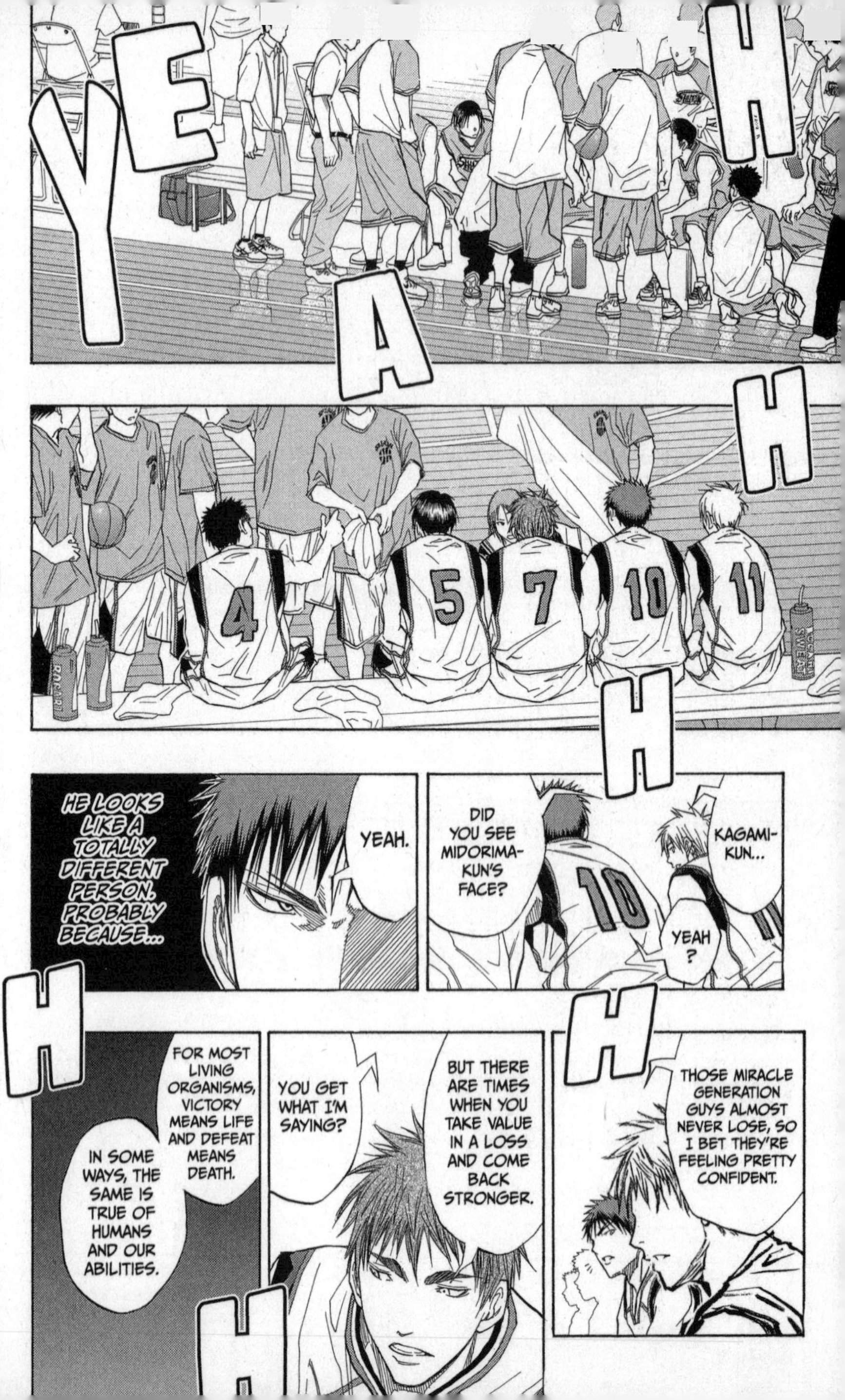
YEAHHHHHH
KAGAMI-KUN...
YEAH?
DID YOU SEE MIDORIMA-KUN'S FACE?
YEAH.
HE LOOKS LIKE A TOTALLY DIFFERENT PERSON. PROBABLY BECAUSE...
THOSE MIRACLE GENERATION GUYS ALMOST NEVER LOSE, SO I BET THEY'RE FEELING PRETTY CONFIDENT.
BUT THERE ARE TIMES WHEN YOU TAKE VALUE IN A LOSS AND COME BACK STRONGER.
YOU GET WHAT I'M SAYING?
FOR MOST LIVING ORGANISMS, VICTORY MEANS LIFE AND DEFEAT MEANS DEATH.
IN SOME WAYS, THE SAME IS TRUE OF HUMANS AND OUR ABILITIES.

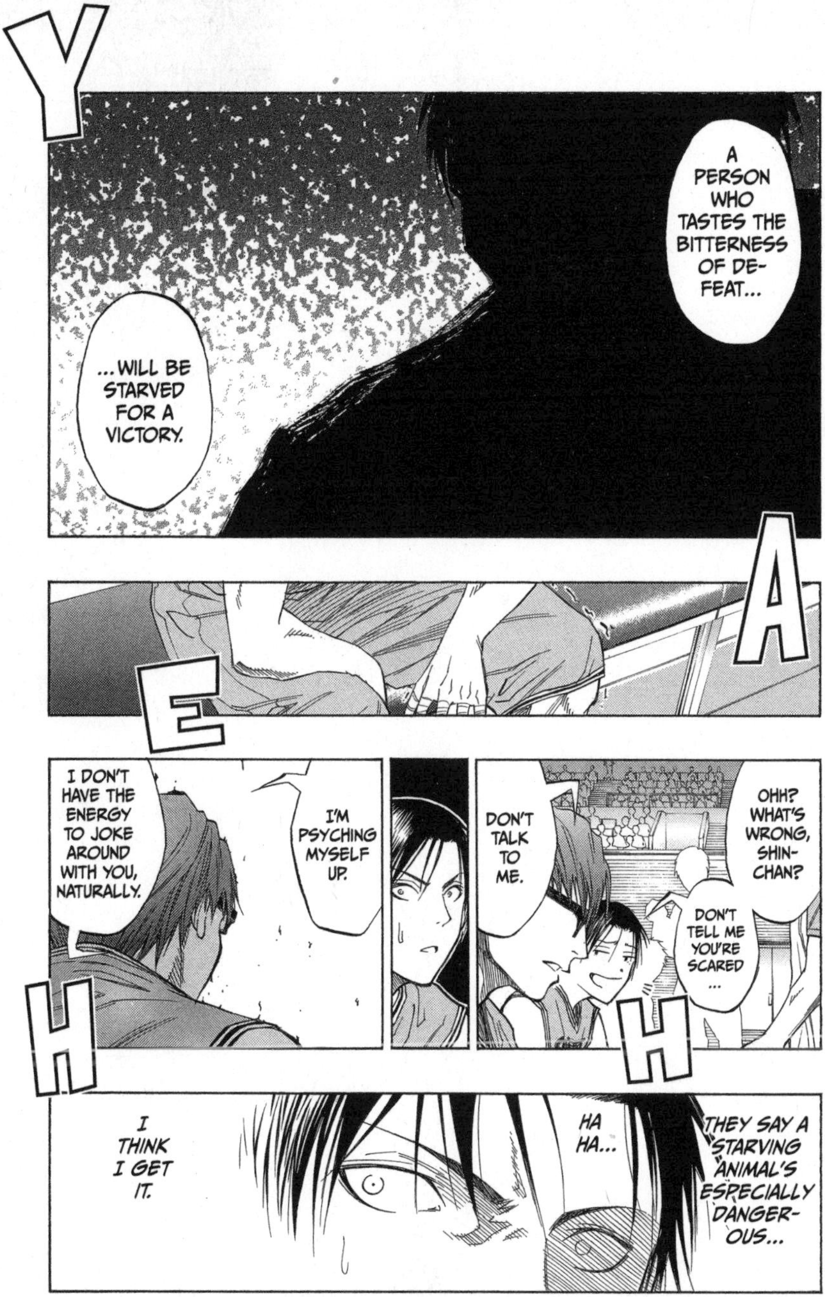

A PERSON WHO TASTES THE BITTERNESS OF DE-FEAT...
...WILL BE STARVED FOR A VICTORY.
YEAHH
OHH? WHAT'S WRONG, SHIN-CHAN?
DON'T TELL ME YOU'RE SCARED...
DON'T TALK TO ME.
I'M PSYCHING MYSELF UP.
I DON'T HAVE THE ENERGY TO JOKE AROUND WITH YOU, NATURALLY.
THEY SAY A STARVING ANIMAL'S ESPECIALLY DANGER-OUS...
HA HA...
I THINK I GET IT.

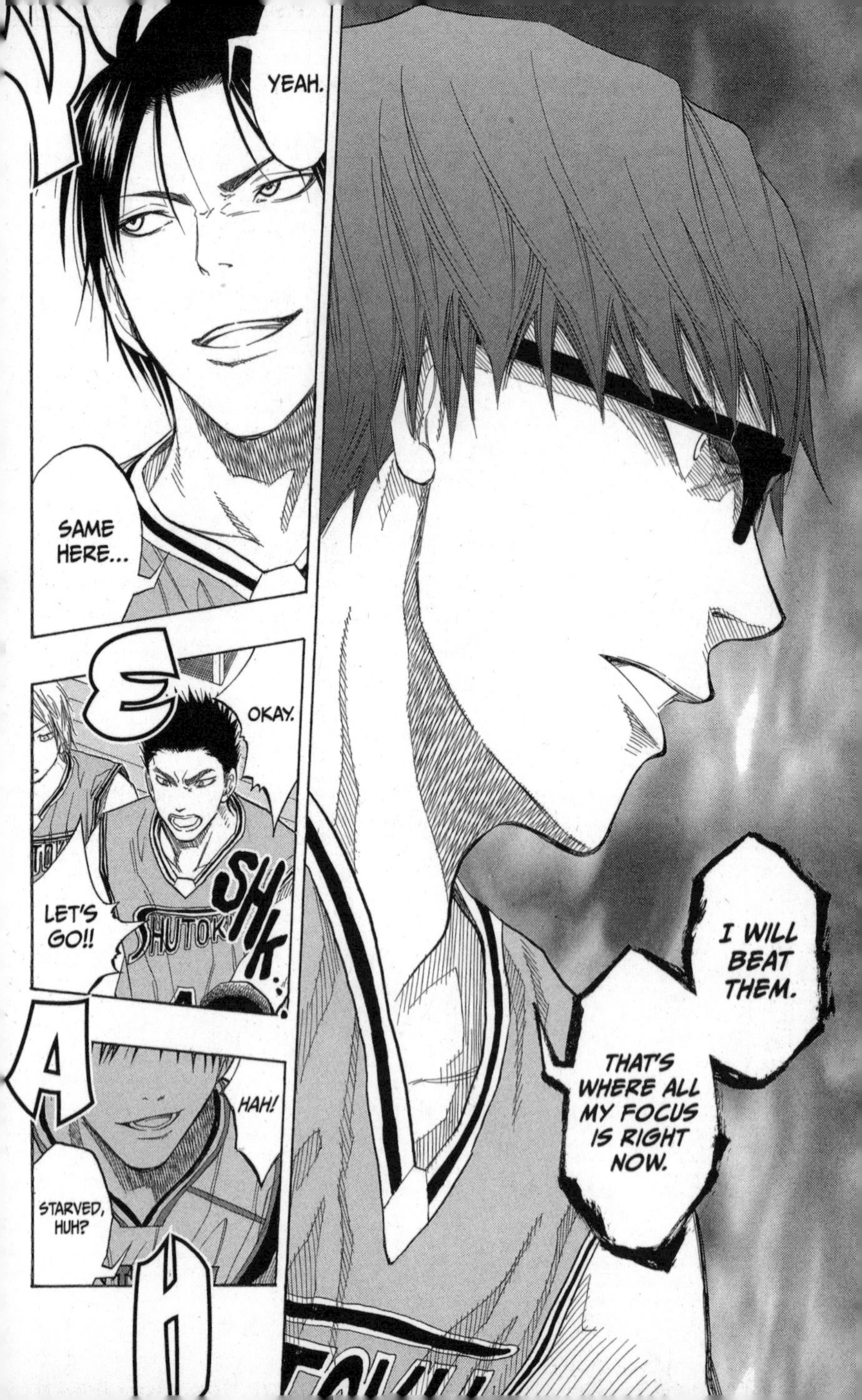
I WILL BEAT THEM.
THAT'S WHERE ALL MY FOCUS IS RIGHT NOW.
YEAH.
SAME HERE...
OKAY.
SHK
LET'S GO!!
HAH!
STARVED, HUH?

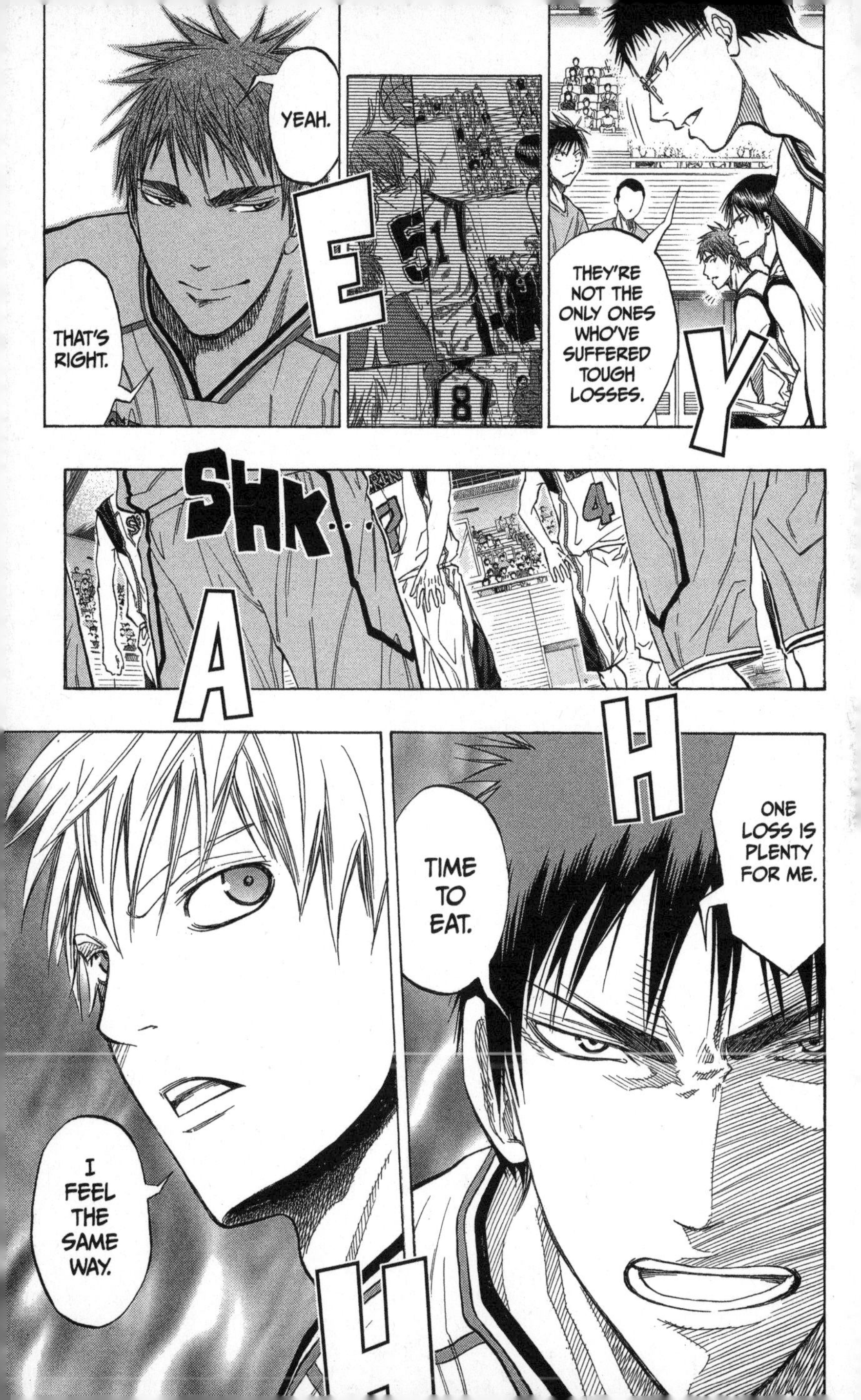
THEY'RE NOT THE ONLY ONES WHO'VE SUFFERED TOUGH LOSSES.
Y
E
YEAH.
THAT'S RIGHT.
SHK...
A
H
ONE LOSS IS PLENTY FOR ME.
TIME TO EAT.
I FEEL THE SAME WAY.
H

KUROKO'S BASKETBALL BLOOPERS TAKE 4

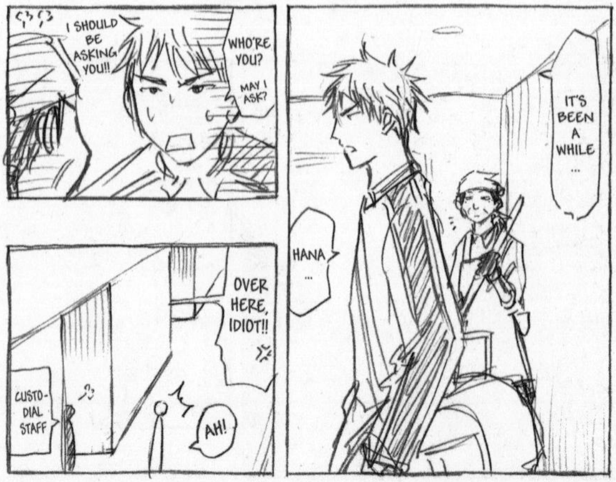
IT'S BEEN A WHILE ...
HANA ...
WHO'RE YOU? MAY I ASK?
I SHOULD BE ASKING YOU!!
OVER HERE, IDIOT!!
AH!
CUSTO-DIAL STAFF

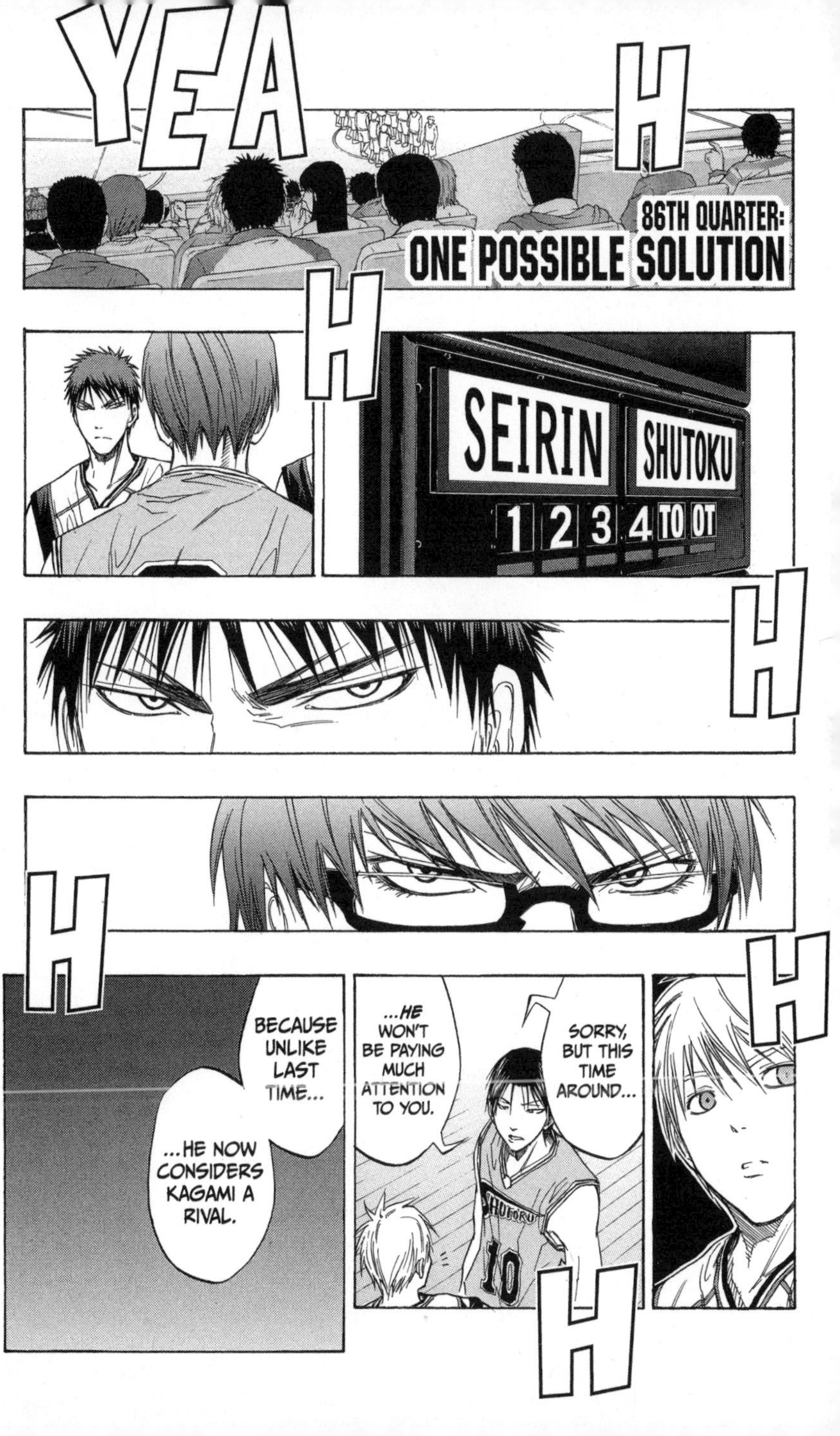
YEAHHHHHHHH
86TH QUARTER:
ONE POSSIBLE SOLUTION
SEIRIN
SHUTOKU
1 2 3 4 TO OT
SORRY, BUT THIS TIME AROUND...
...HE WON'T BE PAYING MUCH ATTENTION TO YOU.
SHUTOKU
10
BECAUSE UNLIKE LAST TIME...
...HE NOW CONSIDERS KAGAMI A RIVAL.

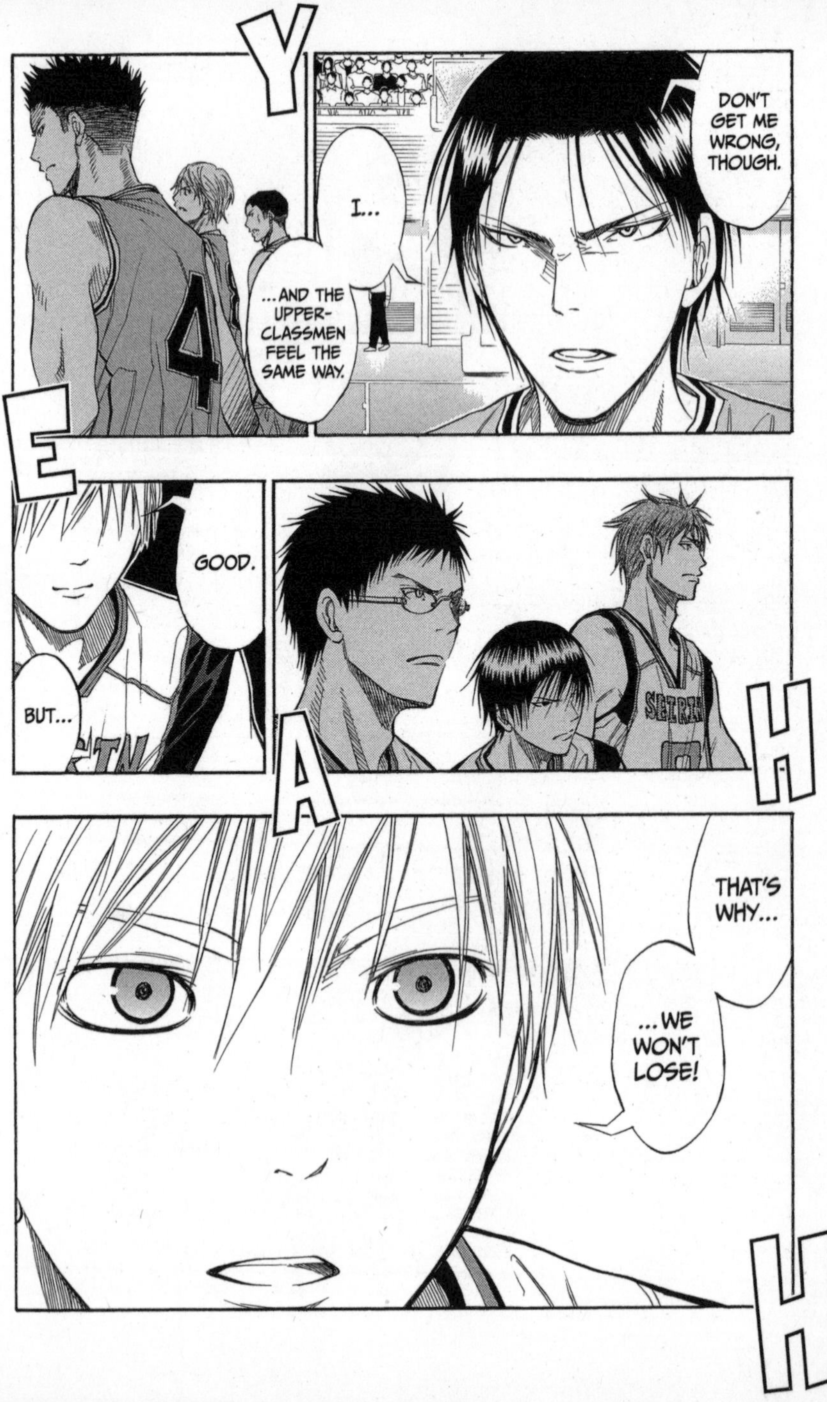
DON'T GET ME WRONG, THOUGH.
I...
...AND THE UPPER-CLASSMEN FEEL THE SAME WAY.
GOOD.
BUT...
THAT'S WHY...
...WE WON'T LOSE!
YEAHH

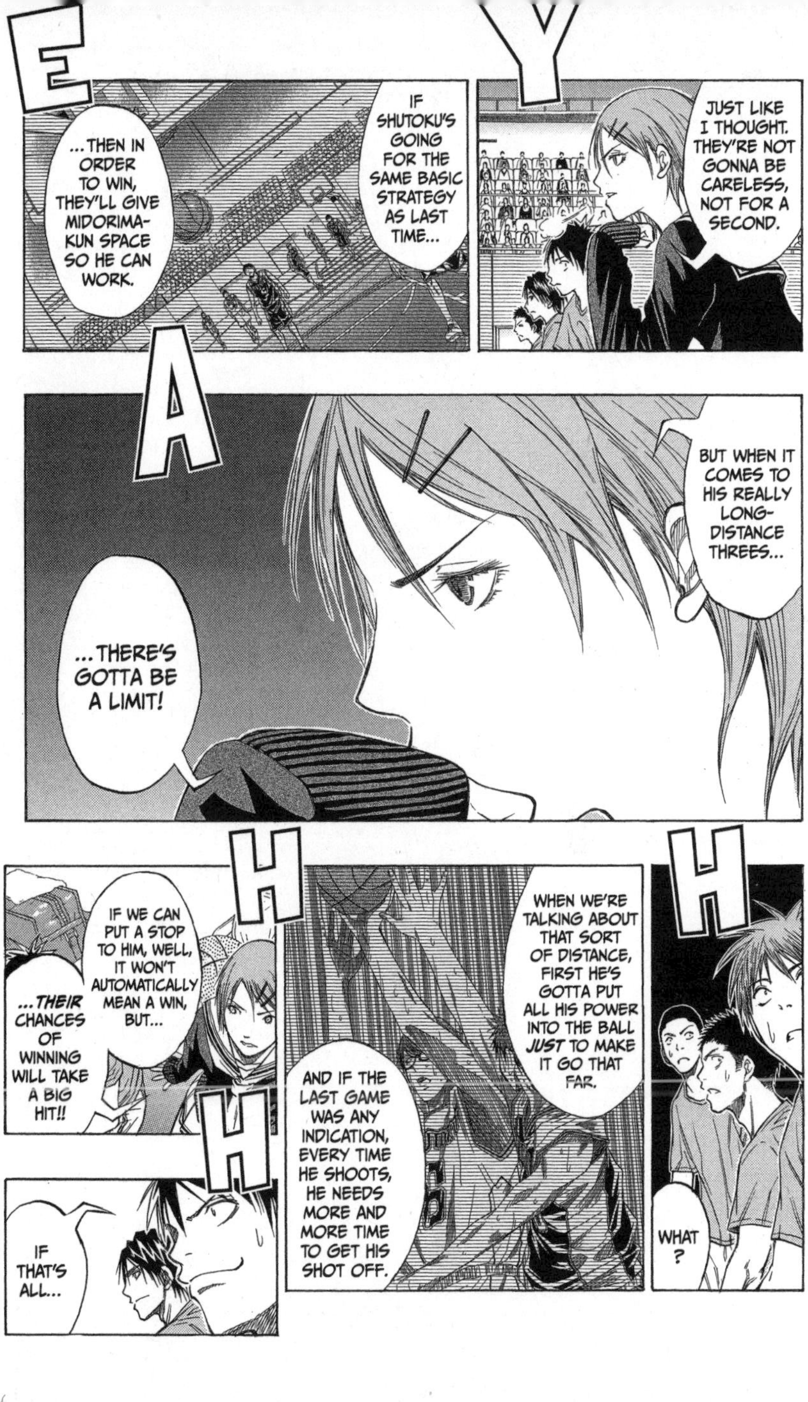
YEAHHH
JUST LIKE I THOUGHT. THEY'RE NOT GONNA BE CARELESS, NOT FOR A SECOND.
IF SHUTOKU'S GOING FOR THE SAME BASIC STRATEGY AS LAST TIME...
...THEN IN ORDER TO WIN, THEY'LL GIVE MIDORIMA-KUN SPACE SO HE CAN WORK.
BUT WHEN IT COMES TO HIS REALLY LONG-DISTANCE THREES...
...THERE'S GOTTA BE A LIMIT!
WHAT?
WHEN WE'RE TALKING ABOUT THAT SORT OF DISTANCE, FIRST HE'S GOTTA PUT ALL HIS POWER INTO THE BALL *JUST* TO MAKE IT GO THAT FAR.
AND IF THE LAST GAME WAS ANY INDICATION, EVERY TIME HE SHOOTS, HE NEEDS MORE AND MORE TIME TO GET HIS SHOT OFF.
IF WE CAN PUT A STOP TO HIM, WELL, IT WON'T AUTOMATICALLY MEAN A WIN, BUT...
...*THEIR* CHANCES OF WINNING WILL TAKE A BIG HIT!!
IF THAT'S ALL...

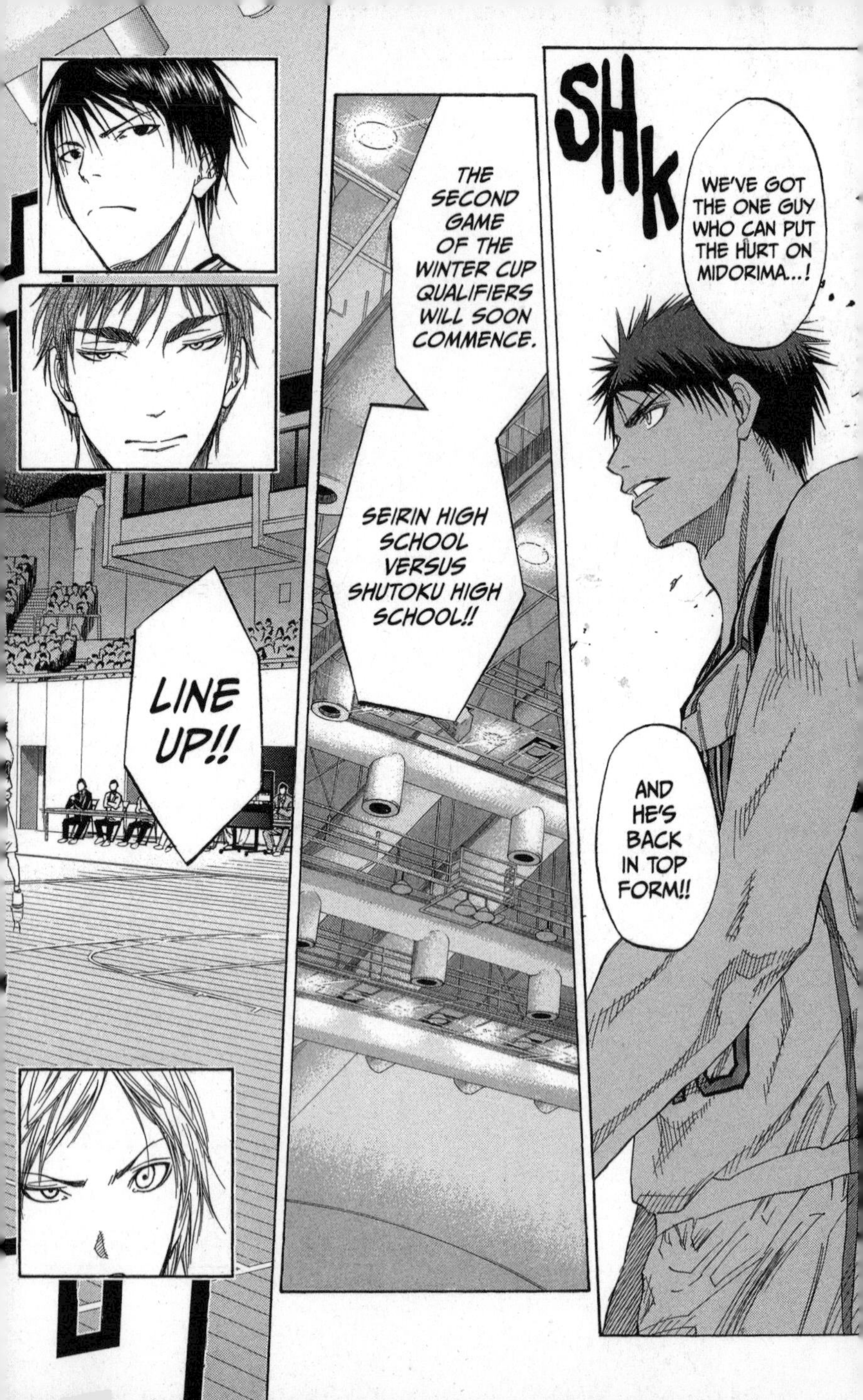
SHK
WE'VE GOT THE ONE GUY WHO CAN PUT THE HURT ON MIDORIMA...!
AND HE'S BACK IN TOP FORM!!
THE SECOND GAME OF THE WINTER CUP QUALIFIERS WILL SOON COMMENCE.
SEIRIN HIGH SCHOOL VERSUS SHUTOKU HIGH SCHOOL!!
LINE UP!!

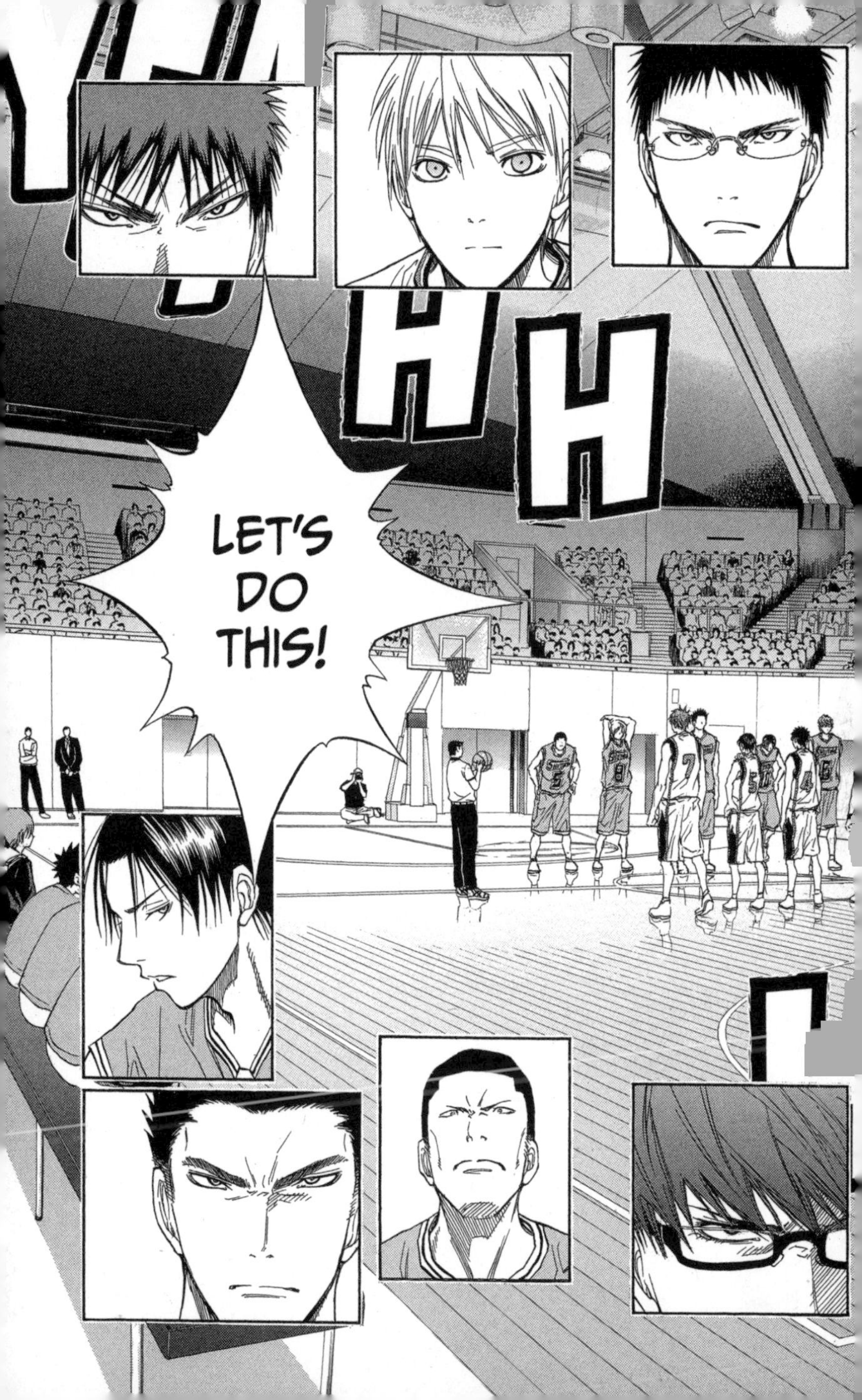
LET'S DO THIS!

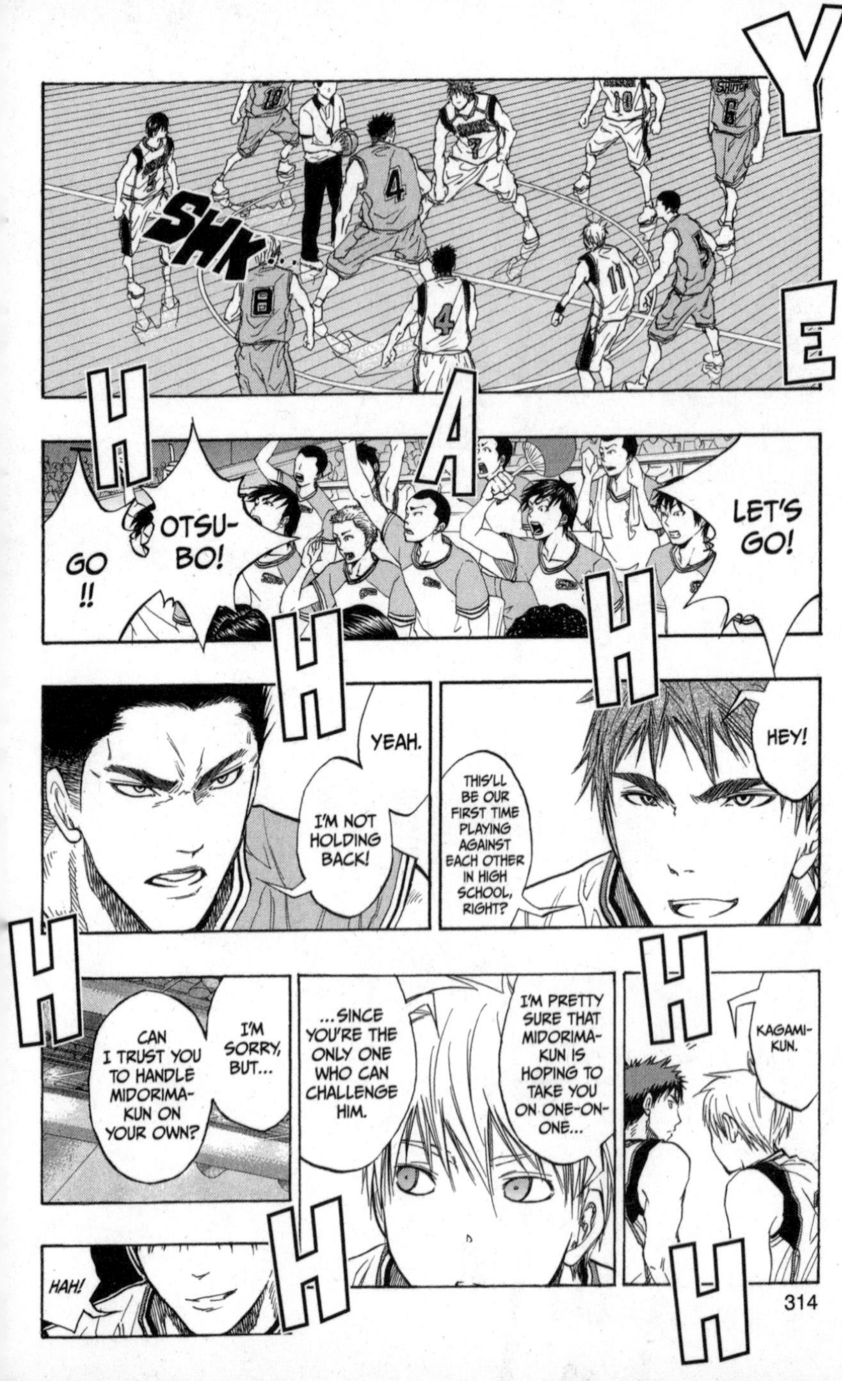
Y
E
SHK...
A
H
LET'S GO!
OTSU-BO!
GO!!
H
H
HEY!
THIS'LL BE OUR FIRST TIME PLAYING AGAINST EACH OTHER IN HIGH SCHOOL, RIGHT?
YEAH.
I'M NOT HOLDING BACK!
H
H
KAGAMI-KUN.
I'M PRETTY SURE THAT MIDORIMA-KUN IS HOPING TO TAKE YOU ON ONE-ON-ONE...
...SINCE YOU'RE THE ONLY ONE WHO CAN CHALLENGE HIM.
I'M SORRY, BUT...
CAN I TRUST YOU TO HANDLE MIDORIMA-KUN ON YOUR OWN?
H
H
HAH!

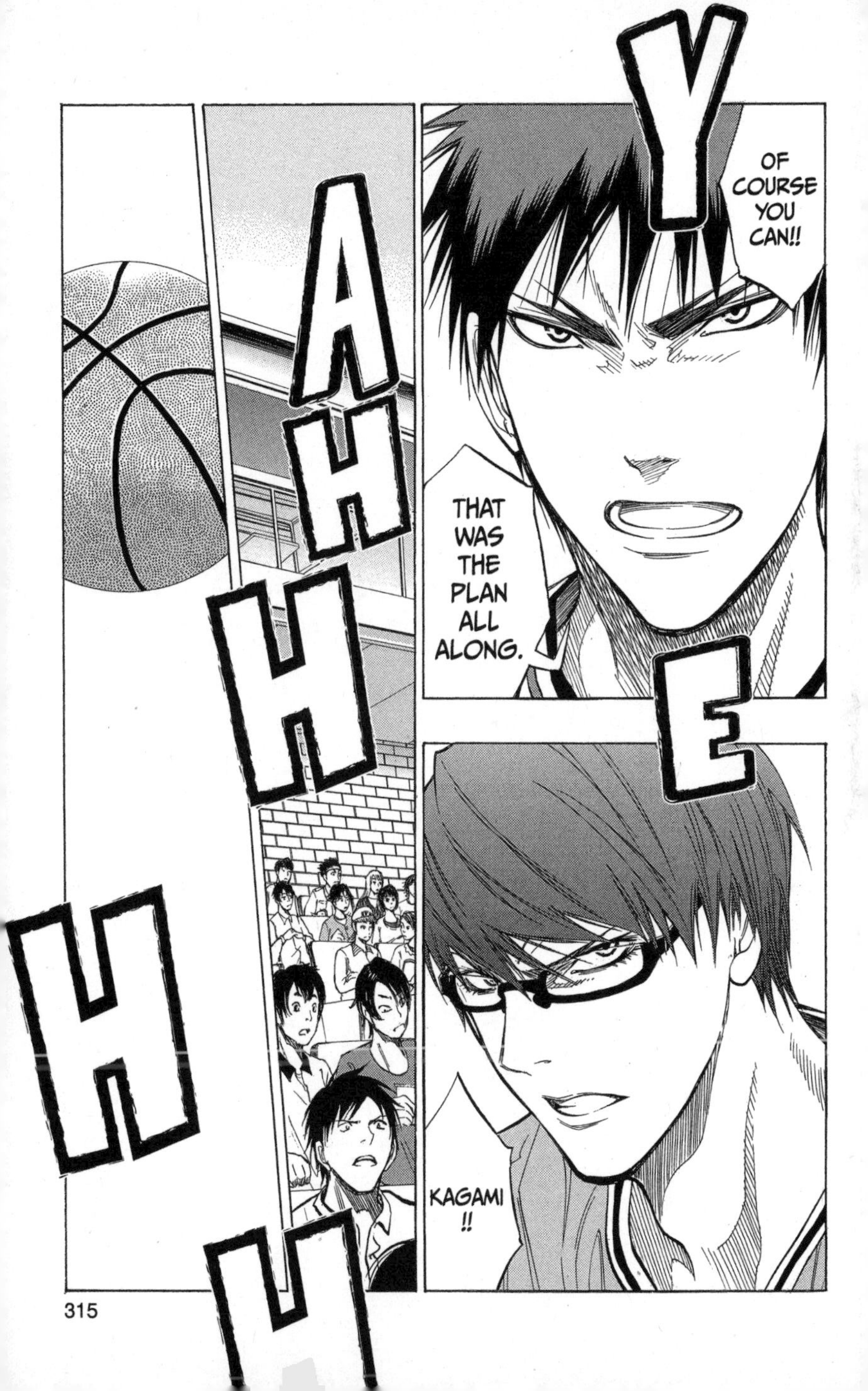
OF COURSE YOU CAN!!
THAT WAS THE PLAN ALL ALONG.
YEAHHHH
KAGAMI !!

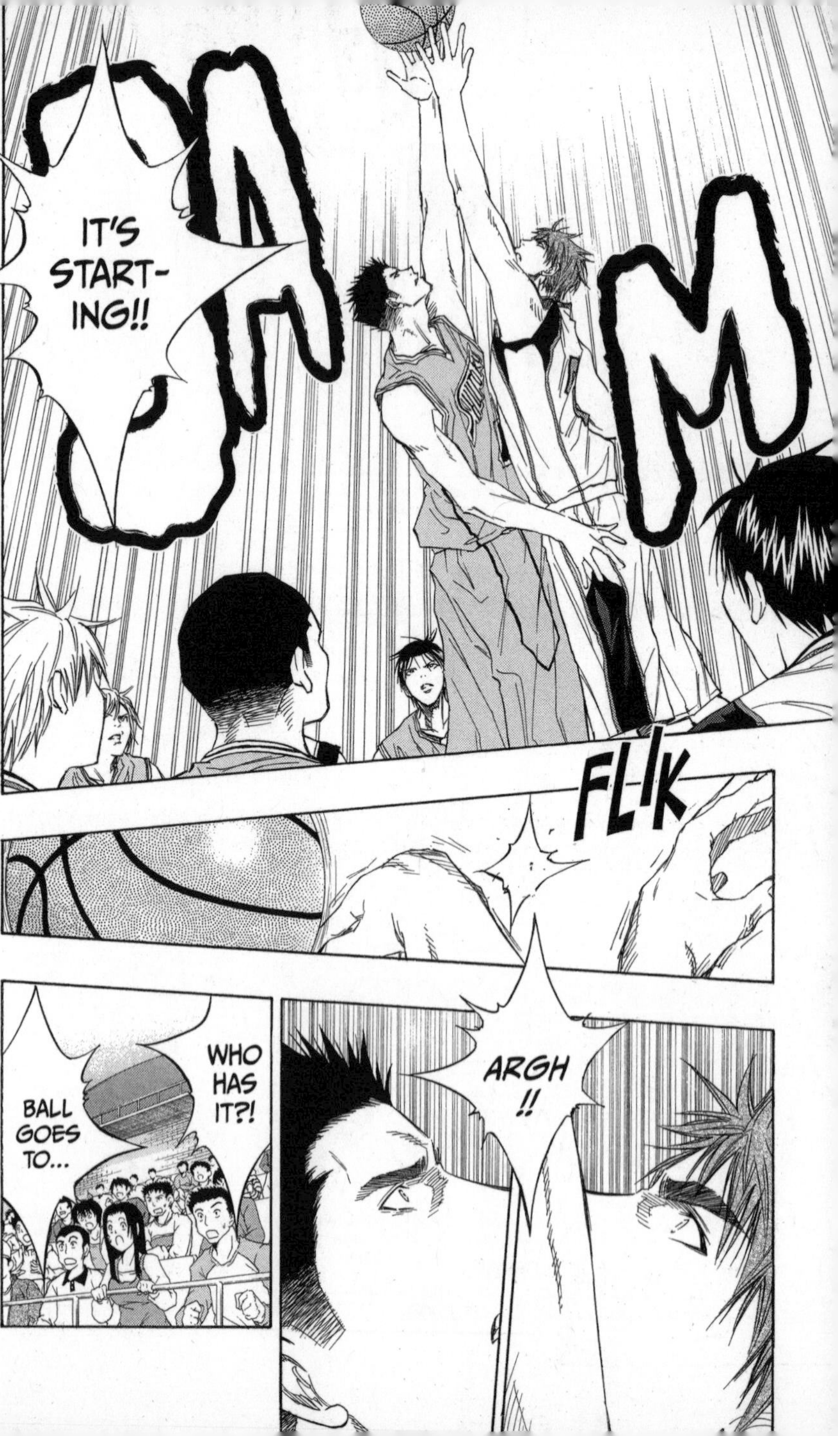
IT'S START-ING!!
FLIK
ARGH!!
WHO HAS IT?!
BALL GOES TO...

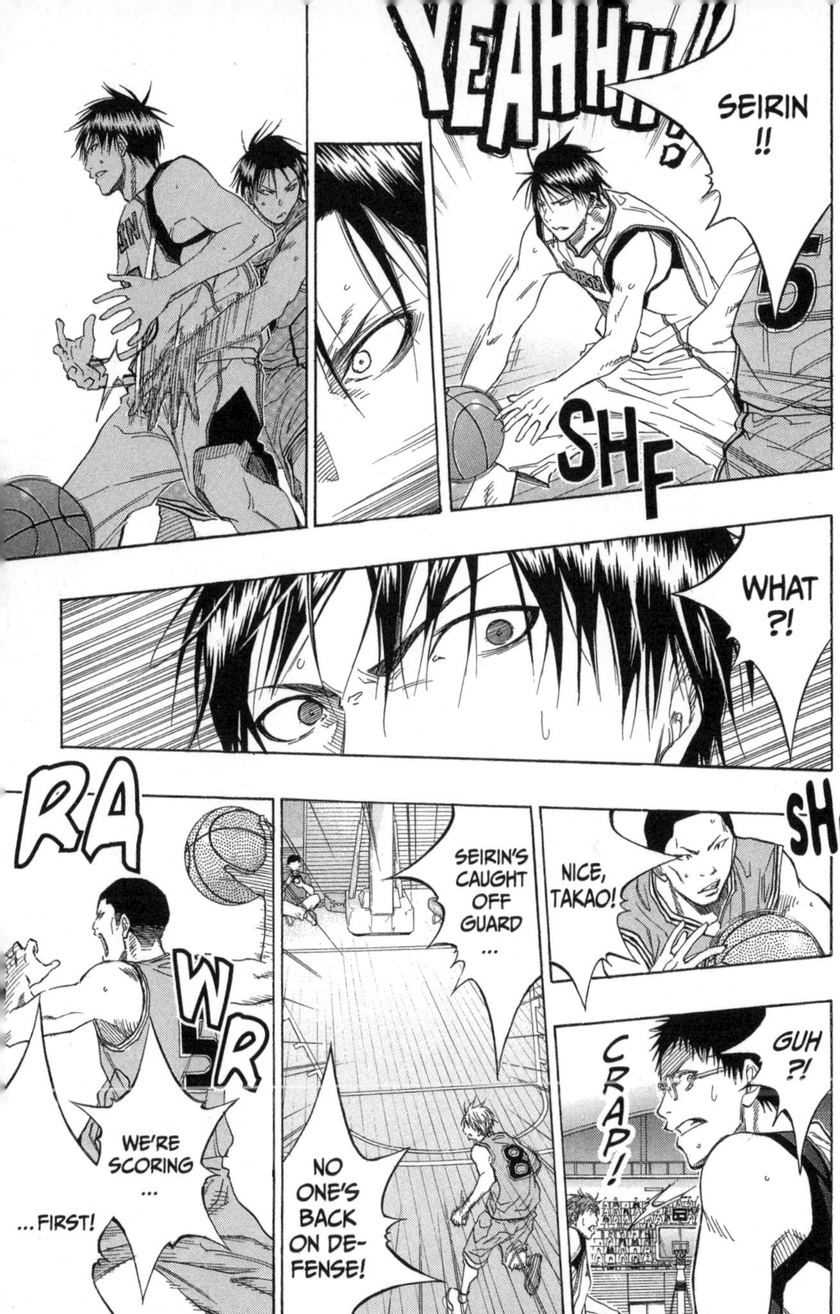

YEAHHH!!
SEIRIN!!
SHF
WHAT?!
SHp
NICE, TAKAO!
GUH?!
CRAP!
SEIRIN'S CAUGHT OFF GUARD ...
NO ONE'S BACK ON DE-FENSE!
RA
WR
WE'RE SCORING ...
...FIRST!

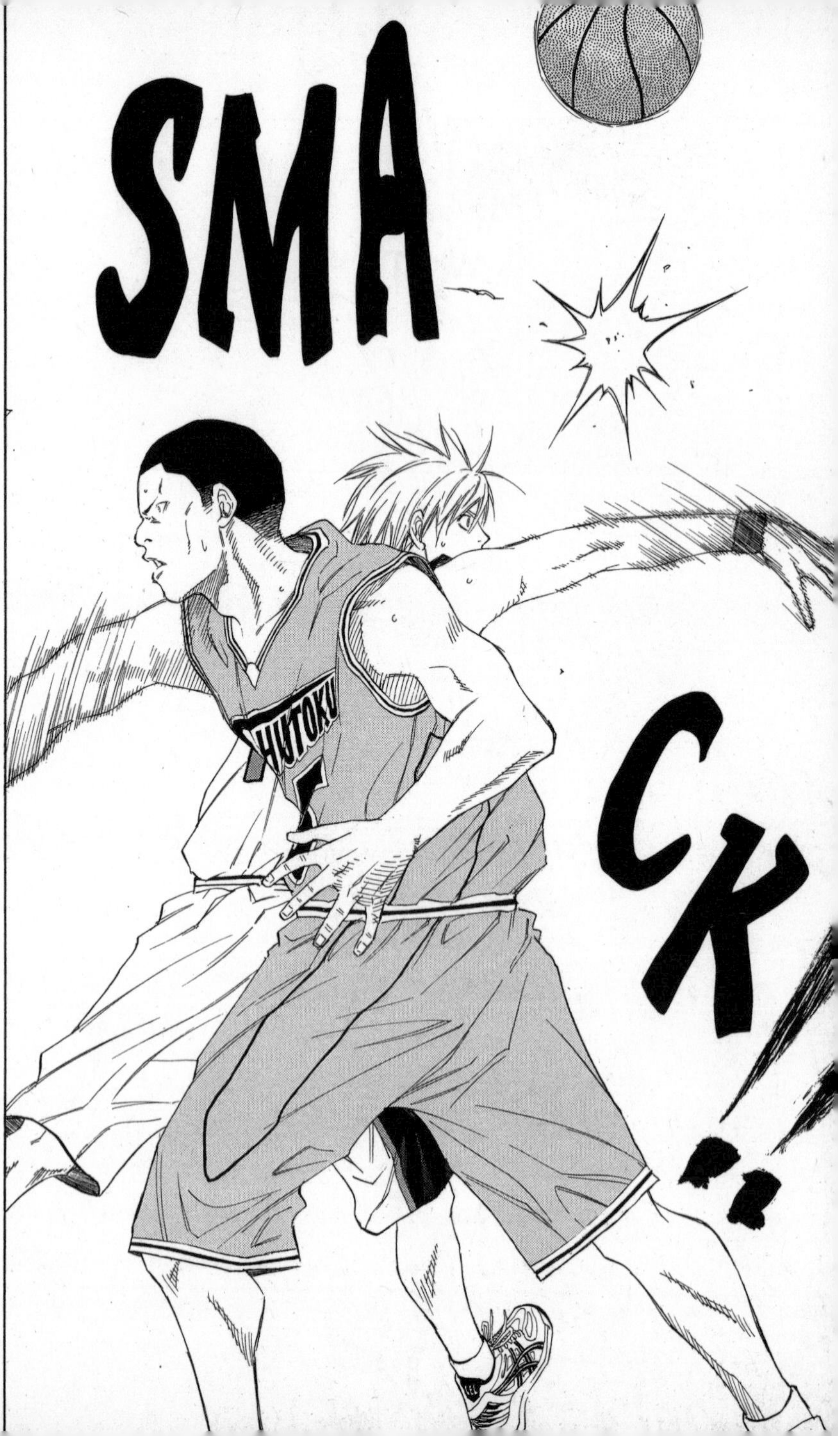
SMA
CK!!
SHUTOKU

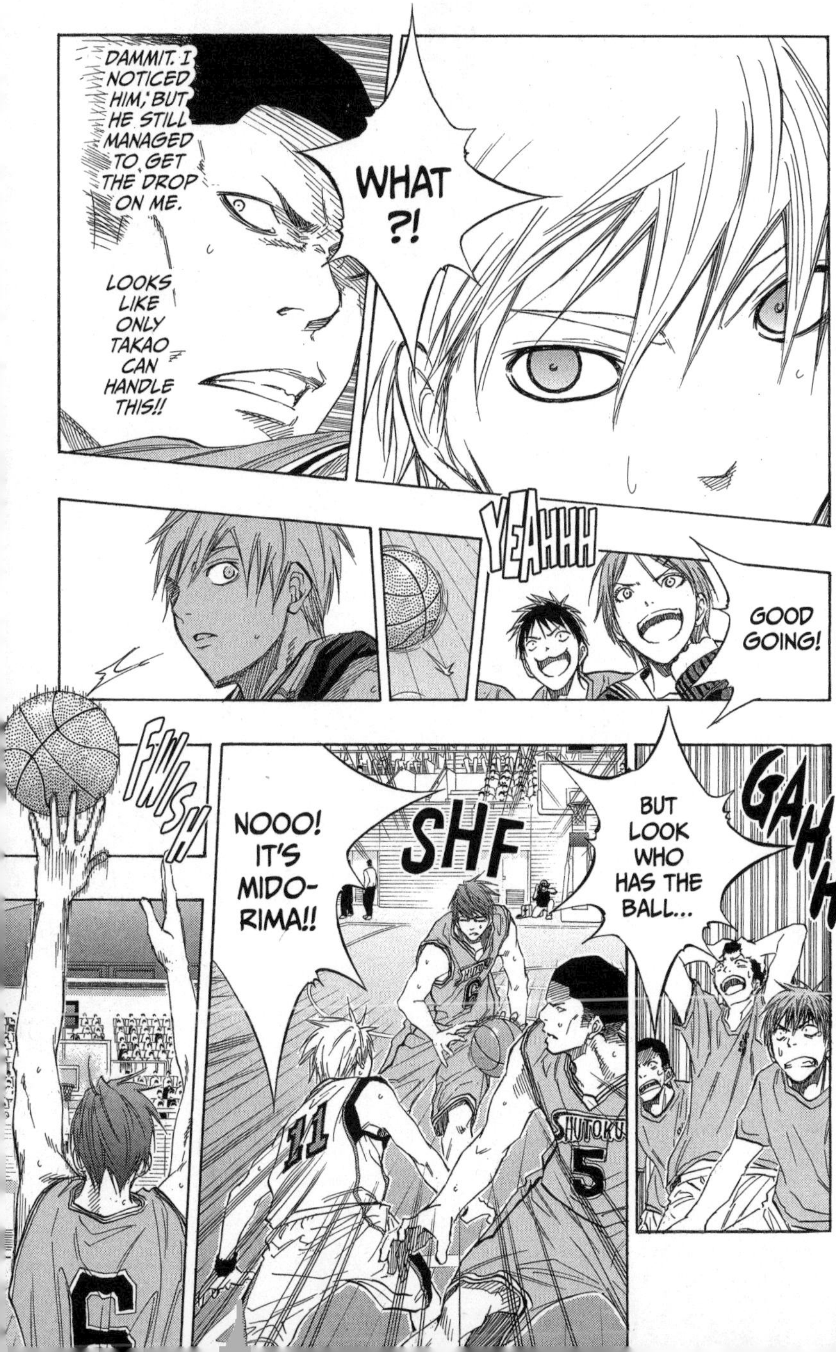
WHAT ?!
DAMMIT. I NOTICED HIM, BUT HE STILL MANAGED TO GET THE DROP ON ME.
LOOKS LIKE ONLY TAKAO CAN HANDLE THIS!!
YEAHHH
GOOD GOING!
GAHH
BUT LOOK WHO HAS THE BALL...
SHF
NOOO! IT'S MIDO-RIMA!!
FWISH

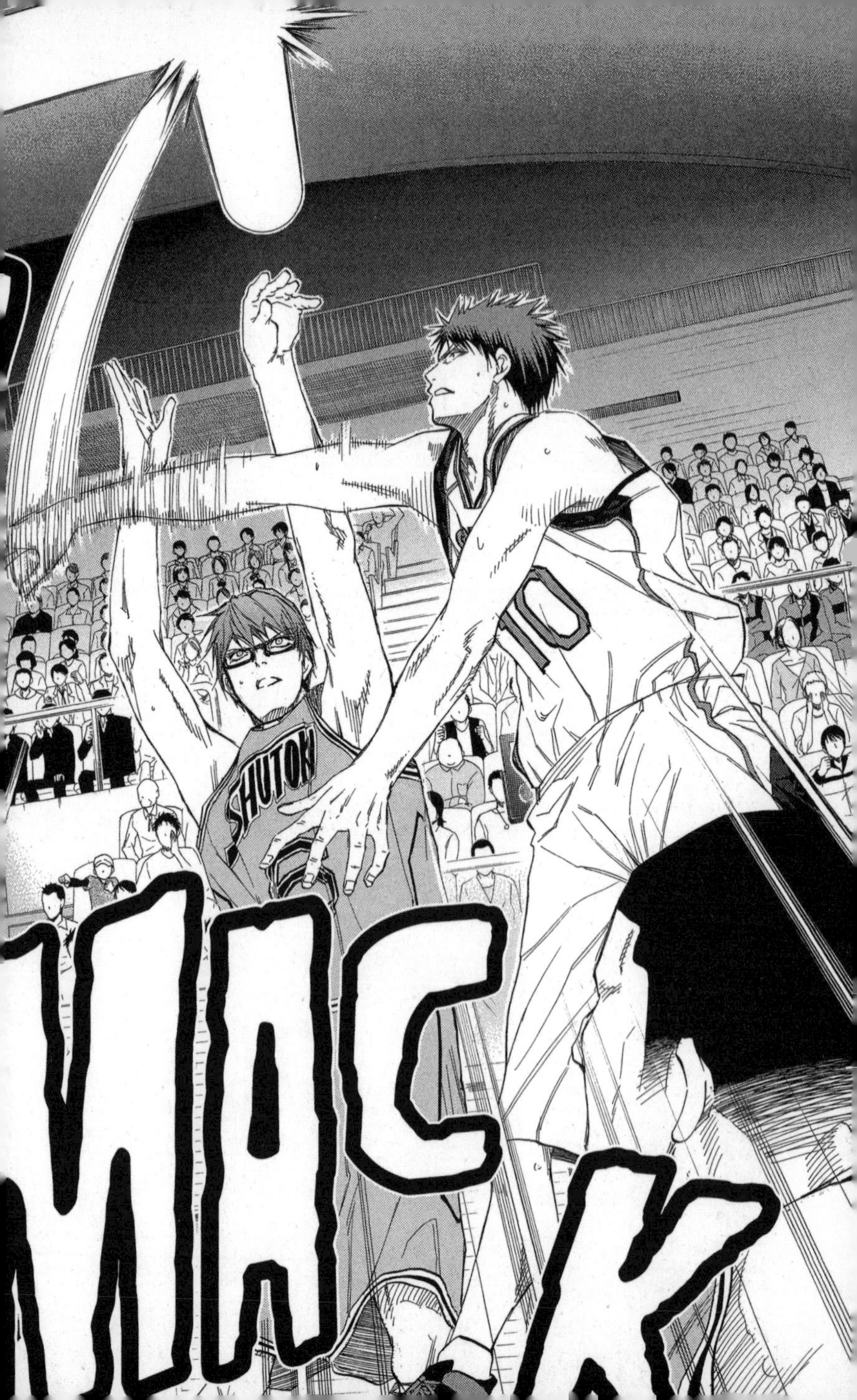
WHACK

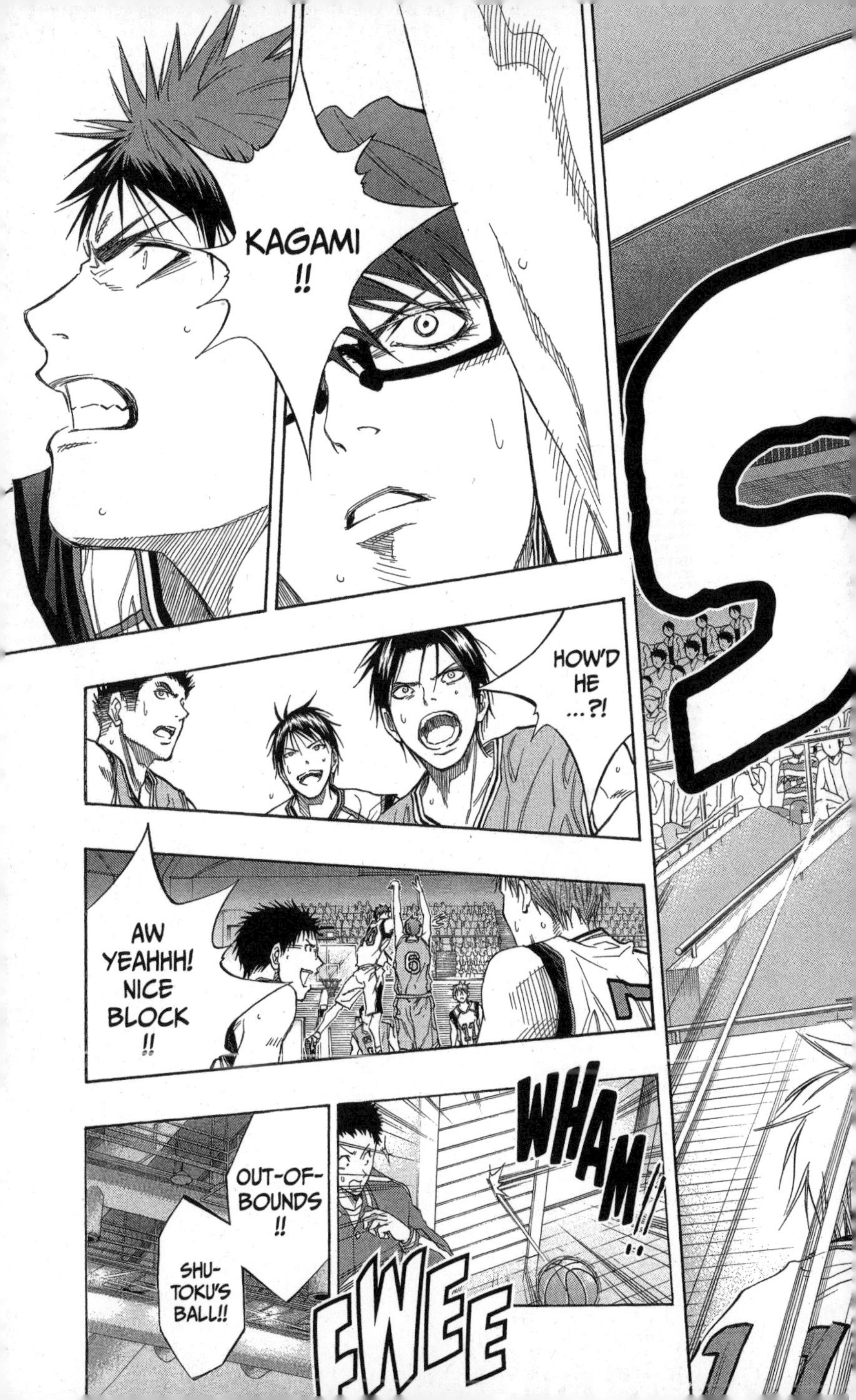
KAGAMI!!
HOW'D HE ...?!
AW YEAHHH! NICE BLOCK!!
WHAM!!
FWEE
OUT-OF-BOUNDS!!
SHU-TOKU'S BALL!!

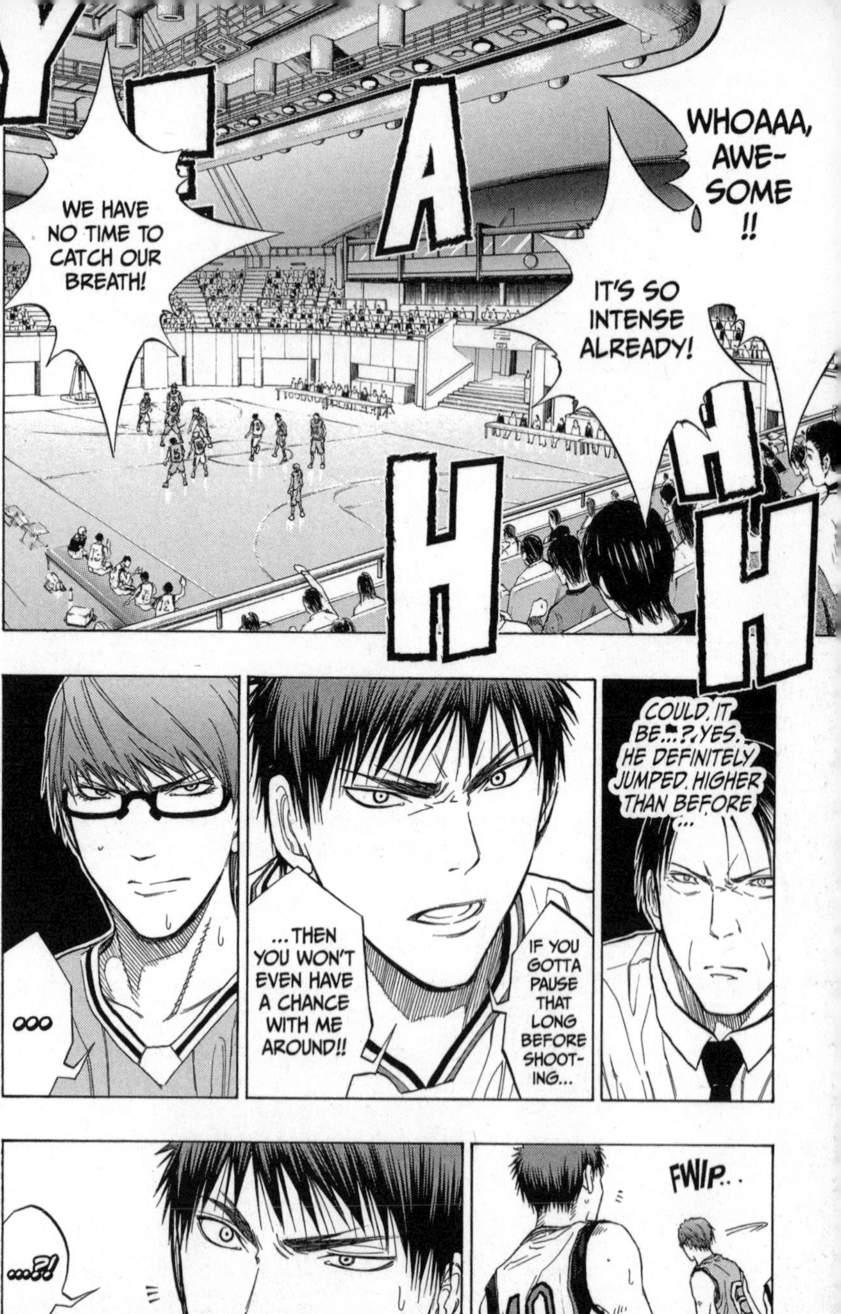

WHOAAA, AWESOME!!
IT'S SO INTENSE ALREADY!
WE HAVE NO TIME TO CATCH OUR BREATH!
Y A H H H
COULD IT BE...? YES. HE DEFINITELY JUMPED HIGHER THAN BEFORE...
IF YOU GOTTA PAUSE THAT LONG BEFORE SHOOTING...
...THEN YOU WON'T EVEN HAVE A CHANCE WITH ME AROUND!!
...
FWIP...
...?!

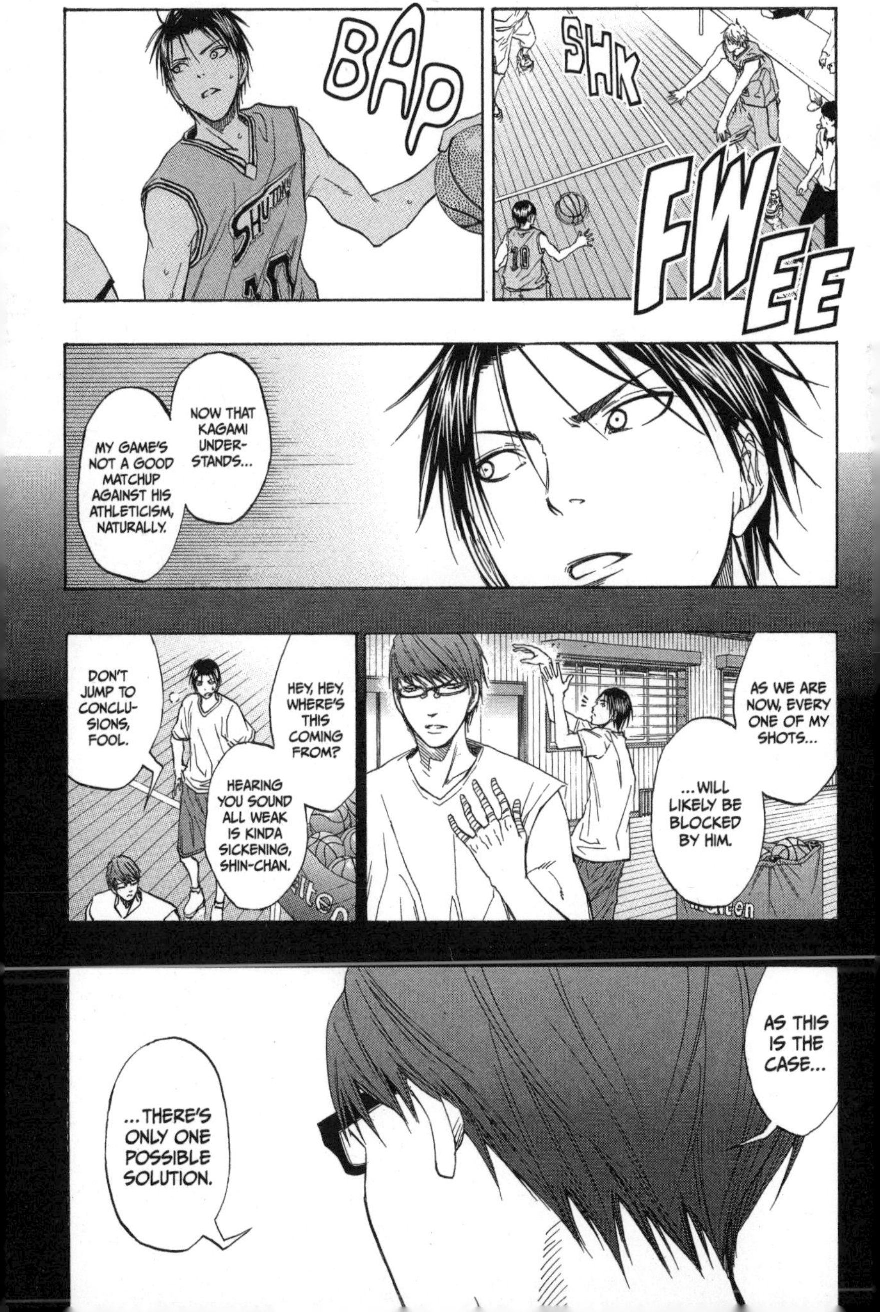
SHK
FWEE
BAP
NOW THAT KAGAMI UNDERSTANDS...
MY GAME'S NOT A GOOD MATCHUP AGAINST HIS ATHLETICISM, NATURALLY.
AS WE ARE NOW, EVERY ONE OF MY SHOTS...
...WILL LIKELY BE BLOCKED BY HIM.
HEY, HEY, WHERE'S THIS COMING FROM?
HEARING YOU SOUND ALL WEAK IS KINDA SICKENING, SHIN-CHAN.
DON'T JUMP TO CONCLUSIONS, FOOL.
AS THIS IS THE CASE...
...THERE'S ONLY ONE POSSIBLE SOLUTION.

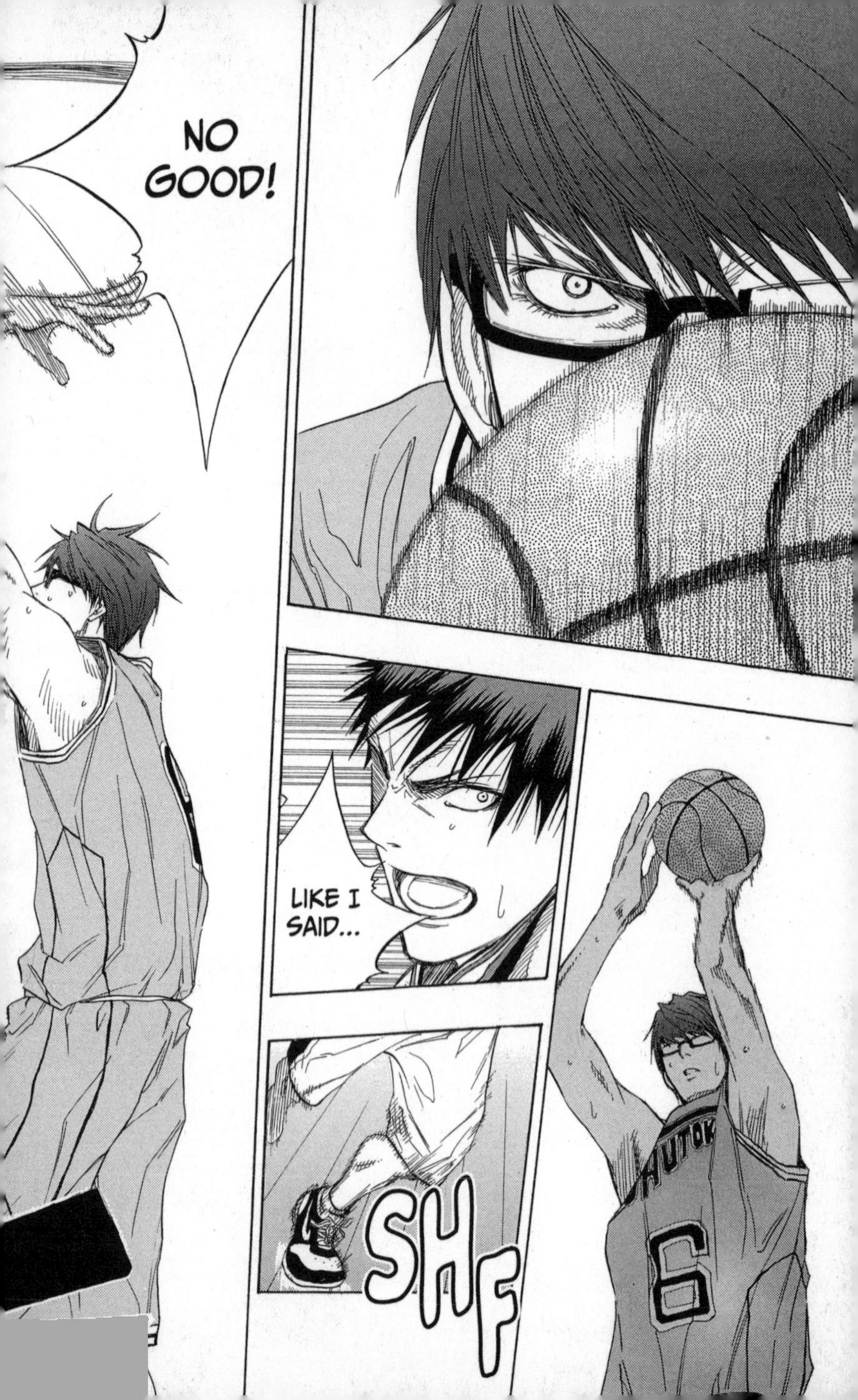
LIKE I SAID...
SHF
NO GOOD!

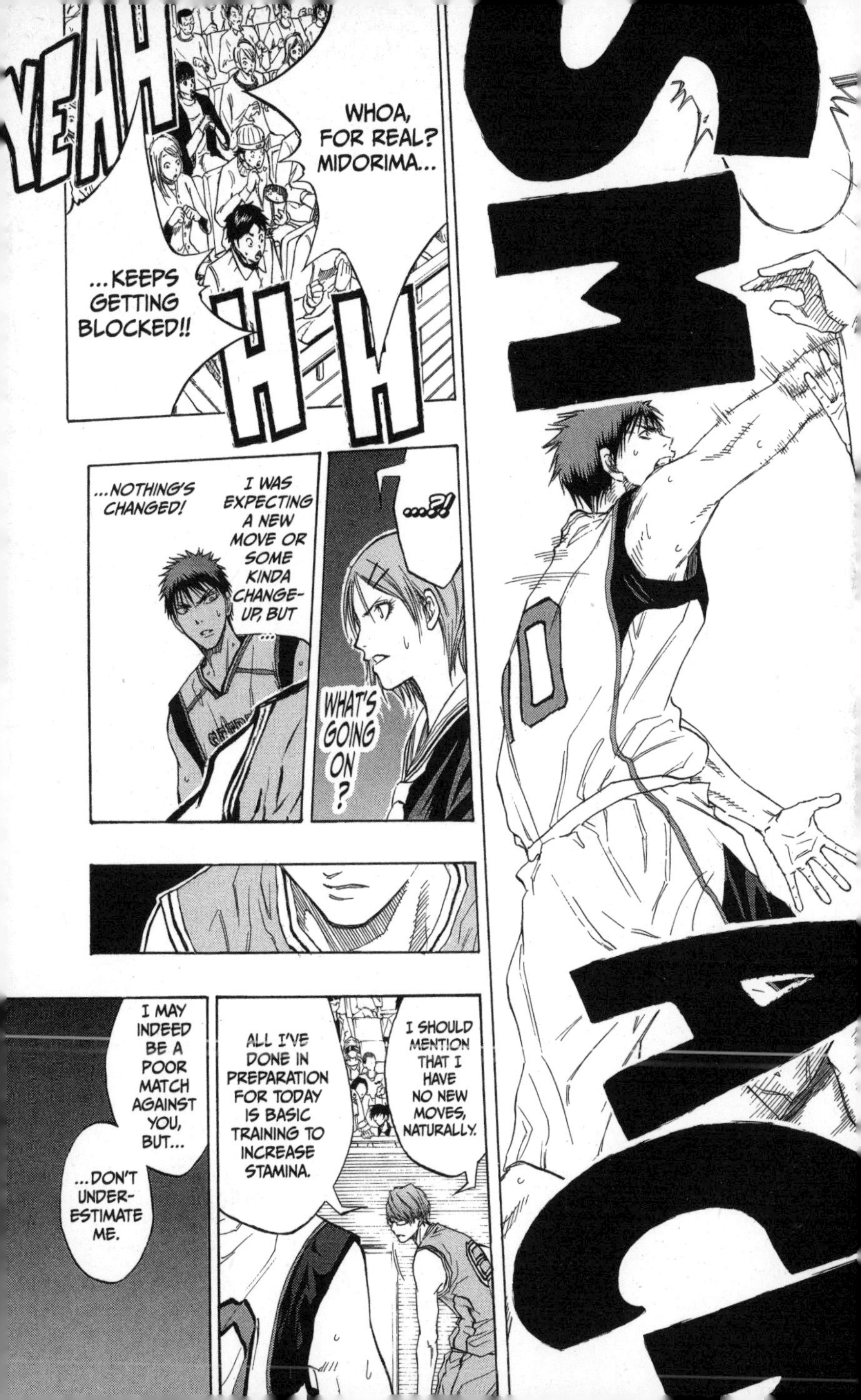

WHOA, FOR REAL? MIDORIMA...
...KEEPS GETTING BLOCKED!!
YEAH
HH
...?!
WHAT'S GOING ON?
I WAS EXPECTING A NEW MOVE OR SOME KINDA CHANGE-UP, BUT
...NOTHING'S CHANGED!
...
I SHOULD MENTION THAT I HAVE NO NEW MOVES, NATURALLY.
ALL I'VE DONE IN PREPARATION FOR TODAY IS BASIC TRAINING TO INCREASE STAMINA.
I MAY INDEED BE A POOR MATCH AGAINST YOU, BUT...
...DON'T UNDER-ESTIMATE ME.

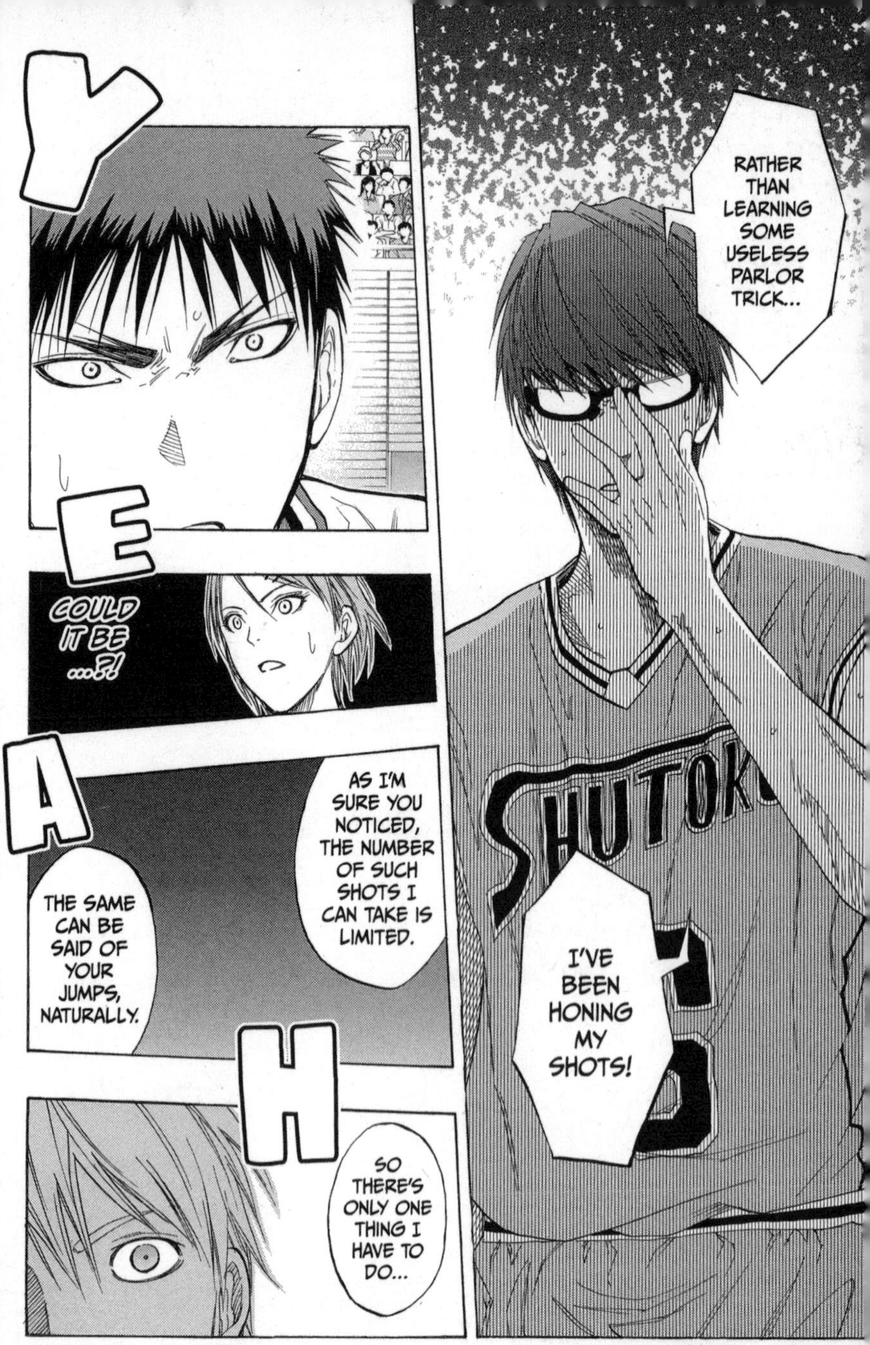
RATHER THAN LEARNING SOME USELESS PARLOR TRICK...
I'VE BEEN HONING MY SHOTS!
Y
E
COULD IT BE ...?!
A
AS I'M SURE YOU NOTICED, THE NUMBER OF SUCH SHOTS I CAN TAKE IS LIMITED.
THE SAME CAN BE SAID OF YOUR JUMPS, NATURALLY.
H
SO THERE'S ONLY ONE THING I HAVE TO DO...

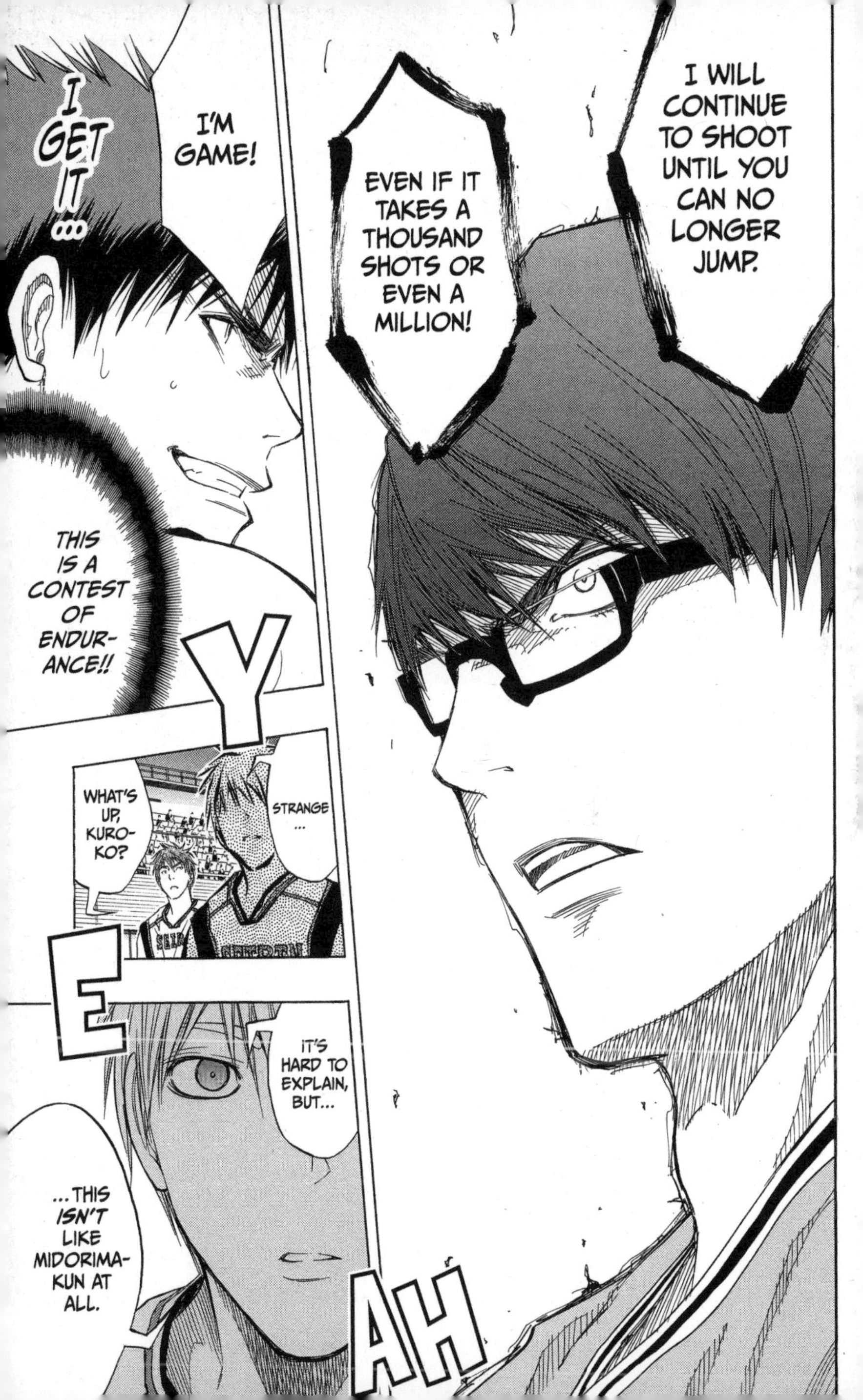
I WILL CONTINUE TO SHOOT UNTIL YOU CAN NO LONGER JUMP.
EVEN IF IT TAKES A THOUSAND SHOTS OR EVEN A MILLION!
I'M GAME!
I GET IT...
THIS IS A CONTEST OF ENDURANCE!!
Y
STRANGE...
WHAT'S UP, KUROKO?
E
IT'S HARD TO EXPLAIN, BUT...
...THIS ISN'T LIKE MIDORIMA-KUN AT ALL.
AH

KUROKO'S BASKETBALL BLOOPERS
TAKE 3

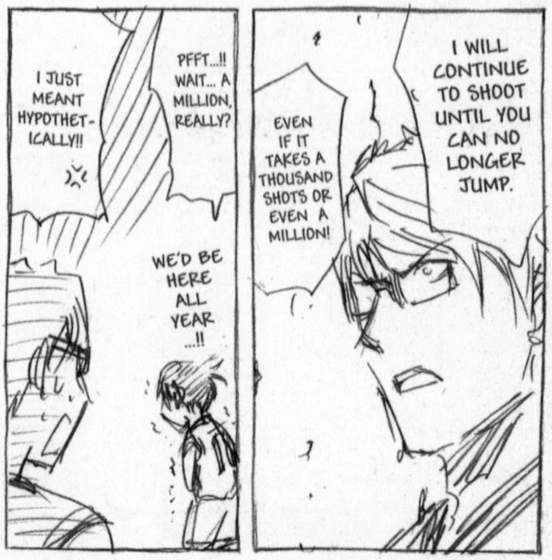
I WILL CONTINUE TO SHOOT UNTIL YOU CAN NO LONGER JUMP.
EVEN IF IT TAKES A THOUSAND SHOTS OR EVEN A MILLION!
PFFT...!! WAIT... A MILLION, REALLY?
I JUST MEANT HYPOTHET-ICALLY!!
WE'D BE HERE ALL YEAR ...!!

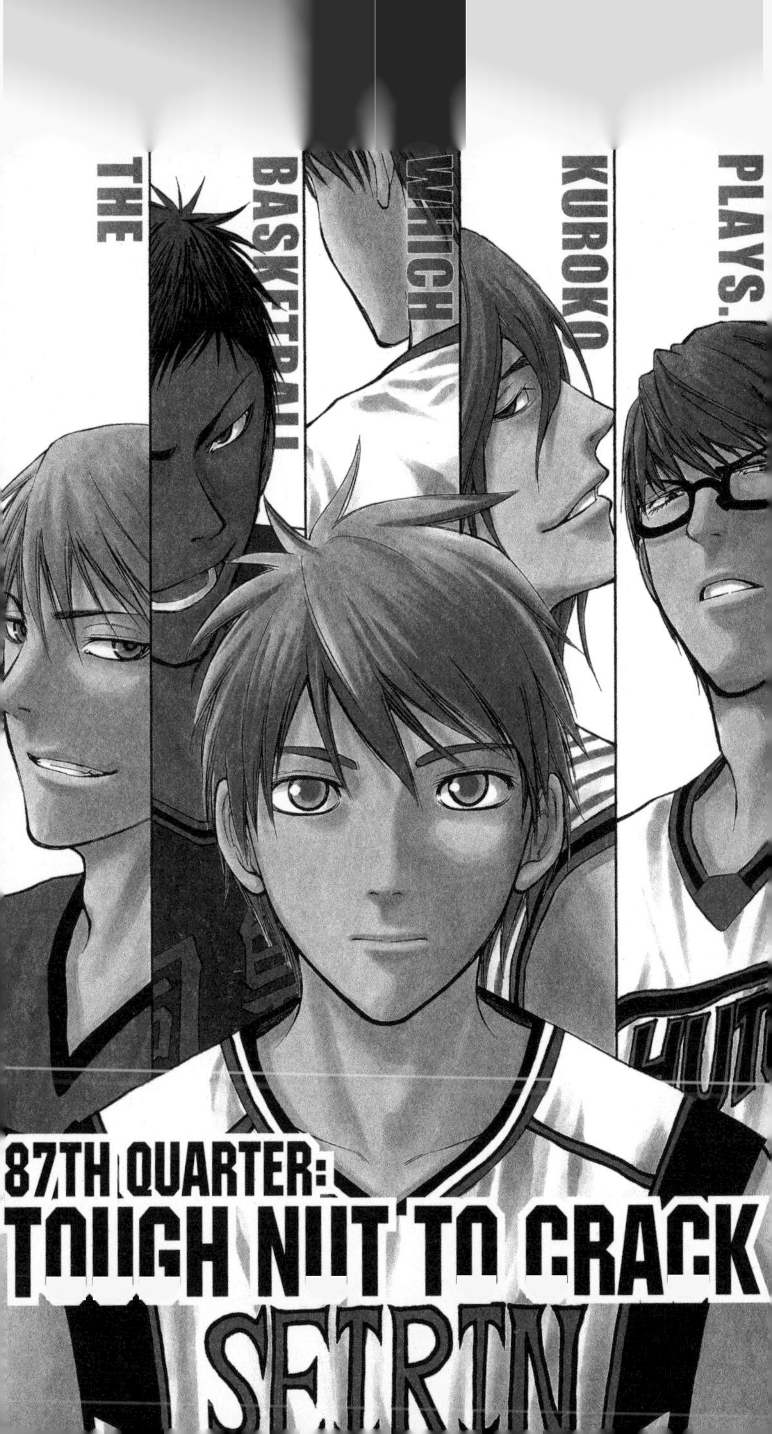
THE BASKETBALL WHICH KUROKO PLAYS.
87TH QUARTER:
TOUGH NUT TO CRACK
SEIRIN

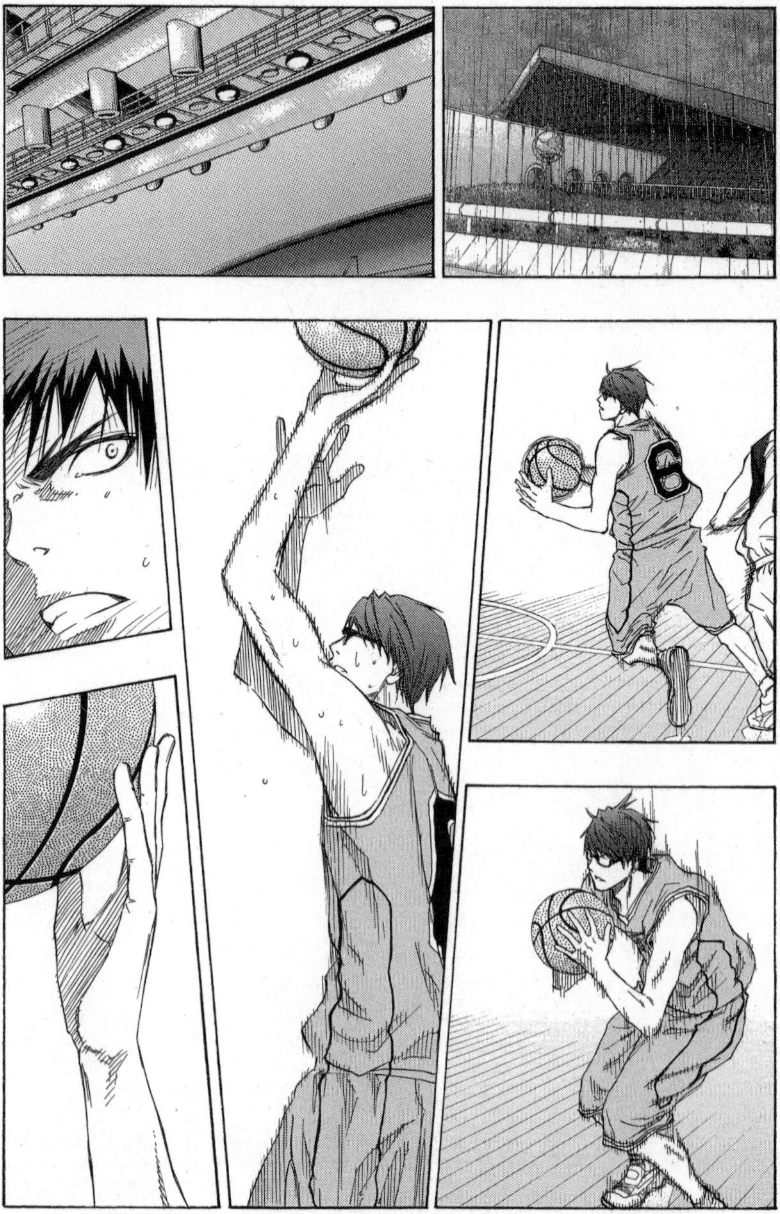

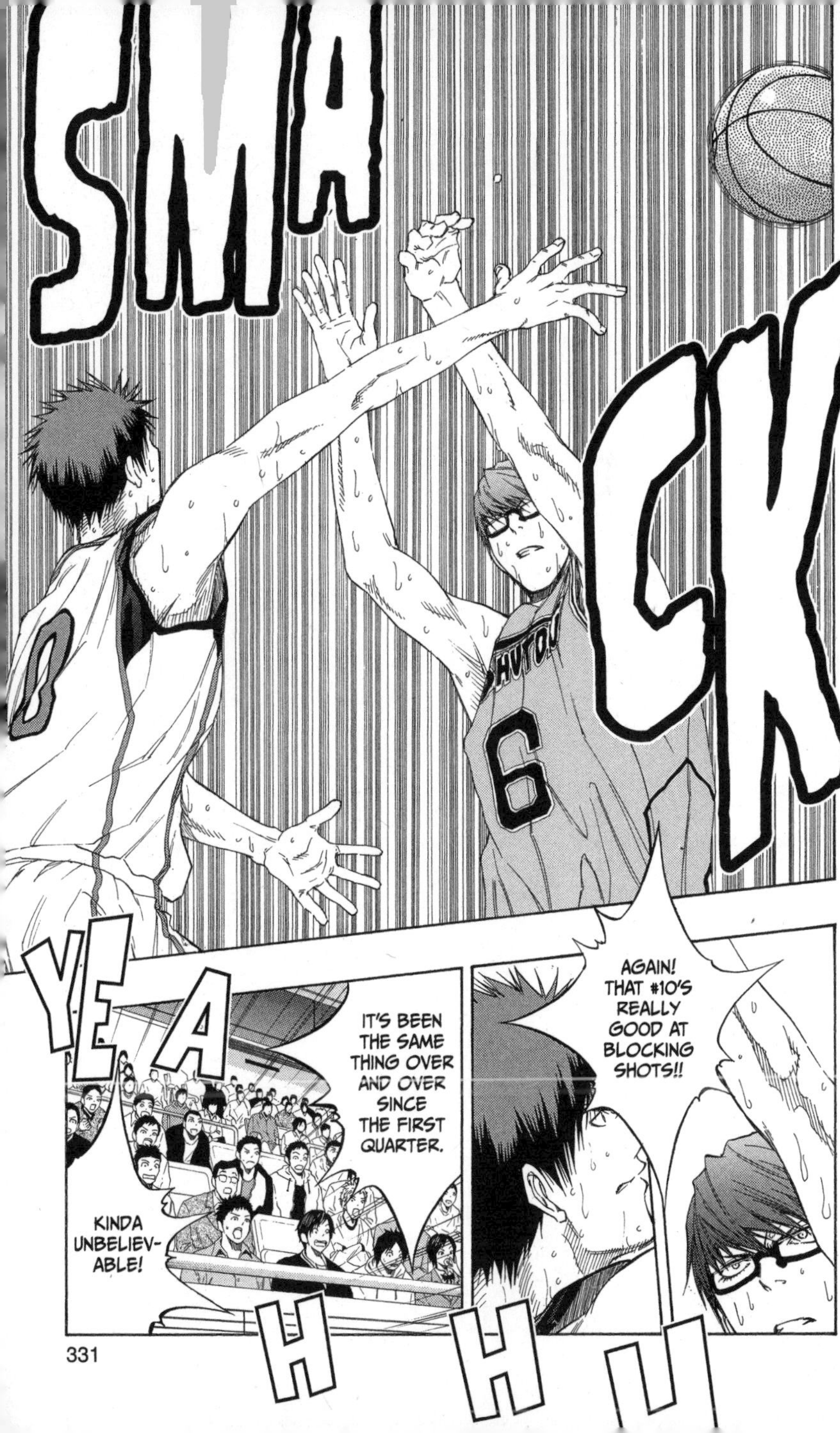
SMACK
AGAIN! THAT #10'S REALLY GOOD AT BLOCKING SHOTS!!
YEAHHH
IT'S BEEN THE SAME THING OVER AND OVER SINCE THE FIRST QUARTER.
KINDA UNBELIEV-ABLE!

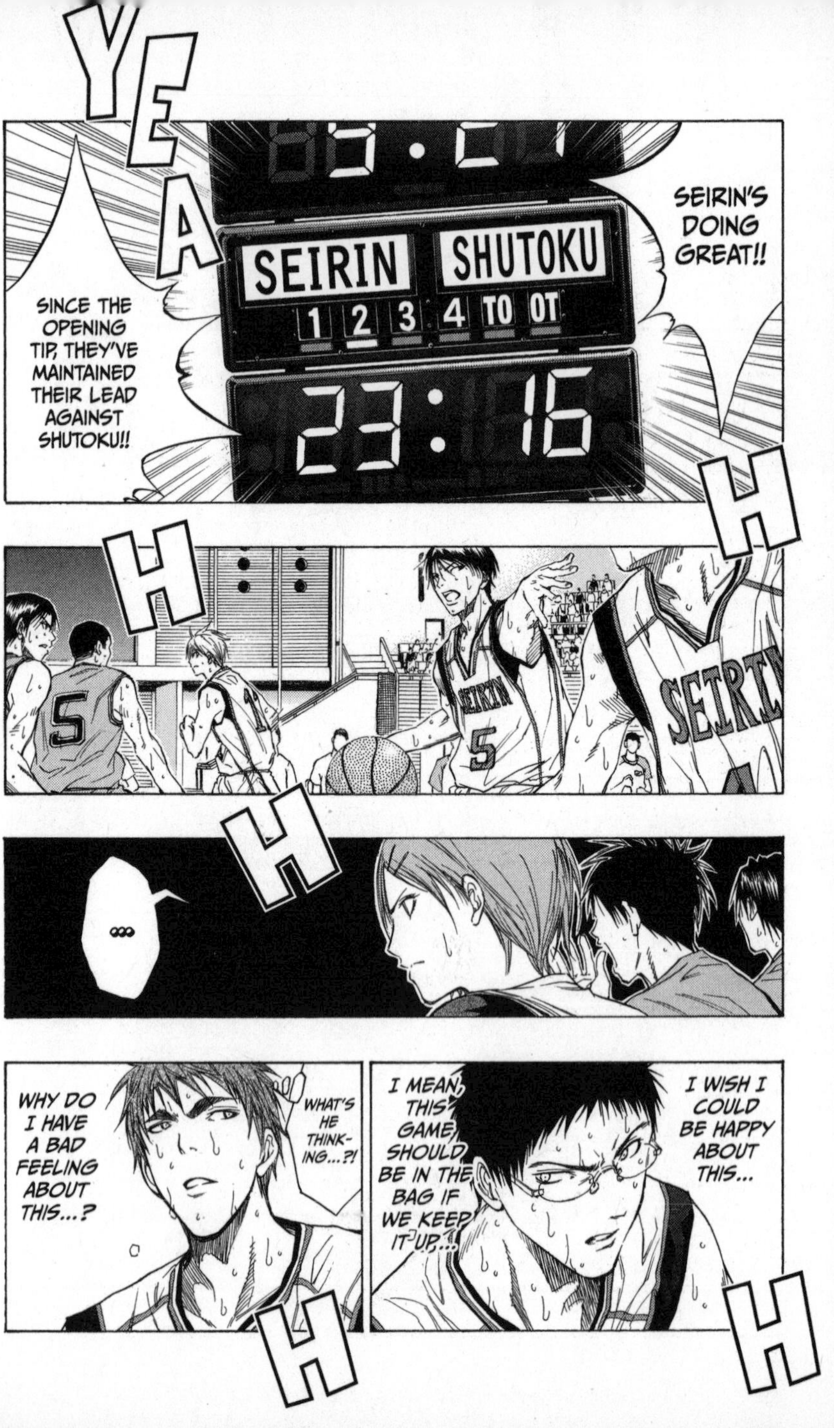
YEAHHHHH
SEIRIN
SHUTOKU
1 2 3 4 TO OT
23 : 16
SEIRIN'S DOING GREAT!!
SINCE THE OPENING TIP, THEY'VE MAINTAINED THEIR LEAD AGAINST SHUTOKU!!
SEIRIN
SEIRIN
5
5
5
...
I WISH I COULD BE HAPPY ABOUT THIS...
I MEAN, THIS GAME SHOULD BE IN THE BAG IF WE KEEP IT UP...
WHAT'S HE THINKING...?!
WHY DO I HAVE A BAD FEELING ABOUT THIS...?

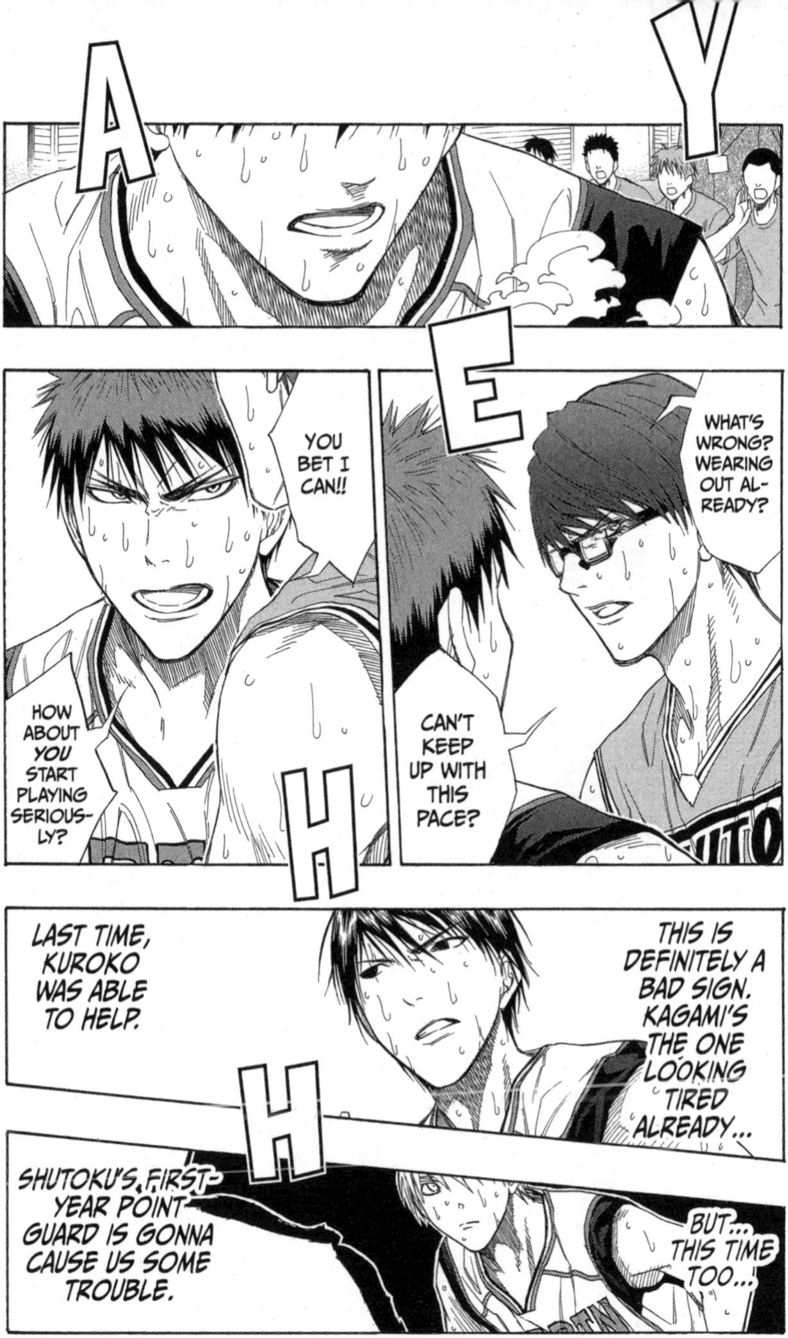
Y
A
E
WHAT'S WRONG? WEARING OUT ALREADY?
CAN'T KEEP UP WITH THIS PACE?
YOU BET I CAN!!
HOW ABOUT *YOU* START PLAYING SERIOUSLY?
H
THIS IS DEFINITELY A BAD SIGN. KAGAMI'S THE ONE LOOKING TIRED ALREADY...
LAST TIME, KUROKO WAS ABLE TO HELP.
H
BUT... THIS TIME TOO...!
SHUTOKU'S FIRST-YEAR POINT GUARD IS GONNA CAUSE US SOME TROUBLE.

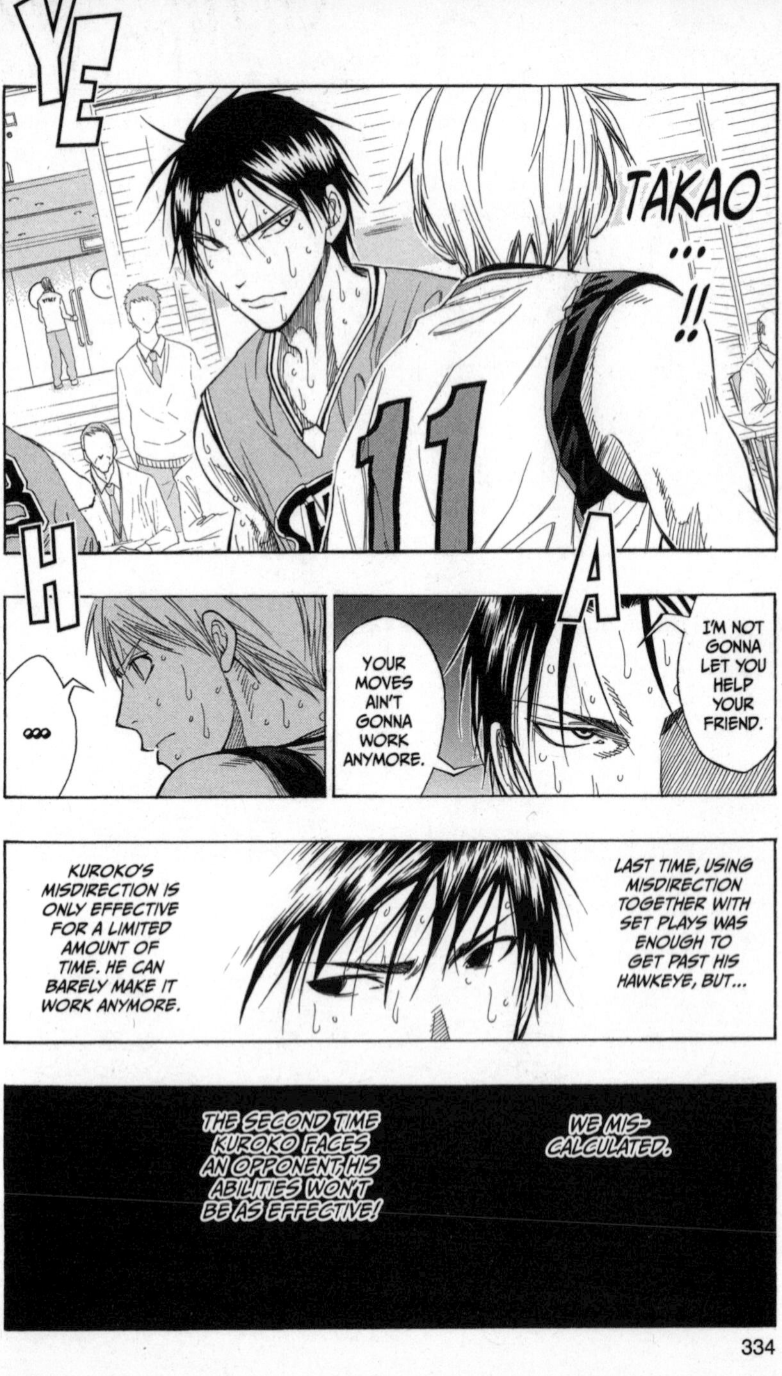
YE
TAKAO ...!!
H
A
I'M NOT GONNA LET YOU HELP YOUR FRIEND.
YOUR MOVES AIN'T GONNA WORK ANYMORE.
...
LAST TIME, USING MISDIRECTION TOGETHER WITH SET PLAYS WAS ENOUGH TO GET PAST HIS HAWKEYE, BUT...
KUROKO'S MISDIRECTION IS ONLY EFFECTIVE FOR A LIMITED AMOUNT OF TIME. HE CAN BARELY MAKE IT WORK ANYMORE.
WE MIS-CALCULATED.
THE SECOND TIME KUROKO FACES AN OPPONENT, HIS ABILITIES WON'T BE AS EFFECTIVE!

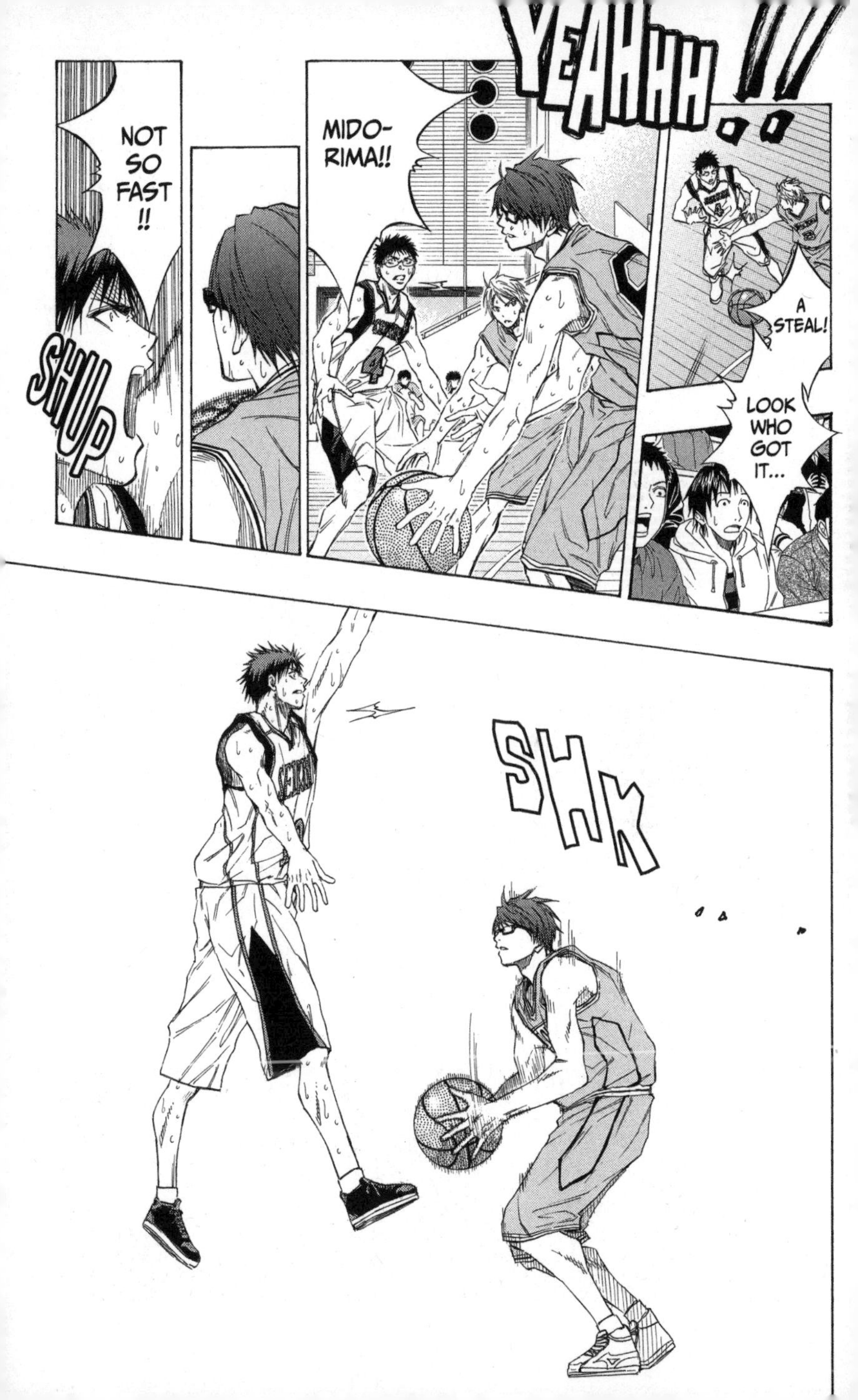
YEAHHH!!
A STEAL!
LOOK WHO GOT IT...
MIDO-RIMA!!
NOT SO FAST!!
SHUP
SHK

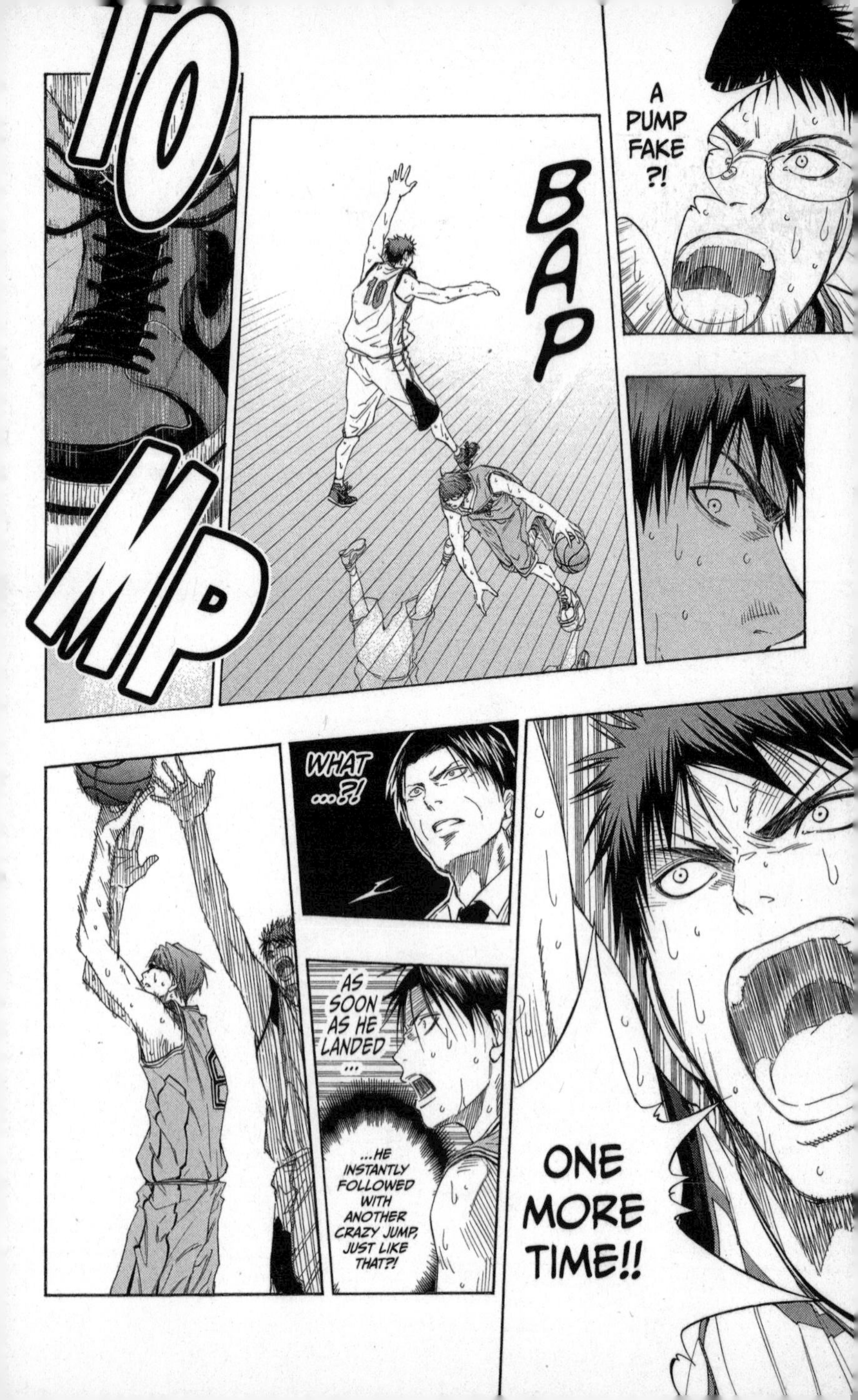
A PUMP FAKE?!
BAP
TOMP
ONE MORE TIME!!
WHAT...?!
AS SOON AS HE LANDED...
...HE INSTANTLY FOLLOWED WITH ANOTHER CRAZY JUMP, JUST LIKE THAT?!

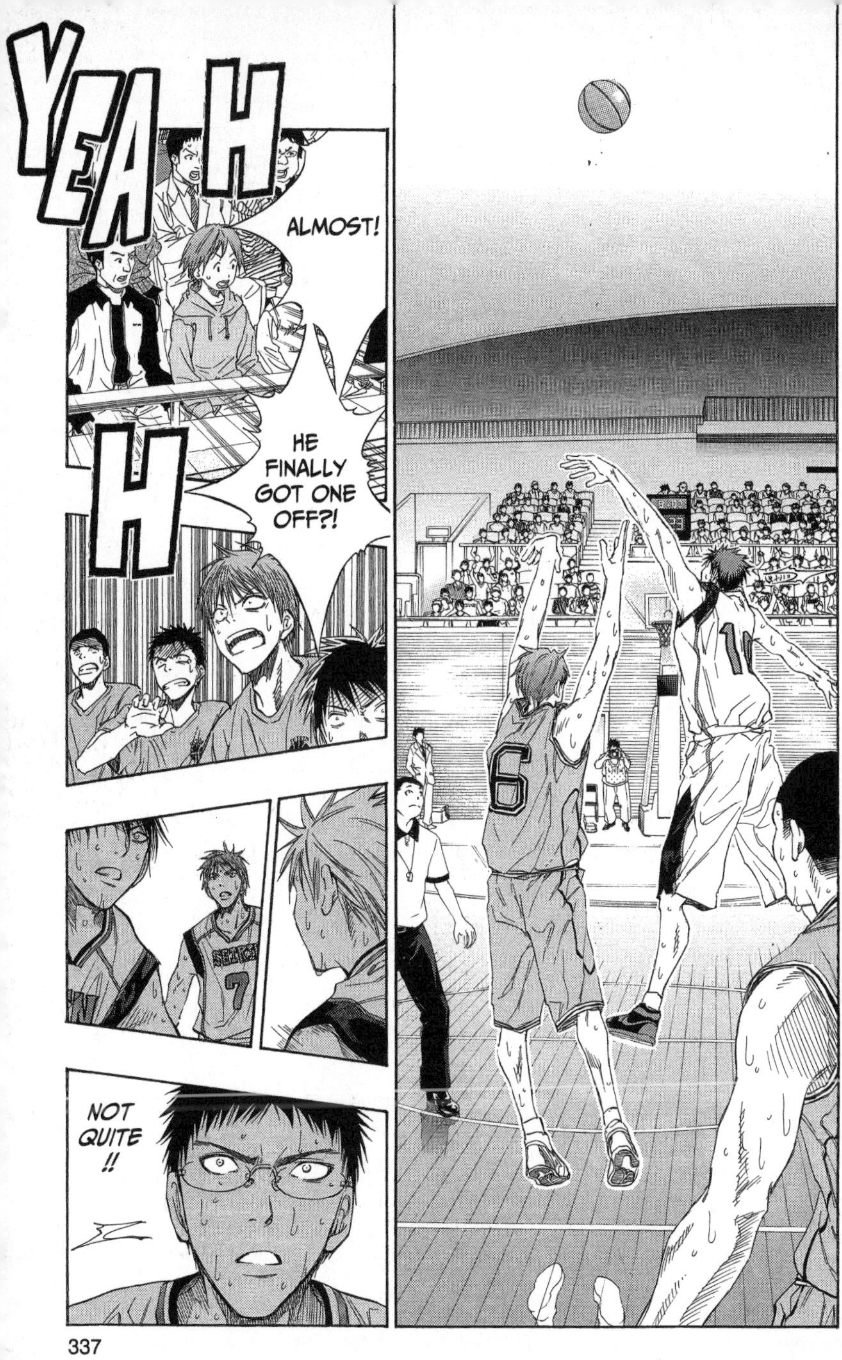
YEAH
ALMOST!
H
HE FINALLY GOT ONE OFF?!
NOT QUITE!!

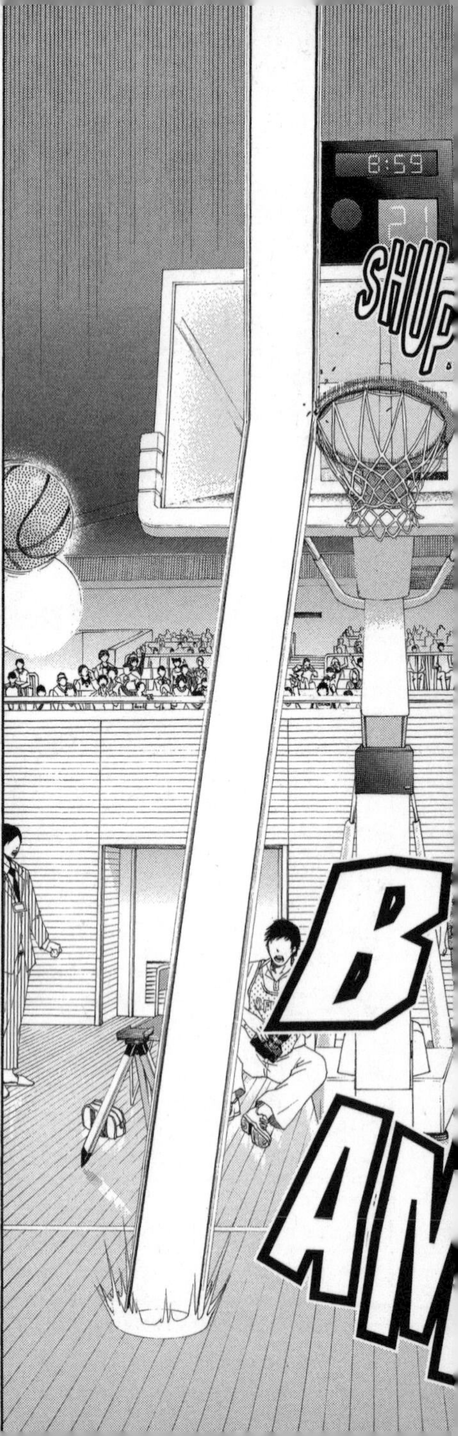
6:59
21
SHUP
BAM

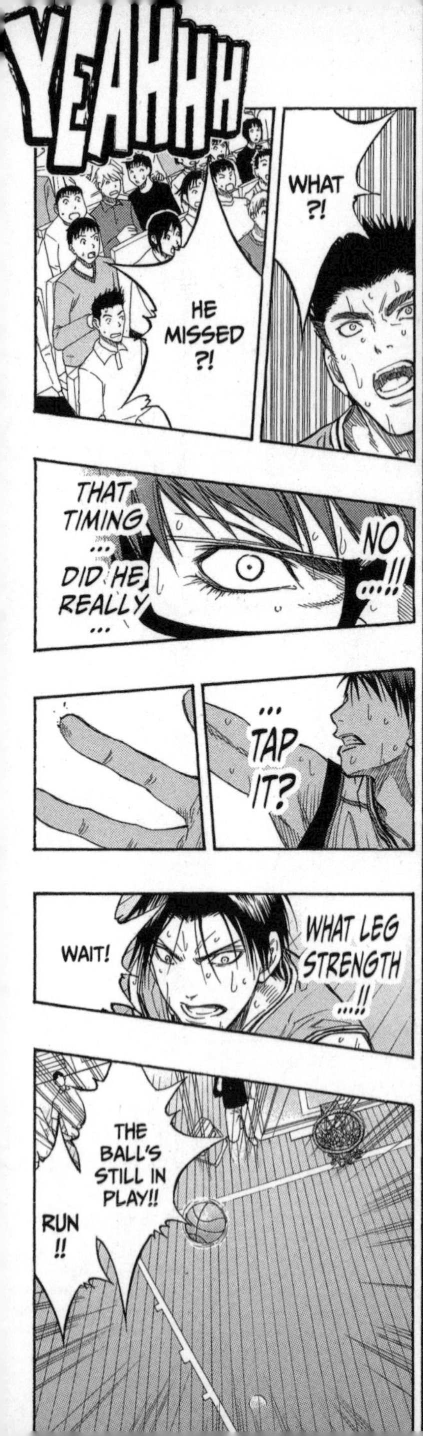
YEAHHH
WHAT ?!
HE MISSED ?!
NO ...!!
THAT TIMING ... DID HE REALLY ...
... TAP IT?
WHAT LEG STRENGTH ...!!
WAIT!
THE BALL'S STILL IN PLAY!!
RUN !!

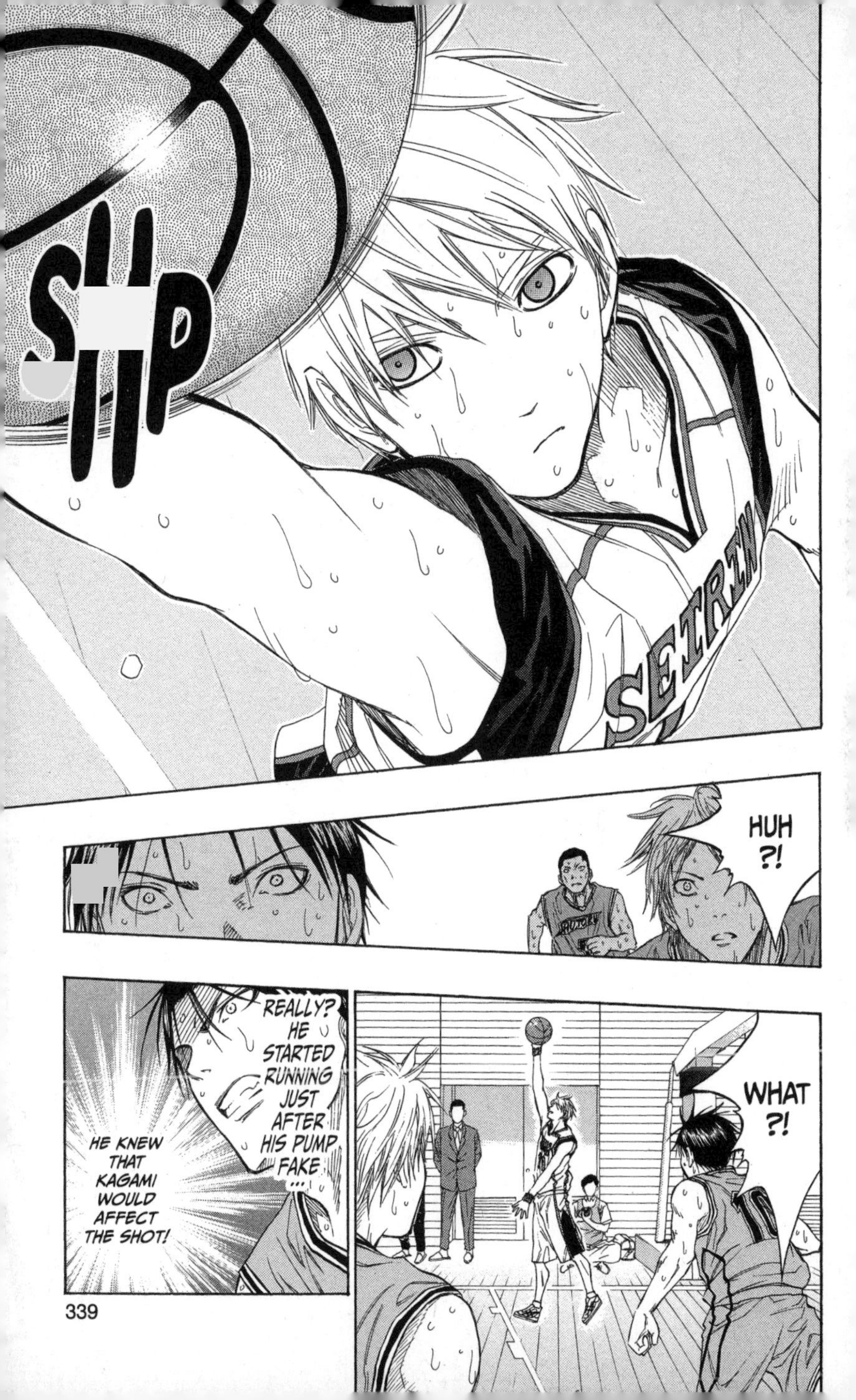
SHP
HUH ?!
REALLY? HE STARTED RUNNING JUST AFTER HIS PUMP FAKE ...
HE KNEW THAT KAGAMI WOULD AFFECT THE SHOT!
WHAT ?!

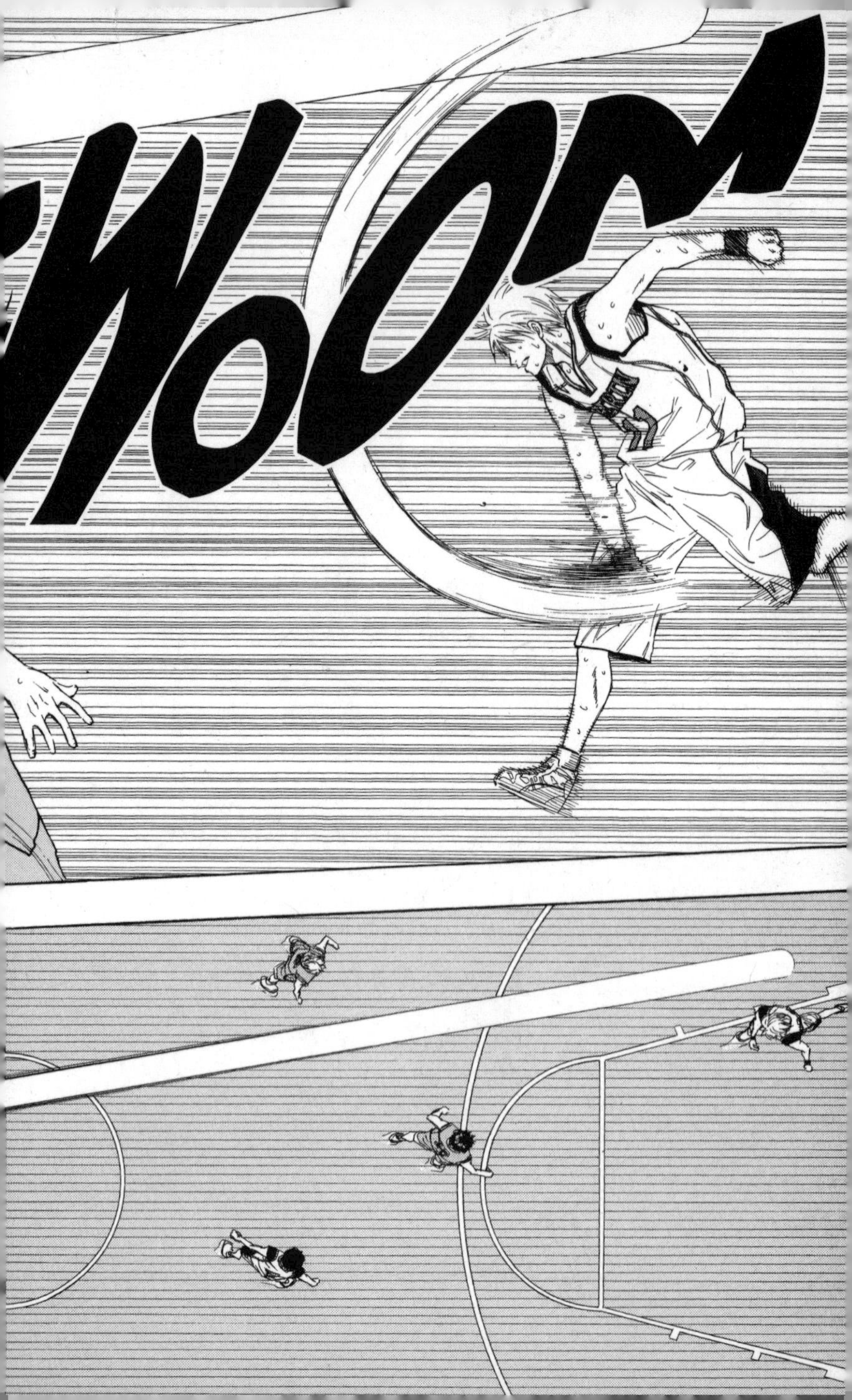
WOOM

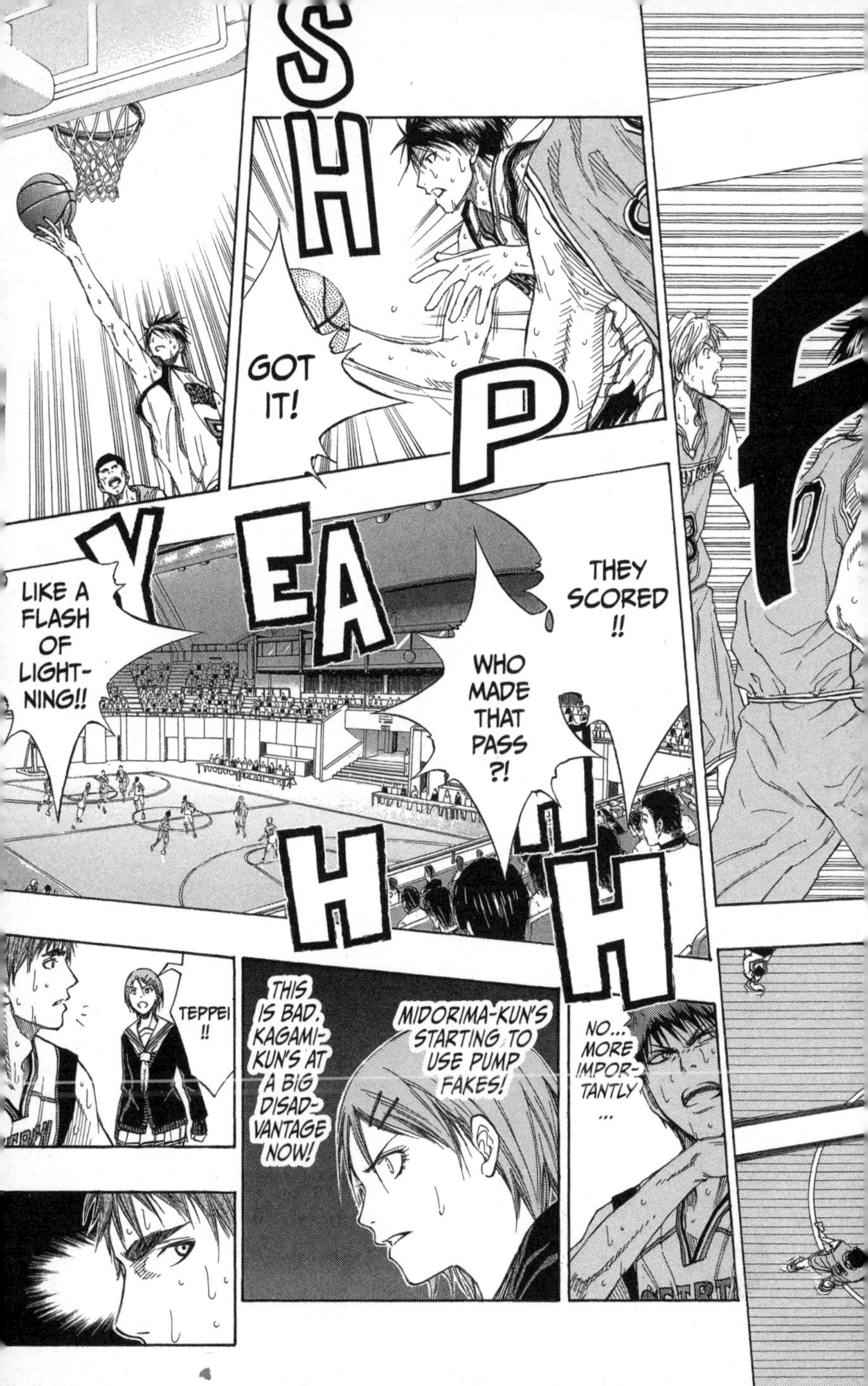
SHP
GOT IT!
YEAHHH
THEY SCORED!!
WHO MADE THAT PASS?!
LIKE A FLASH OF LIGHTNING!!
NO... MORE IMPORTANTLY...
MIDORIMA-KUN'S STARTING TO USE PUMP FAKES!
THIS IS BAD. KAGAMI-KUN'S AT A BIG DISADVANTAGE NOW!
TEPPEI!!

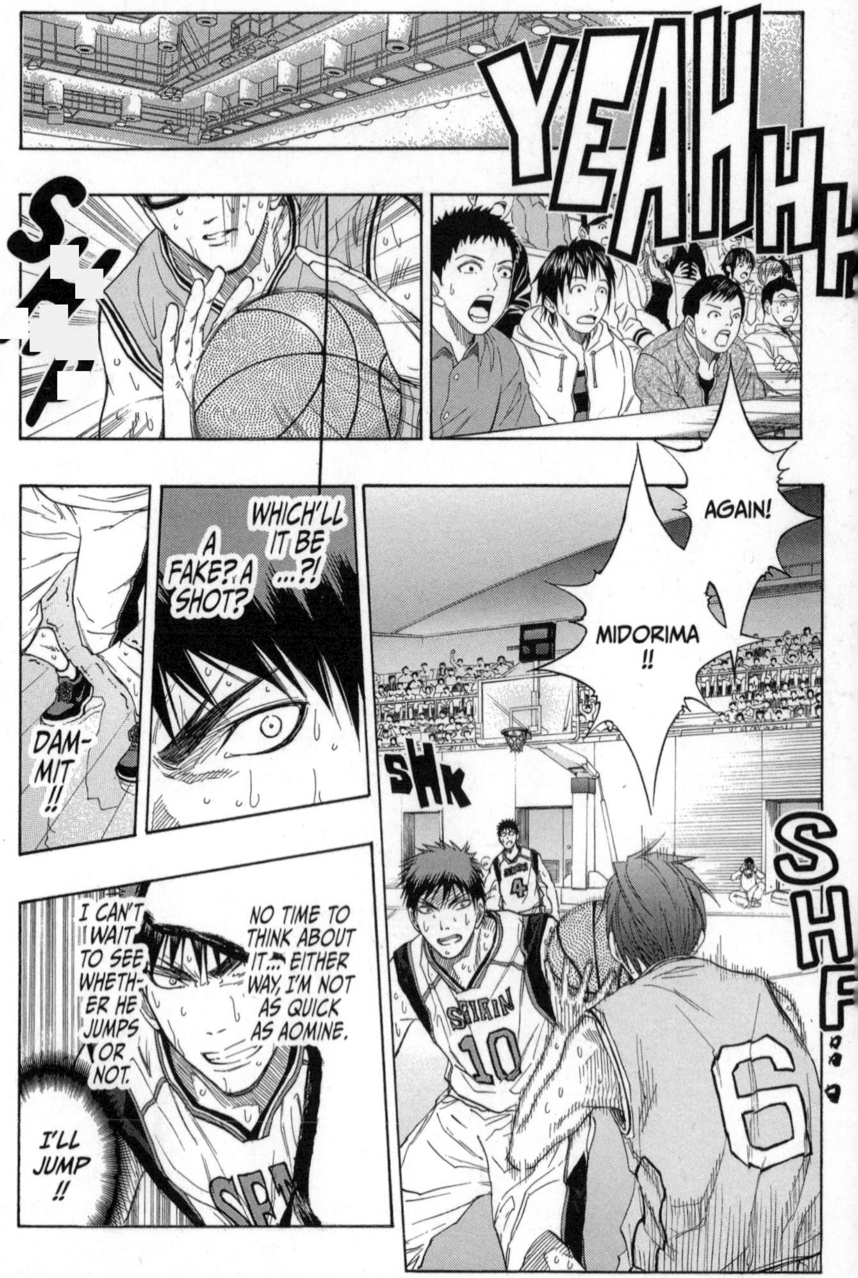
YEAHHH
AGAIN! MIDORIMA!!
SHK
SHF
WHICH'LL IT BE ...?!
A FAKE? A SHOT?
DAM-MIT!!
NO TIME TO THINK ABOUT IT... EITHER WAY, I'M NOT AS QUICK AS AOMINE.
I CAN'T WAIT TO SEE WHETHER HE JUMPS OR NOT.
I'LL JUMP!!

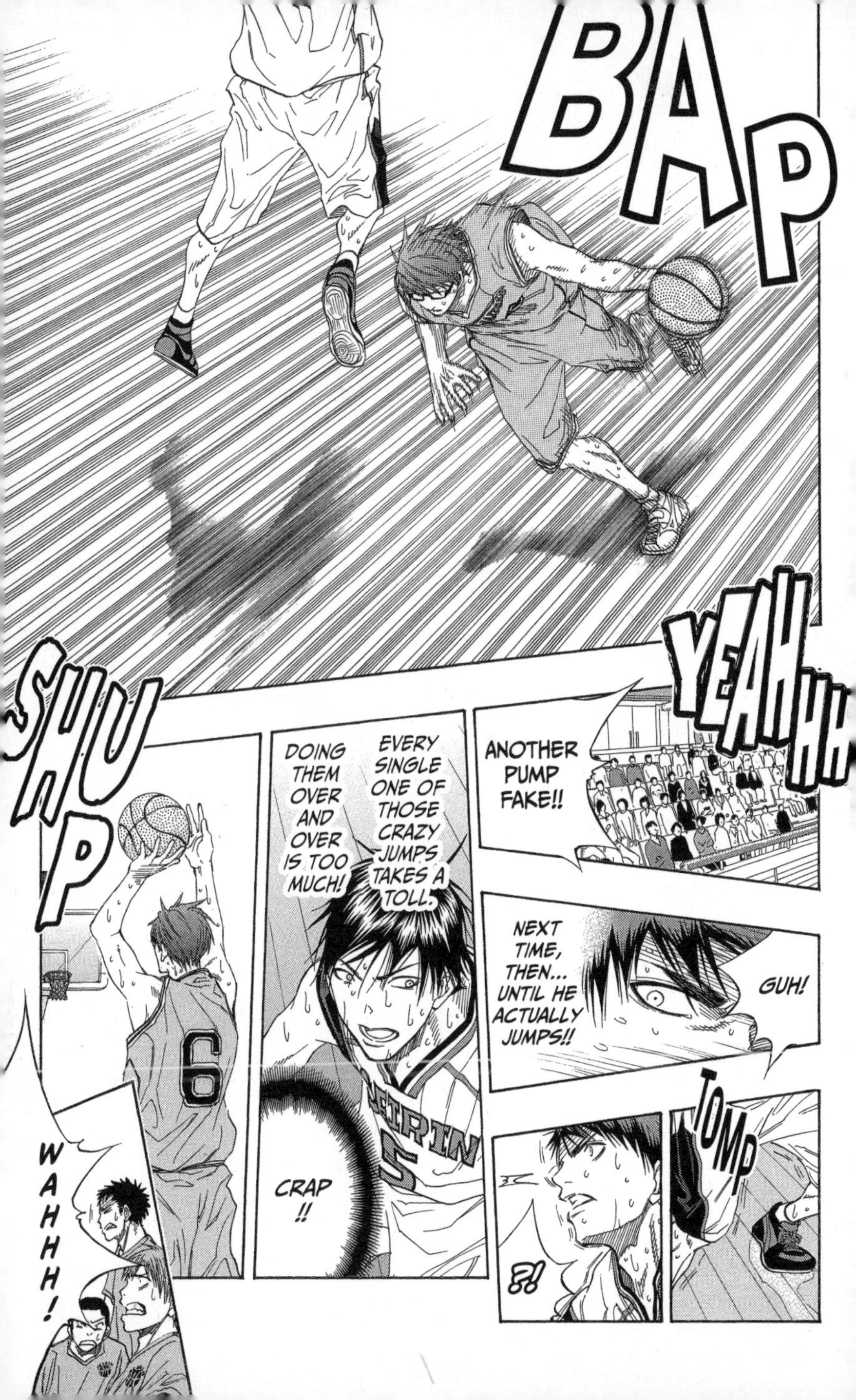

BAP
YEAHHHH
ANOTHER PUMP FAKE!!
NEXT TIME, THEN... UNTIL HE ACTUALLY JUMPS!!
GUH!
TOMP
?!
EVERY SINGLE ONE OF THOSE CRAZY JUMPS TAKES A TOLL.
DOING THEM OVER AND OVER IS TOO MUCH!
CRAP!!
SHUP
WAHHHH!

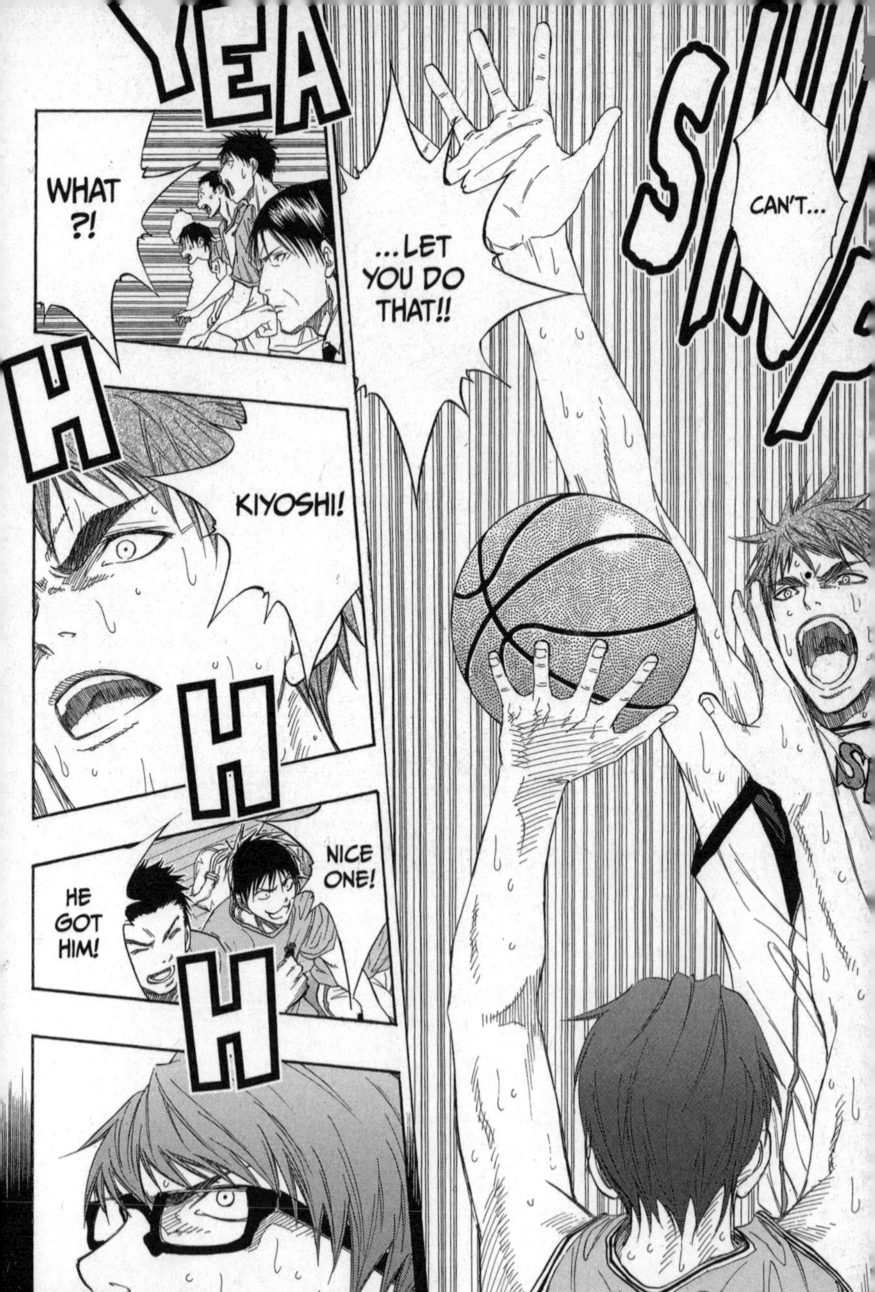

CAN'T...
...LET YOU DO THAT!!
YEAHHH
WHAT ?!
KIYOSHI!
NICE ONE!
HE GOT HIM!

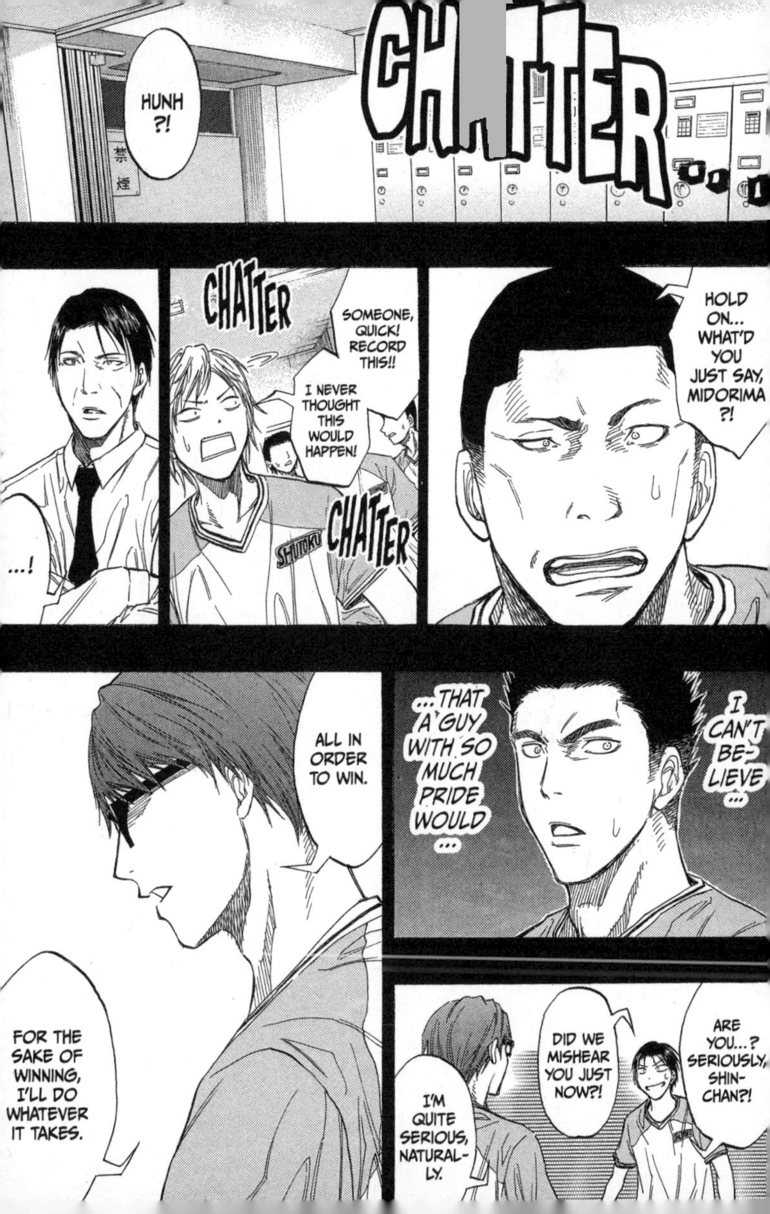
CHATTER...
HUNH ?!
HOLD ON... WHAT'D YOU JUST SAY, MIDORIMA ?!
SOMEONE, QUICK! RECORD THIS!!
CHATTER
I NEVER THOUGHT THIS WOULD HAPPEN!
CHATTER
SHUTOKU
...!
I CAN'T BE-LIEVE ...
...THAT A GUY WITH SO MUCH PRIDE WOULD ...
ARE YOU...? SERIOUSLY, SHIN-CHAN?!
DID WE MISHEAR YOU JUST NOW?!
I'M QUITE SERIOUS, NATURAL-LY.
ALL IN ORDER TO WIN.
FOR THE SAKE OF WINNING, I'LL DO WHATEVER IT TAKES.

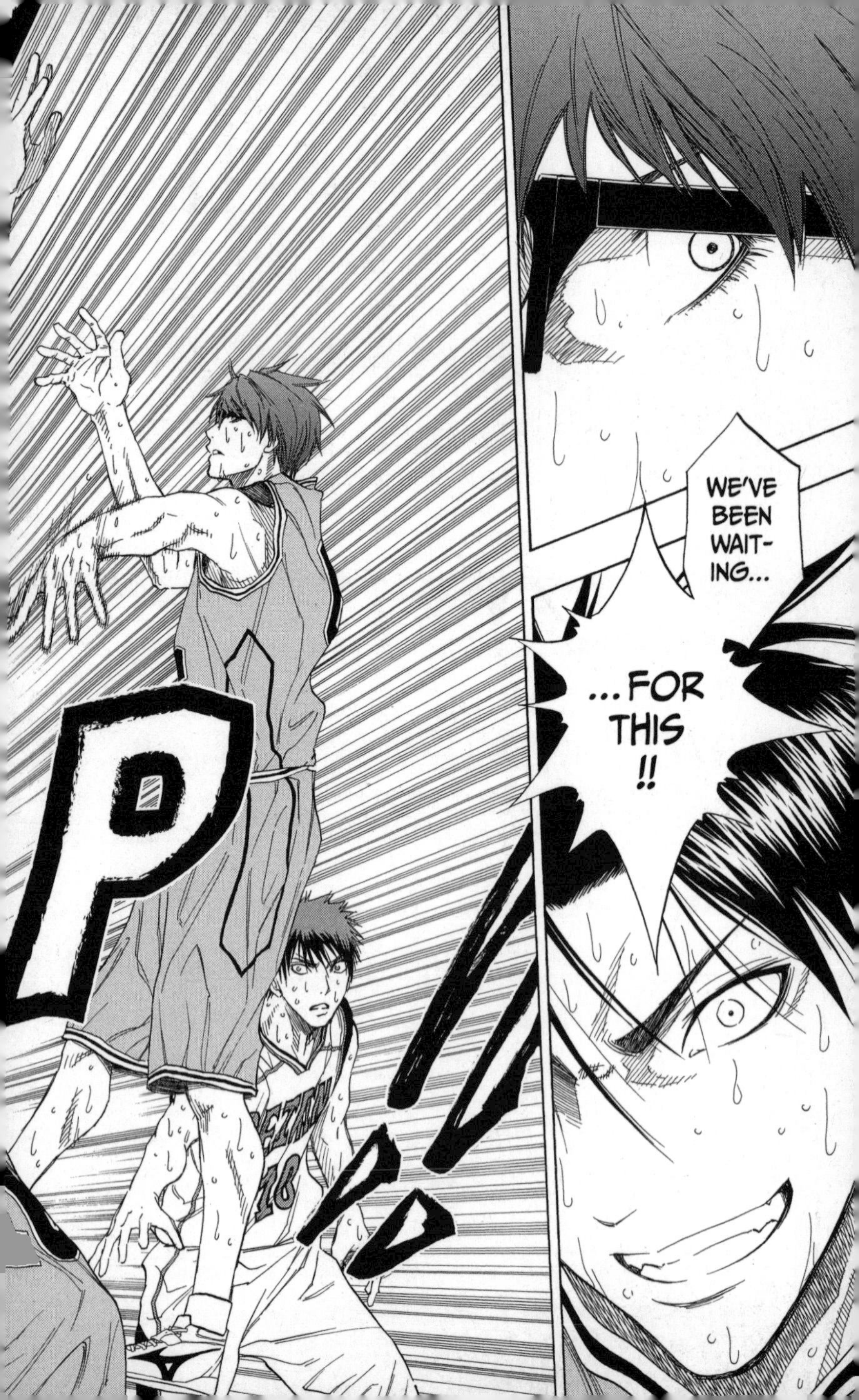
WE'VE BEEN WAIT-ING...
...FOR THIS !!

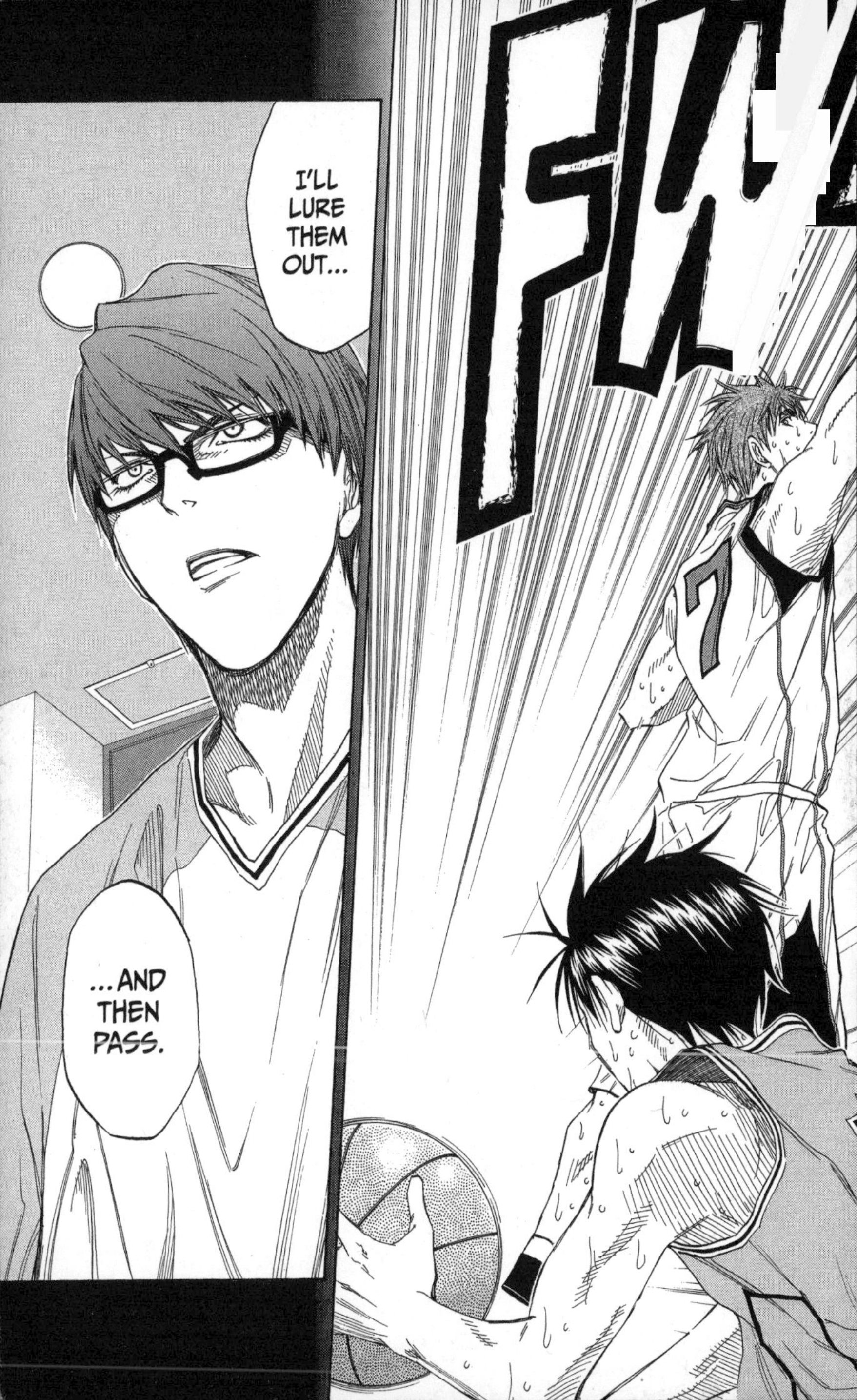
I'LL LURE THEM OUT...
...AND THEN PASS.

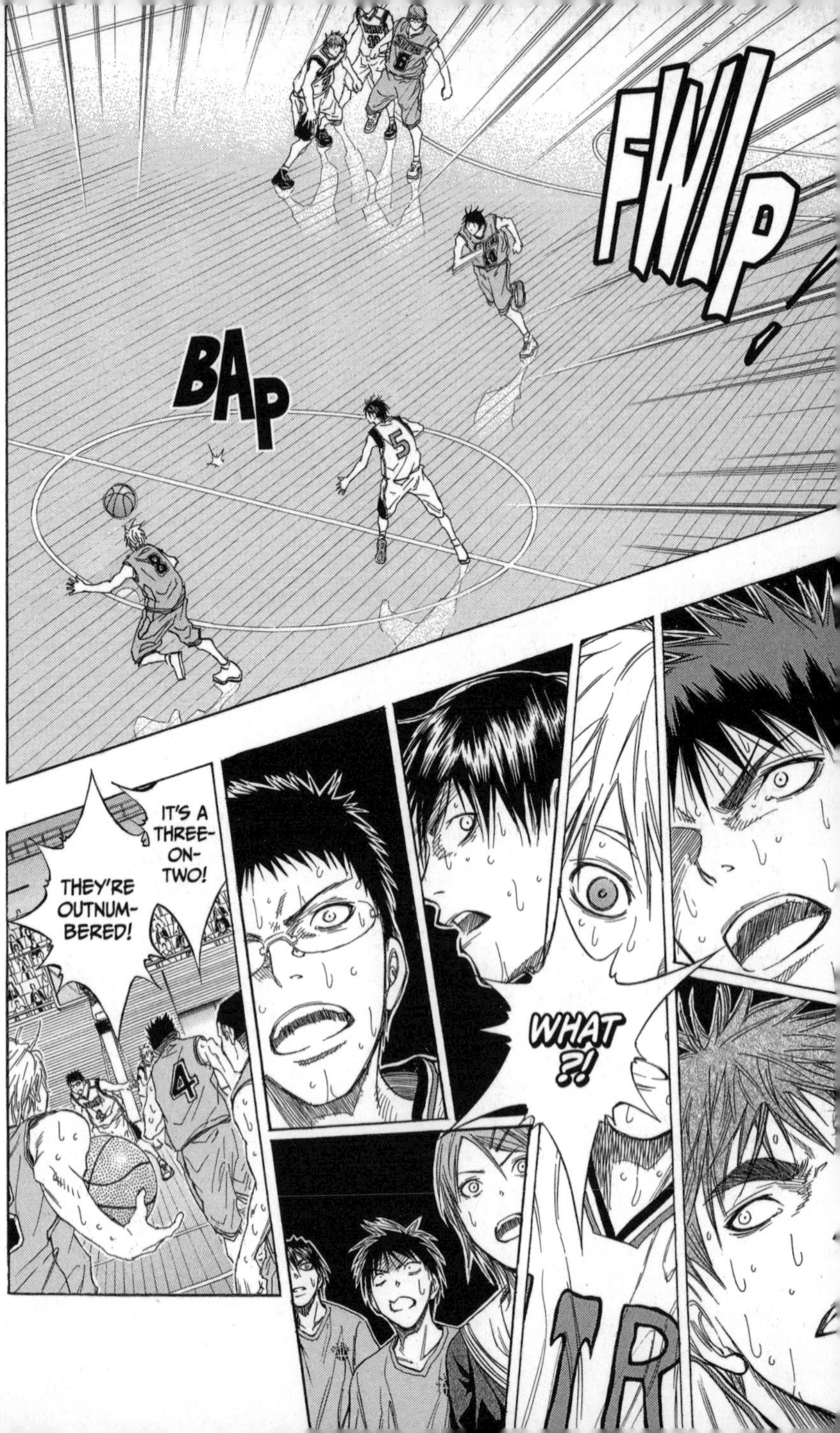
FWIP
BAP
WHAT?!
TR
IT'S A THREE-ON-TWO!
THEY'RE OUTNUMBERED!

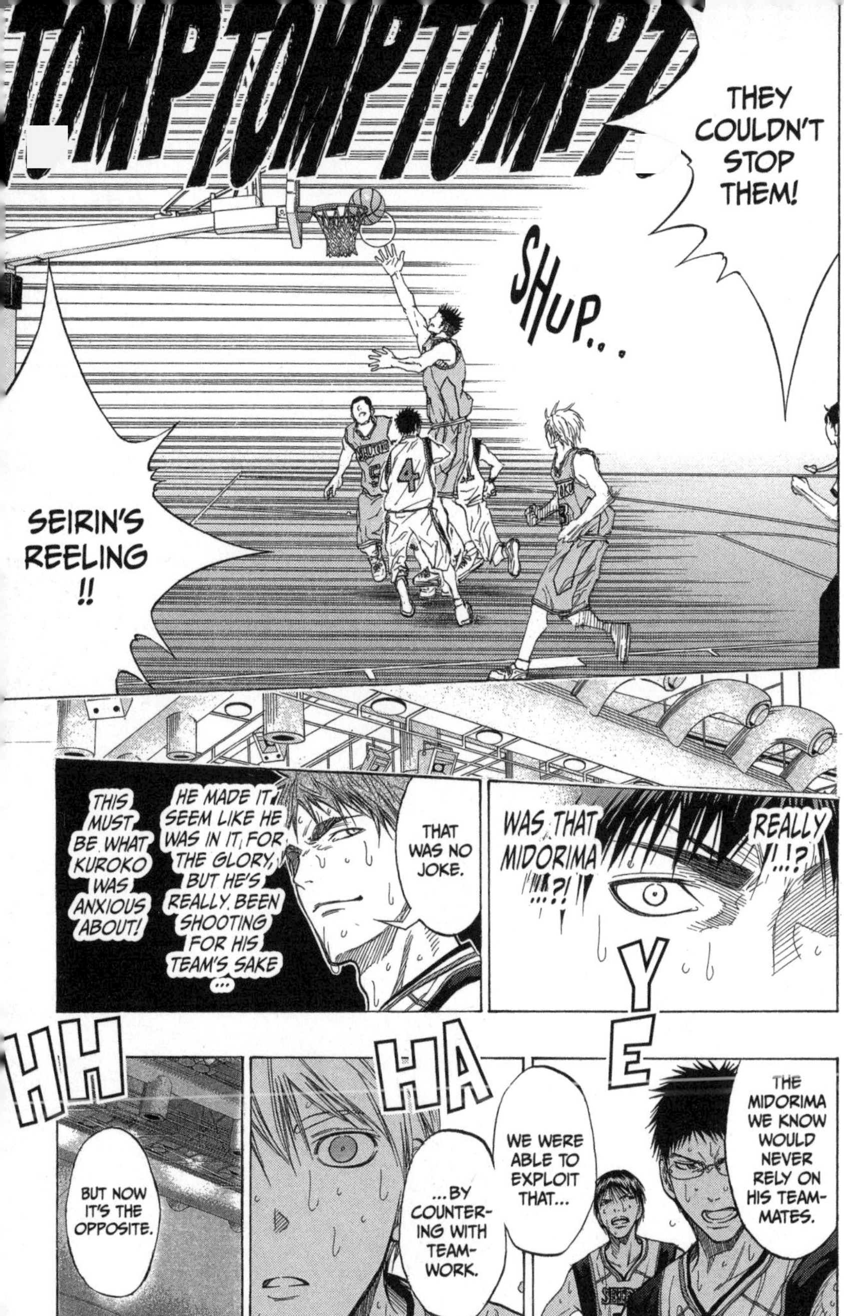
TOMP TOMP TOMP
THEY COULDN'T STOP THEM!
SHUP...
SEIRIN'S REELING !!
WAS THAT MIDORIMA !!...?!
REALLY !!...!?
THAT WAS NO JOKE.
HE MADE IT SEEM LIKE HE WAS IN IT FOR THE GLORY, BUT HE'S REALLY BEEN SHOOTING FOR HIS TEAM'S SAKE...
THIS MUST BE WHAT KUROKO WAS ANXIOUS ABOUT!
YE
HA
HH
THE MIDORIMA WE KNOW WOULD NEVER RELY ON HIS TEAM-MATES.
WE WERE ABLE TO EXPLOIT THAT...
...BY COUNTER-ING WITH TEAM-WORK.
BUT NOW IT'S THE OPPOSITE.

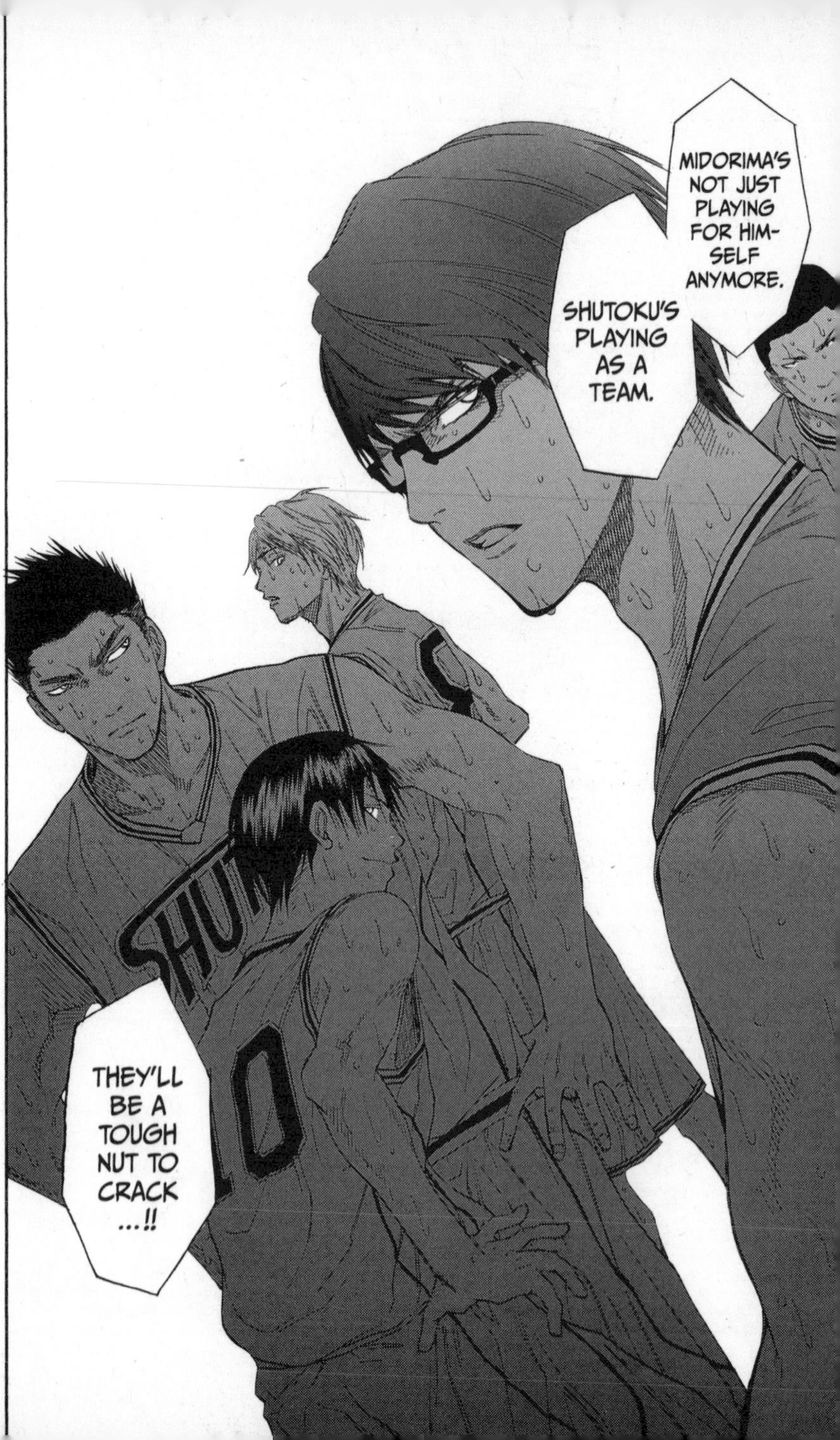
MIDORIMA'S NOT JUST PLAYING FOR HIM-SELF ANYMORE.
SHUTOKU'S PLAYING AS A TEAM.
THEY'LL BE A TOUGH NUT TO CRACK ...!!

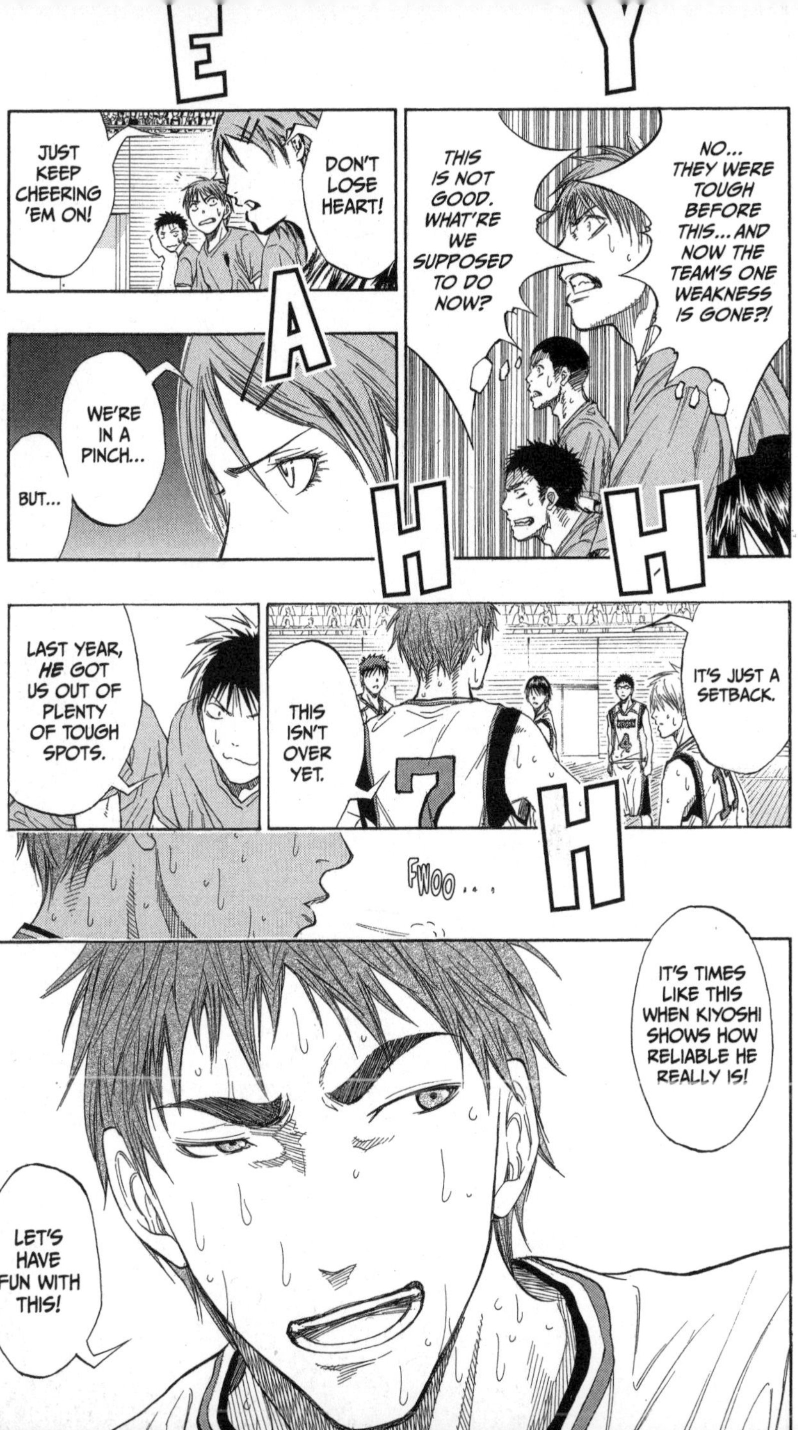
YEAHHH
NO... THEY WERE TOUGH BEFORE THIS... AND NOW THE TEAM'S ONE WEAKNESS IS GONE?!
THIS IS NOT GOOD. WHAT'RE WE SUPPOSED TO DO NOW?
DON'T LOSE HEART!
JUST KEEP CHEERING 'EM ON!
WE'RE IN A PINCH...
BUT...
IT'S JUST A SETBACK.
THIS ISN'T OVER YET.
LAST YEAR, *HE* GOT US OUT OF PLENTY OF TOUGH SPOTS.
FWOO...
IT'S TIMES LIKE THIS WHEN KIYOSHI SHOWS HOW RELIABLE HE REALLY IS!
LET'S HAVE FUN WITH THIS!

KUROKO'S BASKETBALL BLOOPERS

TAKE 2

SOMEONE, QUICK! RECORD THIS!!
GOT IT!
HUH?
I NEVER THOUGHT THIS WOULD HAPPEN!
CHATTER
SHUTOKU
CHATTER
ALL IN ORDER TO WIN.
FOR THE SAKE OF WINNING, I'LL DO WHAT-EVER IT TAKES.
ALL IN ORDER TO WIN.
OOH, AWE-SOME.
WHAT HAPPENED TO YOU, MIDORIMA?
STOP RE-PLAYING THAT CLIP!!

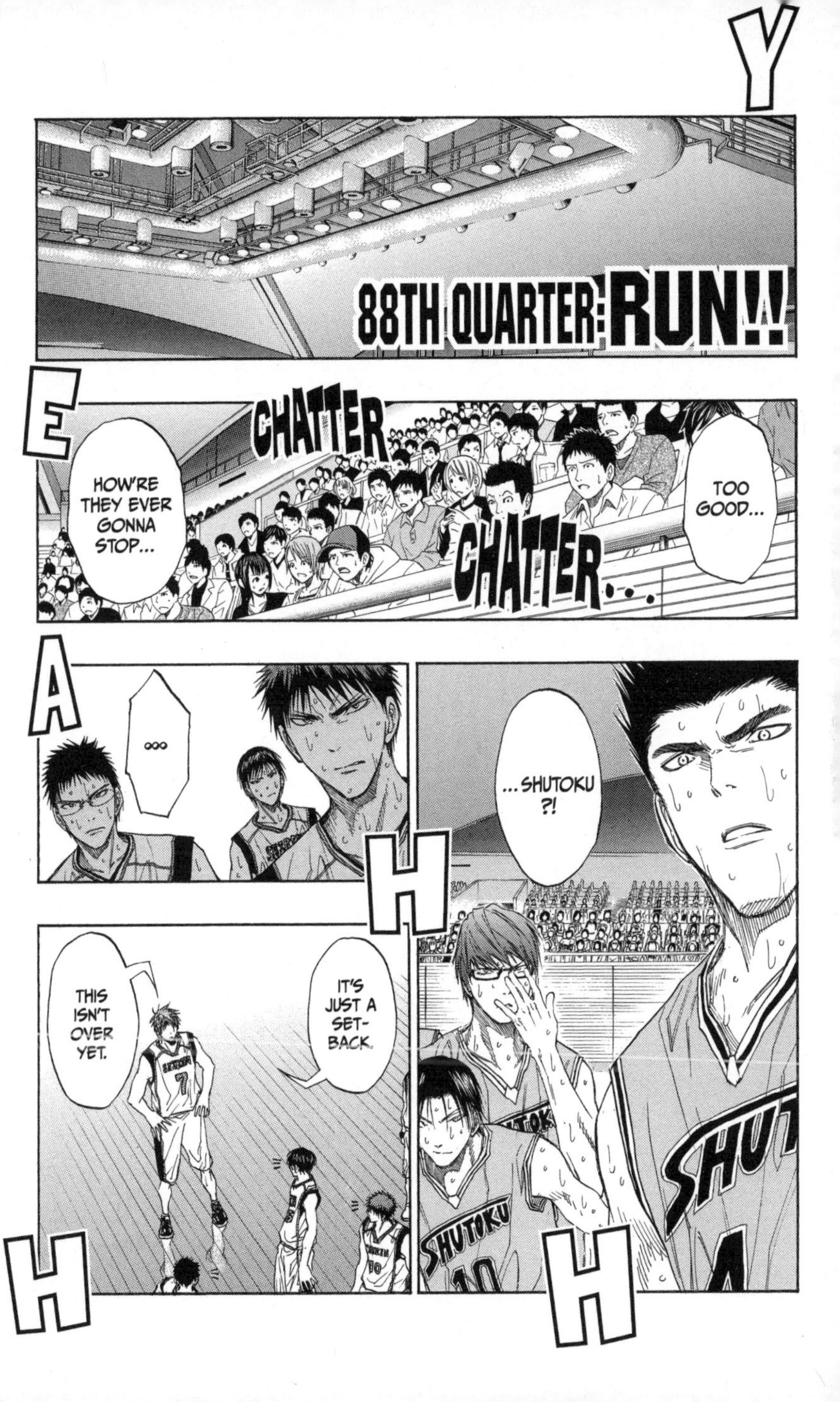
88TH QUARTER: RUN!!
TOO GOOD...
CHATTER
CHATTER...
HOW'RE THEY EVER GONNA STOP...
...SHUTOKU ?!
...
IT'S JUST A SET-BACK.
THIS ISN'T OVER YET.
Y E A H H H

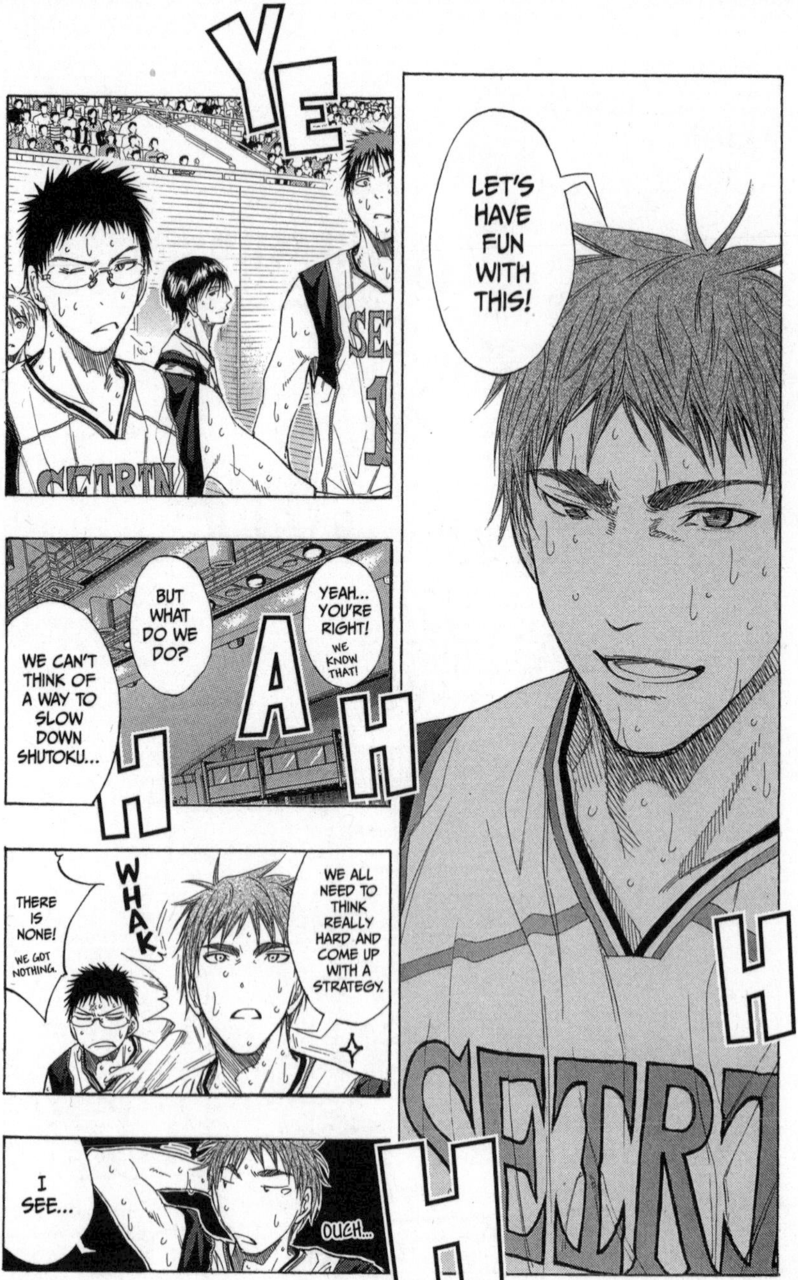
LET'S HAVE FUN WITH THIS!
YEAHHHH
YEAH... YOU'RE RIGHT!
WE KNOW THAT!
BUT WHAT DO WE DO?
WE CAN'T THINK OF A WAY TO SLOW DOWN SHUTOKU...
WE ALL NEED TO THINK REALLY HARD AND COME UP WITH A STRATEGY.
WHAK
THERE IS NONE!
WE GOT NOTHING.
OUCH...
I SEE...

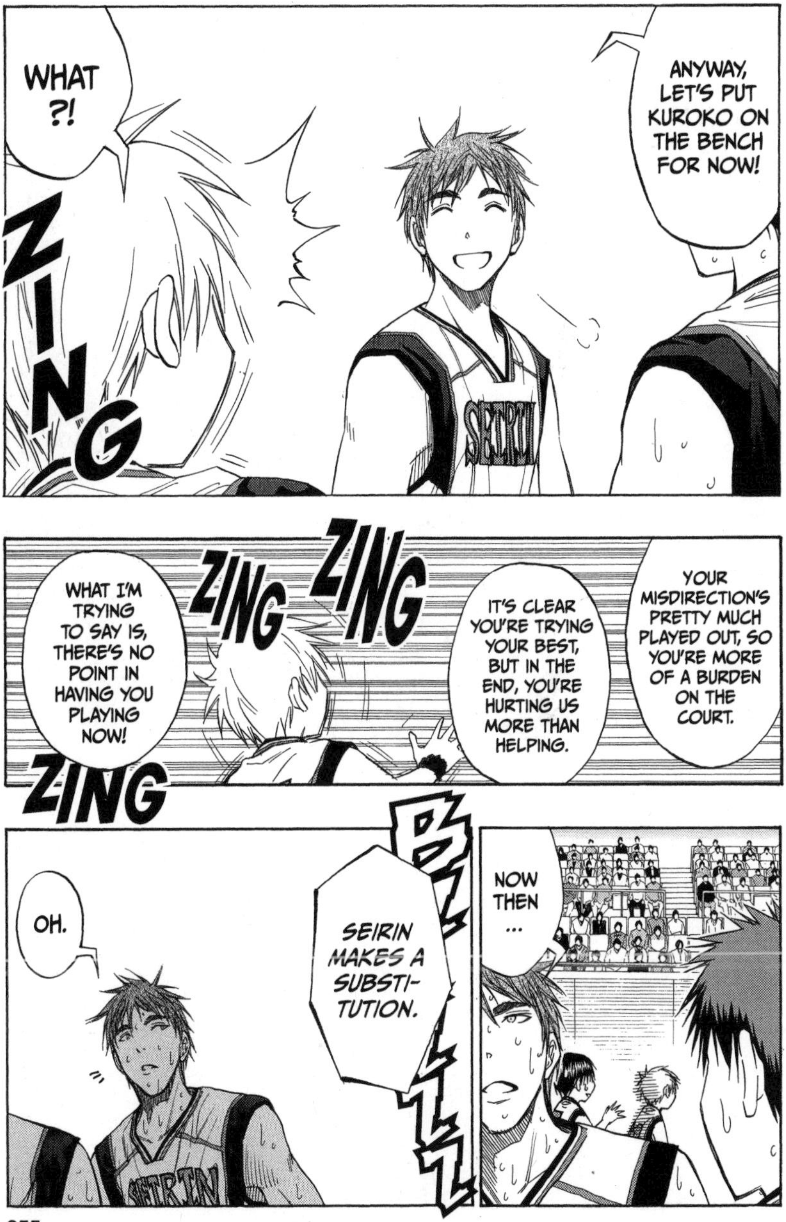
ANYWAY, LET'S PUT KUROKO ON THE BENCH FOR NOW!
WHAT ?!
ZING
YOUR MISDIRECTION'S PRETTY MUCH PLAYED OUT, SO YOU'RE MORE OF A BURDEN ON THE COURT.
IT'S CLEAR YOU'RE TRYING YOUR BEST, BUT IN THE END, YOU'RE HURTING US MORE THAN HELPING.
ZING
ZING
WHAT I'M TRYING TO SAY IS, THERE'S NO POINT IN HAVING YOU PLAYING NOW!
ZING
NOW THEN ...
SEIRIN MAKES A SUBSTI-TUTION.
OH.

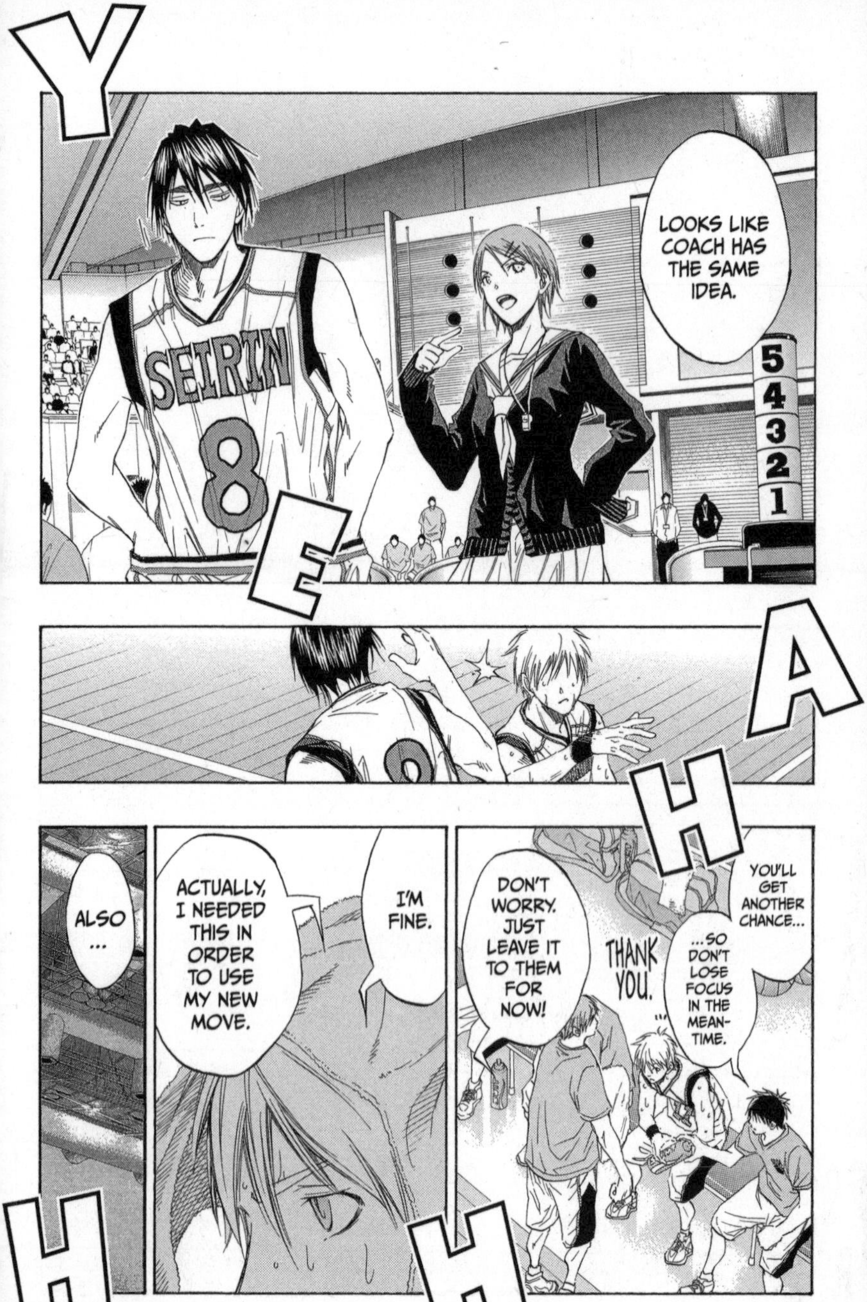
LOOKS LIKE COACH HAS THE SAME IDEA.
5 4 3 2 1
SEIRIN 8
YEAHHH
YOU'LL GET ANOTHER CHANCE...
...SO DON'T LOSE FOCUS IN THE MEAN-TIME.
THANK YOU.
...
DON'T WORRY. JUST LEAVE IT TO THEM FOR NOW!
I'M FINE.
ACTUALLY, I NEEDED THIS IN ORDER TO USE MY NEW MOVE.
ALSO ...

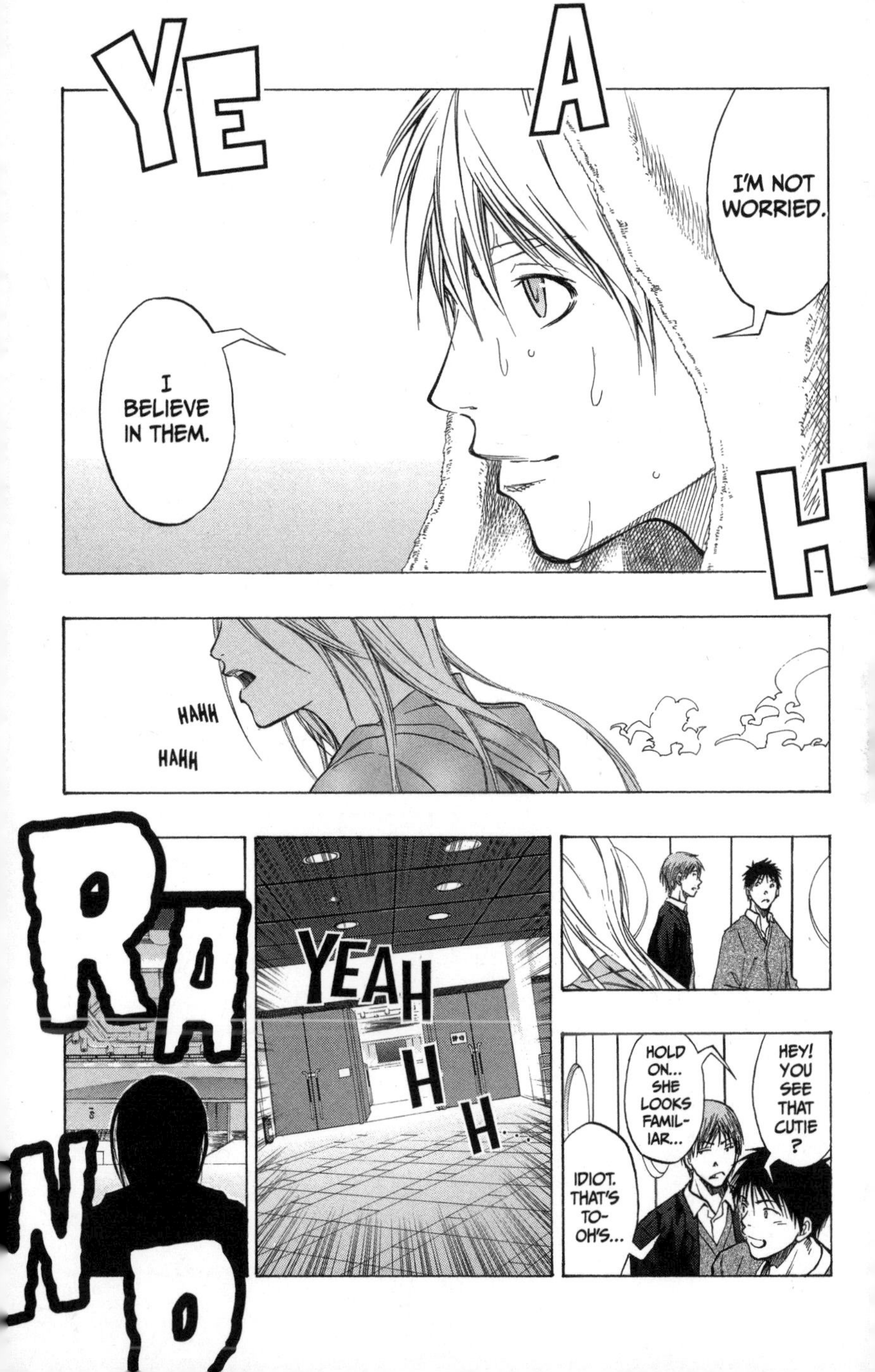

YE
A
H
I'M NOT WORRIED.
I BELIEVE IN THEM.
HAHH
HAHH
HEY! YOU SEE THAT CUTIE?
HOLD ON... SHE LOOKS FAMIL-IAR...
IDIOT. THAT'S TO-OH'S...
YEAH
H
H...
RA
N
D

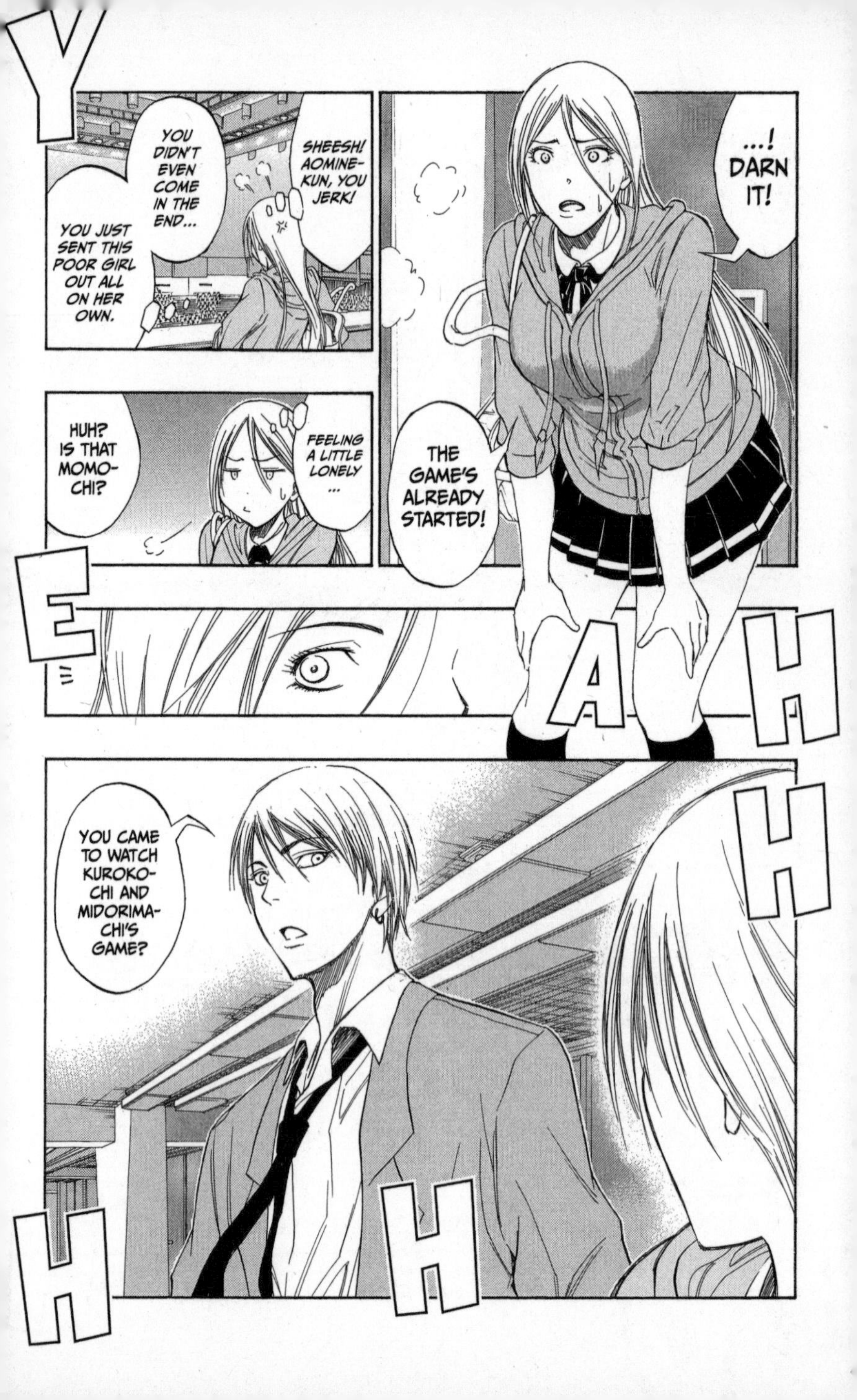
...! DARN IT!
THE GAME'S ALREADY STARTED!
SHEESH! AOMINE-KUN, YOU JERK!
YOU DIDN'T EVEN COME IN THE END...
YOU JUST SENT THIS POOR GIRL OUT ALL ON HER OWN.
FEELING A LITTLE LONELY ...
HUH? IS THAT MOMO-CHI?
YEAHHHH
YOU CAME TO WATCH KUROKO-CHI AND MIDORIMA-CHI'S GAME?

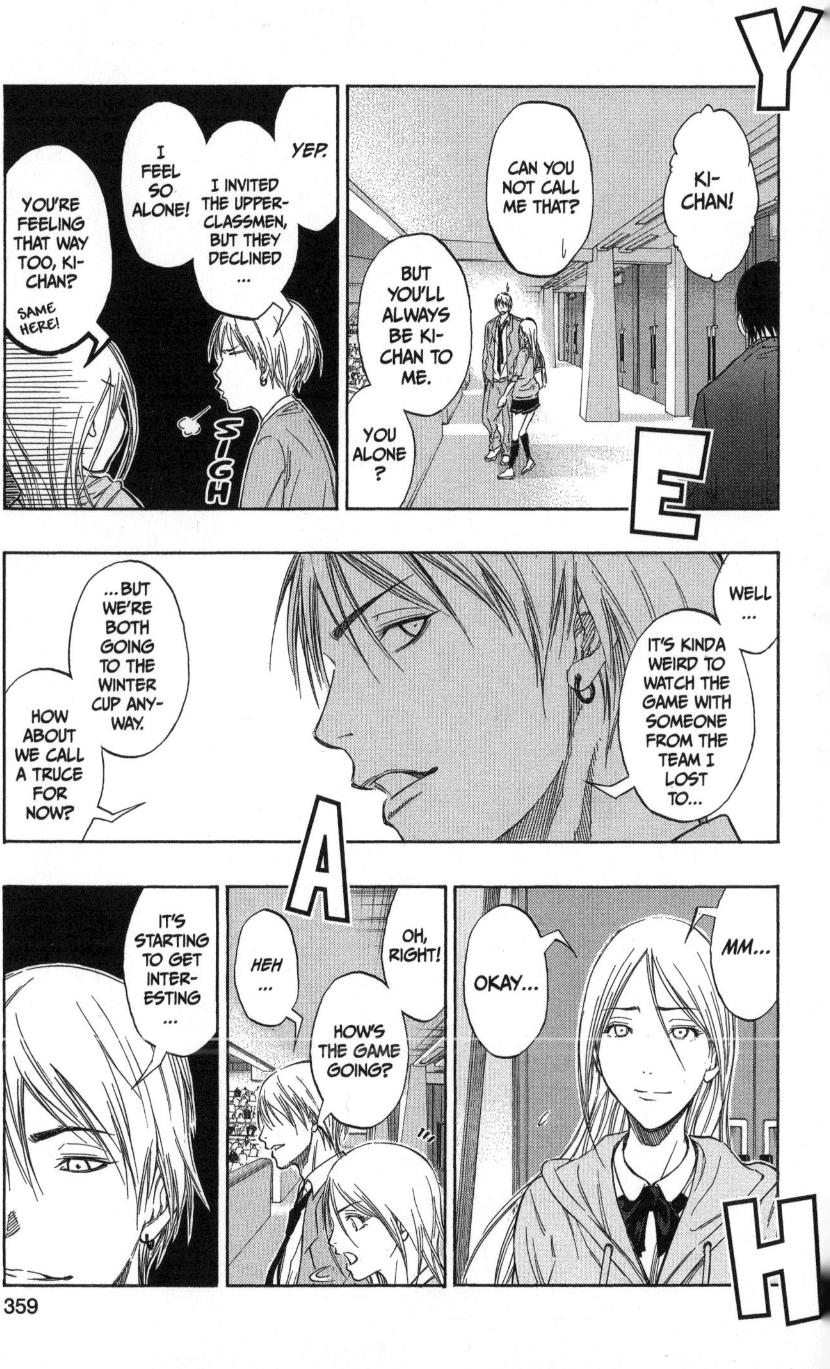
Y
KI-CHAN!
CAN YOU NOT CALL ME THAT?
BUT YOU'LL ALWAYS BE KI-CHAN TO ME.
YOU ALONE?
E
YEP.
I INVITED THE UPPERCLASSMEN, BUT THEY DECLINED...
I FEEL SO ALONE!
YOU'RE FEELING THAT WAY TOO, KI-CHAN?
SAME HERE!
SIGH
WELL...
IT'S KINDA WEIRD TO WATCH THE GAME WITH SOMEONE FROM THE TEAM I LOST TO...
...BUT WE'RE BOTH GOING TO THE WINTER CUP ANYWAY.
HOW ABOUT WE CALL A TRUCE FOR NOW?
A
MM...
OKAY...
OH, RIGHT!
HOW'S THE GAME GOING?
HEH...
IT'S STARTING TO GET INTERESTING...
H

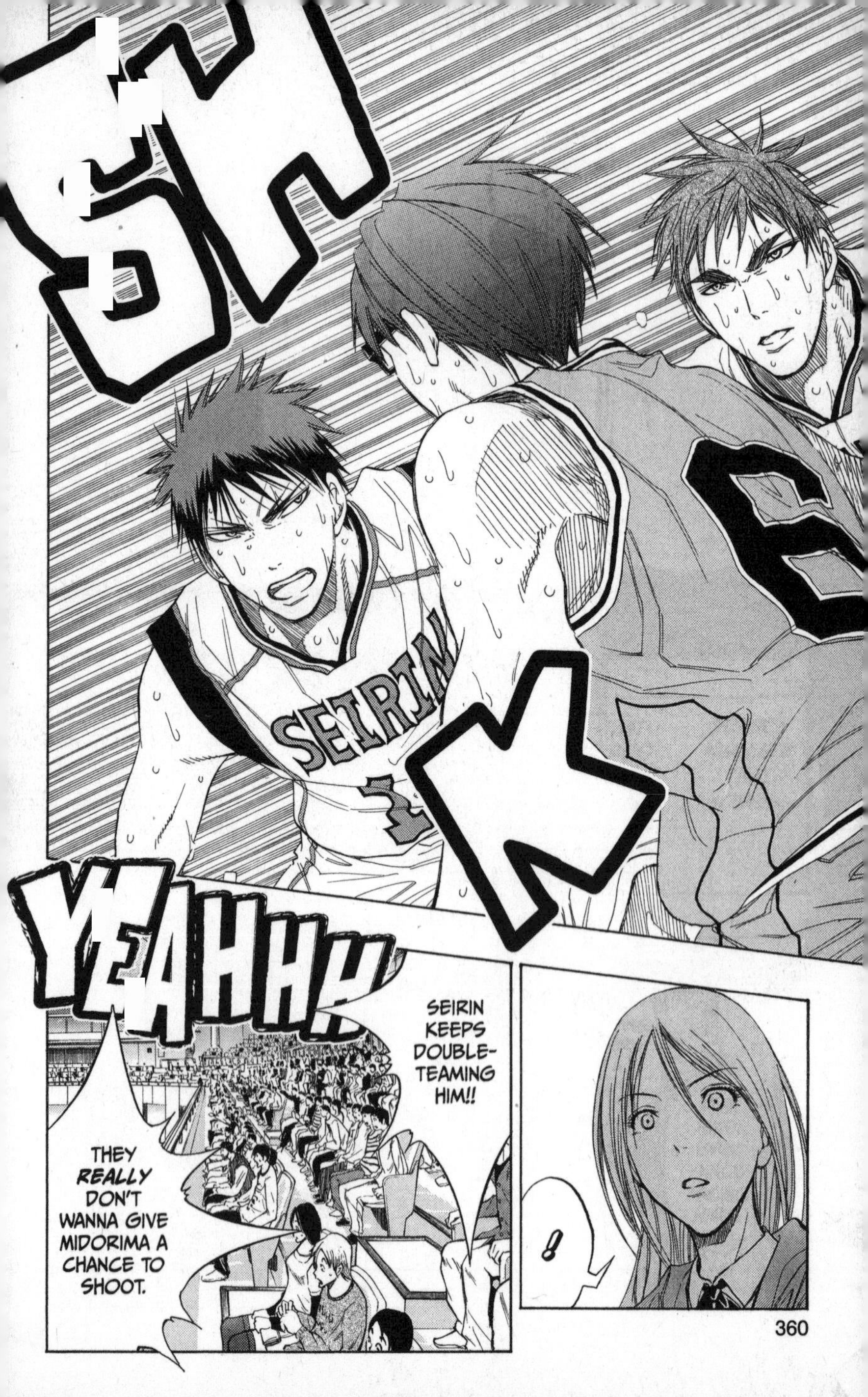
SHK
YEAHHH
!
SEIRIN KEEPS DOUBLE-TEAMING HIM!!
THEY REALLY DON'T WANNA GIVE MIDORIMA A CHANCE TO SHOOT.

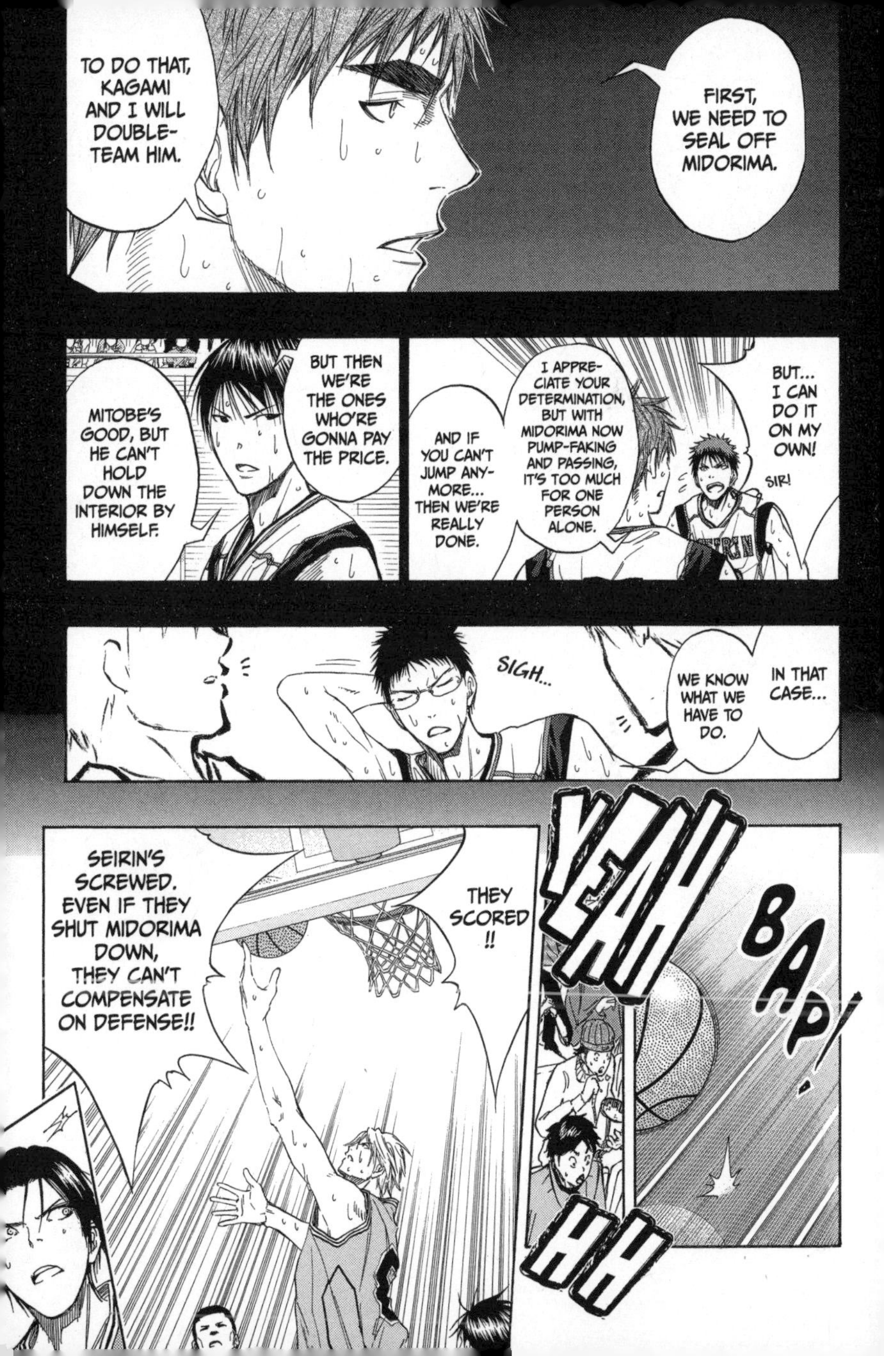
FIRST, WE NEED TO SEAL OFF MIDORIMA.
TO DO THAT, KAGAMI AND I WILL DOUBLE-TEAM HIM.
BUT... I CAN DO IT ON MY OWN!
SIR!
I APPRECIATE YOUR DETERMINATION, BUT WITH MIDORIMA NOW PUMP-FAKING AND PASSING, IT'S TOO MUCH FOR ONE PERSON ALONE.
AND IF YOU CAN'T JUMP ANYMORE... THEN WE'RE REALLY DONE.
BUT THEN WE'RE THE ONES WHO'RE GONNA PAY THE PRICE.
MITOBE'S GOOD, BUT HE CAN'T HOLD DOWN THE INTERIOR BY HIMSELF.
IN THAT CASE...
WE KNOW WHAT WE HAVE TO DO.
SIGH...
YEAHH
BAP!
THEY SCORED !!
SEIRIN'S SCREWED. EVEN IF THEY SHUT MIDORIMA DOWN, THEY CAN'T COMPENSATE ON DEFENSE!!

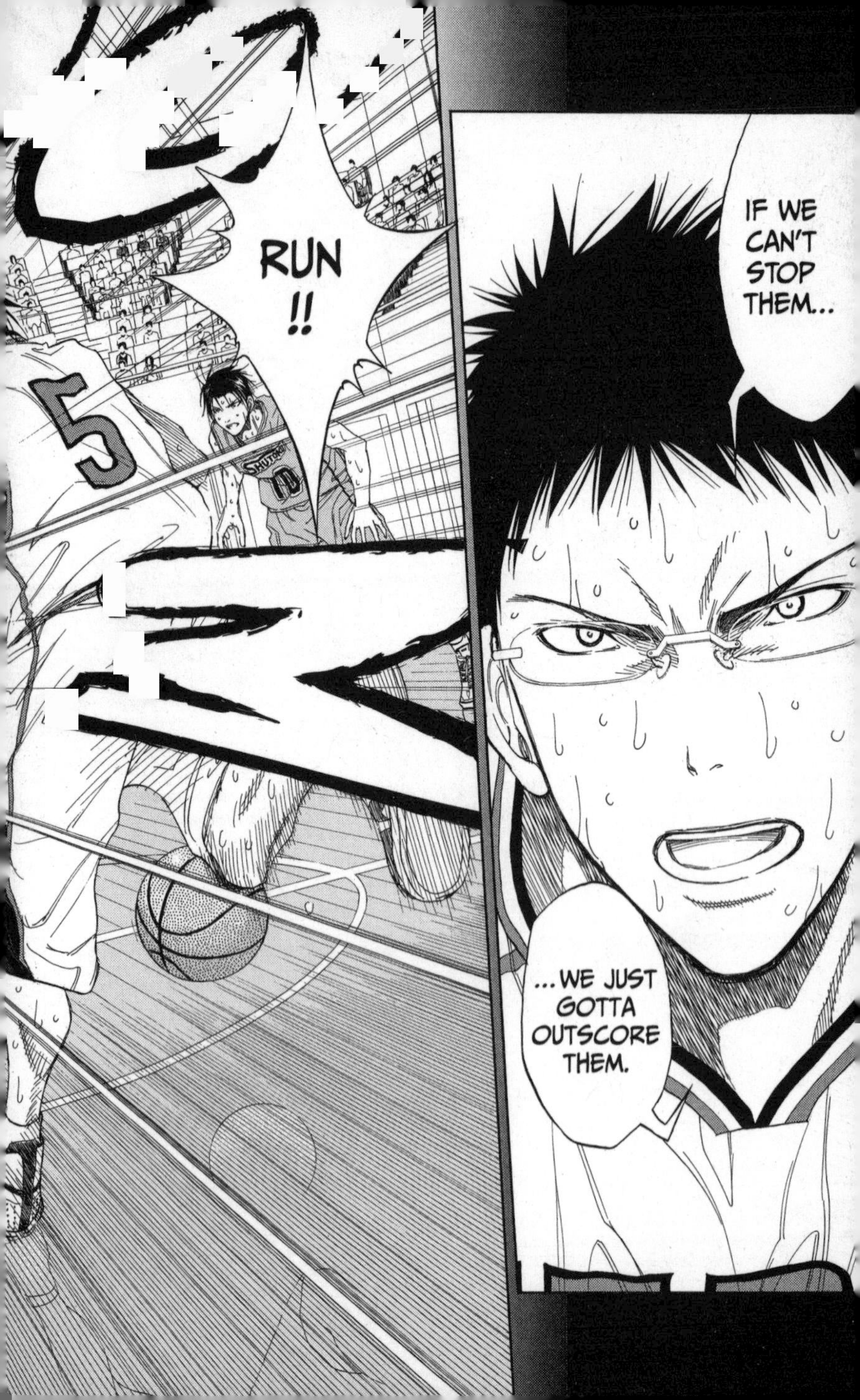
IF WE CAN'T STOP THEM...
...WE JUST GOTTA OUTSCORE THEM.
RUN!!
SHUTOKU

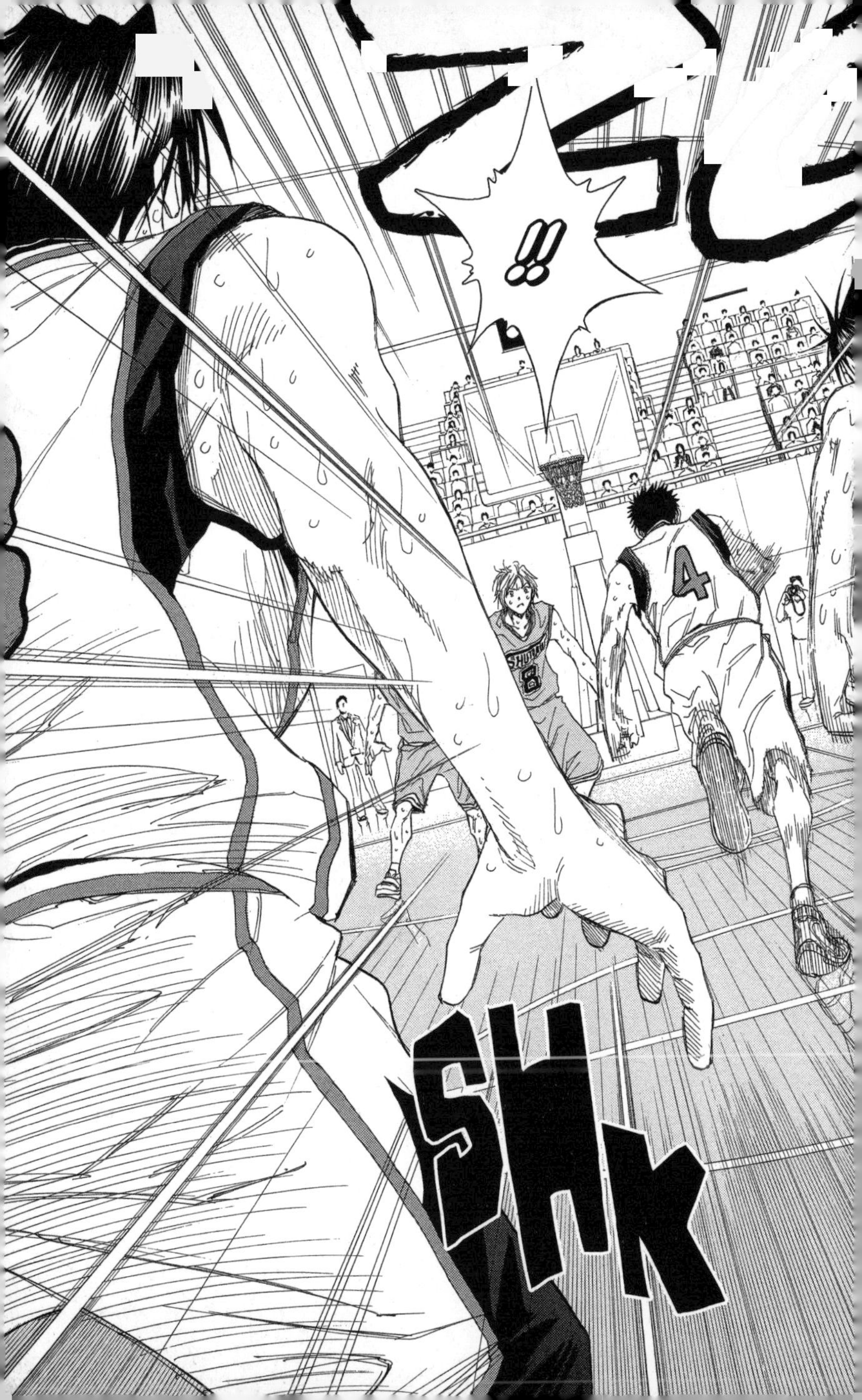
!!
SHK

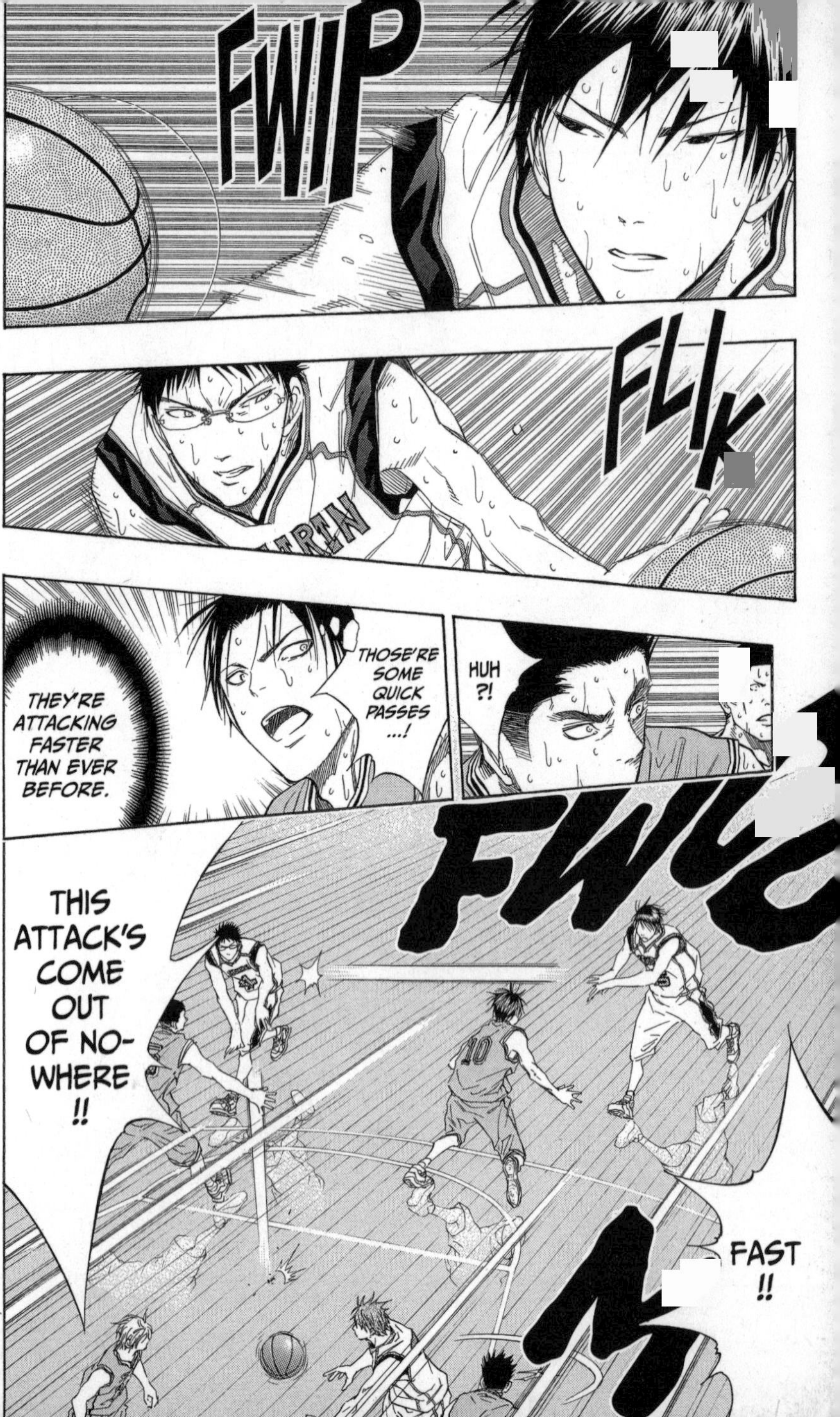
FWIP
FLIK
HUH?!
THOSE'RE SOME QUICK PASSES...!
THEY'RE ATTACKING FASTER THAN EVER BEFORE.
FAST!!
THIS ATTACK'S COME OUT OF NO-WHERE!!

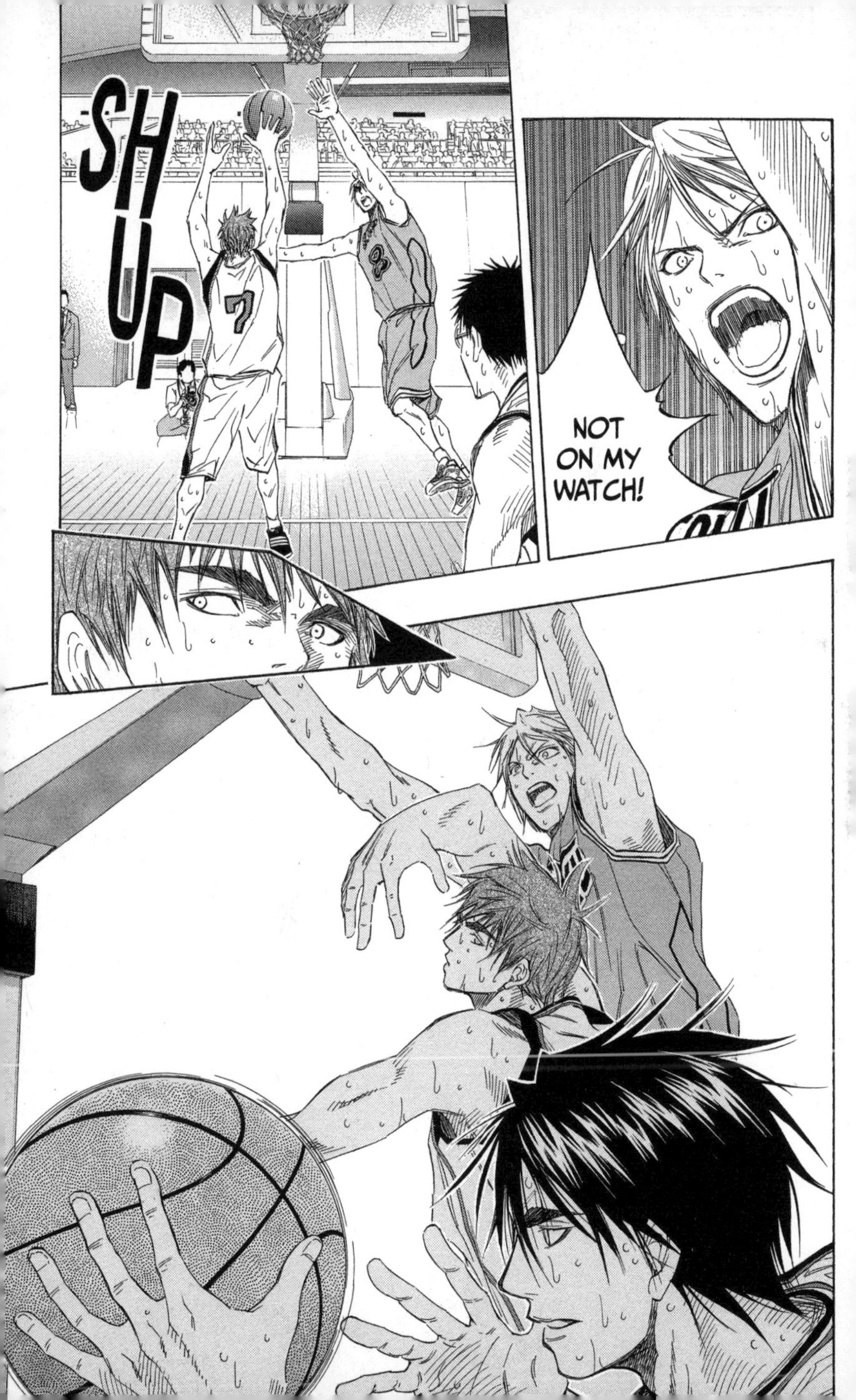
SHUP
NOT ON MY WATCH!

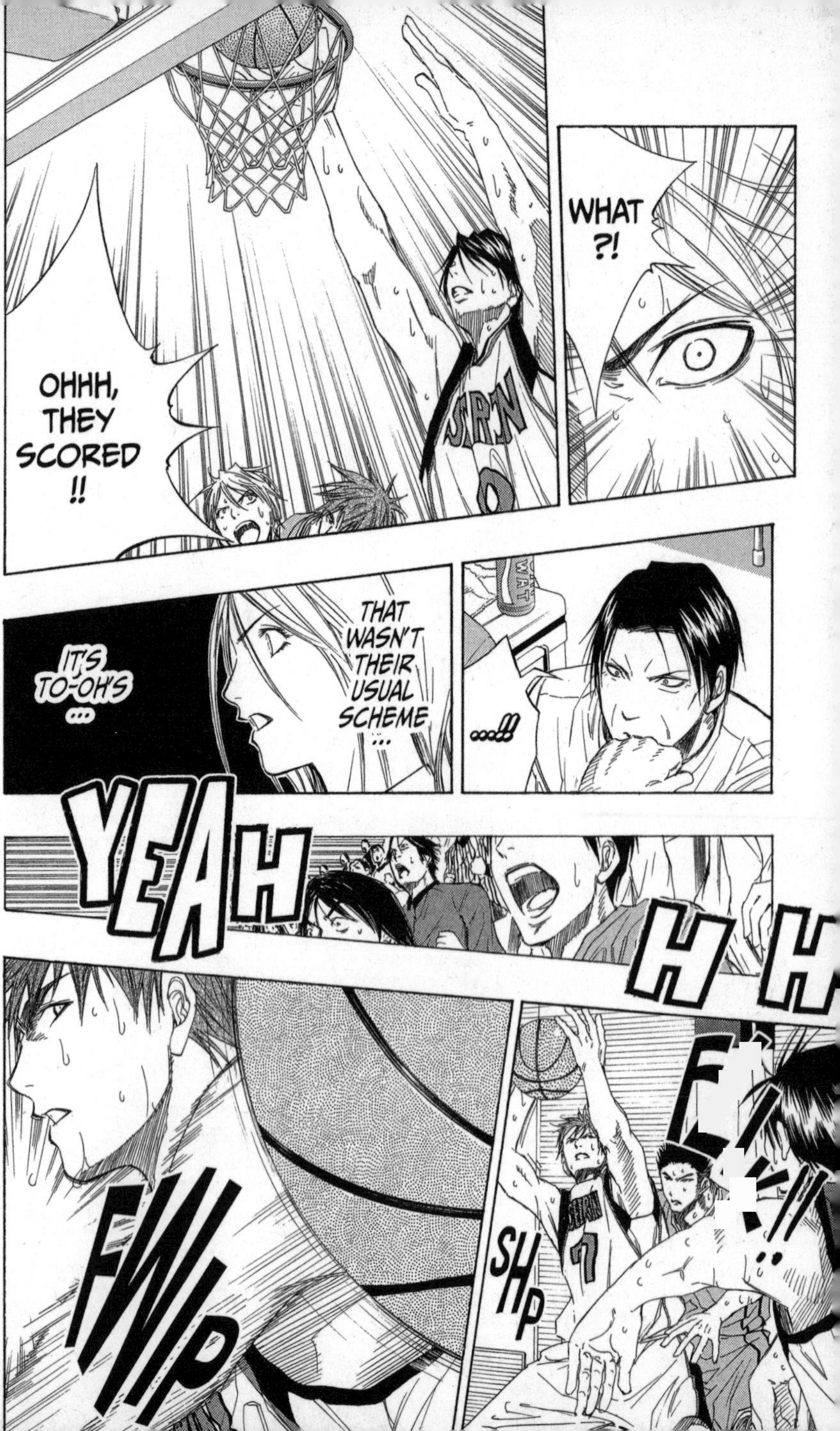
WHAT ?!
OHHH, THEY SCORED !!
...!!
THAT WASN'T THEIR USUAL SCHEME ...
IT'S TO-OH'S ...
YEAHHH
SHP
FWIP

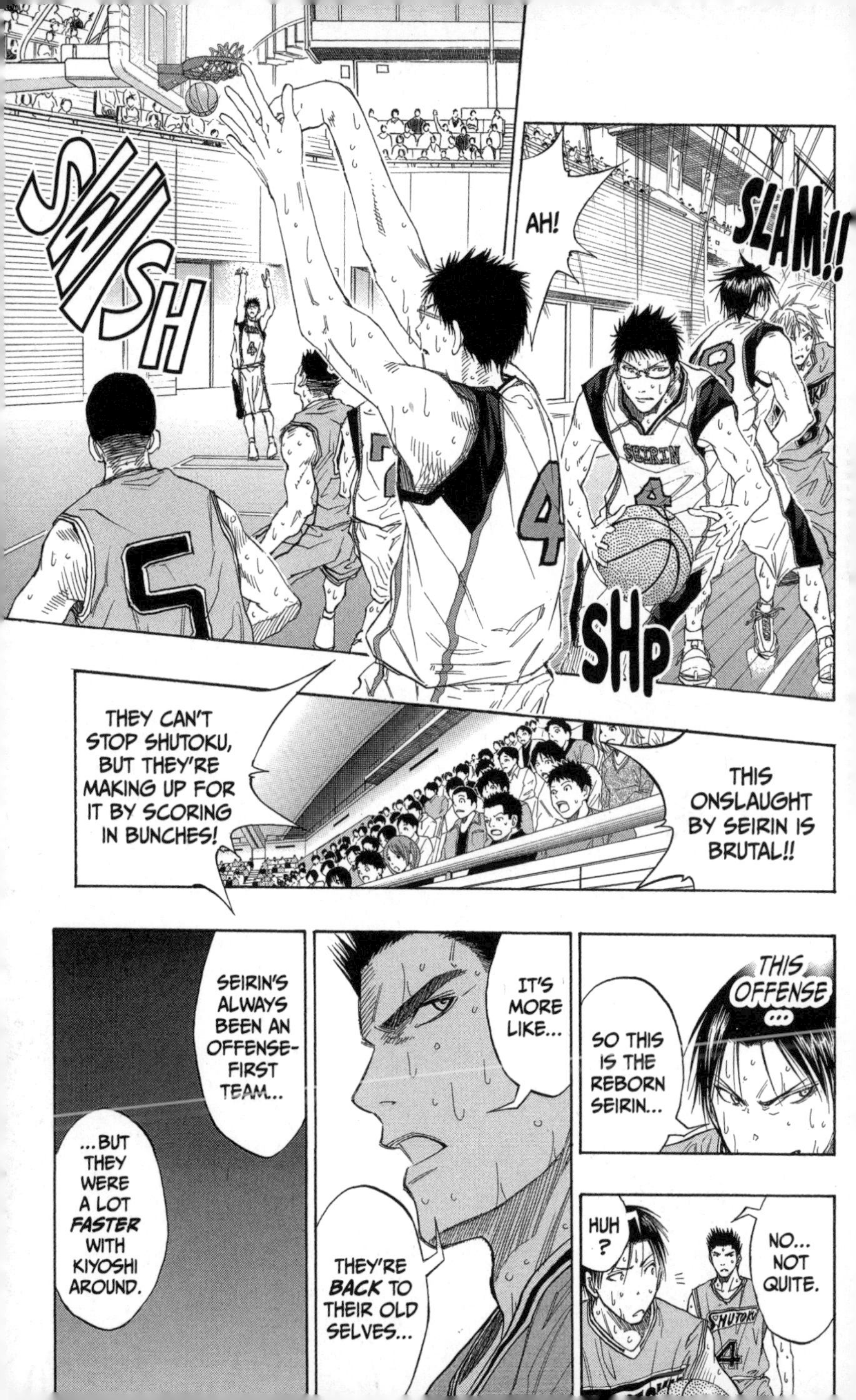
AH!
SLAM!!
SHP
SWISH
THIS ONSLAUGHT BY SEIRIN IS BRUTAL!!
THEY CAN'T STOP SHUTOKU, BUT THEY'RE MAKING UP FOR IT BY SCORING IN BUNCHES!
THIS OFFENSE...
SO THIS IS THE REBORN SEIRIN...
NO... NOT QUITE.
HUH?
IT'S MORE LIKE...
THEY'RE BACK TO THEIR OLD SELVES...
SEIRIN'S ALWAYS BEEN AN OFFENSE-FIRST TEAM...
...BUT THEY WERE A LOT FASTER WITH KIYOSHI AROUND.

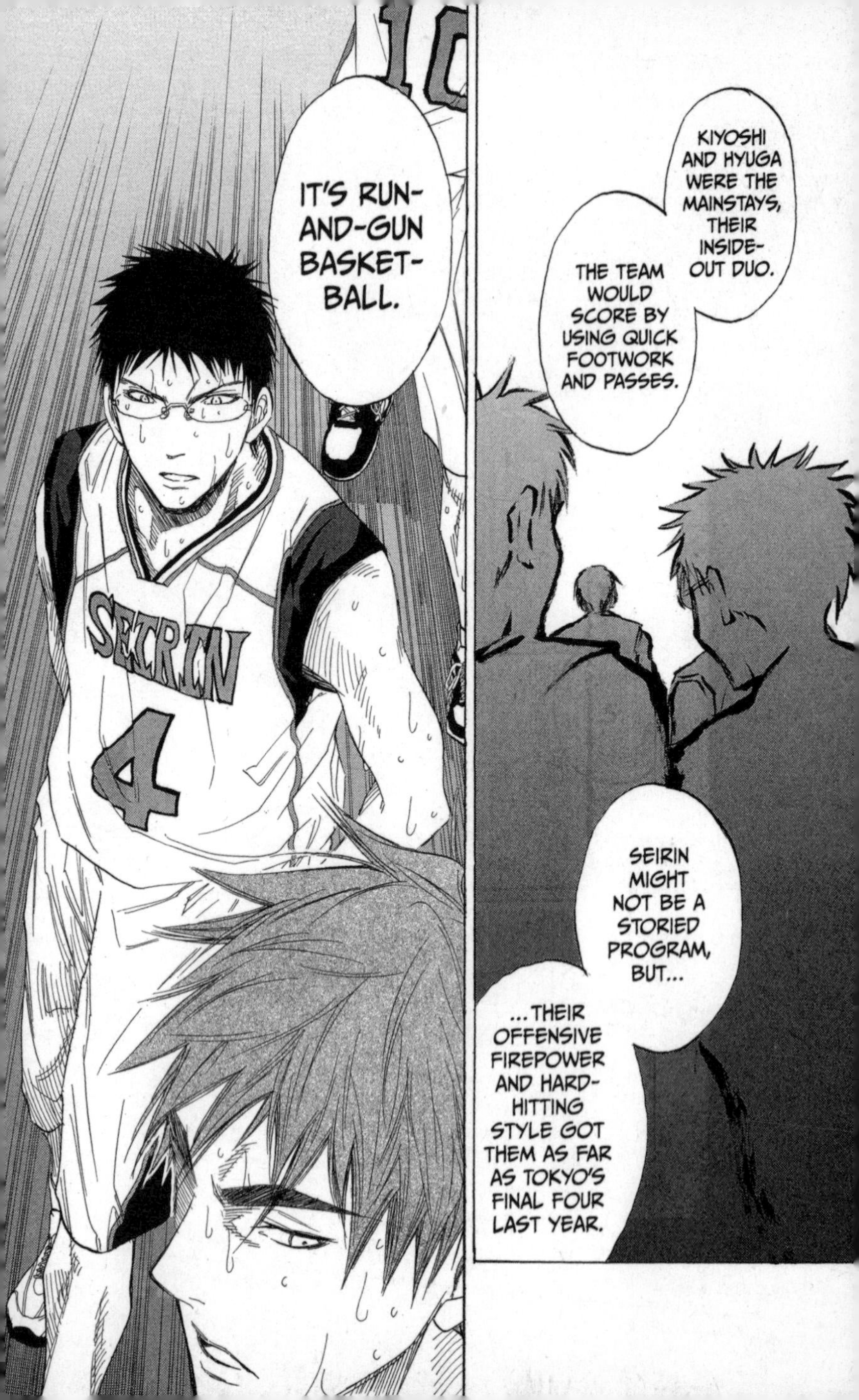
KIYOSHI AND HYUGA WERE THE MAINSTAYS, THEIR INSIDE-OUT DUO.
THE TEAM WOULD SCORE BY USING QUICK FOOTWORK AND PASSES.
SEIRIN MIGHT NOT BE A STORIED PROGRAM, BUT...
...THEIR OFFENSIVE FIREPOWER AND HARD-HITTING STYLE GOT THEM AS FAR AS TOKYO'S FINAL FOUR LAST YEAR.
IT'S RUN-AND-GUN BASKET-BALL.

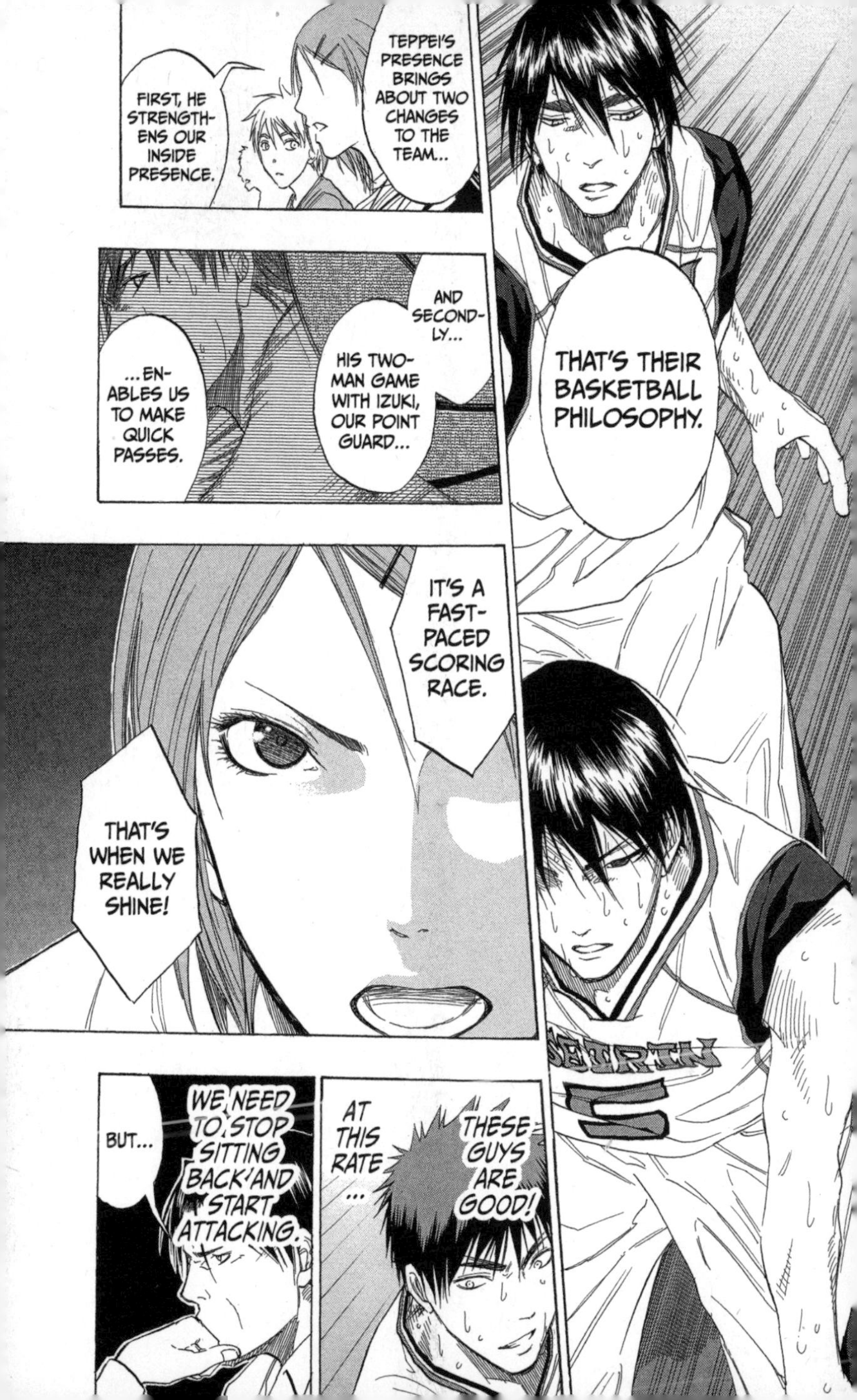
THAT'S THEIR BASKETBALL PHILOSOPHY.
TEPPEI'S PRESENCE BRINGS ABOUT TWO CHANGES TO THE TEAM...
FIRST, HE STRENGTHENS OUR INSIDE PRESENCE.
AND SECONDLY...
HIS TWO-MAN GAME WITH IZUKI, OUR POINT GUARD...
...ENABLES US TO MAKE QUICK PASSES.
IT'S A FAST-PACED SCORING RACE.
THAT'S WHEN WE REALLY SHINE!
THESE GUYS ARE GOOD!
AT THIS RATE...
BUT...
WE NEED TO STOP SITTING BACK AND START ATTACKING.

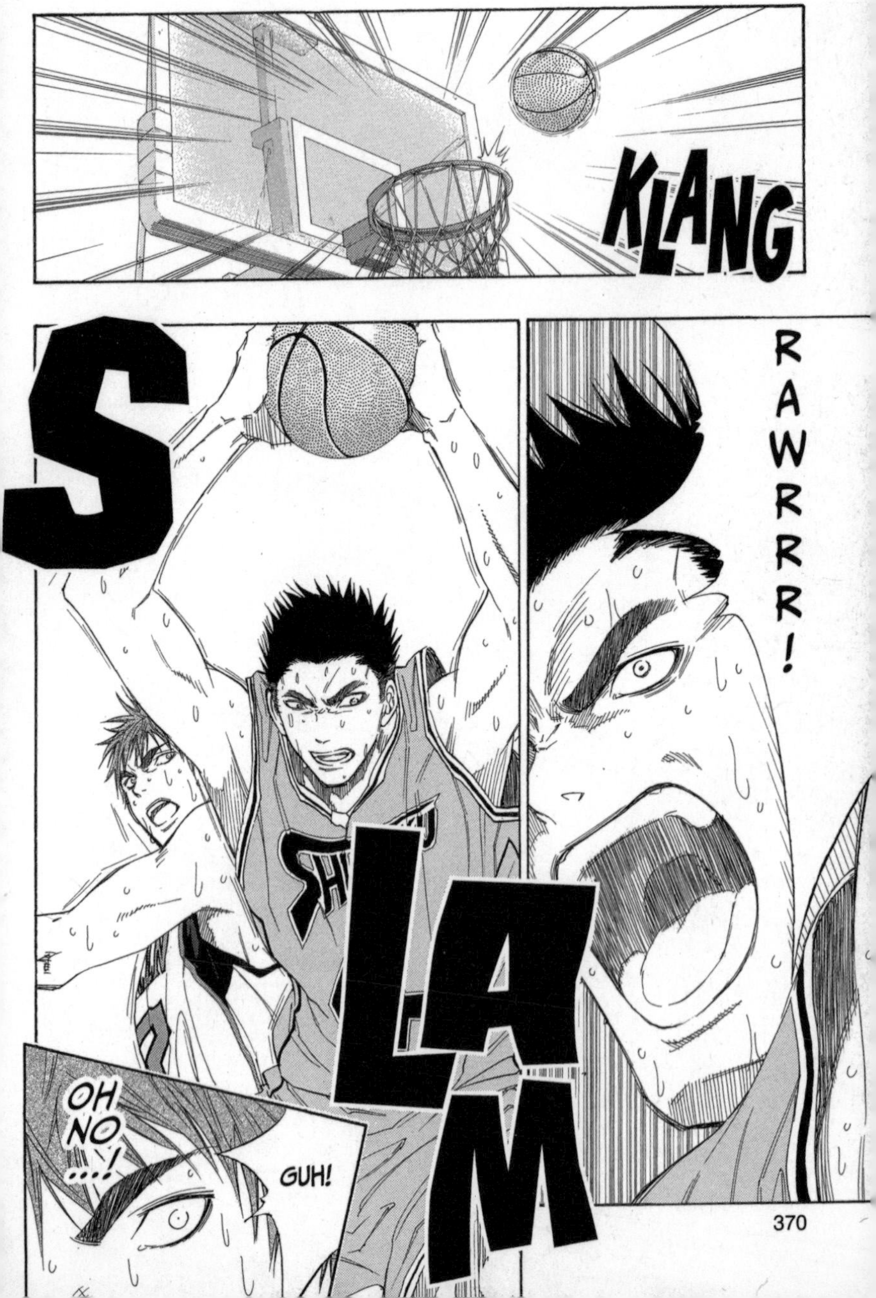
KLANG
RAWRRRR!
SLAM
OH NO...!
GUH!

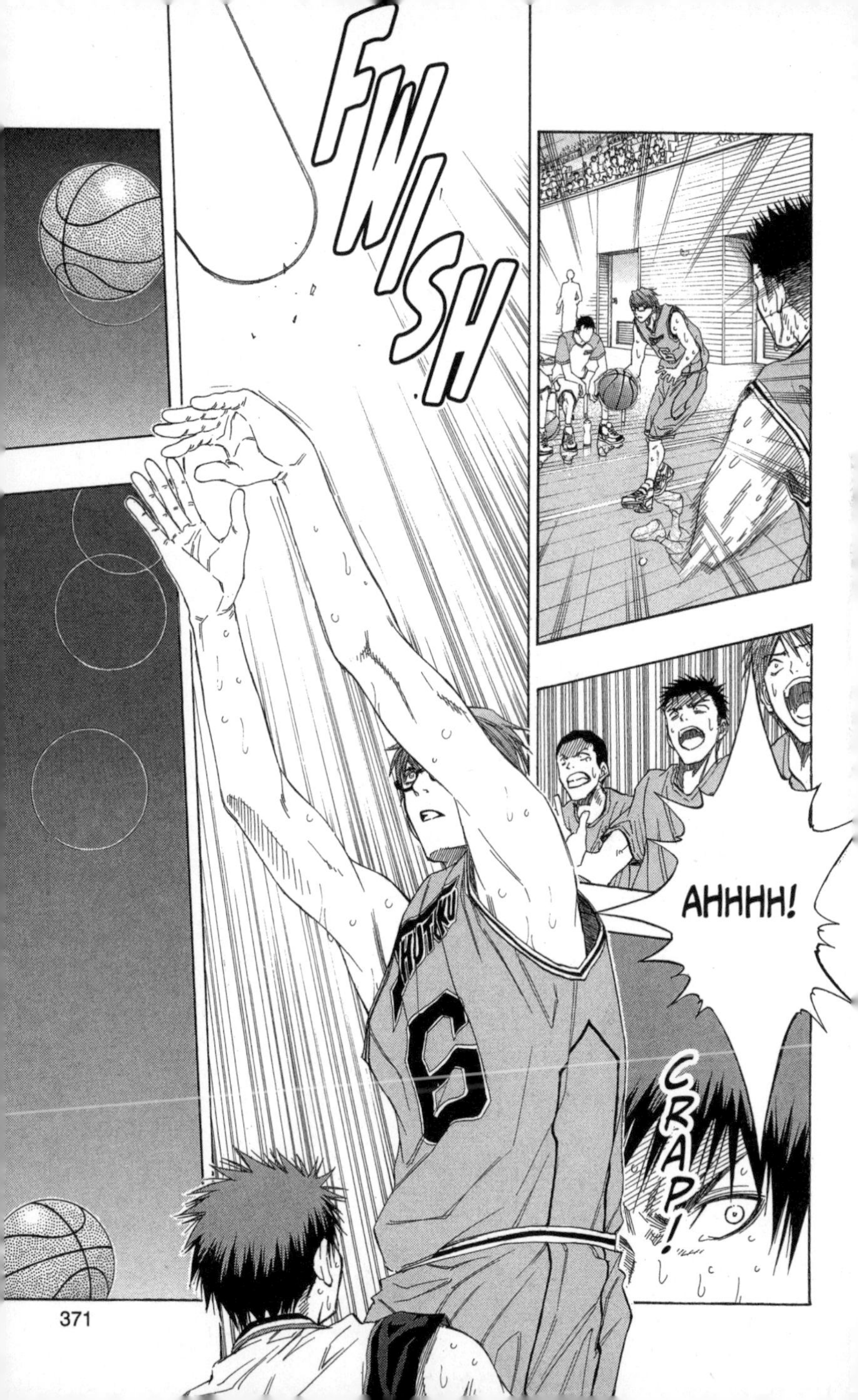
FWISH
AHHHH!
CRAP!

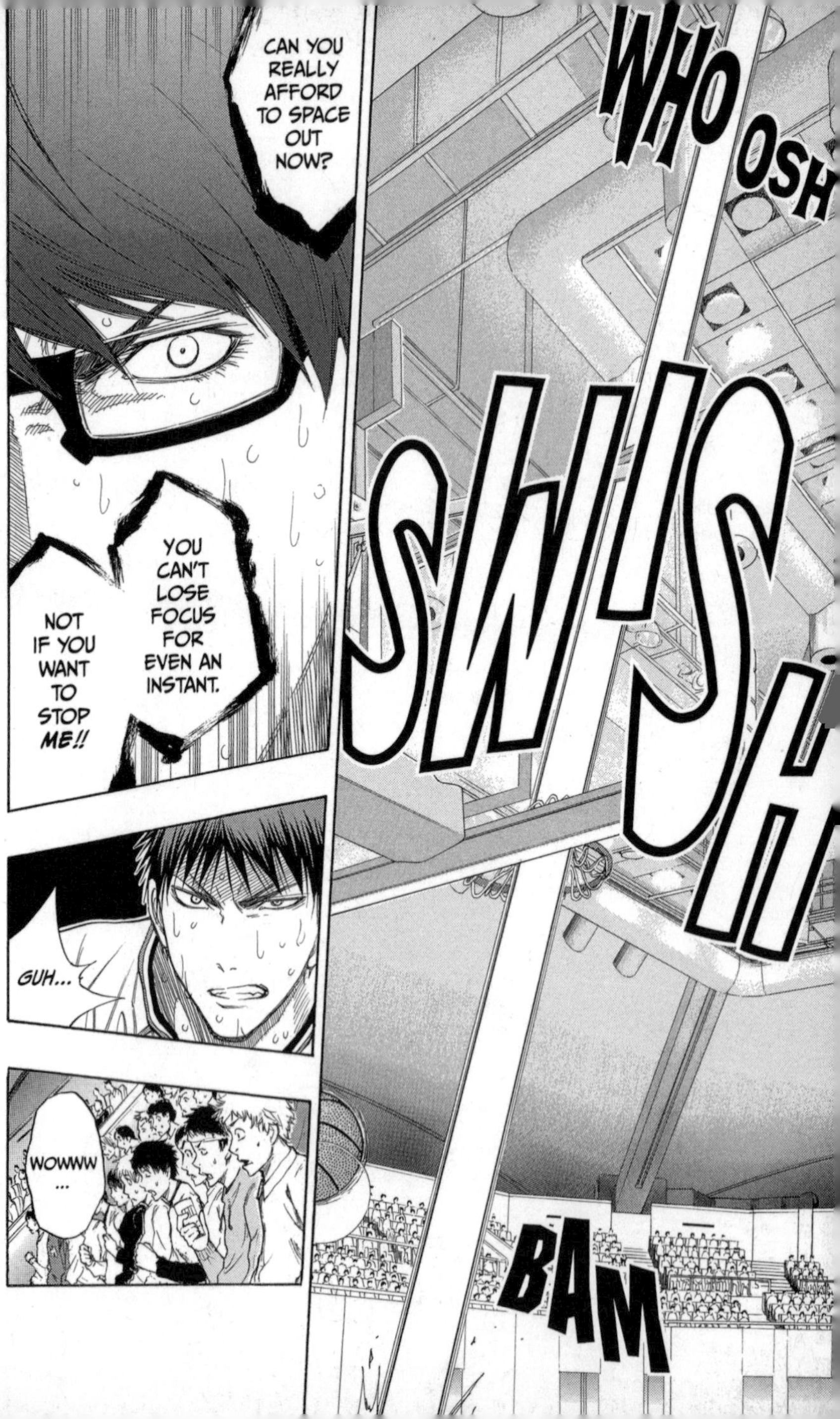
WHOOSH
SWISH
BAM
CAN YOU REALLY AFFORD TO SPACE OUT NOW?
YOU CAN'T LOSE FOCUS FOR EVEN AN INSTANT.
NOT IF YOU WANT TO STOP ME!!
GUH...
WOWWW ...

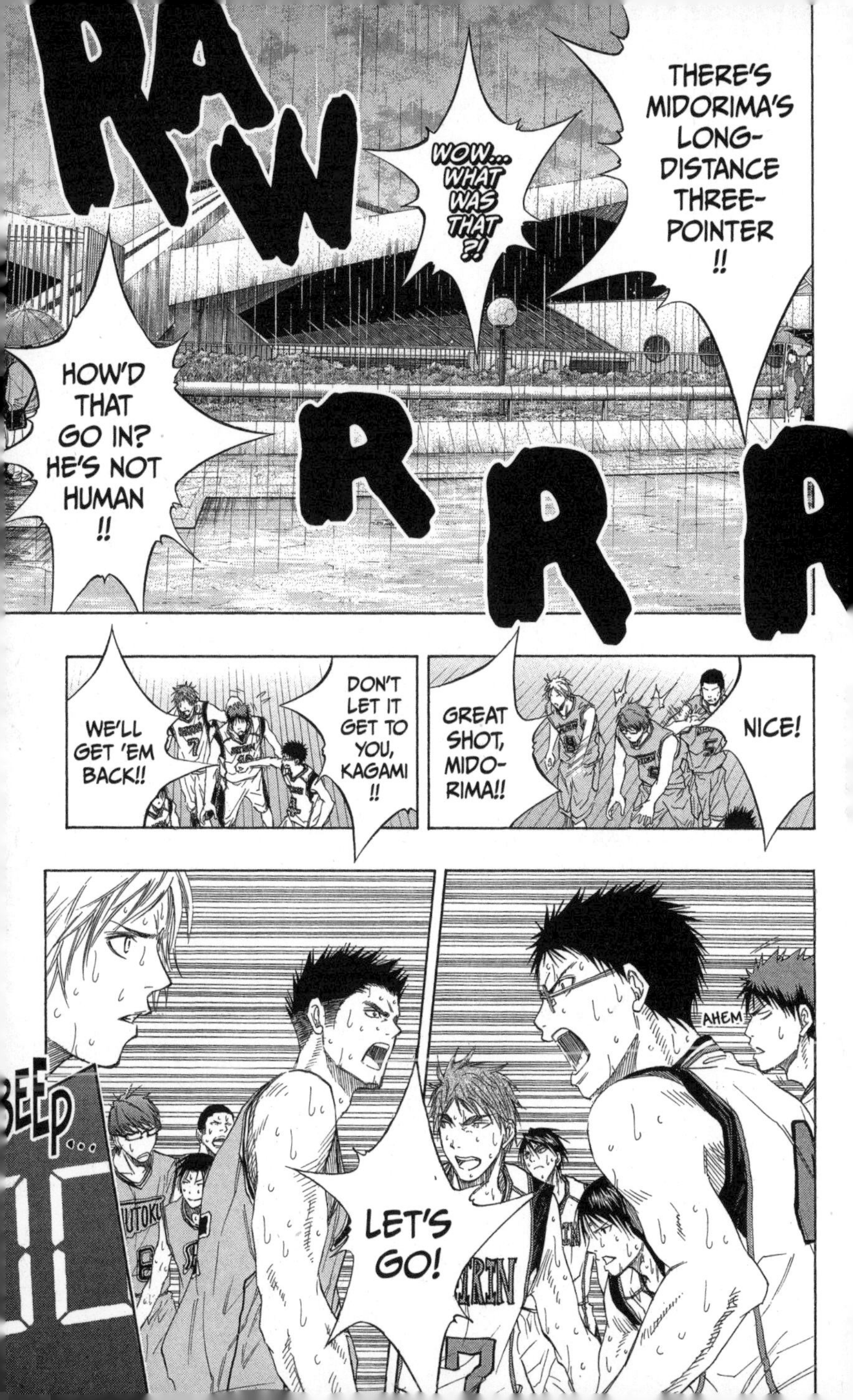
THERE'S MIDORIMA'S LONG-DISTANCE THREE-POINTER!!
WOW... WHAT WAS THAT?!
RAWRRR
HOW'D THAT GO IN? HE'S NOT HUMAN!!
NICE!
GREAT SHOT, MIDORIMA!!
DON'T LET IT GET TO YOU, KAGAMI!!
WE'LL GET 'EM BACK!!
AHEM
LET'S GO!
BEEP...

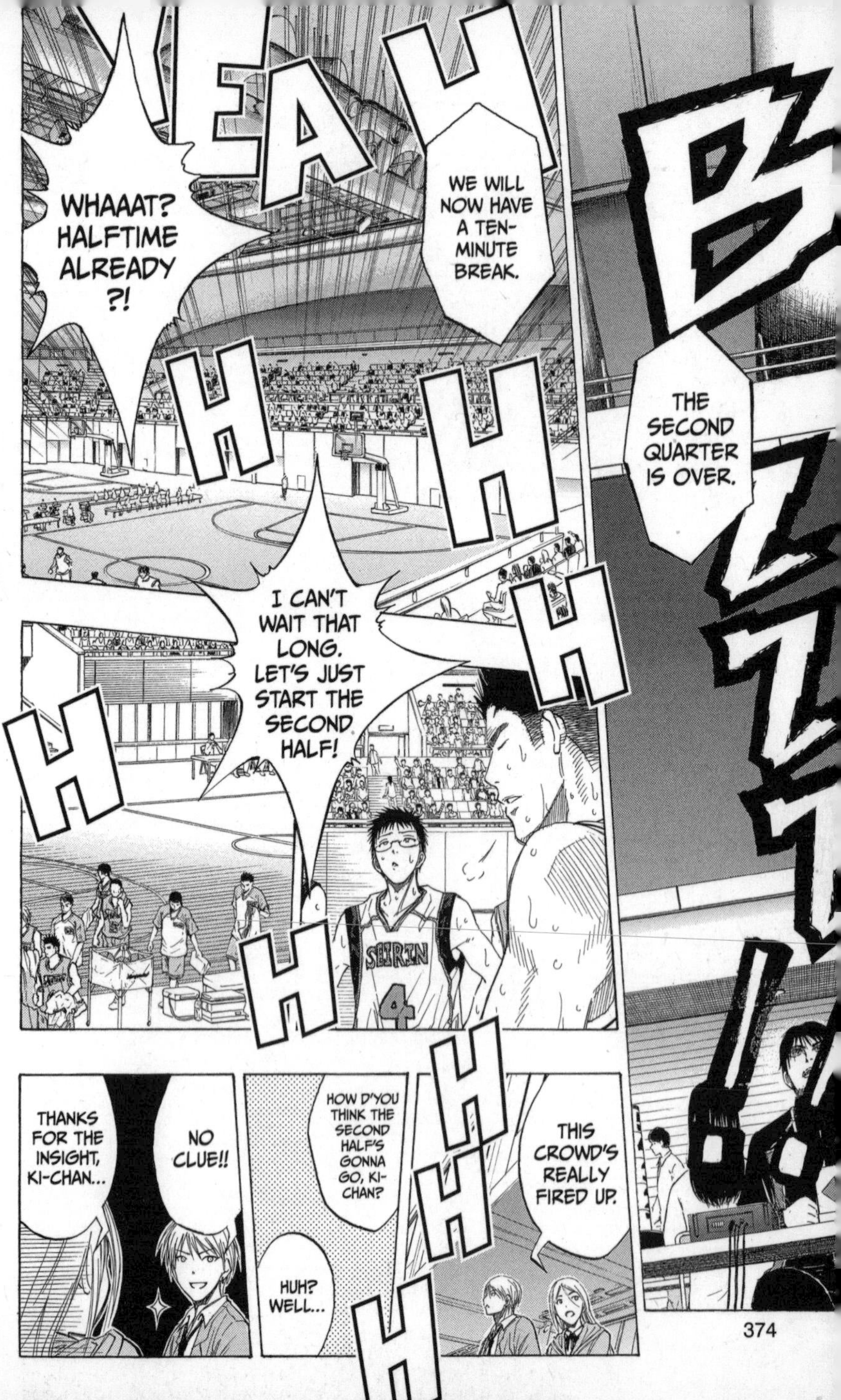
BZZZZZ!!
THE SECOND QUARTER IS OVER.
WE WILL NOW HAVE A TEN-MINUTE BREAK.
YEAHHHHHHHHHHH
WHAAAT? HALFTIME ALREADY?!
I CAN'T WAIT THAT LONG. LET'S JUST START THE SECOND HALF!
SEIRIN
4
THIS CROWD'S REALLY FIRED UP.
HOW D'YOU THINK THE SECOND HALF'S GONNA GO, KI-CHAN?
HUH? WELL...
NO CLUE!!
THANKS FOR THE INSIGHT, KI-CHAN...

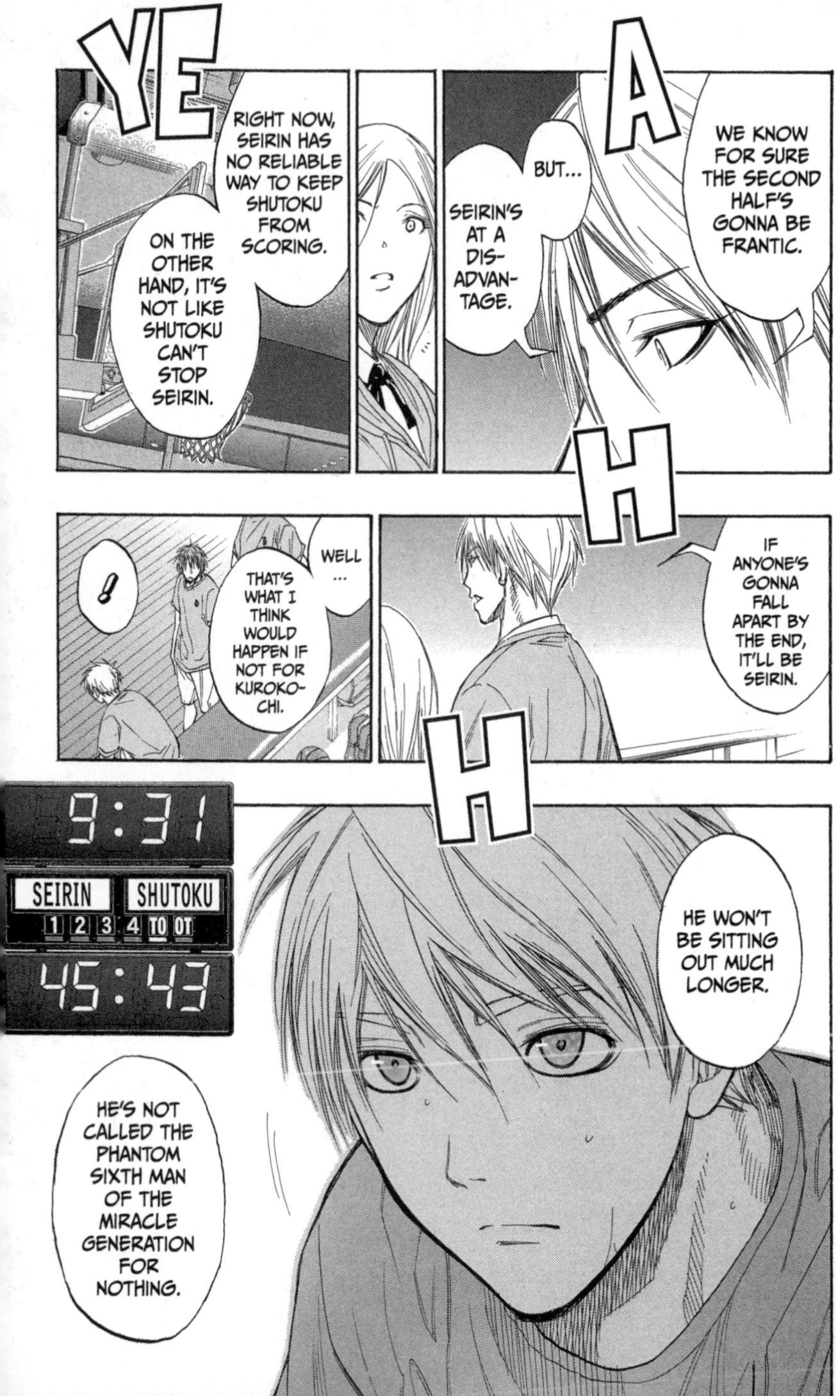
YEAHH
WE KNOW FOR SURE THE SECOND HALF'S GONNA BE FRANTIC.
BUT...
SEIRIN'S AT A DIS-ADVAN-TAGE.
RIGHT NOW, SEIRIN HAS NO RELIABLE WAY TO KEEP SHUTOKU FROM SCORING.
ON THE OTHER HAND, IT'S NOT LIKE SHUTOKU CAN'T STOP SEIRIN.
IF ANYONE'S GONNA FALL APART BY THE END, IT'LL BE SEIRIN.
WELL ...
THAT'S WHAT I THINK WOULD HAPPEN IF NOT FOR KUROKO-CHI.
!
9:31
SEIRIN SHUTOKU
1 2 3 4 TO OT
45:43
HE WON'T BE SITTING OUT MUCH LONGER.
HE'S NOT CALLED THE PHANTOM SIXTH MAN OF THE MIRACLE GENERATION FOR NOTHING.

KUROKO'S BASKETBALL BLOOPERS

TAKE 5

HAHH HAHH
HEY! YOU SEE THAT CUTIE?
HOLD ON... SHE LOOKS FAMIL-IAR...
IDIOT. THAT'S TO-OH'S...
ACK!
TRIP
I JUST SAW MR. BEAR!
MUST BE A POPULAR DESIGN...
SHEESH!
CHATTER...
BADUM BADUM

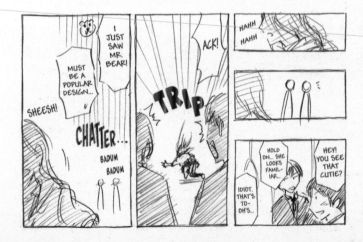

89TH QUARTER: BEEN WAITING

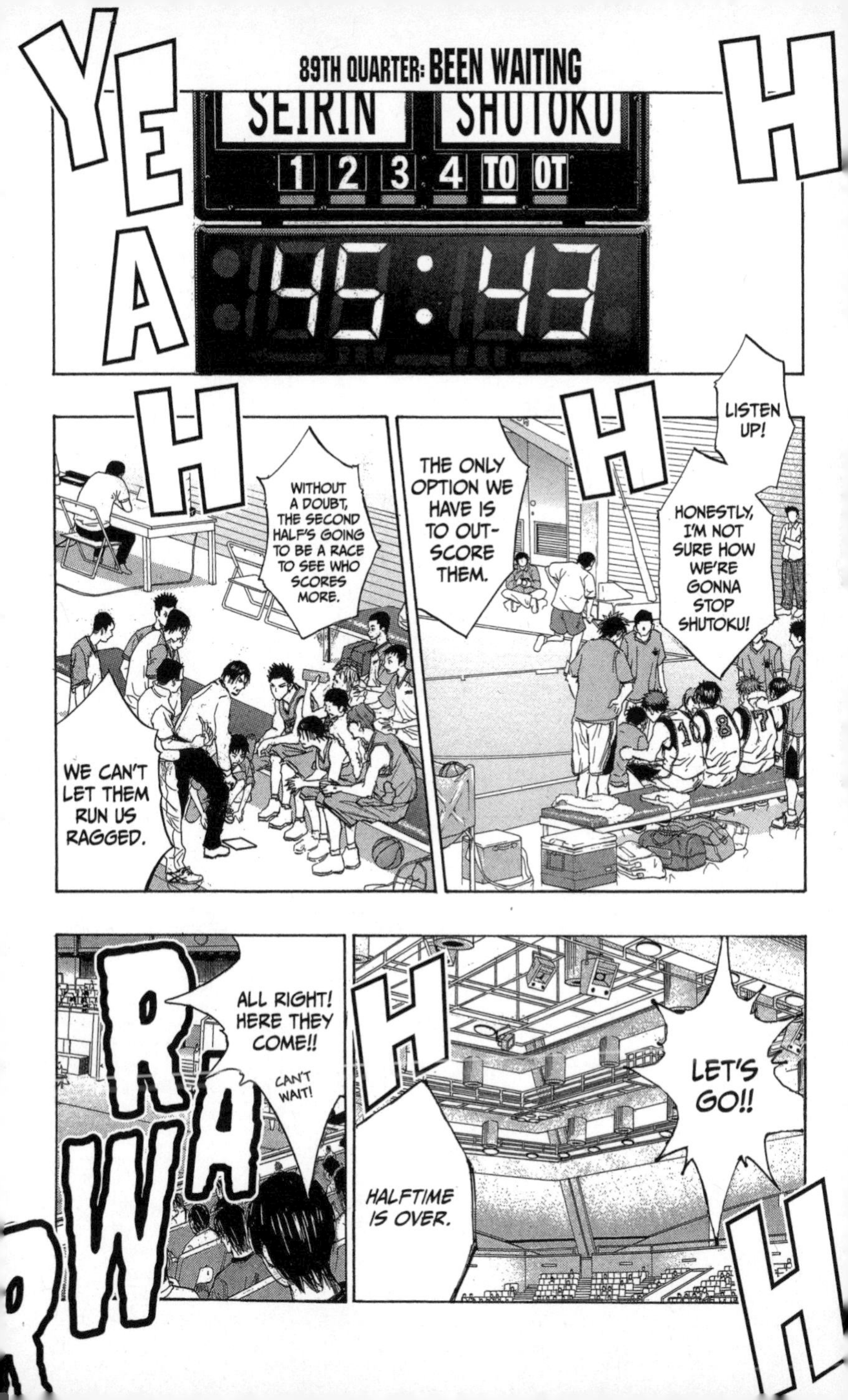
SEIRIN
SHUTOKU
1 2 3 4 TO OT
45 : 43
YEAHHHHH
LISTEN UP!
HONESTLY, I'M NOT SURE HOW WE'RE GONNA STOP SHUTOKU!
THE ONLY OPTION WE HAVE IS TO OUT-SCORE THEM.
WITHOUT A DOUBT, THE SECOND HALF'S GOING TO BE A RACE TO SEE WHO SCORES MORE.
WE CAN'T LET THEM RUN US RAGGED.
LET'S GO!!
HALFTIME IS OVER.
ALL RIGHT! HERE THEY COME!!
CAN'T WAIT!
RAWR

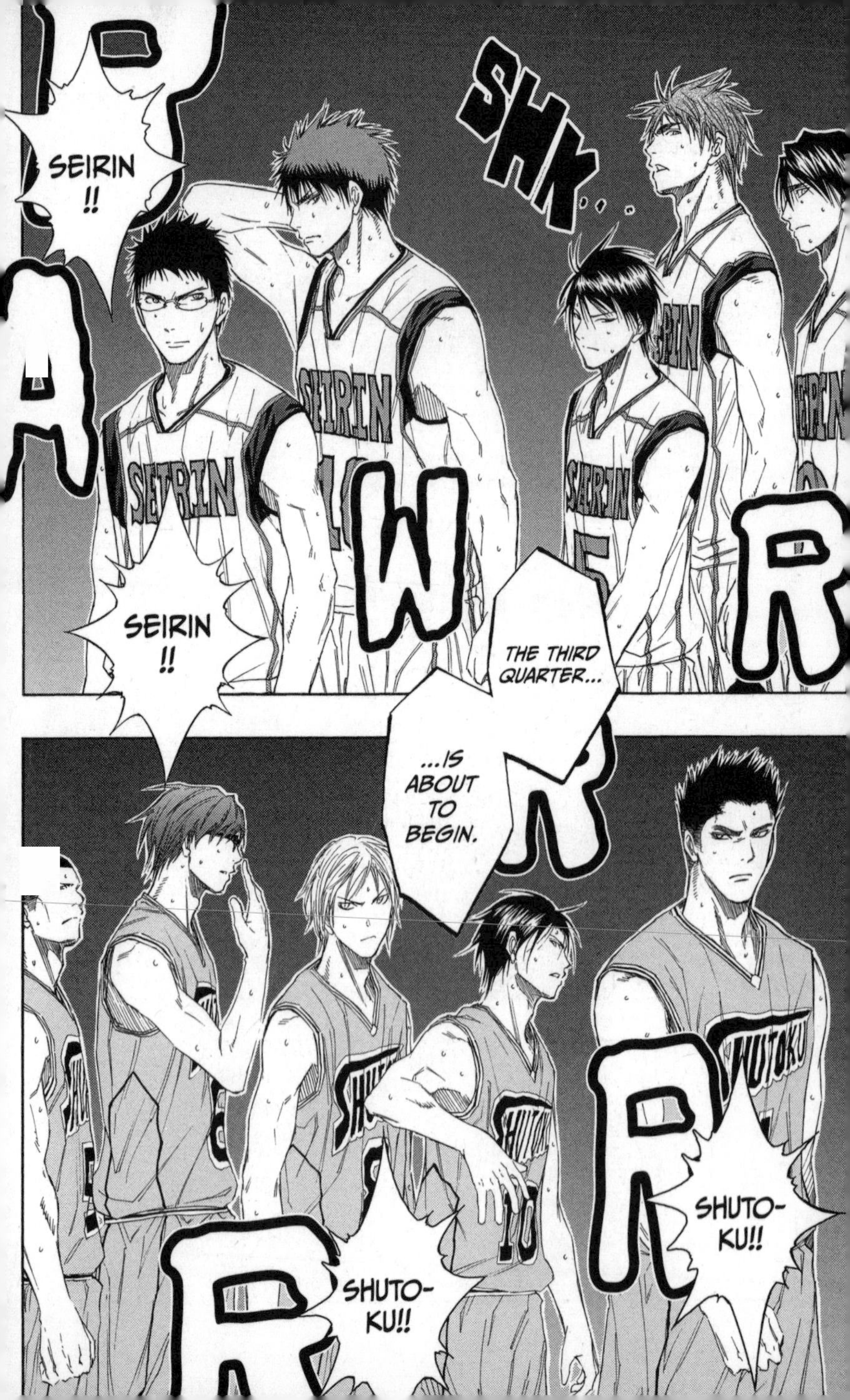
SHK...
SEIRIN!!
SEIRIN!!
THE THIRD QUARTER...
...IS ABOUT TO BEGIN.
SHUTO-KU!!
SHUTO-KU!!

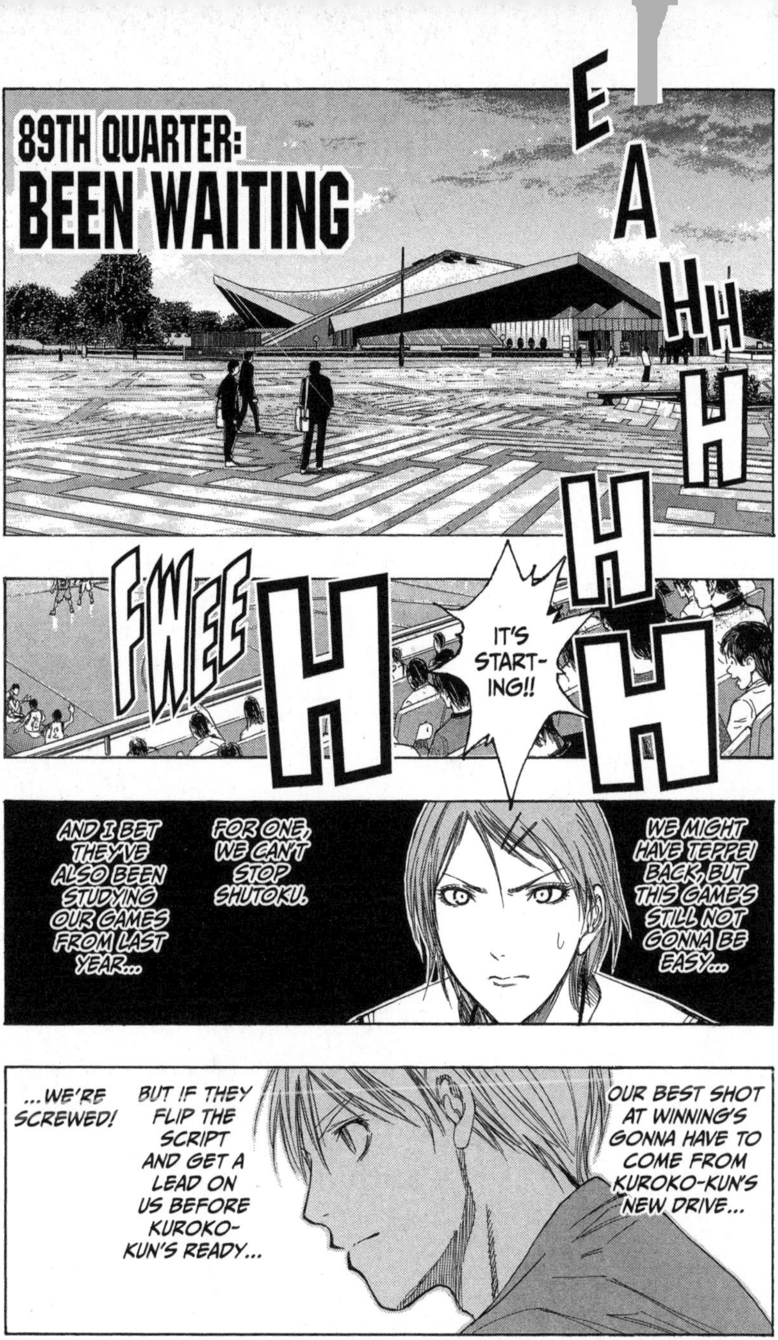
89TH QUARTER:
BEEN WAITING
EAHHHHH
FWEE
IT'S START-ING!!
WE MIGHT HAVE TEPPEI BACK, BUT THIS GAME'S STILL NOT GONNA BE EASY...
FOR ONE, WE CAN'T STOP SHUTOKU.
AND I BET THEY'VE ALSO BEEN STUDYING OUR GAMES FROM LAST YEAR...
OUR BEST SHOT AT WINNING'S GONNA HAVE TO COME FROM KUROKO-KUN'S NEW DRIVE...
BUT IF THEY FLIP THE SCRIPT AND GET A LEAD ON US BEFORE KUROKO-KUN'S READY...
...WE'RE SCREWED!

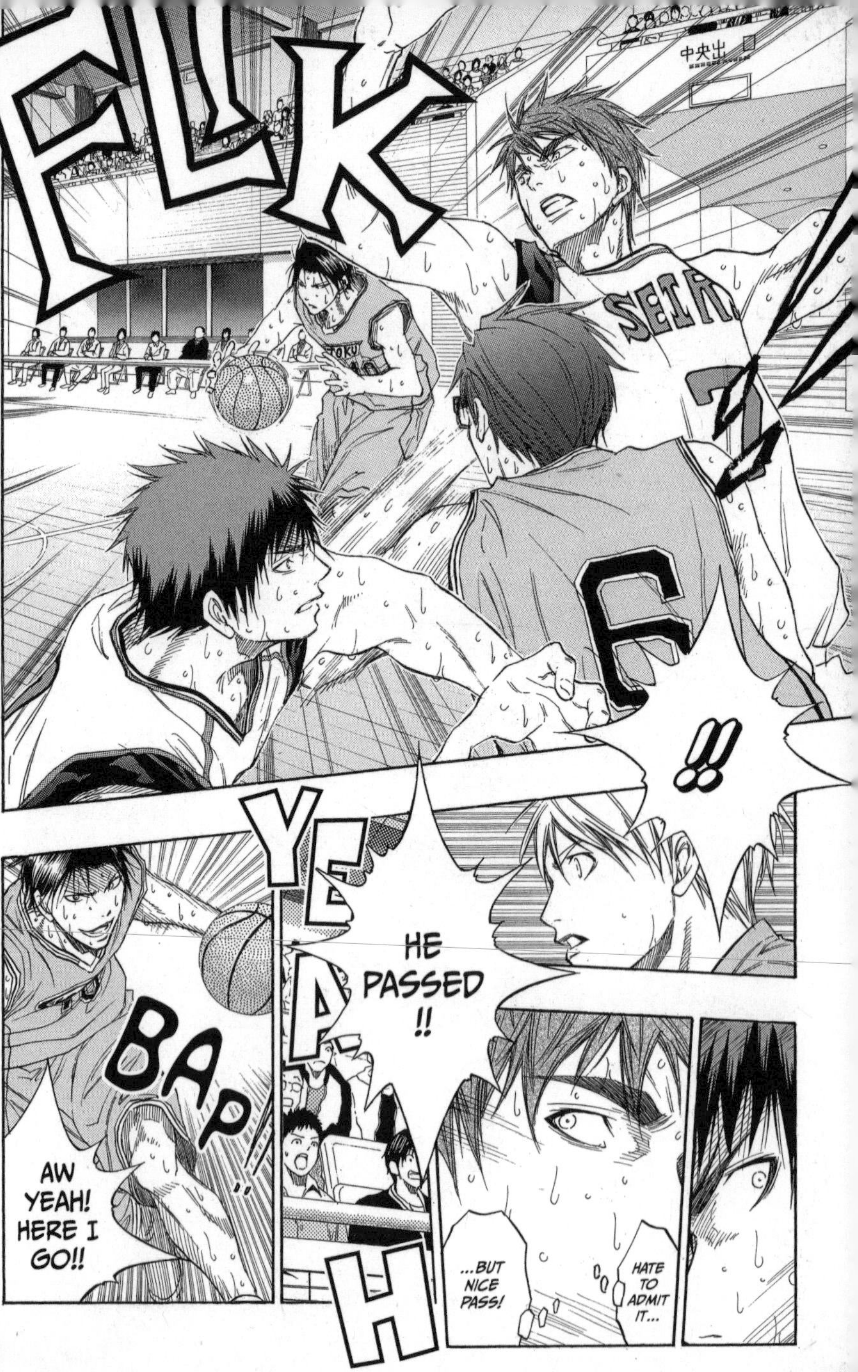
FLIK
!!
HE PASSED!!
HATE TO ADMIT IT...
...BUT NICE PASS!
YEAH
BAP
AW YEAH! HERE I GO!!

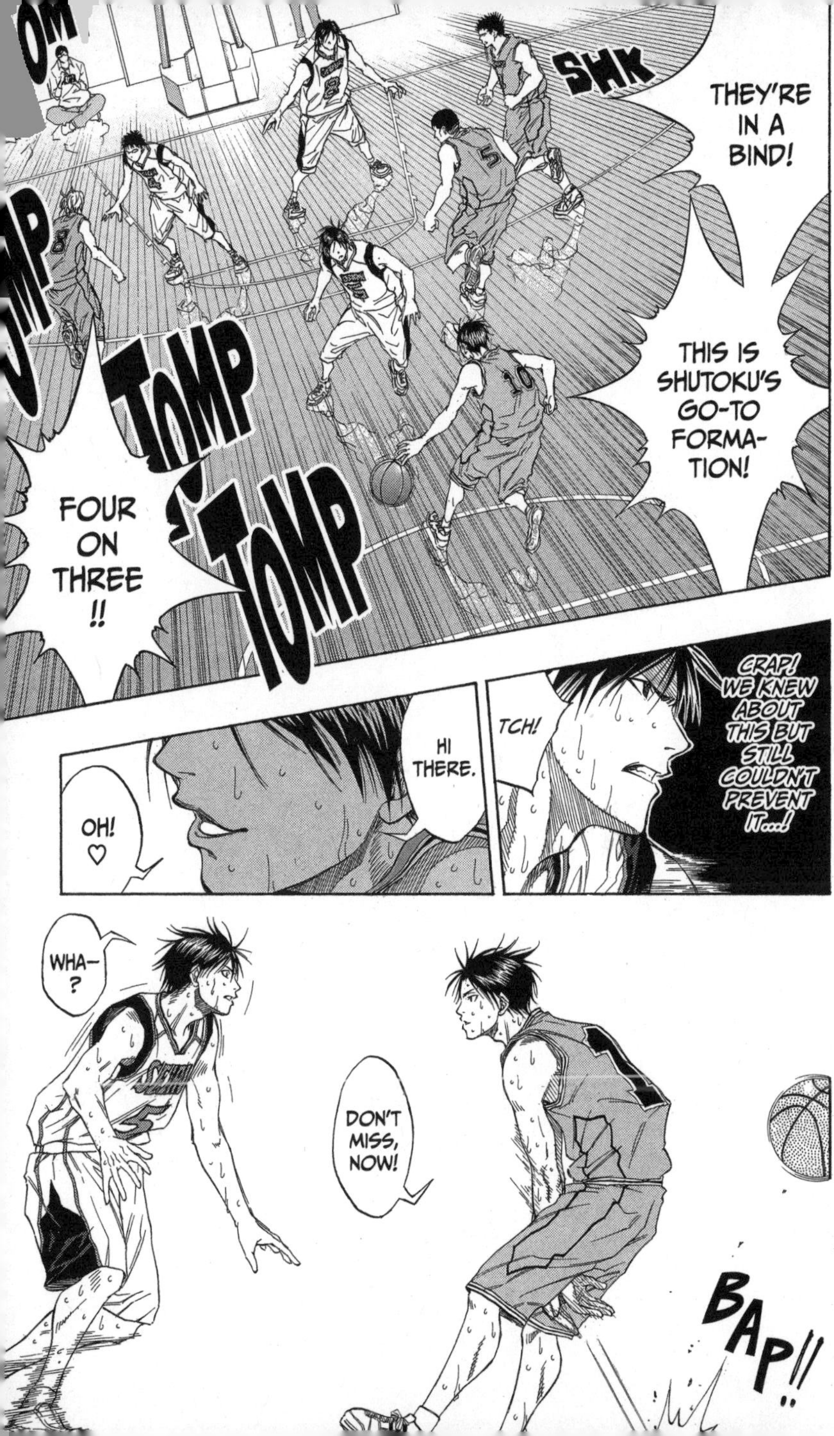
THEY'RE IN A BIND!
SHK
THIS IS SHUTOKU'S GO-TO FORMATION!
TOMP
TOMP
FOUR ON THREE !!
CRAP! WE KNEW ABOUT THIS BUT STILL COULDN'T PREVENT IT...!
TCH!
HI THERE.
OH! ♡
BAP!!
DON'T MISS, NOW!
WHA-?

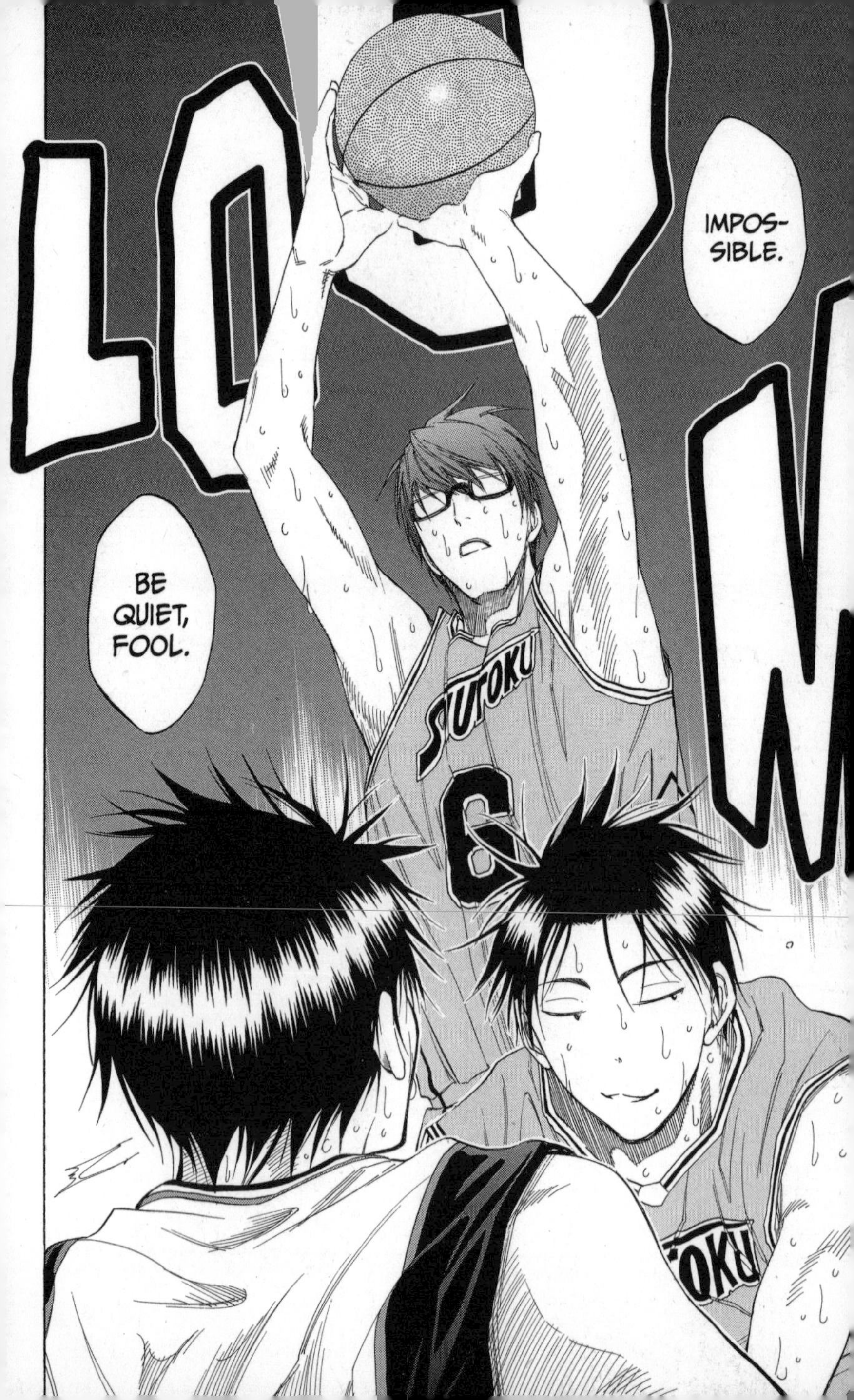
IMPOS-
SIBLE.
BE QUIET, FOOL.

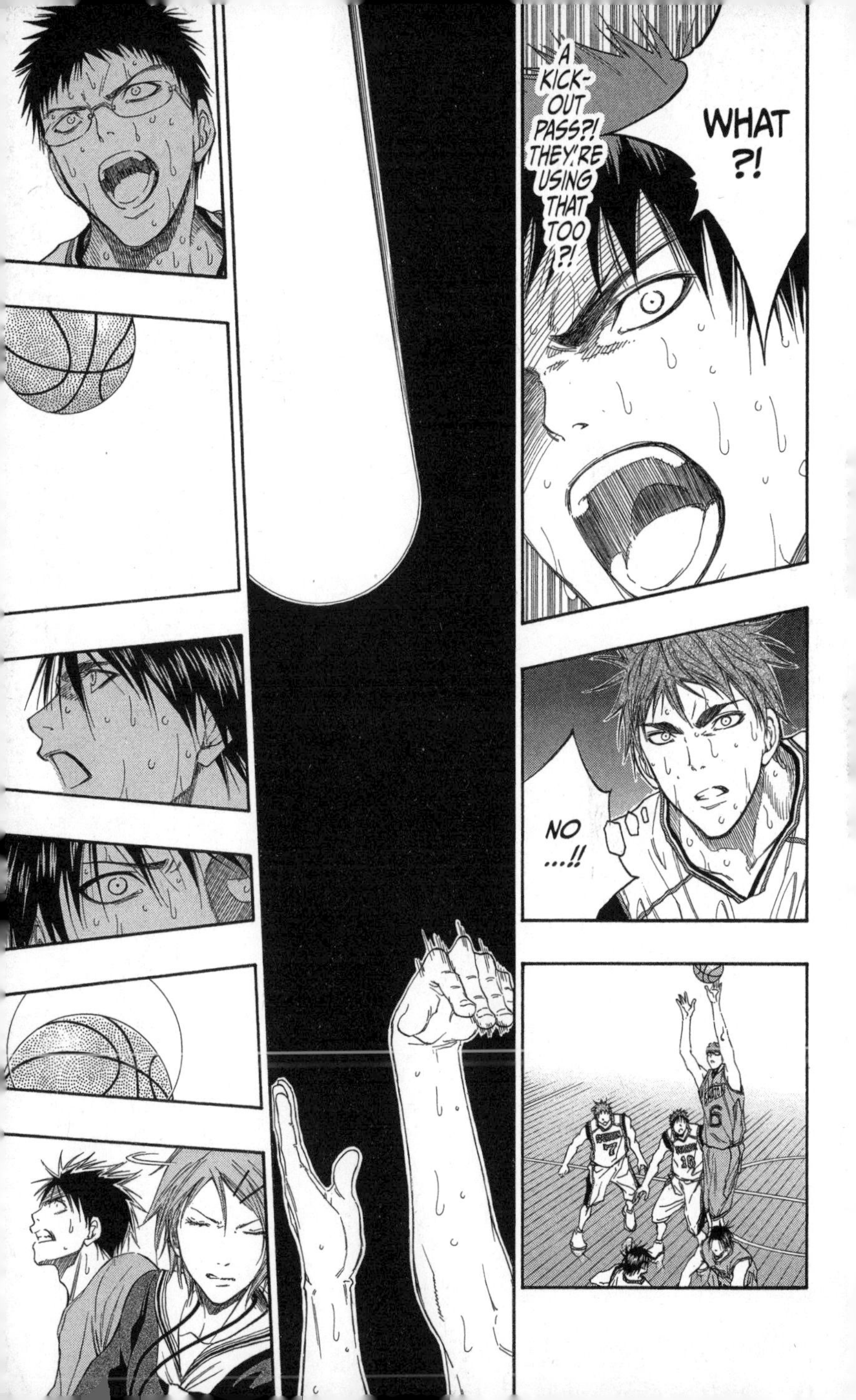
WHAT ?!
A KICK-OUT PASS?! THEY'RE USING THAT TOO ?!
NO ...!!

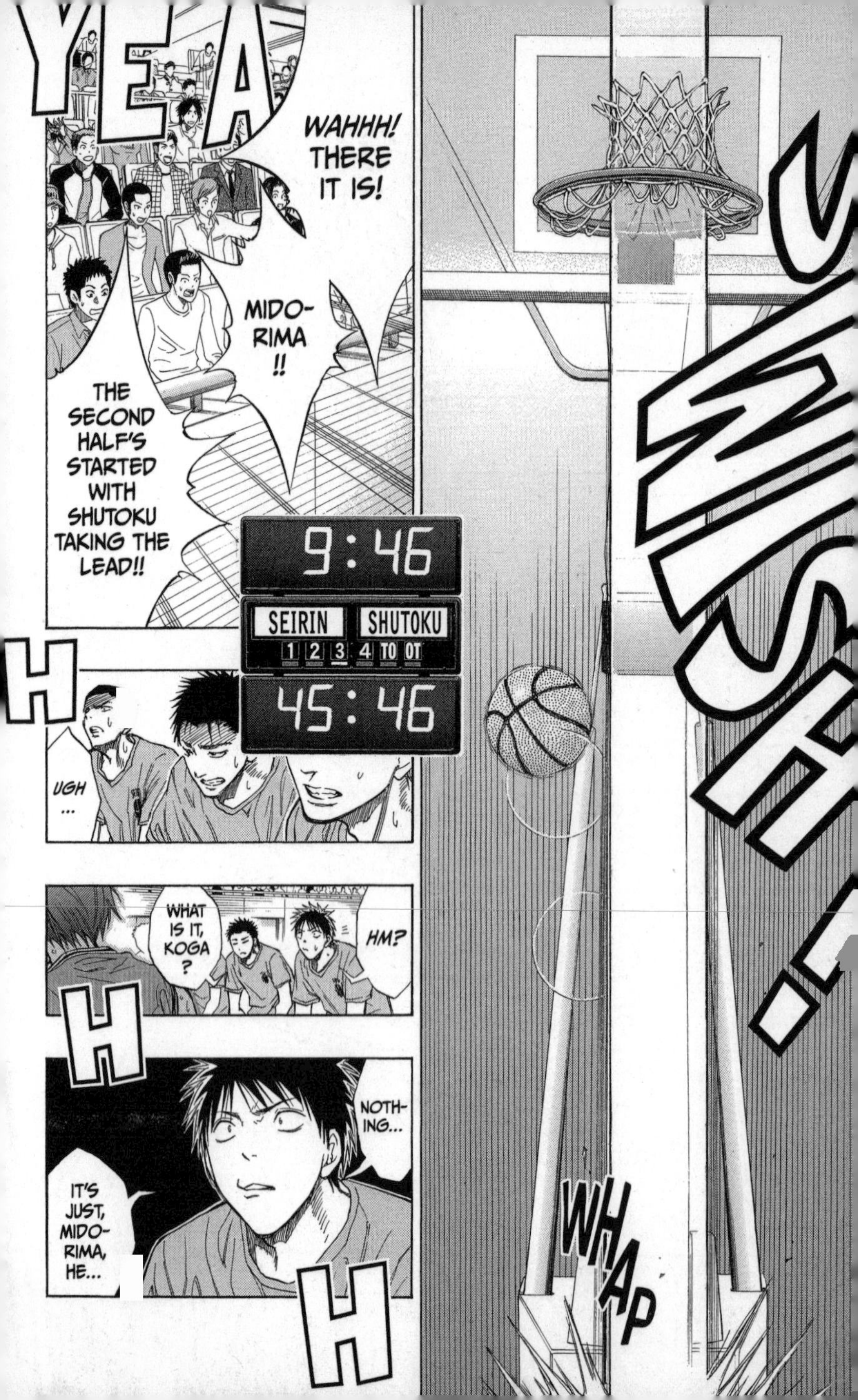
SWISH!
WHAP
YEAHHH
WAHHH! THERE IT IS!
MIDO-RIMA!!
THE SECOND HALF'S STARTED WITH SHUTOKU TAKING THE LEAD!!
9:46
SEIRIN SHUTOKU
1 2 3 4 TO OT
45:46
UGH...
HM?
WHAT IS IT, KOGA?
NOTH-ING...
IT'S JUST, MIDO-RIMA, HE...

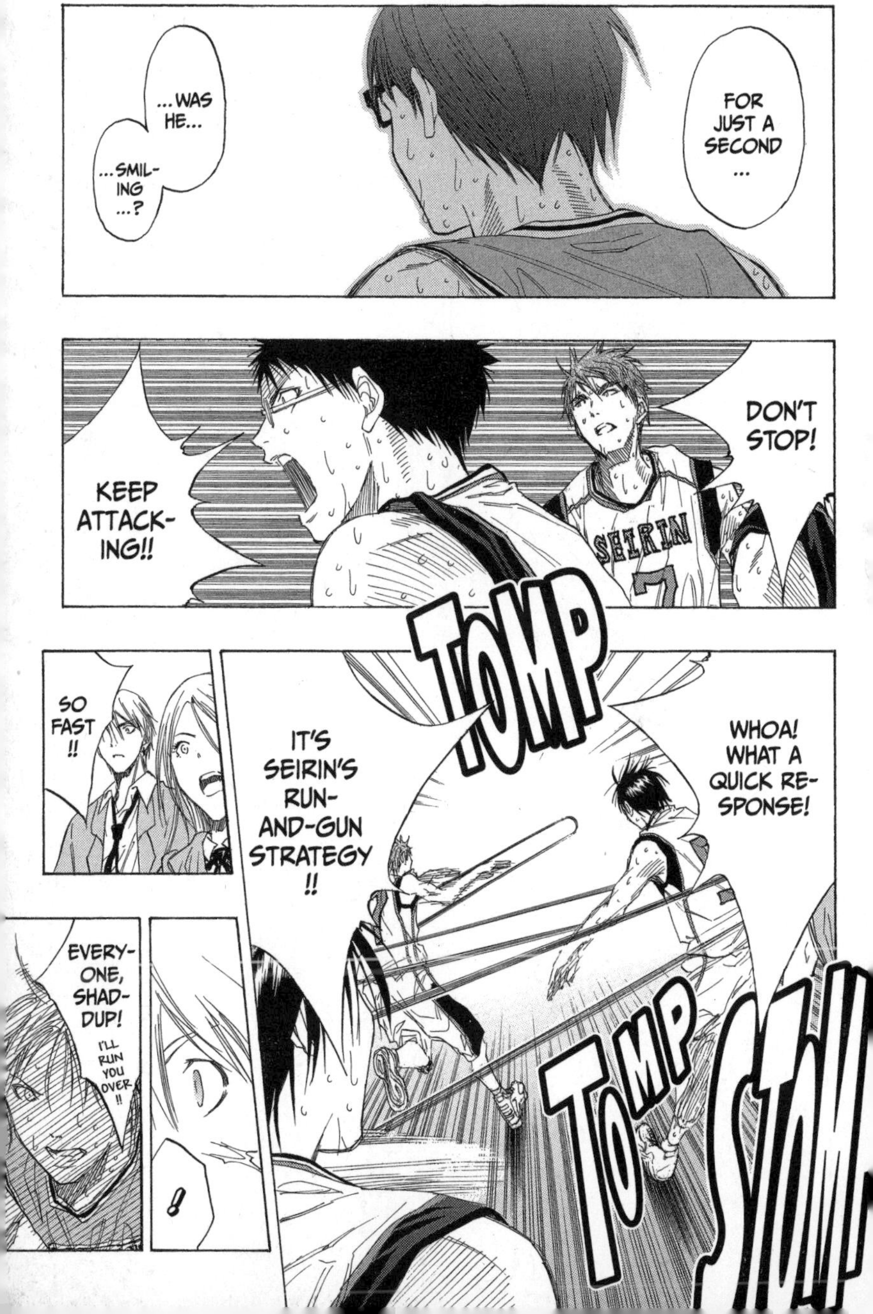
FOR JUST A SECOND ...
...WAS HE...
...SMIL-ING ...?
DON'T STOP!
KEEP ATTACK-ING!!
TOMP
WHOA! WHAT A QUICK RE-SPONSE!
IT'S SEIRIN'S RUN-AND-GUN STRATEGY !!
TOMP
STOM
SO FAST !!
!
EVERY-ONE, SHAD-DUP!
I'LL RUN YOU OVER !!

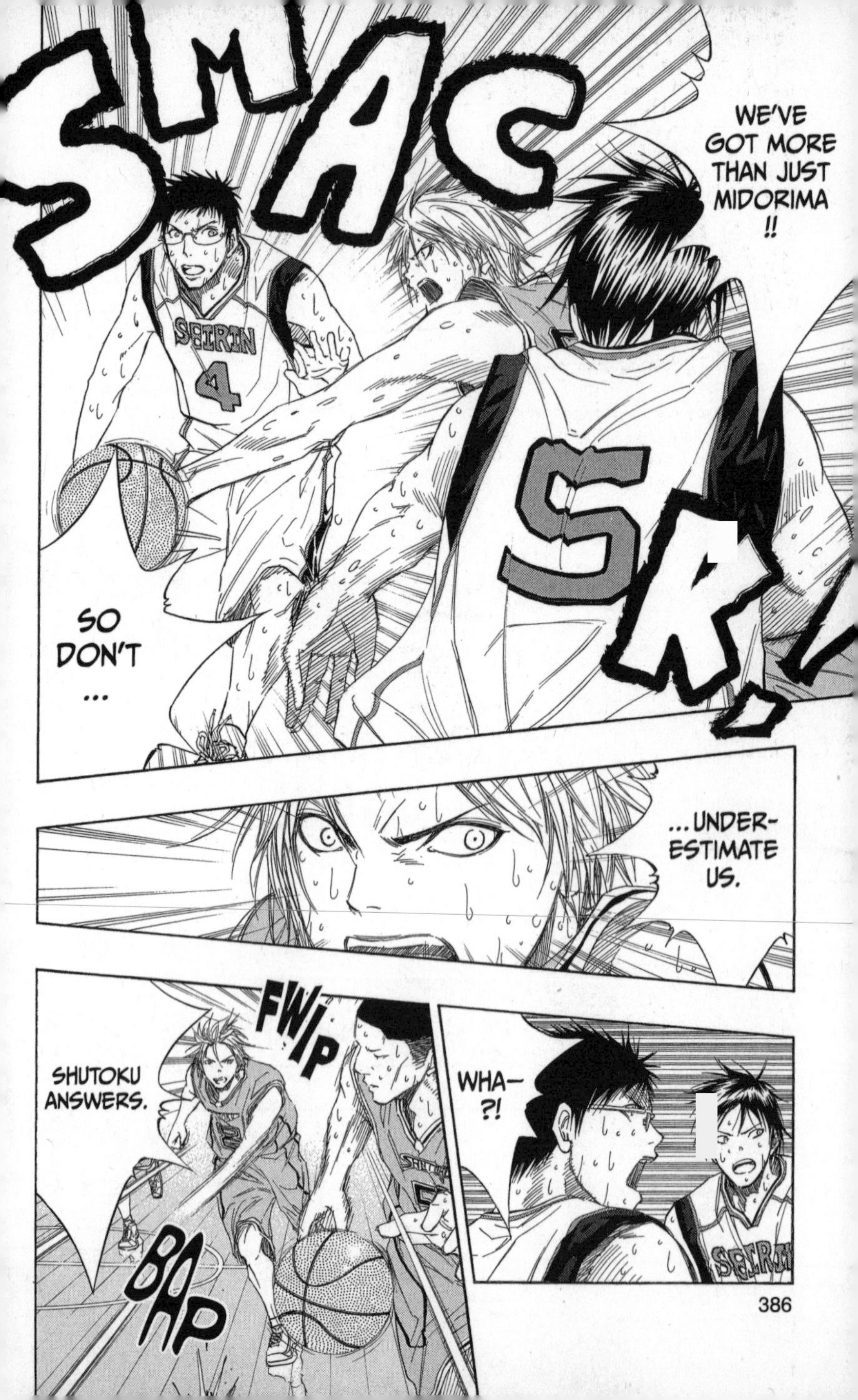
WE'VE GOT MORE THAN JUST MIDORIMA!!
SO DON'T...
...UNDER-ESTIMATE US.
WHA—?!
FWIP
SHUTOKU ANSWERS.
BAP

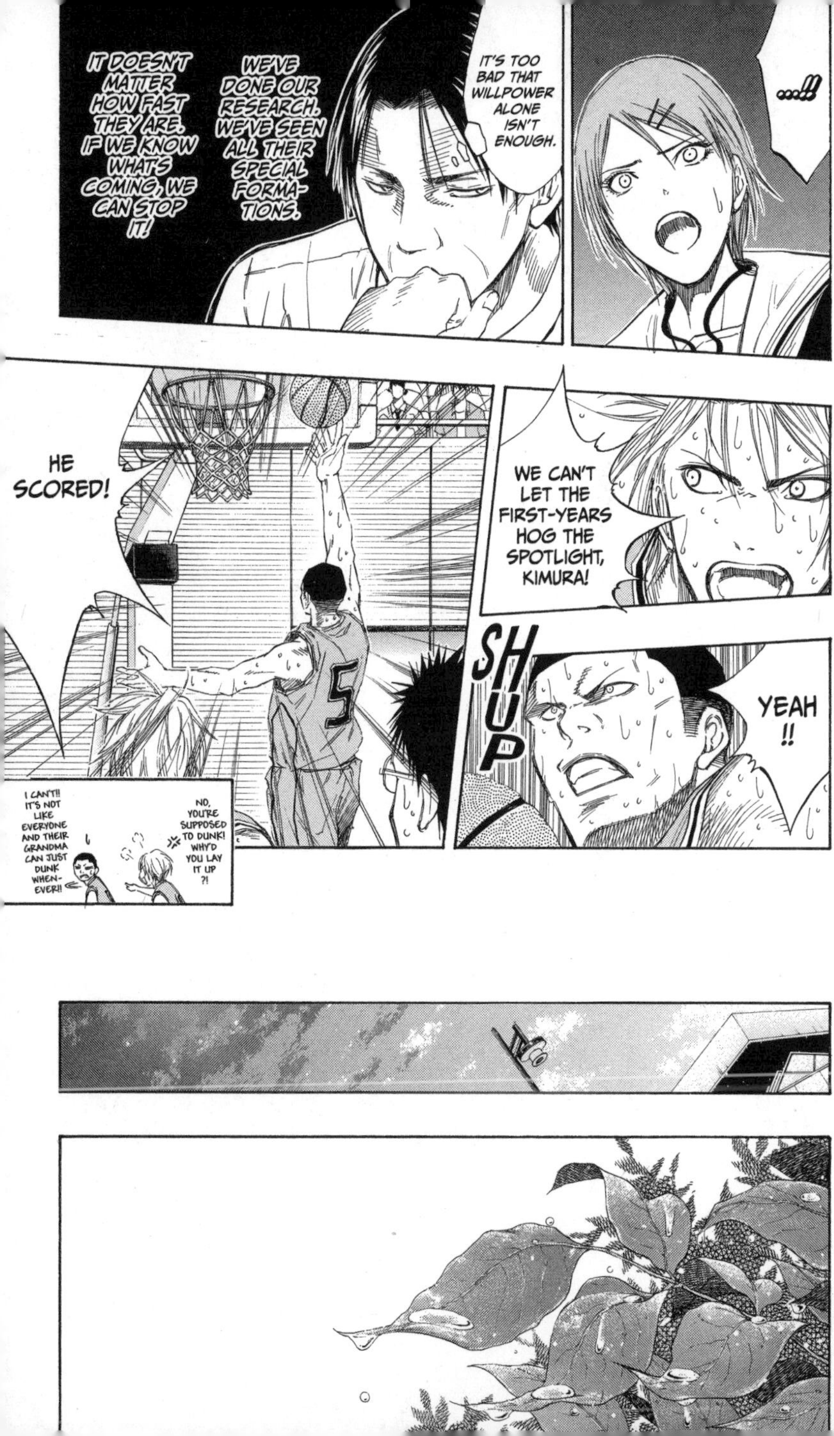
...!!
IT'S TOO BAD THAT WILLPOWER ALONE ISN'T ENOUGH.
WE'VE DONE OUR RESEARCH. WE'VE SEEN ALL THEIR SPECIAL FORMATIONS.
IT DOESN'T MATTER HOW FAST THEY ARE. IF WE KNOW WHAT'S COMING, WE CAN STOP IT!
WE CAN'T LET THE FIRST-YEARS HOG THE SPOTLIGHT, KIMURA!
YEAH!!
SHUP
HE SCORED!
NO, YOU'RE SUPPOSED TO DUNK! WHY'D YOU LAY IT UP?!
I CAN'T!! IT'S NOT LIKE EVERYONE AND THEIR GRANDMA CAN JUST DUNK WHENEVER!!

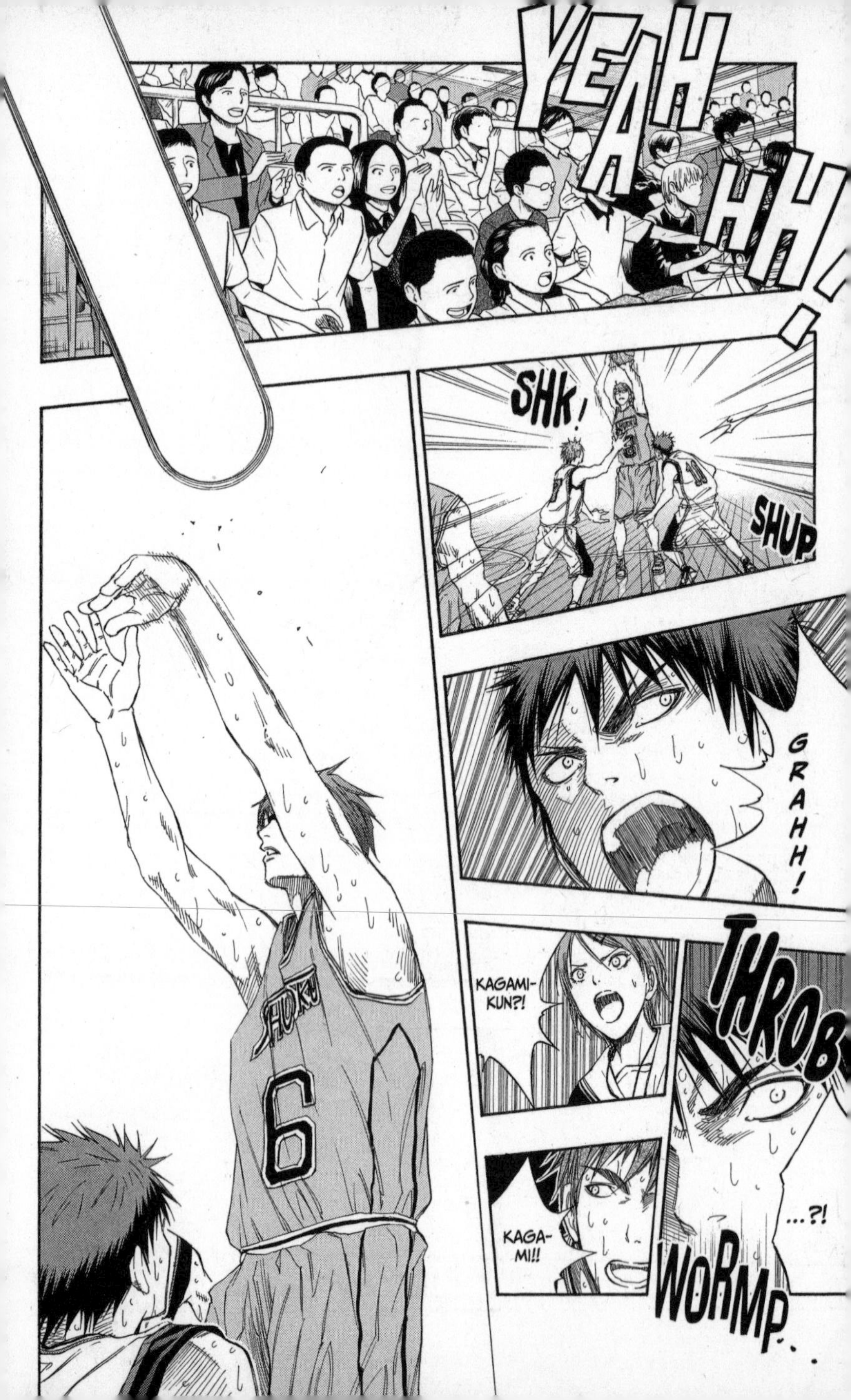

YEAH HH!!
SHK!
SHUP
GRAHH!
THROB
...?!
WORMP...
KAGAMI-KUN?!
KAGA-MI!!
SHUKU
6

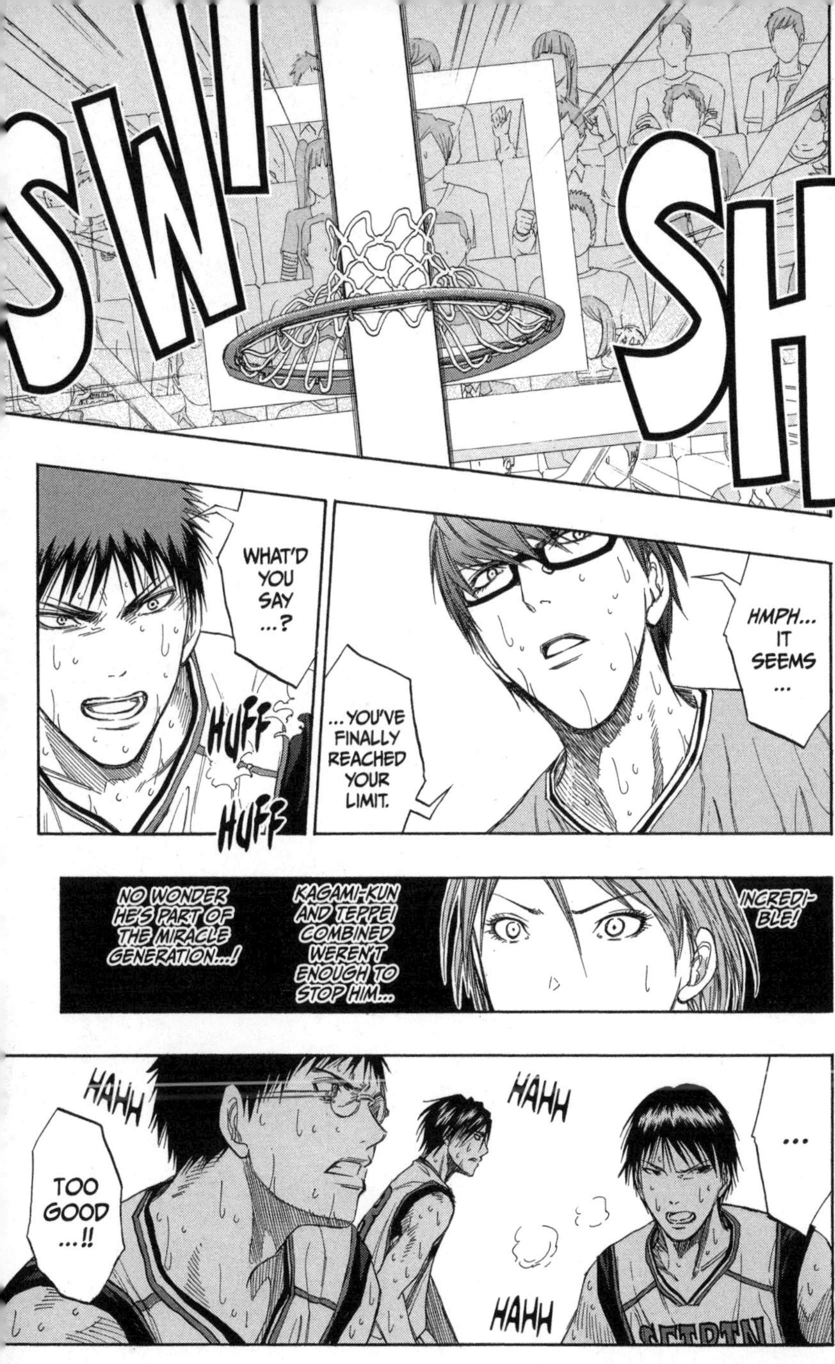
SWISH
HMPH... IT SEEMS...
...YOU'VE FINALLY REACHED YOUR LIMIT.
WHAT'D YOU SAY ...?
HUFF HUFF
INCREDIBLE!
KAGAMI-KUN AND TEPPEI COMBINED WEREN'T ENOUGH TO STOP HIM...
NO WONDER HE'S PART OF THE MIRACLE GENERATION...!
...
HAHH
HAHH
HAHH
TOO GOOD ...!!

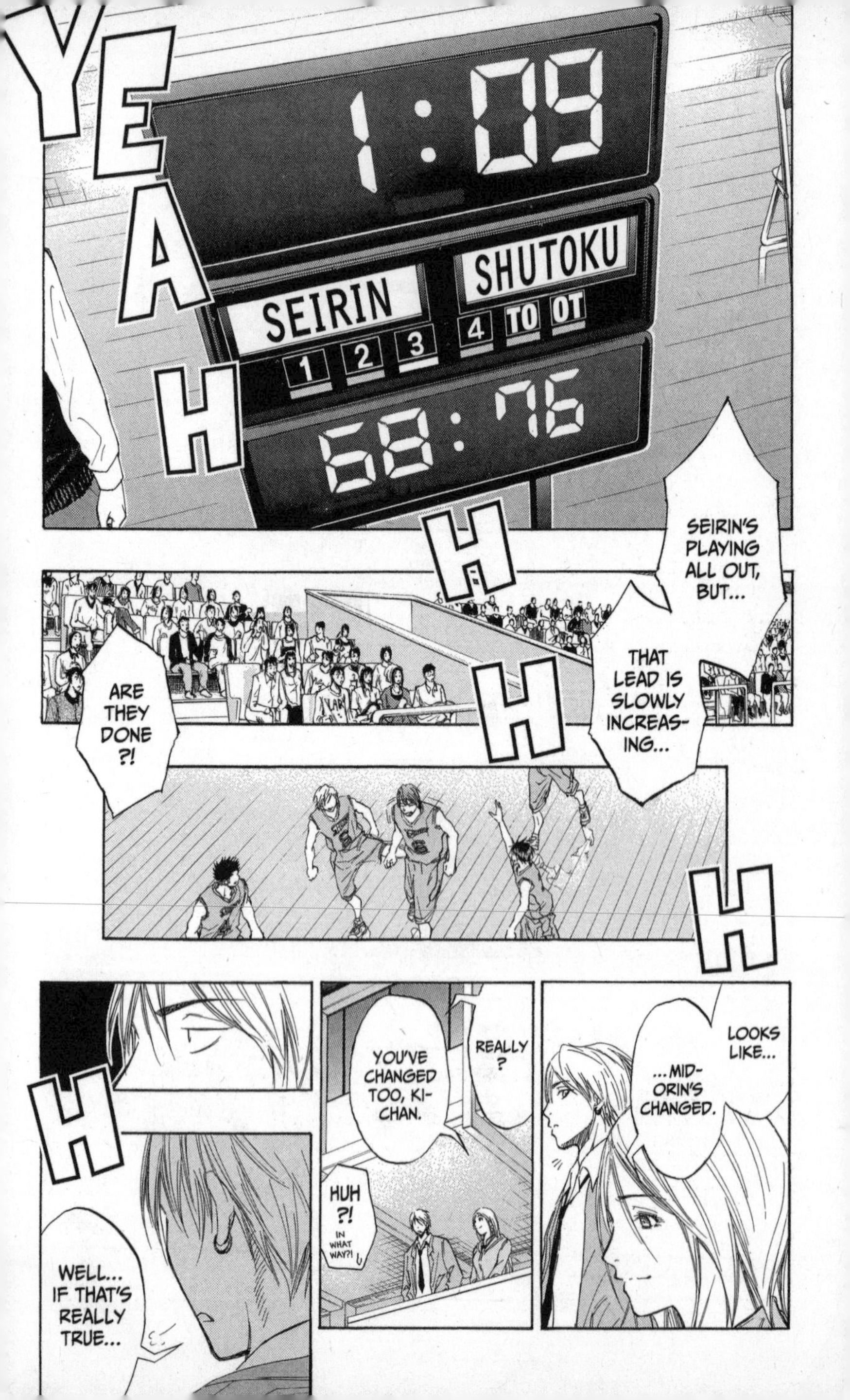
YEAHHHHH
1:09
SHUTOKU
SEIRIN
1 2 3 4 TO OT
68:76
SEIRIN'S PLAYING ALL OUT, BUT...
THAT LEAD IS SLOWLY INCREASING...
ARE THEY DONE ?!
LOOKS LIKE...
...MID-ORIN'S CHANGED.
REALLY ?
YOU'VE CHANGED TOO, KI-CHAN.
HUH ?!
IN WHAT WAY?!
WELL... IF THAT'S REALLY TRUE...

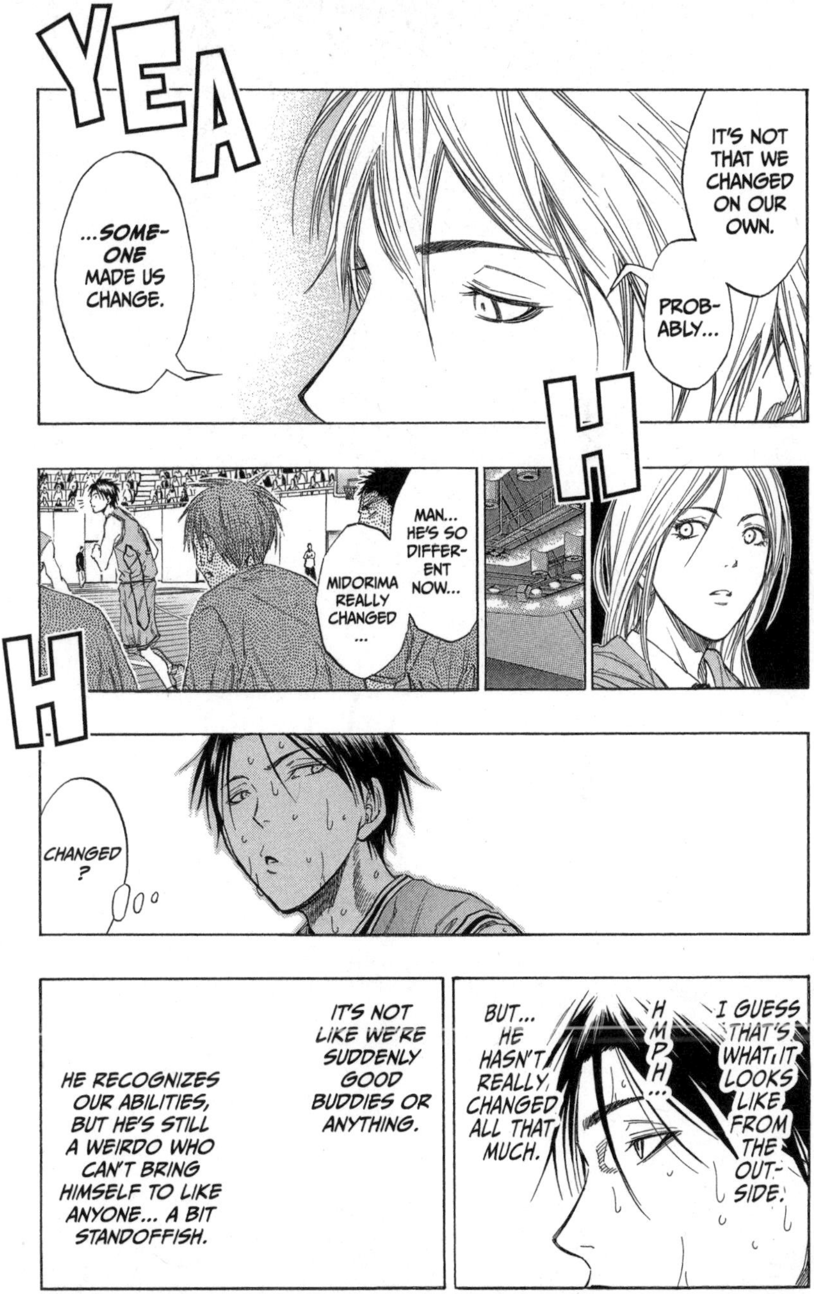
IT'S NOT THAT WE CHANGED ON OUR OWN.
PROBABLY...
...SOMEONE MADE US CHANGE.
YEAHH
MAN... HE'S SO DIFFERENT NOW...
MIDORIMA REALLY CHANGED...
CHANGED?
I GUESS THAT'S WHAT IT LOOKS LIKE FROM THE OUTSIDE.
HMPH...
BUT... HE HASN'T REALLY CHANGED ALL THAT MUCH.
IT'S NOT LIKE WE'RE SUDDENLY GOOD BUDDIES OR ANYTHING.
HE RECOGNIZES OUR ABILITIES, BUT HE'S STILL A WEIRDO WHO CAN'T BRING HIMSELF TO LIKE ANYONE... A BIT STANDOFFISH.

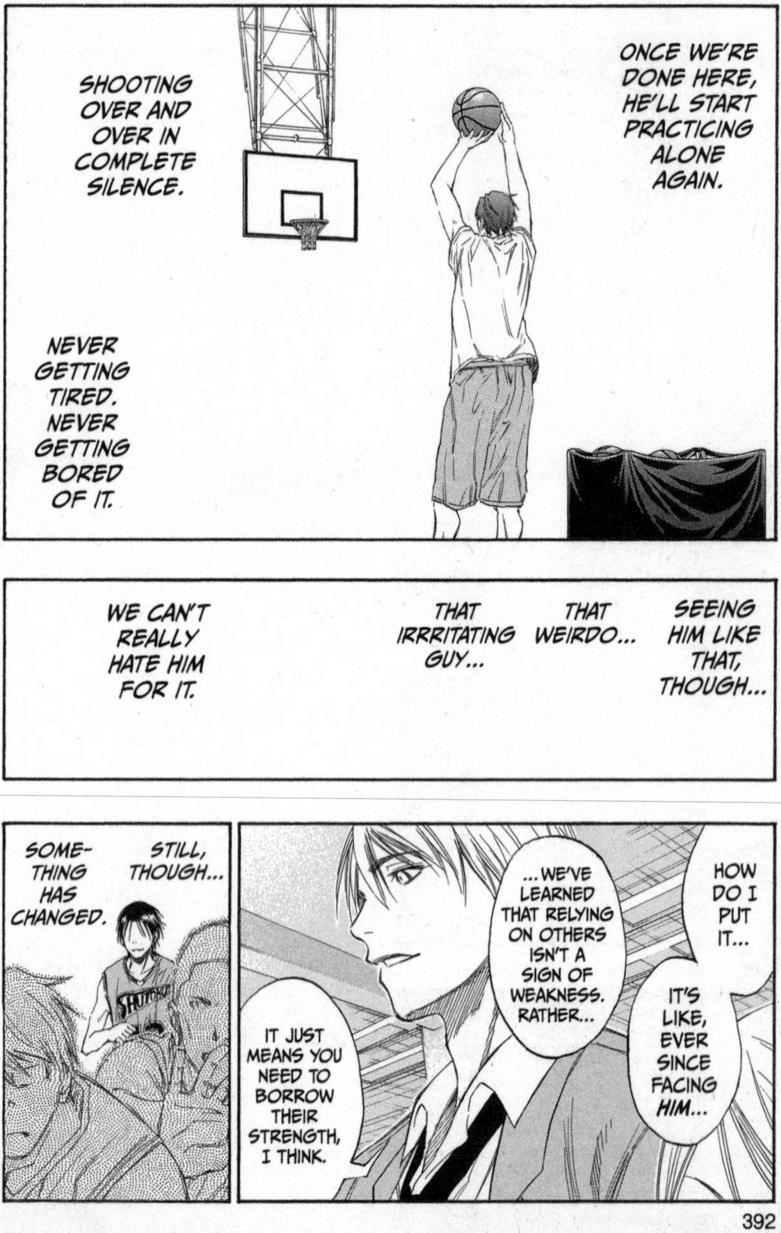
ONCE WE'RE DONE HERE, HE'LL START PRACTICING ALONE AGAIN.
SHOOTING OVER AND OVER IN COMPLETE SILENCE.
NEVER GETTING TIRED. NEVER GETTING BORED OF IT.
SEEING HIM LIKE THAT, THOUGH...
THAT WEIRDO...
THAT IRRRITATING GUY...
WE CAN'T REALLY HATE HIM FOR IT.
HOW DO I PUT IT...
IT'S LIKE, EVER SINCE FACING HIM...
...WE'VE LEARNED THAT RELYING ON OTHERS ISN'T A SIGN OF WEAKNESS. RATHER...
IT JUST MEANS YOU NEED TO BORROW THEIR STRENGTH, I THINK.
STILL, THOUGH...
SOME-THING HAS CHANGED.
SHUTOKU

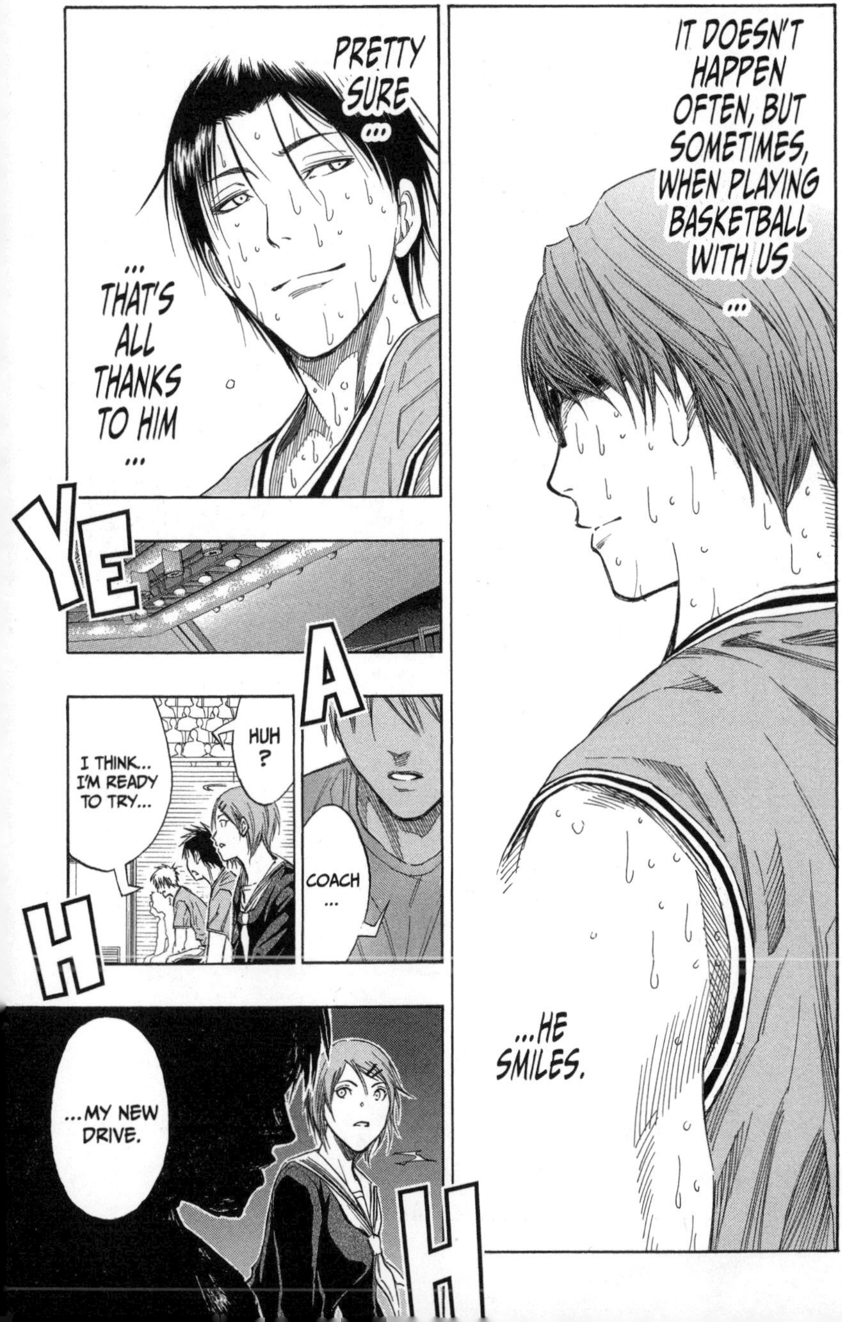
IT DOESN'T HAPPEN OFTEN, BUT SOMETIMES, WHEN PLAYING BASKETBALL WITH US ...
...HE SMILES.
PRETTY SURE ...
... THAT'S ALL THANKS TO HIM ...
YE
A
COACH ...
HUH ?
I THINK... I'M READY TO TRY...
H
...MY NEW DRIVE.
H

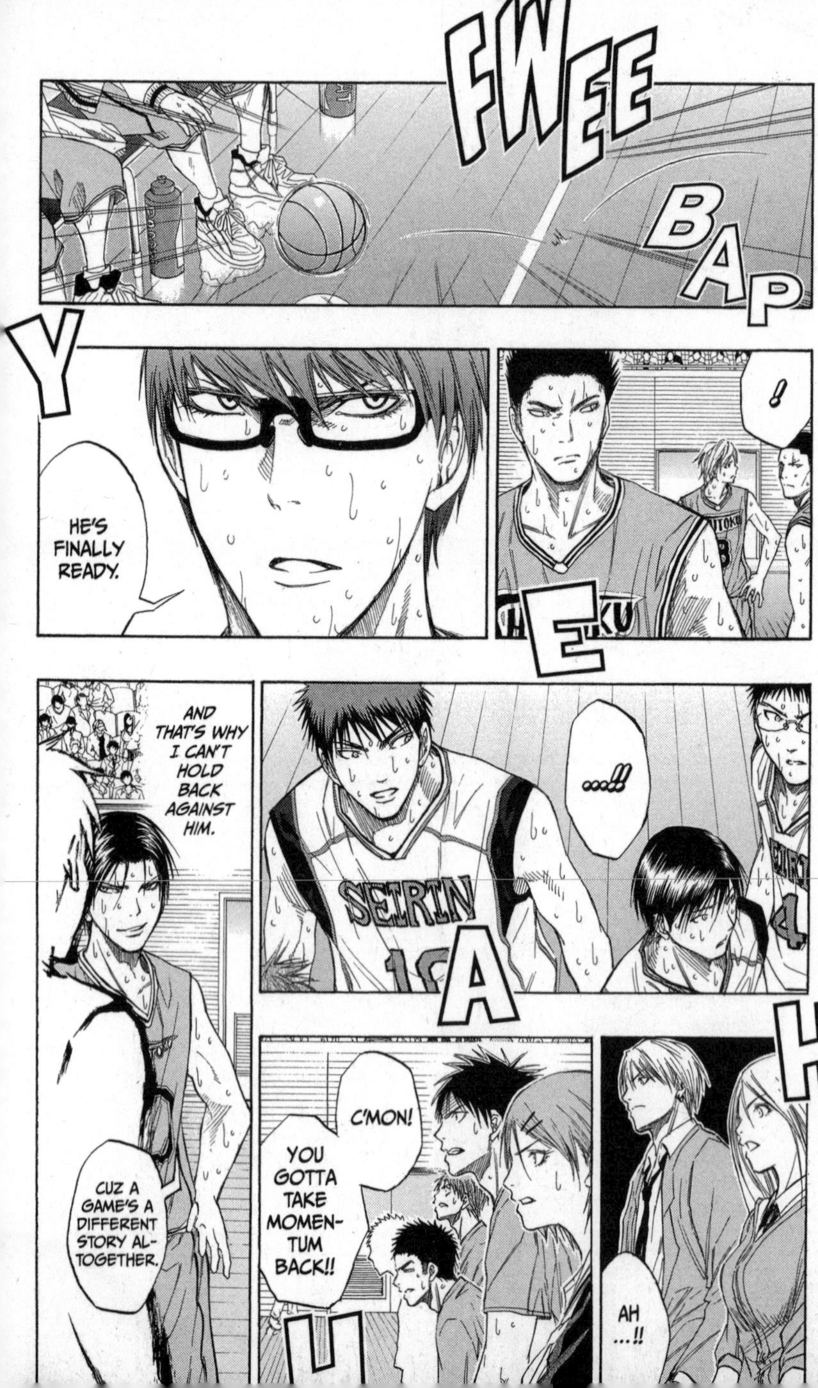

FWEE
BAP
!
Y
HE'S FINALLY READY.
E
...!!
A
H
AH ...!!
C'MON!
YOU GOTTA TAKE MOMEN-TUM BACK!!
AND THAT'S WHY I CAN'T HOLD BACK AGAINST HIM.
CUZ A GAME'S A DIFFERENT STORY AL-TOGETHER.

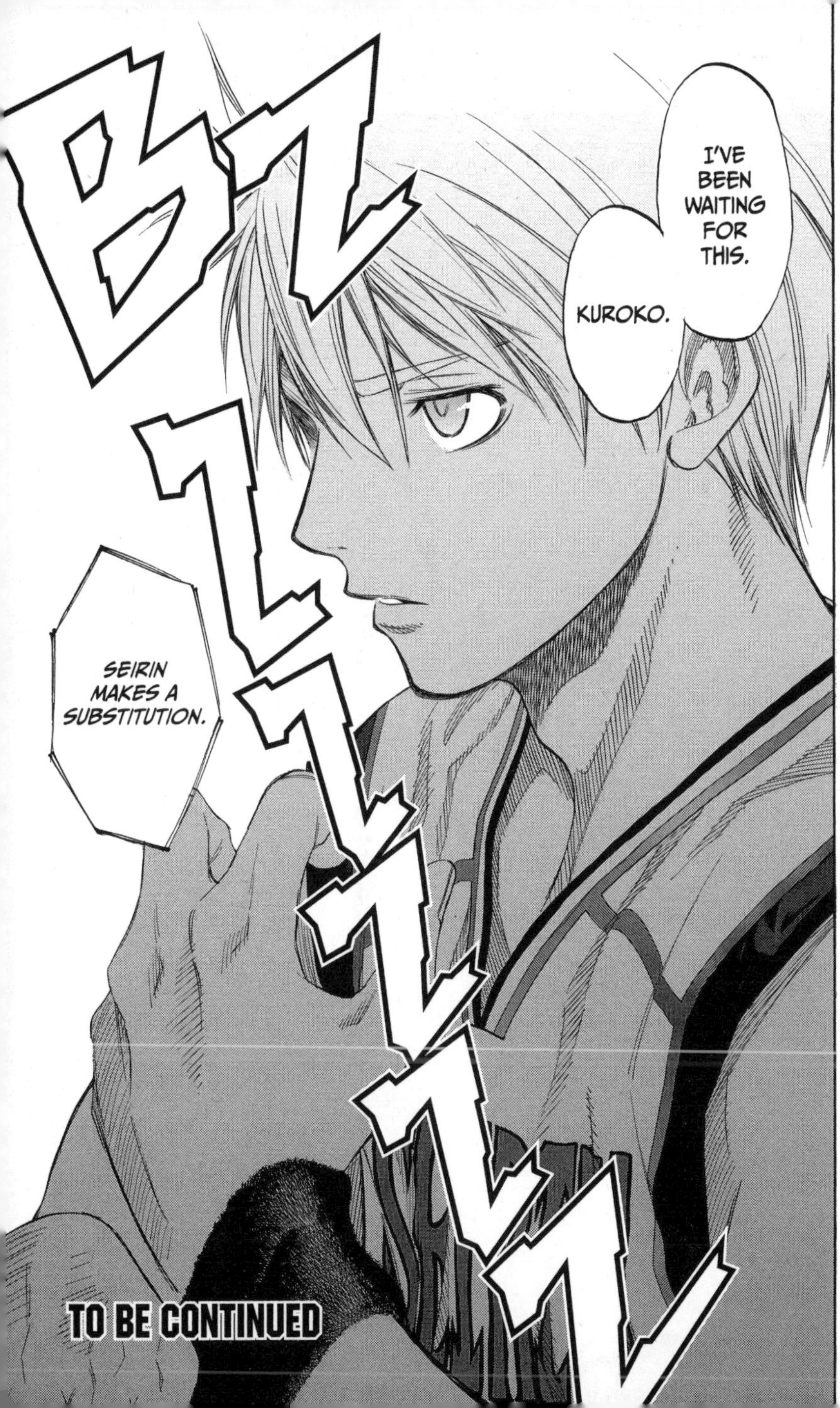
I'VE BEEN WAITING FOR THIS.
KUROKO.
BZZZZZZZ
SEIRIN MAKES A SUBSTITUTION.
TO BE CONTINUED

WE'RE ENDING HERE? THIS IS TOO CRUEL.

JUST AS I WAS ABOUT TO SHINE...

UH...

END-OF-YEAR SPECIAL FOUR-PANEL COMIC

"DON'T WANNA BULK UP"

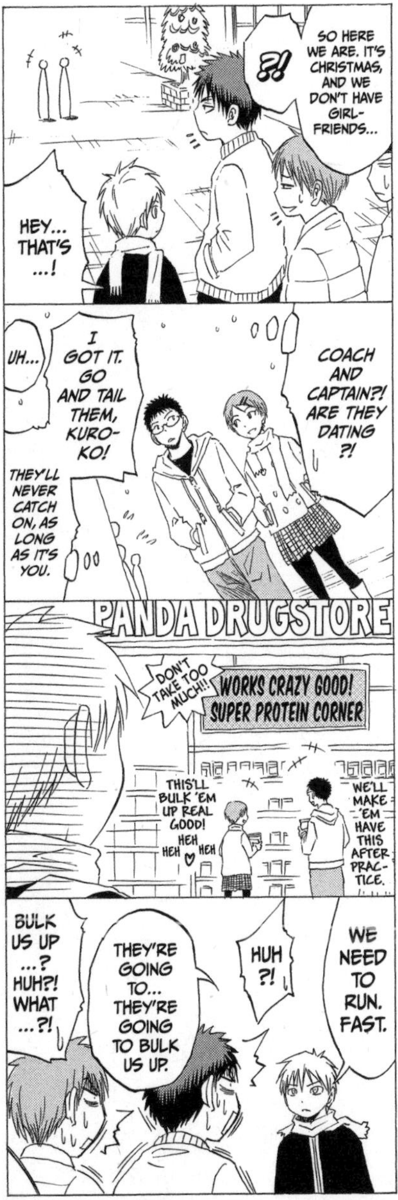
SO HERE WE ARE. IT'S CHRISTMAS, AND WE DON'T HAVE GIRL-FRIENDS...
?!
HEY... THAT'S ...!
COACH AND CAPTAIN?! ARE THEY DATING ?!
I GOT IT. GO AND TAIL THEM, KURO-KO!
UH...
THEY'LL NEVER CATCH ON, AS LONG AS IT'S YOU.
PANDA DRUGSTORE
WORKS CRAZY GOOD! SUPER PROTEIN CORNER
DON'T TAKE TOO MUCH!!
WE'LL MAKE 'EM HAVE THIS AFTER PRAC-TICE.
THIS'LL BULK 'EM UP REAL GOOD!
HEH HEH ♡ HEH
WE NEED TO RUN. FAST.
HUH ?!
THEY'RE GOING TO... THEY'RE GOING TO BULK US UP.
BULK US UP ...? HUH?! WHAT ...?!

ORIGINALLY PUBLISHED IN *WEEKLY SHONEN JUMP*, ISSUE 3/4, 2009

Coming Next Volume

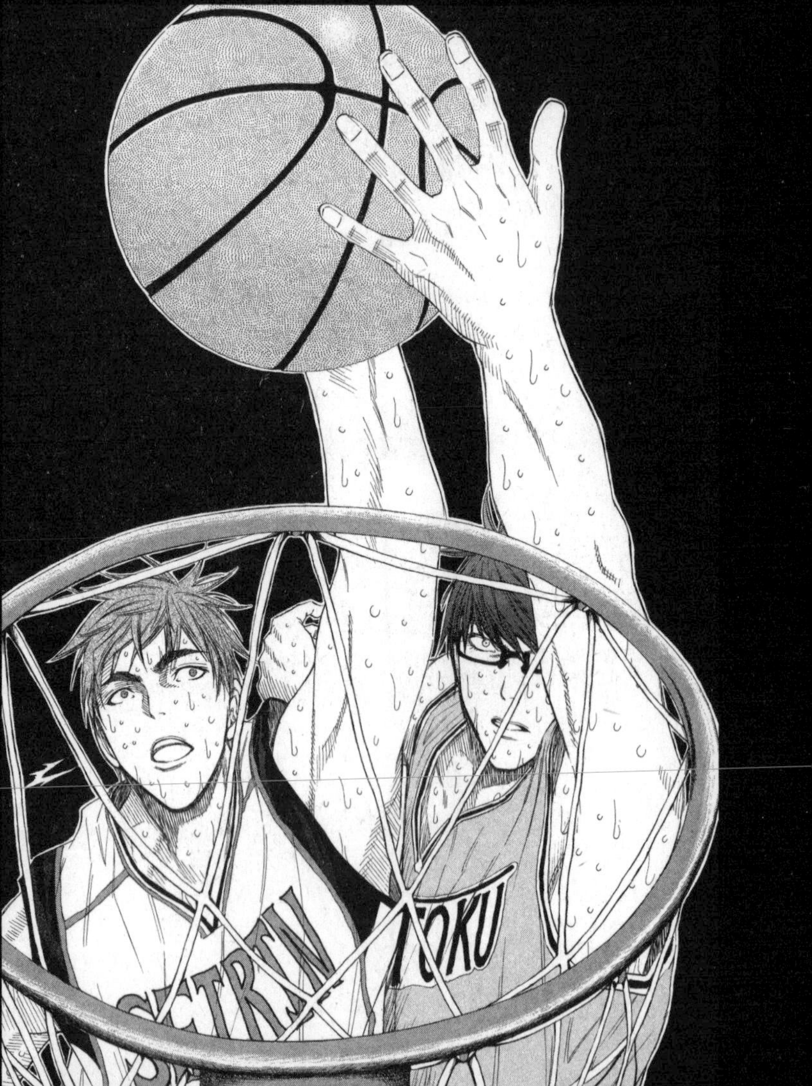

SEIRIN
TOKU

It's down to the wire, as Seirin and Shutoku go toe-to-toe on the hardwood! Who'll be the last team standing at the end?!

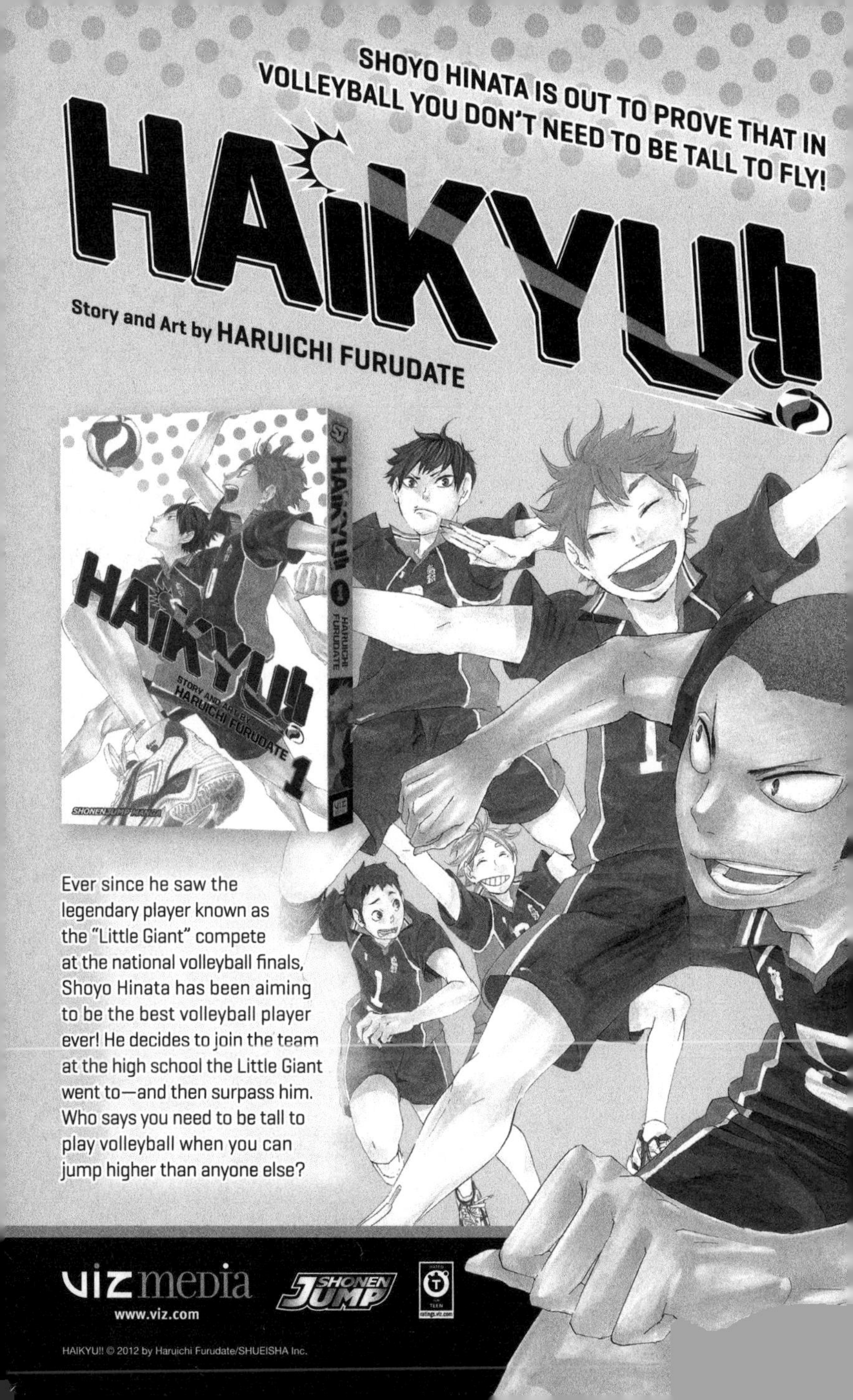
SHOYO HINATA IS OUT TO PROVE THAT IN VOLLEYBALL YOU DON'T NEED TO BE TALL TO FLY!
HAIKYU!!
Story and Art by HARUICHI FURUDATE
HAIKYU!!
STORY AND ART BY HARUICHI FURUDATE
1
SHONEN JUMP MANGA
HARUICHI FURUDATE
Ever since he saw the legendary player known as the "Little Giant" compete at the national volleyball finals, Shoyo Hinata has been aiming to be the best volleyball player ever! He decides to join the team at the high school the Little Giant went to—and then surpass him. Who says you need to be tall to play volleyball when you can jump higher than anyone else?
VIZ media
www.viz.com
SHONEN JUMP
TEEN
ratings.viz.com
HAIKYU!! © 2012 by Haruichi Furudate/SHUEISHA Inc.

YOU'RE READING THE WRONG WAY!

KUROKO'S BASKETBALL reads from right to left, starting in the upper-right corner. Japanese is read from right to left, meaning that action, sound effects and word-balloon order are completely reversed from English order.

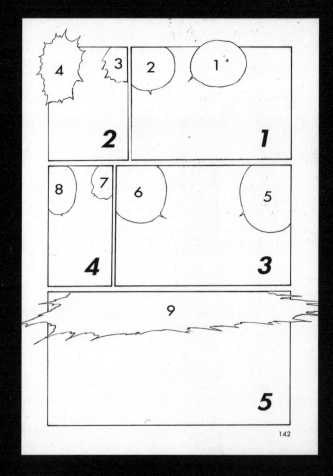

FLIP IT OVER TO GET STARTED!